THE ENTOURAGE OF
KAISER WILHELM II
1888–1918

ISABEL V. HULL

Assistant Professor of History, Cornell University

CAMBRIDGE UNIVERSITY PRESS

CAMBRIDGE

LONDON   NEW YORK   NEW ROCHELLE

MELBOURNE   SYDNEY

Published by the Press Syndicate of the University of Cambridge
The Pitt Building, Trumpington Street, Cambridge CB2 1RP
32 East 57th Street, New York, NY 10022, USA
296 Beaconsfield Parade, Middle Park, Melbourne 3206, Australia

First published 1982

Printed in the United States of America

Library of Congress catalogue card number: 81-17040

British Library Cataloguing in Publication Data

Hull, Isabel V.
The entourage of Kaiser Wilhelm II, 1888–1918.
1. Wilhelm II, *Emperor of Germany*
2. Cabinet officers—Germany
I. Title
943.08′4   DD229

ISBN 0-521-23665-7

THE ENTOURAGE OF KAISER WILHELM II
1888–1918

To my father
and the memory of my mother

Contents

Illustrations

Thanks are due to Fürstlich Fürstenbergisches Archiv, Donaueschingen, for nos. 1, 4 and 5; to Ullstein Bilderdienst, for no. 2; and to Bundesarchiv-Militärarchiv, Freiburg, for nos. 6, 7 and 8

Acknowledgements

It is my pleasure to record here the names of the many people and institutions that have helped me in this project.

I wish to thank the staff of the following archives: the Bundesarchiv in Koblenz, the Bundesarchiv-Militärarchiv in Freiburg i. Br. (especially Dr Gerhard Granier, Dr Gerd Sandhofer and Dr Friedrich-Christian Stahl), the Hessisches Staatsarchiv, Darmstadt, the Historisches Archiv Fried. Krupp GmbH in Essen (especially Dr Köhne and Dr Müther), the Österreichisches Haus- Hof- und Staatsarchiv in Vienna, the Österreichisches Kriegsarchiv (especially Dr Peter Brouczek), the Politisches Archiv des Auswärtigen Amtes in Bonn, the Public Record Office in London, the Bayerisches Geheimes Staatsarchiv in Munich, the Hauptstaatsarchiv in Stuttgart, the Geheime Staatsarchiv Preussischer Kulturbesitz in Berlin-Dahlem, the Fürstlich Fürstenbergisches Archiv in Donaueschingen (especially Prof. Dr Karl S. Bader and Archivar Goerlipp), Sterling Memorial Library at Yale University and the Houghton Library at Harvard University.

For the financial support which made this project possible I thank the Council for European Studies, the Michigan Society of Fellows, Cornell University and particularly the Deutscher Akademischer Austauschdienst and the Danforth Foundation.

My thanks also to Dr Max Bruecher of Freiburg for allowing me to see the diaries of Prince Heinrich and to him and to Mrs. Bruecher for their kind hospitality; and to Mr Klaus Schlegel for allowing me to use his unpublished biographical essays on numerous members of the military entourage.

For their splendid editorial work I would like to thank Lynn Eden, Laura Engelstein, Michael Geyer and Mac Knox.

My greatest debt I owe to three people: to my dissertation director, Hans W. Gatzke, for his steadfast encouragement and confidence, his intellectual enthusiasm and receptivity; to Dr Wilhelm Deist for his friendly support and insightful criticism; and most of all to John Röhl for his generosity in offering information, advice, encouragement, and warm support for this project from its inception, and especially for his continuing friendship.

Unless otherwise stated, all translations of quotations are my own.

In order to avoid the excessive use of italic, roman type has been used for German titles and offices throughout.

Abbreviations

AOK	Armee Oberkommando
BA Koblenz	Bundesarchiv, Koblenz
BGSA Munich	Bayerisches Geheimes Staatsarchiv, Munich
FA	Flügeladjutant
FAD	Flügeladjutant zum Dienst
Fasz.	Faszikel
FFA Donaueschingen	Fürstlich Fürstenbergisches Archiv, Donaueschingen
GHQ	Grosses Hauptquartier
HA Krupp Essen	Historisches Archiv Fried. Krupp GmbH, Essen
HStA Darmstadt	Hessisches Staatsarchiv, Darmstadt
HStA Stuttgart	Hauptstaatsarchiv Stuttgart
HStA Stuttgart, E-73, Verz. 61	Hauptstaatsarchiv Stuttgart, Ministerium der auswärtigen Angelegenheiten II (Berlin), E-73, Verz. 61, volume number
MA Freiburg	Bundesarchiv-Militärarchiv, Freiburg im Breisgau
MA Freiburg RM2	Bundesarchiv-Militärarchiv, Freiburg im Breisgau, Kaiserliches Marinekabinett/volume number
MA Freiburg RM3	Bundesarchiv-Militärarchiv, Freiburg im Breisgau, Reichsmarineamt/volume number
MA Freiburg RM4	Bundesarchiv-Militärarchiv, Freiburg im Breisgau, Kaiserliches Oberkommando der Marine/volume number
MA Freiburg RM5	Bundesarchiv-Militärarchiv, Freiburg im Breisgau, Admiralstab der Marine/volume number
MStGO	Militärstrafgerichtsordnung

Nl.	Nachlass (followed by volume number/page number, where paginated)
OHL	Oberste Heeresleitung
ÖStA Vienna	Österreichisches Haus- Hof- und Staatsarchiv, Vienna
ÖStA Vienna PA III	Österreichisches Haus- Hof- und Staatsarchiv, Vienna, Politisches Archiv des Ministeriums des Äussern, Preussen/volume number
ÖStA Vienna PA IV	Österreichisches Haus- Hof- und Staatsarchiv, Vienna, Politisches Archiv des Ministeriums des Äussern, Bayern/volume number
ÖKrA Vienna	Österreichisches Kriegsarchiv, Vienna
ÖKrA Vienna MKSM, Sep. Fasz.	Österreichisches Kriegsarchiv, Vienna, Militär Kanzlei Seiner Majestät, Separater Faszikel
PA Bonn	Politisches Archiv des Auswärtigen Amtes, Bonn
PA Bonn D 121	Politisches Archiv des Auswärtigen Amtes, Bonn, Deutschland 121
PRO London FO 371	Public Record Office, London, Foreign Office 371/volume number/file number/case number (where different from file number)
RMA	Reichsmarineamt

1

Introduction

The subject of this book is the men who 'surrounded' Kaiser Wilhelm II, his *Umgebung*, or entourage. They were mostly noble, mostly military, and in an unparalleled position because of their proximity to the Emperor to imprint their peculiar vision of the world upon German policy. Theirs is a paradoxical tale, about power and its limits, about social prestige and intimations of its decay. More than anything else, theirs is the story of unintended consequences, efforts to preserve which brought on ruin, or, in Bismarck's colorful phrase, 'suicide for fear of death.'[1]

The story of this elaborate suicide takes place against the background of a profound reinterpretation of the German Empire, which began with the 'Fischer controversy.'[2] In 1961, Professor Fritz Fischer argued, in *Griff nach der Weltmacht,*[3] that Germany had purposely launched World War I in order to establish German hegemony over the European continent. Although such a view was not uncommon among non-German historians, it created a furor among Fischer's conservative colleagues.[4] For one thing, Fischer's argument emphasized the similarities between the Empire's foreign policy and Hitler's and, by extension, suggested that the Second Reich had played an essential role in preparing for the Third. While some of Fischer's assertions (especially those in his second book[5]) remain controversial, he and his allies ultimately routed their conservative opponents and snapped the older tradition of German historiography. In this vacuum a new school soon developed. It selected tools from some of the social sciences (particularly economics and sociology) and applied them to the problems Fischer had raised. It focussed upon continuity, not just in external affairs, but also in the internal socio-political patterns that had caused Germany's ruinous foreign policy. The object was to isolate and to analyze the long-term domestic 'power structures' behind the events of 1870 to 1945.[6] The *Kaiserreich* was to be interpreted according to its role in this larger schema.

This new historiographical school has rapidly become the 'new orthodoxy.'[7] Although it is sometimes called the 'Kehrite' school, after Eckart Kehr, a radical historian of the 1920s,[8] its foremost practitioner is Hans-Ulrich Wehler. Wehler's book, *Das Deutsche Kaiserreich 1871–1918*,[9] presents in one place the main arguments and methodological preoccupations of the group. *Das Deutsche Kaiserreich* is a provocative, polemical, and merciless dissection of the Empire. It provides the first systematic structural analysis of the Second Reich,[10] and does so with such sweep, vigor, and clarity that, for the time being at least, no one can approach the history of the period without engaging Wehler's interpretation.

For Wehler, the Empire's salient structural fact was the continued social and political predominance of Prussia's landed nobility in a time of rapid industrialization and social change. The newly unified Germany was a thinly veiled autocracy, a 'military despotism' designed to preserve Prussia, its monarchy, and its Junker supporters from the political and social challenges of industrialism. Wehler points out that one of the many advantages democracy holds for a modern society is that, by giving every organized group some access to power, it increases cross-class communication and leads to greater legitimacy for the government and greater rationality in its decision making.[11] The Wilhelminian decision makers, however, tried assiduously to avoid the democratic solution. Instead, clinging to power with whitened knuckles, they fought popular and democratic forces, they muffled, frustrated, and twisted them into channels that seemed less dangerous to the monarchy and the Junkers. Wehler's Empire appears to be an almost perfectly ordered hierarchy in which the Junkers subordinated institutions (church, school, the law) and other classes (the bourgeois strata, peasantry and, less successfully, the working class) to their own interests. The attempts of the Junkers and their industrial bourgeois allies to manipulate this hierarchy produced the crucial events of the prewar years: high tariffs, the building of the battle fleet, 'social imperialism,' legislative paralysis, and, finally, World War I.[12] The irony is that these efforts failed to save the monarchy, but succeeded in destroying the democratic potential latent in German society. The Empire is historically important, then, because it paved the way to the Third Reich, both negatively, by eliminating the democratic alternative, and positively, by supporting authoritarianism and hypernationalism.

Wehler's interpretation has naturally elicited opposition. His critics all agree that it is too sweeping. Taken together, they identify three areas in which the breadth of his argument creates problems. The first of these is continuity. Viewing the Empire in the context of the Third Reich inevitably sets a *telos* toward which the whole system seems to be developing. Teleology encourages determinism as well as underestimation both of tendencies peculiar to the *Kaiserreich* and of possibilities inherent in that society which went unrealized after it ended.[13]

Second, there is the problem of uniformity: Wehler's Empire is too much the seamless web. In his account one finds little reference to differences among the ruling strata, of non-Prussian states, of groups whose experience is not easily assimilated into Wehler's analysis,[14] or of independent, non-manipulated activity by autonomous groups.[15] One misses, in short, the complexity and contradictions characteristic of any human society.

Finally, many critics have trouble accepting historical causality located at a level as abstract as Wehler's. He is primarily concerned to explain how Wilhelminian society and government worked to support the nobles and their allies. The actors are the 'ruling elites,' or sometimes 'the upper classes,' but rarely the individuals or organizational fractions that show up in the documents. The tendency is to explain events according to fairly abstract social forces, which does not explain how these forces actually worked, or who, exactly, made them up.

One might sum up these various criticisms by saying that Wehler's necessarily abstract analysis of the Wilhelminian system preceded the minute historical investigations on which it should have been based. Hans-Günter Zmarzlik has compared our knowledge of the Empire to the map of Africa before it was fully explored.[16] Patches of colored information drift in a sea of white ignorance, except, of course, that the mapmakers had the advantage of knowing the outline of their continent, whereas for historians the outline, or interpretation, first emerges from the interaction among all of the parts. The metaphor has its limits, but it does underscore the fact that imperial Germany so far has been unevenly studied at best and that in this sense overarching theories may be premature.

But there are also dangers inherent in some of the criticisms directed against Wehler. Chief among these is the temptation to discard systemic analysis altogether, because it is too abstract, and to revert to the older historical methods that it replaced. Such temptations are already clear in the calls for a return to 'objectivity.'[17] This road leads to a history satisfied with depicting particularity. If it attempts to integrate the pieces of the mosaic, it usually does so in a static way, because

its units are the pieces themselves, rather than the changing relationships among them.

Some young British historians have begun to revise Wehler by other
means. First, they use social history to describe Germany 'from the
bottom up,' a process that helps to fill in some of those white spaces
on the Wilhelminian map.[18] Their efforts contrast with the Wehler-
ites' conception of social history, which concentrates on economic
structures and their translation into political power. This approach
represents a considerable advance over the old idealist historical tradition, but it is still history 'from the top down.'[19] Second, these
younger historians have widened Wehler's theoretical scope by using
other approaches, for example Gramsci's idea of hegemony.[20] Both
of these kinds of revisions will ultimately do much to correct our picture of the Empire, although neither has so far been able to shake
Wehler's basic thesis about the defensive nature of the *Kaiserreich*.[21]

This study also takes Wehler's structural and theoretical preoccupations seriously. It proceeds from the premise that the way to overcome the limitations of the method is not to abandon it, but to expand
it. The chapters which follow do this in a slightly different way from
the one chosen by the young British historians. Rather than adding
other structures to the ones upon which Wehler concentrates, this
study attempts to discover structure or pattern at a level closer to actual
human activity. It tries to connect the social forces so prominent in
Wehler's book to the people whose actions expressed them. For it is
people who make history, but they do so neither as free-willed individuals (as liberals suggest), nor as social automata. Wehler's analysis
errs in the latter direction, because it approaches people's actions from
the outside in. That is, Wehler begins with the functional effects of
activity and then reasons backwards to the origins or causes. On the
abstract, functional plane, his arguments make sense. But they do not
convincingly explain why people did what they did: what their motives
were, how these motives were formed, and how people acted upon
them. For example, Wehler's functionalism allows him to rest content
with the high-level motive of class interest. But class interest is a complicated and ill-understood phenomenon. Even when an individual
articulates class interest in a systematic way, there are other motives
no less real, powerful, and structural, in the sense that they are continuous, patterned, and socially produced. These other determinants
include patterns of personality and friendship, of deference and service, of institutional training and affiliation, and of family network.
These structures close down certain possibilities for action or decision

making and make others likely or probable. And these structures change slowly, as they jostle one another, combine differently, or as circumstances bring some into relief and momentarily overshadow others. In fact, it seems likely that class interest is actually one aggregation of these smaller patterns, the sum total at the end of the complicated process of their interaction. The following chapters will look at that process from the inside out. They will try to reverse Wehler's procedure, or, put another way, they will break down his large structures into the smaller ones that, it is argued, produced them.

Although they differ on how this worked in practice, most historians agree that the discrepancy between the economic and the sociopolitical system was the fundamental dilemma of the *Kaiserreich*. 'The swift industrialization of imperial Germany is one of the commonplaces of contemporary history.'[22] Very shortly after Wilhelm II's accession to the throne, Germany had 'tipped over' into a predominantly industrial economy.[23] But the social and political structures were much slower to change than the economic system.

Under absolutism, the east Elbian nobles, the Junkers, had entrenched themselves with the crown's blessing in the central institutions of the Prussian state: the army officer corps, the higher bureaucracy, the diplomatic corps, and the Court. Their economic base lay in agriculture. The 'agricultural revolution' of the early nineteenth century expanded the wealth of many landowning nobles and allowed them to enter the period of intensive industrialization from a position of strength.[24] Otto von Bismarck added to that position by defeating their main political opponent, the liberal bourgeoisie, and by providing the Junkers with the starring role in the three wars of German unification, through their leadership in the victorious army. Bismarck completed his work by creating an arbitrary constitution, which left the political privileges of the nobles largely untouched.

Despite Bismarck's efforts, the nobles' secure world began to dissolve in the last half of the nineteenth century. The economic basis of their political power collapsed when they were unable to compete with the vast grain exports from America and Russia. Only huge state subsidies out of the consumer's pocket kept the Junkers afloat. As Wilhelm's reign drew on, the discrepancy between what the Junkers produced and what they extracted from society increased. At the same time, the bourgeoisie made increasing inroads into their institutional preserves. More and more untitled names cropped up in the diplomatic service, the officer corps, and the bureaucracy. Typically, the Junkers continued to monopolize the highest, most powerful, and most prestigious positions. But they were more successful in some branches, for example, diplomacy and the army officer corps, than in others, such as the navy or bureaucracy, where the Junkers conducted a rearguard action from the Prussian Ministry of the Interior.[25] In retrospect, we know that the mere replacement of Junkers by bourgeois had no necessarily progressive effect upon these institutions.[26] The Prussian nobility still retained political strength far in excess of its productive role in society. It was still the foremost *Stand*, politically and socially. Nonetheless, the bourgeois march through the institutions frightened the Junkers (and the Crown) with the specter of future powerlessness. By Wilhelm II's reign, the Court remained the last, untouched bastion of Junker hegemony.

Thus, the great paradox of the *Kaiserreich* and the major determinant of its domestic and foreign policy was the discord between its modern economy and its less than modern socio-political structure. This discord produced, through frustration among the 'outs' and fear among the 'ins,' internal tension which the political stalemate could not resolve at that level. The solution to these tensions was sought instead in foreign affairs, with results that culminated in the collapse of the system. One must ask why the representatives of premodern Germany were unable to confront their political problems more directly (and successfully). What factors hindered them from making a smoother adjustment to the demands of the modern industrial world? Historians have addressed these questions in recent studies by examining the diplomatic and officers corps and the bureaucracy.[27] However, they have largely ignored the Court. At most, they have rifled it for an influential individual here or there, but they have never studied the Court as a system. It is important to do so, however, for Bismarck's constitution placed inordinate potential power in the Kaiser's hands. This, in turn, made the Court the home of Wilhelm's most intimate advisers, the fount of overarching policy and the (often unsuccessful) coordinator of the other Prusso-German institutions of government. In addition, the Court was the officer corps' major conduit to the Emperor, and, thus, represented the major way in which the much vaunted military influence became actual. Finally, the Court is our best opportunity to see how the most strategically placed nobles responded to the challenges of the modern age.

The reluctance of historians to deal with the Court is partly a result of their position on the question of whether or not Wilhelm ruled. For if he did not, the argument goes, then it hardly matters who were his friends and advisers or whether they influenced him, or he them.

Contemporaries were convinced that, between the years 1890 and 1908, Wilhelm did indeed rule. The *Daily Telegraph* Affair[28] is the expression of their outrage that Wilhelm not only ruled, but ruled badly. In the early 1920s, historians largely shared their contemporaries' interpretation. Later on, however, this consensus vanished. Until the mid-1960s, Erich Eyck stood virtually alone in his conviction that there had been a personal regime.[29] Many historians have insisted that a 'personal regime' must mean Wilhelm had conscious, logical, political plans, which he consistently effected, often against the constitution and the ministers. Otherwise, although they might grant that Wilhelm had intervened periodically, they could not grant that he had governed. At the same time, it was impossible to show that anyone else had. In that case, it is clear that these standards for personal rule, indeed for governance as a whole, are impossibly rigid, and do not adequately describe the complexity of Wilhelminian decision making.

In 1967, John Röhl reopened the debate on personal rule. He based his work on the vast correspondence of the Kaiser's closest adviser, Philipp zu Eulenburg. These papers have turned out to be the single richest source on imperial decision making during the 1890s. They make clear that, especially in personnel matters, the policies of Wilhelm and his advisers were far more detailed and consistently carried out than historians had previously thought.[30] These personnel changes resulted in government so closely attuned to its Kaiser, that he rarely felt the need to intervene. These are the years when Germany embarked upon Wilhelm's great dreams, the navy and *Weltpolitik*, the dreams which shortly became the Empire's final nightmare. Indeed, a host of the most salient, defining characteristics of Wilhelminian governance in the years before 1914 have the Emperor at their center: the power of the military, the influence of unofficial friends at the expense of ministers, the proliferation of *Immediatstellen* (the right to see the Emperor without a minister being present), the noncoordination of policy which resulted from that, the solutions to problems that were never considered because, to the Emperor and his friends, they were unthinkable.[31] Any historical analysis of Wilhelminian decision making must be able to explain all of these qualities. Whether the whole 'then qualifies as "personal rule" is of secondary importance only.'[32]

The content of the debate on decision making has been changed somewhat by the modern, social-science-oriented focus on 'elites.' This is a progressive step because it recognizes the existence of something more subtle than a monolithic 'ruling class.' It also suggests non-political angles (education, group psychology, group dynamics), which one might study for a more accurate picture of the top of the socio-political hierarchy. This orientation frees one from the limitation imposed by an exclusive focus on the traditional objects of political study, power brokerage and interest politics. However, the potential of this approach has not been fully realized. For if the term 'elite' is not rigorously defined, it is merely a more up-to-date way of repeating the semantic confusion in which the contemporaries indulged when they used the word *Umgebung*.[33] Konrad Jarausch uses 'elite' (undefined) as a kind of *deus ex machina* which periodically intervenes to destroy Bethmann Hollweg's politics, thus exonerating the Chancellor from his failures.[34] For Hans-Ulrich Wehler, 'elite' encompasses the entourage, Chancellor, ministers, the leaders of the interest and agitation groups, and the heads of the military.[35] Wolfgang J. Mommsen includes the 'upper stratum of the governmental bureaucracy, the General Staff, and behind it the officer corps and the conservative entourage of the Emperor.'[36] Mommsen and Wehler thus part ways over the inclusion of specifically industrial interests in their definitions of elite. This is an important distinction because it indicates how far the respective authors believe the military and agrarian interests had relinquished control to the capitalists. Recently, British historians have widened 'elite' still further, because they believe that the Reichstag and the political parties were considerably more important politically than previous historians have granted.[37]

Such profound disagreements about who actually ran the *Kaiserreich* are testimony to its highly complex and diversified character. Leaders of interest and agitation groups, political parties, and large businesses did indeed shape prewar Germany. They are part of its reality. The reader, however, will meet very few of these people in the pages that follow, for the entourage was part of a different Wilhelminian reality. It is therefore worth remembering that the entourage is only one piece, albeit an important one, in an ill-understood, fractured mosaic. As much as the *Umgebung* may at times have been a unity, it never operated in a vacuum. Its influence was circumscribed by external forces, for example, by competing groups and institutions, by the political and social demands of economic industrialization, even by the foreign policies of neighboring states. Many of these forces are the subjects of good studies.[38] However, Wilhelm's entourage was also circumscribed by internal factors: caste narrowness, education, isolation, institutional, and personal conflicts. While not ignoring the external, the following pages will concentrate upon the internal forces, upon 'the stratum-specific systems of social values and norms, processes of political socialization, stereotypic word games, in whose codes the convictions and unconscious premises of the group are set down,'[39] and upon the personalities themselves. The entourage is small enough, particularly when limited to its more permanent members, to allow and indeed oblige one to examine personality as well as sociological categories in order to explain who gets chosen as an adviser in the first place and whose advice is likely to be listened to thereafter. While it is true that the pool from which Wilhelm selected his *Umgebung* was severely limited (and one can make justifiable judgments about the behavior of its members based on these limitations), his choices were not necessarily representative of that pool. It will emerge that the men whom Wilhelm chose fell roughly into three personality types. That is, Wilhelm created a kind of structure of personality which constrained and changed the institutions of Court and Cabinet and affected the decisions which these institutions made.

The term *Umgebung* means not only 'entourage' but also 'milieu.' It includes persons who were not officially members of the retinue. Contemporaries variously used *Umgebung* to mean anyone at Court, the military men attached to Wilhelm's person (his military adjutants, Flügel- and Generaladjutanten), the advisers officially attached to the monarch (Cabinet chiefs and head of the General Headquarters), Wilhelm's friends, or a combination of all of these. Thus the word was often used to designate that group which the critic felt was opposed to his own. More important, the word *Umgebung*, when used pejoratively, seldom meant something specific. It was either used to evoke dark, uncontrollable forces (thus releasing the contemporary critic from complicity in his own political failures), or it was used as a shield behind which one could attack the monarch without actually mentioning him. This method of criticism, the 'evil councillor theory,' is of course as old as the institution of monarchy itself.

The focus of the *Umgebung* was the monarch, Wilhelm. It is in relation to him that it must be defined. Thus, as a rule of thumb, one is or is not a member of the *Umgebung* by virtue of one's attachment to the *person* of the monarch. This study considers as part of the *Umgebung* anyone who, either by filling a post attached to Wilhelm's person, or through friendship with him, spent a considerable amount of time in Wilhelm's presence, or who seems to have exercised influence on him. Excluded from consideration are chancellors, ministers and others whose presence at Court was determined strictly by their position as bureaucrats, unaffected by affectional or personal ties to Wilhelm.[40]

For purposes of analysis and presentation, the *Umgebung* will (somewhat artificially) be broken down into the following groups: (1) those persons who held official posts attached to the monarch, a category which included Court positions (for example, Marshal of the Court, Oberhofmarschall; Master of Ceremonies, Zeremonienmeister; Court Chaplain, Hofprediger; Personal Doctor, Leibarzt), the three Cabinet chiefs (Military, Naval, Civilian), the representative of the Foreign Office, and the adjutants (Flügel- and Generaladjutanten) and occasional military attachés; (2) the intimate friends (for example Philipp Eulenburg and Max Fürstenberg), and those not so intimate (Albert Ballin, Friedrich Krupp); (3) the periodic companions, whose relation might be described as seasonal (participants in the *Nordlandreise,* Kiel Week, hunting trips), technical (naval engineers, archeologists, historians, and others whose interests coincided with Wilhelm's), or artistic; (4) the royal family. Many of these, perhaps the numerical majority, will be dealt with only briefly, because their importance lies merely in the tone they helped to create. The focus is mainly on the persons and institutions in the first two categories, since their presence and effects were long-term.

One cannot begin to consider Wilhelm's *Umgebung* without considering Wilhelm himself. His character and manner of living are therefore the subjects of the second chapter. Wilhelm chose who would surround him according to his own standards. His choices served only so long as they possessed his favor. The peculiarities of Wilhelm's character made demands on his *Umgebung* which were excessive in comparison to the practice in other monarchies of the period. His entourage was forced to spend a huge proportion of its time and energy in efforts to thwart Wilhelm's restless, ill-directed energy, and, where that failed, to undo the effects of his impetuosity. Therefore we will return a number of times to assess Wilhelm's personality, his politics, his prejudices, in order to evaluate to what extent his eccentricities may have caused the *Umgebung* to have been what it was, rather than what many of its critics thought it should have been. The question of who influenced whom in such a symbiotic relationship will naturally be a central one.

Speculation about the possible influence of the *Umgebung* on Wilhelm was rampant almost from the start of his reign. It was a question which sorely exercised contemporaries and upon which they spilled a prodigious amount of ink and an admirable amount of imagination. The kinds of charges they levelled against the *Umgebung* were many and varied, often mutually contradictory. When Wilhelm was just beginning his reign, it was observed that the *Umgebung* was not sufficiently strong to control him.[41] When his reign had ended, it was observed that the *Umgebung* had manipulated the monarch so completely that it had thereby lost the war. One can find Adjutant Major Deines complaining that Wilhelm was 'completely in the hands' of Friedrich von Holstein's camarilla of civilians at the Foreign Office,[42] while at virtually the same time Holstein was complaining that Wilhelm was 'a tool in the hands' of the military men in the entourage (like Deines).[43] From the various critics one learns that the *Umgebung* was excessively civilian and excessively military. It manipulated Wilhelm; it was manipulated by him. It was exclusively Prussian;[44] it was part of the 'Homosexual International.'[45] It was moral; it was immoral.[46] It was blindly loyal;[47] it abandoned Wilhelm.[48] It did not appreciate art;[49] it was full of esthetes.[50] It never rested from political intrigue;[51] it had no political plan.[52] It was unified;[53] it was fragmented.[54] Some of this confusion is due to the point of view of the critic, some to disagreement on whom to include in the *Umgebung*. Charges and countercharges filled the salons, the newspapers, the courtrooms, and, after all was over, the memoirs. What was the real nature of the *Umgebung*? Who influenced whom? These questions were not resolved.

The *Umgebung* was split into military and civilian camps. The civilians were a beleaguered group. They often consisted of only the chief of the Civil Cabinet and the representative of the Foreign Office. They generally supported the views of the chancellor, his ministers, and the Foreign Office. The civilians generally tried to confine the military's influence to military matters. In particular they tried to keep the military from interfering in foreign affairs and from encouraging Wilhelm to launch a coup d'état against the Reichstag. The struggle between these two camps was one of the two major sources of tension in the *Umgebung* (along with the difficulties of tempering the eccentric Emperor). An examination of the differences between the civilian and the military outlook is a central theme of the following chapters.

The numerical majority and, as time went on, the politically most influential members of the entourage were from the officer corps. Their overweening influence is partly a tenacious survival from Prussia's feudal past and partly a reflection of Wilhelm's 'militaristic pathos.'[55] Prussia's military education system steeped its products in narrow caste prejudice. It trained its recruits to approach complex problems in an exceedingly technical manner. Finally, Prussian military education supplemented the political ignorance of its officers with the haughty conviction that they were always right. The reawakened controversy surrounding the origins of the First World War has posed the question of how far such persons could form policies based on (more or less) rational consideration of interests transcending those of their own class and institutions.[56]

The most important member of the civilian entourage was Philipp Eulenburg, who will therefore play a major role in the pages that follow. Eulenburg was thought by contemporaries to be an almost omnipotent intriguer behind the scenes, whose hold over Wilhelm was strengthened by, among other things, spiritism. Eulenburg was the target of the major social scandal of Wilhelm's reign, the Moltke–Harden–Eulenburg trials of 1907–09.[57] The anti-monarchical anger generated by these trials was expressed politically in the *Daily Telegraph* Affair (1908), which shook the government to its foundations. The Moltke–Harden–Eulenburg scandal must be considered at length because it was the occasion for the most vehement, detailed criticism of the *Umgebung* during the period. It resulted in the banishment from Court of a number of influential courtiers, among them Wilhelm's closest (perhaps only) friend, Eulenburg. It crippled the civilian wing of the entourage and proportionally increased the power of the military. The effect of the scandal was so strong that the character of the *Umgebung* and, it is suggested, of the Emperor himself, changed radically after this time.[58]

The accusations raised during the scandal were twisted together from different strands of cultural unease, whose confluence is a fascinating phenomenon for the social historian. These strands reveal a cultural pessimism imbued with intimations of decay, homosexuality, and spiritism (or spiritualism). These preoccupations were not limited to the 'natural critics' of Wilhelminian society. They were shared by the old ruling elites and contributed greatly to the formation of their bleak world view in the dwindling days of peace. We must discover how true these accusations were and, to the extent that a number of them were true, what this says about Wilhelm and his *Umgebung*.

One of the major purposes of this book is to examine why a group of men (the Kaiser and his entourage) so securely anchored in power should have tried to preserve its position in such an obsessively rigid way. Why did it adamantly refuse to acquiesce to even the smallest concessions which it might have used to placate its enemies? What were the consequences of this obstinacy? What drove the entourage to run the risk of beginning the war that ultimately destroyed it? What prevented the entourage from curbing the excesses of the Kaiser? The answer to these and other questions lies in the way three elements acted to limit each other. These elements, which operated in patterned ways, were: monarchical institutions (the Court offices, the Cabinets, the Hauptquartier), individual personality and psychology (the entourage, thanks to Wilhelm's own peculiar needs, was composed not of a random selection of personalities, but of a select constellation of types), and the social values and expectations of class.

For a majority of the members of the entourage, social values and class norms were contained in the officer's honor code, which prescribed not only the proper *Weltanschauung* of the noble officer, but also his comportment down to the smallest detail. The specificity of the code enables the historian, in turn, to be quite precise in evaluating the effects of the officer's life on the attitudes and assumptions of the people who lived it. Even in the best of times, the honor code predisposed its holders to rigidity and narrowness. In times of stress, this predisposition seriously weakened the ability of the entourage to respond to pressure flexibly.

The social values and class norms of the smaller, civilian entourage are not to be found neatly collated in a handbook. In the case of Philipp Eulenburg and the Liebenberg Circle, however, these values emerge clearly from their letters. These reveal how, under the guise of idealist esthetics, the Liebenbergers reformulated and strengthened typically conservative values in an artistic and personal mode. In the case of the other civilians (and a few of the military men), their attitudes were fundamentally affected by the official positions they held. The bureaucratic need for efficiency and policy continuity demanded that they be more critical of Wilhelm and more insistent that he change than were other people at Court.

The social values of the men of the entourage, the constellation of their personalities, and the peculiar demands and limits of the monarchical institutions in which they served acted upon each other to form a dangerous syndrome. On the one hand, their privileged position at the top of society made them arrogant. On the other, it made them anxious lest they lose their eminence. That anxiety was reflected in the increasing rigidity of both the honor code and of Court etiquette and operation. This was not a healthy sign, for it meant that the entourage was concentrating more and more on control and repression and less and less on adaptation. The more the Junkers, including those in the entourage, became addicted to control and repression, the more they felt it necessary to display their strength. They became gripped by the need to demonstrate to their enemies (external and internal) and to themselves how strong and self-sufficient they were. These displays of strength were not limited to parades and other ceremonies. They spilled over into policy making. As Wilhelm's reign continued, the tone within the entourage, in Wilhelm's speeches, and in government policies became more desperately strident. The syndrome in which arrogance shared sovereignty with anxiety spawned, first, rigidity and control-mania. It overvalued strength and, finally, it produced belligerent aggressiveness. Politically this syndrome meant that policy was hardly formulated in a rational way, in Weber's sense.

The syndrome was not merely psychological, not merely the product of individual personality. It was grounded as well in the institutions of monarchy and in class values of the Prussian nobility. Since these three elements formed an interacting complex, they have, as far as possible, not been considered separately from one another. Thus the reader will find biographical sketches intermingled with discussions of institutions and of political crises. The outcome should be a balanced analysis and portrait of a specific stratum of the old ruling elite. It should expose who these men were, how they were chosen and what backgrounds they brought with them to their posts. The study surveys the dynamics of their position in society at large (where most were members of the declining agrarian–military aristocracy) and the dynamics in the smaller society of the Court. Within that smaller society it weighs the constraints upon men who constantly had to deal with Wilhelm and with each other, burdened by limitations imposed on them by education, caste, and *Männerbund*. This book, then, is a detailed study of an elite which was not only in decline but under great pressure to adapt itself to a future it may have scorned, but which, most of all, it feared.

2

Wilhelm and his Court

Kaiser Wilhelm II was a bafflingly complex person. The caricature of the saber-rattling warrior, he broke down when war actually began. Endowed with a high intelligence and an excellent memory, he was capable of the most crashing stupidities. Fascinated by the latest technological advances, thoroughly at home in a fast-moving, modern world, Wilhelm clung to medieval notions of divine right. Enormously energetic and ambitious, he proved utterly unable to work hard. The contradictions were so numerous and startling that before Wilhelm had spent two years on the throne people wondered if he were quite sane.[1]

This line of thought usually centered around two characteristics: *Cäsarenwahnsinn* (paranoia accompanied by delusions of grandeur, thought to be typical of supreme autocrats) and hypernervousness. The former trait was particularly fastened upon by the public, especially after Ludwig Quidde's celebrated pamphlet, *Caligula, Eine Studie in Cäsarenwahnsinn*,[2] in which Quidde cleverly, but unmistakably, equated the Kaiser with the crazed Emperor Caligula.[3] Persons closer to Wilhelm also worried about *Cäsarenwahnsinn* (Georg Hinzpeter, the Kaiser's tutor, for example[4]), about his 'egotism,'[5] and about his 'unfortunate vanity.'[6] But mostly the members of the entourage worried about his nerves. This was the phrase invariably used by contemporaries. It is hardly an analytical term, but it is the best description of how Wilhelm behaved.

Indeed, Wilhelm's mental and physical constitution was not robust. Excitement, prolonged work, anxiety or responsibility rubbed him raw and threatened to unloose a breakdown. 'His Majesty has no nerves, he won't bear up' under a crisis, Wilhelm's good friend Admiral Friedrich Hollmann warned Bernhard Bülow.[7] Wilhelm's doctor, Rudolf von Leuthold, worried constantly that Wilhelm would 'overtax his nerves and break down.'[8] The best efforts of Leuthold, General Plessen,[9] and Eulenburg,[10] among others, did not prevent Wilhelm from succumbing to nervous strain. In addition to his well-known breakdown following the *Daily Telegraph* Affair, Wilhelm suffered prolonged nervous disturbances in 1893,[11] 1900, 1903,[12] 1913, and throughout the war.[13] He suffered more minor collapses at numerous points in his reign.[14] After a particularly violent scene with Wilhelm, War Minister Walther Bronsart von Schellendorff[15] concluded that Wilhelm was 'not quite sane.' When he told this to Chancellor Chlodwig von Hohenlohe, Hohenlohe did not disagree.[16] Two years later, Holstein reported that the *Bundesfürsten* agreed with Bronsart that Wilhelm 'was "not always sane." '[17] This assessment was shared by most informed close observers of the Kaiser. One such was Alois Frhr Klepsch-Kloth von Roden. Klepsch-Kloth was Austro-Hungarian military attaché to Berlin from 1902 to 1908 and then served as Austro-Hungarian delegate (and then plenipotentiary) to the General Headquarters from 1915 to 1918. Klepsch-Kloth was an excellent observer and was afforded ample opportunity to scrutinize the Kaiser.[18] Although Klepsch-Kloth was well-disposed toward Wilhelm, he nonetheless summed up Wilhelm's character in those same words, '*not quite sane . . .* he had, as one says, a screw loose [*dass er – wie man zu sagen pflegt – einen starken Hieb hatte*].'[19] Chancellor Theobald von Bethmann Hollweg, looking back in 1920 over events 'before and during the war,' also became 'overcome by the feeling that our Emperor had many traits that oppressed us like a nightmare.' Bethmann was even moved to wonder 'why this burden, which we clearly recognized as such, was not removed in time.'[20]

Why Wilhelm developed into such a burden is a fascinating question, but one which must be left to his biographers.[21] We shall be concerned here with the broad patterns of Wilhelm's personality and the way these affected his milieu, his entourage, and his reactions to them. Wilhelm's bad nerves and the tumultuous inner struggle he constantly waged against himself were the two aspects of his character that had the greatest impact in determining his behavior.

The effects of Wilhelm's nerves were immediate and obvious. Wilhelm's attention span was extremely short. This meant that both official correspondence and verbal reports (*Immediatvorträge*) had to be short and, if possible, gripping. There was no place for longer background reports or for intricate detail.[22] A second problem was Wilhelm's restlessness. His reign was a carousel of trips, which interrupted even the most pressing affairs. Separated from chancellor and ministers for weeks at a time, Wilhelm carried on business through his Civil Cabinet chief or the representative of the Foreign Office, whose messages to Berlin might finally arrive there only after two or more days via courier. As if this were not bad enough, Wilhelm's nervousness conspired to prevent him from working at all. Government officials and the Cabinet chiefs complained bitterly that Wilhelm avoided hard, concentrated work or difficult decisions. They excoriated the Kaiser (privately, of course) for his self-indulgence, his 'hobby-horses and moods.'[23] 'He is not dutiful,' wrote Admiral Georg von Müller, who would later become Wilhelm's long-time Naval Cabinet chief,[24] 'or else he would devote his free time to the more serious duties of his calling.'[25] Wilhelm was self-indulgent, it is true, but it would be a mistake to attribute his poor work habits strictly to laziness. Daily governing and decision making were genuine tortures to Wilhelm. The war years, the best example of this difficulty,[26] lead one to question how much improvement Wilhelm's constitution might have allowed even with the best of advisers. The pressure of governing was not even the most important weight which Wilhelm bore, however. A worse burden was the one he imposed on himself.

Wilhelm lived out his life in an elaborate masquerade. He paraded as the consummate soldier–warlord, always in uniform, always fierce, hard, decisive, steady, an amalgam of the 'masculine virtues.' Wilhelm was actually none of these. Slightly feminine in appearance, with delicate health, hypersensitive, squeamish, nervous as a caged animal, and steady as an aspen leaf, Wilhelm, in fact, could not have been farther removed from his ideal. Walther Rathenau later recalled how surprised he had been when he first met the Kaiser.

How different from what I had expected. I knew the energetic, youthful pictures with broad cheeks, bristled mustache, threatening eyes; the dangerous telegrams, the speeches and mottos which exuded energy.

There sat a youthful man in a colorful uniform, with odd medals, the white hands full of colored rings, bracelets on his wrists; tender skin, soft hair, small, white teeth. A true Prince, intent on the impression [he made], continuously fighting with himself, overcoming his nature in order to wrest from it bearing, energy, mastery. Hardly an un[self]-conscious moment; unconscious only – and here begins the part which is humanly touching – of the struggle with himself; a nature directed against itself, unsuspecting.

Many have seen this besides me: neediness, softness, a longing for people, a childlike nature ravished, these were palpable behind athletic feats, high tension and resounding activity, these people grasped and sympathized with. This man must be protected, guarded with a strong arm, against that which he feels but does not know, that which pulls him into the abyss.[27]

Another man in another time might have acknowledged his 'softness' and still have been able to rule. Not Wilhelm, not at the turn of the century. Instead, he ruthlessly suppressed his softness. Wilhelm accepted society's judgment that such characteristics were unnatural in a man. He grasped every opportunity to prove his masculinity and, hence, his worthiness. Wilhelm copied the venomous marginalia style of his ancestor, Frederick the Great. He gloried in fierce speeches. He preened and strutted at countless ceremonies until his soldierly bearing was stamped in everyone's mind. He adopted a 'Potsdam lieutenant's view'[28] of the world because that was the epitome of German masculinity. He married and had six sons and a daughter.

But Wilhelm's successful propaganda image did not make him rest easily. The tension resulting from pretence made Wilhelm even more nervous. He chafed at the programs, the balls and other public functions where he was open to the scrutiny of persons he did not trust.[29] Wilhelm's marriage may have stood 'in our memory as an example of a deep and pure, truly German family happiness, like the picture of the noble Kaiserin as an ideal picture of a German wife and mother,' as War Minister Karl von Einem wrote, echoing the sentiments of much of Germany.[30] But this rosy portrait was filled with thorns. The Empress did indeed possess qualities that won her contemporaries' praise. Where the Kaiser sacrificed his official obligations for trips and private amusements, the Kaiserin's devotion to duty was legendary.[31] Where he epitomized showy ostentation, her sincerity and directness shone through all the brighter.[32] Where he flirted with modern heresies like ruthless *Machtpolitik* or biblical criticism, she remained true to the piety of earlier times. And where Wilhelm had to force his masculinity, Auguste Viktoria seemed the image of what her age regarded as natural femininity.[33] In fact, the adulation that the Empress elicited stems in good measure from the fact that she was many of the things which her imperial husband was not, but, many felt, should have been.

However, her virtues were also weaknesses. Her piety, for example, was ultra-orthodox and intolerant. She disliked Roman Catholics, Jews, divorcé(e)s, indeed anyone who was not a conservative Lutheran with a spotless, conventional past. Her love of Germany was provincial and xenophobic. Bernhard Bülow summed up the Empress's politics and, in a way, her character in his remark that hers was the

standpoint of an orthodox-protestant conservative with an instinctive preference for the agrarians as the surest support of throne and alter. . . . She would have won widespread respect and love had she been the wife of a commanding general or of a provincial governor . . . people would have said 'Splendid woman [*tadellose Frau*], dutiful through and through, and so completely German!'[34]

As Empress, however, Auguste Viktoria was narrow, rigid and colorless. Her public time she divided among official representations and numerous charities. But she always felt that, befitting her gender, her major duties lay in the private sphere, in devotion to husband and children.

Despite her conscientious efforts, or perhaps because of them, Auguste Viktoria's effect upon her family was not entirely positive. The Empress 'bored and agitated' Wilhelm,[35] as she ultimately bored most people with whom she was in constant contact.[36] She had perfected the domestic virtues to the exclusion of worldliness or curiosity. She shared none of Wilhelm's enthusiasms, not art or sport, not archeology or history, not science or technology. Religion was her one passion and Wilhelm and her seven children the other. She doted on the Kaiser like a mother, paid him constant attention and tried to smooth out the difficulties he encountered by suppressing political discussion when she was with him[37] and by surrounding the Kaiser with her naive optimism.[38] These last efforts, combined with her arch-conservatism, had unfortunate political effects during the war.[39] But even in peacetime Auguste Viktoria strongly influenced the milieu in which Wilhelm lived and worked, even though she rarely intervened in politics directly. The more the Kaiserin tried to calm, the more she contributed to the Kaiser's nervousness.

Brittle and anxious, Auguste Viktoria concentrated her nervous energy upon her family. Major General Adolf von Deines, the overseer of the princes' education, was driven to distraction. 'I have to deal with a nervously ill woman and an unreasonably anxious mother [*planlos ängstlichen*], who, despite many excellent qualities, hurts at least as much as she helps – strictly from anxiety.'[40] The pattern was clear. The Empress worried, pried and intervened until, as in December 1897, 'H.M. broke down from exhaustion and suffered not only a slight influenza attack, but such a nervous shock, that simply taking it easy will no longer help [*dass gar nicht Vernunft zu reden ist*],' Oberhof- und Hausmarschall August Eulenburg reported. The Kaiser wanted to send her to a southern clime. She resisted (she never liked to leave Wilhelm, even for reasons of health[41]), 'and now,' Eulenburg sighed, 'we find ourselves in the familiar *Tiraillement*.'[42] The Kaiserin's nervous attacks elicited the same from her equally anxious husband. Wilhelm, the Court knew, 'cannot stand it at home,'[43] and sought every opportunity to escape. As Philipp Eulenburg reported before Wilhelm's annual summer trip in 1899, 'the farewell was very difficult for the Empress, less so for the Emperor, who longs for peace and recuperation.'[44]

But Wilhelm longed to escape not merely from his wife's particular characteristics, but from the fact that she was a woman. As a young man of twenty, Wilhelm wrote (in English), to his old friend Marie Gräfin von Dönhoff,[45] how dreadful he found all the women (but one) in Berlin society, who only talked of dresses and flirtations. 'I hope that you know me well enough to know that I am a serious enemy to such kind of thing as well as to such kind of ladies, who want to be flirted with. I think that is something beneath a real man and gentleman, especially I think beneath myself, don't you think so too?'[46] Wilhelm never changed his mind. Eulenburg wrote that the *Nordlandreise*, Wilhelm's annual trip with his male companions, was Wilhelm's ' "*Saison*," . . . without female conversation, which he does not like.'[47] When Auguste Viktoria once accompanied Wilhelm on the *Nordlandreise* in 1894, Alfred von Kiderlen-Wächter, the representative of the Foreign Office, reported how subdued the atmosphere became.[48] The presence of women meant that the *Männerbund* would be constrained by 'all sorts of considerations and etiquette.'[49] These had made Berlin society 'dreadful' for Wilhelm, even as a young man of nineteen. He hated to visit there, he wrote. 'I never feel happy, real[l]y happy at Berlin. Only Potsdam that is my "el dorado" and that is also where Mama mostly likes to live, where one feels free with the beautiful nature around you and soldiers as much as you like, for I love my dear Regiment very much, those such kind nice young men in it.'[50] Wilhelm often told Eulenburg how, before he entered the regiment, 'I had lived through such horrible years when no one understood my individuality. . . . Here I found my family, my friends, my interests, everything that I had previously missed.'[51]

The regiment, then, was Wilhelm's first refuge. He imported it into the entourage via the Flügeladjutanten, or aides-de-camp.[52] He ate several meals a week at regimental *Kasinos* when he stayed in Potsdam as Kaiser. But regimental life satisfied only one of the poles of Wilhelm's nature. It provided him with an ideal to which to aspire and with comrades of the proper masculine stamp. But it did not satisfy the Wilhelm that Rathenau noticed. The soft, the vulnerable, the emotional Wilhelm gravitated to Philipp zu Eulenburg and his friends, the so-called 'Liebenberg Circle.' From Eulenburg Wilhelm received both tenderness and stimulation, a combination he never found with anyone else.[53] The basis of the relationship, from Eulenburg's side, was love. From Wilhelm's it is less clear. Wilhelm never resolved his feelings for Eulenburg, never understood them, and certainly never labelled them. Eulenburg was closer to Wilhelm than was any other man, and where Auguste Viktoria made Wilhelm nervous, Eulenburg made him happy and calm.[54] Wilhelm seems to have remained unconscious of the homoerotic basis of his closest friendship and, by extension, of the homosexual aspects of his own character. Despite speculation to the contrary,[55] it is unlikely that Wilhelm engaged in overt homosexual activity. Such an acknowledgement of 'unmasculinity' would have been too threatening for someone so unsure of himself as Wilhelm. It would also have flown in the face of Wilhelm's utter acceptance of current social values.

Wilhelm was in some respects as straightlaced as his grandmother, Queen Victoria, or his wife. He was very proud of his record of marital fidelity, for example, and was furious at the inevitable rumors which idle tongues spun.[56] However, in the 1880s, before his accension to the throne, Wilhelm had engaged in a couple of brief extramarital flings of the sort that were practically a *rite de passage* for a young prince. These were one of the initiations that Wilhelm had doubtless neglected because of his uncommonly early marriage (he had been barely twenty-two years old at the time). Whether they were caused by Wilhelm's desire to be one of the boys, by a need to escape his boring and almost continuously pregnant wife, or both, these sexual encounters soon ceased. After he became Kaiser, Wilhelm held steadfastly to his marriage vows and went to great lengths to cover up his youthful dalliances.[57] In fact, one of the major reasons why Wilhelm so disliked Edward VII was that Edward's sexually freewheeling lifestyle 'shocked' Wilhelm.[58] It must also have fascinated him, since he discussed the subject so insistently that even King Edward heard of his remarks.[59] Wilhelm's prudery seems indeed to have been the proper Victorian mix of censure and prurient interest. After all, Wilhelm loved 'strong' stories and felt cramped when his wife's presence forbade them.[60] Altogether, Wilhelm had internalized the lessons of his youth, even when he obviously suffered under them. As a final example of the Kaiser's conventionality and its cost one might mention Georg Hinzpeter, Wilhelm's tutor, who had blackened Wilhelm's boyhood with his rigidity and dourness.[61] Yet when the time came for Wilhelm's sons to be educated, he insisted that Hinzpeter be consulted, because his method 'was the only correct one.'[62]

Wilhelm, then, was saddled with an enormous burden. He adhered to the prevailing conception of the proper man and the proper monarch, yet he was unable to live up to the stereotype. He struggled mightily to conceal his inadequacy from the world and from himself. This latter struggle was one of the reasons why Wilhelm was so resolutely unself-reflective, so eager to rob himself of any opportunity for self-discovery. Wilhelm could tolerate neither solitude nor silence. Even when he was reading a book, Wilhelm refused to let his companions retire. '*Kinder,* why are you all running away? You're acting as if I were poison!'[63] Wilhelm's fear of being alone was easier for the entourage to take than his constant chatter. The Emperor's compulsion to talk increased during the years, until in the war it became a veritable torture for innocent bystanders.[64] But even before the war, the unfortunate results of his predilection were worrisome. Wilhelm's good intentions were often ruined by it.[65] He talked in front of persons before whom he should have kept silent. He could not keep secrets.[66] Worse, he never allowed others to speak and therefore rarely learned anything from those he met.[67] Through constant talking, Wilhelm rigidly controlled his milieu and thus guarded himself from the new or unexpected, which might have damaged his fragile sense of self.

Another tactic that Wilhelm used in his conspiracy against self-understanding was to choose entourage members whose own personalities tended to confirm his own, rather than to challenge it. As we shall see, these persons fell roughly into three groups: the *forsch,* manly soldiers, who provided Wilhelm with guidelines for his own behavior; the 'weaker' or less forceful men, upon whom Wilhelm could practice being *forsch;* and the artistic and sensitive souls who struck chords of recognition and tenderness within the imperial breast. This constellation of personalities in the entourage had personal and political effects which are the subjects of the next chapters.

When the eccentric Wilhelm acceded to the throne at the age of twenty-nine, he found Court and Cabinet structures which soon would have to accommodate themselves to the demands of his personality. The tense and unsteady balance that the Kaiser maintained between his positive characteristics (intelligence, energy, ambition, interest in the modern world, articulateness) and his negative ones (anxiety, inability to work, impulsiveness, self-delusion, ignorance) challenged these structures. In general the men in the official institutions at Court tried to translate Wilhelm's internal paradoxes into consistent behavior and policy. They tried to protect him from himself and from outside currents which might disrupt his precarious balance. They tried to maximize his kingly qualities and to change or dampen his human frailties. How they did this and with what results depended not only upon Wilhelm, but upon the duties of their office, upon the bureaucratic dynamics internal to it, and upon their own personalities and political opinions. All of the men were the Emperor's choice. Some of them inhabited for years the most important offices of Court and Cabinet and therefore left their indelible impression upon the way in which these offices functioned.

The highest ranking Court official was the Oberstkämmerer (High Chamberlain).[68] The persons actually responsible for running the Court inhabited four other positions, however. The Minister of the Royal House[69] managed Wilhelm's and his family's personal affairs as well as the royal income. These duties kept him out of the public eye. The Oberhof- und Hausmarschall[70] was responsible for the expenditures of the entire Court, Court festivities, ceremonial questions, audiences, trips, management of the seventy-six royal palaces, and the behavior of all five hundred servants. He was assisted in these tasks by the Hofmarschall,[71] who superintended the royal kitchen and its forty cooks, ceremonial matters and invitations during Court affairs, and all of the arrangements for trips and excursions, and by the Hausmarschall,[72] who dealt chiefly with the royal family and its possessions. Of these last three courtiers, one was always on duty. The Oberhof- und Hausmarschall met daily with the Emperor at about 9 a.m. to map out the order of the day. Afterwards he would confer with the Hof- and Hausmarschälle to straighten out the arrangements. On trips, Wilhelm was always accompanied by at least one, and frequently by two, of these people.[73]

The orchestrator of this tangle of positions and jurisdictions was Count August Eulenburg.[74] He was the only courtier to serve during Wilhelm's entire reign. Bismarck once called Eulenburg 'the most intelligent man in Berlin,'[75] an opinion shared by a wide variety of people.[76] Eulenburg was not merely intelligent, he was also experienced and tactful. His ability to handle difficulties was little short of amazing. These qualities made him irreplaceable at Court even though his talents led others to consider him for diplomatic posts and even as a possible chancellor.[77] The only complaint offered against Eulenburg's capacities was that he arranged things at Court so smoothly that it was too easy for Wilhelm to lead his undisciplined and capricious existence.[78]

August Eulenburg was the only Court functionary who had political influence. He used his influence subtly, though constantly, for agrarian–conservative ends. Eulenburg was a confirmed *Bismarckianer*. He worked for a reconciliation of Wilhelm with Otto von Bismarck[79] and for an end to the New Course,[80] the relatively pro-industrial, progressive policies of Bismarck's successor, Chancellor Leo von Caprivi[81] and his ministers, Adolf Frhr Marschall von Bieberstein (Foreign Secretary),[82] Artur Graf von Posadowsky-Wehner (Interior)[83] and Karl Heinrich von Bötticher (Vice Chancellor).[84] These policies included some social legislation for the working class and low tariffs on agricultural products.[85] While low tariffs encouraged trade and made food cheaper, they also hurt the economic position of the Junkers, who quickly became steadfast enemies of both the New Course and its authors. August Eulenburg was pleased when Bernhard von Bülow took over the reins of government. Bülow raised tariffs, although not enough to satisfy the most rabid Junkers on the land. Both Bülow's and August Eulenburg's politics in this matter were characteristic of the right-wing bureaucracy, not of either the agrarian or industrialist pressure groups.[86] Wilhelm told Philipp Eulenburg that his cousin August had been lobbying for the Bülow tariffs incessantly for six months, though Wilhelm claimed to have ignored these pressures.[87] Hutten-Czapski writes that Eulenburg intervened on Bülow's side in other ways up to 1909.[88] Max von Mutius was another observer of Eulenburg's influence. Mutius was a first cousin of Chancellor Bethmann Hollweg and an aide-de-camp [FAD] from 1910 to 1915 and thus was in a good position to watch August Eulenburg at work. According to Mutius, Eulenburg was the only non-Cabinet, non-ministerial person to whom Wilhelm turned for political advice. He also writes that Bethmann Hollweg consulted the Oberhof- und Hausmarschall as well.[89] Unfortunately neither Mutius nor Hutten-Czapski tells us anything further about these matters.

Unlike other irresponsible advisers, August Eulenburg never became the target of public criticism before the war for his covert political activities. This was due partly to his undeniable intelligence and tact, and partly to the fact that, despite his conservative views, he was never fanatical. Further, it did not appear that August Eulenburg used his position to shut Wilhelm off from outside influences or to topple personal enemies.[90] Nonetheless, he was not above advancing himself and his brother, Botho.

Eulenburg's predecessor was Eduard von Liebenau, who had come to Crown Prince Friedrich's attention when Liebenau was serving as chief of the prestigious *Leibkompagnie*. The Crown Prince appointed Liebenau Hofmarschall to young Prince Wilhelm. When Wilhelm became Kaiser, Liebenau became Oberhof- und Hausmarschall, passing over August Eulenburg, who had been Hof- und Hausmarschall under Kaiser Friedrich III and who continued to serve Wilhelm II in the first two years of his reign as Vize Oberzeremonienmeister (Vice

Chief Master of Ceremony). Eulenburg lost no time in trying to unseat his rival. This was not an easy task, because Liebenau enjoyed intimate relations with the Bismarcks, cordial ones with Holstein[91] and the complete trust of the Kaiserin.[92] Eulenburg brought in two big guns to help him: his cousin Philipp Eulenburg, the Kaiser's closest friend, and General Alfred von Waldersee,[93] who longed to remove Liebenau, because 'he serves at the same time and even more [than the Kaiser] the house of Bismarck and is therefore a traitor.'[94] These three intrigued for months before Liebenau finally fell in the summer of 1890.[95] It was precisely his identification with the Bismarcks which hastened his fall once Bismarck himself had departed. Liebenau's end was also helped along by his venomous personality, which alienated scores of people, including the House Minister, with whom he had to collaborate closely.[96] Eulenburg may have won the Oberhof- und Hausmarschall post through intrigue, but he kept it through talent; he was in fact a much better Court manager than Liebenau had been.[97] After 1890, Eulenburg never again conspired on his own behalf. He did, however, push hard (unsuccessfully) to secure the chancellorship for his brother, Botho. All the same, nepotism was not his motive. Conservatism was. It was the red–white–black thread uniting all of August Eulenburg's covert interventions into politics.

The war brought out the latent extremism in Eulenburg's conservative *Weltanschauung*. He did not support the moderate Bethmann. Unlike many of the anti-Bethmann fronde, Eulenburg was uncomfortable with the thought of Bernhard von Bülow as Bethmann Hollweg's successor, because he feared Bülow would relinquish Poland and Courland in an effort to reach a separate peace with Russia.[98] August Eulenburg reluctantly embraced Bülow's candidature in 1917.[99] The extent of his opposition to Bethmann Hollweg is clear from the lengths to which he went in order to scotch the Prussian electoral reform[100] and to remove Bethmann's major supporter in the entourage, Civil Cabinet Chief Rudolf von Valentini.[101] Finally, Eulenburg was one of the few genuinely well informed persons who refused to counsel Wilhelm to abdicate in October/November 1918. As late as 7 November, Eulenburg told Admiral Georg von Müller (who favored abdication) that he could not ask Wilhelm to do this, especially since Wilhelm had been so cheered by his recent trip to the front.[102] Chancellor Max von Baden, who also tried to persuade Eulenburg to intercede with Wilhelm on behalf of abdication, received the impression that Eulenburg thought that abdication was unavoidable, but that the monarchical cause would best be served by waiting until the Allies forced Wilhelm out. This would be an honorable exit and would play on xenophobic sentiment to win support for the monarchists.[103]

Admiral von Müller felt that Eulenburg's political vision had been dimmed by staying 'too long in Court life.'[104] Reischach had noticed similar signs in 1908.[105] But Eulenburg had spent the war not in the isolated General Headquarters, but in Berlin, where the bad effects of war could not be overlooked. Eulenburg's wartime advice was perfectly consistent with the political line that he had advocated since 1888. It was only during the war, however, that the utter bankruptcy of such policies became so glaring.

In addition to the Court functionaries over whom August Eulenburg presided, there were the companions to the Empress.[106] Ernst Frhr von Mirbach (1844–1925), the Oberhofmeister, was the highest ranking man, but he was completely overshadowed by the three women whom Berlin termed the 'Hallelujah-Aunts.' They were Oberhofmeisterin Therese Gräfin von Brockdorff (1846–1924), and the two Hofstaatsdamen, Mathilde Gräfin von Keller (1853–1946), and Claire von Gersdorff (1858–1926). All three were 'conservative, agrarian and strictly evangelical,'[107] and thus mirrored Auguste Viktoria's politics exactly. And all three got on Wilhelm's nerves. While he teased Gersdorff, who tended to be naively silly, he could only become angry at Brockdorff, who tended more toward ferocity.[108] The three women served Auguste Viktoria devotedly throughout her married life. Permanent fixtures at Court, Brockdorff, Keller, and Gersdorff strongly reinforced the airless stodginess and narrow conservatism from which the Kaiserin never emancipated herself and which weighed so heavily upon the rest of the entourage and upon the Kaiser. Ambassador Karl Treutler, in an effort to be sympathetic to Auguste Viktoria's entourage, described them in this way: 'They did innumerable good works, and if they were perhaps not very young, not very elegant, not overly intelligent, and not very modern, this was all compensated for in that they gave their all in the service of their mistress and shielded the Court from any not quite correct note.'[109]

The Cabinets were the other archaic institution that Wilhelm inherited in 1888. The Cabinet chiefs had their origin in the monarch's house government as his personal servants and go-betweens. Several reforming efforts failed to subjugate the Cabinets to the power of the Staatsministerium.[110] They remained outside the constitution, monuments to unbridled monarchical power. To the older Military and Civil Cabinets, Wilhelm added the Naval Cabinet.[111] These three institutions were supposed to provide the bureaucratic link between the King-Emperor and his armed services and civil administration. Their two major tasks were (1) to transmit, explain, and complete reports from the services or administration to Wilhelm and his orders back to them; and (2) to choose the personnel who staffed the officer corps and bureaucracy.[112] Officials whose reports were being handled or mishandled by the Cabinets could only complain. They could in no way effect a change in the proceedings since the Cabinets were responsible only to Wilhelm, not to the chancellor, the Reichstag or to any other body. Furthermore, the Cabinet chiefs met with Wilhelm several times each week, usually alone. Ministers (except the war minister and the head of the Imperial Navy Office [Reichsmarineamt – RMA]) were lucky to see the Emperor once a year, and then always in the presence of the Civil Cabinet chief.

Obviously the Cabinet chiefs held considerable potential power. This potential had a greater chance of becoming actual under three conditions: (1) when Wilhelm did not work hard and therefore depended upon the facts which the Cabinet chief presented; (2) when Wilhelm had no opinion of his own; and (3) when opposing views of other institutions were not reaching Wilhelm. Since conditions 1 and 3 frequently obtained, it is no wonder that contemporaries complained so vociferously about the illicit influence of the Cabinets. Chapters 8 and 9 below examine the extent to which this was true for the Military and Naval Cabinets and for the Civil Cabinet after 1908.

The putative activities of the Civil Cabinet before 1908 were the subject of much speculation at the time. This was not surprising, since the Civil Cabinet chief sat like a spider, monitoring the entire web of non-military matters that required the Emperor's attention. These matters included everything pertaining to

filling of offices, bestowing of titles and honors, pardoning of guilty persons, granting of funds from the state or from the all-highest [i.e. the Emperor's] treasury, suggestions for laws or bills to be voted upon by the law-giving bodies [Reichstag and Bundesrat] and the execution of laws and ordinances, and finally also the matters of the royal family and the court administration.[113]

From this lengthy list the chancellor had managed to exempt only the political and personnel affairs of the imperial and the Prussian foreign offices and the personnel of the State Secretariats.[114]

Wilhelm's first Civil Cabinet Chief, Hermann von Lucanus,[115] worked for twenty years in the post. He had perfected his considerable bureaucratic skills in the Prussian Ministry of Culture, where he served equally well five ministers with very different policies. Despite his administrative abilities, public opinion in the 1890s held a dim view of Lucanus. He was thought responsible for dismissing chancellors and ministers because it was his job to deliver the 'blue letters' which spelled their doom.[116] Lucanus' evil reputation was heightened by the number of his enemies. Otto von Bismarck thought that Lucanus had helped to topple him.[117] Bismarck's larger-than-life hatred was echoed on a smaller scale by the numerous members of the 'fronde' and by the military entourage, which idolized the first chancellor.[118] The men of the New Course were no more kindly disposed to Lucanus – not surprisingly, since by 1897 he was vigorously involved in the efforts to unseat them all.[119] The Cabinet chief, the son of an apothecary, was never accepted by the upper nobility, either. A witness reported how Lucanus had fallen from his horse during a hunt and had to be carried from the field. His fall was greeted by the *Jagdgesellschaft* 'with more amusement than regret.'[120]

Lucanus' actual political role is difficult to disentangle from the web of rumors and insinuations. He burned his papers,[121] and the official *Akten* of the Civil Cabinet do not disclose his part in decision making.[122] We can learn something from the fact that the rumors of Lucanus' power reached their height in 1897 and declined thereafter. By Lucanus' death in 1908, one merely heard that Wilhelm had frequently consulted him in matters outside the jurisdiction of the Civil Cabinet, but that Lucanus 'was generally reckoned a conscientious and dutiful official.'[123] Lucanus' zenith had indeed occurred in 1897, because the power of the chancellor and the secretary of the Foreign Office was then at its nadir. Philipp Eulenburg, Bülow, and Wilhelm were preparing to end the New Course by a sharp tack to the right in personnel and policies.[124] Lucanus aided them because his conservatism was as pronounced as their own.[125] He favored the fiscal policies of Johannes von Miquel[126] and Alfred von Tirpitz's large naval plans.[127] Lucanus was even a little to the right of Eulenburg in his candidate for chancellor (Botho Eulenburg), but he soon made his peace with Bernhard von Bülow, who faithfully pursued the proper conservative course.[128] Once Bülow had taken over, Lucanus no longer found himself opposed to the *Reichsleitung*. For the remainder of his term, he 'achieved great services' for Bülow.[129]

Lucanus' isolation before 1897 explains why the rumors never accused him of advancing favorites; he had none. Lucanus was completely devoted to Wilhelm. Most of his administration was consumed not by intrigues, but by smoothing over Wilhelm's mistakes.[130] As he had no favorites, Lucanus also had no independent policy. He was a consummate bureaucrat who merely tried to put Wilhelm's ideas into effect. His actions against State Secretary Marschall and Admiral Friedrich Hollmann and for Miquel and Tirpitz were exactly what Wilhelm wanted.

Lucanus' loyalty to Wilhelm had one other effect which was typical of the entourage. It moved Lucanus to try assiduously to placate the Kaiser's feelings, to let him have his way on small matters so that Lucanus' equity could then be used to advantage in large questions.[131] It was, however, not always easy to tell which problems were large and which small, just as it was not always easy to break the pattern of compliance. After nine years' service under the difficult Kaiser, Lucanus was reduced to an even more submissive posture than Bernhard von Bülow, the notorious flatterer, had been when he was preparing to become chancellor. Bülow began his tenure as Secretary of the Foreign Office by trying to rein in Wilhelm's oratorical flights, at least in their printed, public versions. Lucanus was appalled.

'For God's sake, don't start right out upsetting the Kaiser. Where will that lead?' [Lucanus asked Bülow.] I [Bülow] kept silent, since this was the first experience of its kind, but I decided in future to keep a more alert eye on the Kaiser.[132]

For his successor, Lucanus carefully groomed Rudolf von Valentini.[133] Valentini came from a long line of bourgeois scholars, one of whom followed accepted seventeenth-century practice by latinizing his German name, Velten, into Valentinus, which eventually became Valentini. At the beginning of the next century, one of the Valentinis, a doctor, became ennobled. Thereafter most of the family pursued military careers more in keeping with its new status. Rudolf Valentini's father, too, was an officer, but resigned his commission early to devote himself to agriculture. He was also a Progressive representative in the Prussian House of Deputies, but gradually aligned himself with the agrarian–conservative supporters of Bismarck. His son followed him in espousing conservative politics.[134]

Rudolf Valentini, an excellent student, entered the Prussian civil service in 1879 as a jurist. He later transferred to administration where he made such a name for himself as Landrat of Hameln (Hannover, 1888–99) that the minister of the interior asked him to assist Lucanus in the Civil Cabinet. Because he did not relish the restrictions of Court life, Valentini only reluctantly accepted this post, hoping it would soon lead to higher positions in the civil administration.[135] Unfortunately for these plans, he soon became indispensable as the obvious successor to the aged and ailing Lucanus. Lucanus recognized in his young associate an efficient and meticulous bureaucrat like himself. Indeed, Valentini's devotion to duty was extraordinary. As he prepared himself in 1907 to become Civil Cabinet chief, he noted some guidelines for his future office.

You must quit all other activities, interests and hobbies, just as if you were entering a monastery [he wrote to himself]. You will cement your position if you make yourself objectively *indispensable*. You must always be perfectly informed about everything which comes up, [you must] be oriented about personnel, [you must] be informed on trips (about historical points of interest, etc). To do this requires much work and careful preparation.[136]

Valentini's zealous attention to duty earned him the respect even of those who disagreed with him.[137]

Lucanus carefully schooled Valentini to regard the Civil Cabinet chief strictly as the mediator between the Kaiser and his chancellor, ministers and bureaucracy. This injunction was doubtless congenial to the career bureaucrat, who, in any case, obeyed it until his dismissal in January 1918. Lucanus' modest view of the task of the Civil Cabinet acted as a brake to his and his successor's independent political influence, but it also placed the Civil Cabinet firmly on the side of the civilian policy makers. This was true even though the chancellor played no role in selecting Civil Cabinet officials. Valentini, through his tireless mediation efforts, developed into Chancellor Bethmann Hollweg's most important spokesman in the entourage. His toil on behalf of civilian policy was particularly crucial during the war and earned him the undying enmity of the military conspirators in the German High Command.[138]

The chief of the Civil Cabinet was always something of an anomaly because he was one of the few civilians around the Kaiser. Of the persons who served at Court for two years or more, Egloffstein, August Eulenburg, Gontard, Maximilian Lyncker, and Reischach were all military men who transferred into the Court. Only Wedel-Piesdorf and Zedlitz-Trützschler were unconnected with the officer corps. Even Auguste Viktoria's entourage was heavily military; Mirbach was an officer and both Brockdorff and Gersdorff were the daughters of officers. When, either through illness or vacation, Court positions became temporarily open, they were routinely filled by substitutes from the army.[139]

Besides the Court functionaries and Cabinets, which were military enough, there was the actual 'military retinue' (*Militärisches Gefolge*). This consisted of those who were on permanent duty with the Kaiser, the Hauptquartier (HQ), and those who, although they were adjutants of one rank or another, were stationed elsewhere in other positions.[140] A Commandant[141] headed the Hauptquartier and directed the young adjutants, the Flügeladjutanten zum Dienst (FADs), who performed personal service for Wilhelm. They were the Cerberuses at the gate past whom one had to pass to reach the Kaiser.[142] The ubiquitous FAD was the epitome of the Court's military character.[143]

When Wilhelm became Kaiser in 1888, he patterned his daily routine after that of his beloved grandfather, Wilhelm I.[144] Kaiser Wilhelm I, while hardly the 'Wilhelm the Great' whom his grandson idolized,[145] was nonetheless a diligent, sober, and unostentatious sovereign. The old man arose at 8 a.m., had his coffee at a small table where he often was already working. On Mondays, Wednesdays, and Saturdays promptly at 11 the Civil Cabinet chief began his personal report [*Immediatvortrag*]. It lasted between one and one and a half hours. The *Vortrag* of the Military Cabinet chief, Tuesdays, Thursdays, and Saturdays, usually lasted about two hours. At one o'clock Wilhelm I had a warm meal, to which he devoted little attention. The afternoon mixed audiences and work with a ride in an open carriage. In the late afternoon Wilhelm I would have dinner alone with his wife and afterwards would often go to the theater from which he would return at about 9 p.m. A handful of men, usually officers, but now and again a scholar, would join the Emperor and Empress in non-controversial conversation until 11 p.m., when everyone retired. Wilhelm I seldom deviated from this schedule. His year was divided by four events, all of them military: the spring parade in Potsdam, the autumn parade at the Tempelhof field,[146] the annual spring troop reviews, and the fall maneuvers. Even Wilhelm I's advanced age changed the rhythm of his life only slightly. Out of concern for his health, his Civil Cabinet chief cut back his weekly *Vorträge* from three to two.[147]

Wilhelm II kept his grandfather's routine but, as might befit a man sixty years younger, added to it. Significantly Wilhelm never restored the third Civil Cabinet *Vortrag*. Instead he added three military reports, one each for the chief of the Military Cabinet (Tuesday), the War Minister (Thursday), and the chief of the General Staff (Saturday).[148] Gradually, two more joined this list until Wilhelm's official schedule became: Monday – Civil Cabinet; Tuesday – chief of the Admiralty and the Military Cabinet; Wednesday – Civil Cabinet; Thursday – War Minister and Military Cabinet; Friday – free; Saturday – Naval Cabinet, Imperial Navy Office, chief of the General Staff, and Military Cabinet.[149] The chancellor and ministers (except the War Minister and Naval Office head) were received irregularly. Bernhard von Bülow met with Wilhelm almost daily from 1897 to 1909. Other chancellors and heads of the Foreign Office averaged once or twice a week, ministers once or twice a year. In addition to the *Immediatvorträge*, Wilhelm received military reports (*Militärische Meldungen*) twice a week and granted audiences daily. These activities were squeezed into the minutes before the midday meal.

Had Wilhelm followed this schedule he would have been a very busy man indeed. During the first months of his reign he made the effort, but could not sustain it. By the time Caprivi became chancellor, Wilhelm's actual working day bore only a faint resemblance to its Platonic Ideal. Caprivi complained that

service is made materially more difficult by His Majesty's schedule [*Taseseinteilung*] which undertakes too much and too many different things. Under Kaiser Wilhelm I each Minister had his fixed *Vortrags*-day and His Majesty himself took care of written reports with the greatest punctuality. Now there is no rule. The *Vorträge* are fewer and take place at the most unbelievable times. The written reports are taken care of now and again by adjutants and remain unfinished for long periods of time.[150]

Lieutenant von Müller (later chief of the Naval Cabinet) noticed in 1890/1 that Wilhelm spent less and less time on *Vorträge*. Although he was cordial to the *Vortragender* and asked intelligent questions, he never ceased fiddling with objects on his desk or pressing his officials to make their reports even shorter. At the same time, Wilhelm was fatally attracted to details, and thereby made reports needlessly long.[151] Wilhelm's improvisational lifestyle meant that *Vorträge* were often cancelled at the last moment and rescheduled, frequently to take place in a train, boat or car while Wilhelm was travelling. Friedrich von Holstein was one of many who felt that official reports given under such conditions were 'mostly not very thorough.'[152] Permanent *Vortragende* became inured to such proceedings.[153] Postponed *Vorträge* were just as often crammed into other days. The usual victim of this was the Civil Cabinet chief who repeatedly found himself squeezed into Saturday mornings along with the four others whose regular day that was.[154] By 1910 Hofmarschall Zedlitz-Trützschler reported that the Civil Cabinet chief 'for weeks at a time has the greatest difficulty being heard once [a week].'[155]

What did Wilhelm do with the time he spent not working? In 1888 Wilhelm's day looked much like his grandfather's. He awoke an hour or more earlier, however, and went riding with the FADs, sometimes for as long as two hours. After breakfast he worked until 1.15 when lunch was served. Wilhelm was as indifferent to this activity as Wilhelm I had been. Since Wilhelm did not eat much either at 'second breakfast' or lunch, he filled this time by talking.[156] In the afternoon Wilhelm had audiences, paid visits, went to museums, perhaps did more work, and always took a long walk, usually with his wife. After dinner, the royal couple would entertain a small group of people, often family, until eleven.

It was not long before afternoon activities (visiting exhibitions or artists' ateliers, greeting famous persons) began to creep into the morning hours. The rides, walks, and meals lengthened. Waldersee observed in 1890 that Wilhelm

no longer has the slightest desire to work. Distractions, whether it's playing games with the Army, or more likely the Navy, trips or hunting, these are the things most important to him. . . . It is truly scandalous how the Court Reports [in the newspaper] fool the public about Wilhelm's activity. According to them he is busy working from dawn to dusk.[157]

No wonder, since the FADs were the authors of the Court Reports. By 1910 this process had gone so far that Wilhelm was

arising between 9 and 10 a.m., having a rich, warm, three-course breakfast; then comes a ride, a short walk, perhaps with the Chancellor or Foreign Secretary. At twelve noon there are *Vorträge,* around one, lunch, then another little trip, then a one- to two-hour nap. Dinner is around eight, followed by guests or theater. In either case, conversation goes until twelve or one o'clock in the morning.[158]

Even this truncated schedule only applied consistently to three and a half to four months out of the year. Travels consumed the rest. Wilhelm's peripatetic habits sparked much speculation about how much time the Kaiser actually spent in Berlin. Were one to discount Potsdam, this amount would be quite small, since Wilhelm only lived in Berlin from 1 January to the end of May. Otherwise, Potsdam, forty minutes by train from Berlin, was his official residence. Although this short trip was not especially convenient for the *Vortragende,* it did not stand in the way of the business routine, particularly since Wilhelm often travelled back and forth himself. In his first six months as Emperor, Wilhelm spent a career high of 65 percent of his year in Berlin or Potsdam. For the next five years, he averaged 60 percent. Beginning in 1894, Wilhelm settled into the pattern he retained until the war: he was present in Berlin or Potsdam less than half the year, or 47 percent of the time. During the war, the Kaiser insisted upon residing at Supreme Headquarters, which was never located in Berlin. As a result, Wilhelm was in the capital for only ten months out of four and one-quarter years (that is, 20 percent of the war).

Despite Wilhelm's peregrinations his year ran regularly. On New

Year's Day the royal family moved to Berlin for the *Saison*. Wilhelm rarely left the capital in January, and February was punctuated by one-, two- or three-day jaunts to Wilhelmshaven, where Wilhelm swore in the naval recruits. After 1897 this duty was pushed into March and replaced by a week's vacation at the royal hunting estate in Hubertus- stock, Mark Brandenburg. The last half of March and April became increasingly reserved for long trips to Italy (1893, 1894, 1896), the Mediterranean (1904, 1905), and Corfu (1908, 1909, 1911, 1912, 1914).

Wilhelm purchased the estate Achilleion on the island of Corfu in 1907. Renovation and furnishings cost almost 600,000 Marks, while the yearly upkeep was 50,000.[159] In addition were the travelling costs for one hundred servants, officials, and guests, plus five automobiles. This extravagance was too much for Hausminister Wedel-Piesdorf, who quit his position in protest.[160] The purchase turned out to be a great mistake. Except for natural beauty, Corfu offered only one diversion: the archeological excavation of a ruined temple. After the novelty wore off, boredom and frustration set in, especially for the entourage, most of whom were considerably less interested in archeology than Wilhelm was. Fürstenberg recorded that the 'mood was bad' already in 1908.[161]

Wilhelm's trips typically froze after the first occasion, the guests and the activities remaining almost exactly the same regardless of how many times the experience was repeated. Corfu usually consisted of Auguste Viktoria, Viktoria-Luise, and August Wilhelm (and suites), the three Cabinet chiefs, Frhr von Rücker-Jenisch (representing the Foreign Office), August Eulenburg, Plessen, two FADs, and Wil- helm's doctor. The guest list was short: Hofprediger Georg Göns,[162] Wilhelm's good friend Max Egon Fürst zu Fürstenberg, and seascape artist Willy Stöwer,[163] who was replaced by another seascape artist, Hans Bohrdt,[164] in 1914. 'Each day passes completely routinely, one just like another,' wrote Plessen.[165] Admiral Müller finally stopped recording in his diary: 'It didn't pay to make any entries whatsoever, life was too dull [*stumpfsinnig*]. The Kaiser's ruthlessness and egoism lay like an alp on everybody. These characteristics were only sur- passed [in their ill effect] by his avoidance of hard work.'[166] Twice a week the arrival of the courier (three days out of Berlin) forced Wil- helm to work. This method of governance was not only inadequate, it was expensive. The Naval Cabinet alone spent 183 Marks on tele- grams while on Corfu in 1908.[167] Otherwise, Wilhelm 'concentrate[d] his life on the excavation of the miserable temple ruins and demand[ed] that his entourage do the same. No one does this from inward motivation, and only a few adhere to the outward appearance of doing so.'[168] Wilhelm chafed at his wife's presence and 'treated her worse' than usual.[169] The imperial clouds made even Fürstenberg's sunny disposition gloomy, and he longed for home.[170]

Wilhelm devoted the rest of April and over half of May to a series of visits to Alsace-Lorraine, Karlsruhe, the theater in Wiesbaden, the estate of Wilhelm's friend, the ruling count and sculptor Emil Graf Schlitz gen. Görtz,[171] and finally to the Dohna's hunting lodge at Prökelwitz, in East Prussia. Wilhelm returned to Berlin in time to take up official residence in Potsdam for the spring parade. Two weeks later he was off to Kiel Week, the international yacht races.

Every year the international jet-set, or in this case yachting set, met at Kiel, ostensibly to see the races, actually to see and be seen themselves. Kiel Week had a heavy Anglo-American accent, since, until Wilhelm II, Germany had been a nation of landlubbers. Wilhelm's love for yachting was an inheritance from his English relatives. It cost him dearly: in money (6,079,384.51 Marks total to 1914);[172] in self-confidence (Wilhelm seldom won the races and was often seasick); and in respect from his entourage (who found the enterprise foreign and shockingly bourgeois). In 1904 Wilhelm's close friend Axel von Varnbüler, who was also Württemberg's representative to Berlin, reported his acidulous observations of Kiel Week.

Yachting [he began] is an expensive amusement. Those German castes [*Ständen*] in which one could find suitable people, passion, nerve, and muscles for such a masculine sport lack financial means. High finance, big business, and heavy industry have to be included in order to defray the expenses for the docks, clubs, and lodgings (where just now the memorial to its builder, Krupp, is being unveiled), and to bring the requisite number of German ships to the starting line. That is, those ships which sail under German flag, because the ships themselves are mostly built in America or England and are manned by English captains and crews. Meanwhile, their owners, like Krupp, [Albert] Ballin,[173] [Carl Frhr von] Stumm[-Halberg],[174] [Adolf von] Hansemann,[175] [Hugo Graf von] Douglas,[176] [Friedrich von] Friedländer[-Fuld],[177] etc., make sure that they do not lie wet to the skin ... in narrow boats threatened by breaking masts. It is not the sport that draws them here, but the social position, the indirect business advantage, the favor of the Kaiser, which they hope to win. Thus in this Regatta week, Kiel harbor becomes an arena less for fresh and happy competition of seamen's strength and skill, than for social climbing [*Strebertum*], pushy snobbism, and international sport fanaticism [*Sportfexerei*].[178]

Varnbüler then proceeded to a lengthy display of disdainful anti-Semitism directed at Ballin, who acted as host for the Regatta.

1 Wilhelm II and his companions on the *Nordlandreise,* 1905. The inscription 'Prosit Neujahr, 1905' is in Wilhelm's hand, and the card was sent to Fürstenberg.

Admiral Tirpitz's disgust was less wordy than Varnbüler's, but just as typical. 'Kiel Week was dreadful as usual. The worst parts can't be set to paper.'[179]

When Wilhelm had finished visiting with the rich British and Americans, he departed for his month-long cruise along the Norwegian coast, the *Nordlandreise.* This tradition began in 1889 and was only ended by war. The original guests were divided between a military and an artistic party. The former consisted of Adjutants Gustav von Kessel, Friedrich Scholl, the younger Helmuth von Moltke, Dietrich von Hülsen-Haeseler, Karl Ferdinand von Grumme, Hans Boehn, Hausmarschall General Max von Lyncker, and Naval Cabinet Chief Gustav von Senden-Bibran. Art, music, and conversation were safeguarded by Philipp Eulenburg, Kuno Moltke (who later became FA), Professor Paul Güssfeldt,[180] painter Carl Saltzmann,[181] Georg von Hülsen, and Emil Görtz. In later years Albert von Schleswig-Holstein[182] and Prince August Sayn-Wittgenstein[183] joined as regular voyagers, together with a host of one- or two-time guests.[184]

The *Nordlandreise* was originally designed to help Wilhelm recover from the strain of politics and Court etiquette. Work was therefore deliberately deemphasized. The Civil Cabinet chief was never aboard, and some years even the Military Cabinet chief was represented by one of the guests.[185] The communication problem was knotty, since the imperial yacht lay for days in isolated fjords. Political work was coordinated by the various representatives of the Foreign Office: Philipp Eulenburg, Alfred von Kiderlen-Wächter, Heinrich von Tschirschky-Bögendorff, and Karl Treutler.

The tone of the *Nordlandreise* befitted Wilhelm's idea of comfort. Etiquette was relaxed, so that juvenile behavior became the order of the day.[186] Wilhelm indulged in practical jokes, while his shipmates attempted to amuse him by storytelling, musical performances, and outlandish theatrical productions. After illness removed Eulenburg from the company in 1903, music and theater were replaced by cards and games. But these efforts were to no avail. Wilhelm generally returned to Wilhelmshaven more tired and nervous than when he had left. 'His Majesty is physically and mentally upset by the long voyage, diet and exhaustion of different kinds. . . . [Wilhelm's doctor] says that it is crazy to make the *Nordlandreise* longer than three weeks. It harms His Majesty more than it helps him.'[187]

The entourage suffered more than Wilhelm did. It was impossible to keep the restless and insatiable Kaiser happy. Since the guest list remained virtually unchanged, one became quickly bored. One participant felt as though he had been imprisoned in 'a petrified circle.'[188] The daily routine and even the itinerary were as petrified as the guest list, and even the beautiful surroundings could not revive flagging spirits. The rampant guards' lieutenant juvenility was not to everyone's taste either. Admiral von Senden-Bibran tried to get older men invited to prevent youthful high jinks,[189] while Helmuth von Moltke was relieved to find in 1908 that the mood was 'not so stupidly silly as usual.'[190] The *Nordlandreise* made Eulenburg so nervous that, upon returning, he hastened to his own vacation to recover from Wilhelm's.

Wilhelm himself did not return to Potsdam. From 1888 to 1895 he sailed instead to Cowes, England, for the yacht races there. After 1895 Wilhelm spent most of August at the imperial residence in Wilhelmshöhe. The Kaiser and family left this retreat in time for the huge military parade at the Tempelhof Field in Berlin in early September. From there he rushed off to the army and navy maneuvers, which lasted two weeks. When these ended he headed for the hunting lodges, Rominten, Hubertusstock, Cadinen, and Prökelwitz, where he frequently stayed a week or two into October. Auguste Viktoria often, but not always, accompanied him. From 15 June to 7 October Wilhelm averaged twelve days in Berlin/Potsdam.

Rominten, Prökelwitz, and Hubertusstock were very different from Wilhelm's other retreats. They were the only places which actually offered him rest. Prökelwitz was the East Prussian hunting estate owned by Richard Graf (later Fürst) zu Dohna-Schlobitten. Here in 1886 Wilhelm first met Philipp Eulenburg, and here every year in May/June the two friends would relive the beginning of their friendship, along with Dohna, his brother Eberhard, Wilhelm's doctor, and FAD Kessel. Admiral Friedrich (von) Hollmann later joined the circle.[191] This small group met again in September/October at Wilhelm's two East Prussian estates. Auguste Viktoria would sometimes come for part of these trips, in which case the salutory effect was often lost. Rominten, Hubertusstock, and Prökelwitz helped Wilhelm because he had no one before whom he had to perform: no women to demand solicitude or propriety, no military phalanx to demand toughness, no cheering crowds. Wilhelm arose early, devoted himself to hunting, worked little, retired early, and repeated the cycle the next day. Social intercourse occurred only at meals, and even that was truncated.[192] This was just what Wilhelm needed, for it is the only time during his reign when he could be described as 'completely human.'[193]

Cabinet chiefs and ministers commuted from Berlin. The most important naval questions of the year – building schedules and ship types – were always decided at Rominten. But even *Vorträge* were not permitted to disturb Wilhelm's hunting. As on the *Nordlandreise,* Eulenburg managed politics while Wilhelm played. After Eulenburg's fall, Rominten/Hubertusstock became not quite the intimate experience that it had been before. Hofmarschall Zedlitz-Trützschler, August Eulenburg, the Cabinet chiefs, and one or two FADs increased the crowd, while Auguste Viktoria and assorted royal children made it more of a family experience. We would not be wrong in guessing that Wilhelm regretted this turn of events.

Wilhelm usually spent the rest of October in Berlin or Potsdam. The Kaiser fragmented November with the official Court hunts, his annual visit to Philipp Eulenburg's estate, Liebenberg,[194] two- and three-day hunting excursions to Silesia, and, after 1905, trips to Donaueschingen, the German estate of Max Egon Fürst zu Fürstenberg.[195] The Court hunts were gigantic affairs, often with thirty guests, drawn from the upper-level bureaucracy, generals, and diplomats, as well as the highest ranking members of the entourage. These persons met at the imperial hunting preserves at Letzlingen, Göhrde, Springe, and Königswusterhausen, where they ran through a never varying program designed to dispose of a maximum number of animals in a minimum amount of time. As befitted the stations of the hunters, talk tended to be political, although the large number of guests meant that conversations were often hasty and superficial.[196]

The atmosphere in Silesia was more *gemütlich*. That province harbored an uncharacteristic nobility, which was both extremely wealthy and successfully engaged in capitalist enterprises. These gentlemen took turns hosting the Kaiser, the Eulenburg circle (Philipp Eulenburg, Kuno Moltke, Axel Varnbüler), Emil Görtz, Wilhelm Hohenau, one or two FADs, and each other at their different estates. The most weighty of these magnates were: Guido Graf (Fürst in 1901) Henckel von Donnersmarck (1830–1916) at Neudeck; Franz Hubert Graf von Thiele-Winckler (1857–1922) at Moschen; Christian Kraft Fürst zu Hohenlohe-Oehringen, Herzog von Ujest (1848–1926) at Slawentzitz; Hans Heinrich XV Fürst von Pless (1861–1938) at Pless; Hermann Fürst von Hatzfeldt (1848–1933) at Trachenberg; Mortimer Graf von Tschirschky-Renard (1844–1909) at Gross Strehlitz; Friedrich Fürst zu Solms-Baruth (1853–1920) at Klitschdorf; Viktor Amadeus Prinz zu Hohenlohe-Schillingsfürst, Herzog von Ratibor und Fürst zu Corvey (1847–1923) at Rauden; and Karl Max Prinz (1901 Fürst) von Lichnowsky (1860–1928) at Kuchelna. Three held Court positions: Hohenlohe-Oehringen and Solms-Baruth as Oberstkämmerer, and Hatzfeldt as Oberstschenk. Lichnowsky was Bernhard Bülow's long-time protégé, who crowned his diplomatic career as Germany's ambassador to England from 1912 to 1914. Pless was 'an unimportant man absorbed by appearances,'[197] who put up Wilhelm and the German Headquarters at Pless during the war. Henckel was a late convert to the last Kaiser. At first a staunch Bismarckianer, he joined Herbert von Bismarck behind the scenes of the 1894 *Kladderadatsch* attacks on Wilhelm, his advisers and the New Course. As the infighting intensified, Henckel wanted to withdraw, so Philipp Eulenburg arranged for him to switch sides. So deeply involved was he, however, that it took four years to extricate himself entirely from the Bismarck-fronde.[198] Except for the *Kladderadatsch* Affair, Henckel was noteworthy only for his enormous wealth. The same was true of Thiele-Winckler, who once stocked his estate with 20,000 pheasants for the imperial hunt. Even Wilhelm thought this extravagant. Presumably Thiele's neighbors agreed. Lichnowsky claimed that another imperial visit would drive him into bankruptcy.[199]

Wilhelm enjoyed himself at these gatherings, not merely because

he liked the company of the very well-to-do, but because he felt at ease
with these particular people. Axel Varnbüler reported that these Silesian magnates were

mostly trusted acquaintances, before whom His Majesty could completely let
himself go. He could say anything without danger of misunderstanding or
misuse. This gave a comfortable character to the gathering and reminds one,
despite all the external differences, of the Liebenberg circle, from which several representatives were present.[200]

The difference, of course, was that in Silesia there were 'trusted
acquaintances [*vertraute Bekannte*],' while at Liebenberg there were close
friends. The Silesians were at least one circle removed from the intimacy which bound Wilhelm to the Liebenbergers.

The Silesian hunts often stretched into the first week of December.
Wilhelm spent the rest of the month in Potsdam. The royal family
celebrated Christmas in exactly the same way each year. Seven days
later they moved officially to Berlin, and the cycle began again.

Wilhelm's contemporaries often speculated upon the reasons behind
his incessant travelling. Not a few concluded that he was driven by a
desire to change his surroundings, to meet and converse with new
people.[201] This can hardly have been the case. As we have seen, the
guest lists, itineraries, and activities seldom varied. Wilhelm did not
enjoy seeing new faces, quite the contrary. It was at his insistence that
the same persons were invited on the same trips year after year.[202] As
with people, so with geography. Wilhelm visited the same fjords, castles, islands, *Kasinos,* parks, exhibitions, and dances. He disrupted plans
by arriving at a different time, by staying longer, or leaving sooner,
but never by searching for somewhere new. Wilhelm travelled in order
to find some respite from his constant companion, anxiety. He sought
escape from the things which made him ill with nervousness. The few
places which approximated happiness, ease, or rest for Wilhelm tell
us what these things were: women – especially Wilhelm's wife, family,
and politics or governing (particularly non-military matters). Wilhelm's travelling was an elaborate attempt to control the forces which
threatened his balance. When Wilhelm was away he could avoid the
unexpected by controlling his surroundings. *Vorträge* were fewer and
shorter because they were regulated by Wilhelm's (hunting, visiting,
sailing) schedule, rather than vice versa. Wilhelm did not have to play
the dutiful father, loving husband, or fierce warrior, because there
was no one to impress. He knew exactly what to expect from his
friends. There was no challenge to which Wilhelm had to rise, because
there were no challenges.

Ceremonies offered Wilhelm the same control and therefore the same security.[203] They unfolded with carefully planned precision. He could play the dashing autocrat without preparation, without responsibility, and without consequences. The only surprises came from Wilhelm himself in the form of frequently startling utterances. The time that Wilhelm and his entourage spent on ceremonies was astounding. The Kaiser swore in recruits, dedicated regimental colors, unveiled monuments, launched ships, opened buildings, consecrated churches, reviewed troops, led parades, ate farewell dinners, inaugurated galleries, pinned medals, and performed a hundred other such activities in dizzying succession. This concern for show was severely criticized on two accounts: inflated pomp degraded the historic value of ceremonies, medals, and other monarchical symbols, and was irrelevant to the real tasks of the monarchy.

Symbolic inflation was indeed one of the hallmarks of the Wilhelminian era. Under Wilhelm the Court 'developed . . . a huge luxuriousness,'[204] criticism of which we have already seen on the occasion of Kiel Week. When Wilhelm created a large number of *Fürsten,* for example, the response among the *Hofgesellschaft* was 'laughter, shoulder-shrugging, and a few derisive comments.'[205] Helmuth Moltke was ashamed to have received the Order of the Black Eagle for maneuvers, when Moltke the elder had had to win the Franco-Prussian war to acquire his.[206] Worse, thought Moltke, the obsession with symbols distracted the monarchy from essential duties. It was the folly of weakness.

Next Sunday there will be a large flag-nailing [a military ceremony – see below] at the Zeughaus [in Berlin]. We still seem to think that we can win victory in a life-and-death struggle with a patch of embroidered cloth! We are caught in a dreadfully peaceable frame of mind. It makes me sick when I see this nonsense that makes us completely forget the main thing, which is to prepare ourselves earnestly and with bitter energy for war. And so we deck people with multi-colored ribbons as insignia, which only get in the way of handling the weapons. We encourage ambition through every possible external symbol, instead of developing a sense of duty. Uniforms become more and more flashy instead of camouflaged for war. Maneuvers are now parade-like theatrical productions. Decoration is the order of the day, and behind all this folderol [*Firlefanz*] grins the Gorgon head of war.[207]

Wilhelm encouraged this state of affairs. He constantly tinkered with the uniforms. He forced the entourage to wear them when 'we would have much preferred to wear suits.'[208] He stipulated the speed at which the cavalry was to move at parades.[209] He became indignant upon observing that officers at Court balls were removing their gloves, when it was well known that only after the last dance could the right-hand glove alone be removed.[210]

But Wilhelm's childlike enthusiasm for pomp and circumstance were not, in fact, the source of the weakness that Moltke thought resulted from them. Nor did they serve merely as psychological crutches for Wilhelm. Symbolic trappings, even luxurious display, were not luxuries at all, but necessities, for a monarchy.[211] They were rubrics of self-definition. They legitimized the monarchy through appeals to tradition and stabilized society by cementing hierarchies which determined appropriate behavior. At the apex stood the monarch, to whom all symbols ultimately referred. The perpetuation of rigid, ceremonial symbolism served a twofold propaganda function, vis-à-vis the masses and vis-à-vis the monarch and the ruling elite.

The masses were to be entertained, enlightened, and impressed by public spectacles like parades, national holidays, and monuments. Many were invented by the monarch and by bourgeois civic leaders after 1871 to inculcate 'order and decency,'[212] or as one proponent of the Bismarck statues put it, 'high patriotic sense . . . , noble spirit, joy in self-sacrifice, social harmony, and contentment,' i.e. the virtues of quiet subjects.[213] This was the reason why Wilhelm was imprisoned at his desk, literally for several hours per week, signing orders, commendations, promotions, and so forth. The Cabinets had made several attempts since 1871 to reduce the number of these. The last attempt, in May 1911, specified, for example, that the monarch was only to sign the following medal-patents: the Order of the Black Eagle, Pour le Mérite, the Wilhelm Order, Service Order of the Prussian Crown, the Great Cross, the Order of the Red Eagle First Class, the Crown Order First Class, and the House of Hohenzollern Orders, through the Cross and Eagle of the Commander (of the Order), and the Red Cross Medal First Class.[214] Obviously this was not much of an improvement. Wilhelm's personal signature was retained on so many documents, because 'it actually created a kind of personal union [between] the sovereign' and the recipient.[215]

Wilhelm I had been so anxious to save the recruits from the influence of subversive forces that he began administering the oath to them personally.[216] Wilhelm II continued this practice. The events of Wilhelm's reign clearly added to monarchical unease, for in October 1908 he began distributing his own and the two military chaplains' speeches to each recruit so as to make the greatest possible impression.[217]

The ceremony of consecration and nailing (of battalion colors) combined three motifs typical of Wilhelminian rituals: religion, military honor, and fidelity to the royal family. *Nagelungen* took place when a battalion's old flag had to be rededicated to a new monarch, when it had just replaced its old flag, or when a new battalion with new colors had just been created. The two-part service consisted first of the consecration, a religious act performed by the evangelical chaplain 'in the presence' of his Roman Catholic colleague (as a sop to the South German and Rhenish *Bundesbrüder*). Then followed the *Nagelung*, during which Wilhelm hammered the first nail that held the flag to the staff. Wilhelm was followed by a string of luminaries, who nailed the second nail, the third, and so forth, until the flag was secured or the luminaries exhausted. At one such *Nagelung* on 2 May 1889 Wilhelm was followed by his wife, mother, and grandmother, several imperial sons, numerous princes and princesses of Prussia and then of other states. They performed these duties before the chief of the General Staff, the Commander of the Mark, the war minister, Field Marshall Moltke, the chief of the Military Cabinet, the Commandant of the Hauptquartier, all of the Kaiser's adjutants who were in Berlin, and the Emperor's entourage. The instructions for the ceremony filled ten pages.[218] In other *Nagelungen* the chancellor was also present.

The identification of the monarchy with its military arm had become so strong that the military predominated even at civilian ceremonies. When the Empress dedicated churches the music was usually provided by the local regiment. In fact, the militarization of public celebrations had gone so far that it threatened the original purpose: successful propaganda.[219] Admiral Wolf Graf von Baudissin suggested in 1912 that more civilians, bureaucrats, and notables take part in the forthcoming unveiling of a national monument. His advice was not only accepted but was expanded to include the participation of local organizations and even children's groups.[220]

Despite these efforts, establishment-inspired ceremonies were rigid and lifeless. Like Wilhelm's trips, they duplicated themselves with nary a change. They were 'a bore for the Emperor as well as for his guests.'[221] The only occasion which was any fun for the entourage or the participants was the annual *Krönungs- und Ordensfest*. The recipients of the medals awarded on this occasion were not limited to the nobility, and its format was therefore not so rigid. 'It has the advantage,' remarked one FAD, 'that one can see and speak to people.'[222]

The entourage and its Emperor were unhappily imprisoned in a thicket of formalities, customs, etiquette, and ceremony. Although they chafed at these chains, they were loath to abandon them, because these chains were thought to hold the Empire together. Wilhelm even created new ceremonies or resurrected old ones to strengthen the protective aura surrounding the monarchy.[223] Moltke was, however, correct in noting that the overvaluation of the symbolic was not a sign of strength. The monarchy attempted to do with ceremony what it should have done with politics, namely, integrate large sections of the population comfortably into a stable but changing order. Not only did the propagandistic use of symbols substitute poorly for genuine political solutions, but it was also not without effect on the propagandizers, as we have seen. Ceremonies boosted Wilhelm's sense of self by allowing him to playact. At the same time, they oppressed him by their rigidity and ubiquity, hence he fled to his friends' retreats. Ceremony bored the members of the entourage, while it also fettered them. It locked them into a symbolic world whose every detail signified either order or chaos. It encouraged inflexibility and control mania. It made a sense of proportion exceedingly difficult to maintain. Only an officer's life was more restricted, more rigid, more anxiety-ridden. Since most of the courtiers were officers as well, their lives were doubly straitened.[224]

3

Philipp Eulenburg and the Liebenberg Circle

In the 1890s Philipp Count zu Eulenburg was the most powerful man in the entourage. He was the leader and chief manipulator of the civilian faction of the entourage as it jockeyed with the military men for influence over the Kaiser and over policy. While in the short run Eulenburg managed successfully to outmaneuver the military entourage, he simultaneously set the stage for its final triumph. Thus, Eulenburg's importance reached beyond the years of his own activity.

Eulenburg also differed from any other adviser or member of the entourage because his relationship with Wilhelm was unique. No one was ever closer to the Kaiser. No one was ever in a position to influence him more for better or worse. Eulenburg's career illustrates like no other the limits placed on an imperial adviser by Wilhelm's personality, by the structure of the entourage and its other personnel, by other monarchical institutions like the army or the Staatsministerium and by the attitudes and prejudices of the Wilhelminian nobility, which formed Eulenburg as they did Wilhelm's other advisers.

The twenty-seven-year-old Prince Wilhelm met Eulenburg for the first time in May 1886, while he was hunting at Prökelwitz, the huge, East Prussian estate owned by Richard Dohna-Schlobitten. Wilhelm was accompanied by one Flügeladjutant. Besides Dohna and his brother, Eberhard, Eulenburg was the only guest. He had been invited by his friends the Dohnas in order to entertain the young Prince.

What instantly drew Wilhelm and Eulenburg together was not politics or power, but personality. Each discovered in the other his complement. Each had found a boon companion, soul mate, and friend, who seemed so suitable that the Prökelwitz hunt took on the character of a whirlwind courtship. During the day the five men hunted. In the evening they were entertained by Eulenburg, who accompanied himself on the piano, singing his own ballads, while Wilhelm turned the pages. Wilhelm was so taken with the Count that he induced him to stay longer than Eulenburg had originally planned. In later years,

2 Prince and Princess Philipp zu Eulenburg

Wilhelm would occasionally sign himself 'Hokan,' a character from one of Eulenburg's ballads, 'How They Became Friends.'[1]

At the time, of course, neither Wilhelm nor Eulenburg had an inkling of what was in store for either one of them. Everyone expected Wilhelm's father, Friedrich, to succeed the aged Wilhelm I and to embark on a long and energetic reign. Prince Wilhelm, it was thought, would spend most of his life waiting in the wings as Crown Prince.

Wilhelm's and Eulenburg's friendship was firmly cemented by the time it was discovered that the reign of Wilhelm's father would be drastically cut by cancer and that Wilhelm would shortly accede to the throne. Eulenburg feared that his friendship with the Prince would have to end. 'I am tortured by the thought that the gulf which separates us socially, but which our friendship has bridged, must, with the imperial crown, become ever wider and deeper.'² As it turned out, Eulenburg need not have worried. With the isolation that came with the throne, Wilhelm was more than ever in need of a friend and confidant. In any case, the gulf that separated the two lessened as Wilhelm engineered Eulenburg's diplomatic rise. But more important, the gulf which had once been bridged only by friendship was now also spanned by politics. Eulenburg slowly added the role of adviser to that of friend.

In particular, his intimacy with the Emperor allowed Eulenburg to manipulate personnel appointments and, through them, policy. He made and broke chancellors, ministers, and diplomats. He elevated his own friends, who later were vilified as the 'Liebenberg Round Table,' to positions of influence. The specter of his strength haunted his colleagues, kept them nervously wondering if they were about to become sacrifices to his power. Eulenburg's meteoric rise from third-level diplomat to power broker, however, was excelled only by the suddenness and completeness of his disgrace. In 1907 Eulenburg's enemies were finally able to destroy him. Since his personal relationship to Wilhelm was the foundation of his political power, they made that relationship socially impossible by charging that Eulenburg and a number of his friends were homosexual. These charges precipitated the largest social scandal of the Wilhelminian period. The political reverberations were far-reaching, not only because numerous prominent members of the entourage were banned from Court, but also because it was generally recognized that Eulenburg had merely been used as a lightning rod to deflect criticism actually directed at the Emperor and his policies.

Before going on to discuss Eulenburg's political career, we must examine his own character and the personal relationships that formed the basis for his political importance. This discussion must include Eulenburg's sexual life. There are doubless many persons whose sexual tendencies, in whatever direction, are irrelevant to their careers, their ideas, even to the structure of their social lives. Eulenburg, however, was not one of these. His love of men was the central, shaping impulse of his private and public self. If one ignores or misunderstands this aspect of Eulenburg's character, one will also misinterpret his political activity and importance.

Even Eulenburg's critics were forced to share Wilhelm's appreciation of his friend's abundant good qualities. Eulenburg was an unusually charming, broadly interesting man. He could converse knowledgeably on a variety of subjects in which Wilhelm meddled with enthusiasm and about which the members of his military entourage evinced not the slightest interest. These subjects included painting, sculpture, architecture, theater, music, poetry, opera, history, travel, Nordic culture, and spiritism. Indeed, Eulenburg gave Wilhelm the opportunity to indulge himself in all those areas which were irrelevant to the proper concerns of a Prussian militarist. In addition, Eulenburg was a fine raconteur with a good sense of humor. He was, in marked contrast to most of the persons at Court, amusing. But Wilhelm's attachment to Eulenburg was too strong to be explained merely by Eulenburg's amusement value.

Wilhelm and Eulenburg cemented their friendship very quickly. Wilhelm was immediately attacted to Eulenburg because he found him 'congenial and warm-feeling,' quite unlike the 'flatter[ers] and intrigue[rs]' who usually gravitate to princes.[3] Georg Hinzpeter, Wilhelm's tutor, shared this view. 'You are the first person who loves the Kaiser for his *own* sake,' he commented.[4] Eulenburg's unselfish and uncritical devotion to Wilhelm as a person was so clear that even that ultimate cynic, Holstein, recognized that it was genuine.[5]

Eulenburg became very swiftly the Kaiser's 'bosom friend – the only one I [Wilhelm] have'[6] – the only one he was ever to have. It was Eulenburg's picture that Wilhelm had on his desk at Rominten.[7] It was a volume of Eulenburg's ballads, *Skaldengesänge*, which rested lonely among the naval technica on Wilhelm's bookshelf aboard his yacht, *Meteor*.[8] And most significantly, it was with Eulenburg that Wilhelm wished to be, when he was 'himself,' among his male friends away from official Berlin. Eulenburg was not only the central figure at the exclusive hunts at Prökelwitz and Rominten. He was also *Hauptperson*[9] on the summer *Nordlandreisen*. Eulenburg usually rode beside Wilhelm during their forays on land as well. The two men had adjoining rooms aboard the yacht *Hohenzollern* (and at Rominten),[10] and Eulenburg was usually the last person to see Wilhelm at night and the first to see him in the morning.[11]

A glance at Eulenburg's sociological profile would scarcely have revealed the character who so charmed the Kaiser, for on paper Eulenburg differed little from the majority of the contemporaries of his class. He was born, the eldest of three children, into a branch of one of Prussia's oldest noble families. Despite the fact that numerous Eulenburgs had played significant roles in Prussian history,[12] the family, or at least Philipp's father, was not particularly well-to-do. Not until Eulenburg was eighteen did his mother inherit enough to make them anything more than comfortable.[13] Even with the Hertefeld inheritance and later with his own diplomatic salary, Eulenburg's financial position was never quite adequate to his needs (which included frequent travel and the collection of objects d'art).[14] Eulenburg was better off than most of the other members of the entourage, but still not nearly so wealthy as Wilhelm's Silesian friends. When Wilhelm elevated Eulenburg to the rank of Prince in 1900, everyone agreed that, other considerations aside, Eulenburg was not sufficiently rich to deserve the honor or to be able to maintain the requisite manner of living.[15]

Unlike some of the military members of the entourage, Eulenburg had received a *Gymnasium* education. Although he served several years in the prestigious Garde du Corps, including a stint during the Franco-Prussian war, he soon abandoned the military to pursue a career in the Prussian civil service. To this end he earned a doctorate in law, which turned out to be less useful than the friends he acquired while preparing for it. Eulenburg soon tired of the civil service, however, and switched careers once again, this time to the diplomatic corps, where he was to remain until his retirement in 1902.

The disparity between the spare, Prussian background and the 'idealist and phantast . . . , musician, poet, *Schöngeist*, enthusiast for all things good and beautiful'[16] disturbed contemporaries. This polarity was mirrored in Eulenburg's own feelings about his parents. The father was hard-working, cold, Prussian, businesslike, frugal, distant, unartistic. Father and son eyed each other mistrustfully from opposite sides of a deep chasm. Eulenburg felt his father was narrow and unreasonable. Philipp Konrad Eulenburg, for his part, could barely conceal his disappointment in his son's dilettantish pursuits. 'My good father . . . never wanted to understand me in my individuality and therefore suffered a lot on my account,'[17] Eulenburg later admitted.

By contrast, the person to whom Eulenburg was closest, indeed the one woman in his life, was his mother. Alexandrine Eulenburg was everything Philipp Konrad was not. Warm, understanding, artistically gifted, she was Eulenburg's confidante and solace. She conciliated between the 'father, who stood soberly with his feet on the ground, and the son, whose artistic temperament swung fantastically in the clouds and indulged in extravagant feelings, often of *Weltschmerz*.'[18] It was with her that Eulenburg identified. He attributed his own nervous constitution, artistic sensibilities, indeed his 'whole essence and individuality [*Eigenart*]' to his mother. Throughout his adult life, Eulenburg wrote to her every day. He dropped his official duties in an instant to be at her side when she was ill. His devotion to her was extraordinary even in that age of extraordinary filial piety.[19] When she died in 1902, Eulenburg wrote to the Kaiserin that he was desolate because 'something had bound me to her since early childhood, something which came from heaven and is incomparable with anything else.'[20]

Eulenburg's romanticized view of his mother became his Platonic Ideal of womanhood,

I also have a selfless mother [he once wrote to Herbert von Bismarck], who only lives for her children and I hang on to her with the same love which you do to yours. . . . What greatness lies in the self-sacrifice, in the selflessness of such a woman! We have both truly understood through the examples of our mothers, what a female character is and should be. How false it is to search for the character of a woman in *energetic* demeanor.[21]

Most of Eulenburg's close friends eventually married. Marriage was, after all, an expected part of the life of any proper Wilhelminian. When Eulenburg followed suit in 1875 (his schoolfriend Emil Count von Görtz had become engaged six months previously), he found a woman who embodied the self-abnegating ideal his mother represented. Eulenburg's bride was the Swedish Countess Augusta von Sandels.[22] His male friends found his choice disappointing. She is 'good,' Görtz wrote, 'but *terribly* boring.'[23] Alfred von Bülow was also impressed with her 'purity of heart and goodness,' but was forced to admit that she 'has little mental vivacity.'[24] Axel Varnbüler went into greater detail:

in no way remarkable, her conversation negligible, in address always asking, in answer always agreeing . . . she didn't intrude but was never, even in household matters, important. She was entirely eclipsed by the brilliant Phili, whom she looked up to in idolizing love and wonderment. She was only his shadow and echo.[25]

Eulenburg seems to have wanted and expected nothing more. Certainly the letter he wrote to Varnbüler on the occasion of his engagement betrays no overweening passion:

Dearest Axel, I am at the goal! I have become engaged to the only daughter of Count Sandels. That's enough for today. I will write you more another time, but do not expect any 'Brideletter' – I am just as I was, completely calm and not at all silly.[26]

Eulenburg quickly tired of ideal family life. Two years after his marriage he wrote, 'I enjoy the family little. I gladly go my way, like a peculiar sheep, who avoids the herd with a scowl. The dog which ceaselessly and pitilessly drives him back is an acquired sense of duty. Heaven knows it's not innate.'[27] Augusta's unquestioning support of her husband bored him as it had his friends. It took on 'a monotonous character, which fills [me] with indifference,' an indifference which Eulenburg admitted he was too 'lazy and indolent' to fight.[28] While it is true that Eulenburg was in many respects a devoted father, it is nonetheless clear that his primary emotional attachments lay outside his family. This becomes particularly clear in Eulenburg's response to the calamities which beset him in the early 1880s.

In March 1881 Eulenburg had to look on helplessly as his tiny daughter died of diabetes. She was the second child of his to die in infancy. Her death, perhaps in combination with other things of which we are ignorant, pushed Eulenburg first into a kind of emotional paralysis and then into apathetic despair which was dispelled only in 1886. In the darkness of this depression Eulenburg turned for solace to three sources: to his mother, his friends, and to art.

Eulenburg's adult emotional life revolved around what his friend Varnbüler called 'highly idealized, effusive, male friendships.'[29] Often the participants saw little of each other, carrying on the relationship by fervent letters written in a style more typical of the earlier, than the latter part of the nineteenth century, that is, romantically passionate, rather than conventionally reticent.[30]

Friendship was Eulenburg's coin of the realm. He knew an enormous number of people, many of whom he called 'friend,' rather than the more usual, and more cautious, German term 'acquaintance' [*Bekannte*].[31] As it turned out, not all of these persons deserved Eulenburg's trust. His superior at the Foreign Office, Friedrich von Holstein, once warned him that it would be his fate 'to be left in the lurch by people you consider friends.'[32] But Eulenburg would not listen to such cold advice, because friendship was sacred and politics was not.

Not all of Eulenburg's attachments were one-sided, however. The Count's 'highly idealized, effusive, male friendships,' whether of a more literary or merely incidental nature, were patterned after his relationships to a core group of intimates. His closest boyhood friends were Edgard von Wedel[33] and Eberhard Count von Dohna, the latter of whom introduced him to Prince Wilhelm in 1886. During his *Gymnasium* days he formed such a strong alliance with a student named Scherer, that they were known as the 'inseparables.'[34] This attachment, however, does not seem to have survived Eulenburg's entrance into the army in 1866. The 'hard core' of Eulenburg's friends were those he met in the army and in the university years which followed his army service. These included his two most intimate friends, Kuno Count von Moltke,[35] later Flügeladjutant and Commandant of Berlin, and Axel Baron (Freiherr) von Varnbüler,[36] the diplomatic representative of Württemberg to Prussia from 1894 to 1918. The others were Karl von Dörnberg[37] and Konstantin von Dziembowski[38] – neither of whom lived to reap any benefits from their association with the Kaiser's friend; Baron Boris von Wolff;[39] Alfred von Bülow,[40] brother of the chancellor; Emil Count von Schlitz (gen. von Görtz),[41] ruling sovereign at Schlitz and sculptor; and Bolko Count von Hochberg,[42] who would later become Intendant of the Berlin Court Theater.

Some of these long-term friends later became part of the so-called 'Liebenberg Round Table.' This designation covered those whom Eulenburg, with Wilhelm's approval, regularly invited to the *Kaiserjagd* held in Liebenberg every October or November. The intimate confederation, which included such guests as the relatives, neighbors, or in-laws of the Eulenburgs',[43] centered on a core group consisting of Eulenburg and his two closest friends, Varnbüler and Kuno Moltke, who were all invariably present. The next concentric circle was made up of Eberhard Dohna,[44] Georg von Hülsen,[45] and Emil Görtz.

Other men occasionally participated in the imperial hunt, without being real members of the Liebenberg Circle. Among them were Helmuth von Moltke,[46] the Chief of Staff; Oskar von Chelius,[47] who sometimes contributed his piano playing to the evening entertainments; and Jan Baron von Wendelstadt,[48] a Munich artist, who figured prominently in the scandal that brought about Eulenburg's fall. In addition, there were three courtiers who always accompanied the Kaiser to Liebenberg: Adjutant Gustav von Kessel,[49] Oberhof- und Hausmarschall August Eulenburg and Walter Baron von Esebeck,[50] Deputy Master of the Imperial Stables. All three were Eulenburg's cousins, but none was his intimate (Eulenburg distrusted Kessel, in particular). Finally, the wives of the hunters were in evidence at meals and sometimes during the evening, but otherwise the atmosphere was distinctly masculine.

The Liebenbergers were a small circle, despite the journalist Maximilian Harden's allegations.[51] As he inflamed the Eulenburg scandal, he inflated his list of Liebenbergers to include Heinrich von Tschirschky-Bögendorff, Raymond Lecomte, Wilhelm von Hohenau, Paul von

Below, and Johannes Count von Lynar.[52] Lecomte[53] was a good friend
of Eulenburg's and was a guest several times at Liebenberg, but was,
nonetheless, not a constant companion of the group. Tschirschky[54]
had a pleasant business relation with Eulenburg and that was all.[55]
Hohenau,[56] Below[57] and Lynar[58] were never guests during the *Kaiserjagd* although Eulenburg did know them all. The Knights of the
Liebenberg Round Table were six: Eulenburg, Varnbüler, Kuno
Moltke, Eberhard Dohna, Georg Hülsen, and Emil Görtz.

If Harden's lists were not quite right, his other theories were more
convincing. When in 1906 he levelled charges of homosexuality at
Eulenburg and his friends, this accusation provided contemporaries
with an explanation both for Eulenburg's seemingly divided character
and for the particularly intense nature of his relationship with his
male companions. Neither Eulenburg nor any of his friends ever
admitted to being homosexual. Their surface lives belied the suggestion. Most were married, many had children, and Eulenburg, especially, was a devoted father. But beneath this surface some of them
led other lives which they hid resolutely from the world and from
themselves. Both the deception and the self-deception obscure the
historical record and make it difficult to reconstruct the exact nature
of their relationships and the way they understood or rationalized
them. To compound the interpretive difficulties facing the historian
in sexual matters, most of the Moltke–Eulenburg correspondence was
fed to the flames in 1907 when the scandal broke.[59] The material
collected by the prosecution was destroyed in 1932.[60] The material
that Harden uncovered has, with few exceptions, not survived the war
and its dislocations. Fortunately, however, some illuminating letters,
mostly to and from Axel Varnbüler, have survived. These, in combination with the Harden evidence that was published and a close
examination of the pattern of Eulenburg's (and Moltke's) friendships,
leave little doubt about the homoerotic nature of the bond among the
core members of the group.

As close as he was to the rest of the Liebenbergers, Eulenburg's love
for Kuno Moltke and Axel Varnbüler puts them in a separate category. They formed an unbreakable triumvirate. They were each
other's helpers and confidants; they shared each other's secrets.
Whether the love between Eulenburg and Moltke ever found physical
expression may be impossible to determine. Harden proved conclu-
sively that Eulenburg had carried on long-term sexual affairs with
lower-class men,[61] and it is possible that the count followed the widespread practice of restricting active homosexual relations to persons

3 The Liebenberg Circle: Kaiser Wilhelm II and other hunters at Eulenburg's estate in 1892. (*Key*: 1 August Count zu Eulenburg; 2 Walter Baron von Esebeck; 3 Axel Baron von Varnbüler; 4 Emil Count von Schlitz, gen. von Görtz; 5 Alfred von Kiderlen-Wächter; 6 Botho Count zu Eulenburg; 7 Kuno Count von Moltke; 8 Kaiser Wilhelm II; 9 Georg von Hülsen; 10 Heinrich von Keszycki; 11 Leopold Count Kalnein; 12 Prince Richard zu Dohna; 13 Prince Philipp zu Eulenburg; 14 Gustav von Kessel; 15 Eberhard Count zu Dohna; 16 Major von Zitzewitz; 17 Friedrich Count zu Eulenburg; 18 Generalarzt von Leuthold; 19 Baron von Werthern; 20 Karl Count Kalnein-Kilgis)

beneath his social station. It is clear, however, that Moltke's and Eulenburg's mutual attraction was both deep and rich in erotic overtones.[62] Varnbüler, on the other hand, is more ambiguous. He was a kind of father-confessor to the other two. He understood them and their passions completely and, as he once explained to Moltke, he loved them 'for precisely those qualities which others label your fault.'[63] Varnbüler's broadmindedness and his bohemian manner of living suggest that he might have allowed himself a brief homosexual liaison with either of his two friends, perhaps in the days when they studied together at the university.

Moltke and Varnbüler, in their letters to one another, often referred to Eulenburg by a feminized form of his name, 'Philine.'[64] Shortly after their friend 'Chacha' Dörnberg died, Moltke wrote to Varnbüler that he was on his way to visit Eulenburg in Stuttgart.

I long for the old Philine. I must chat and gossip with *her* about our little one [Dörnberg]. [I] must see *her* out of the feeling that we must hold each other doubly tightly after this tear in our intimate circle.[65]

Moltke's tender feelings for Eulenburg were fully reciprocated. Eulenburg was appalled when Moltke married.[66]

This marriage was extremely *gruesome* to me, and I'm afraid that the 'young bride' noticed it. Nonetheless I shouldn't form a lasting judgment on a first, short meeting. Kuno looked like a man *in despair* – and that was for me the most painful experience on this wide earth.[67]

Eulenburg liked Moltke's wife even less as he got to know her. Eulenburg's jealousy is reflected in a letter he wrote to his mother, describing a visit he had just had with Moltke and Varnbüler: 'Kuno appeared a bit depressed. Was it disquiet because of his wife's poor health – or doesn't she like it when he goes to his friends?'[68]

In August 1897, Wilhelm appointed Moltke military attaché to Vienna, where Eulenburg was ambassador. The man Moltke replaced, Dietrich Hülsen-Haeseler,[69] suspected Eulenburg of having engineered the switch and thereafter was Eulenburg's implacable foe. Such a maneuver is not impossible. Eulenburg had written to Wilhelm that Hülsen's rough, Berliner style had alienated him from Viennese society and intimated that this had made him less effective as a military attaché. While the first part of this may have been true, the latter part was not. Hülsen was highly regarded by Austrian military figures and maintained good rapport with them until his death.[70]

Eulenburg was, of course, *selig* [ecstatic] about Moltke's impending arrival. 'But the wife! I actually intend to suggest to Kuno that he come to Vienna for the first winter *without* [his] wife. She should visit him in the spring – in a hotel. Then they would not need an apartment until the autumn of 1898.'[71] Unfortunately for them all, Lily von Moltke moved to Vienna with her husband. There she became entirely embroiled in her own and Eulenburg's mutual jealousy.[72] She and Moltke had a number of loud, attention-attracting fights, and the marriage quickly ended in divorce. To avoid more scandal, Moltke was removed to Berlin. Lily von Moltke later went to Harden with some revealing letters exchanged by Moltke and Eulenburg and also with her own account of Eulenburg's possessive jealousy. She would later testify in court that Eulenburg had pressured Moltke to leave his wife only two days after the wedding and had then importuned her to 'release my friend, give me back my friend.'[73]

Moltke had tried to hide the difficulty he had been having in his marriage even from his friends. Axel Varnbüler finally wrote to reassure Moltke that this silence 'even vis-à-vis your best friend' was not necessary.

I know now, through Philli, what I saw coming for a long time. . . . If you had succeeded in truly carrying this through, in transforming yourself so completely inside, in denying the ideals which you've held all your life, in climbing down from these pure heights and feeling at home in the oppressive atmosphere of the normal [*Gewöhnlichkeit*], then, *mein Dachs,* and only then would you have lost yourself, and I, you. That you must not, you cannot, be allowed to do – and I thank God, that the excess of intolerableness led you to this recognition and to liberation, before you had injured your innermost being.

And now, *mein Dachs*, that you are free, now come back to my wide-open heart, without mistrust, without hesitation, without false shame. I will not hurt you with questions. I do not want to know anything further, you need not worry about me. Everything is simply the way it always was, only that, if it is possible, I love, treasure and honor you even more.

He compares Moltke to Dostoevsky's Idiot:

yes, the majority of mankind, what one calls the world, laughs haughtily at such figures, because they don't understand. Many people, even among those who wish you well, have never taken you quite seriously – you were not manly, not vigorous, not worldly-wise enough for them.

They had made Moltke an object of their pity, Varnbüler wrote, as they had done to the researcher into homosexuality, Albert Moll.

But those people, who know you and love you for precisely those qualities which others label your fault, we have only anger and contempt for the injustice that has been done to you – and pity also, yes, pity – but not of the kind which could hurt you or make you ashamed, but rather innermost empathy with your soul's torture. And it is these few who understand us who count, *mein Dachs*, not the judgment of the world. And they are not so few, it is not merely the clique [*gelichteter Kreis*] of friends – think of the departed, whose

souls I feel so near to here [in Bielau, Schlesien] . . . and the many people
who only fleetingly crossed your life's path, but whose hearts you have won
forever by the good which you had done to them. I have heard many touching words of care and sympathy . . . from small, simple people, whom you
have probably long forgotten, but who have remained thankful to you. And
also the One, *mein Dachs*. I am probably not mistaken that it is an intensifica-
tion of your pain not to be able to hide all the ugliness from him, from the
darling [*Liebchen*] [this refers to Wilhelm]. But do not torture yourself unnec-
essarily on this account, he is man enough to silence harmful gossip, and he
knows and loves you too well in your individuality, to let even a shadow of
guilt fall upon you.[74]

This remarkable letter could hardly be clearer. The language in
which Varnbüler couches his love and his understanding reveals more
than the mere fact that he knew Moltke to be primarily homosexual.
He cannot use the term 'homosexuality'; he must give it a more honorable name – 'the ideals which you've held all your life,' 'these pure
heights,' 'your individuality,' which is contrasted to 'the oppressive
atmosphere of the normal,' the many who do not understand the few.
In other words, Varnbüler removed the sexual aspects from these
homoerotic feelings and elevated them to the level of cultural sensibility open only to a select few. This was not an uncommon tactic for
homosexuals of the nineteenth century to use.[75]

Varnbüler's deception was part of an elaborate system that the core
members of the Liebenberg Circle used to cloak their homoeroticism.
Their code words were friendship, peculiarity or uniqueness [*Eigenart*], idealism, and art. Closely connected with these four, as we shall
see, was their mutual fascination with spiritism. These words and the
concepts behind them fused into the Liebenbergers' *Weltanschauung*.
They formed the basis especially of Eulenburg's belief and became
the platform from which he acted upon his surroundings. The code
was, then, not merely instrumental, nor was it entirely hypocritical.
Almost all of the Liebenbergers were in fact talented artistically, and
Eulenburg's circle originally formed around their shared involvement
in art. Varnbüler drew gifted caricatures, Moltke composed music and
played the piano, Alfred Bülow was an enthusiastic amateur actor,
Görtz was a serious and talented sculptor, Hülsen became a professional stage director, and Eulenburg composed both music and poetry.

More than either Moltke or Varnbüler, Eulenburg considered himself primarily an artist who had been forced (by his father) into the
prosaic career of diplomat. As we have seen, he identified his artistic
inclinations entirely with the influence and personality of his mother.
He also subscribed to the current stereotype of the artist as

hypersensitive neurasthenic, tortured by bad nerves and ill health.[76] Eulenburg was all of these things, so it is difficult to know whether his own susceptibilities made him affirm the stereotype or if he perhaps patterned himself after it. In any case, Eulenburg's recurrent neurasthenia rescued him more than once from the penalties society exacted for homosexuality. This is true in the literal sense, when in 1902 poor health gave him the excuse to retire before his blackmailers closed in, and in 1909, when disability prevented the conclusion of his trial. It is also true in another sense, because the excuse of the artist's delicate sensibility allowed Eulenburg to explain some of his physical and emotional anomalies without considering their sexual origins.[77]

Eulenburg's first published effort was 'Out of the Ordinary,'[78] a short story of adolescent rebellion against a father. The hero is an artistic, dreamy youth, who is a failure in the eyes of his harsh father, because he cannot meet the latter's Prussian standards of practicality and hard work. The boy develops a strong, emotional attachment to a peer, who embodies the active, manly virtues which he lacks. When the father and the object of his son's affection clash, the latter is driven away. The son, in despair, commits suicide. It is not reading too much into the story to recognize the autobiographical elements in it. Eulenburg's later works were less direct, but still serve the purpose (among others) of legitimizing his own 'difference' from everybody else on the basis of artistic ability, rather than of forbidden sexuality. The themes Eulenburg chose to write about are interesting from this viewpoint. Eulenburg did not pick ancient Greece as his model, but rather the Nordic realms. His eight volumes of *Skaldengesänge* (ballads) were paeans to Nordic culture, replete with heroes as dedicated to male friendships as they were to valor in battle. Wilhelm was particularly fond of these ballads, through which he first came to understand their composer.

Eulenburg was not a mere dilettante in the world of art. Indeed, he might actually have been able to fashion a comfortable career out of his work. The *Rosenlieder,* for example, were a great popular success and in 1910 went into their 300th printing.[79] The resolutely romantic style of these *Lieder* reflected Eulenburg's taste. For him, art was an expression of the good and the beautiful, or at the very least a didactic spur to these perfections. Social criticism could never be art because its subjects were squalid and its tone harsh. Similarly, since Nature was at once the ideal and the muse of art, abstractions, which shattered Nature's forms, were also disqualified. Eulenburg therefore militantly opposed the modern movement in all its manifestations.

His art, in this respect, was consistent with his politics, indeed, as we shall see, both reinforced each other.

The ideas of art, idealism, the uniqueness of both the artist and of the friendship between artists fused into a symbolic complex which was more than merely a justification for homoeroticism, but also a positive, creative force. This cluster of ideas inspired works of art that persons far beyond the Liebenberg Circle enjoyed. It also produced a form of social intercourse which most people at Court found vastly more pleasant and entertaining than the usual royal fare.[80]

But this fusion, or symbolic complex performed another function that one should not forget: it gave an esthetic base to the inherited conservatism of the noble class from which all the members of the Liebenberg Circle came. That is, it allowed them to recognize, even to revel in, their uniqueness without in the slightest rejecting the society from which they stood apart. They merely saw themselves as 'better' members of their own class. Their artistic sensibilities elevated them from their boorish, *Krautjunker* peers. At the same time this elevation lifted them even farther from classes lower than their own. Nowhere is the esthetic credo of the circle, as well as its unconscious sexual base and its concrete political result, better expressed than by Eulenburg himself in a letter to Moltke written just after the scandal had broken.

Our idealism has actually become an anachronism and therefore has elicited opposition. Twenty years ago, when we were already forty!, in the Munich years with Karl Stieler, Kaulbach, and so forth, when we went through city and countryside making music, excitedly awakening excitement, we had just passed the high point of our thinking and feeling. Since then and for twenty years the new age has advanced across our country, whose noblest, best sensibility [*Empfinden*] we thought we had given expression to in our cult of the beautiful and good.

They had not realized that 'our way of feeling' was saved from ridicule only by their high station.

In the moment when the freshest example of the modern age, a Harden, criticized our nature [*Wesen*], stripped our ideal friendship, laid bare the form of our thinking and feeling which we had justifiably regarded all our lives as something obvious and natural, in that moment, the modern age, laughing cold-bloodedly, broke our necks. . . . The new concepts of sensuality and love stamp our nature as weak, even unhealthily weak. And yet we were also sensual [*sinnlich*], not any less so than the moderns. But this area lay strictly segregated; it did not impose itself as an end in itself. Family, art, friendship and all our ideals were completely divorced from sensuality and from that which we regarded only as dirt, even if it might have ruled us here or there in those unconscious reciprocal effects [*Wechselwirken*], which describe 'mankind'. . . .

Sensuality now overwhelms everything in crass materialism . . . it is the destruction of the ideal in materialism. . . . Our idealism is 'weak,' 'sickly sweet,' 'unmanly' – because the new idealism means only: 'power,' 'activity of manliness and femininity in ruthless right.'

This victory of the 'social democratic concept' means

a denial of culture, whose representatives we are, we, whom one cannot use, pests [*Schädlinge*], weaklings, who must be ripped down, as one smashed icons in the sixteenth century.[81]

He and his friends were the true representatives of culture by virtue of their idealism as they lived it in their lives ('ideal friendship') and in their art ('our cult of the beautiful and good'). These spheres 'were completely divorced from sensuality.' But Eulenburg admits that there might have been an 'unconscious' lapse 'here or there,' because, after all, they were only human. This is one of the few clear intimations that Eulenburg (and Moltke) might have crossed the line dividing 'idealism' from physicality. But Eulenburg obviously felt that the mere effort to control 'sensuality,' that attempt represented by the code words, was in itself noble. The 'modern age,' he thought, opposed that nobility, mocked it. 'Sensuality now overwhelms everything in crass materialism.' In standard conservative fashion, Eulenburg linked modernity with sensuality, materialism, and all of these with social democracy. Against this 'denial of culture' stood the anachronistic Liebenbergers and their imperiled idealism.

This discussion of the Liebenbergers' self-conception and why they developed it has centered on Eulenburg, Kuno Moltke, and Varnbüler. How true is it for the other men in Eulenburg's circle? Harden, of course, thought that it was completely so. But Eulenburg's schoolfriends and the narrower Liebenberg Circle that developed from them were informal networks. Nobody subscribed to a charter or endured initiation rites. Time wrought its changes, too. Friends died, or drifted closer to some people and further from others. And, finally, the newest friend, Kaiser Wilhelm, imposed his tastes and needs upon the group.

The surviving evidence on homosexuality is not conclusive, but it does strongly suggest that, at the very least, homoeroticism permeated the atmosphere around the schoolfriends. Eulenburg and Moltke were not the only Liebenbergers whom scandal later touched. Jan Wendelstadt became widely suspected as a homosexual and, when the shock waves that Harden touched off finally reached him, he committed suicide before the police investigation could be completed.[82] Georg Hülsen managed his problems more happily. Twice accused of the same thing by different people, he was able to exonerate himself each time.[83] Such publicity did not illuminate the private lives of other Liebenbergers, but scattered letters hint at strong, same-sex attractions holding the group together. One of the most enduring of these was the bond between Eulenburg and Eberhard Dohna, which lasted undiminished from early boyhood to Dohna's death. When Richard Dohna, Eberhard's brother, had a major falling-out with Eulenburg at the turn of the century, only Eulenburg's 'intimate relations [*innige Beziehungen*]' with Eberhard, he wrote, stopped him from exposing Eulenburg.[84]

Alfred Bülow and Karl Dörnberg were another close pair. Roommates at the university, they were tutored together for their law exams, and passed them sitting next to one another.[85] There was some question about where they would go next. There was no question that they would go together. 'I can't decide whether to complete my Prussian *Lehrsemester* in Hanau or Wiesbaden,' Bülow wrote to Görtz. 'In any case, Karl Dörnberg will accompany me.'[86] He finally chose Hanau, where he and Dörnberg shared rooms at a hotel. They were inseparable. 'In the mornings we sit next to our judge and finish the cases. . . . At noon [we take] a walk to Wilhelmsbad or Philippsruh castle. . . . In the evening one sits with a glass of wine or visits some wealthy family.'[87] Six months later they moved again, to the district court at Neu Ruppin. 'Dörnberg and I have a nice apartment in Ruppin,' Bülow reported. 'Eulenburg lives in [nearby] Wulkow, but comes daily to the court sessions here; we frequently spend the afternoons with him in Wulkow.'[88] However Bülow may have rationalized his own life, he had few illusions about Eulenburg's. In these same letters, he commented to Görtz that Eulenburg 'is unfortunately *very* little made for marriage [*leider ist er aber* sehr *wenig für die Ehe geschaffen*].'[89] At this point the detailed information dries up, but Dörnberg and Bülow both lived in Berlin until 1880, when they moved to Breslau within six weeks of one another.

Although they remained close friends until Dörnberg's death in 1891,[90] sometime in the early 1880s Bülow decided to change his manner of living. In 1884 he entered a marriage which seems to have made him happy, and he saw less of his male friends. Bülow was an excessively pious and conventional person, whose conservative Protestantism dominated his judgment. He once told Görtz that the most important ingredient for a happy marriage was that the couple should share 'their God and their Redeemer together.'[91] Sensuality made him uncomfortable if it escaped from its proper social context. Bülow was relieved, for instance, when a friend of his finally became engaged: 'his sensuality [*Sinnlichkeit*] is very ennobled by his engagement and now is completely held in the right confines [*in den richtigen Schranken gehalten*].'[92] Not surprisingly, given these attitudes, Bülow's relationship with the Liebenbergers had made him feel guilty. After a tumultuous week with Eulenburg, Varnbüler, Dörnberg and three other male friends, Bülow complained to Görtz:

during the whole time . . . I had to think about what you would have said about the whole business. I doubt very much that you would have liked it [*dass es dir zugesagt hätte*]. In any case you would have tried to bring a more serious and better tone to the society. On such occasions I unfortunately howl *much* too much with the wolves, but basically still feel unhappy about it.[93]

Years later, he still felt the same way. 'Your friendship,' he told Görtz, 'aroused pure and noble viewpoints and thoughts in me. I cannot say that this happened in the same way with my other friends.'[94]

Whatever the physical reality behind Bülow's relationship with the Liebenbergers, its emotional content, the all-absorbing quality of the same-sex bond, is clear. There can be little doubt that the homoerotic, or homosocial, aspect was a primary attraction for the original members of the group. For some of them, however, that attraction later faded. Whether this was due to a late discovery of genuine heterosexuality or to a desire to avoid the stigma associated with homosexuality or for other reasons is hard to say. But these early, intense friendships created, even in those who later drifted away, an enduring warmth and devotion. Nine years after his marriage had removed him from constant contact with his male friends, Bülow wrote to Eulenburg that 'your friendship is, next to the blessing which I found in my marriage, that possession on earth which I need most for my inner happiness and well-being.'[95] Even the scandal of 1907–9 did not shake Bülow's affection for Eulenburg, or his loyalty.[96]

If some Liebenbergers found the group's homoerotic component less alluring than others, at least one member seems not to have found it alluring at all. There is no information in any of the voluminous correspondences that links Emil Görtz to such matters. This may be the origin of Alfred Bülow's remark that Görtz, in contrast to his other friends, 'aroused pure and noble viewpoints.' Görtz's interest in the group stemmed from its other main common denominator: art. Groomed by his father and his tutor Hinzpeter for a life of public service, Görtz found few things less congenial than jurisprudence and politics.[97] Drama and sculpture were his loves and he pursued them enthusiastically and diligently at the University of Strassburg. These were the ties that bound him to Eulenburg and his friends. Görtz, too, chafed under the chains of duty. He was also a bohemian, an outcast, an artist. When he announced his plan to pursue the artist's life seriously, Hinzpeter warned Görtz's father that 'such a choice is often misused as an excuse for a life of personal pleasure.'[98] Hinzpeter's and his father's disapproval dogged Görtz for years, until he finally managed to combine artistic with administrative responsibilities.[99] How different was his experience with the Liebenbergers. There he found enthusiastic support for his artistic endeavors; he found an audience and collaborators all at once; and he found a refuge from the continuous criticism he received from home. The Liebenberg *Weltanschauung,* with its glorification of art, uniqueness, and friendship, served Görtz for reasons quite apart from those that had caused the core group to formulate it in the first place.

Were one to sum up the Liebenbergers, one might say that they were all male, all noble, all university-educated and entirely conservative. Most of them found men more attractive than women. All of them thought themselves unique by virtue of artistic talent or sensibility, idealism, capacity for friendship, or alienation from the prosaic world of common duty. The Liebenberg ethos epitomized this self-conception, and it and the shared experiences of their youth bound them together even when their later careers diverged.

It is not difficult to see why Prince Wilhelm found Eulenburg and his friends so appealing. For the young prince's uniqueness was like theirs, only far more burdensome. He suffered under the isolation of approaching kingship. His entourage contained no personal friends in whom he could confide, just bureaucrats or courtiers. His wife, like Eulenburg's, was devoted, but boring. His duties, except for the military ones, did not interest him. They stood in the way of his many and varied interests. They oppressed him as their own occupations oppressed Eulenburg and Görtz. With the Liebenbergers, Wilhelm escaped his onerous obligations at the same time that he assuaged his need for personal friends and for justifying his eccentric enthusiasms. He basked in male comradeship and attention unencumbered by demands that he be kingly or warrior-like. He found intuitive understanding for his homoerotic longings, plus a disinclination as complete as his own to acknowledge that that is what they were. The Liebenberg connection was the best of all worlds. And it not only suited Wilhelm's character, it was also perfectly natural or at least socially inevitable as well. For the Liebenbergers belonged to distinguished noble families, their political and aesthetic views were unimpeachably conservative and several of them, Görtz and Hülsen, for instance, had often played with Wilhelm when he was a child.

Wilhelm rarely set his heart to paper. The telegram was the closest he usually came to recording his feelings. As a consequence, it is easier to cite how the Liebenbergers felt about him, than vice versa. Wilhelm's complete trust in them, though, is clear from a remark he made to the Empress, when he introduced her to Varnbüler. The Liebenbergers, he told her, 'are the honest people.'[100] But Wilhelm's greatest tribute to his friends rested in his actions, not his words, in his unflagging desire to be with them on the *Nordlandreise,* at Liebenberg, at the Silesian hunts in autumn, at countless intimate evenings in between, indeed at all the times when the fierce, public Kaiser made way for the vulnerable, private Wilhelm. His constant invitations throughout the years and his attempts to relocate his friends nearer to him in Berlin testify to the depth and strength of Wilhelm's end of the friendship.

As we have seen, Wilhelm was closer to Eulenburg than to anyone else, male or female. Because of Eulenburg's tendencies and because Wilhelm surrounded himself with a remarkable number of men, who were, if not exclusively homosexual, then at least ambisexual, one is naturally led to wonder if Wilhelm and Eulenburg had a physical relationship. Though one cannot be absolutely certain, it is most unlikely, Harden's suspicions notwithstanding.[101] Wilhelm's need to deny his real feelings is the strongest evidence against the supposition. Wilhelm stood paralyzed between his conventionality, which labelled male homosexuals weakly effeminate non-men, and his fear that he could not live up to society's masculine stereotype. The physical expression of homosexuality would have dealt Wilhelm a severe blow. His overt relations with male comrades bear the strong stamp of repression: juvenile pranks (such as squirting men in the face with soda, or cutting their suspenders with a penknife), constant touching, behind-swatting, physical sadism under the guise of 'exercises' and so forth.[102] Wilhelm's capacity for self-delusion was almost limitless. It is difficult to imagine a person who knew himself less well. The reason why he preferred to surround himself with all-male circles of hyper-masculine military men or sensitive esthetes remained hidden from him.

Not all of the Liebenbergers were equally close to the Kaiser, nor were they important to him in the same ways. Wilhelm lavished his greatest affection on Eulenburg, and it was entirely reciprocated.

Contemporaries often misunderstood Eulenburg's intense devotion to the Kaiser, partly because they did not wish to interpret the relationship as in any way homoerotic and partly because they could not grasp the place of friendship in Eulenburg's *Weltanschauung*. They chose rather to believe that Eulenburg had ulterior motives of personal gain and status. There was undoubtedly an element of self-seeking on his part, particularly after Wilhelm became Kaiser, but this was never a major factor in the relationship.

What bound Eulenburg to Wilhelm was the immediate, instinctive feeling that they were kindred spirits. Eulenburg felt that Wilhelm, and Wilhelm 'alone,' understood 'innately' what Eulenburg termed his 'old-fashioned sensibility.'[103] Wilhelm was 'the person who understands me and what moves my heart completely.'[104] To Eulenburg, who generally felt misunderstood and unappreciated, Wilhelm was a heaven-sent discovery.[105] And Eulenburg responded in the way most natural to him: he fell in love with Wilhelm. Wilhelm became the 'beloved Kaiser,'[106] the 'Darling,'[107] whom Eulenburg loved 'above everything.'[108] Eulenburg described the relationship in the same disguised language he generally used: 'the *ideal* sphere forms the basis for our connection,' he wrote.[109] But his friends knew better.

Kuno Moltke shared Eulenburg's adoration. The last Liebenberger to meet the Kaiser, Moltke swiftly ingratiated himself with his music and gentleness.[110] He surrounded Wilhelm, in turn, with the romantic haze through which Moltke characteristically viewed the world. In Eulenburg's phrase, Moltke was 'of a tenderness [*Zärtlichkeit*] and love for the Kaiser, which was truly uplifting.'[111] Eulenburg later claimed that it was Moltke who first began the practice of calling Wilhelm 'the Darling' to his two trusted friends.[112]

As usual, Varnbüler was the least romantic of the three. He found Eulenburg's and Moltke's attachment rather amusing. 'With half-embarrassed joy and excitement Philly showed me countless photographs taken by Kistler of the *Nordlandreise!*' he wrote to Moltke. 'Your beloved Kaiser and he always in thickest union. H.M., as Dörnberg says, looked mostly rather fat and common, but I didn't have the heart to say so to Philly.'[113] Although a loyal supporter of the Kaiser's, Varnbüler always maintained a certain critical distance appropriate to his position as Württemberg's diplomatic representative to Berlin.[114]

Wilhelm saw less of the other active Liebenbergers, Eberhard Dohna, Emil Görtz, and Georg Hülsen, at least until Hülsen took over the Royal Theater at Berlin in 1903. Dohna was present at the biannual hunt in Prökelwitz, but otherwise kept the lowest profile of the group.

Hülsen, whose father had been Generalintendant of the Berlin Court
Theater, had grown up around the Court and knew the young prince
before he knew the Liebenbergers. Like Moltke, Hülsen was a somewhat passive character, whom the world threatened to overwhelm. In
addition he was sickly, or at least hypochondriacal,[115] which moved
Wilhelm and Eulenburg to alternate in efforts to take care of him.
Although his real talent, like his father's, lay with the stage, Hülsen
had wandered into a military career which ill-suited him. Wilhelm
first rescued him from this in 1892 by transferring him to the comfortable military attaché post in Munich, at which, not incidentally,
Eulenburg was currently serving as Prussian diplomatic representative. When Eulenburg left for Vienna, he nudged Wilhelm into
appointing Hülsen Theater Intendant at Wiesbaden.[116] From there,
Hülsen advanced to his father's old position at the Court Theater in
Berlin. Eulenburg's putative role in this precipitated a scandal which
turned out to be the dress rehearsal for the one that ended Eulenburg's career several years later.[117] Hülsen did not use his position to
impose his own esthetic ideas on the capital. Just the opposite. Widespread criticism of the byzantinist variety contended that he was much
too subservient to the Kaiser, whose frequent interventions bore poor
dramatic results.[118]

Emil Görtz had also been a youthful friend of Wilhelm's and without this connection it is unlikely that he would have become a Liebenberger. For Görtz, like Alfred Bülow, had steadily drifted away from
his university friends, and from Wilhelm, too. It was only when Wilhelm became Kaiser so unexpectedly early that Görtz picked up the
threads he had dropped, and resumed his old place.

By all rights, Görtz should have been Wilhelm's Eulenburg. Their
mutual tutor Hinzpeter constantly schemed to bring the two boys
together, in hopes that the older would improve the young prince's
character. Hinzpeter held an extravagantly positive opinion of Görtz,
just as he nurtured an extravagantly dismal one of Wilhelm. While
teaching the future Kaiser at Potsdam, Hinzpeter informed Görtz's
father that 'I cannot and will not relinquish the thought, that he [Görtz,
not Wilhelm] is called to do great things,' and he went on to suggest
that this might very well concern 'redirecting and using differently a
[coming] repeat of the moment of 1789.'[119] After much engineering,
Hinzpeter arranged in 1874 the first social visit outside Court confines that young Wilhelm and his brother Heinrich had ever under-
taken.[120] They went, of course, to Schlitz (the Görtz estate). Another
such visit made Hinzpeter ecstatic:

in Schlitz I received a much better impression of my tutee than I had before. I had thought him less able to find a taste for good things and [good] people than he showed there; and I would never have believed that he could discover the kind of passion for a person that he showed for Count Emil.[121]

Hinzpeter's plans foundered on two rocks: Görtz did not have the instinctive empathy for Wilhelm that came so naturally to Eulenburg, and, although Görtz 'dream[ed] of his great political–social role as friend of the Kaiser, . . . his legal studies and his political interest and understanding were so faulty [*mangelhaft*].'[122] So, Görtz neglected to visit Wilhelm as he grew older, and, in the meantime, Wilhelm and Eulenburg captivated one another. When he read the guest list for the first *Nordlandreise* in 1889, Görtz had second thoughts. His mother contacted Hinzpeter to find out why the Kaiser had not invited her son. Hinzpeter explained that the *Nordlandreise* was a pleasure cruise and Wilhelm invited guests

with whom he can completely let himself go. Why Count Eulenburg seems to him more suitable for this purpose than Count Emil, I don't understand; why Count Eulenburg, whom the Kaiser calls his friend, and who calls Count Emil his special friend, did not suggest [Görtz], if he wanted to go along, is even less understandable. . . . In my imagination [Görtz] could and should already have taken the place which Count Ph. Eulenburg now has, and not only on this trip, but in life.[123]

Hinzpeter was, in fact, furious that Görtz had not done more to cultivate Wilhelm's friendship, after Hinzpeter had gone to such trouble 'intentionally and artificially' to implant it.[124] Nonetheless, Hinzpeter swallowed his anger and intervened. He pointed out to Görtz that, in the next few months, both he and Wilhelm would have recently completed trips to the Orient and that would provide a 'favorable conjuncture' to renew their acquaintance.[125] This strategem worked. On 1 May 1890, Wilhelm made a return visit to Schlitz as a last test before admitting Görtz to the *Nordlandreise* company. The visit was clearly much more successful than Görtz had dared to hope. 'It was *extraordinarily* nice and comfortable,' he reported to his mother. 'I can't say *how* comfortable and nice he was; you could see and feel that he *enjoyed* being together with us. He is now also completely at home with Sophie [Görtz's wife], and it is a very *pretty* relationship with her – it pleases me very much.'[126] 'For us it was truly a *beautiful, good* day. He [the Kaiser] told me to hold myself ready at the *end* of June for the *Nord*[*land*]*reise*.'[127] Görtz was thenceforth back in the inner circle with both Wilhelm and the Liebenbergers.

No sooner had Görtz reestablished himself than Hinzpeter launched his last attempt to make over the Kaiser under Görtz's influence. 'I would like you to swear that you will do everything in your power to make something out of [this relationship]. Above all show him, if you can do it with good conscience, that you like him, have sympathy for him for his own sake, for his own individuality. That is seldom the case.' 'If you cannot [find this sympathy], . . . then it can only become an interesting acquaintance, whose fruits will be essentially of purely personal value.' But if Görtz had this genuine sympathy and if, in the course of his experiences, he had 'found a deeper sense in human existence,' then he must act as 'the sighted one amongst the blind. Above all, preach . . . that from those to whom much is given, much is also demanded and that the more one has, the less one has for oneself alone.'[128] Had Görtz followed this noble advice, the friendship would have died a quick death. Instead, Görtz sidestepped the political possibilities. It is not clear whether he did so because of his old antipathy to politics or because he discovered that there really were limits to his compatibility with the Emperor. In any case, he and Wilhelm were satisfied with a friendship of 'purely personal value.'

Only the three core Liebenbergers had a direct political impact on Kaiser Wilhelm, and, of these three, only Eulenburg's influence made a palpable difference to the course of events. But the Liebenbergers had oblique effects which stemmed from their position as an alternate court. Wilhelm's peculiar personality made such an alternate court necessary, especially since the official court, stifled between the Empress's piety and the FADs' narrowness, left him bored and restless. Into this breach stepped the multi-talented Liebenbergers. Their object was to regulate Wilhelm's uneven moods, to jolly him out of his depressions, to distract him from his anxieties or to calm his brainstorms and rages.

One did this through a combination of controlling Wilhelm's tastes and accommodating them. The word 'entertainment' hardly describes this difficult task, but, however it is called, the job was Eulenburg's. At Prökelwitz and Rominten, where there were very few guests, Eulenburg had to manage alone. Georg Hülsen and Emil Görtz assisted him at Liebenberg and on the *Nordlandreise*, where the entertainments were sometimes elaborate. The Liebenbergers amused Wilhelm with all manner of presentations: sketches, puppet shows, plays, silhouettes, magic, poetry, and music. One evening's fare aboard the *Hohenzollern* in 1891 began with Hülsen singing, accompanied by Görtz and FA Zitzewitz. Then Görtz played a 'self-instructed' man reciting 'Über allen Gipfeln,' followed by a Max-und-Moritz sketch starring Görtz and Hülsen; then Görtz as an Italian tenor in Nordic garb, and so on until the last sketch in which Paul Güssfeldt (the marine painter) and Alfred von Kiderlen-Wächter (the representative of the Foreign Office) played Siamese twins whom Eulenburg put through their paces.[129]

Not all of the productions were either so elaborate or so tame. The Liebenbergers devoted no mean effort to satisfying Wilhelm's taste for the vulgar and grotesque. Shortly before the 1892 Liebenberg hunt, Hülsen had an inspiration. 'Like Athena from Jupiter's head, an idea springs out of mine,' he told Görtz.

I'll parade you like a clipped poodle! That'll be a 'hit' like nothing else. Just think: behind *shaved,* in front long bangs out of black or *white* wool, in back under a real poodle's tail, a noticeable rectal opening, and, as soon as you stand up on your hind feet, *in front* a fig leaf. Just think how terrific [it'll be] when you bark, or howl to music, shoot off a pistol or do other foolish things. It'll be simply splendid!! Nobody can make a costume as good as you can; you can model the head yourself – I already see in my mind's eye H.M. laughing like us – [*sic*] and I'm counting on a *succès fou.*[130]

Such sketches were possible when there were no women present, which was often the case at Liebenberg and almost always so on the *Nordland-reise.* That circumstance also allowed another of Wilhelm's favorite forms of entertainment: transvestism. Many of the short plays and skits contained female characters that, in the absence of the real thing, the male guests had to portray. The more unlikely the better. Eberhard Dohna was rather more than corpulent and when he was scheduled to take his turn, Hülsen commented, 'Eberhard Dohna as a woman!! – it's useless [*es hilft nichts*]!'[131] One should avoid linking transvestism too firmly with the Liebenbergers. For one thing, Georg Hülsen regretted the limitations that all-male casts imposed on his repertory, since numerous plays were 'unthinkable without women.'[132] For another, Wilhelm found cross-dressing so richly amusing that it was a not infrequent part of imperial entertainments elsewhere. The most famous example occurred in 1908 at Max Egon Fürstenberg's before a mixed audience, and starred Dietrich Hülsen-Häseler (who stood several inches over six feet tall) attired as a *balleteuse.* It became famous only because Dietrich Hülsen died of a heart attack directly after his performance. Otherwise it was scarcely noteworthy, since Hülsen occasionally danced in a tutu before the Kaiser, and the assembled guests, men and women from the Berlin Court (but not the Empress) and some of the grandees of the upper Austrian nobility, found it merely funny, not scandalous. 'Everyone was highly amused, because the count danced wonderfully, and there was something unique about seeing the Chief of the Military Cabinet perform ballet costumed as a lady.'[133] One should also recall that Dietrich Hülsen, despite his brother Georg's connection with the group, was a vociferous enemy of Eulenburg's and the Liebenbergers'.

Even at its most risqué, the Liebenbergers' entertainments never went beyond the juvenile. Because of the number of guests and the length of the voyage, the atmosphere aboard the *Hohenzollern* was considerably more raucous than at the Prökelwitz, Rominten, or certainly the Liebenberg hunts. The prosaic truth, particularly about Liebenberg, would have disappointed contemporaries, who liked to imagine the dark goings-on dreamed up by the tainted esthetes and occultists there. In fact, what distinguished Liebenberg during imperial visits from the usual atmosphere at Court was its informality, levity and musicality, not depravity. The Kaiser typically arrived around dinner time on a Thursday, stayed to hunt on Friday and Saturday, and returned to Berlin on Saturday night. The hunting was never particularly good and was not infrequently abandoned for walks, rides, tennis, or billiards.[134] In later years, Eulenburg's musically gifted children played a greater part in the evening entertainments. The aura at Liebenberg was, in fact, so harmless and enjoyable that even that arch-puritan, Rear-Admiral Müller, who was very quick to criticize Wilhelm's entourage and the imperial milieu, could only remark upon the 'nice tone' of the evening he had spent there.[135]

Another aspect of the Liebenberg ambience that disturbed contemporaries was spiritism. This had enjoyed considerable vogue in the mid-nineteenth century, in the form of séances, mediums, and interest in preternatural phenomena. For most people spiritism was a diversion that soon exhausted its fascination. For others it was very serious business. Varnbüler, Moltke, and Eulenburg were all deeply involved in it. They took part in séances, visited mediums, read books on the subject, met with famous 'scientists' of the supernatural, and talked to their friends about their experiences. Varnbüler seems to have become less absorbed after a while, though he never repudiated his early interest. Eulenburg, however, remained a true believer, as did most of his family.[136]

Eulenburg discovered in himself a taste for the mystical when he was quite young. At the age of seven or eight, he had the unpleasant experience of having a snake fall on him from a branch over his head. His response to this, apart from developing a life-long fear of snakes, was to believe that he could sense their presence even without seeing them.[137] This readiness to believe in phenomena on the basis of feelings or intimations rather than empirical proof evolved into an acceptance of spiritism, which also had the advantage of connecting religion and friendship. Eulenburg, who was strongly evangelical and thought of himself as orthodoxly religious, viewed spiritism as a completion of Christianity. He wrote to Wilhelm in March 1888:

Spiritistically, I have just experienced some pretty remarkable things – all things which make individual life after death a complete *certainty*. How narrow and limited is the opinion of those, who, in their pious pride, deny phenomena which are incontestable. And how wonderfully uplifting [*erhebend*], how evangelically Christian are the messages which I have experienced.[138]

In another place he refers to spiritism as a 'wonderful elucidation of our Christian belief.'[139]

Religious spiritism, like art or idealism, also served to disguise Eulenburg's passionate male friendships, to purify them into something non-material and, thus, non-sexual. By these lights, friendship was not merely a pleasure, but a mystical sacrament and sacred trust. Eulenburg felt he possessed a God-given 'deep, holy sensibility for friendship.'[140] Spiritism consoled him that these 'related sentiments, earthly relations between people of many kinds live on, miraculously transfigured.'[141] This was a solace not only when death intervened (as with Dziembowski and Dörnberg), but also when melancholy darkened Eulenburg's life and only consciousness of 'a solidarity of allied souls . . . [and] strong memory of similarly inclined sentient beings' heartened him.[142]

Eulenburg confined his spiritism to his private life. He used it as a mechanism to reassure himself that his friends were not lost to him. He used it to try to cure himself of his myriad neurasthenic complaints. He does not seem to have used it to determine either the nature or execution of his politics. Nor did he use it to exercise power over Wilhelm.

Eulenburg's belief in spiritism preceded his acquaintance with Wilhelm, and was one of the many things they had in common from the very beginning.[143] Wilhelm was fascinated by tales of the supernatural and never tired of hearing other people's 'ghost stories.'[144] Eulenburg was by no means the only person in the entourage with whom Wilhelm shared a taste for the supernatural. Wilhelm's brother Heinrich recorded in his diary for 31 August 1888 that Wilhelm held a séance in Adjutant Usedom's rooms, with the adjutants and Friedrich Grand Duke of Mecklenburg-Schwerin and told *Spukgeschichten* until 11.30.[145] Nonetheless, Wilhelm's enthusiasms did not reach quite so far as Eulenburg's. Wilhelm saw doctors, instead of magnetisers,

when he was sick. He did not consult signs, numbers, or mediums
before he made decisions. Spiritism for Wilhelm was more in the
nature of a hobby than a religion or belief system.

Exactly how far Eulenburg and Wilhelm went in their mutual spiritistic adventures is difficult to determine. From their first acquaintance on, they avidly traded experiences, less frequently in letters,
however, than in private conversation.[146] Because Eulenburg was quite
open about his enthusiasms, it was well known in government circles
that he was a spiritist. As soon as Wilhelm became Kaiser it was feared
that Wilhelm's interest in mysticism could subject him to evil influences. The Prussian experience in this regard had not been happy.
Wilhelm II reminded many people of Friedrich Wilhelm II, who had
numbered among his many eccentricities a strong tendency toward
the mystical and who, partly as a consequence, was one of the worst
Hohenzollerns to inhabit the throne.[147] Shortly after Wilhelm became
Emperor, his personal physician, Dr Leuthold, asked Eulenburg if he
discussed spiritism with the Kaiser. Leuthold was afraid 'that a man
like the Kaiser, who tended toward mysticism, might be pushed in a
"too internal direction" by such conversations.'[148]

Eulenburg had anticipated such criticism. In August 1887 he had
written to the Prince that he should be careful to whom he confided
his own and Eulenburg's interest in spiritism. 'If Y.M. were to divulge
your true opinions in *larger* circles, many people would become alienated from Y.M., or at least a *suspicious* regret would ensure. Hostile
elements would trumpet about that Yr Royal Highness had gone over
to the "Spiritists".'[149] Eulenburg recommended that Wilhelm wait until
spiritism had become a large religious movement before he announced
his beliefs. A year later, when Wilhelm had apparently received several offers from mediums to hold séances for him, Eulenburg urged
the Kaiser to reject them all and to deal only with persons he himself
had recommended, lest Wilhelm be deceived by charlatans.[150]

As a result of the warnings he had received, Eulenburg became
more circumspect in his spiritistic practices, although he by no means
gave them up. After 1889, there is no mention in his letters to Wilhelm of spiritistic adventures. However, the mystical continued to
appeal to them both and to be part of their discussions when they
were together. In 1900, for instance, Eulenburg told his friend Bernhard Bülow that he, Admiral von Hollmann, and the Kaiser had passed
the time at Rominten conversing about, among other things, spiritism.[151] Conversation is probably the extent of the Kaiser's and Eulenburg's mutual spiritistic involvement after the early years of Wilhelm's

reign. General Alfred von Waldersee heard rumors that Eulenburg had taken Wilhelm to a séance as late as September 1891.[152] Whether or not this was true, it is the last specific rumor of its kind, although, despite Eulenburg's care, more general rumors dogged him to the end of his career. They surfaced in 1894 during the *Kladderadatsch* campaign, again just before Eulenburg's retirement in 1902, and finally during Harden's successful attack. The rumors always charged that Eulenburg manipulated the Kaiser through mysticism. The written evidence available today reveals only that Eulenburg used spiritism as a subject of conversation to keep Wilhelm amused.[153]

Eulenburg was not the Rasputin the public feared. Nevertheless, he and his coterie did have other, if less lurid, effects upon the Kaiser. Quite apart from the overt political influence that is the subject of following chapters, Eulenburg and the Liebenbergers surrounded Wilhelm with a thicket of spoken and unspoken assumptions with repercussions on the Kaiser's own *Weltanschauung*. Art might serve as a best first example, since esthetics was one of the ways through which the Liebenbergers expressed their conservatism. Harden later accused Eulenburg of ruining Wilhelm's nascent modernism by his own reactionary romanticism.[154] He was right. Wilhelm was enough inclined toward certain aspects of modernity (for example, technology, advances in science, and other academic subjects) that one could at least imagine that under different tutelage these tendencies might have extended to the art world. Eulenburg always felt that he was merely confirming Wilhelm's taste, but he in fact seems to have done a bit more. The restoration of Burg Hohenzollern, the family's original castle and one of the Kaiser's pet projects, bears the unmistakable stamp of Eulenburg's romanticism.[155] In the same way, Eulenburg's language shines through Wilhelm's speech when dedicating the monstrous *Siegesallee* in Berlin in 1901. Art, the Kaiser declared, follows

the law of beauty, the law of harmony and the law of aesthetics. . . . Sculpture has for the most part remained pure of the so-called modern tendencies . . . may it remain so. . . . Art must contribute to educating the people, it should give the lower orders . . . the possibility to reorient themselves to ideals. These ideals have remained the abiding property of the German people, while they have become more or less lost to other peoples. . . . The cultivation of the ideal is the greatest duty of culture.[156]

Although Eulenburg could not have expressed the Liebenberg esthetic ethos better, Görtz was more directly involved in the *Siegesallee*. He sculpted the statue of Markgraf Ludwig the Roman.

The Liebenbergers also introduced the Kaiser to new influences.

Wilhelm did not care much for literature, preferring instead technical books or military and naval history. The few literary works he did read were usually recommended to him by his friends. More important than books, however, were people. Eulenburg thought his biggest coup was inviting Houston Stewart Chamberlain, the Germanophile author of *Foundations of the Nineteenth Century*[157] to the *Kaiserjagd* at Liebenberg in 1901. 'I had finally succeeded in doing what I had wanted: to provide the Kaiser some stimulation from one of the spheres of learning, which would elicit better thoughts in him than politics does.'[158] Before the visit, Eulenburg had Wilhelm study the book, so that together the Emperor and Chamberlain spent two days deep in discussion of the racialist, social Darwinian theories it advanced. Eulenburg noted[159] that Wilhelm 'stood completely under the spell' of Chamberlain, an impression borne out by Wilhelm's later correspondence with the writer[160] and by many of Wilhelm's remarks.[161] Varnbüler reported that Chamberlain had particularly entranced Wilhelm with the idea that 'the Germanic race alone was the most vital and that the present and future belonged to the German Reich, which was its strongest political organism.'[162] Chamberlain's theories also nourished Wilhelm's conviction that the German Kaiser had a mission 'on the basis of personal power.'[163]

The Chamberlain episode illustrates well the oblique effects of the Liebenberg Circle. Chamberlain did not make the Kaiser a racist, any more than he made him suddenly an advocate of personal regime. Wilhelm had been inclined for years to accept a social Darwinist view of politics, just as he had believed in divine right since he was a young man. Chamberlain's visit merely justified Wilhelm's opinions further and lent them a pseudo-scientific sheen. It was the same way with the Liebenbergers. Their milieu reinforced the narrowest and most conservative aspects of Wilhelm's eclectic *Weltanschauung*. None of them encouraged his flashes of liberalism, his early concern for the working class, for example, or his preference for an industrial rather than an agrarian Germany. In the matter of anti-Semitism, the Liebenbergers had a sharply negative impact. Eulenburg, Varnbüler and Görtz saturated Wilhelm with a vehement and principled anti-Semitism that he had not held before. But, more serious than any particular attitudes they fostered, the Liebenbergers perpetuated the habits that produced these attitudes. Hinzpeter called them *Standesfehler*, shortcomings of class: 'distracted thinking, unreliable work habits, irresolution in fulfilling [one's] duties.'[164] The Liebenbergers did not challenge Wilhelm to become better than he was. Their goal was not to subject Wilhelm to the discomforts that personal growth demands, but, on the contrary, to make his life easier by shielding him from unpleasantness. They were friends, not advisers or tutors. Wilhelm picked them for this purpose and they fulfilled it.

The Liebenbergers contributed in one other unintended way to preserving Wilhelm's *Standesfehler*. As a group, they were more successful than anybody else in 'handling' the difficult Emperor. Critics labelled this activity either 'manipulation' or 'byzantinism,' depending on their point of view. They did not understand, however, that the alternative to sensitive intervention was to abandon the Kaiser to his ungovernable moods. That route promised quick disaster for the government. Although at least one high official briefly advocated such a policy,[165] it is not surprising that upper-level bureaucrats and advisers refused to run the risk. Instead, they tried to defuse Wilhelm's volatility by sparing his nerves. Before their eyes they had the example of the Liebenbergers, who did such a good job, because they understood Wilhelm so well. Not all the men at Court who learned how to manage the Kaiser learned their skill from Eulenburg's circle, of course. But it would be astonishing if many did not, particularly since Eulenburg dispensed free advice to those whose success he wished to ensure.[166] The friendship network, then, bequeathed to political advisers a patterned way of dealing with Wilhelm based upon the dictates of friendship, not of politics.

Finally, Kaiser Wilhelm made his closest friend into his most intimate political adviser. With that, Philipp Eulenburg, the man who loved the Kaiser 'above all else,' became the strongest civilian voice in the entourage.

4

Philipp Eulenburg prepares 'personal regime'

Eulenburg's diplomatic career had been quite undistinguished until he met Wilhelm. Bismarck did not think highly of his abilities 'he has no political judgment, does not distinguish between the important and the unimportant, listens to gossip and whispering campaigns, and can do a lot of damage.'[1] Eulenburg himself approached his job with the utmost indifference and even hostility. He was a close personal friend of Herbert von Bismarck, but up until 1886 this fact had had little impact on Eulenburg's career. Eulenburg became a power at the Foreign Office only after he had established his friendship with Wilhelm and only because of it. At the time (1886), he was first secretary to the Prussian legation in Munich. Both Friedrich von Holstein and the Bismarcks felt that Eulenburg's friendship with and possible influence on the young Prince would be useful in their coming fight with Wilhelm's father, whom they suspected of unPrussian liberality. Holstein immediately began a correspondence with Eulenburg, which lasted until 1899.[2] Eulenburg was given access to the Foreign Office files[3] and was showered with information and advice in foreign and domestic politics by the indefatigable Holstein.

Eulenburg's antipathy towards politics had been waning since early 1886. Alfred Bülow reported to his brother Bernhard that Eulenburg had finally recovered his equilibrium,[4] and with it came a renewed interest in his diplomatic career.[5] As his enemies alleged, Eulenburg did indeed pull strings for his own advancement, although his goals were much more limited than they imagined. He wanted to become envoy to Bavaria and later, when he had outgrown that post, ambassador to Austria. With the help of Holstein and Bernhard Bülow, and of course of Wilhelm, he finally attained both these goals. Around 1900/1 and again in late 1906 rumors claimed that Eulenburg wanted to become Statthalter of Alsace-Lorraine.[6] Eulenburg's sympathetic historian, Johannes Haller, later wrote that Eulenburg had never concealed the fact that he had found the Statthalter position attractive, but that he had never actually taken steps to obtain it.[7] None of the rumors were specific, and until new evidence should surface the matter must rest in the realm of conjecture. While Eulenburg may not have aspired to higher office, he did indeed aspire to higher rank. The only other prize which he may have engineered for himself was the title 'Fürst,' granted to him by Wilhelm in 1900. Chancellor Hohenlohe reflected public opinion in thinking that Eulenburg had requested this honor.[8] Eulenburg, however, always denied this, and, in his letter of thanks to the Kaiser, described how surprised and 'perplexed' he was by Wilhelm's action.[9]

Once Eulenburg's friendship with Wilhelm had given him entrée to Holstein, he lost no time in trying to secure himself the Bavarian legation. While first secretary to the Prussian legation in Munich, Eulenburg wrote to Holstein (16 July 1886) to describe the characteristics which a successful Prussian envoy to Bavaria should have. The description sounded curiously like Eulenburg himself, and Holstein was not fooled for an instant by Eulenburg's protestations that he had written the letter 'with no thought whatsoever of a particular personality.' In fact, Holstein thought Eulenburg would be rather good in the position,[10] especially since he wanted to prevent Bismarck's son-in-law, Kuno von Rantzau,[11] from obtaining the post. Holstein and Eulenburg therefore embarked on almost two years of machinations.

The tactics which Eulenburg used were various and often clever. The count let Wilhelm know that he was comfortable in Munich and wished to stay there. Aware that Rantzau was the main contender, he suggested that it was not necessary to fill the post immediately. Eulenburg could conduct business as interim-envoy for a long time, from which position he could not only make extra money, but could also insinuate himself into the job and then virtually inherit it.[12] He tried to blacken Rantzau's name by claiming that Rantzau was unwelcome to the Bavarians and had intrigued against the former representative.[13] He tried to make Herbert von Bismarck bow to pressure from Wilhelm, but did so very gently so as not to appear to be pulling too many strings.[14] Already in 1887, he began to drop the first of many hints about Vienna: 'If something in Vienna could be made for me later, remember me,' he asked Herbert. 'For financial reasons other large cities would be hard for me to bear for the time being.'[15]

Despite Holstein's and Eulenburg's efforts, Rantzau became Prussian envoy to Bavaria in 1888, while Eulenburg was appointed envoy to Oldenburg. A scant two years later, Wilhelm advanced Eulenburg to the same position in Stuttgart. The fall of Bismarck in March 1890 at last cleared the way for Munich. Wilhelm waited only eight months before informing the new chancellor, Caprivi, that Eulenburg was going to Munich.[16] Indeed, Wilhelm's unseemly haste in fulfilling his wishes made Eulenburg nervous. The new envoy rightly feared the number of persons who would feel slighted by his own meteoric rise and by the knowledge of how he had engineered it. For its part, the Bavarian government was pleased to have Eulenburg back because many of the officials liked him and because they felt that there might be advantages to having the Emperor's closest friend in their capital.[17]

The road to the embassy in Vienna was just as rocky as the one to Munich had been, and it took Eulenburg almost as long to reach it. He continued to drop hints that he wanted the post. Holstein, again, was in favor of the idea in order to forestall the appointment of Carl Wedel,[18] an ex-military man, who was the candidate of the military entourage. It was doubtless through Holstein that Caprivi heard of the possibility of appointing Eulenburg, which he then recommended to Wilhelm early in the summer of 1892.[19] Wilhelm was of another mind, however. The Emperor felt that Vienna was not important enough for his friend. Clearly Wilhelm wanted Eulenburg in London. Eulenburg was, however, unsure of the language and in any case disliked the English. He could only reply that Vienna was where he wanted to be and the matter was dropped for the time being.[20]

Meanwhile, Eulenburg recruited another conspirator with whose help he was ultimately successful. Bernhard von Bülow and he had been growing closer by leaps and bounds. Now they each began to work for the other's appointment as ambassador: Eulenburg's to Vienna and Bülow's to Rome. In early September 1892, Bülow had a long talk with Austrian Foreign Minister Gustav Graf Kálnoky[21] about who would succeed the current German ambassador, Prince Heinrich VII Reuss.[22] Kálnoky pointed out that Reuss was well-liked and thoroughly trusted by Franz Joseph. He realized that Reuss soon would retire, but saw no reason to hurry the process, and, besides, Carl Wedel was the name one heard in Berlin, not Philipp Eulenburg. Bülow assured Kálnoky that Wedel was merely the military's favorite but Eulenburg was actually the best candidate.[23]

Bülow spoke to Kálnoky again at the end of April or the beginning of May 1893, and this time Kálnoky was more receptive. Bülow hoped that Eulenburg would press harder for the post and wanted to know if he should write Kiderlen-Wächter[24] to point out how ill Reuss was and that Eulenburg was the only possible successor.[25] The Eulenburg papers do not provide an answer to this question, but Eulenburg seems to have hesitated to throw his whole weight into the fray. On 29 June, he relayed to Holstein some information on the rabidly pro-Bismarckian (and therefore anti-Wilhelminian) views of Reuss's wife. These would have been sufficient to have rocked Reuss's position badly, but Eulenburg asked Holstein not to leak the information.[26] Eulenburg finally made up his mind in the summer when Wilhelm confronted him with a choice of embassies, hoping that the count would opt for England. Eulenburg, however, still wanted Vienna.[27] With the help of his 'sorcerer's apprentice,' Prince Karl Max von Lichnowsky,[28] who was then second secretary at the German Embassy in Vienna, Bülow set up a dinner for 16 December 1893 at which Eulenburg charmed Kálnoky with amusing stories. The next day the two of them discussed politics for an hour,[29] and Eulenburg composed an official report of the conversation, just as if he had been ambassador.[30] On 29 December, Eulenburg informed Bülow that Wilhelm was going to announce Eulenburg's appointment on 27 January. This meant that Bülow and Anton Monts would have to apprise Reuss of the situation and get him to resign.[31] They accomplished this task on the 31st.[32]

Eulenburg's hesitation to push harder for Vienna had not come from doubts about whether he wanted the post, but from fear of the consequences of 'the path over corpses' which led there. The legion of his enemies grew with each step. They now numbered among them Carl Wedel, who had accepted a post at Stockholm, with the understanding that he would fill the Austrian Embassy when it became vacant.[33] Prince Reuss was, naturally, most depressed at the unceremonious way he had been pushed aside.[34] Chancellor Caprivi had played no part in the selection of Germany's ambassador to its most important ally and complained to Wedel that he was 'powerless' against Eulenburg.[35] Finally, Emperor Franz Joseph was heard to lament the departure of the man 'with whom I could talk like a friend.'[36]

For the first few years after 1886, Eulenburg loyally carried out the Foreign Office line, as it was interpreted by Friedrich von Holstein.[37] He acted merely as go-between for the Foreign Office and kept it well informed of his communications with the new Emperor. Only when the unity in the Foreign Office itself began to dissolve, was Eulenburg forced to make decisions on his own. The conflict that first drew Eulenburg into the political fray was the struggle that preceded Bismarck's fall in 1890. The struggle had begun even before Wilhelm's accession in June 1888 and grew in intensity in direct proportion to

Wilhelm's desire to be his own ruler. Bismarck countered Wilhelm's plans by increasingly complicated and dangerous schemes designed to create enough chaos so that Wilhelm would be forced to defer to the Iron Chancellor. These schemes included opposition to a conciliatory policy towards the working class, an anti-socialist bill so harsh that it was unacceptable to the Reichstag, the destruction of the government's coalition in the Reichstag (the *Kartell*), alliance with the Catholic Center Party, introduction of an unacceptably large army bill, a closer foreign policy orientation toward Russia (at the expense of Austria, or so many diplomats and military men feared), and finally the artificial dissolution of Germany itself in preparation for a coup d'état. The story of Bismarck's fall has been told elsewhere.[38] Eulenburg's role in it, however, is interesting for the pattern it reveals.

Like almost everyone else in his generation, Eulenburg was a great admirer of Bismarck. He had close personal ties to the family (through his Uncle Fritz) and especially to Herbert, whom he had befriended when Herbert was enmeshed in an unhappy love affair. But, like many Prussian conservatives, Eulenburg blamed Bismarck for introducing universal manhood suffrage and for the *Kulturkampf,* the divisive and unsuccessful struggle against the Catholic Church. In Eulenburg's view, the former had created the socialist movement and the latter, the Catholic Center Party. Together, these groups were the two strongest opponents of the Junkers. But these reservations were not enough to put Eulenburg into the anti-Bismarck camp. Eulenburg's primary substantive disagreements with Bismarck were more personal than political. In the first place, Bismarck was responsible for blocking Eulenburg's plans to remain in Munich. This does not seem to have bothered Eulenburg nearly so much, however, as his growing conviction that both Bismarcks were intentionally poisoning Wilhelm's relations with his own mother. Wilhelm was in fact a pawn in the Iron Chancellor's struggle against the presumed liberality of the Kaiser's father and mother. One of Bismarck's tactics, designed to alienate Wilhelm from his parents, was to sow distrust and even hatred between the stubborn and impetuous son and his equally stubborn and impetuous mother. Eulenburg, to whom filial devotion to one's mother was a sacred duty and sublime pleasure, was incensed at this process. He never forgave the Bismarcks for it.[39]

Despite these early differences, Eulenburg's conversion to the anti-Bismarck forces was gradual and unwilling. Wilhelm's habit of discussing important matters of state with whomever was in hearing distance would eventually have pulled Eulenburg into high politics in any case. But it was Holstein who set the specific course, and Eulenburg trailed along in his wake. Holstein used Eulenburg chiefly as a contact with the Emperor, to warn Wilhelm of Bismarck's impending maneuvers, to influence Wilhelm on how he should counteract these maneuvers, and to gain support for Wilhelm among other high ranking persons (such as the Grand Duke of Baden and the King of Saxony). Eulenburg received Holstein's daily political advice and then acted upon it.

Eulenburg began to emerge from Holstein's shadow only in early 1890 and then only tentatively. On 13 January 1890, Wilhelm and Eulenburg had their most extensive talk to date on politics.[40] A week later, Eulenburg sent Paul Kayser's[41] detailed plan for a government initiative on behalf of the workers to the Emperor. Holstein had previously cleared both this and another plan drafted by Franz Fischer of the *Kölnische Zeitung*. Eulenburg chose to send the more conservative of the two to Wilhelm. When the Kaiser and Bismarck had a showdown the next day at the Crown Council over the Kayser Plan, Bismarck emerged the winner. Early in February, Eulenburg carried on the fight by urging Wilhelm to appoint Kayser under secretary of state. Holstein learned of this move only two days later.[42] Eulenburg went out on his own twice more during the crisis. Later in February, he tried to use his personal connections with the Bismarck family, through a cousin, to coax the old man into a good mood for an important audience with the Emperor.[43] Five days later, Eulenburg briefly toyed with the notion of allowing Bismarck to precipitate a coup d'état from which Wilhelm and Bismarck might both profit.[44] This trial balloon burst immediately when Eulenburg realized that any chaotic situation would benefit only the chancellor at the expense of the Kaiser.

When the actual moment came, Eulenburg seems not to have been involved in causing Bismarck's dismissal. He was, however, instrumental (again on Holstein's instruction) in getting Marschall appointed foreign secretary and in keeping Holstein at his desk. Whether or not he was involved with the selection of Caprivi is not clear. Eulenburg maintained that he was not, though in that case it seems odd that he met with Caprivi barely two weeks before the latter's appointment as chancellor.[45]

The stakes in the Bismarck crisis were high: the power of the chancellor or the power of the Kaiser. Many of the anti-Bismarckians supported the power of the Kaiser merely because it was the strongest, most legitimate weapon with which to depose the old chancellor.

Others felt that Wilhelm actually showed promise both in native ability and in political direction. Persons like Holstein, who backed the
Kaiser for such reasons, were soon disappointed. But there was a third
reason to stand on the Emperor's side, the reason Eulenburg did so.
Eulenburg wrote that he was in an uncomfortable position 'because I
had to choose between two friends [Herbert Bismarck and Wilhelm].
In the deciding moment the Kaiser, despite his royal power, was the
weaker and I could not disappoint his deep conviction that he had
support in adversity in my loyalty. I stood by his flag.'[46] This sentiment, support for the Kaiser as friend, had in fact already begun its
transformation into a more political mode, support for the Kaiser as
Kaiser, that is, as an end in itself. Eulenburg was beginning to develop
a concept of kingship motivated by his love for Wilhelm, but based
neither on a realistic appreciation of Wilhelm's abilities nor of the
exigencies of rule in a modern nation.

Along with nascent notions of 'personal regime,' Eulenburg developed other patterns of thought and of political strategy that were to
characterize his outlook and behavior after the Bismarck crisis had
receded. The main part of the anti-Bismarck strategy had consisted
in keeping the chancellor in office, at the same time diminishing his
authority while adding to Wilhelm's until the balance should tip and
the chancellor could easily be dismissed. This strategy involved juggling numerous personalities, papering over differences until the right
time, holding back the over-eager and so forth. Eulenburg proved to
be more than gifted in these matters of personal diplomacy. The techniques he developed between 1888 and 1890 would be his main tools
for the coming political struggles.

We have already seen how Eulenburg was gradually becoming less
dependent on others for his political opinions. Nonetheless, he was
sufficiently unsure of his own political judgment to act more as Holstein's messenger than as his master. But Eulenburg never trusted
Holstein as a friend; Holstein was too cold and calculating for that.
So Eulenburg found another source for advice on foreign policy, a
source which would combine expertise and friendship: Bernhard von
Bülow. During the height of the Bismarck crisis Eulenburg wrote to
Bülow: 'how often I think of you, when questions and decisions of a
serious nature come upon me and I wish [I had] your experience by
my side.'[47] Eulenburg already thought of Bülow as the future head of
the Foreign Office.[48] This friendship was to have fateful consequences in the political and personal spheres. It is enough at this point
to indicate that the seeds of later developments were already sown
by 1890.

On Bismarck's dismissal, Eulenburg was placed squarely in the midst of high politics. His access to the Kaiser was limited only by the necessity to visit occasionally the capitals to which he was Prussia's accredited representative.[49] He was privy to the secret documents at the Foreign Office and more important to the scheming mind of *Geheimrat* Holstein. He had begun his role as coordinator of the disparate arms of high-level government. Eulenburg's career as central manipulator and imperial mastermind between 1890 and 1898 has been painstakingly recounted in John Röhl's *Germany without Bismarck*. I do not intend to repeat the detailed contents of that book. Instead, the following pages will assess the broader themes of Eulenburg's political activity, dipping down into detail as example or explanation may warrant.

The charge which many contemporaries levelled against Eulenburg was that he manipulated Wilhelm for his own purposes, or at the very least, screened Wilhelm from other, presumably 'better,' influences. A close examination of Eulenburg's political dealings, however, clearly reveals that when Eulenburg intervened to prevent Wilhelm from acting, his purpose almost invariably was to change the form, rather than the content of Wilhelm's action. Until 1898, moreover, Eulenburg and Wilhelm had no major policy disagreement. To be sure, Eulenburg would chide Wilhelm into toning down the fiery rhetoric of his speeches, or urge him to refrain from insulting the Bavarians, as he was wont to do.[50] He might even warn Wilhelm against interfering in foreign affairs, as he did during the Crete crisis in March 1897.[51] But even here, the aim of Eulenburg's policy was not to stop the Emperor or to change his politics, but to make his politics more successful. Ultimately, the aim was to reestablish the power of the Emperor to run the government himself, using his ministers and the bureaucracy as his pliant tools. This was the way Prussia had been and the way it should be again:

It is difficult to admit, but the establishment of the German Empire, that is, the blending of liberal and south German with Prussian blood, *the combination of a ruling statesman* [Bismarck] *and a sleeping Kaiser-Hero* [Wilhelm I] have ruined the old Prussian kingdom. A King who rules by himself, despite the fact that this is his perfect right, is unthinkable in the eyes of the 'educated, progressive' people. . . . When Wilhelm appears as an actual ruler, that is only his perfect right. The only question is whether the consequences can be endured in the long run.[52]

Eulenburg answered this question with a firm 'yes,' but only if certain conditions were met. A successful war was one way to gain the necessary royal prestige. But how could one guarantee that a war would be successful? This course was too risky, and Eulenburg not only did not advocate it, but tried to prevent others, notably the military, from doing so. Eulenburg felt slightly more comfortable with the risks presented by internal war. We have already seen how he toyed with the idea during the Bismarck crisis. In principle, Eulenburg favored a revolution from above which would definitively wipe out such democratic concessions as universal suffrage and reestablish the rights of historic Prussia. But in order to be a success, the coup d'état would have to occur when hostile foreign powers could not take advantage of Germany's preoccupation with internal chaos and when Wilhelm had the undivided support of the other German states and of at least some political parties and interest groups. Such a fortuitous constellation never materialized. This did not stop certain military hotheads or the Emperor from sporadically threatening a coup.[53] It did, however, stop Eulenburg.

Imperialism was another way to legitimate the resurgent power of the Emperor. But imperialism, Eulenburg felt, pandered to the people. It would redirect popular enthusiasms and thereby strengthen them. It was a policy dangerous to the status quo, because, if the establishment lost control of the forces it had encouraged, these could easily transform themselves into revolution. Eulenburg saw that imperialism 'would mean the end of the monarchy, if not for Him [Wilhelm], then for his successor. H.M. would never go over to this form.'[54]

And so Eulenburg came by a process of elimination to the policy he would follow consistently throughout the 1890s. Wilhelm must ally himself with his natural allies in Prussia, the Conservatives.[55] This presented a problem in the Reich, because the parties who supported unification, who could be counted on to quash particularism, were the liberal parties. Therefore the national policy Eulenburg recommended was based, to be sure, on Prussian dominance, but a veiled and tactful dominance, in which power would be wielded as unobtrusively as possible. In the Reich, the liberal parties were to be supported against Catholics, Welfs and other irredentist groups. As time went on, Prussia's hegemony over the Reich and the fact of unification itself could be taken more and more for granted. Consequently, Eulenburg concentrated on the Prussian wing of his policy, what he saw as the reorientation of Prussia towards the Conservatives. This was a *re*orientation because Bismarck's dismissal had necessitated a shift to a more liberal, pro-industrial program, which was enthusiastically carried out by Chancellor Caprivi, Secretary Marschall, Holstein, and, at first, Eulenburg himself.[56] For Eulenburg, however, this was merely a tactic which had to be adhered to until a reassumption of power by the Bismarcks was out of the question, that is, until Bismarck was dead, or until Wilhelm had sufficient personal prestige to go it alone. From the beginning of 1894, Eulenburg felt that point had been reached. It was time to shift from the negative holding action of the Caprivi administration to the positive thrust of personal regime.

The political tone of personal regime in internal affairs would be primarily agrarian. Eulenburg felt that industry had 'attained everything attainable' and agreed with Miquel that it was time to lavish attention on the rural estates.[57] Eulenburg was, however, not prepared to give in to the most outrageous agrarian demands and was particularly anxious to avoid the impression that the government was bowing to Junker pressure. Nonetheless the political and economic orientation of the government would be decidedly pro-agriculture, while industry would be left to fend for itself. In external affairs the anchor of the Reich was to be Austria, whose continued friendship and stability would be maintained at all cost. The preservation of Austria dictated a cautious foreign policy, one that would avoid adventures which might upset the delicate system of balances inside the creaky Dual Monarchy.

On both these points Eulenburg was more conventionally conservative than his master. Eulenburg was undoubtedly correct that personal regime instituted at this late date required either conventional conservatism (agrarianism) or 'revolutionary conservatism' (imperialism and nationalistic caesarism) to legitimize itself. Unfortunately for Eulenburg, Wilhelm (and, in fact, the entire Wilhelminian system) tended more toward the latter than toward the former.

The Emperor was frankly bored by the agricultural depression and could be brought to consider the subject only with great difficulty. His sympathetic attention to the matter was fitful at best. Usually he was neglectful, if not hostile. Wilhelm felt the Prussian Conservatives were unduly shrill and demanding. Their recalcitrance offended his imperial pride, and he responded to them with anger and ridicule. After Caprivi's dismissal in 1894, the policy of the government did shift in favor of the East Elbian estates. But neither Eulenburg nor the other pro-agrarians at Court succeeded in weaning the Emperor away from his infatuation with technology and industry.

Similarly, a German foreign policy which had the Austrian alliance at its core was too sedate for the reckless Kaiser. We shall see how this disagreement between Wilhelm and his friend disrupted their relationship more and more as the 1890s drew to a close.

At the time Eulenburg was most active in political manipulation, however, he still believed that Wilhelm's better instincts would prevail and that the Emperor would follow the conventionally conservative paths which Eulenburg preferred. Fortified by friendship's faith, Eulenburg overlooked Wilhelm's wayward tendencies and concentrated upon providing the Kaiser with pliable instruments for the imperial hand. The major instrument of personal regime was to be Bernhard von Bülow. Bülow seemed to Eulenburg to combine three essential qualities: he favored a cautious, anti-Russian, pro-Austrian foreign policy; he would be acceptable to the agrarians but not at the same time anathema to the industrial groups; and most important, he was absolutely loyal to Wilhelm.

Bülow and Eulenburg came to know each other in 1880 when they were second and third secretary respectively in the German Embassy in Paris. Bülow was apparently quite kind to Eulenburg while Eulenburg's daughter was dying and he was slipping into depression. Eulenburg returned the favor several years later when he helped smooth the social waves caused by Bülow's marriage (9 January 1886) to the divorced wife of a fellow diplomat.[58] Despite these mutual kindnesses, the friendship developed much more slowly than was usual with Eulenburg. In fact, until the early nineties, Bülow's letters were considerably warmer than Eulenburg's: his salutations, for instance, were always 'My dearest Philipp,' while Eulenburg's were merely 'My dear Bernhard.'[59] Eulenburg valued Bülow first of all for his political knowledge and talents, for Eulenburg always felt that he himself lacked the necessary hardness for politics. 'I do not possess your knowledge,' he once wrote to Bülow, 'but belong more to the intuitive diplomats.'[60] In Bülow he saw his political alter ego:

How often I think of you [he wrote during the Bismarck crisis], when questions and decisions of a serious nature crop up and how I wish I had your experience at my side. I do not deny that I see in you, not only my support, but the support of a good many people and let no opportunity pass to mention you. . . . Write me what you advise. . . . If only *you* were in Berlin.[61]

Bülow played up this aspect of their relationship and thus underscored his indispensability to Eulenburg:

[I am] through disposition and education more oriented towards historical, legal, and economic studies, [and] am able to hand you from my gradually built-up storehouse, many pieces for the construction which you (thrown into the political struggle against your actual inclination, but to the good of the Emperor and country) direct with a light but sure hand. You are perhaps more German–Hellenic, like the second part of Faust, while I am more Prussian–Roman; you are more knightly, I more military; you are more individualistic, while I am more the 'political animal' [in Greek] of Aristotle.[62]

Unlike Holstein, Bülow did not restrict himself to the role of sober, political helpmate in relation to Eulenburg.

It is difficult to avoid the conclusion that Bülow intentionally pulled Eulenburg's heartstrings. Bülow's capacity for personal manipulation is legendary. It would probably be incorrect, however, to ascribe to him only motives of personal gain, for Bülow did reckon Eulenburg among his four closest friends.[63] He once wrote that 'my wife, you, and Alfred [Bülow] are actually the only people with whom I would always like to be and who never get on my nerves.'[64] Nonetheless, Bülow's letters could not have been better tailored to fit the complex ins and outs of Eulenburg's personality. He never failed to mention Eulenburg's 'muse.' He invariably inquired after Eulenburg's mother. When Eulenburg's old friend Karl Dörnberg was attached to the same embassy as Bülow, Bülow exclaimed how much he liked him, 'not only because he is so close to you but by virtue of his own personality.'[65]

Eulenburg's warm letter (cited above) during the Bismarck crisis emboldened Bülow to greater heights of effusiveness. He remarked how curious it was that Eulenburg, 'who seemed predestined as few others by inclination and development for an aesthetic existence' should be embroiled in politics. He flattered Eulenburg by writing:

> You have the intuition and the eye of the poet, which notice and see what reason misses. . . . You also have poetic openness, which does not anxiously calculate and differentiate; you have a rare lack of selfishness, in short, everything which is humanly likeable and noble and which seldom springs from the green table [of bureaucracy]. Therefore do not complain about the many difficulties and disputes of your current position of trust. Precisely you are able to fill such a position and only because of your singular inclinations and characteristics. I regard it as a particularly happy dispensation of heaven that you are standing by the side of our Kaiser as a loyal disciple. I am convinced that no one [but you] can understand and interpret many [aspects] of our master – perhaps precisely the innermost and most beautiful sides.[66]

In these passages Bülow has cleverly echoed back many of Eulenburg's pet ideas about himself and about Wilhelm. He has even picked exactly those phrases ('aesthethisches Dasein,' 'Intuition,' 'eigenartigen Anlagen und Eigenschaften,' 'innerlichsten und schönsten Seiten') which Eulenburg himself used and which rang the most responsive chords of his *Weltanschauung*. In fact, Bülow possessed a remarkable sensitivity to the homoerotic needs of other men and he knew how to respond to them in sympathetic ways. This was one of the secrets of his success with Eulenburg and, later, with Kaiser Wilhelm II.

In the letters after 1890, Bülow began more and more to emphasize

still another theme: how wonderful he thought Eulenburg's friend
Wilhelm was.

His ideas and plans are almost always right, often brilliant; they rise up from
the well of singular and splendid individuality, which combines rare energy
and prudent consideration with remarkable understanding for the requirements of the time, [an individuality] that wants the best and usually perceives
what the best is. It is another question whether the All-Highest intentions are
always efficiently carried out [he added].[67]

Although many persons would agree that Wilhelm had a 'singular
personality,' few of Bülow's intelligence would have accused him as
late as 1891 of 'remarkable understanding for the requirements of
the time,' much less of 'prudent consideration.' Bülow repeated these
sentiments in letter after letter, long after they should have seemed a
cruel mockery.[68]

Eulenburg, however, succumbed to this long-distance seduction
completely. Because Eulenburg was two years older than Bülow, the
strict rules of German intimacy required that he, rather than Bülow,
propose that the two friends use the familiar form of address, 'Du.'
Eulenburg did so very delicately in a letter of 28 February 1893: 'Do
not be surprised, dear Bernhard, if some day I should call you "Du,"
because that is how I feel about you.' Bülow responded in the idiom
he knew was characteristic of Eulenburg himself:

My dearest Philipp, . . . When you addressed me with the brotherly *Du* you
met the wishes and the feelings of my heart. . . . It seems so natural to me,
that we call each other *Du*, as if it could never be otherwise. Although externally we are in many respects different, internally we are truly *wahlverwandt*
[kindred souls]. . . . I found you congenial since I first met you and I love you
from my heart; I have come to understand your nature better through my
wife; may you remain with me a long, long time; as long as I live, my dear
Philipp, you will have in me a loyal friend.[69]

In every letter Bülow gave Eulenburg just the right impression. He
represented himself as the political version of Eulenburg, the esthete.
He assured Eulenburg tirelessly of his absolute devotion, not only to
him but more important to Wilhelm. He made it increasingly clear
that the touchstone of his politics would be the establishment of personal regime. 'I would be a different kind of chancellor from my
predecessors. . . . I would regard myself as the executive tool of His
Majesty, so to speak his political Chief of Staff. With me, personal rule
– in the good sense – would really begin.'[70] It seemed to Eulenburg
that Bülow's expertise, energy, and political inclinations, by transforming the government completely, would make him the perfect
person to relieve Eulenburg of the burden of holding the government

together. Bülow thus became the cornerstone of Eulenburg's political plans.

Eulenburg began steadily but determinedly to elevate Bülow to the chancellorship. He began by bringing Bülow to Wilhelm's attention as often as possible, by sending portions of Bülow's letters on to the Kaiser, accompanied by messages like 'whoever ignores Bülow's knowledge and ability in the political sphere is nothing but jealous.'[71] Once Wilhelm was apprised of Bülow's virtues, Eulenburg went to work on the two most important figures in the Foreign Office, Holstein and Kiderlen-Wächter, neither of whom was well disposed towards Bülow. Eulenburg could report that Kiderlen was won over as early as February 1893.[72] Holstein presented greater difficulties. Although Bülow noticed that Holstein was much friendlier towards him,[73] no one was sure until the moment actually came whether Holstein would consent to work under the younger man.

The next step was to provide a platform, in the shape of a major embassy, from which Bülow could spring into the foreign secretary's chair. After six years of exile in darkest Romania, Bülow was becoming impatient and complained that the foreign service was turning into an institution for the aged and infirm.[74] Less than three months later (in December 1893) Bülow was appointed ambassador to Italy. Eulenburg managed this by playing off Wilhelm, Marschall, Caprivi, Holstein, and Kiderlen against one another. Wilhelm wanted Col. Engelbrecht, the military attaché there, for the post. Secretary Marschall wanted another military personage, General Wedel. Holstein and Kiderlen-Wächter both feared an increase in the military's influence in foreign affairs, and Holstein converted Caprivi into a Bülow supporter on this basis. Once Caprivi backed Bülow's candidature, Eulenburg, behind Caprivi's back, told the Kaiser that Caprivi would resign if Bülow did not become ambassador. Wilhelm relented.[75]

As soon as Bülow was installed in the Palazzo Caffarelli, Eulenburg encouraged him to send some reports, in the form of private letters, directly to Wilhelm.[76] Caprivi was furious at this subversion of his authority, but Wilhelm ordered the practice to continue.[77] Once Bülow was in a position to develop a formidable reputation for himself, Eulenburg could concentrate on clearing Bülow's future path to Berlin.

From March 1894 on, Eulenburg uninterruptedly followed the same plan. The men of the New Course were to be dismissed as soon as possible. Bülow would become head of the Foreign Office under an interim chancellor. This arrangement was necessary because the political bills to pay for a sudden switch to the right might be quite high and might even include a coup d'état. The interim chancellor would use himself up politically in these struggles, while Bülow was establishing himself as the master of foreign policy. Bülow could then easily succeed to the chancellor's position, while Johannes Miquel[78] and the agrarians would set the domestic tone. The hard-headed men of the New Course would then be out, their political support in the nation defeated, while the new leaders would be traditional supporters of the unfettered power of the Crown.

Ultimately, Eulenburg achieved precisely these goals. But circumstances forced him to take longer doing it, and to do it in a slightly different way than he had hoped. The stumbling blocks proved to be the opposition of Holstein and Caprivi and the political power of Secretary Marschall.

Holstein and Eulenburg began to fall out politically in 1894. By that time Eulenburg had achieved his political security (the Viennese embassy) and had developed confidence in his own political judgment, which he proceeded to exercise independently of his former tutor, Holstein. Bernhard Bülow gradually usurped Holstein's place as political confidant. Until 1894, both Holstein and Eulenburg by fantastic epistolary feats had managed to protect Wilhelm from himself, by toning down his speeches and telegrams, by delaying actions he wanted taken, by preventing the appointments of rabid military men to diplomatic posts, by counteracting the advice of the military entourage, and so forth. Doing this caused Holstein to lose very quickly his initial admiration for the Kaiser, whereas Eulenburg's awe continued unabated until 1898. Holstein's clarity on the defects of Wilhelm's character in turn caused him to support institutional curbs (parliamentary and ministerial) on imperial power. Eulenburg's desire to enhance imperial power persisted, however, because his love for Wilhelm prevented him from realizing the seriousness of those defects.

Throughout 1894 relations between Eulenburg and Holstein gradually worsened as they realized more and more the political gulf which separated them.[79] The crisis surrounding Chancellor Caprivi's fall in October brought their differences into sharp focus for the first time.[80] Eulenburg had decided that it was time to remove Caprivi and to end the New Course by the appointment of his hard-nosed, reactionary cousin, Botho Eulenburg, as chancellor. Botho Eulenburg was the candidate of the Junkers, Conservatives, agrarians, and of those who wanted a repressive policy against the Social Democrats, including, perhaps, a coup d'état. The choice of Botho leaves little doubt that Philipp Eulenburg was at least willing to risk a coup, although his repeated calls for 'compromise' between his cousin and Caprivi indicated that he preferred to inaugurate the new conservative policy in a less risky fashion.

Throughout the summer and autumn, Eulenburg strengthened Wilhelm's dislike for his chancellor general while he groomed Botho Eulenburg for the new position. He was helped in his endeavors by Botho's brother, August Eulenburg, who lobbied unceasingly on Botho's behalf and who helped arrange the final showdown between Caprivi and the minister president.[81] Ranged firmly against the family Eulenburg were Holstein and Marschall, who wanted Caprivi to hold firm, indeed to expand his power by forcing Botho's resignation from his office of minister president of Prussia. Botho's resignation would do two things. It would be a convincing blow against the Junker–Agrarian–Conservative bloc, which housed the strongest opponents of the New Course. And it would be a stunning defeat of the Kaiser's power, because he stood squarely behind the repressive, anti-Socialist policies advocated by Botho but opposed by Caprivi, a position Wilhelm had adopted after spending the summer with Philipp Eulenburg on the *Nordlandreise*.

Caprivi at first won a series of political victories over Botho Eulenburg and his supporters. In the end, however, the furious scheming of Holstein, Marschall, and Philipp Eulenburg maneuvered everyone into an impasse from which the only way out was to dismiss both Caprivi and Botho. Philipp Eulenburg had wanted the next chancellor to be a strong man capable of carrying out a successful, armed reorganization of government. Under the circumstances, Eulenburg had to settle for an interim chancellor too weak to cross the Kaiser as Caprivi had done. He arranged that Caprivi's successor would be the liberal, venerable Prince Chlodwig zu Hohenlohe, whose major advantages in Eulenburg's eyes were his advanced age and crippling asthma.

The Caprivi crisis caused Holstein and Eulenburg to exchange a series of letters in which they both defined their political views vis-à-vis royal power.[82] Holstein observed (correctly) that Eulenburg had left the ranks of the 'simple royalists for the Court conservatives of the newest observance.'[83] Eulenburg denied that he was anything but a 'moderate conservative' and claimed that the vehemence which characterized his defense of Wilhelm was solely due to the fact that he 'lov[ed] the Kaiser and [was] personally close to him.'[84] Holstein was not quite ready to give up on Eulenburg, although he had entirely given up on his imperial friend. The *Geheimrat* still hoped that Eulenburg might come to Berlin as a 'mediator,' because without such a person, the autocratic (and, he hinted, probably insane) ruler would not be able 'to make a go of it much longer.'[85]

The following two and one half years (January 1895 to June 1897) were the most politically troubled of Wilhelm's peacetime reign. The innumerable intrigues, the continuous tension and uncertainty wore down the various combatants until they no longer had the strength to hide from each other their real plans. Holstein expressed his irreconcilable difference with Eulenburg this way: 'you tend instinctively to an autocratic regime. . . . I am for the moderate use . . . of a system of constitutional cooperation.'[86] Eulenburg, in response, tried to make the spurious distinction between politics and personality, but was not convincing:

The exhaustion [from continuous political upheavals] is so great that I would have either physically collapsed or withdrawn to Liebenberg, if I had not through personal intercourse with the Kaiser been filled by a firm trust both in his undeniable gifts and in his thoroughly high idealism which will struggle to final clarity. You lack this trust. Herein is a contradiction – [but] not at all in political opinions.[87]

Despite Eulenburg's denials, the situation was clear to all. Holstein had become convinced that the only way to stop Wilhelm was to allow him to follow one of his wild notions to its conclusion and then to confront him with the mass resignations of his ministers. The resulting débâcle, he felt sure, would be the only way to save the monarchy. When Holstein broached his plan to Eulenburg in February 1896, Eulenburg answered 'that I would not deny my nature. I would only follow the path along which my instinct leads me, I hope, for the good of the Kaiser, whom I tenderly love.'[88]

Holstein was probably right from his own point of view. A cold water cure, for all the risks it brought with it, was still the best resort – though a last resort – for anyone who wanted responsible government. The more Eulenburg was successful in patching over differences, in putting off the final reckoning, the more demoralized and divided became those persons (Caprivi, Hohenlohe, Marschall, Bötticher, Holstein, Kiderlen) who might have stopped personal regime. Indeed, Holstein and Eulenburg would doubtless have parted ways much earlier than they did had it not been for Bülow's efforts to keep them together. It was, of course, in Bülow's interest to prevent a *Krach* which might pull him prematurely into office and then use up his political capital cleaning up the debris. Accordingly, Bülow ceaselessly advised Eulenburg to continue his 'mediating role' and to try to keep everyone in office and on civil terms with one another. At the same time he performed the same service which Eulenburg had once done for him: he acted as Eulenburg's go-between with Holstein and encouraged the suspicious *Geheimrat* to find other explanations for Eulenburg's behavior than the ones which were obviously true,[89] that is, that Eulenburg was firmly determined to establish personal regime. Holstein, for all his paranoia, had correctly appraised both the Kaiser and his friend and had reached the logical conclusion about what had to be done. Unfortunately, he shrank from doing it.[90] Holstein remained in office until 1906, but had no contact with Eulenburg after January 1899. By that time, of course, Eulenburg's plans had been quite fulfilled.

In his struggle to establish personal regime, Eulenburg found Secretary of the Foreign Office Marschall von Bieberstein to be a far more irritating problem than Caprivi had been, and it took Eulenburg longer to bring about his fall. Eulenburg was thwarted by Marschall's strong support in the Reichstag, the prestige he gained first from successfully concluding the tariff and trade agreements,[91] and later from the Tausch trial.[92] Again, it is interesting to note Eulenburg's tactics. Since Marschall was too well entrenched to dislodge formally from his position as secretary of the Foreign Office, Eulenburg tried to achieve this end informally, by restricting Marschall's activities to trade questions. 'If Marschall is smart,' Eulenburg wrote to the Kaiser, 'he will leave foreign politics to Hohenlohe and Holstein and regard trade questions as his domain. The effort to be on top of foreign questions and to determine the personnel [of the diplomatic corps] could gradually lead to tensions, as I see it.'[93] The fact that these two duties were the essence of Marschall's job did not deter Eulenburg. Eulenburg further wrote that he would hint to Marschall that the Secretary would be wise to follow his instructions.[94]

Marschall had been the target of Court intrigue for some time. Kuno Moltke, August Eulenburg, and Lucanus, who were most active in poisoning Marschall's reputation with Wilhelm, had two motives for wanting to be rid of the secretary. The underlying one was simply that Marschall was too liberal, a south German who had made his peace with both industrialism and parliamentarism. The second motive, which provided the ammunition for most of their pot shots, was anti-Catholicism. In order to get Reichstag support for various government measures, Marschall had developed ties with the Catholic

Center Party. He was quite willing to undo the vestiges of the *Kultur-kampf* in exchange for Catholic votes in the Reichstag. The entourage was virtually unanimous in considering Catholics a contemptible, untrustworthy, 'international,' and therefore treacherous bunch with whom one seldom dealt and upon whom one never relied. Wilhelm tended in this direction himself, so that Marschall's politically neces-sary Center Party dealings were a nice excuse for acid comment. This constant *Minenarbeit* from persons who were *en suite* was intermit-tently successful with the Kaiser, whose growing distrust for his sec-retary was punctuated by emotional outbursts against him. But Wil-helm did not feel nearly as uneasy around Marschall as Eulenburg thought he should.

The 'Lieber Affair' illustrates how eager Eulenburg was to foster the growth of Wilhelm's antagonism toward Marschall, even if it meant taking advantage of the Kaiser's weaknesses.[95] In early February 1895 there was a Court ball at which the head of the Catholic Center Party, Dr Lieber, was present. Marschall suggested to the Emperor that he speak with Lieber, since the naval appropriations depended for pas-sage on the support of Lieber's party. Wilhelm refused and instead spent some time talking with an anti-Catholic ex-Jesuit introduced to him by Lucanus. The whole business was unremarkable enough and would have passed into oblivion had it not been resurrected a week later by Wilhelm's two aides-de-camp, Hans von Arnim[96] and Gustav von Kessel. They had accompanied the Emperor, alone, to his hunt-ing retreat at Hubertusstock and used the opportunity to snipe at Marschall. At this point, Wilhelm suffered an attack of retrospective rage at the incident and fired off an hysterical letter to Eulenburg, in which he distorted the truth of the affair. Wilhelm complained that Marschall had had Lieber invited behind his back and had then rudely tried to force Wilhelm to speak with the gentleman. Wilhelm added that Marschall would soon have to go.

As we have seen, Eulenburg's usual tactic when confronted by extreme emotional outbursts from his friend was to calm Wilhelm down and prevent him from taking precipitate action. Wilhelm's vio-lent moods usually passed if given a bit of time. But in this case, Eulenburg leapt at the chance to burn Marschall before the flames died down. Eulenburg had received his master's letter, plus one each from Arnim and Kessel, at his ambassadorial post in Vienna. Eulen-burg wrote back that Holstein would probably leave with Marschall. The trick was to prevent Chancellor Hohenlohe from doing so as well. To this end, Eulenburg wrote a long letter to the chancellor, which relayed Wilhelm's side of the story.[97] As a further measure, Eulenburg wanted to bring in Bülow as a prop for Hohenlohe. To make peace with the Bismarcks he would offer Herbert the post of ambassador to London, thereby gaining the Bismarcks' support for the government reorganization.

The next series of letters which Eulenburg received in Vienna forced him to abandon his plans, however. Eulenburg learned from Marschall and Holstein what fabrications Wilhelm's complaints had been and how weak the government would be in the Reichstag if Marschall, its chief spokesman there, were dismissed. Eulenburg's next letter retreated to an acceptance of the status quo. Wilhelm responded by retreating even further: he blamed Eulenburg for stirring up trouble about something he had 'long ago' forgotten. 'Unhappy one, leave me in peace with such stuff! . . . Let all those people whom you caused to dance around like puppets remain quietly seated in their offices.'[98]

There are several conclusions to be drawn from the 'Lieber Affair.' The first is that, while both Eulenburg and Wilhelm were tending in the same direction, Eulenburg was pushing the Emperor considerably faster than he wanted to go. Eulenburg showed that he was willing to take advantage of Wilhelm's impetuosity, so long as the effects of this rashness would help to establish personal regime. By doing so, Eulenburg risked encouraging Wilhelm to retain habits of thinking and action with which Eulenburg otherwise did not agree and which were inimical to wise and steady government. In this case, the habits were reliance upon politically ignorant military men, mindless anti-Catholic prejudice translated without intervening steps into harsh policy, and abrupt changes of civilian officials regardless of their popularity or ability. Encouragement of these habits was a short-sighted policy indeed, for their continuance would make personal regime a disaster.

Second, Eulenburg's advocacy of reconciliation with the Bismarcks marks a move to the right on his part, a closer orientation with the politics of those at Court, namely Kuno Moltke, August Eulenburg, and some of the military people.[99] These figures exerted influence on Wilhelm daily. Eulenburg could reasonably assume that since they were all humming the same tune, Wilhelm would begin to pick it up. But, finally, the 'Lieber Affair' illustrates the limits of Eulenburg's power at this time. Since the Emperor could appoint and dismiss his ministers at will, his irreconcilable opposition to someone would almost certainly spell that person's doom. With this in mind, Eulenburg pressed in the next years to convert the Kaiser's distrust for Marschall into irremediable dislike. But so long as the targets of

Eulenburg's intrigues supported each other and had a political base independent of the Kaiser or the Court (in the Reichstag, for example), they could prevail. And in this case, Wilhelm's fitful anger could not crack their solidarity.

Eulenburg's plans suffered another setback at the hands of ministerial solidarity in the Köller crisis of November 1895, when Chancellor Hohenlohe and the Staatsministerium forced the resignation of Minister of the Interior Köller.[100] The Köller crisis placed the Kaiser in a *Zwangslage,* that is, the ministers compelled Wilhelm to act against his will by threatening mass resignation. Eulenburg was at his position in Vienna during the affair and played a role only afterward, by working to keep the chancellor and Holstein in office, thus preventing the crisis from spreading. However, Eulenburg was 'incensed' at the humiliation that Wilhelm had received at the hands of his own ministers and felt that the ministry was 'discredited' by its lapse into parliamentarism. Eulenburg henceforce redoubled his efforts to institute personal regime.[101]

After their success in the Köller crisis, Eulenburg was sure that Holstein, Marschall, and War Minister Bronsart[102] had agreed to curb Wilhelm's power permanently. Even before Holstein confirmed his suspicions, Eulenburg knew that they planned to repeat the Köller crisis on a scale so large that Wilhelm would never recover. Eulenburg's counterplan was: (1) to postpone all controversial policy decisions for as long as possible, specifically until Eulenburg's personnel changes had taken effect, (2) to split Hohenlohe from Holstein and Marschall, thus making it possible to oust the latter without the large scandal another change in chancellor would entail, and (3) to proceed with the original plan to bring Bülow to Berlin as secretary of foreign affairs in preparation for his future elevation to the chancellorship.

Wilhelm's anger at his humiliation in the Köller crisis made him more eager than ever before to support Eulenburg's political plans. Wilhelm wrote to Eulenburg in December 1895 that he firmly intended, should Hohenlohe fall ill or die, to appoint Bülow chancellor, vice president of the Staatsministerium, and head of the Foreign Office, to dump Marschall into an embassy, and to replace Bötticher by Posadowsky.[103] With the Emperor fully committed to the proposed changes, it became merely necessary to wait for the appropriate moment.

Eulenburg let matters rest until summer 1896 when he went into high gear again. The occasion for his renewed activity was a flare-up of excitement over Military Court Reform.[104] Eulenburg tried to use

Wilhelm's anger at War Minister Bronsart and Chancellor Hohenlohe to bring about the desired personnel changes. The plan was the same: to replace Bronsart, Marschall, and Bötticher, while keeping, if possible, Hohenlohe. If Hohenlohe could not be persuaded to remain, Eulenburg wanted Botho Eulenburg as interim chancellor. In any case, Bülow would become head of the Foreign Office. These changes all were to take effect before the Reichstag reconvened.[105] The residual solidarity of the ministers was, however, still too great to allow such sweeping changes. But this time the Kaiser and his friend were strong enough to exact one sacrifice: Bronsart. Under the compromise which Eulenburg proposed, Bronsart was promoted upstairs and replaced by a lackey of Wilhelm's, Heinrich von Gossler,[106] who had sworn 'only to be his Kaiser's General.'[107] Everyone else remained in his old position for the time being.

In November 1896 the military entourage[108] pressed Wilhelm to dismiss the Reichstag and carry out far-reaching governmental changes through a coup d'état. Eulenburg, prodded by Holstein, warned Wilhelm against such a course on the grounds that Wilhelm lacked the necessary political support for such a grand step.[109] Marschall's political power would have to be destroyed first. Fortunately for Eulenburg, Marschall was in the process of accomplishing this by himself. He had rashly become embroiled in a court case, the Tausch affair,[110] which sapped his energy and created a new phalanx of enemies for him. Eulenburg advised Wilhelm to wait until the Tausch trial had thoroughly exhausted Marschall, at which time he would fall of his own weight and bring the other ministers with him. In June 1897 this is exactly what happened.

The precipitate personnel changes of June 1897 marked the establishment of personal regime and a sharp shift to the right in government policy. The liberal Marschall was replaced by Bülow, heir apparent to the chancellorship, whose stated goal was to be the 'tool' by which 'personal rule – in the good sense – would truly begin.'[111] Interior Minister Bötticher, the other pillar of the Caprivi economic system, was replaced by Posadowsky. These and the five other changes which accompanied them were exactly what Eulenburg had prescribed.[112] The June 'revolution,' moreover, had actually been preceded by another personnel coup of which the public learned only a few months later: Admiral Hollmann, defender of the small navy, was driven out of the Reichsmarineamt by Admiral Tirpitz, evangelist for the huge, 'risk' fleet. Hollmann's departure was the result of collaboration between the Emperor and his Naval Cabinet chief,

Senden-Bibran, precisely in order to enable Tirpitz to build a fleet large enough to launch *Weltpolitik*. Eulenburg's role in this was negligible. However, the changes Eulenburg brought about and the appointment of Tirpitz formed the two pillars of German policy thereafter: conservative–agrarian *Sammlungspolitik* internally and aggressive *Weltpolitik* externally.

The successful conclusion of the personnel changes of June 1897 was due primarily to the weakness of Eulenburg's opponents. Chancellor Hohenlohe had allowed himself to be split off from and stripped of his political allies, Marschall and Bötticher, through indecision, the weaknesses of infirm old age, and considerations of pecuniary gain.[113] Marschall was physically exhausted by his exertions in the Tausch trial and undoubtedly by years of combat with his enemies at Court. Bötticher was simply tired of office.[114] Why Holstein abandoned his principles is not clear.[115]

Although each person had his different reasons for capitulating, there were two elements at work which made the capitulation likely. The most important was mental and physical exhaustion suffered by the men of the New Course. Eulenburg, civilians at Court like August Eulenburg and Lucanus, and almost the entire military entourage had worked tirelessly for years to undermine the position of Marschall in particular, but secondarily of everyone whom Marschall could call an ally. By the time they had won over the Kaiser to their point of view, the endless struggle, day after day, had finally become too much for their enemies. It was too hard to fight everyone all the time. This explains why the Caprivi ministers were relieved to quit office. It does not explain why they did not make more political capital out of their departures. Had they made more waves in June they could have prevented the easy transition to the personal regime which they opposed. The genie behind their convenient acquiescence was Eulenburg. In 1894 Eulenburg had supported Hohenlohe's candidacy for chancellor precisely because he thought the old man could be manipulated in this way. Eulenburg literally tricked Marschall into cooperation by promising him a comfortable embassy, which, unbeknownst to the minister, he would have received anyway.[116] With the submission of these two, everything else fell into place.

Eulenburg's overall success was also in good measure due to the active, behind-the-scenes support he received from the entourage, particularly from Lucanus. During the struggle to turn away from the New Course Eulenburg had been drawn much closer to the entourage than he had been before or would be again. But his tactical success, the easy transition, was due to his own efforts and points up the limits of his cooperation with certain factions of the entourage. For its part, the military, particularly Senden, Plessen, and Waldersee, had pressed during the spring of 1897 for a violent transition. They planned to take advantage of the quiescent external situation to quieten the internal one permanently. The emotional Kaiser seemed at several points eager to go along. A coup was prevented by the stern warning from Eulenburg and Bülow that the risks were too great and that the coming Bülow chancellorship might be ruined forever by such haste.[117] Eulenburg's solution was therefore the less radical of the two most likely outcomes.

1897 marked the zenith of Eulenburg's political influence. Its decline thereafter was at least partly intentional. Eulenburg had championed Bülow because he would inaugurate the personal regime that would relieve Eulenburg of the burden of holding together the disparate elements of government. Increasingly Eulenburg had complained that he could no longer act alone as coordinator. It was too much for one man, and Eulenburg's frail health was buckling under the strain. So it was with great relief that Eulenburg ushered in the new era, which was to make him obsolete. 'Oh my dearest Bernhard,' he wrote, 'what a difference in terms of work and burden for me, *since you have been in office.*'[118]

Eulenburg may have marginally regretted his sudden retirement; indeed, he wrote in the same letter that he almost suffered under his freedom 'because I would like to help you [Bülow] bear [the burden of governing].'[119]

But Bülow clearly was not about to allow this lest Eulenburg upstage him. Bülow did not keep Eulenburg as well informed, particularly on internal matters, as he had been before 1897. Eulenburg's main source of information throughout the nineties had been Holstein. This spring dried up entirely in 1899 when Holstein stopped speaking (and writing) to Eulenburg altogether. Holstein's antipathy was reflected, albeit more mildly, by Hohenlohe as well. The most important repositories of information were therefore largely closed to Eulenburg. He still had his sources at Court, of course, for the count continued to be on good terms with his cousin August and with the chief of the Civilian Cabinet, Lucanus.

In 1902, Eulenburg's relations with the Military Cabinet, which as we have seen were uncertain at best, took a decided turn for the worse when his old enemy,[120] Dietrich Hülsen, succeeded Hahnke as Military Cabinet chief. It is difficult to tell exactly what news Eulenburg received and from whom because of a peculiarity in his surviving papers. For the years 1886 through 1897 the *Nachlass* contains a tremendous wealth of letters, diary entries, memoranda, and notes on both personal and political topics. From 1898 to 1902, however, the personal documents are missing, for reasons which will be discussed below, and the number of political items drops off sharply.[121] Omitting personal letters after 1898 and halting the collection at 1902 were decisions made by Eulenburg.[122] It is possible that he deliberately thinned out his political correspondence after 1898 as well, though this seems hardly likely. The paucity of the collection more probably reflects Eulenburg's political inactivity. One should not get the impression, however, that Eulenburg was suddenly an ill-informed, political outsider. He was not. He was merely no longer a necessity without which things would fly apart. And, not being required, Eulenburg was content to let the affairs of state flow as the new team of hand-picked ministers determined, intervening only now and again as his diplomatic office or intimate friendship with Wilhelm dicated.

A measure of Eulenburg's contentment with the new order is the warmth and trust he continued to feel for Bülow. For Eulenburg, Bülow was unique and irreplaceable: 'Another person could not, or further would not do the work for him [the Kaiser] that you do. No one besides you has the mixture of genius, knowledge, and loyalty which you combine.'[123] Shortly after Bülow finally became chancellor in 1900, Eulenburg wrote proudly that 'one of the best duties for which God called me was my intervention in your life's course, this intervention which I have *always regarded as a mission.*'[124]

Even after his disgrace, when he had good reason to think Bülow might have been involved in his fall, Eulenburg did not turn against his old friend and protégé. Instead, he chose to believe that if Bülow had failed him as a friend, it was because Holstein had pressured him to do so and Bülow had at last weakly given in. This saddened Eulenburg, but did not fill him with the hatred which one finds in his other, post-scandal assessments of former friends.[125] Eulenburg's constant trust for Bülow shows something beyond his capacity for friendship. It shows the extent to which his political designs were, however misguided, selfless. He did not aspire to be chancellor or, ultimately, even to be the power behind the throne. He wanted power to reside in the throne itself, independent and stable. With the accession of Bülow to office, Eulenburg hoped that he had achieved that goal.

Before proceeding to the tangled events of Eulenburg's fall, two things remain to be considered: the extent to which Eulenburg advanced his friends, and the ways in which he influenced or did not influence the Kaiser.

Bernhard Bülow was the most important person who owed his job to Eulenburg, although it is also clear that he would have gone far, at least in the diplomatic service, even without Eulenburg's help.[126] Karl Dörnberg was another diplomat whom Eulenburg disinterestedly espoused. In 1890 the count lobbied on Dörnberg's behalf with Wilhelm to get for him the post of first secretary in the embassy in Rome.[127] Instead, Marschall and Caprivi insisted he go to the more sensitive post in Russia.[128] Holstein and Bülow both thought Dörnberg remarkably capable.[129] Only his early death prevented him from taking his place among Germany's top diplomats.

The case is different with Varnbüler and Moltke. Eulenburg almost singlehandedly maneuvered them both into potentially important political positions. Varnbüler might possibly have acceded some day to the post of Württemberg's envoy to Berlin into which Eulenburg propelled him with such haste in 1893/4.[130] Varnbüler's father had been Württemberg's minister president from 1864 to 1870. His brother-in-law had for many years represented that state at the Berlin Court, so Varnbüler was well connected politically. His own way was blocked, however, by the opposition of the Bismarcks,[131] and the powerful Bavarian envoy to Berlin, Hugo von Lerchenfeld-Köfering.[132]

While Eulenburg continued to pull strings, Varnbüler's career was given a boost by another friend, Baron Boris von Wolff, who recommended to the King of Württemberg that Varnbüler become Württemberg's representative to Russia.[133] Varnbüler, who had up until then been in the Prussian civil service as *Landrat* of Tarnowitz in Silesia, now left the Prussian service for the Württembergian so that he could take the position. One and a half years later, Varnbüler moved on to Vienna. Holstein accused Eulenburg of having brought about this change. Eulenburg, of course, denied it.[134] Despite these rapid advances, Varnbüler's career remained mired in the opposition of Lerchenfeld, Caprivi, and Marschall, to which Varnbüler added a complication by his impending marriage to a Russian divorcee of whom everyone disapproved. In fact, a not inconsiderable amount of resistence to Varnbüler centered around his roué's life and his rough manners.[135]

In 1893 Eulenburg earnestly set about to remove these obstacles. He planned to clear the way to Berlin by bringing about the fall of Minister President Hermann Freiherr von Mittnacht.[136] His replacement would be Württemberg's current representative to Berlin,

Moser,[137] who could then in turn be replaced by Varnbüler. Eulenburg tried to discredit Mittnacht in Caprivi's eyes by making it appear that Mittnacht was being deceptive in the crisis concerning Prussian army maneuvers in Württemberg that fall. Mittnacht wriggled out of the trap by framing Moser. The result was the same. While Kiderlen-Wächter worked on Caprivi,[138] Eulenburg talked Wilhelm into requesting Varnbüler's appointment.[139] This done, Eulenburg could assure King Wilhelm of Württemberg[140] that Varnbüler's private life was not really so shameless as gossip would have it.[141] Holstein became reconciled to Varnbüler's selection because Varnbüler was not a particularist and because Holstein's enemies were castigating Kiderlen, Eulenburg, and Varnbüler, along with Holstein himself in satirical articles in the *Kladderadatsch*.[142] In Holstein's eyes, Varnbüler's appointment became a slap in the face of the Bismarck faction. In this spirit, Holstein then mollified Marschall.[143] Varnbüler finally took up his post in April 1894 and held it until 9 November 1918.

In conducting this maneuver, Eulenburg had more on his mind than nepotism. Varnbüler's appointment was another step toward the creation of personal regime. Eulenburg explained to Wilhelm the importance of Varnbüler's advancement. Lerchenfeld's view could be summed up this way, he explained:

[Varnbüler] is disgusting to the entire Bundesrat, first because of his manners, and then as *Mignon* of the Kaiser. It is quite unpleasant for the other state representatives when they know that there is one among them who perhaps will not hold tight with them against the Kaiser!!!! Axel is admittedly first and foremost Your Majesty's servant. ... He will regard things more through Your Majesty's eyes than through Stuttgart's spectacles. ... I have briefed him exactly and explained the task which he must fulfill: that is, as I indicated before – the necessity to weaken Bavaria in the Bundesrat.[144]

Kiderlen agreed that the appointment had 'great advantages for the imperial government.'[145] In fact, Varnbüler went on to develop fairly good relations with Lerchenfeld.[146] Neither Mittnacht nor King Wilhelm II were in any case inclined to join in small state plots against Prussia. King Wilhelm was a devoted admirer of Kaiser Wilhelm and of the Prussian army. He was, moreover, not overly energetic and preferred to see Reich policy run from Berlin. Although Mittnacht occasionally dabbled in particularist waters, he basically supported national unity, and neither he nor his successors posed a real danger to Berlin. While Varnbüler represented Württemberg in Berlin, relations between that state and Prussia were therefore quiescent. Kaiser Wilhelm, Eulenburg, and the men of the New Course exhibited an almost paranoic distrust for Mittnacht because he was a strong supporter of Bismarck. The Kaiser thought Mittnacht was a 'disguised red democrat, who steered a specifically Swabian particularist politics.'[147] These groundless fears made Wilhelm happy to have a trustworthy servant in the viper's nest.

Varnbüler lived up to Wilhelm's – and Eulenburg's – hopes. Wilhelm considered him 'one of my best friends.'[148] Varnbüler's loyalty, in turn, was unquestionable. His conservatism and unabashedly pro-Prussian stance is well illustrated by his response to the Zabern affair.[149] After accurately reporting the parliamentary ire caused by this archetypal exercise of Prussian militarism, Varnbüler went on to admire the physical presence and 'stiff bearing [*stramme Haltung*]' of the Prussian war minister as he tried to browbeat the Reichstag into silence. Had Chancellor Bethmann Hollweg been more aggressive, Varnbüler thought, he could have intimidated the parliamentarians. He then referred to the Social Democrats as 'such Hereros' against whom only 'disdain' of the kind exercised by the military at Zabern would suffice.[150] Varnbüler's detailed reports to Stuttgart made him valuable to his home state as well.[151] And unlike other members of the 'Liebenberg Round Table,' Varnbüler managed to keep a low profile in Berlin; although he was mentioned at the beginning of the Eulenburg scandal, he never actually became a target of it. His name soon dropped from public view, and he continued at his post until Wilhelm fled the throne.

Axel Varnbüler may have brought 'great advantages' to the imperial government, as Kiderlen suggested, but what Kuno Moltke contributed, beyond musical ability, is highly questionable. Indeed, Kuno Moltke is the one person whom Eulenburg advanced of whom it can fairly certainly be said that, without his protective angel, he would have languished forever in some lowly position.

Moltke was singularly ill-suited to his chosen career in the military. Neither his bearing nor his personality was soldierly. He projected an image of weakness, sensitivity, and ineffectuality. We have seen that he was never taken quite seriously, politically or militarily.[152] Admiral von Müller did not even consider Moltke part of the military entourage: 'in the predominantly militarily brought up entourage of the Kaiser, he was indubitably a very worthwhile supplementary element' because of his musical gifts.[153] Indeed Moltke owed his position in the *Umgebung* largely to those gifts. Wilhelm must have known Moltke fleetingly as he knew all the officers who served under him. Still, the first record of an extended meeting is on 23 May 1892, when Moltke arrived at Prökelwitz by Wilhelm's invitation and stayed for several days with Eulenburg, enchanting the Kaiser by his piano playing and by a march of his own composition. Wilhelm was so taken with the latter that he ordered the trumpet corps of the Leib-Husaren Regiment from Danzig to come and perform it for him.[154] A month later, when Eulenburg feared he would be unable to attend the *Nordlandreise,* Wilhelm called Moltke to replace him, clearly as a musical substitute.[155] When Wilhelm journeyed to England that August (the first to the sixth), Moltke accompanied him. Eulenburg wrote that he was 'happy, though actually not surprised, that Y.M. likes Kuno. It is a humanly justified feeling, to wish that two persons to whom one is particularly close, should like each other.'[156]

Eulenburg professed to be surprised when, in April of the following year, Wilhelm appointed Moltke Flügeladjutant.[157] To Varnbüler Eulenburg wrote that 'it is good that we have him in Berlin.'[158] In the next several years, however, Eulenburg discovered that it was not always so 'good.' The one area in which Moltke exhibited any political independence was in precisely that area in which he and his friend disagreed: whether or not Wilhelm should seek a reconciliation with the Bismarcks. Moltke was an emotional admirer of the old chancellor. It was his fondest dream that harmony should once more reign between Friedrichsruh and Potsdam. Moltke was, of course, not alone amongst the entourage[159] in these feelings, but his naïveté about how reconciliation could weaken Wilhelm's power infuriated Eulenburg. Eulenburg tried to disabuse Moltke of his romantic view of politics, but those few letters which Eulenburg included in his papers do not indicate a large degree of success.[160] Under the influence of his entourage, Wilhelm suddenly in January 1894 sent Moltke with two bottles of wine to Friedrichsruh as a gesture of friendship toward Bismarck. This move paved the way toward limited reconciliation, but only by going behind the backs of Wilhelm's ministers, who were not pleased with the maneuver.[161]

After this episode, Eulenburg warned Wilhelm that Moltke had an 'impulsive nature,' which made his judgment untrustworthy in matters concerning the Bismarcks.[162] Apart from the Bismarck affair, Moltke does not appear to have engaged in politics to any significant extent. Harden subjected Moltke's imperial career to minute scrutiny and found nothing discreditable. If he had a political effect it was as just another reed which bent to the more conservative, agrarian, Bismarckian, military, racialist,[163] anti-Foreign Office wind which whistled through the entourage.

Eulenburg's role in Moltke's appointment as military attaché to

Vienna in 1897 has already been examined.[164] When Moltke and his temporary wife made a hash of that career possibility, Wilhelm gave him the command of his old regiment, the Leib-Kürassier. Eulenburg evidently feared that Moltke might botch that chance as well and supplied Wilhelm in advance with excuses to explain that possibility.[165] Moltke advanced to the command of the 11th Cavalry Brigade (1901), through section chief in the General Staff (1903), to Kommandant of the city of Berlin (1905), where he was when the Eulenburg scandal toppled him into the law courts. He had attained the rank of major general (1906) but had not achieved any greater degree of public esteem than he had enjoyed at the beginning of his career. He remained a musically talented, rather nice nonentity.

A vast majority of persons (and there were many) whom Eulenburg caused to be shifted around were not personal friends of his. Most were career civil servants or diplomats whose advancement or relegation to the backwaters Eulenburg felt was beneficial to Wilhelm and to the establishment of personal regime. Almost all were already candidates for the specific post in question, and Eulenburg merely pushed them over their few competitors. Most appointments were also favored by Holstein, Kiderlen, often by Marschall and Caprivi, although very often their support was for other reasons than Eulenburg's. In diplomatic appointments Eulenburg was successful time and again because he favored civilians, and Holstein and company went along in order to forestall the military possibilities who were continually thrown up by the military entourage and/or by the Emperor. Similarly, in civil service appointments, as long as the deciding factor was the candidate's relation to the Bismarcks, then Eulenburg, Holstein, Caprivi, Hohenlohe, and Marschall were usually in agreement.

It was frequently observed at the time and has been since that the pool for high offices after 1890 was mediocre at best. Admiral Müller and Chancellor Bethmann Hollweg discussed 'the lack of great personalities in that age group which is now occupying the higher positions. This is true for all branches: army and navy, administration and diplomacy.'[166] Partly this was due, as Norman Rich has noted, to the all-pervasive bureaucratic system, which stifled personal initiative and thus rerouted creativity from policy making to intrigue.[167] Primarily, however, mediocrity was the costly price which the *Kaiserreich* paid for stability. Since the founding of the Empire personnel policies had been consciously designed to winnow out the socially and therefore politically unacceptable from the bureaucracy.[168] The resulting bureaucratic *Stand,* while different from the Junkers, nonetheless was an essential cog in the interlocking system, bureaucracy–officer corps–diplomatic service–Court, that ultimately sustained the Junkers' (and the monarch's) power. Reform, either in terms of new blood or new policy might upset that balance.[169] So reform was impossible, and the bureaucracy became increasingly relegated to a strictly supportive role in the system at large. The bureaucracy became less and less involved in policy innovation, more and more in mere administration, even at the ministerial level. This trend made Eulenburg's self-appointed task much easier, since he wanted Wilhelm to decide policy and his ministers to carry it out more or less unquestioningly. The pattern of his choices points uniformly in this direction. The consequences of Eulenburg's efforts to advance a few friends pale in comparison to the cumulative political effect of the many other personnel changes which he brought about.

As for the charges of flattery, it is true that Eulenburg was particularly sensitive to the isolation, loneliness and pressure which surrounded his imperial friend. Consequently, he did everything in his power to make Wilhelm's personal and political existence both more successful and easier. He did flatter Wilhelm. He did try to mitigate the impact of setbacks. But he also squeezed in more criticism than Wilhelm received from any comparably important member of the entourage during the 1890s.[170] But Eulenburg was never merely critical. This was one of the sources of his success. He always sweetened the bitter by preceding (or succeeding) praise, by long-winded regret or by jokes.[171] He could make his barbs quite sharp, however. He effectively ridiculed Wilhelm's occasional approval of duels in matters of honor, the Emperor's anti-Catholicism, and the stupidly violent ways of the military entourage by suggesting once when Wilhelm was loudly excoriating the Pope that he should send Plessen to challenge His Holiness to a duel. Wilhelm laughed, but the message was clear.[172] Eulenburg often protected himself from the reaction to his own criticism by attributing it to public opinion or by forwarding critical letters from other people to Wilhelm with a mild disclaimer that Wilhelm would know which was the correct course.[173] His own more censorious latters were not infrequently sent to the secretary of the Foreign Office in hopes that they would either be incorporated anonymously into an *Immediatvortrag* or would be received as an official, rather than a personal report.[174]

The best summation of Eulenburg's techniques for handling the difficult Emperor are contained in the advice he gave to Bülow in

June 1897, just before Bülow travelled to Berlin to inaugurate personal regime.

This is my last word, my last request of you. . . . Only if you handle the Kaiser psychologically correctly can you be of use to the country. You are Kaiser Wilhelm II's last card. Wilhelm II takes everything personally. Only personal arguments make an impression on him. He likes to teach others but does not like to be taught. He cannot tolerate boredom; ponderous, stiff, thorough people get on his nerves and achieve nothing with him. Wilhelm II wants to shine, to do, to decide everything himself. Unfortunately, what he does himself often turns out wrong. He loves fame and is ambitious and jealous. In order to get his approval of an idea, one must act as though it is his own. One must make everything comfortable for Wilhelm II. He will encourage others to be rashly vigorous but will let them lie in the holes they fall into as a consequence. Never forget that H.M. needs praise now and then. He belongs to those who become mistrustful if they do not hear recognition from important people now and again. You will be granted all your wishes if you do not fail to utter appreciation where H.M. deserves it. He will be thankful for it like a good, smart child. He will finally see ill-will in continued silence where he deserves appreciation. Both of us will not step over the border of flattery.[175]

Eulenburg here shrewdly recapitulated Wilhelm's character. By scrupulously following this advice, Bülow ensconced himself closer to Wilhelm II than any other chancellor or minister did during his reign. But this advice also opened yawning pitfalls. It encouraged Wilhelm to continue to personalize politics and to delude himself about his own genius. It encouraged advisers to shorten reports, sweeten criticism and cater to Wilhelm's self-delusions. In short, this psychologically astute and personally understanding method of handling the Kaiser never gave him the opportunity to grow out of being a 'good, smart child.' How much of a possibility growth actually was is questionable. Nonetheless, the attempt to make Wilhelm's life both successful *and* easier could not work. Wilhelm's temperament presented his advisers with a choice. Making Wilhelm comfortable meant at most some short-run successes,[176] but ultimately, failure.

Eulenburg's political legacy was not what he had intended it to be. He thought that by furthering personal regime he was ensuring conservative, monarchical continuity against change. But by focussing so much responsibility on to the Kaiser, he actually laid the foundation for military adventurism. Eulenburg's love for Wilhelm made him disregard for too long the probably fatal effects of the Kaiser's character. Wilhelm's neurotic compulsion to be manly and his inability to work, in particular, virtually assured that, in a time of crisis, the military entourage would gain the upper hand. Furthermore, a time of crisis was highly likely to follow the inauguration of Wilhelm's dream, *Weltpolitik,* which threatened to upset the balance of international relations.

In effect, personal regime encouraged the common denominator of the Prussian governmental system. That is, in the absence of a strong chancellor, Wilhelm alone was unable to unite the various threads of policy. The Cabinets, the Hauptquartier, the Court, the bureaucracy, and the General Staff began to move independently of one another. The degree to which any institution was able to initiate (as opposed to execute) policy on its own, without the Kaiser, always depended upon how interested he was in its domain. In any case, since the Kaiser was never entirely absent, these institutions were not simply left to fight among themselves. Instead, over time Wilhelm's sporadic interventions assured that that institution became dominant which seemed to be the strongest and therefore seemed to offer the best hope of preserving the monarchy unchanged. This institution was, of course, the military, which, apart from claiming to be the natural support for the monarchy, was also the perfect tool for a class which was determined to rule by control and repression. Personal regime thus reinforced the fundamental tendency of the Bismarckian system to rely ultimately upon the military.

5

Philipp Eulenburg: decline and fall

There were other events besides the inauguration of personal rule which weakened Eulenburg's political effectiveness. 1897/8 marked a turning point in Eulenburg's private relations to Wilhelm. At the same time that Kuno Moltke's marriage was breaking up, so was Friedrich Eulenburg's. Friedrich (Fredi) was Philipp's younger brother[1] and had been married for more than twenty years to Klara von Schaeffer-Voit,[2] the daughter of a rich industrialist.[3] As in the Moltke case, it was the wife who sought the divorce. And, as in the Moltke case, she did so because of her husband's homosexuality. But Lily Moltke had been content to charge only cruelty and to pursue the homosexuality aspects of the case privately with the journalist Maximilian Harden. Klara Eulenburg was not so easily put off. Along with cruelty, she openly charged Friedrich with 'unnatural passions.' He was called before a military court-martial in October 1897 and resigned from his regiment before the decision was handed down.[4]

In contrast to his response to the Moltke divorce scandal, Wilhelm reacted to Friedrich's case with extreme hostility.[5] The most obvious reasons for this difference are the public nature of the charges and the fact that Friedrich was in Berlin, while Kuno was in Vienna. Friedrich's affair was therefore more immediately embarrassing to Wilhelm. Wilhelm also felt closer to Moltke and thought highly enough of him to have appointed Moltke his Flügeladjutant, thus putting Moltke in a class of persons whom Wilhelm regarded as untouchable.[6] Although Wilhelm knew Friedrich personally, there are no indications that they were close.

Wilhelm's vehemence suggests that other factors were also at work. That Friedrich Eulenburg had to quit the officer corps indicates that the evidence against him was strong. This impression is strengthened by the defendant's passivity in his own case: he did not request an investigation in order to clear his name, but allowed himself to be called before the court. Then he summoned his influential

brother from Vienna to try to persuade Wilhelm to dismiss the proceedings before they reached a conclusion.[7] Wilhelm's position on the
officer's honor code was clear. He expected his officers to take the
initiative in clearing their names. Failure to do so was almost worse in
his eyes than any crime or dishonor of which they might have been
accused. As we will see, this situation would repeat itself with brother
Philipp in 1907.

Friedrich Eulenburg's swift demise also suggests that he did not
have much support from his brother officers, and/or that some members of the military establishment were trying to 'get' Philipp through
his brother. These persons would have been in a position to convince
Wilhelm of Friedrich's guilt. Thus, Philipp Eulenburg's anticipated
intervention would not only come too late to be successful, but would
tend to discredit him in the Emperor's eyes. This would explain why
Philipp was desperately anxious to conceal his efforts on his brother's
behalf from the military: 'I would like to ask Your Majesty to keep all
of this information, which are *military secrets,* secret, especially from
the military authorities.'[8] If Wilhelm were being constantly worked
on by anti-Eulenburg forces in his military entourage, it might also
explain the extraordinary demand he made of Eulenburg. The Kaiser wanted Philipp to break off all contact with his brother. This
remarkable requirement enraged Eulenburg, as it was undoubtedly
meant (by others) to do, and he did not abide by it.[9] Eulenburg's own
interpretation[10] was that Klara had charmed or bribed several officers, presumably the chief of the military court-martial, Wartensle-
ben, whom she later married, into supporting her, and that Wilhelm
was particularly upset at the heavy attacks which Philipp Eulenburg
levelled at his sister-in-law. Eulenburg did indeed react to Klara in as
vociferously misogynistic a fashion as he had to Lily Moltke and later
would do to Auguste Viktoria,[11] but this hardly explains Wilhelm's
vehemence.

The rift between the Kaiser and his friend was deep and lasted into
the summer of 1898. For Eulenburg the psychological strain played
itself out on the physical plane, in a series of ailments that bothered
him throughout the spring. He wrote Bülow that he felt 'very poorly.
I feel as if I were morally stretched out on a medieval rack. The fate
of my poor brother exhausts me.'[12] Eulenburg's personal contact with
Wilhelm withered to a few letters. The count, pleading illness, did not
accompany the Kaiser on the customary pilgrimage to Prökelwitz for
the annual celebration of the beginning of their friendship. While
Eulenburg's seeming fall from grace delighted gossips and, of course,

Eulenburg's enemies, it deeply distressed Bülow, whose concern stemmed from both friendship and career considerations. 'I am convinced that everything will be as before between His Majesty and yourself as soon as you have been together with him for a few days,' he wrote optimistically to Eulenburg. But he was careful to insist emphatically that Eulenburg meet him and discuss the matter before Eulenburg embarked as the Foreign Office representative on the royal *Nordlandreise* that summer.[13]

As it turned out, Bülow's optimism was not unfounded. The feud was officially closed and the friends reconciled after a long talk between the Kaiser and his adjutant, Kuno Moltke, aboard the *Hohenzollern*. Whether or not Bülow suggested such a talk or whether Moltke took the initiative on behalf of his friend is not known. At any rate, Wilhelm considered the matter closed and 'did not want to hear any more about it.'[14] Both Eulenburg and Moltke were deeply touched by Wilhelm's efforts to be friendly with Eulenburg. As to Friedrich, Moltke reported Wilhelm speaking of him 'without any bitterness,' but Eulenburg was not sure if Moltke had not merely told him this to spare Eulenburg's feelings.[15] Eulenburg's lingering uncertainty about Wilhelm's true sentiments indicates what the episode had cost them both. Eulenburg never again trusted Wilhelm with the blindness which love had enabled him to preserve through a decade of changing political fortune. The almost religious devotion, the unshakeable faith had been deflated and slowly descended toward the earth. Henceforth Eulenburg was more critical of Wilhelm's character, his politics, and his capacity for growing. One might say that the foliage of the relationship had been broken off, although the roots remained. For both men, the relationship with the other was still of deep importance. But for Eulenburg at least his immense capacity for self-delusion about his friend had finally become limited. It was still perhaps not small, but it was no longer boundless.

The focus of Eulenburg's criticism was Wilhelm's character. After all his years on the throne, Wilhelm was still

unchanged in his explosive nature. [He is] even harder and more impulsive in a self-reliance upon [his] mature experience – which is no experience [*Sogar härter und plötzlicher in einem Selbstgefühl gereifter Erfahrung, die keine Erfahrung ist*]. His individuality is stronger than the workings of experience.[16]

These same observations about Wilhelm's character had persuaded Holstein years before that the Kaiser's power must be curbed by other institutions. Personal regime, under the circumstances, could only be a short-lived and dangerous experiment. Now, after his own bitter experiences, Eulenburg was finally prepared to agree. When Wilhelm pontificated against the Reichstag and threatened to crush parliamentary government, Eulenburg countered not with his usual argument that Wilhelm needed more political support among the princes and states before he could safely do this, but that the whole idea was impossible: 'Germany cannot and does not wish to live without a parliament.'[17] Eulenburg was filled with 'fearful and torturing worry' about the future to which Wilhelm's tendencies might lead.[18]

Eulenburg even began to share Holstein's doubts about Wilhelm's mental health.[19] 'I felt as if I were sitting on a powder keg,' he wrote to Bülow during the 1900 *Nordlandreise*. He begged Bülow not to send Wilhelm any political news which might provoke further outbreaks of the uncontrollable royal temper. At Kiel, before the embarkation, Wilhelm had exploded at Eulenburg over a political disagreement. Wilhelm's wild behavior worried Eulenburg so much that he discussed the matter with Bülow. The 'vacation' trip had made Wilhelm only more irritable. After another splenetic scene (to which Eulenburg was only a witness), he reported to Bülow that

H. M. *no longer has himself under control.* . . . Leuthold [Wilhelm's personal physician in attendance] just told me that he is at a loss. . . . I also see no way out but to wait quietly and pray to God that no complicated things come before H. M. Because more scenes, such as we had in Kiel, would lead to some sort of nervous crisis, whose form is difficult to predict.[20]

Three years later Eulenburg thought the situation was, if anything, worse. But this impression was not merely the product of his own disillusionment. The traits which Eulenburg had overlooked or downplayed in the past had indeed been exacerbated with time. Wilhelm's extreme nervousness was now aroused not merely by high politics, but by virtually every topic including the weather. Eulenburg spoke again with Leuthold about the condition of the Kaiser, 'who wanders around as if in a dream world and [whose] ego develops into an ever greater phantom.'[21] Leuthold was also vexed by Wilhelm's 'increasingly evident nervousness and ever-weakening self-control.' Eulenburg's reports on this score are in the same vein as the ones from 1900. His method of handling the situation was also the same (and was shared by the rest of the entourage): he tried to distract the Kaiser with amusing, harmless tales, tried to calm his nerves. In no case did he allow himself to become involved in an argument. All the while he prayed fervently that the nervous spells would pass. Eulenburg felt he had nothing more to offer his suffering friend than 'compassion and sympathy.'[22]

Eulenburg's compassion for Wilhelm encouraged him to label Wilhelm's condition somewhat curiously. While admitting that 'not healthy' was the 'mildest' conclusion one could reach concerning Wilhelm's state, he drew the spurious distinction between 'mental disturbance' and 'nervous breakdown.'[23] Wilhelm was not mentally ill, he merely suffered from weak nerves which were apt to snap under strain:

In a total breakdown, the Kaiser's nature would collapse in terrible convulsions, whose effects on governmental business and dealings with the highest officials of the Empire cannot be predicted. The crisis would bear the *character* of abnormality, without being it.[24]

It is not clear exactly what Eulenburg meant by this distinction except to spare Wilhelm the stigma of mental illness. We have seen how gifted Eulenburg was at such label-juggling in relation to himself. Nonetheless, this slight dishonesty regarding Wilhelm did not prevent Eulenburg from making other, more perceptive and more disquieting observations. He reported to Bülow that Wilhelm was prone to lapse into pathological lies, lies which had no purpose and which were easily discoverable. He wrote worriedly of numerous instances in which Wilhelm exploded in rage and demanded all sorts of fantastic things from his entourage, including the shooting of unarmed civilians. Eulenburg pleaded with Bülow to force Wilhelm to rest. Otherwise the crisis, he thought, would soon be upon them. He doubted that Wilhelm would consent to rest on his own or that Dr Leuthold would be likely to succeed in persuading him to do so. Eulenburg was pessimistic enough to add, 'unfortunately, it is probably questionable whether it [the crisis] can be stopped by hard-won rest.'[25]

Eulenburg's concern about and fears for Wilhelm were primarily personal. It tortured him to see his friend tormented by demons of his own making.

I frequently feel tears welling up inside me when I hear the dear, good Master (to whom I am *so* thankful, especially for his loyalty, despite the many sufferings he has caused me) in extreme attacks against all sorts of windmills and see his face distorted with rage.[26]

'A deep sadness fills me.'[27]

The political lessons which Eulenburg drew from his reassessment of Wilhelm's personality and mental health, however, he drew haltingly. At first, he could think of no other remedies than rest and the minimal restriction of royal power afforded by already existing institutions. After Wilhelm's betrayal of Eulenburg in 1907 had snapped the personal bonds between them, Eulenburg reread his le'- ters to Bülow and added a passage more specifically critical of Wil- helm's politics and of his political steadiness.[28] Apparently Eulenburg also felt that with the information he had had as early as 1900, he should have reached political conclusions more quickly than he did.

Nonetheless, despite the slowness of the process of Eulenburg's political disillusionment, by 1898 Eulenburg and Wilhelm had come for the first time to disagree on some fundamental matters of policy. Eulenburg's traditional conservatism became more pronounced in reaction to the notions of internal governance and *Weltpolitik* that per- sonal regime now allowed Wilhelm to pursue. Wilhelm's frequent outbursts against the Conservatives, on the occasion of the canal bill and the fleet, for example, frightened Eulenburg with the nightmare that Wilhelm might actually throw them over in order to rule with a more liberal Reichstag coalition.[29] Eulenburg's sympathy for the agrarian conservatives was the basis for his support of Miquel's *Sammlungspolitik*. That is, he was willing to endure the advantages which industry derived from *Sammlungspolitik*, advantages which might have an expansionary character ultimately harmful to the conservative causes, as a trade-off for the short-run preservation of the agrarians. Eulenburg was even prepared to put up with the *Bund der Landwirte*. In 1893 Eulenburg had opposed the group as demogogic and dan- gerously 'democratic.'[30] Six years later, when Wilhelm and Hohen- lohe tried to break the influence of the *Bund* in Prussia after the defeat of the canal bill, Eulenburg opposed this policy. Precisely the growth of 'democratic influences' moved him to accept the *Bund*, or more exactly, the membership of the great estate owners of East Prussia in it, as a bulwark against further erosion of the conservative position. Any effort to destroy the *Bund*, he felt, would only drive it to greater political extremity.[31]

Eulenburg's nervousness about increasing democratic extremism heightened in the years after 1897. Characteristic of his frame of mind was his reaction to a series of mysterious fires which broke out in Liebenberg in 1900. Eulenburg immediately imagined a socialist con- spiracy of intentional pyromaniacs. The culprit turned out to be a deranged local man who enjoyed fires. This story, which Bülow cites with amusement in his memoirs, illustrates Eulenburg's overly acute sense of Germany's internal instability and his perception of the weakness of his class. This siege mentality, however, made Eulenburg cautious where it made others desperately bold.

The difference between caution and boldness formed the most important area of disagreement between Eulenburg and Wilhelm when it came to *Weltpolitik*. Eulenburg, as we have seen, considered imperialism too risky a course for the monarchy to take. However, he compromised on his beliefs somewhat by supporting the establishment of a German navy in 1897–8. This position was at variance not only with Eulenburg's policies (in 1893 he wrote that he would regret it, if a naval bill were introduced to the Reichstag),[32] but also with his esthetics. He found Wilhelm's naval companions crude and boorish[33] and preferred dry land to rocking ships, cramped quarters, and seasickness. He also shared Miquel's and Holstein's doubts about the effect a navy would have on German finances and on the political balance in the Reichstag. Far from championing Wilhelm's dream, Eulenburg played an uncharacteristic role on the periphery of the maneuvering. As late as 1896, Eulenburg was still cautioning Wilhelm not to overburden the Reich and to use the navy for more or less conventional purposes. This was a veiled warning not to challenge British naval hegemony.[34] The following year, however, Eulenburg began to write Wilhelm of his warm interest in the fleet bill[35] and even went so far as to advise Wilhelm how best to get it passed.[36] One is forced to assume that Eulenburg's new-found enthusiasm stemmed from his loyalty to Wilhelm, whose most ardent desire and only concrete accomplishment the fleet was. Opposition to his dream fleet was tantamount in Wilhelm's eyes to treason and is perhaps more than one could reasonably expect from his most devoted admirer. Even Eulenburg's warmest outpourings, however, were tempered by nervousness about England's reaction.[37] He never shared the boundless optimism that many Wilhelminians pinned on naval politics.

Furthermore Eulenburg's belated support for the fleet did nothing to expand his continental view of politics. The heart of German foreign policy remained for him the Austrian alliance, which he thought should be maintained above everything else. Eulenburg's unswerving devotion to the Austrians brought him into increasing conflict with the Emperor and the Foreign Office (notably Holstein), who felt that the ramshackle, multi-national empire was a drag on the modern, energetic Reich.

As is often the case with Eulenburg, it is difficult to separate the political from the personal motivations behind his pro-Austrian stance.

Personal questions were indeed quite important. Eulenburg had become close to Count Goluchowski, the Austrian foreign minister,[38] close enough that Eulenburg practically enlisted Goluchowski's aid in his intrigues against Marschall in 1897.[39] Substantive disagreements between Eulenburg and the Foreign Office focussed on Eulenburg's unflagging support for Goluchowski and his colleagues. Holstein suspected Goluchowski of using Eulenburg's unquestioned support as a tool against himself and by extension against the German government.[40] It is not clear whether or not Goluchowski actively tried to split Eulenburg from the German Foreign Office and from Holstein. This was, however, certainly the effect of the string of arguments between Eulenburg and his diplomatic superiors, that resulted from the former's defense of the Austrian foreign minister. The last, and most important of these arguments occurred in the winter of 1901/2. Goluchowski's position in Austria had been shaken by large Polish nationalist demonstrations. The German government, and Wilhelm in particular, reacted badly to the disorders because they feared that they might spill over into Posen and disrupt the very fragile balance there between the growing Polish and the dwindling German populations. Wilhelm thought Goluchowski and his colleagues had not been stern enough in suppressing the riots and he wanted to say so in his emphatic way. Such criticism from Austria's major ally was likely to bring down the foreign minister, who was himself Polish. Eulenburg's course on the other hand was to hold on to Goluchowski at all cost. This discord contributed to Eulenburg's resignation later in the year.

Eulenburg's identification with Goluchowski and the Austrians underscored his isolation from Holstein and the Foreign Office. At one point Eulenburg was so furious with the manner in which the Foreign Office was treating Austria, that he claimed that 'the entire *Dreibund* rests at the moment upon Goluchowski, Schratt [Franz Joseph's female companion, previously a popular actress and as far as one can tell an innocent in foreign relations], and me.'[41] Eulenburg consistently overvalued his personal indispensability to the alliance.[42] He never changed his mind on the subject,[43] probably because he felt so isolated. In any event, Eulenburg's concerns were not unfounded. Austro-German relations had deteriorated considerably during the 1890s. His own absences from Vienna were partly to blame,[44] but most fundamental was the increasing power disparity between the two allies, which strained the relationship by changing its terms.

Eulenburg was caught in the middle. The strain from this, from pressures in Eulenburg's life, which we shall examine in a moment, and from the death of his mother, took its toll on Eulenburg's health. Throughout 1901 and 1902, Eulenburg pleaded with Bülow to let him resign. Finally, in August 1902, the Emperor and the chancellor relented. Eulenburg explained to his cousin August the reasons for his resignation from office:

> Last winter there were a number of episodes (particularly the Polish question) which showed where a strict adherence to one's own convictions could lead under certain circumstances. And therefore I believe that, as regards the well-known relationship between His Majesty and me, it is better *also for the Kaiser*, if I go my way *in peace*. I am no longer up to the tempo which is being maintained in Berlin, truly not.[45]

The next day in another letter of explanation to Max Fürstenberg,[46] he added that he no longer 'had the nerves to fight against such a tempo.'[47]

And so Eulenburg's official political career came to its anticlimactic end. Its high-point had been passed in the summer of 1897. Since then Eulenburg's political influence had been eclipsed by the slippery management of his protégé, Bülow. The basis for that influence, his relationship with Wilhelm, had been shaken and, though restored, never regained its former solidity, at least not in Eulenburg's eyes. Once Eulenburg had set up the instrument for personal rule, that is, the Bülow government, he became less interested in political questions. His letters to Wilhelm from Vienna became more and more devoted to Court gossip. His view of politics, always personal even in the best of times, became only more so. The man who left office in November 1902, though perhaps better informed of the twists and turns of policy and personnel than other officials, stood nonetheless on the periphery of politics. But the memory of his former power had grown into a myth which dogged him from the early 1890s until it finally felled him in 1907. The waves from Eulenburg's fall rocked the Emperor, the entourage, and the careers of numerous other highly placed persons. To complete Eulenburg's story we must now consider the other, personal reasons for his resignation in 1902 and proceed to his twilight career and the 'Eulenburg scandals' of 1907–8.

Perhaps Eulenburg's arguments with Wilhelm and his deteriorating health would have been sufficient to drive him from office, but there were many persons in Germany who were more than happy to help the process along. Indeed the number of persons who were jealous of Eulenburg's position, who felt he was the architect of their own career misfortunes, or who disagreed with him politically had become huge, especially since 1900, when Eulenburg was made prince.[48] As it became clear that Eulenburg's position with Wilhelm was not what it once had been, these people became bolder in expressing their opposition. By 1901/2 there were several schemes afoot to blackmail Eulenburg into resigning.

The first of these occurred in the summer of 1901, when Wilhelm received an anonymous letter from Munich recounting Eulenburg's interest in spiritism when he was envoy there. Wilhelm questioned Eulenburg about it. Eulenburg denied having pursued his interests after the late 1880s.[49] Eulenburg later was convinced that there was no letter, that Wilhelm was merely inquiring for his own purposes.[50] This is unlikely to have been the case, since Harden got wind of the same thing and used Eulenburg's spiritism as the main *leitmotiv* in an article attacking the prince in November (1901).[51]

The reawakened interest in Eulenburg's spiritist activities coincided with another setback in Eulenburg's emotional concept of friendship. Two of his oldest friends, Bolko Hochberg, Intendant of the Royal Theater, and Richard Dohna-Schlobitten (brother of Eberhard), suddenly turned against him in extreme bitterness. The cause of their enmity was Hochberg's replacement by yet another of Eulenburg's old friends, Georg Hülsen. Hochberg's had been until 1901 a mediocre career. The lack of artistically distinguishing productions unfortunately had not been compensated for by financial success.[52] The money situation was made worse by either the incompetence or malfeasance of one Pierson, Hochberg's close collaborator and trusted colleague at the theater. Wilhelm followed theatrical matters closely. He was as incensed at Hochberg's bungling as he was impressed by Hülsen's management at Wiesbaden, where Wilhelm made annual, week-long pilgrimages to view the performances. It is therefore unnecessary to think Eulenburg was much involved with Hochberg's replacement, though it is impossible to prove one way or the other, since the correspondence surrounding the affair had already disappeared during Eulenburg's lifetime.[53]

One must admit that Eulenburg's story is rather complicated.[54] According to him, Wilhelm found out about Pierson's financial misdeeds from Hausminister Wedel, who had jurisdiction over the *Hoftheater*. Wilhelm asked Eulenburg to use his influence to split Hochberg from Pierson so that the former's position could be saved. Eulenburg wrote twice to Hochberg, warning him to dissociate himself from Pierson, but did not tell Hochberg that the information was coming from Wilhelm and the Hausminister. Eulenburg claimed that the reason for his reticence on this point was that it was improper for Wilhelm to use Eulenburg to go behind the Hausminister's back and that, should Wedel discover what had occurred, Wilhelm would have been forced immediately to dismiss both Pierson and Hochberg in order to appease Wedel. Thus, Hochberg would lose his job anyway. Whether or not this was really Eulenburg's motive, Hochberg not surprisingly reacted to the letters as if they were a threat. Hochberg's close friend, Dohna, was equally incensed and shot off a vitriolic letter to Eulenburg complete with innuendoes about his character. Although Eulenberg's intimate friendship with Eberhard Dohna prevented Richard from publicizing the information he had at hand, the prince was frightened enough to plead with Chancellor Bülow to intercede on his behalf.[55]

A further indication that the scandal had widened to include other, more intimate allegations was Eulenburg's terror that the matter would end in the courts. When Pierson sued Eulenburg for slander in January 1902, Eulenburg immediately wrote to Bülow pleading with him to get Lucanus to quash the suit before it could reach the public arena. It took Lucanus less than a month to accomplish this, for which Eulenburg was eternally grateful.[56] Pierson then obligingly committed suicide, which brought the affair to a close. But Eulenburg had already succumbed to the pressure he was receiving from this and/or other quarters, and had asked Bülow to be able to resign. He said the reason was his health, but he added a paragraph, which made the real reason unmistakable: 'Also certain people must be told that my health requires a life in the south, far from Berlin and its social intercourse – I therefore would go to Oberbayern.'[57]

Pierson's death did not end the pressure on Eulenburg to resign. One of the 'certain people' whom Eulenburg wanted Bülow to assure that Eulenburg would not remain in Berlin was Maximilian Harden. Harden's latest campaign to rid the Court of its most accomplished courtier had culminated in early 1902 with a veiled ultimatum to Eulenburg to resign quickly.[58] In the spring of 1902 Harden had received more damaging information in the form of letters confirming Eulenburg's and Moltke's homosexuality. Harden alluded to these briefly in an article in terms which would have been unmistakable to those involved. Harden's pressure continued even after Eulenburg's resignation, which he celebrated with the observation: 'Hochberg plus Munich [had] worked together with smaller items,' including Holstein, to drive Eulenburg from office.[59]

The various intrigues against Eulenburg were more successful than

their authors had dared to hope. Although he did not fulfill his promise to go south permanently, Eulenburg was a prisoner of his bad
health for three years following his resignation and engaged in little
or no political activity. He lived in Liebenberg, occasionally making
unsuccessful forays to Gastein or Karlsbad to regain his health. In
1903, just after his resignation, he tried to make himself available to
Wilhelm as he had in the old days, but was too sick to carry it off. He
accompanied Wilhelm on the *Nordlandreise,* but was ill the entire time,
which made him a moody and unenjoyable companion.[60] He went
with Wilhelm to Rominten the same year but lasted only a day before
severe rheumatic pains forced him to retire to his bed and finally to
Liebenberg. In 1904, Eulenburg saw Wilhelm twice and spent some
days with the Emperor in Rominten. Their relationship, however, was
still tense. Tirpitz, who was also present, noted in his diary how upset
Eulenburg was at Wilhelm's instability and at the irresponsibility of
his entourage (chiefly of Admiral Hollmann). Eulenburg exclaimed
that he had never appreciated so much the efforts of the higher-level
bureaucracy and selected members of the officer corps, upon whose
shoulders fell the onerous task of 'setting everything right again and
taking responsibility for all the nonsense [that Wilhelm created].'[61]
A few months later Bülow remarked that Wilhelm had such a
catastrophic effect on Eulenburg's shattered nerves that the prince
was forced to take to his bed for several days after an imperial
visit.[62]

This state of affairs continued until late August 1905, when Eulenburg's health and spirits took a turn for the better. On the 26th,
Eulenburg wrote Wilhelm from Gastein to break a long silence and to
report that finally his depression had lifted and that he had regained
a sense of himself. He asked the Emperor if he might not accompany
him to Rominten. 'How I long to see Your Majesty again! I hope that
my health is now recovered so that I am not a gloomy companion.'[63]
Eulenburg gave a few, broad, general views of the foreign situation,
but mentioned nothing about domestic politics. Wilhelm was in any
case delighted and returned to Liebenberg on 30 October 1905 for
the annual *Kaiserjagd.* The following month, the Kaiser not only invited
Eulenburg to Rominten, but assigned him the political task of conducting informal talks with visiting Russian Minister President Sergei
Witte.[64]

These talks were part of the preliminaries to the Conference of
Algeciras. Witte had just come from a meeting with Chancellor Bülow,
where the two had agreed upon an agenda for the conference. Eulen-

burg was present during the time Witte spoke with the Kaiser, but neither Eulenburg nor Wilhelm said anything which disagreed with Bülow's views. In fact, the Rominten conversation was a rubber-stamp for decisions Bülow had already made. Thus, Eulenburg acted under orders of the Emperor and with the approval of the chancellor.[65] In no sense was he pursuing his own politics or interests, nor did his presence change the course of German policy at all.[66]

Rominten 1905 marked Eulenburg's delicate reentry into the world outside Liebenberg. In the first five months of 1906, Eulenburg saw Wilhelm as often as he had the entire previous year, but this amounted to only five times. Moreover, these meetings were hardly intimate, an occasional lunch or dinner, a wedding, and so forth. In May, Eulenburg accompanied Wilhelm on a foray through Alsace-Lorraine and then on to Prökelwitz, for the first time in years. Eulenburg was even on the list to rejoin the *Nordlandreise,* but at the last moment was crossed off. He was again present in Rominten in the autumn of 1906, which was also the last year in which the Liebenberg *Kaiserjagd* took place.

Eulenburg's reappearance set off spasms of terror and dismay among his all too numerous enemies. It was generally suspected that Eulenburg's physical recovery would enable him to begin to spin the webs by which he could once more exercise the power he had had in the 1890s. Three charges in particular finally combined to end his career forever. Holstein, as well as Harden, believed that Eulenburg had caused Holstein to be removed from his position in May 1906. Bülow believed that Eulenburg was trying to oust him in favor of a chancellor more susceptible to manipulation. And any number of people believed that Eulenburg had been instrumental in Germany's defeat at Algeciras by pushing a 'soft line' toward the French.

The first of these allegations is easy to dispose of: Holstein was dismissed by Bülow, who had grown weary of juggling the powers of Europe and Holstein too. Their repeated disagreements in the Moroccan crisis were the immediately precipitating factor. Characteristically, Bülow covered his tracks well and, uncharacteristically, Holstein's paranoia did not ferret out the cause of his misfortune. Of course, Bülow could not have ousted Holstein without Wilhelm's approval, but Wilhelm's approval could hardly be primarily ascribed to Eulenburg. Wilhelm and Holstein had disagreed about foreign policy for a number of years, and Wilhelm's efforts during the Moroccan crisis had only deepened the chasm between them. Holstein had almost as many enemies as Eulenburg, a number of whom were in Wilhelm's entourage and kept the royal ear well supplied with complaints. In any case, Holstein and Eulenburg had not spoken for years (since 1899), and Holstein's position was perfectly secure until he slipped from Bülow's graces.[67]

The second charge, that Eulenburg intrigued against Bülow in 1906/7, is less easy to dispose of since nothing is so elusive as a failed intrigue. That is, events typically leave behind documentary evidence, but non-events leave only tangled rumors. The rumors in this case were rife and were faithfully repeated to the chancellor by Eulenburg's old enemies, Carl Wedel and Dietrich Hülsen-Haeseler, joined by Hans von Plessen.[68] It is hardly surprising then if Bülow gradually came to believe them.

Bülow's suspicions were strengthened when Eulenburg urged him to resign on account of health shortly after the chancellor collapsed in the Reichstag in April 1906. Eulenburg's concern for Bülow's health was certainly not appreciated,[69] but it is unusual behavior for an intriguer to try to remove his opponent face to face. An equally likely explanation is simply that Eulenburg was projecting his own precarious health and hypochondria upon Bülow and sought to protect his old friend from the same fate that had befallen him. Eulenburg frequently warned both Bülow and Wilhelm of the dangers of overwork, and this conversation was probably another in that long line.[70]

Bülow returned to his duties in October 1906. The next month the German press crackled with rumors that, after Algeciras, the Kaiser wanted to dismiss Bülow, and had asked Eulenburg to keep an eye open for the next chancellor. These reports claimed that Eulenburg wanted Heinrich von Tschirschky, whom Harden called a creature of Eulenburg's,[71] to run foreign affairs, with Chief of Staff Helmuth Moltke becoming chancellor.

In the case of Tschirschky at least, contemporary sources do not substantiate the rumors. Tschirschky had replaced Richthofen as state secretary of the Foreign Office in January 1906 over the objections of both Holstein and Bülow. Tschirschky's appointment was solely due to Wilhelm,[72] who knew him personally, liked and trusted him from the days when Tschirschky had accompanied the Kaiser as Foreign Office representative on various imperial trips. The few relevant scraps in the Eulenburg papers indicate that Tschirschky and Eulenburg were on cordial, but hardly intimate terms.[73]

Austrian Ambassador Szögyényi thought that Harden's allegations concerning Tschirschky were 'entirely incorrect,'[74] and Lerchenfeld agreed.[75] Ambassador Monts, who was even better informed than Lerchenfeld, was equally astonished.[76] Tschirschky himself was furious at the implication that he was a creature of Eulenburg's but evidently felt it to be so groundless that he soon cooled down and did not bother to reply to it.[77] Indeed, the Tschirschky papers are entirely silent on Eulenburg.[78] In short, there is no evidence to support Harden's claim that Eulenburg had raised Tschirschky to the Foreign Office; Wilhelm's attitude, formed during the years after Eulenburg's retirement, would alone have been more than sufficient for that. In the absence of proof that Eulenburg had anything to do with that appointment, or that the two men were close, it is difficult to justify the notion that Tschirschky figured in Eulenburg's alleged plans for a governmental shake-up.

Helmuth Moltke was supposed to be the other lynchpin of Eulenburg's plan. The sources for the story were the same newspaper accounts, capped by an official denial, and Bülow's memoirs.[79] If the rumor were true, then Eulenburg never cleared his scheme with Moltke, who was horrified by the idea of becoming chancellor.[80] There is little question about one aspect of the incident, however: Bülow, through his press chief Hammann, orchestrated the publication of the story in order to discredit in advance any Court attempts to replace him.[81]

Whether or not the plots were real, Bülow had good reason to be nervous, because his position, especially after the setback at Algeciras, was indeed shaken. Imaginative improvisation has only a limited life-span in politics. By 1906, Bülow had frittered away his political and personal capital, just as the cracks in Wilhelminian Germany were beginning to gape open for all to see. Conjecture about Bülow's imminent departure filled the political atmosphere from April 1906 through June 1909. Eulenburg was not by any means the only person implicated in putative plots to overthrow the chancellor.[82]

The shakiness of Bülow's position was the background for the rumors which then developed from the memory and fear of Eulenburg's political power in the early 1890s and from the supposition that Eulenburg and Bülow had been on bad terms since Eulenburg's retirement from active service.[83] The projection of Eulenburg's political influence beyond 1897 is, as we have seen, unjustified. Eulenburg's reemergence onto the political scene after 1905 was tentative and limited to foreign affairs.[84] The question, then, is whether Eulenburg really was on bad personal terms with Bülow, and/or if Eulenburg disagreed with Bülow politically to the extent that he would have wanted to remove the chancellor. The answer to both these questions is no.

Eulenburg had been forced from office in 1902 by a combination of ill-health, weariness, and blackmail. Throughout that ordeal, Eulenburg used Bülow as his confidant.[85] The tone of Eulenburg's letters becomes strident as his nervousness increases, but the letters make clear that when Eulenburg finally left public life he still considered Bülow one of his very closest friends. While Eulenburg was living as a recluse in Liebenberg, his wife and children would sometimes visit the Bülows in Berlin or Norderney, behavior highly improbable had there been a rupture in 1901–2. Finally, Bülow is one of the very few persons whom Eulenburg spares in the vengeful and acidic essays which he wrote in bitter isolation after the scandal. He does not blame Bülow for his own resignation in 1902, for the scandals, nor for the subsequent trials. In these essays, Eulenburg is embarrassingly free with his hatred; had Bülow been a target, he would certainly have been gored by Eulenburg's pen, as was everyone else Eulenburg held responsible for his misfortunes. In fact, had Eulenburg actually been plotting against Bülow, it is reasonable to suppose that Eulenburg would have been suspicious that Bülow might retaliate. As it was, Eulenburg was one of the few people who did not imagine that Bülow had helped Harden in some fashion.[86]

Rumors of political disagreements between Bülow and Eulenburg had begun late in 1901.[87] They were remembered and elaborated upon five years later. At their origin, these rumors probably reflected Eulenburg's frayed nerves, which caused him to criticize irritably the tactics Bülow was currently using to handle the Austrians. However, the imputed tension between the two men did not, ultimately, encompass policy. Both the chancellor and the ambassador viewed the Austrian alliance as the cornerstone of German foreign policy, and both thought it would be wise to continue to support the current Austrian personnel (i.e. Goluchowsky).[88] Similarly, during the Moroccan tangle, Eulenburg and Bülow were considerably closer in their assessments of the situation than were Bülow and Holstein.[89] If anything, Eulenburg and Bülow were in even closer agreement on internal policy. After all, Bülow was Eulenburg's creature. Eulenburg had chosen him to be Germany's leader precisely because his own views dovetailed so nicely with Bülow's. Terence Cole has recently argued that Bülow gradually became estranged from Eulenburg's policies, because, during the course of his chancellorship, Bülow moved steadily away from personal regime, in favor of parliamentary fetters on the unpredictable Kaiser. Cole maintains that Eulenburg's political activity after 1905 aimed to restore personal regime.[90] This line of argument may very well be correct for Bülow, but it ignores Eulenburg's own changes since 1898. In fact, Eulenburg's disillusionment with the Kaiser went deeper and came earlier than Bülow's.[91] Unless it could be shown that Eulenburg unlearned his hard-won lessons between 1903 and 1906, it is very unlikely that personal regime was his object in 1906, or that he and Bülow disagreed on this subject.

If rumors of a split between Eulenburg and Bülow did not come from politics or from animosity on Eulenburg's part, whence, then, did they originate? It is fairly clear that they were Bülow's work. Eulenburg's decision to leave office was taken at the very beginning of 1902 and was firm and unalterable. But Bülow made Eulenburg's resignation sound like dismissal. Perhaps in order to appear in control of the events, the chancellor told the Austrian ambassador as late as 29 August 1902 that Bülow was planning to replace Eulenburg, but that he knew nothing of the latter's plans to quit.[92] Lies of this kind made it easier for people to believe in a rift and therefore in the possibility of revenge on Eulenburg's part. It is difficult to tell whether or not Bülow's misstatements were only an example of the lies he felt compelled to tell even when there was no need for them, or whether these lies actually reflected his desire to neutralize Eulenburg's influence.

The latter wish was first of all a response to immediate circumstances. It must have been hard for Bülow to juggle Eulenburg's absences from Vienna, Wilhelm's tactlessness vis-à-vis the Austrians, plus Eulenburg's whining insistence that he be allowed to retire.[93] Once Eulenburg was safely ensconced in Liebenberg, this source of trouble evaporated. A more serious underlying motive for Bülow's behavior, however, was his enormous suspicion of possible competition from any quarter, and his jealousy of the prince's power in particular.[94] Eulenburg, the extent of whose power in the 1890s Bülow knew only too well, was an obvious focus for his wariness. When Eulenburg emerged from retirement, Bülow's fear, assiduously nourished by Holstein and Eulenburg's many enemies at Court, quickened. His preventive action in November 1906, the press campaign exposing Eulenburg's putative plans for Helmuth Moltke,[95] reinforced contemporary suspicions and convinced some historians that Eulenburg actually was intriguing once more. This is not impossible, although, as I have tried to show, it is unlikely.[96] Eulenburg's mere reappearance was all that was necessary to set off the anti-Eulenburg machinery, so laboriously built up over the years. The old charges surfaced again, unchanged: personal regime, spiritism, even the accusation that Eulenburg aspired to become Statthalter of Alsace-Lorraine.[97] As understandable as Bülow's suspicions were, their repetition in newspaper accounts, the only surviving traces of Eulenburg's 'conspiracy,' does not constitute proof that it actually existed.[98]

The third charge, the one that caused Harden to attack Eulenburg publicly, concerned Eulenburg's role in foreign policy. Eulenburg was supposed to have affected German policy in Morocco in two ways: by encouraging Wilhelm to be conciliatory toward France and by giving the French government, through its first secretary in Berlin, Lecomte,[99] inside information which assured them of Germany's pacific intentions and therefore aided their efforts to maintain a 'hard line.' Eulenburg's role in the first Moroccan Crisis and the Algeciras Conference will never be entirely clear.[100] However, it is possible to sketch the limits of his possible influence. Eulenburg was, relative to Holstein, pro-French, and his view of the crisis was decidedly pacific. It is true that he saw Wilhelm from time to time (though not nearly so frequently as it was thought) and that he discussed Morocco with the Emperor. His influence would indeed have tended in the direction alleged. However, Wilhelm's friendly attitude toward France was something the Kaiser had followed consistently since 1904, when he and Eulenburg were barely in contact. In other words, Eulenburg may have helped sustain views that Wilhelm already held, but he certainly did not change Wilhelm's mind. Wilhelm changed his own mind in February 1906, abandoning the pacific stance just as Bülow had reembraced it. Germany's policy from February until the end of the conference (April) was made by Bülow, who pulled the Kaiser along in tow.[101]

We will never know what, if anything, Eulenburg may have told Lecomte, for Lecomte destroyed his own papers.[102] Haller writes that Eulenburg met Lecomte in Berlin by chance in the fall of 1905. Lecomte complained that the French Government feared Germany would go to war over Morocco. Eulenburg relayed this information to Deputy Chief of Staff Moltke and to Bülow, both of whom denied that it was true. Haller claims this was Eulenburg's only role.[103] Harden's accusation that Eulenburg invited Lecomte to Liebenberg in 1905 while Wilhelm was there is so far unverifiable. It is possible that, in his zeal, Harden leapt to this conclusion after he learned that Lecomte attended the *Kaiserjagd* the following year (7 and 8 Novem-

ber 1906), seven months after the Algeciras Conference was concluded.[104] In any case, the French had no need of whatever secret
information Eulenburg may have had. Wilhelm's attitudes in the matter were hardly a secret. On 22 March 1905 Wilhelm gave a speech in
Bremen which underlined his pacific intentions in colonial matters.[105]
The Foreign Office was appalled because this seriously undercut its
policy.[106] Wilhelm did it again in May 1905, when he told the French
military attaché that he would not fight for Morocco.[107] Obviously
even a moderately well-informed diplomat should have had little
trouble ascertaining the opinions of the outspoken and careless Wilhelm.

In any event, the strengths of the French position and the cause of
French success at the conference table did not rest upon knowledge
of Wilhelm's mind, but upon the determined support of France's allies.
German policy was unrealistic. Its conception was based on a woeful
misreading of the relative strengths of the participants and on the
mistaken notion that colonial diplomacy, backed by the mere threat
of war, was an appropriate tool with which to try to pry apart the
Entente. By 1905, Germany's isolation was already too great for it to
achieve major victories by diplomacy alone. If Germany wished to
dismember the Entente, it could do so either by ceasing to appear as
a threat to Great Britain, that is, by abandoning the fleet race, or by
annihilating the other Entente partner, France, when Russia was too
weak to rush to its aid. Either of these two policies would have been
more effective than the path actually taken. France's strengths were
greatly enhanced by Bülow, who failed to develop a consistent position. He allowed himself to be buffeted about between the Kaiser and
Holstein. When the wreckage was too great to salvage, Bülow at last
took over the helm and sank as gracefully as he could manage. Bülow
was not helped by Wilhelm's adherence to a more pacific policy than
Holstein's, but it was nonetheless the chancellor's job to mediate as
best he could between the two and to present a consistent line to the
outside world. His failure to do so remains his own. It was not the
execution of the policy, however, which is to blame for Germany's
defeat at Algeciras, but the unrealistic conception of the policy itself.
Therefore Eulenburg is at most guilty of helping Wilhelm to confuse
the implementation of the program, but he is several degrees removed
from responsibility for its failure.

The German defeat at Algeciras marks a turning point in the history
of the Wilhelminian period. As A. J. P. Taylor observes, 'it shattered

the long Bismarckian peace.' The adversaries in the coming war were firmly ranged against each other and, for the first time in thirty-five years, had seriously contemplated war.[108] The complacency of the late nineteenth century was fast being replaced by the *Angst* of the twentieth. This nervousness on the international stage was reflected and compounded inside the Second Reich. The political consensus which had made Bülow seem so successful now broke apart. The over-exuberant optimism of the Bülow years from 1897 on gave way to an equally unrealistic pessimism, which, though generally felt, was most pronounced among the upper classes. Volker Berghahn, the historian of Tirpitz's navy, finds it 'astounding how strongly the military men and politicians were struck by these pathological moods.'[109] Without considering their widespread fatalism, he writes, one cannot understand the origins of the war. Berghahn attributes the psychological malaise after 1905/6 largely to the defeat of German naval strategy by the appearance of the *Dreadnought* (10 February 1906). But contemporaries grasped even more immediately the meaning of the defeat at Algeciras. Nonetheless, the German navy was the essence of Wilhelminian optimism, its concrete tool to reach world power, and its most flamboyant symbol. Once it was clear that expansion was going to be blocked at sea by Great Britain and at the conference table by almost everyone else, the stage was set for the reemergence of the internal social, political, and economic contradictions which had been papered over in the hope that the fruits of expansion would cure them, or that they would miraculously disappear if ignored long enough. As Varnbüler put it, bold strokes of *Weltpolitik* could 'compensate for many grievances in the internal, socio-political sphere.'[110] But when these strokes were everywhere frustrated, the disillusionment was all the greater. 1906 was the beginning of a crisis of confidence in Wilhelminian leadership, on the part of the led and of the leaders themselves.

For Hofmarschall Zedlitz-Trützschler, March 1906 marked a sharp decline in his confidence in Germany, a decline which continued steadily until he resigned his office out of sheer depression. He noted

On the whole I have become more pessimistic. The autocratic part of the Kaiser's personality increases and we are encountering difficulties with this system both internally and externally. . . . I believe that the outlook for entirely positive developments has receded, and while I used to give my pessimistic interpretations only a twenty-five percent chance [of becoming real], today I give them fifty percent.[111]

Zedlitz-Trützschler was surprised to find that Tschirschky, who knew more about politics than he did, but who could also do more about it, had an even darker outlook than his own. About Algeciras Tschir-schky told him, 'we find ourselves ranged as enemies against not only the whole of Europe (except Austria-Hungary) but also against the entire world. We have had to retreat a step at a time, and we shall naturally have to weaken further.'[112]

Foreign observers noted Germany's sudden nervousness with alarm. They wondered what effects it might have on the leaders and their policies. A British diplomat reported perceptively from Saxony on the German mood:

It has been said . . . that 'Fear was born when first man awoke in the dark.' Germany has awakened from her pleasing dream that the Emperor and his Chancellor were past masters in the art of diplomacy, and that nothing could be done in Europe without their permission.

The extent to which the prestige of the Emperor and of the central author-ities has declined in the last year can hardly be exaggerated. Germany (or this part of it at any rate) has not only awakened, but has found herself in the dark and practically alone. It is hardly too much to say that she is afraid. But Germany is undoubtedly strong, and the combination of fear and strength is dangerous.[113]

Very dangerous indeed. The paranoid conviction that Germany was being 'encircled,' the projection of aggressive intent upon others, as in the 'Copenhagen Complex'[114] – these were some of the politico-psychological results of the new perception of German weakness. '[E]verywhere I note a more or less pronounced discontent with the recent foreign policy of the Empire,' an astute British observer wrote, 'and at the same time the newspapers show an anxiety to make for-eign countries understand that Germany is powerful and that if driven to the wall she will fight with determination.'[115] The loss of the obvious diplomatic superiority of Bismarck's time made Bülow afraid that any pacific statements on world affairs made by Germany would be inter-preted by others as weakness. He thus felt forced to appear tougher than usual.[116] Similarly, Wilhelm's marginalia became even more pugnacious than before.[117] His speeches reflect his preoccupation with encirclement, popular pessimism, German strength. In short, after Algeciras, German public life became marked by what might be called compensatory bellicosity.

The new nervousness was deep and broad enough to be expressed in a number of ways. The leadership busied itself with excoriating a series of scapegoats. Germany's isolation was blamed on each of the European powers in turn, though the weight of censure came finally to rest on the British.[118] Bülow embarked on a series of parliamentary gymnastics, dusted off the *Kulturkampf*, dragged the specter of revo-lution across the stage and hoped no one would notice the paucity of ideas these tricks were designed to cover. The extent of the failures was too great to hide. 'If a certain malaise was discernible for some time . . . still, the public first surrendered to it when it saw in the conclusion of the Morocco Affair a weakness in the prestige of the Empire,' the Austrian military attaché reported. 'The considerable rise in food prices, a result of the agrarian policies, has encouraged the psychological depression.'[119]

The politically aware quickly identified many of Germany's problems with the existence of personal regime and with the personality of the Emperor.[120] Editorial comment, which had been noisy on the subject in the 1890s[121] but had subsided after 1897, revived again. Partly in order to avoid charges of *lèse majesté*, and partly no doubt out of sincere monarchical loyalty, much of the criticism of personal rule fell not on the monarch but on his advisers. The critique of personal rule had been from the beginning mixed up with visions of one or several camarillas. This mix did not make for clear analysis or vigorous political action. It was all too easy to fall into personal vendetta, to forget that the real villains were a too-strong monarch and a too-weak parliament. Nonetheless, the renewed criticism of personal regime was the most concrete reflection of the post-Algeciras uncertainty.

Criticism of personal regime and the almost pathological concern with weakness combined to destroy the first victim of the growing malaise, Prince Philipp zu Eulenburg. As the Kaiser's closest friend and the instigator of personal regime, Eulenburg was a proper target for the post-Algeciras criticism, but it was his personal life that left him open to destruction. One of the surprising things which came to light during the scandal was that Eulenburg's homosexual tendencies had been rather widely known or suspected for years. Harden had been treated to Bismarck's caustic views on the subject in 1892.[122] The police in Berlin had had Eulenburg on their lists for some time.[123] This was possible, since the lists were voluminous and the police rarely acted upon them without an outside stimulus. In 1900 Chancellor Hohenlohe wrote to his son that Eulenburg had just visited him. 'He made a thoroughly unfavorable impression on me. I wonder that I did not feel this aversion to him earlier.'[124] His son agreed completely. 'Mama had good judgment and recognized him from the first moment. I only later understood, how right she was.'[125]

Holstein voiced his suspicions only after he felt Eulenburg had intrigued to have him removed from the Foreign Office. 'I am now free,' he warned Eulenburg, '. . . to handle you as one handles a contemptible person with your peculiarities [*Eigentümlichkeiten*].' Holstein ended his note by daring Eulenburg to duel him over the charges.[126] To avoid a scandal, Bülow and the Foreign Office arranged a compromise under which Holstein withdrew his charges, though his later correspondence with Harden leaves no doubt that he never changed his mind.[127]

Bülow always claimed that Harden's allegations against Eulenburg completely surprised him.[128] This can hardly have been the case. When, in March 1902, Eulenburg wrote a letter to Bülow detailing the medical reasons that impelled him to seek early retirement, Bülow jotted down the following skeptical notation in pencil, which included frank mention of Eulenburg's sexually aberrant appearance:

Leuthold [Wilhelm's personal physician], who examined Eulenburg thoroughly (against his will and on orders of His Majesty) said to me that he suffered only from neurasthenia, brought about by an irregular life, uncareful diet, effeminization [which Bülow misspelled *Verweichlung*] and _____[sic]. All his organs are entirely healthy. Renvers [the famous Berlin physician, who examined Eulenburg on the advice of Bülow and Wilhelm] believes the same thing. Also the doctor at Karlsbad [where Eulenburg took a month rest in 1902] wrote in the same sense.[129]

It is unlikely that this note was written too long after Bülow received the letter, since he wrote an answer to Eulenburg based upon the note later in March.[130]

Chancellors Hohenlohe and Bülow and the doctors who examined Eulenburg about this time were not the only persons who noticed that his physical presence seemed more effeminate than it had been. Barrère, Eulenburg's French colleague during his Munich years, reported that while Eulenburg had seemed unremarkable enough then (prior to 1894), 'the later *Fürst* [Eulenburg became *Fürst* on 1 January 1900] seemed to him *détraqué* and his [Eulenburg's] sweet, affected piety had repulsed him.'[131] Eulenburg himself was aware of the change and explained it to his Viennese friend Nathaniel Rothschild in this way:

I look back upon the last years, since our parting [in 1902, when Eulenburg retired as German Ambassador to Vienna] as though upon a bad dream. At a certain age, men go through a period of bodily change, just as women do. I think that men who in their sensitivity and finer organization have, next to their masculine activity, a kind of feminine sensibility [*Empfindung*] suffer much more during this period than the manly – cannons. I try to console myself with these 'periodicity-thoughts' and have similar comforting flights of thought about you. . . . Thank God, that we are conscious of a solidarity of allied souls, that we still have to console us the strong memory [*Hindenken*] of similarly inclined sentient beings [*gleichgearteten empfindenden Wesen*].[132]

If Eulenberg's secret was so widely known, why had not his numerous enemies at Court or in the ministries used their information to
discredit him earlier?[133] There is a complex of reasons why this did
not happen.

Because sexuality in general and homosexuality in particular were
such strong taboos during this time, it was thought indecent to mention such matters unless one was absolutely forced to do so. This had
the effect that people would choose to remain ignorant of things they
could easily have known had they devoted the slightest thought to
them.[134] This also meant that the acts which were defined (however
vaguely) as legally punishable were in fact rarely prosecuted and then
only for ulterior reasons.

Even when a motive existed for proving sexual delicts, evidence was
hard to come by. 'Victimless' sexual acts, when they take place privately, leave no witnesses other than the participants. It is in their
interests to deny that anything happened. If the persons remain
friends, as was the case with Moltke and Eulenburg, then one is left
with merely circumstantial evidence, such as letters, behavior patterns, and so forth. Thus Harden's case rested on personal testimony
only in those instances where Eulenburg had been careless enough to
venture outside the safe confines of his social circle. Much of Harden's
evidence pertained to the early 1880s, that is, before Wilhelm became
Kaiser. It would stand to reason that Eulenburg became more circumspect when Wilhelm's rising star began to throw more light on his
circle of friends than Eulenburg had heretofore been subject to. Bülow
maintained that the Berlin police had told him they had nothing on
Eulenburg after Wilhelm's accession.[135]

Another factor that made the anti-Eulenburg contingent of the
entourage hesitate to bring charges was Wilhelm himself. Wilhelm
had, after all, chosen Eulenburg and the Liebenbergers, and one could
not be sure what his reaction would be, since charges against them
reflected in some measure upon himself. Wilhelm's earlier responses
to news of homosexuality among his circle of friends had been ambi-
valent. On the one hand he could be violently homophobic, as he was
when he learned of Friedrich Eulenburg's troubles in 1898. But he
had been more than understanding about Kuno Moltke's marital
problems the same year, and had braved public criticism to show his
solidarity with his friend Friedrich Krupp by attending the latter's
funeral in 1902, after Krupp had been driven to suicide by revelations
of the same nature.[136] Krupp was, if anything, more notorious than

Philipp Eulenburg. That Wilhelm dropped Eulenburg so quickly doubtless surprised many persons in the entourage.

There are other reasons to deter highly placed persons from using sexual scandals to discredit their enemies. Scandals, once loosed, are difficult if not impossible to control. The net cast out to snare the foe may snag friends as well, or even oneself, since few people lead lives of blameless purity. The Eulenburg affair spun dizzily through German society, and before it finally came to rest it had touched the chancellor, one official in the Foreign Office, a Kammerherr and Zeremonienmeister, one of the Kaiser's sons, General Kessel's son, several officers of prominent regiments, hitherto anonymous country gentlemen, servants, and fishermen. Eulenburg's network of friends extended into the families of his political opponents: Alfred was Bernhard Bülow's brother; Eberhard, Richard Dohna's; Georg, Dietrich Hülsen-Haeseler's, and so on. As soon as Eulenburg's character was called into question, so might the nature of his friendships. Therefore, the fear of unintended consequences of scandal undoubtedly protected Eulenburg for a long time.

In 1906, however, Eulenburg's luck deserted him, and he had the misfortune to become a symbol for all that ailed Germany. Maximilian Harden had opposed Eulenburg and his politics since the early 1890s. He had assiduously collected information about him and had repeatedly attacked him in the pages of his journal, *Die Zukunft*. Since 1902, he had 'hard' evidence, that is, evidence he felt would stand up in a court of law, about Eulenburg's homosexuality. Harden used his inside information only after he became convinced that Eulenburg (through Lecomte) had been the cause of Germany's defeat at Algeciras.[137] His reasons for removing Eulenburg were therefore political, but it was not merely for convenience's sake that the means he used were sexual. By doing so, he was reflecting a dominant theme in current political discourse. Much of the language of compensatory bellicosity was in fact sexual. The virtues of strength, military preparedness, courage, hardness, aggression, vitality, comradeship, productivity, and so forth were all virtues associated with masculinity. Even Zedlitz-Trützschler, whose views on these matters were much more sensible than many of his contemporaries, betrayed the same prejudices when he took refuge from his pessimism only in the growing population figures, which, he thought, reflected the 'strength' of the people.[138] Thus to seize on the question of Eulenburg's masculinity was to touch a raw metaphoric nerve with the hot iron of actual sexual scandal.

Harden was actually more 'enlightened' on the subject of homosexuality than most of his contemporaries. He had read in the latest scientific literature (this included works by Magnus Hirschfeld, Albert Moll, Emil Kraepelin, Richard von Krafft-Ebing, and so forth),[139] had had discussions with Hirschfeld, who was the founder of the Scientific Humanitarian Committee in Berlin, the first organization dedicated to the legalization of (male) homosexuality, as well as to the education of the public on matters sexual.[140] Harden favored abolition of Paragraph 175, which forbad certain sexual acts between men.[141] Nonetheless, Harden subscribed to virtually the same stereotypes of homosexual men that everyone else did in the period. He repeatedly used the words 'sickly sweet' (*süsslich*), 'unmanly,' 'sickly' (*kränklich*), 'weak' to describe them.[142]

I cannot recognize the equality of homosexual persons in every direction [he wrote]. . . . They almost always have the unpleasant sides . . . of femininity. . . . A certain tendency to duplicity (perhaps as a result of the law, which forces them to a life of dissemblance) and to intrigue and such. . . . They do not belong in every position. . . . Where several of them are gathered together they can unconsciously do damage. Particularly at Courts, where complete men have a hard enough time.[143]

He felt that homosexuals were cliquish, that they typically tended toward spiritism and mysticism, and therefore were 'unfit for hard times' such as the ones in which the fatherland found itself.[144]

Harden's views were fortified by the medical literature then current. Harden cited Dr Emil Kraepelin, the founder of pre-Freudian German psychiatry and author of the standard psychiatric textbook, *Psychiatrie*,[145] on the typical characteristics of homosexuals:

Their character is mostly weak, suggestible, dependent. . . . Undependability, lack of veracity, tendency to boastfulness, and petty jealousy are typical vices. . . . In cases of predominant homosexuality the manner of living frequently changes in the direction of the opposite sex. The man becomes feminine in his movements, walk, bearing, taste. He shows a sickly sweet, fragile essence, becomes vain, flirtatious, lays much worth on externals, clothes himself with care . . . writes tender letters on perfumed paper . . . etc. There is not the slightest doubt, that contrary sexual tendencies develop from the foundation of a sickly degenerate personality.[146]

Men and women were regarded as polar opposites, equipped with exactly opposite characteristics, of which men, it was thought, possessed the lion's share of what were actually regarded as virtues. Male homosexuals were slightly worse than women in this schema because, while they failed to be men or had through sickness degenerated from that exalted state, they had failed also to be women, that is, exhibited few of the virtues of the female (nurturant qualities, selflessness, and so forth). Instead, they exemplified all the worst characteristics of the feminine and precisely those which were invariably cited as disqualifying women from participation in political life. Since the 1890s, it was widely feared that (male) homosexuality was on the increase, particularly among the upper classes, and that this was both a portent and a cause of national decay. The link between ideas of decadence and of homosexuality in people's minds was quite strong. The concern with decadence was part of the complex of pessimistic cultural criticism of the late nineteenth and early twentieth centuries, part of the fear and confusion caused by rapid change and potential social upheaval. Homosexuality was a wonderful symbol for aspects of this complex of criticism because it cut so many different ways.

Homosexuality was a violation of one of the strongest organizing principles of society, namely, sex roles. It reduced fundamental order to uncertain chaos. It seemed symbolically to undermine the family, which was both the primary unit of social organization and the most important instrument of socialization. It flew in the face of religion and, by extension, of the state. For religion had bequeathed its moral principles to the state, where they became imbedded in law (including Paragraph 175). Since the rise of the nation state, religion had come to be regarded as the repository of patriotic virtues. Far from being patriotic, homosexuals, it was thought, were loyal only to their kind. This meant that they formed a kind of international. But this international was even more repulsive than the International of the working class. Instead of being based on crass materialism and class hatred, which was bad enough, this international was based on sexual desire, that base, all-devouring, all-destroying, ill-understood urge whose existence in women was so feared that it was completely denied and whose existence in men was blushingly acknowledged, though rarely spoken of. Homosexuality was so terribly threatening because it called into question so many assumptions upon which the stability of society seemed to depend. At a time when that very stability was being attacked both externally and internally, the addition of this particular assault was to some unbearable.

In many ways, the case of Maximilian Harden, Wilhelminian Germany's foremost critic (cultural and otherwise) provides the most fascinating example of the power of a symbol. He began as a relative liberal on the question of homosexuality, and he launched his public attacks with an aura of Olympian detachment. He was actually indifferent to the sexual lives of people, he wrote, except when, as in this case, they had a deleterious political effect.[147] He chided Holstein not to overestimate the power of homosexuals at Court, nor to ascribe all of Germany's problems only to them.[148] But as he was drawn deeper and deeper into the judicial morass which followed his disclosures, he became increasingly convinced that the web he had attacked was stronger than he, that its threads reached through the courts, wound round the prosecutor, leaving no office untouched or untouchable. Harden became obsessed.

In 1908 I first learned of the terrible propagation of homosexuality, felt clearly . . . 'the levelling effect of the common efforts of the forbidden through all classes,' [felt this] in the mound of threatening letters from cities near and far, in the sign of comradeship which is stronger than that of brothers in an order or of freemasons, and holds more tightly together, which links together a band beyond the divisions of belief, state or class. . . . Everywhere men of this tribe sit, in courts, in high positions in the army and navy, in ateliers, in the editorial rooms of large newspapers, in the chairs of merchants, teachers and even judges. All united against the common enemy.[149]

His had become a crusade.

The state which allows this chain of the most infamous breaches of justice in favor of a Pompadour *masculini generis,* deserves to perish. In Germany these injustices are not only possible, they are deliberate. I will say everything necessary next week in the Bock brewery to loose an even larger scandal. As long as I have the strength [I shall] go through the land to brand this infamy. It is wonderfully appropriate, that at the same time the whole stupid duplicity of our politics should also break down internationally. . . . I am determined, with Scythian brutality to rage against this black band of allied criminals.[150]

Harden's rage ruined the lives of a number of persons (Johannes von Lynar, Wilhelm von Hohenau, Edgard Graf von Wedel, Paul von Below, the younger Kessel) who were politically unimportant. His biggest catch was Eulenburg, but his victory had come over ten years too late.

The complex and twisted tale of Harden's attacks and the resulting trials has been fairly well unravelled by Helmuth Rogge, Harry Young, and Norman Rich.[151] This is not the place to recount all of the twists and turns. After a brief summary, the rest of this chapter will instead consider the role of Eulenburg's intimates (friends and enemies) in his fall and the effects of the scandals on the Emperor and his entourage.

Harden did not at first intend to create a scandal. He merely wanted Eulenburg to quit the area around Berlin so that he could be sure the Fürst was not engaging in politics. He attacked (17 November 1906) Eulenburg sharply but in such a way that only the initiated could read the message: leave Liebenberg, which was only one hour away from Berlin, or else your 'abnormal sexual instincts' will be exposed. Eulenburg left. He returned, however, in January 1907. In April, Harden began his attacks again. Receiving no response from Eulenburg or Moltke (it was through Moltke that Harden could get at Eulenburg), Harden became more obvious. No one in the entourage dared tell the Emperor. Finally, on 2 May 1907, the Crown Prince laid the articles before his father. Wilhelm was furious that no one had told him sooner and that neither Eulenburg nor Moltke had instituted proceedings to clear themselves. Moltke, Hohenau, and Lynar resigned their commissions on 3 May. Eulenburg and Moltke spent the rest of the month trying to find a way to extricate themselves without actually confronting Harden's evidence. Hahnke and other officers advised Moltke to challenge Harden to a duel. The editor, however, refused to accept. Moltke then asked the state prosecutor to bring charges against Harden. The state prosecutor refused on the grounds that the state did not have sufficient interest in the case. Moltke, as a last resort, sued Harden in a civil suit for libel (6 June).

Meanwhile, Wilhelm had asked Eulenburg (through Kessel) what he intended to do about the charges. Eulenburg answered that he 'felt completely free' of guilt in the matters.[152] When he was informed that he could not institute disciplinary proceedings against himself, as he wished, in his capacity as a member of His Majesty's service, he elected to have the state prosecutor of his local district (*Kreis*) begin an investigation of his past life. Neither of these methods was as rigorous (or risky) as a libel suit would have been. In a letter to Bülow (12 May 1907) Eulenburg again employed the curious phrase 'I feel myself clean of the dirt into which they are trying to pull me'[153] rather than the more direct 'I am not guilty.' Wilhelm was well-disposed toward Eulenburg as late as 12 May,[154] but soon after was told of incriminating evidence against Eulenburg: his and Moltke's correspondence, the same letters which Harden had received from Moltke's ex-wife, plus the information that Eulenburg's friend, Jan Wendelstadt, who had been with Wilhelm at the *Kaiserjagd* on several occasions, had such a bad reputation as a homosexual that he could not be invited to official functions in Munich. Wilhelm was irate. He demanded that Eulenburg resign from the diplomatic service and clear his name in some way. Eulenburg's resignation was accepted on 11 June. The local investigation, which not surprisingly turned up nothing, continued until 28 July. After that, Eulenburg stayed in Liebenberg and watched the trials unfold in ghastly succession.

The first Moltke–Harden trial (23–29 October 1907) ended in Harden's acquittal. Public opinion supported the verdict. The government, and particularly Wilhelm, did not. The verdict was quickly overturned on a technicality, and the prosecution of the case shifted to the state prosecutor (who had originally turned the case down in May). The verdict of the second Moltke–Harden trial (19 December 1907 to 3 January 1908) was more pleasant to Wilhelm: Harden was found guilty of libel. In between, the Bülow–Brand trial had taken place (6 November 1907). Adolf Brand, a strident voice for homosexual emancipation, received eighteen months in jail for alleging without legal evidence that Chancellor Bülow had committed homosexual acts with an underling. Eulenburg testified in both the Brand and the second Moltke–Harden trials. During the latter, he answered directly under oath that he had never transgressed Paragraph 175 (which judicial opinion had narrowed to mean only anal intercourse). When pressed to deny that he had ever committed any homosexual acts, Eulenburg replied enigmatically that he had 'never done anything dirty [*Schmutzereien habe ich nie betrieben*].'[155]

Thus, in early 1908, both Moltke and Eulenburg stood practically vindicated. While he appealed, Harden set about collecting information that would finish off Eulenburg once and for all. He found it in Starnberg, in the form of two locals, a fisherman and a laborer, who swore that they had had sexual relations with Eulenburg in the late 1880s. Harden presented his evidence on 21 April 1908 in Munich, out of reach of the Prussian authorities, in a libel trial which he and an editor friend named Anton Städele had staged for the purpose. Städele 'accused' Harden of not being able to prove that Eulenburg was homosexual and of having been bribed by Eulenburg not to present his evidence. Harden's evidence, however, convinced the Munich court on both counts.

The reaction in Berlin was immediate and electric. Bülow ordered Eulenburg to be arrested and his castle searched. Eulenburg was charged with perjury. His trial took place from 29 June to 17 July 1908, when Eulenburg collapsed and was declared by the court doctors to be physically unfit to continue. The trial was temporarily postponed. Eulenburg was allowed to leave the court's custody on 25 September 1908 after posting a large bail.

In May 1908, the Leipzig Supreme Court found the second Moltke–Harden trial to have been invalid. That duel now had to begin from scratch, although the state prosecutor was left in charge. A trial date was set for 24 November 1908, but suddenly postponed. The third and last Moltke–Harden trial finally took place on 20 April 1909 and ended the same day with a verdict against Harden, who was ordered to pay a fine of 600 M plus court costs for all three trials, a sum amounting to 40,000 M. Harden appealed. By this time everyone (involved and not) felt the trials should end. After much negotiation among Harden, Bülow, Moltke, Ballin, Walther Rathenau, Eugen Zimmermann, and their attorneys, a settlement was reached. Moltke recognized Harden's patriotic motives in writing the articles and withdrew his suit. Harden withdrew his appeal. Ballin paid Harden's fines and costs and was reimbursed from a fund from the Reichskanzlei, on Bülow's orders.

On 7 July 1909 the second and last Eulenburg trial began and ended like the first with Eulenburg's collapse. Until 1919 Eulenburg was examined biannually by court doctors who always found him too ill to stand trial. His case was finally indefinitely postponed. From May 1907 to July 1909, Moltke, Eulenburg, Lynar, W. Hohenau, Below, and Gustav Kessel's son resigned or were removed from their posts. Jan Wendelstadt committed suicide.

Most people found Harden's evidence convincing. So did Varnbüler, whose neat system dividing the esthetes of the 'pure heights' from those who engaged in crude sex was shattered during the Städele trial. 'He is lost, hopelessly,' Varnbüler wrote to Eulenburg's lawyer.

That he lied to us, swore falsely – that one could *forgive*, as the act of desperate necessity, of one harassed to death, had he done it not to save himself, but to save the honor of his family and his name. But then he should have judged himself before he was judged [by society] and quietly, as his illness allowed him to, left this life.[156]

Varnbüler was at first afraid to visit Eulenburg because of possible repercussions to his own family and official position. He even authorized Eulenburg's lawyer to use his, Varnbüler's, name to convince Eulenburg to commit suicide, though Varnbüler wondered if 'he lack[ed] the manly energy.'[157]

One must suspect that at least part of Varnbüler's extreme reaction was due to fear that he himself might be implicated in the scandal were it not cut off immediately. When he calmed down, he retraced his moral steps and no longer demanded that Eulenburg kill himself. In the following years he visited Eulenburg at Liebenberg, corresponded with him and, finally, stood by him when Eulenburg had been abandoned by almost everyone else. But Varnbüler was never under the illusion that Eulenburg's continued protestations of innocence were true. He wrote to Moltke:

He [Eulenburg] lives by the fiction that he is innocent and that I believe this. I accept this fiction, although I do not believe it. . . . This pose before his family and a couple of friends is his last support. He hopes they will stand by him through this belief [in his innocence]. I haven't the courage to break this support. Nor have you.[158]

Harden had presented no direct evidence of Moltke's homosexual activities. Judging by Varnbüler's letter, this lack of evidence was sufficient for him to keep Moltke in the category of the 'idealists,' from which Eulenburg, by his indiscreet lapse, had fallen. Public opinion was not so lenient at first. Bülow's official observer at the first trial reported to him that 'the scenes from Moltke's married life, which is being discussed in open court, would seem to prove his abnormality and destroy him completely as a person.'[159] Even after the second trial had ended in Moltke's exoneration, the British ambassador reported that he felt the majority of people 'hold that the finding of the first court was correct . . . and, in fact, that the second trial was practically an affair arranged by the Court in order to put an end to the scandal.'[160] But as the trials continued, people grew heartily sick of the whole business. Moltke was in any case not the true target of Harden's attacks; he was merely caught in the cross fire. Besides, as Varnbüler had written in 1898, Moltke was never taken quite seriously and was better liked than Eulenburg, probably on that account. And so Moltke was gradually rehabilitated. The *Hofgesellschaft* was as prepared as Varnbüler was to shut its eyes to Moltke's sexual proclivities. His peers cleared his name in a military court-martial, and Moltke returned as a guest to Court functions after 1911. He even visited the exiled Kaiser at Doorn.[161]

Although most people were convinced of it at the time, Harden was not the tool of either Holstein or Bülow. Harden acted alone, out of his own convictions. His most important pieces of evidence came from many people, from his own observations, and from hard detective work. Once the campaign was begun, Holstein offered moral support and advice, which tended in the direction of moderation, rather than of excess.[162]

Bülow's role is less clear. As we have seen, he viewed Eulenburg at least partially as a rival and in 1906 thought Eulenburg was trying to remove him from office. Bülow held much potentially damning information about Eulenburg,[163] including letters in which Moltke and Eulenburg referred to Wilhelm as *'das Liebchen.'*[164] And Bülow tried to collect more. In 1904 or 1905 he asked Police Commissioner Tresckow for police information on Eulenburg's homosexuality, which

Tresckow refused to divulge.[165] In February 1907 Bülow gave Holstein other incriminating bits of information, apparently in the hope that Holstein would pass them along to Harden, which, however, he also did not do.[166] However, Bülow did not bring the *Zukunft* articles to Wilhelm's attention nor did he push Eulenburg and Moltke to resort to trials which would make a small scandal into a huge affair. Bülow may have been behind the state prosecutor's refusal to take the Moltke case in May.[167] If, however, Bülow's aim was to neutralize Eulenburg, it was already accomplished by that date.

In many respects, limbo was the situation most advantageous to Bülow because his political rivals were nullified, but embarrassing questions which might involve him were unasked and unanswered. Bülow's actions once the trials began seem consistent with his general method of governance, neglect which was not quite benign. Bülow could have intervened in two ways, either in favor of, or against, Moltke and Eulenburg. In either case, prosecution would have been swift and the trials soon over. On the whole, Bülow did neither, with the result that the trials dragged on in suffocating legal complexity. In only one document, a telegram to Wilhelm during the first Moltke–Harden trial, did the chancellor betray any eagerness to get on with it, and this was clearly because Bülow knew what Wilhelm wanted to hear.[168] Bülow was of course being pressured from both sides to interfere. Both sides were unhappy that he did not do a better job, and he received frequent complaints. His excuse was that his efforts to intervene always went awry somewhere between the darkest Justizministerium and the state prosecutor's office.[169] There is probably some truth to this, for Harden repeatedly discerned friction between those two institutions.[170]

Nonetheless, in the two cases where Bülow clearly intervened, results came quickly. The first was at Wilhelm's insistence after the first Moltke–Harden trial, the verdict of which shocked the Kaiser and was overturned in a matter of days, and control removed to the prosecutor's office. The second was when Harden (through Holstein) blackmailed Bülow into postponing the date (24 November 1908) for the third Moltke–Harden trial. Harden had evidence which linked Wilhelm (but not necessarily sexually) to Jakob Ernst, the fisherman in Starnberg with whom Eulenburg had had sexual relations.[171] Harden shuddered, he wrote, 'at the unreserved discussion which will be necessary: political strife (Lecomte, *funditus*); Bundesfürsten and princes; Kistler–Ernst–H. M.; Moltke himself; Kessel–Eberh. etc., etc.'[172] But he was forced to go ahead, because 'this monarch will never change and is simply in the hands of blackmailers.' It might become necessary to force Wilhelm from the throne by 'privately using the strongest means (I could say by becoming "earnest") [*Ich könnte auch sagen: "Ernst" gemacht werden muss*].'[173] This is, of course, a play on Jakob Ernst's name. Holstein made the point clear to Bülow.[174] Bülow quickly responded with positive results.[175]

Once Eulenburg's fate was virtually sealed by the Städele trial, Bülow was consistent in his efforts to avoid further litigation by encouraging a private settlement between Moltke and Harden.[176] Axel Varnbüler came closest to characterizing Bülow's role correctly. The idea that Bülow had planned the scandals of 1907/09 gave the chancellor both too much and too little credit, he wrote. Bülow was neither unscrupulous enough nor decisive enough for this. Varnbüler considered him 'a man of opportunity, of small resources, of clever exploitation of given situations, and, admittedly, in these things he was of the most inventive agility and the most exact calculation . . . and rare luck.' Bülow merely 'tolerated and used' what he found.[177]

The most important actions of the military entourage for its part came at the beginning of the scandal and made possible the course of events which followed. The most decisive actor was Dietrich Hülsen, Chief of the Military Cabinet, who had hated Eulenburg since 1897. Hülsen furnished Harden with information about Eulenburg.[178] He had tried to convince Bülow in 1906 that Eulenburg was intriguing against him. Hülsen was after Moltke, too, whom he considered Eulenburg's microphone in the entourage. He had suggested Moltke's elevation to Commandant of the city of Berlin in order to get him out of the *Umgebung*.[179] Once Harden began his campaign, Hülsen leapt at the chance to destroy his foes.

He pushed from the beginning the hard line that both Eulenburg and Moltke should defend themselves by bringing charges against Harden in court.[180] Hülsen knew that Harden's evidence would destroy them. Thus, Hülsen forced the scandal into the open by blocking the more discreet paths. Hülsen's insistence on rapid, decisive action could be defended as eminently soldierly and was bound to appeal to Wilhelm for that reason.

Hülsen was assisted in his efforts by Hahnke, Plessen, Löwenfeld,[181] and at long distance by Carl Wedel and Max von Fürstenberg, whom Eulenburg had up until that moment considered a friend of his.[182] Hülsen testified at Eulenburg's first trial and regretted that 'unfortunately, I could not say much against him.'[183] Löwenfeld felt the same way: 'in my opinion, the misfortune would not have been so great if Eulenburg had had to stay under fire in court.'[184] Plessen was somewhat milder, but was still convinced of Eulenburg's guilt and glad to see him go.[185] Throughout the long ordeal, the military men continued to sing the song of complete exoneration or ruin by trial. Their insistent chorus made it difficult for Wilhelm to weaken and try to interfere to rehabilitate his friends. Wilhelm was tempted to do so after Moltke's victory in the second trial, but the military entourage stopped him.[186] August Eulenburg, who supported his cousin's rehabilitation in 1908, appears to be the only person around Wilhelm who stayed loyal to the fallen Fürst. The others kept silent.

Wilhelm's response to the Eulenburg scandals is enigmatic unless one keeps in mind the advice he constantly received from his *maison militaire* that the only honorable and manly course was to proceed with public trials. It took the military men at Court almost a month to move the Kaiser to their position. Wilhelm at first favored mere disciplinary procedures,[187] which offered a greater chance of clearing his friends' names. It was not until 31 May 1907 that Wilhelm's tone suddenly changed. He demanded that Eulenburg deny Harden's charges, sue him or otherwise take decisive action.[188] The following day Hahnke advised Moltke to challenge Harden to a duel.

The Kaiser's toughened stance was a direct result of Dietrich Hülsen's efforts. The Military Cabinet chief met Wilhelm alone and showed him reports from the Prussian envoy in Munich which said that Wendelstadt was so notorious a homosexual that the envoy could not invite him as a guest to the legation. Hülsen also informed the Kaiser of the incriminating Moltke–Eulenburg letters that Moltke's wife had given to Harden. It is not clear whether Wilhelm actually read the letters or was merely apprised of their contents.[189] In either case, they were enough to make Wilhelm abandon his earlier, conciliatory course. The letters seem to have made a vivid, but nonetheless passing impression. Friendship proved stronger than Harden's evidence. Wilhelm was therefore astonished and furious at the results of the first Moltke–Harden trial. His marginalia to news-clippings on the trial confirm that he thought it unfair, prejudiced 'against the crown and its officials' and abject towards the 'plebs' and 'the mob.'[190] Hence, Wilhelm's intervention to ensure, not that the trials would end, but that they would continue to a satisfactory conclusion in other, less 'prejudiced' forums.[191]

Thus, when the verdict from the second Moltke–Harden trial was favorable, Wilhelm was immediately prepared to rehabilitate fully both Moltke and Eulenburg. As far as he was concerned, they had fulfilled the requirements of the military code of honor. At this point, the military entourage in the voice of Field Marshal Hahnke hastened to point out that they had not, since court-martial proceedings were still outstanding against Moltke.[192] Wilhelm's haste to overlook the honor technicalities makes it clear how much he wanted his friends back. Edgard Wedel told how Wilhelm had a 'growing yearning' for Eulenburg. 'He could not and did not want to do without him.'[193]

Wilhelm's deep desire to believe in the provable innocence of his friends also explains why he felt so crushed and then angry when the results of the Städele trial became known.[194] In a fury, Wilhelm demanded that Eulenburg return the Order of the Black Eagle. When the first Eulenburg trial was indefinitely postponed, Wilhelm was

very unpleasantly surprised. . . . The trial must go forward, even if Eulenburg stays in the fire. That would be better for him anyway than vegetating for months under arrest, with the trial threatening in the background which will then begin from the beginning.[195]

Despite the imperial imperative, the trial did not go forward, and everyone had to live with irresolution.

For Wilhelm the limbo was a negative resolution; he had lost his one friend. The nature of the charges, of Wilhelm's own unclear feelings in the matter, the contradiction between the rigorous clarity demanded by the military and the fact that at some level Wilhelm did not really wish to know the truth, the personal attacks on himself, his own guilt at having abandoned his friends so quickly, the triumph of the critical press – all of these things combined to push Wilhelm into emotional turmoil. He was angry at Eulenburg and Moltke for getting tangled in such a net, but he was equally angry at the way Hülsen and Plessen had handled matters, and of course angry at Harden for starting it all.[196] The emotional confusion settled into depression.[197] Wilhelm was not paralyzed, just duller than usual, disinclined to be active. His doctors and people at Court urged him to travel to England in November 1907 in hopes that his spirits would pick up.[198] Their prescription worked, so well, in fact, that Wilhelm was loath to return.[199]

The Städele trial, however, brought another assault on the royal nerves. The preceding year and a half of grief set the stage for the nervous breakdown which Wilhelm suffered during the *Daily Telegraph* Affair in November 1908. It is doubtful that Wilhelm would have been hurt so deeply by that conflict had he not just suffered through eighteen months of what he felt was personal betrayal and perfidy. Wilhelm never did straighten out his emotional reaction to the Eulenburg scandal. Admiral Müller, who spent ten years in the inner entourage, never was clear on how Wilhelm felt about Eulenburg. Now and again, however, he would utter a wistful remark about 'poor Phili.'[200]

The French, Italian, and British newspapers and their diplomats reacted as the Germans feared they would, with remarks about German degeneracy and moral decay.[201] The German newspapers responded in kind.[202] Persons at Court and in society reacted in much the same way, only without the same *Schadenfreude*. They were sickened by the details and depressed by the sheer duration of the affair.[203] Even the police commissioner in charge of such matters was delighted to get away from it and 'for a week to hear nothing about pederasts and perversity.'[204] Hugo Reischach, the aged Oberstallmeister, was deeply depressed. After a visit to the shattered Hohenau family, he recorded his feelings: 'I have no confidence in myself any more. I feel old and used up. I don't think that I am up to this endless turmoil.'[205]

But for all the noise and pain, the political catharsis was missing. The Eulenburg scandals occasioned much criticism, but criticism that was diverted into personal vendetta instead of into political reform. The power of the monarch remained untouched, yet everyone knew that that was where the problem really lay. This is the explanation for the swiftness and the vehemence of the public response to the *Daily Telegraph* Affair. Eulenburg's messy demise had crystallized opposition to personal regime and to the person of the monarch. It had collected around the symbol of the Kaiser the just anger at ten years of misrule, but had given the anger no outlet. When the *Daily Telegraph* interview was published, people were so anxious to get at Wilhelm that they overlooked the fact that, for once in his life, he was not actually to blame, that he had followed constitutional procedures. Without the preparation of the Eulenburg scandal, the *Daily Telegraph* Affair, the one truly momentous political scandal of Wilhelm's reign, the one which nearly toppled him from the throne and which changed the character of personal regime, would not have been possible.

Eulenburg's fall was not itself of immediate political importance. By 1907 it was no longer necessary to liquidate Eulenburg. He had already done his worst and was no longer important. The other victims were small fry. But the long-term consequences of the affair were negative. His enemies, who thought he was still powerful, had attacked him because he favored a relatively pacific foreign policy. Eulenburg became a symbol of unmanly weakness and pacifism. His fall removed one more voice against saber-rattling and against military influence in foreign affairs. Inside the entourage, the balance now tipped decisively in favor of the military.

6

Other civilians: Fürstenberg, Ballin, and Krupp

Philipp Eulenburg and his circle were not the only civilians in, or reckoned in, Wilhelm's entourage. There were others who might have influenced the Kaiser in ways different from Eulenburg. For Eulenburg labored under constraints peculiar to his own personality, social class, and convictions. His love for Wilhelm made him persist in his plans for personal regime long after he should have known that the Kaiser's weakness and instability would make personal regime, in fact, military regime. Eulenburg's social class did not help him to see the situation with greater clarity. He was an arch-conservative royalist, just as Holstein had accused him of being, whose dreams of archaic, Prussian monarchy were historically consistent with immoderate military influence on political affairs. One is tempted to ask what might have happened had Eulenburg been less an integral part of the Junker system. What if he had been more of an outsider, bourgeois, or perhaps even a foreigner? What if he had been more in sympathy with industrialism?

These questions are answered by a look at the careers of three men: Max Egon Fürstenberg, Albert Ballin, and Friedrich Alfred Krupp. Fürstenberg was an Austrian, Krupp, an indistrialist, and Ballin, both a businessman and a Jew. All were prominent figures in their own right, who need not have been beholden to the Kaiser. All could claim (some with more justice than others) to be the Kaiser's friend, but none loved him. All were widely (but not always correctly) considered to be members of the entourage. And all did try to influence Wilhelm politically, although not in the same direction. Fürstenberg generally restricted himself to lobbying on Austria's behalf. Krupp's highly conservative politics, as well as his business interests, put him close to positions taken by the military. Ballin was the only one of the three whose convictions were somewhat progressive. Despite their eminence and despite the variety of the politics that they advocated, none accomplished nearly so much as had Eulenburg. The wealth, power, and influence of each man were counteracted by the forces which are the focus of this study. That is, their impact on the Kaiser and on policy was limited by Wilhelm's personality and its interaction with their own, by the weight of the monarchy as an institution (or, in other words, by the way one felt one was expected to behave around an Emperor), and, particularly in the case of Ballin, by the form and personnel, the opinions and policies favored by the rest of the entourage. Fürstenberg, Krupp, and Ballin are three exceptions which prove how difficult it was even for powerful and independent individuals to break through the bounds set by the Kaiser and the organizational and personal framework of his entourage.

As Philipp Eulenburg retreated more and more into private life after 1900, Maximilian Egon II Fürst zu Fürstenberg[1] began to replace him as Wilhelm's chief friend. Fürstenberg was born and raised on his father's estates in Bohemia. He graduated from a *Gymnasium* in Prague and went on to study at the university there and later in Bonn and Vienna. After he had passed the *Staatsprüfung* in the history of law, he served one year as a volunteer with the K. u. K. Husaren Regiment No. 8 and then returned to Vienna to pass the state judicial exams. In the interim he had married the eminently Austrian Irma Gräfin von Schönborn-Buchheim. In all likelihood Fürstenberg would have remained in Austria without ever coming to Wilhelm's attention had not the German line of the family suddenly died out in 1896.[2] Along with his property in Bohemia, which made him one of the largest landholders in Austria-Hungary, Fürstenberg now added an enormous amount of territory in Baden and Württemberg.[3] He became an hereditary member of the upper houses of Baden, Württemberg, Austria-Hungary, and Prussia.

Wilhelm and Fürstenberg met in Vienna in 1893, but numerous social meetings occurred before either appreciated the other. In April 1900 Wilhelm first visited Fürstenberg at Donaueschingen. Their friendship ripened quickly thereafter. That October Wilhelm sent Fürstenberg birthday greetings in verse.[4] The next year they were on a 'Du' basis.[5] Wilhelm appointed Fürstenberg his Oberst-Marschall in February 1904, the only official position which Fürstenberg held in the Berlin Court. After Philipp Eulenburg's disgrace in 1907/8, Fürstenberg was widely viewed as the new Eulenburg.

He did share with Eulenburg the ability to put Wilhelm completely at ease. The Fürst managed this with his 'inexhaustible, optimistic

4 Portrait by László of Max Egon II Fürst zu Fürstenberg (*c.* 1899, Donaueschingen)

humor.'[6] After a visit to Donaueschingen, Wilhelm described his pleasure at the Fürstenbergs' company:

As always you have once again understood how to create a cosiness [*Behaglichkeit*] which I can hardly find elsewhere. You possess the talent to lend a refreshing peace to the convivial atmosphere around you, even with all the elegance and all the princely comfort. In [this peace] I find my recovery among the nice, happy people of this skillfully matched circle. Not just the terrific hunting, or the special air from the charming Black Forest hills, but especially the unrestrained conversation in such pleasant company does me good and makes me thankful.[7]

Wilhelm never forgot the haven which the Fürstenbergs prepared for him during the *Daily Telegraph* Affair. Although his visit ended in another sorrow, the death of Dietrich Hülsen-Haeseler, Wilhelm was always grateful for the friendship he had received. 'You laid balm on my aching heart,' he wrote, 'and gave me the courage and energy to believe in myself.'[8]

In the later years of his reign, Wilhelm frequently needed distraction and rest. Fürstenberg performed one service after another to these ends. He amused Wilhelm by what a non-admirer termed 'rude and often silly jokes,'[9] or by his impressive repertory of dirty stories, which Wilhelm loved, but which Fürstenberg only recounted if ladies were absent.[10] 'I miss you very much,' Wilhelm cabled Fürstenberg after they had been together at Corfu. 'Your humor helped me this time as always and has accompanied me after you left.'[11] Not only the Fürst's sunny personality, but also his steady nerves calmed Wilhelm. The members of the entourage were usually sorry when Fürstenberg left, because none of them could handle Wilhelm nearly so well as he could.[12]

The Donaueschingen hunt each November was the most elegant such event of the year.[13] Each day was meticulously, but unobtrusively planned to include, besides the hunt, diversions like music, fireworks, theatrical presentations, and so on. More than anything else, Wilhelm liked the company,[14] which, with the exception of a few notables from Baden, was exclusively made up of the highest Austro-German nobility. Among the regulars were Fürstenberg's old friends Erwein Nostitz, Gottfried Prince zu Hohenlohe-Langenburg,[15] Ernst Graf Silva-Tarouca, Rudolf Graf von Colloredo-Mannsfeld, and Paul Almeida, all of whom were accompanied by their wives and often by children as well.

Wilhelm's new friendship seems to have been untouched by homo-eroticism, despite Eulenburg's claim that Wilhelm was 'smitten with [Fürstenberg's] appearance.'[16] Irma Fürstenberg was a more integral part of the atmosphere at Donaueschingen than was usual for wives at other imperial hunts.[17] Unlike Eulenburg, Fürstenberg got on extremely well with Auguste Viktoria. She found him pleasant and amusing.[18] He felt sorry for her because Wilhelm treated her badly and he did everything he could to smooth over the resulting unpleasant situations.[19] Wilhelm's mother was equally charmed by the Fürstenbergs,[20] as was Wilhelm's second wife, Hermine,[21] who felt that

Fürstenberg was 'the best and truest friend' that Wilhelm ever had.[22]

Friendship with Wilhelm induced in Fürstenberg the same stress it had induced in Eulenburg before him. Keeping up with the peripatetic Kaiser was a physical strain, even for the robust.[23] Worse was Wilhelm's suffocating grasp on his chosen friend. The Emperor wanted Fürstenberg constantly at his beck and call. He begrudged the time Fürstenberg wished to spend with his own family, work, or friends. On Corfu after several weeks as the unrelieved focus of Wilhelm's attention, Fürstenberg would gradually pry himself loose. 'I am so thankful to you for each day that I have you with me,' Wilhelm told him once, 'but I do understand that I am not the only one with a right [*Anrecht*] to you.'[24] Life with Wilhelm was also difficult for Fürstenberg in a way in which it had never been for Eulenburg: Fürstenberg was Roman Catholic. As Wilhelm's only Catholic friend, Fürstenberg was sensitive to the not always faint anti-Catholicism of the evangelical Court milieu. This made Sundays tense, even on idyllic Corfu.[25] Wilhelm, however, made every effort to make Fürstenberg feel at home and was, on the whole, as warm with him and as thoughtful as he was capable of being.

Not everyone was so pleased by Wilhelm's friendship with Fürstenberg. A FAD wrote:

It has never been clear to me why the Kaiser, after [Eulenburg's] tragic fate, picked this boisterous and not always tasteful Austrian as a substitute for Fürst Eulenburg, who was in many ways highly talented and attractive. . . . Fürst Fürstenberg's character was hotly disputed. . . . Always cheerful, a joke-maker, downright noisy in his behavior, he gave a first impression of a superficial, unimportant, happy *causeur* and *bon vivant*. But this [description] did not exhaust his character. While it is true that he was not brilliant, he did combine very sound appreciation of people with good nerves and experience in many areas of life. Admittedly, he was a gambler, and one without much luck, as his repeated financial collapse, despite his colossal wealth, documents.[26]

Hutten-Czapski, who had studied with Fürstenberg, agreed that Fürstenberg was no genius, but he did not agree with the prevailing opinion 'that the Fürst used Wilhelm's love for his boisterous manner and comfortable humor to advance Austrian interests.'[27]

There are several reasons why such a likeable person as Max Egon zu Fürstenberg should have had so many enemies: jealousy; fear that Fürstenberg would encourage Wilhelm in his juvenile, irresponsible behavior; fear that Fürstenberg's judgment was impaired; and fear that Fürstenberg was not impaired at all, but was cleverly working for Austria. The first two points were shadows cast by Eulenburg's suspected influence (which the suspicious supposed had been transferred automatically to the substitute Eulenburg) and by the *Daily Telegraph* Affair. German public opinion was incensed when Wilhelm fled to Donaueschingen to be entertained by hunting and by Berlin cabaret artists, when the greatest storm of his reign was breaking in Berlin.[28] After 1908, however, Wilhelm's visits to Donaueschingen were no longer a matter of controversy.

Fears about Fürstenberg's judgment came less from political than from financial events. Fürstenburg was involved in the best-known bankruptcy in the Wilhelminian era. He and Christian Kraft zu Hohenlohe-Oehringen, Wilhelm's erstwhile Oberstkämmerer and owner of gigantic estates in Upper Silesia and Hungary, had formed a corporation, the Handels-Vereinigung, or popularly, the Fürsten-Konzern. This octopus-like firm was active in Berlin construction and transportation, coal and potash, banking, steamships, trade and expansion in Turkey, and one newspaper. Its business connections included the Deutsche Bank, Dresdener Bank, Hamburg–American Lines, North German Lloyd, Krupp, and Bleichröder. By 1909 collapse threatened on several fronts. As reorganization followed reorganization, the partners fell to bickering, and finally a large lawsuit beckoned. By this time (1914) even financial experts had difficulty disentangling the affair. Wilhelm stuck firmly to his belief that Fürstenberg was the wronged party. According to Axel Varnbüler, to whom Hohenlohe-Oehringen had shown numerous documents, the opposite was true. Varnbüler was convinced that Fürstenberg had acted in ways 'incompatible with his conceptions of *Stand*,' and reported that 'the vast majority of high finance' shared this conviction.[29] The scandal had gone so far that Wilhelm's current Oberstkämmerer, Solms-Baruth, a Silesian friend of Hohenlohe's, asked Wilhelm to intercede.[30] Wilhelm did so by getting Arthur Gwinner of the Deutsche Bank to liquidate the Fürsten-Konzern with as little damage as possible.[31] Fürstenberg emerged poorer, but with his estates intact. The unfortunate Hohenlohe-Oehringen was not so lucky. In order to raise money for the interest on his debts, he was forced to sell his home estate, Slawentzitz. 'He invited his friends for the last time and touchingly took his leave from them as master of the hunt.'[32] The whole business underlined Fürstenberg's reputation as a risk-taker, which he had acquired from his fondness for jokes. The Austrian ambassador took a less drastic view of the affair than most Germans. He only noted that 'mere dilettantism' was no longer sufficient to manage large estates in a capitalist world.[33]

Fürstenberg's political judgment was better than his financial sense.

Throughout his political career, Fürstenberg was affiliated in the Austrian Herrenhaus with the 'Verfassungstreue Grossgrundbesitzer.' These great landowners were strongly pro-German and centralist. Originally, in the 1870s and 1880s, they were also economic liberals and, in religious matters, often free-thinkers. As the German minority in Bohemia came under increasing nationalist competition from the Czechs, the Verfassungstreue dropped the economic and religious aspects of their program in order to work politically with their counterparts to the right, the conservative landowners.[34] The Verfassungstreue were led by four of Fürstenberg's closest friends: Joseph Baernreither,[35] Erwein Graf Nostitz,[36] Alain Rohan[37] and Ottokar Graf Czernin.[38] Fürstenberg's other boyhood friend, Heinrich Graf Clam-Martinic[39] was one of the leaders of the conservatives.

Fürstenberg made his political debut in 1900 at the German–Czech conference called to arrange a mutually acceptable answer to the prickly language question.[40] According to Baernreither, the delegates quickly recognized Fürstenberg's talent for compromise. Although clearly a German nationalist, Fürstenberg never showed anti-Czech prejudice and even spoke Czech with the delegates on occasion.[41] His reputation continued to grow. The Verfassungstreue soon made him their steward. In 1908 Fürstenberg became First Vice President of the Herrenhaus, a position he filled until the fall of the monarchy. Fürstenberg's political eminence was due strictly to his ability to get along with almost everyone, regardless of native language, political conviction, or religious persuasion. In the multi-national Empire, this was surely not a small gift. On the other hand, it was an inadequate substitute for political insight or organizational ability. Fürstenberg took his cues from Baernreither and Czernin, his 'political alter ego.'[42] The ideas which Fürstenberg espoused were theirs. He was their intermediary, the hail-fellow-well-met who could smooth the way to the goals that they had chosen. As a result, Fürstenberg was in the thick of Viennese politics, he was minutely informed, but he was not active as an initiator of policy.

Once Fürstenberg became close to Kaiser Wilhelm, his potential political influence increased considerably. 'Fürstenberg is destined through his double position in Germany and Austria to accomplish important services for the alliance,' Baernreither noted in 1900.[43] This was exactly what people in Berlin feared, for Fürstenberg was clearly first an Austrian and then a German.[44] Would not Fürstenberg's influence only work in one direction?

A definitive answer to this question is difficult to piece together.

Fürstenberg's papers contain a seemingly haphazard selection of correspondence addressed to him. Only rarely did he keep copies of his own letters. It is therefore easier to discover who tried to influence him than how he tried to influence others. Nonetheless a pattern does emerge from the scattered information. It shows that Fürstenberg's activities regarding Austria and Germany were similar to his role inside Austria itself, that is, he was primarily a mediator, not an initiator. Fürstenberg favored Austria heavily, just as his enemies imagined, but his prejudices left few marks on relations between the two countries.

Austria's ambassador to Berlin, Ladislaus Graf von Szögyényi-Marich, used Fürstenberg as early as January 1899 to patch up a misunderstanding between heir to the throne Archduke Franz Ferdinand and Wilhelm.[45] Through the years Wilhelm frequently called upon Fürstenberg to transport letters to and from the Archduke.[46] Superintending the relationship between the Kaiser and the Austrian heir was Fürstenberg's most consistent service for the alliance. Oddly enough, Wilhelm seems to have made greater use of Fürstenberg in this connection than did Franz Ferdinand, with whom the Fürst was on cordial but hardly intimate terms.[47]

In early 1900 Fürstenberg was in Berlin when a serious rupture threatened the Austro-German alliance. The Dreyfus Affair in France had embroiled the German military attaché there in charges of spying, which forced Germany to recall him. That meant that Germany would be unrepresented at the French army maneuvers. The German government expected Austria to support its German ally by boycotting the maneuvers. Instead, Austria planned to send its usual military representative. Wilhelm's fury expressed itself in expletives directed against Agenor Graf von Goluchowski, Minister of the Imperial and Royal House and of External Affairs. When these remarks reached Goluchowski, Austro-German relations took a sharp nose-dive. Wilhelm sent Fürstenberg to mollify Goluchowski. This done, German Ambassador Philipp Eulenburg advised Fürstenberg to encourage Franz Joseph to travel to Berlin. Fürstenberg managed this as well and the whole affair ended amicably.[48]

After this success, Fürstenberg's role changed from one of personal intervention to something like a quasi-ambassadorship. Both Szögyényi and Eulenburg consulted him. When Heinrich von Tschirschky became Germany's secretary of foreign affairs, he urged Fürstenberg to continue advising Wilhelm with his 'open eye for all relationships and with [his] rich experience,' especially in Austro-German affairs.[49] Chancellor Bethmann Hollweg also valued Fürstenberg's opinions. At the beginning of 1913 he wrote to ask Fürstenberg if Tschirschky, who had become Germany's ambassador to Austria in 1907, should be replaced. Bethmann's question was prompted by a remark Fürstenberg had made to Foreign Secretary Kiderlen-Wächter that Tschirschky and Franz Ferdinand did not get along. Kiderlen-Wächter's death in December 1912 made it possible to shuffle the high diplomatic posts. Bethmann wanted to know if Tschirschky should be removed, and, if so, whom Fürstenberg could recommend who was compatible with both Franz Ferdinand and Wilhelm.[50] Unfortunately no record of the meeting between Fürstenberg and Bethmann, which occurred on 18 January,[51] has been found in the Donaueschingen archive. The point, however, is clear. The German government was fully aware of Fürstenberg's peculiar situation and used him as a resource, particularly in personality–personnel matters.

As a result of his quasi-ambassador ship, Fürstenberg was quite well-informed. He, of course, received a continuous flow of information from the Austrian camp, to which he added his correspondence with the German ambassador to Austria, Foreign Secretary Jagow, and, occasionally, the chancellor. Fürstenberg's best source, however, was his imperial friend. In 1909 Wilhelm showed Fürstenberg secret German fleet plans and other sensitive documents.[52] Three years later, Fürstenberg saw the top secret material surrounding the Haldane mission and Wilhelm's fight with Chancellor Bethmann and Foreign Secretary Kiderlen-Wächter.[53] Bülow and others feared that everything Fürstenberg found out he relayed directly to Vienna.[54] To a large extent this is probably true. But Fürstenberg was not entirely indiscreet, especially about Wilhelm's private, personal conversations. Fürstenberg's wife at one point asked her husband if she might show his diary to his childhood friend Ottokar Czernin. Fürstenberg agreed but was careful to except any sections which contained the Emperor's conversations or confidential discussions.[55]

Furthermore, Wilhelm was most likely to divulge state secrets when he was in direct contact with someone. Of the almost fifty telegrams in the Donaueschingen archive which Wilhelm sent to Fürstenberg in the two years before the war, only one contains a political reference. It is therefore hardly surprising that the two examples mentioned above of Wilhelm's political intimacy both occurred on Corfu. Even had Fürstenberg faithfully repeated every imperial utterance to Vienna, the messages would have been sporadic, since Fürstenberg saw Wilhelm for extended periods alone only in Corfu and Donau-

5 A caricature, by W. A. Wellner, of the Kaiser and his advisers, Fürstenberg
and Hans Graf von Oppersdorff, anxiously watched by Bülow and Bethmann

eschingen. Fürstenberg was also in Berlin for part of the *Saison* at the
end of January each year and for the huge September maneuvers,
neither of which were occasions of much intimacy. Otherwise, he spent
most of his time in Vienna.

Only once before the war does Fürstenberg appear to have pushed
a policy different from that of the German Foreign Office, which
rebuffed him sharply, although his and other official efforts were not

without effect. Characteristically, Fürstenberg relayed the opinions of others, and, equally characteristically, he did not go behind official channels, but through them. This episode occurred in 1912 at the time of the first Balkan war. Germany restrained Austria-Hungary from a bellicose posture, which frustrated the Austrians and caused them to wonder if Germany would fulfill its alliance duties.[56] Fürstenberg's old friends, Heinrich Clam, Erwein Nostitz, Ottokar Czernin, and Fürst Karl Schwarzenberg[57] urged Fürstenberg to let it be known that high Austrian circles felt that a deep rupture threatened the alliance. They asked for assurance that Germany still supported its ally.[58] This was a polite way to chastise Germany for its pacific policy, and by implication to urge Germany to adopt a more warlike stance. Fürstenberg informed Tschirschky on 17 November 1912 of Austrian sentiments. Two days later Tschirschky received Foreign Secretary Kiderlen-Wächter's sharp reply,[59] which he forwarded to Fürstenberg.[60] Kiderlen-Wächter 'urgently' requested Fürstenberg 'energetically to protest the thought among [his] *Standesgenossen* of a loosening of [Germany's] relations to Austria-Hungary.' Without abandoning Germany's caution in this instance, Kiderlen-Wächter nonetheless assured Fürstenberg that Germany would stand by the Austrians 'in further events.' It would be interesting to know if Fürstenberg sent his and his colleagues' thoughts on the alliance to Kaiser Wilhelm, for it was just at this time that Wilhelm performed an about-face. He switched suddenly, on 21 November 1912, from non-intervention in the Balkans ('non-intervention at any price') to such vociferous and potentially warlike support for the Austrians that the German Foreign Office became worried.[61] Wilhelm later calmed somewhat, but German policy makers in 1913 and 1914 expressed greater concern for Austro-Hungarian sentiments than they ever had before, though they continued to restrain Austria in the Balkans.[62]

When the war began, Fürstenberg greeted it with an enthusiasm soon dampened by disappointment at not being able to serve at German headquarters. Fürstenberg was the first victim of General Hans von Plessen's assiduous efforts to isolate the Emperor from any influence other than that of the General Staff. In late July Fürstenberg had written to Plessen, who as Commandant of the Hauptquartier was in charge of such matters, to ask Wilhelm whether Fürstenberg should serve near Wilhelm in the German army or in the Austrian army. Plessen replied that the Kaiser and he had already decided the subject and that 'His Majesty thought' the Austrian army would be nearer Fürstenberg's heart.[63] Fürstenberg journeyed to an audience with the Kaiser on 3 August. Wilhelm was very friendly, and even embarrassed,[64] but stuck with Plessen's advice. 'It was a difficult moment,' wrote Fürstenberg,[65] who spent the next two years with the Austrian army at the front.

Fürstenberg's front experience, added to the news he received from his well-connected friends in Vienna, convinced him early on that an overwhelming victory such as the Germans foresaw was impossible.[66] The war had to be ended soon lest the Dual Monarchy collapse under the strain. Finally, on 9 December 1915, Wilhelm granted Fürstenberg's request to be transferred into the 14th German Army.[67] This gave Fürstenberg the chance to see Wilhelm about twice a month, when he could discreetly lobby on Austria's behalf. His Austrian orientation placed Fürstenberg on Bethmann Hollweg's side in the political disputes at General Headquarters,[68] although his political role during the war was about what it had been before: messenger between the two governments.[69] Fürstenberg's most important service occurred on 24 June 1918, when he delivered Kaiser Karl's letter (of 20 June 1918) to the Emperor, which stated that Austria could no longer continue the offensive and must soon sue for peace.[70] Fürstenberg considered the calmness with which the Germans received this news a great success for Austria-Hungary.

Again more as a spectator than an actor, Fürstenberg took part in the final, frantic hours of the monarchy at Spa. Although he knew that abdication was inevitable, he found it hard to advise the step, so he remained in the background of the consultations. Wilhelm's and Fürstenberg's friendship continued unhindered by exile. Fürstenberg frequently visited the ex-Kaiser at Doorn, and their correspondence continued until Wilhelm's death on 4 June 1941, a few weeks before Fürstenberg's.[71]

Albert Ballin,[72] owner of the Hamburg–America Line, and Friedrich Alfred (Fritz) Krupp,[73] owner from 1887 to 1902 of the steel and armament firm of Fr. Krupp, were Kaiser Wilhelm's most prominent friends from the business sphere. Fritz Fischer repeats a common assertion when he writes that

Men like Krupp and his son-in-law Bohlen und Halbach, like the brothers Stumm, like Gwinner and Helfferich of the Deutsche Bank, like Max von Schinkel and Carl Fürstenberg, or like the Upper Silesian industrial magnates Henckel-Donnersmarck, Pless and Hatzfeld were as much part of the Emperor's entourage as the officers and senior civil servants who came mostly from Prussian Junker families.[74]

He goes on to add that Ballin and several other Jewish financial and industrial notables were received by Wilhelm, who also listened to their advice. The place within the entourage of the Upper Silesian magnates has been discussed elsewhere. Fischer's elevation of the other businessmen to a regular position in Wilhelm's entourage is excessive, however. They appeared at Court only sporadically, and their influence on Wilhelm depended upon timing and luck. In neither scope nor depth of influence were they comparable to the officers of the entourage. Only Friedrich A. Krupp and Ballin established a personal relationship with Wilhelm which placed them near, although not quite in, the *Umgebung*. Nonetheless, since Krupp and Ballin were the only non-landed businessmen who were close to the Kaiser, they form an interesting contrast to the rest of the entourage. In addition, they were both thought to be powerful influences upon the Kaiser, and, finally, Krupp's acolyte, Admiral Hollmann, was an important member of Wilhelm's entourage. For all these reasons, Krupp and Ballin deserve closer inspection.

As was frequently the case in his life, Wilhelm found Fritz Krupp personally attractive because his personality echoed parts of Wilhelm's own, while Krupp's interests and experience were wider than those of the Kaiser's customary suite. Fritz Krupp, like Wilhelm, was robust in neither body nor spirit.[75] A severe asthmatic, he was also plagued by extreme nervousness which made prolonged work a torture[76] and frequent travel a necessity. Widely curious but narrowly educated, the heir to the Krupp fortune became a ferocious dilettante in the subjects of marine biology and archeology. Besides the latter subject, Krupp and Wilhelm shared an avid interest in technological progress and inventions of every sort. And, like so many of Wilhelm's friends, Fritz Krupp was probably homosexual, although the mere suggestion of this possibility drove the Emperor into a rage.[77] Krupp, who was doubtless helped along the road to neurasthenia by his willful and overpowering parents, was overwhelmed by the restless exuberance of the Kaiser. The timid and inarticulate industrialist was no match for the flashy Wilhelm.

Although both Wilhelm and Fritz Krupp came to like each other, friendship was not the bond between them. Theirs was an almost official relationship of national duty and business necessity, respectively. Fritz Krupp's place was unique for this reason. Two years before his own death, Alfred Krupp admonished his son 'to be to the future Kaiser what I have been to the present one, and then no swindler can hurt the factory.'[78] Indeed, Fritz Krupp was already at work plying the young prince with invitations and sending him technical reports and photographs of the firm's accomplishments. Although Wilhelm did attend an artillery demonstration at the Fr. Krupp testing range at Meppen in June 1878, the prince's entourage stopped Fritz Krupp's other entreaties cold. FAD Jacobi, for instance, refused Krupp's request that Wilhelm send him his photograph, on the grounds that such things were never sent to corporations.[79] However in the ensuing years, Wilhelm's entourage slowly weakened against the flood of technical publications and personal greetings that Fritz Krupp passed along through them to the prince.[80] Even so, Wilhelm does not appear to have invited Fritz Krupp to Potsdam until 1885,[81] and he did not visit another company establishment until 1890.[82] After Wilhelm became Kaiser, he saw Fritz Krupp on almost yearly, two-day visits to the Krupp estate (Villa Hügel in Essen), at occasional testings at Meppen, during Kiel Week each June, and when Krupp happened to be in Berlin. These mutual visits rarely amounted to over six per year, and were often fewer, particularly after 1898, when Krupp began spending several months a year on the Italian island Capri.

Fritz Krupp was not near Wilhelm enough to penetrate beyond the dazzle. In 1896 he described an 'unforgettable' evening they had spent together in Berlin.

There were only five persons present and I sat next to Him; we stayed until 11 p.m. at one and the same table. For almost the entire time the Kaiser spoke on the most interesting subjects. . . . He is a man of great importance, and I was enormously touched by how he begins to moderate his remarks and opinions. The main themes were x-rays, the Conservative party and a few of its leaders, the Kanitz bill, navy, the bad feeling vis-à-vis England and Stöcker.[83]

This was the sort of conversation that quickly tired the entourage. But if Krupp ever became seriously disillusioned with Wilhelm, his correspondence does not reflect it. However, his was not the infatuation borne of love, but loyalty underwritten by necessity. At the time of widespread attacks against himself and the firm, Krupp wrote, 'I can bear my fate with equanimity so long as I am sure of H. M.'s trust and so long as the attacks against me glance off His affectionate sentiments [for me].'[84] For in the end, Krupp did not go to Kiel to be with Wilhelm 'for his own sake,' but in order to cement the relationship between Fr. Krupp and the government. As he put it, 'I have to go to Kiel, because I do not want to miss the opportunity to speak with the Kaiser.'[85]

Wilhelm's relationship to Fritz Krupp was not really based on friendship, either. The Kaiser regarded Krupp as his industrial counterpart, a kind of bourgeois king whose meaning to Germany's strength, internal and external, was practically as important as his own. Richard Owen quite rightly points out that 'Krupp "was . . . in his kingdom the successful representative of a socio-political system" and his factories served as "a bastion against the infiltration of social revolutionary ideas." '[86] For his part, the Kaiser barely recognized the difference between Fr. Krupp and the German Empire. After Fritz Krupp's death in 1902, Wilhelm wrote to his daughter, the new owner of Fr. Krupp, offering his 'advice and help at anytime, and hopefully you will one day show me the same openness and trust as your beloved father [did] for the benefit of the works and of the Fatherland.' He advised her to go every day into the factories and houses of the workers. 'The worker should and must know that he is dependent upon Fräulein Bertha *Krupp* and not a board of directors or managers. That was the secret of your father, of his belovedness and greatness!'[87] This was of course sheer nonsense regarding Fritz Krupp, who, particularly at the end, was very much the absentee owner, but it was precisely the picture that Wilhelm held in his mind's eye about himself, the workers' Kaiser who singlehandedly steered the ship of state through revolutionary rapids. Wilhelm's relationship to Fritz Krupp, then, sprang from his identification with Krupp's position and from his acceptance of the firm as symbol and guarantor of German national strength.

The real place of Fritz Krupp as head of the firm was less grandiose than Wilhelm imagined. Fr. Krupp's official historian, Wilhelm Berdrow, argues that after the first few years after his father's death in 1887, Fritz Krupp became less subservient to his board of directors (*Direktorium*).[88] But the documents he cites and others in the Krupp archive seem to show instead only Fritz Krupp's sporadic efforts to reassert himself against a dominant *Direktorium*.[89] Which is not to say that the owner did not have his own ideas, or that he did not have final say on large policy questions, but he did not run the firm as his father had.

It is naturally not my wish to learn assorted details [he informed the *Direktorium* in 1896], but it is necessary that I receive notice of important changes. In particular I want to know about each change in the method of production, improvements in machinery, changes in technology, further, each expansion or transfer of particular plants, new buildings and alterations.[90]

This is one of several letters in the 1890s complaining about lack of information or control. Wounded pride was not the reason for the complaints. Discrepancies between what Fr. Krupp did and what Fritz

Krupp said it would do were dangerous. After one such incident in 1891, Fritz Krupp explained why. 'It has uncommonly weakened my position vis-à-vis the Kaiser.'[91] In 1899 he repeated that if such occurrences 'should put me in a bad position [*eine schiefe Lage*] with H.M. the Kaiser, I will hold my entire *Direktorium* responsible.'[92] Wilhelm's view of Fritz Krupp as Kaiser of the company demanded that Krupp keep better informed than he might otherwise have wished. That is, Fr. Krupp's special position with the German government entailed mirroring, however imperfectly, Wilhelm's conception of personal regime.

The burden which thus fell on Fritz Krupp's shoulders was too great for him to bear. He had neither the personality, time, nor energy for the constant personal attention that Fr. Krupp's imperial benefactor demanded. Fritz Krupp was fortunate to find someone who did: Admiral Fritz Hollmann. Like many officers in the German navy, Hollmann was bourgeois (he was ennobled in 1900). Hollmann became an intimate of both the Kaiser and Krupp through his official position: state secretary of the Imperial Navy Office (1890–7). Wilhelm came to like him quite apart from his naval affiliation, however. He told good stories, knew interesting people and shared Wilhelm's enthusiasm for spiritism.[93] Hollmann was *Stammgast* at Rominten even after Tirpitz replaced him in the Navy Office. Affable and pliant, Hollmann was also firmly bourgeois. He did not use 'von' on his stationery, and avoided gatherings of nobles, who made him nervous.[94] The Court made him uncomfortable, too. After a couple of weeks at Rominten with the Kaiser, Hollmann sighed at how well he felt in the 'complete enjoyment of my freedom after the long constraint. Each long stay in the Court atmosphere strengthens anew my thankfulness that I was not born to serve in this higher region.'[95] Although Hollmann was conventionally monarchist and even mildly anti-Semitic,[96] his perspective was nonetheless different from that of his fellow entourage members. His heart beat to industrial Germany, and he felt happier with bankers and self-made businessmen than with officers. These sympathies doubtless helped inscribe him in Wilhelm's imagination, precisely because they were so underrepresented at Court.[97] Hollman was also free-thinking enough to read the liberal *Vossische Zeitung*, and during his periodic visits to Albert Ballin, the retired admiral even enjoyed catching up on back issues of Harden's *Zukunft*.[98]

Under these circumstances, it is perhaps surprising that Hollmann did not develop a critical stance toward Wilhelm and his Court in the way his fellow bourgeois Admiral Georg Müller did.[99] Two factors prevented him from taking this path. First, after he left office in 1897, Hollmann did not have to conclude pressing business at Court. The Kaiser's impetuosity and unsteadiness therefore weighed less heavily upon him than they did upon working bureaucrats. Second, where Müller's bourgeois tastes made him censorious, they made Hollmann insecure. He could not believe his own social success, and for all his dislike of the *Hofluft*, the Kaiser remained for him an untouchable object of awe. Hollmann once set down his impressions after nine days together with Wilhelm at Hubertusstock:

Since I accompanied H. M. many times in the wagon and on foot, I [was able to say] a number of intelligent things [*manches kluge Wort*], but I heard a thousand times more intelligent things. If I were not such a lazy and comfortable fellow, and above all if I had a better memory and were more articulate than I am, I could indeed write memoirs that would be very useful in the long years when we are no longer alive. ... Because when H.M. warms to his remarks, he in fact knows no bounds and speaks of past, present and future with such mighty words and in such seductive dialectic, that one becomes carried away by his magic. It becomes clearer to me that he is a completely important man who is becoming more and more serious and energetic in his conception of his self-appointed goals. How is it that someone as unimportant as I, has won to such a large degree the trust of this man? I have *no* answer to this; but I want to enjoy [this trust] as long as it remains to me, and I shall never become immodest, because I am clearly conscious that I have done nothing to deserve this.[100]

In keeping with this modesty, Hollmann treated Wilhelm with kid gloves. He did not contradict or argue. He waited patiently for the opportune moment to discuss a subject.[101] Even when the Kaiser clearly erred, Hollmann avoided correcting him. 'I could move him [Wilhelm] with the documents to admit that he is wrong, but that would not be a victory; I would not like to use facts to prove him incorrect [*ich möchte ihn mit den Thatsächlichen nicht ins Unrecht bringen*].'[102] So, for different reasons from Philipp Eulenburg, Admiral Hollmann also failed to clear the web of self-delusion that Wilhelm spun around himself.

If Hollmann felt out of his depths at Court, he felt much more at home in the Villa Hügel. Apparently Hollmann was a self-convinced admirer of the Krupps' accomplishments even before he took office in 1890. What cemented the relationship between Fritz Krupp and the State Secretary, however, was Hollmann's role in cajoling the young Kaiser to observe personally the superiority of Krupp's nickel steel plates at the company's firing range.[103] Wilhelm came, saw and was conquered. Krupp's nickel steel won the monopoly over government naval contracts thereafter.[104] In gratitude, Fritz Krupp invited Hollmann to the Villa Hügel. 'I believe that I cannot better express my thanks to you,' Hollmann wrote afterwards to the *Hausherr*, 'than by the assurance, that in your house, I felt like an old friend and guest returning to much loved surroundings. . . . I simply felt incredibly comfortable with you.'[105] From this beginning, Hollmann became a standard figure at Fritz Krupp's hunting lodge, Sayneck, and aboard his yacht at Kiel. When Krupp visited Berlin, he was a frequent dinner guest at the Hollmanns'. Their relationship became closer still in 1897, when Tirpitz replaced Hollmann as naval secretary. The latter was naturally most upset and Krupp tried to comfort him and his wife with a five-week vacation aboard his yacht.[106] This trip seems to have spawned a new nickname for Hollmann, 'Onkel Zückerchen,' as the admiral frequently signed himself thereafter.[107]

Even while he was still in office, Hollmann often acted as though he represented Fr. Krupp. He went to great lengths to smooth over imperial displeasure when the firm's deliveries were late,[108] and he conspired with company officials to outmaneuver opposition within the Prussian War Ministry. 'We'll make it,' he assured them, underlining his identification with Essen against Berlin.[109] The admiral saw no conflict of interest in his actions, because he was convinced of Fr. Krupp's utter superiority over its competitors. He once remarked, when Fr. Krupp's product emerged the winner in a test with another company, 'I see in this a victory of the good side, the good against evil [*des Guten gegen das Böse*].'[110] Furthermore, he accepted completely Wilhelm's idea that the Kaiser and Fritz Krupp represented the same principle in their different spheres, and that therefore a solid personal relationship between them was necessary. 'It is absolutely indispensable,' Hollmann told Fritz Krupp, 'that you and H.M. always be on intimate terms [*auf dem besten Fusse stehen*] and mutual trust prevail, and I hope that this shall always be so, in the interests of our armed forces, particularly the navy.'[111]

Hollmann was thus the perfect intermediary for Fritz Krupp and Wilhelm once he no longer filled an official post, but it was not until 1899 that he succeeded to this predestined role. In the meantime inactivity told on his nerves, and his wife wrote in despair to Fritz Krupp, begging him to counsel his friend to accept the job that Albert Ballin had offered him with the Hamburg–America Line. 'You have such a great influence on Fritz [Hollmann],' she wrote, 'and if you tell him to do something, he'll do it.' So far he had hesitated because 'he can't make himself free of his Kaiser.' 'Please don't hold up the Kaiser's friendship against me, that consists only of pretty words and means nothing to me,' she added.[112]

The Kaiser's friendship meant more to Krupp and her husband, so, for the moment, Frau Hollmann's entreaties were vain. The next year, however, Hollmann's enforced retirement finally ended. It was apparently Civil Cabinet chief Lucanus who suggested that the admiral head the Berlin chapter of the Navy League.[113] Fritz Krupp had (not so secretly) helped to found the League in 1897 in order to saturate Germany with propaganda and raise public support to build a huge battle fleet. The League was designed to spead the wishes of big industry and the Imperial Naval Office throughout the land.[114] Hollmann was flattered and expressed his debt to Fritz Krupp, 'If I did not know that you stood behind Schweinburg [Secretary of the Navy League] I would certainly have declined. You alone would give me the security to venture out onto such dangerous terrain.'[115] Fritz Krupp made it clear why he wanted Hollmann: it is necessary 'that the chairman in Berlin have close connections to the Kaiser.'[116]

Krupp's venture into national propaganda turned out to be a dreadful mistake. Public support was indeed aroused, but so was public ire. Attacks against Krupp and his profits multiplied until he sought refuge by withdrawing from the League.[117] Consequently, Hollmann's tenure with it lasted only a year. But in the same letter in which Fritz Krupp urged Hollmann to accept the Navy League post, Krupp also brought the admiral for the first time into company affairs. He put Hollmann into direct contact with Director Jencke, the most powerful member of the *Direktorium,* and with Admiral Barandon, head of Fr. Krupp's shipbuilding arm, the Germania wharf.[118] Thenceforth, Hollmann mediated between the *Direktorium* and the Germania wharf, and between the company as a whole and the government, via the Kaiser (particularly regarding naval affairs). Hollmann did not officially work for Fr. Krupp, nor was he paid for his efforts. He construed himself merely as a personal friend of Fritz Krupp's.[119] Hollmann's conception of his role reflected the same self-effacement that he felt toward the Kaiser. He told Krupp:

I am happy, when I have the opportunity to be useful to you, and that of course can only be to intervene as interpreter of your ideas, when you cannot bring your own voice to be heard. The agreement of our ideas in all things, [my] complete understanding for your way of doing things makes me particularly suited to this task.[120]

Contemporaries naturally imagined that Fritz Krupp, because of his great wealth and many connections, exercised considerable influence over the Kaiser and his government. Rumors that Wilhelm owned large blocks of stock in Fr. Krupp suggested a material basis for this influence. However, Fr. Krupp did not become a stock company until

1903, after Fritz Krupp's death. Bernt Engelmann claims that between 1908 and April 1914, the Kaiser owned 50,000 M worth of Krupp bonds, but he cites no source for this allegation.[121] No evidence of any financial connection has survived in the Krupp archive,[122] nor is it necessary to explain the complex relationship between Wilhelm, the government and Germany's best known business in so simplistic a fashion.

The question of influence is best broken down into political and economic influence. By far the greatest share of influence that Fritz Krupp and his company exerted in Berlin lay in economics, not politics. Krupp, as both an ultra-conservative and an industrialist, was in a difficult position politically during the Caprivi years. On the one hand he naturally supported the Caprivi tariffs, which favored industry, but at the same time he rejected the social policies and liberal ministers[123] who went with them. Krupp's serious disagreements with the Kaiser on imperial policy toward the working class in the early 1890s are well known.[124] Krupp was in fact so incensed at Wilhelm's conciliatory social program that he threatened to sell the company. The Kaiser was shocked and tried to mollify Krupp.[125] How far the industrialist's threat dampened Wilhelm's enthusiasm for social projects cannot be determined, but Krupp remained unhappy about the official attitude toward workers and strikes at least until 1897. He once complained that Wilhelm was 'deaf' on the subject and avoided all discussion of it, so that Krupp resorted to occasional written reports which he hoped would be effective.[126] By 1897, Wilhelm had indeed swung around to the conservative side, but Krupp was hardly the only individual pressing in this direction, so it is difficult to say how instrumental he was in scotching the New Course's progressive legacy. There are very few documents from after 1897 in the Krupp archive, which reflect similar over-intervention of the kind that Caprivi elicited. We may surmise that the inauguration of *Weltpolitik* and the navy robbed Krupp of the temptation to interfere, since he approved of the new tenor of government. In general it is clear, however, that Fritz Krupp did not have a happy hand in pure politics, either in the Reichstag, with the young Kaiser, or in nationwide propaganda.

Economics was a different matter, however, for here Fr. Krupp did indeed enjoy an unprecedented 'special relationship' with the German government.[127] Furthermore, both Fritz Krupp and Wilhelm inherited this relationship, although together they deepened and widened it. Fr. Krupp's power in Berlin rested upon its undeniable size and accomplishments, plus the careful cultivation of strategically placed bureaucrats and officers.[128] Numerous ex-officers joined the Krupp payroll as liaisons to their old posts, while swift technological changes forced military and civilian bureaucrats to seek expert technical assistance from business. By 1890 this interlocking effect was far advanced and it is questionable how much the firm really needed the Kaiser's active intervention.[129] Nevertheless, Wilhelm's good graces brought the firm enormous profit.

As we have seen, the Kaiser viewed Fr. Krupp less as a business than as a patriotic enterprise. Wilhelm did not recognize here the line dividing public from private, any more than he did in his own life. He passed along government secrets to Fritz Krupp,[130] informed him personally of government contracts,[131] and even intervened himself on the firm's behalf with the recalcitrant Artillery Testing Commission.[132] The Kaiser took an active interest in all aspects of Fr. Krupp, and Fritz Krupp responded by clearing major company decisions with Wilhelm (for example, the purchase of the Gruson works),[133] and by keeping him *au courant* via annual reports and intermittent oral communications.

Boelcke writes that the Kaiser's main contribution to Fr. Krupp's profits lay in two areas: encouraging foreign business for the company and steering its way an undue proportion of orders for the new fleet.[134] The navy was the more important of the two,[135] but until 1896, Fr. Krupp did not own a shipyard. Although the company had now and again contemplated acquiring one,[136] there is little doubt that Wilhelm and Hollmann were behind the final decision to go ahead. This episode marks the Kaiser's most spectacular intervention into the company's fortunes. In the space of a few months, the *Direktorium* made an about-face from opposing such a move, on grounds that it expanded the firm too quickly, to ardent support.[137] Fritz Krupp himself remained opposed until Hollmann pressured him. 'The opinions of the State Secretary were so positive about this undertaking, that in the end I could no longer maintain my standpoint. . . . [Hollmann] assured me before the conclusion [of the deal] that H. M. approved.'[138] Hollmann had wired the news to Krupp directly after his audience with the Kaiser, on 25 August 1896.[139] Richard Owen is quite right that Fr. Krupp's expansion into shipbuilding was entirely in line with general company policy (capturing a solid domestic market and enlarging the business),[140] but Wilhelm's and Hollmann's prodding enabled Fr. Krupp to get in on lucrative fleet contracts from the very beginning, which the *Direktorium* could otherwise not have done.

Although he might have wished it, Wilhelm could not spend all of his time on armaments questions. Day to day business and actual contracts went through the Prussian War Ministry and the Imperial Naval Office. Fritz Krupp and his directors were hypersensitive to complaints and injustices that they felt these two institutions meted out. Earlier relations with the War Ministry had indeed been rocky,[141] but by Wilhelm's accession to the throne, Fr. Krupp's special relationship was smoothly cemented. In 1892 and 1893, critics of the company within the Artillery Testing Commission and the Weapons Department were replaced and their tasks supervised by Heinrich von Gossler, who became war minister in 1896.[142] Gossler was not only 'the Kaiser's General,'[143] he was also Krupp's. Fritz Krupp was pleased that he 'was of an astonishing openness and filled with goodwill for the company.'[144] Gossler himself admitted to Fritz Krupp, 'I would feel completely unsure in technical questions, if I could not rely on your trust.'[145]

Even before Gossler became war minister, however, it had been standard practice for the Technical Department to let Fr. Krupp know exactly how far to underbid competition. Furthermore, in order to assure Fr. Krupp a hefty profit, the Department purposely did not name the lowest possible price.[146] Under the circumstances it is perhaps surprising that the company found anything worthy of complaint about the War Ministry. Yet, especially in the early 1890s, there is enough record of such dissatisfaction that the official Krupp historian, Berdrow, believed the relations between the firm and Ministry were bad, even under Gossler.[147] On the contrary, the friction developed precisely out of the unique place that Fr. Krupp enjoyed. For Fritz Krupp and his directors became distressed whenever the War Ministry treated the company as a mere business, that is, according to contractual criteria, which are implicitly adversarial. The company took it as a sign of bad faith whenever the War Ministry questioned prices, awarded contracts to competitors or insisted that artillery demonstrations be made on government testing ranges instead of at Meppen. 'In the past,' Fritz Krupp once complained, 'this country was proud of the achievements of the firm of Krupp. Both the army and the navy were grateful for the firm's cooperation and were happy that it allowed them to be independent of foreign producers.'[148] This was another way of saying that Fr. Krupp was a national institution, not merely a factory. Furthermore, Fritz Krupp saw no conflict of interest between patriotism and profit. There may even have been more self-delusion in this view than cynical hypocrisy,[149] for businessmen are no more immune to ideology than emperors. And, Fr. Krupp had even occasionally sacrificed profit for patriotism, as when it rejected expanding into England 'despite the large pecuniary advantages,'[150] because 'the Krupp tradition and our position of trust with the state and particularly the continuous, high degree of favor and kindness that H. Majesty shows me [Fritz Krupp] exclude cooperation with English firms.'[151]

The quasi-official status of Fr. Krupp also caused minor irritations with the Emperor, just as it had with the War Ministry, but again, these were simply the price of the company's exalted position. Wilhelm was, in a sense, caught in the middle. On the one hand, he wanted Essen to receive the major armament contracts, while on the other, he wanted good merchandise, promptly, at good prices for the armed forces. The result was a constant stream of imperial questions, proddings, indelicate telegrams, and unwanted suggestions. Had Fr. Krupp made an excess profit from Germany's involvement in the Boxer Rebellion?[152] Was Fr. Krupp slowing work on a German battleship in order to finish a Russian one?[153] Was Fr. Krupp aiding the British war effort against the Boers?[154] Had the company fixed the price of shrapnel?[155] Why was the Germania wharf always slow to deliver, and so sloppy at that?[156] Such questions were the price of imperial favor, and although they cost time to answer, the Kaiser declared himself satisfied in virtually every case, except for the perennial Germania problem. Admiral Hollmann succeeded time and again in deflecting Wilhelm's anger on to the war minister or the naval state secretary. On one such occasion the Kaiser even burst out, 'I've canned three War Ministers because of Krupp, and still they don't catch on!'[157] This, it is true, was mostly hyperbole: War Minister Verdy (1889–90) fell over a technical issue that involved Fr. Krupp, but not in the way Wilhelm intimated;[158] Bronsart (1893–6) was a victim of Court politics;[159] Kaltenborn (1890–3) may actually have departed in the way Wilhelm claimed.[160] Nonetheless, there could be no doubt that Wilhelm favored the company outrageously. Therefore, while Fr. Krupp may not always have welcomed the imperial queries and demands, these showed Wilhelm's unflagging esteem for the firm, and even his complaints usually ended in victories for it.

The same is true for the largest anti-Krupp crusade, Tirpitz's turn-of-the-century press campaign against the 'Krupp monopoly.'[161] Tirpitz's allegations did considerable damage to the firm's public reputation and provided ammunition for Krupp opponents for years to come. But once again, Fr. Krupp's predominance in shipbuilding remained untouched. As he had in the 1890s, the Kaiser again took Fritz Krupp's renewed threat to sell the company seriously. Wilhelm enforced a compromise which lowered Fr. Krupp's prices, but retained its monopoly. Tirpitz never again attacked the firm publicly.

From these and other incidents it is clear that Fr. Krupp exercised its greatest influence on the specific economic areas closest to its interest: contracts, prices, types of weapons. Its influence on larger questions of policy, domestic and foreign, was not remotely as great. Nor was it as direct. There are few traces of attempts to intervene in central political questions through the Kaiser or highest-level officials. As in the early 1890s, the attempts that were made were not always successful. Further, there are more examples of influence going the other way. For instance, it was only after energetic government pressure that Fr. Krupp entered two of its most lucrative fields: armor-plating[162] and shipbuilding. Wilhelm even appears to have chosen the (rather inept) first head of the Germania wharf himself, and tried repeatedly to pick his successor, but Frau Krupp, a much more forceful individual than her husband, stood firm.[163] All of which is not to say that Fr. Krupp had no political impact in Germany. Of course it did. But its political influence was oblique, through its many connections in the lower-level bureaucracy, in banks and in pressure groups, through the workplace, through the atmosphere of public opinion, through the Krupp myth, but not, for the most part, through direct wire-pulling at the apex of power around the Kaiser and his advisers.

Indeed, in the last three years of his life, Fritz Krupp pulled fewer and fewer wires altogether. The 'Krupp monopoly' attack and other public criticism increasingly dispirited the industrialist, who tried to recover with ever longer vacations on the island of Capri. In Krupp's absence, Admiral Hollmann's role necessarily widened, and with it, Wilhelm's as well. Scarcely a year after Fritz Krupp made Hollmann the firm's unofficial representative in Berlin, the admiral found himself in constant contact with the directors, expected to take immediate action of which the troubled industrialist learned only afterwards in letters sent to his retreat.[164] There is no indication that Fritz Krupp disapproved of this situation. On the contrary, he consulted Hollmann on the most important and delicate issues.[165] It was an open secret in Berlin that if one wanted to contact the reclusive Krupp, one went through Admiral Hollmann.[166]

Toward the end of 1902, Hollmann ran across the first serious problem that he could not resolve. This was the scandal which ended in Fritz Krupp's death. Its similarity to the Eulenburg case and the continuing speculation about Wilhelm's and Hollmann's parts in it, required at least a brief discussion of the circumstances. For at least a

year, Krupp had received blackmail threats stemming from his paedophile activities on Capri.[167] Similar rumors began to spread and
finally appeared in the Italian press. Exactly what happened next, and
the Kaiser's and Hollmann's roles remain obscure. Historians critical
of the Krupp legend have repeated an account published at the time
in the *Münchener Post*.[168] According to that article, sometime in October 1902 Frau Krupp received anonymous letters detailing her husband's activities on Capri. With Fritz Krupp in England, she turned
to the Kaiser, and told him of the stories. He suggested declaring Fritz
Krupp incompetent, thus removing the firm from his control.[169] When
Hollmann discovered what the Kaiser had said, he intervened immediately and turned the tables on Frau Krupp. Hollmann discredited
her by maintaining that she was under great mental strain and needed
to go to a sanitorium. He recalled Krupp from England. Shortly
thereafter Frau Krupp was taken against her will to Jena and put
under the care of Dr Otto Binswanger, a physician long connected
with the Krupp family. She was only released after her husband's
death.

Some historians have added incorrect elaborations to the *Münchener
Post's* account. For example, Frau Krupp could not have spoken to
Wilhelm in Berlin,[170] because he was in Rominten and Cadinen (East
Prussia) from 28 September to 16 October. And she would not have
been committed to the Jena institution on 2 November,[171] because
Admiral and Frau Hollmann visited her there on 31 October.[172] In
addition, if Frau Krupp really did journey almost to the Russian border to speak to the Kaiser, she must have told him more than the
Italian rumors, because he had known about those since June, when
he and Fritz Krupp had discussed who might be behind them.[173]

Nevertheless, it is clear that Wilhelm and Hollmann were active in
taking Fritz Krupp's part against his wife, who seems to have talked
openly about the Capri rumors when he, the *Direktorium* and the Kaiser were trying to keep them secret.[174] Whether their activity included
forcing Frau Krupp into an asylum is uncertain. Fritz Krupp insisted
(curiously) in two different letters that she had gone 'voluntarily.'[175]
Frau Krupp's later hostility toward the Kaiser and the admiral is certainly consistent with the *Münchener Post's* account, but then it is hard
to explain why she continued on such friendly terms with the two
doctors involved, Binswanger and Vogt.[176] The Krupp archive unfortunately does not contain solutions to these ambiguities. It has just
enough scraps to suggest that other material may have been removed,
but not enough to provide a definitive account of the last six months
of Fritz Krupp's life.

On 15 November the Social Democrats outflanked whatever machinations may have occurred by publishing the Italian newspaper stories in *Vorwärts*.[177] Fritz Krupp began immediate legal proceedings, but died on 22 November, before the truth or untruth of the allegations could be established. Krupp's death was as mystery-shrouded as the other events of 1902. His doctors claimed it was a natural death (stroke), but they allowed no autopsy, so suicide seemed then and seems now the more likely explanation.[178]

About one thing there is no doubt, however, and that is Wilhelm's opinion on the matter. He felt that the Social Democrats had libelled Fritz Krupp and then hounded him to death. The Kaiser demonstrated his contempt for them by attending his friend's elaborate funeral with a large contingent of the military entourage. He also made an impassioned funeral oration, which public opinion found excessive.[179] In the years after 1902, Wilhelm's paternal concern for the company continued undiminished by Fritz Krupp's death or by Wilhelm's antipathy toward Frau Krupp.[180] Nothing could make clearer that the real basis of the relation between Fritz Krupp and Kaiser Wilhelm II had been the firm.

Albert Ballin[181] contrasts sharply with Fritz Krupp. The Hamburg–America Line, while large and the object of Wilhelm's interest and goodwill, was neither the core of Germany's defense industry nor the basis of Wilhelm's and Ballin's connection. It was Ballin himself who attracted the Kaiser; and Ballin was considerably more a friend to Wilhelm than Krupp was. For if Krupp was more like Wilhelm in his weaknesses (nervousness, hypochondria, the need to escape pressure), Ballin shared more of the Kaiser's strengths.[182] A self-made man, Albert Ballin harbored great plans for the future, and set about realizing them with inexhaustible energy. He was as brilliant a conversationalist as Wilhelm was, and both men therefore enjoyed each other's company, particularly when they discoursed on their mutual loves: ships, travel, the sea and Germany's glorious future upon it. The Kaiser could not dominate Ballin as he had Krupp. But the Emperor and Ballin also shared weaknesses, especially moodiness. Ballin, too, leapt to premature judgments based on hunches. He too swung from unrealistic optimism to blackest despair. In short, the Junker Kaiser and the Jewish shipowner had more in common than anyone would immediately have guessed.

The two men do not seem to have become close until 1899.[183] Like Krupp, who had donated the land for the Imperial Yacht Club, Ballin was a mainstay at Kiel Week. Each year he entertained the Kaiser and his guests on luxury liners belonging to the Hamburg–America fleet. Throughout the rest of the year, the shipowner and his Emperor met intermittently in Hamburg, where frequent naval inspections lured the Kaiser, or in Berlin, when Ballin was in town. All told, Ballin saw Wilhelm about a dozen times per year,[184] or twice as often as Krupp did.

Contemporaries were much interested in Ballin's putative influence over the Kaiser and, in order to explain it, they entertained the same idea that they had about Krupp: the Emperor must own stock in the Hamburg–America Line. Historical investigation has discovered no more evidence of this in Ballin's, than in Krupp's case, however.[185] Nonetheless, Wilhelm was indeed interested in the fortunes of the company. But his actions were infrequent and not remotely so proprietorial as they were vis-à-vis Fr. Krupp. Ballin discovered that Wilhelm's good wishes were a two-edged sword. On the one hand, imperial intervention helped the Line make a handful of advantageous settlements with foreign shipping companies and with the government.[186] On the other hand, Wilhelm's impetuosity not infrequently disturbed the internal functioning of the company and its relations with its customers and host countries. One of Ballin's board members asserted that 'Ballin's friendship with the Kaiser hurt more than it helped the Hamburg–America Line.'[187]

If Ballin was intermittently successful in pursuing economic interest at Court, he was uniformly a failure when he tried to do the same in politics. For although Ballin was a more forceful person than Fritz Krupp, he was in a worst position vis-à-vis the entourage because he was a Jew and, by Junker standards, a political gadfly. Ballin's only admirer at Court was Admiral Georg Müller, who was hardly popular there himself.[188] Without a Hollmann in more or less constant touch with the Emperor, Ballin's lone voice could not hope to compete with the daily conservative chorus at Court. The shipowner's naïveté also weakened his political impact. Although Ballin disagreed with the government's reactionary and pro-agrarian tax and tariff policies, although after 1908 he favored a naval agreement with England and after 1914 a quick, non-annexationist peace, these fundamental objections to the status quo did not move him to develop a coherent political critique of the Wilhelminian system. He did not draw the logical conclusions that Wilhelm had to be restrained, the political system modernized, and the Junkers displaced, until 1918, when it was too late. Without the guidance of such a coherent plan, Ballin's political activities at Court were sporadic, undirected, often fantastic, and almost always failures.[189] Ballin agreed with many aspects of the Second Reich, for instance, its hostility to social democracy, and this fact, plus his anomalous social position, doubtless inhibited him from developing a critical stance. But Ballin's friendship with Wilhelm also lamed his political effect.

Like virtually everyone who served near Wilhelm for long, or who liked him, or even who felt sorry for him, Ballin was overcome by Wilhelm's fragility. Ballin could not bring himself to hurt so vulnerable a person. 'We were all too weak toward the Kaiser,' he wrote in 1915. 'No one wished to disturb his childlike, happy optimism, which could shift at once into an almost helpless depression if anyone criticized one of his pet projects.'[190] When on 5 September 1918 Ballin screwed up his courage to tell the Kaiser that the war was lost and that peace negotiations had to begin immediately, he discovered that Wilhelm had just recovered from a breakdown. 'His Majesty was in such a sunny disposition that it seemed to me quite impossible to spell out, or even to intimate, the seriousness and the frightful danger in which Germany found itself. My determination collapsed.'[191] So Ballin, despite the fact that he was an outsider and a relatively progressive one at that, was as much a prisoner of Wilhelm's character as anyone else in the civilian (or military) entourage. In political matters, he bowed, as had Krupp and Fürstenberg, to the limitations imposed upon them by Wilhelm's personality and by the structure and personnel of the entourage. None of them pursued a political program with the tenacity that Eulenburg had. All of them were too busy, too far from Berlin, to have a lasting impact on how decisions were made or who made them. In the end, their influence on policy was far, far less than anyone looking at their wealth or prestige would have imagined.

These three negative examples, although different from each other in many ways, illustrate several fundamental principles operating in the imperial entourage which determined whose influence weighed most heavily with the Kaiser. First, one had to be in nearly constant attendance, either personally or through an intermediary (or preferably intermediaries). Wilhelm's impetuosity, indiscriminate confidences and inability to make decisions based upon long preparation or sustained reflection guaranteed the importance of those nearest him when he struck a choice. Second, one had to know how to handle Wilhelm's moods to best advantage. Third, in order to exercise lasting, not just spasmodic, influence on policy, one had to have a consistent political *Weltanschauung* that one promoted on several different levels: personnel, domestic and foreign policy, even symbolic matters, such as medals and titles. If one narrowed one's focus to a single arena (such as particular business gains), the decisions taken constantly in other spheres might soon undercut the effects of earlier, but limited victories. Finally, the politics one pushed stood a better chance of acceptance if Wilhelm either already agreed with them (obviously), or believed that he ought to agree with them, for his own sake, the monarchy's, or the nation's. The appeal to tradition (familial, monarchical, and Prussian) was the strongest lever in the battle to persuade Wilhelm of what he ought to believe. Once Eulenburg departed the scene, only the military entourage fulfilled all these conditions. Who these men were, how they used their opportunity and the limits they encountered are the subjects of the next chapter.

7

The military entourage

Kaiser Wilhelm's military entourage [*militärisches Gefolge*] consisted of his own, his father's and his grandfather's generals *à la suite*, general adjutants, Flügeladjutanten (aides-de-camp, or FAs) and Wilhelm's Military and Naval Cabinet chiefs. The term 'military entourage' is used in the following discussion the way the contemporaries used it, that is, excluding the military retinues of Kaisers Friedrich III and Wilhelm I. Wilhelm II's military entourage was further divided into those generals *à la suite*, general adjutants and FAs who performed personal service for their Emperor and those who did not. Wilhelm rather bellicosely called the former his Hauptquartier [Headquarters]. In addition, the Hauptquartier consisted of three other posts: Commander of the Schlossgardekompagnie, Commander of the Leibgendarmerie[1] and the Commandant of the Hauptquartier itself. The AKO of 7 July 1888 which defined the Hauptquartier did not include the Cabinet chiefs,[2] although a supplementary directive of 3 December 1888 mentions the Military Cabinet chief as a member.[3] The *Handbuch über den königlichen preussischen Hof und Staat* for the 1890s follows the supplementary directive in excluding only the Naval Cabinet chief from the Hauptquartier. Despite the official confusion, both the Military and Naval Cabinet chiefs were in fact integral parts of the Hauptquartier and will be considered such in the discussion that follows.

The two Cabinet chiefs were politically the most influential members of Wilhelm's Hauptquartier. Their power was part of the resurgence of the army as an independent force within the state after the wars of unification. The Military Cabinet had originally been the bureaucratic arm of the king in military affairs. Through proximity to the throne, the Military Cabinet had developed immense influence. The Prussian reformers of the Napoleonic period had reined in the Military Cabinet by subjecting it to the war minister. In that way they hoped to promote the responsible power of the ministers against the irresponsible power of the king's private advisers.[4] Once the period of reform had ended, however, the Military Cabinet began to creep back to its former position. This process was aided by the vast prestige the army won in the successful wars of 1864, 1866, and 1870/1.

Even more important to the resurgence of the Military Cabinet was the establishment of the democratically elected Reichstag, which the Junkers feared that liberal reformers would use as a wedge to dislodge the army from its central position in state affairs. The King/Kaiser was now more concerned than ever before to guard his army from the prying eyes of the legislature. Since the Reichstag could interpellate the Prussian war minister, Kaiser Wilhelm I and his military advisers began to strip him of power. The less the war minister controlled, the less he would be compelled to tell the people's representatives. The major conspirators, General Alfred von Waldersee at the General Staff and General E. L. von Albedyll, Chief of the Military Cabinet, concocted the fiction that the Kaiser's right to command the armed forces, his *Kommandogewalt,* was set in the constitution and not a matter for debate in the Reichstag. Therefore, they reasoned, all matters which stemmed from the *Kommandogewalt* should fall, not under the purview of the responsible war minister, but under the Kaiser's own men, his Military Cabinet. In 1883, after a long struggle, they succeeded in divesting the war minister of jurisdiction over everything except administration in the narrow sense and budget matters.[5] The General Staff now emancipated itself from the War Ministry and won the right to report to the Kaiser without the war minister's presence. The Military Cabinet also became once again independent. But its victory in some ways was even greater than that of the General Staff.

After 1885, the Military Cabinet controlled matters pertaining to the honor code, the so-called *Gnadensachen* (medals, citations, ennoblement, and grants from the Kaiser's personal funds) and, most important, personnel. The latter included all personal orders: promotion, transfers, commands, dismissals, resignations, retirements, vacations, and so forth. One observer described the Military Cabinet's power over personnel like this:

In our country there are very few families of the higher ranks which are not represented in the army by at least one member and therefore who have nothing to hope or fear from the chief of personnel affairs. The ruling princes are as little exempt from this rule as the respectable and otherwise independent magnates or the numerous princely proletariat. All signs of personal favor from the monarch, like the bestowal of high honors, attachment to a regiment, the right to wear a becoming uniform, go through the Military Cabinet. Despite their seeming worthlessness, regardless of their absurdity, they are useful instruments of power. Disposition over the pleasant adjutant positions and other commands, for which there are no exact prerequisites, gives [the Military Cabinet] the opportunity to extend its influence in very wide circles and also very high up.[6]

In addition to these powers, the Military Cabinet had reserved to it any matter which could conceivably fall under the rubric of the imperial *Kommandogewalt*. Even in 1883, War Minister von Kameke had caustically noted that its boundaries were potentially unlimited.[7] Under Wilhelm II, the Military Cabinet strove ceaselessly to expand this area, until, as a Progressive Reichstag member put it, *Kommandogewalt* had become a 'fetish.'[8] The Military Cabinet used *Kommandogewalt* not merely to extend its own influence, but primarily to increase monarchical power vis-à-vis the Reichstag. This reactionary and anti-constitutional purpose made the Military Cabinet the focus of much criticism throughout Wilhelm's reign. Criticism, however, had no effect on the most conservative institution of the monarchy.[9]

As his first chief of the Military Cabinet, Wilhelm appointed Wilhelm von Hahnke.[10] Hahnke was not a scion of an old noble family. His father, an officer, had been ennobled in 1836.[11] After an education in the *Kadettenanstalt*, Hahnke followed his father into the military and advanced through two prestigious guard regiments, the Kaiser Alexander Grenadiers and the 3rd Guard Grenadier Regiment-Elisabeth. In 1881 as commander of the 1st Guard Infantry Brigade, he became Prince Wilhelm's superior. The young Prince was impressed by Hahnke's experience and attention to detail. The older man saw Wilhelm often as he taught him 'the technical details of the General Staff Officer's duties.'[12] Wilhelm noted with favor Hahnke's utterly soldierly bearing: he was tall and striking in appearance, with what the Kaiser later described as a 'crystalline character ... [and] remorseless strickness [*unerbitterliche Strenge*].'[13] These quintessentially 'Prussian' qualities were somewhat sweetened by a sense of humor. In addition, the Kaiser prized Hahnke's 'clear view of all questions concerning the honor and *Stand* of officers,'[14] which is merely to say that he held tight to thoroughly conservative social standards.

Hahnke's qualities, which might be summed up by the phrase 'perfect soldier,' led Wilhelm to consider his former superior 'predestined' to become Military Cabinet chief.[15] As soon as Wilhelm ascended the throne, he put through Hahnke's appointment. It soon became clear, however, that precisely those characteristics which Wilhelm so admired in Hahnke – his conservatism, his utter loyalty to the Kaiser, his attention to detail – conspired to make him a poor Cabinet chief. Philipp Eulenburg, leader of the civilians in the entourage, complained that Hahnke was a one-sided soldier, 'without any diplomatic capacity.'[16] On the other side, the military men around Alfred Waldersee felt that Hahnke was a poor administrator, was badly informed and allowed Wilhelm to go his way with too little guidance.[17] By the time Hahnke retired as Cabinet chief in 1901, most informed observers thought that both Eulenburg and Waldersee were correct. The acutely perceptive Bavarian representative to Berlin, Hugo von Lerchenfeld-Köfering summed up Hahnke's accomplishments upon his retirement:

General von Hahnke leaves His Majesty the Kaiser's closest entourage as an able and conscientious worker and a man of reliable and clear character, who filled his office with fairness and good will. He lacked, however, larger vision. He belonged to the men of the old school, who have difficulty adjusting themselves to new ideas and trends. His influence on his imperial master did not exceed that which his office brought with it. He sought to hinder and to mediate much, but understood how to give in when there was no alternative. This [tendency to give in to Wilhelm] may have been due partly to the fact that General von Hahnke, as a man without means but with a numerous family, lacked the independence [which] external [that is, non-Court-connected] means [would have given him.][18]

As a man of the old school, however, Hahnke spent his tenure conducting a highly successful rearguard action against the encroachment of liberal or progressive influences on the army.[19] He also managed to enhance the Military Cabinet's power within the army by convincing numerous commanders who had the right to report to the Kaiser personally to submit written reports instead. Hahnke thus gained the opportunity to interpret these to Wilhelm.[20]

In 1889, Wilhelm established the Naval Cabinet and granted it the same powers as its military counterpart.[21] Wilhelm's particular love for the navy meant that it did not suffer from its newness relative to the army and its institutions.

The long-time chief of the Naval Cabinet was Gustav Frhr von Senden-Bibran.[22] His father was a Silesian landowner who served in the Austro-Hungarian cavalry. Senden-Bibran joined the navy at fifteen as a cadet. He never married, nor did he allow any other interest to compete with a devotion to his service so great that Bülow called it 'fanaticism.'[23] Whereas Military Cabinet Chief von Hahnke directed his efforts toward conserving the position which the army already possessed, the virtual non-existence of the navy forced Senden-Bibran to dedicate his energy to building the fleet from scratch.[24] The enormity of this task did not discourage him because he had the Emperor on his side.

The Naval Cabinet chief's unceasing attempts to promote a large navy put him in direct opposition to the civilians, especially to Chancellor Hohenlohe, Foreign Secretary Marschall, Friedrich von Holstein, and Philipp Eulenburg. According to Holstein, Senden-Bibran was 'one of the most influential men in the entourage.'[25] He acquired this position because he was an enthusiastic tool for developing Wilhelm's naval plan and because he gave Wilhelm access to the technical arcana which the Kaiser aspired to know. As originally with Hahnke,

Senden's importance for the Kaiser lies in the fact that H.M. has only a superficial knowledge of the navy, but, since he wants to rule by himself, he cannot ask questions or demand to be taught. If he has a plan for the navy, or any desire or thought, Senden has to put it in the correct form. With [Senden-Bibran] the Kaiser is not embarrassed to ask or to allow himself to be taught.[26]

Thus, Wilhelm's desire to rule personally caused him to depend upon one-sided technocrats.

Senden-Bibran made no secret of the ultimate goal of the fleet: it was to aid the process begun by German industry, to wrest economic and political power from Great Britain.[27] The Cabinet chief's anti-English bias was only excelled by his political ignorance and lack of tact. The German Ambassador to France, Georg Count von Münster,[28] had the misfortune in 1898 to dine with Senden-Bibran, whom he sarcastically called 'one of our rabid naval heroes.' 'It was horrendous [*geradezu himmelschreiend*] to have to listen to the political nonsense, the delusions of grandeur which he babbled.'[29] Eulenburg considered him an 'abortion.'[30] Chancellor Hohenlohe, who opposed Wilhelm's huge naval plans, wrote that 'so long as Senden has the upper hand, my position is unsure.'[31] Eulenburg tried to remove Senden-Bibran from the entourage. He warned the Kaiser that Senden-Bibran's constant talk of a large naval bill harmed the political position of the government and ultimately of the Emperor himself.[32]

In the end, Senden-Bibran outmaneuvered the civilians. Admiral von Tirpitz was both the Kaiser's and the Cabinet chief's candidate for creating the new fleet. Although the Cabinet chief and Tirpitz later fought each other over matters of jurisdiction,[33] Senden-Bibran supported Tirpitz wholeheartedly in the latter's original fleet plan.[34] Tirpitz's appointment to the Imperial Naval Office in 1897 spelled

Senden-Bibran's success, and marked the greatest extent of his power. Thereafter the initiative in naval matters passed to the Imperial Naval Office, while Senden-Bibran was relegated more to the background.[35]

At the beginning of Wilhelm's reign there were twenty men in his military entourage. This number rose to a high of forty-four in 1914 and declined slightly in the war years. The average per year was thirty-three. In the thirty years of his reign, only 108 men served in the military entourage, a low rate of turnover, particularly in comparison to the civilian ministers.[36]

Most of the 108 held the position of FA, general *à la suite* or general adjutant. Those who found imperial favor, advanced successively through these positions. One generally became a FA (or, if one performed personal service, a diensttuender Flügeladjutant – FAD) around the age of forty-four or forty-five, as a captain, major or lieutenant colonel in the army (depending upon when one had entered the army and whether one had served with the General Staff and had thus been promoted ahead of others). Naval officers were usually captains (Kapitän zur See). As one advanced to brigadier general (rear admiral), the title changed to general (admiral) *à la suite;* when one reached major general, it changed to Generaladjutant. Only a handful of men (13) entered the Hauptquartier at the top of this ladder. We will therefore turn to the most numerous and most important members of the Hauptquartier, the Flügeladjutanten.

The FAs enjoyed a personal relationship with the Emperor. He became their direct superior, through whom even the most trivial bureaucratic arrangements (such as vacations) had to be approved. In this manner they were lifted above their comrades and distinguished from them by ostentatious epaulettes and a cumbersome but flashy sash. This was not mere show, however, for their monarch treated the FAs with even more respect and friendliness than he showered upon the regular officers. Philipp Eulenburg remarked that Wilhelm believed his FA to be a higher form of human being. Whether or not a FA took advantage of the personal relationship with Wilhelm depended upon a number of things, not the least of which was his own personality. Those FAs who were simultaneously military attachés or who were stationed in Berlin or Potsdam had better opportunity (and more temptation) to meddle in politics. There were other FAs whose appointments were merely honorific. Those among them who were in the provinces might come into contact with the Kaiser only rarely. Those FAs who were constantly around Wilhelm and who were

6 Wilhelm von Dommes in the uniform of Flügeladjutant

accused of forming a ring around him were the diensttuende Flügeladjutanten.

The task of the FAD, as one of them put it, was to be the Kaiser's
'shadow.'[37] 'While he is on duty, the FAD must always [*unausgesetzt*]
stay in closest proximity to His Majesty; he is to accompany Him at all

occasions and stands at every instance at the disposal of His Majesty.'[38] Two always had duty together, twenty-four hours a day. They accompanied Wilhelm on his customary walks in the morning and afternoon and on the numerous trips he undertook. They ate the midday and evening meal with the monarch and his wife. During the rest of the day they hovered close to the Kaiser, announcing the entrance of ministers and others who had audiences, answering questions and telegrams, relaying messages from Wilhelm to government officials, composing the condolence and congratulatory messages from the monarch to his subjects, running errands and keeping the imperial log. The number of FADs fluctuated between four and eight per year. One of two diensttuende general adjutants or generals *à la suite* supplemented the FADs, so that the pool of persons serving Wilhelm directly was always between six and eight. The Commandant of the Hauptquartier determined the schedules of the FADs. In the 1890s, a FAD normally served two days and then had two days off.[39] Later, this was changed to service three or four times a month, three days in a row.[40] Time of service could be vastly longer on trips, when Wilhelm was never accompanied by fewer than two FADs, the Commandant of the Hauptquartier, and his personal doctor.

In theory, Wilhelm chose the FAs and FADs in consultation with the Cabinet chiefs, who were in charge of personnel matters for their respective services. Theoretically prerequisites were good qualification reports, the respect of one's comrades, and manners suitable to the imperial Court.[41] In practice, things did not always work out this way. The qualification reports contained the annual judgments of an officer's superiors upon his character, intelligence, and performance. As one advanced in rank, these reports tended to become more glowing and consequently less reliable.[42] Even when they were reliable, the reports concentrated on qualities which were not necessarily those required by an officer in a politically responsible position. The qualities most valued in an officer were 'character, compatibility, spiritual direction, general knowledge, external and social appearance, financial situation, comradeship, ambition ... and only *then* ... professional performance and aptitude.'[43] 'Character' was the euphemism used by the officer corps to describe persons compatible with the sociopolitical prejudices of the nobility.

Even if the qualification reports winnowed out the deserving few and the Military Cabinet chiefs selected the best of these, Wilhelm did not always follow the Cabinet chiefs' suggestions. Wilhelm exercised his imperial power more frequently in personnel matters than in other areas and was particularly adamant about choosing the persons with whom he would come into frequent contact.[44] The persons he picked were usually officers he already knew and liked or who had caught his eye in some way. It is not surprising, then, that just over half the FAs came from the small number of prestigious Guard Regiments stationed in Potsdam and Berlin, regiments which came most frequently under the admiring eye of their monarch. Nor is the proportional representation of the different services within the entourage surprising. No naval officer had been a FAD before Wilhelm appointed Senden-Bibran in 1888. Wilhelm's love for the navy brought its percentage of officers among the FAs to fourteen for the entire reign. Within the army, Wilhelm's preferences were quite clear: the cavalry was more dashing than the infantry, which was, in turn, more respectable than the rather technical and bourgeois-infiltrated artillery. These branches contributed, respectively, 43, 36, and 7 percent of the total FAs. Wilhelm's prejudices mirrored those of the nobility, which chose the cavalry (when it could afford the higher expenses) over the infantry and almost never joined the artillery.[45] The celebrated Foot Guards provided the preponderance of infantry officers and doubtless elevated the infantry's representation among FAs considerably over what it might otherwise have been.

Wilhelm thus reified the nobility's estimation of the various service branches in his military entourage, and in doing so he undermined one of the original purposes of the FAs. Originally, the FAs were supposed to represent each different branch of the military. After brief service at Court, they would return to their unit for active duty. Wilhelm's peculiar appointment system changed the very structure of the *Adjutantur*. Not only did the FAs no longer reflect the army's technical diversity, but the FAs after years at Court became estranged from the operational realities of the branches they did represent.[46]

Wilhelm's preference for the familiar over the unfamiliar face and his consequent predilection for Guard officers meant that the pool of candidates eligible for FA shrank to a group endowed with certain peculiar characteristics, which we shall detail in a moment. But this spectrum of possibilities narrowed still further when Wilhelm applied other, even more idiosyncratic criteria, designed to select for traits that satisfied the Kaiser's personal tastes, but did not necessarily make for competent FAs. This, too, was a break with the original *Adjutantur* structure, which formerly had contained FAs singled out for their military knowledge and proficiency.

In Wilhelm's eye, one of the most important prerequisites for FA was appearance: it was a great advantage to be either good-looking, tall, or preferably both. Some of the adjectives used by others to describe officers in the entourage were: 'good-looking,'[47] 'elegant,'[48] 'a giant,'[49] 'very pleasant appearance,'[50] 'good-looking, large figure,'[51] 'pretty exterior.'[52] Three of the tallest specimens, Hülsen, Lippe, and Scholl, were also three of Wilhelm's favorites. Eulenburg claimed that good looks were a precondition of admittance to the Leibkompagnie of the First Foot Guard Regiment, which had close ties to Wilhelm and which accounted for more than its share of FAs.[53] For naval officers one of the stepping stones to the *Adjutantur* was the command of Wilhelm's yacht, the *Hohenzollern*. Five of its commanders, or one-third the total naval contingent in the entourage, later became FAs. The 'Regulations concerning personnel appointments aboard H.M. Yacht *Hohenzollern* and the royal pleasure craft at Potsdam' make clear what Wilhelm found essential. Note the order of the regulations: the crew 'must have served at least a year and have one and a half year's service remaining; they must be of good height and appearance, have a military bearing, good intelligence, and be of exemplary behavior and capacity. The sailors must especially be well-trained in seamanship.'[54] The admonition to appoint only good-looking persons was repeated at least twice, in 1898 and again in 1908.[55] In addition to comeliness, Wilhelm favored the lively, sporty, and agile to the slower-moving, and overlooked well-qualified persons whom he failed to find attractive.[56]

Wilhelm's preferences were not limited to the physical; he also was attracted to certain personality types. Here, the contemporary critics point out a duality of Wilhelm's, which was replicated in the men he chose for his entourage. The critics vacillated for thirty years between believing, on the one hand, that Wilhelm's entourage manipulated him shamelessly and, on the other, that they spinelessly followed his commands. In other words, some thought the men of the entourage were too forceful, some thought them too weak. Wilhelm, in fact, seems to have been drawn to both types. Wilhelm's baffling complexity and contradictoriness have already been described. Whatever their psychological origins (and there were doubtless many), these traits caused Wilhelm both to be attracted to strong, outspoken persons and at the same time to feel threatened by them. As a result, the Kaiser surrounded himself with men who tended to cluster either at one end of the spectrum or the other, that is, they were either explosively arrogant and tactlessly energetic (qualities which Wilhelm and others prized as 'masculine'), or they were tactful, quiet, 'nice,' and unobtrusive.

The vast majority of the FAs falls into the latter category; they mixed blandly together to create a tone typical of their social background, unrelieved by kinks or twists of personality. The Cabinet chiefs, the Commandant of Hauptquartier, and the FAs active in the Military or Naval Cabinets also were likely to be on the conciliatory side. Their jobs were more conventionally bureaucratic than those of the other FAs and were less suitable for 'characters' than were the usual military commands. The necessity to transact business routinely with the Emperor made them anxious to preserve whatever steadiness Wilhelm possessed, rather than to encourage his uncontrollable spontaneity. Daily contact also made Wilhelm less likely to endure abrasiveness, a quality more appealing at a distance than close up. The careers of General Adolf v. Wittich[57] and Hans v. Plessen[58] are illustrative in this connection.

Wittich was generally considered one of Prussia's most intelligent and capable generals. Although educated at a *Kadettenanstalt,* he had gone on (through the General Staff and his own studies) to amass considerable technical knowledge.[59] Wittich was outspoken, self-assured, energetic, and untouched by politeness, all qualities which suited him to a career as active officer.[60] He impressed the Kaiser and, upon his accession to the throne, Wilhelm appointed Wittich diensttuender General Adjutant and Commandant of the Hauptquartier. It quickly turned out that the virtues of a line officer did not easily coincide with those of a courtier. Barely seven months after his appointment, it was already public knowledge that Wittich felt constrained and unhappy at Court.[61] Wilhelm, however, hated to make changes in his intimate entourage. He held on to Wittich until the general made himself intolerable by withdrawing as much as possible from Court life, and by criticizing his surroundings in the most frank and pessimistic manner.[62] Wilhelm found pessimism utterly unbearable and finally brought himself in 1892 to replace Wittich with the infinitely more congenial Hans von Plessen, who remained in that central position until the collapse of the monarchy.

The choice of Plessen was characteristic of Wilhelm's *Personalpolitik.* No one every argued that Plessen was Wittich's equal, either in intelligence or in strength of character. But Plessen possessed a military aura wrapped around a courtier's soul, the perfect combination for the appearance-conscious Emperor. Plessen was 'as elegant and nimble as he was youthfully fresh.'[63] He had been FAD to Wilhelm's grandfather for nine years and, to Wilhelm's eye, 'represented . . . the military tradition of Kaiser Wilhelm I.'[64] As a young man, Plessen was

remarkably different from the older Generaladjutant, who, after 1879,
served almost exclusively in Court positions. Plessen apparently had
had a temper and was capable of vehemence on occasion. Carl Wedel
felt (hoped?) that these characteristics would limit the general's tenure as head of the Hauptquartier.[65] But Plessen soon learned to control himself. One no longer heard of temperamental outbursts, but
rather of his 'conciliatory manners'[66] and his cavalier's ways. Plessen's
efforts at self-restraint were so successful and his subsequent manners
so indiscriminatingly friendly, that he acquired the reputation of an
insincere flatterer,[67] an opinion shared even by some FAs.[68] Certainly
he took great pains to avoid making enemies. It would be difficult, if
not impossible, to discover at this late date whether Plessen's tendency
toward harmony was disingenuous or not. Admiral Müller, a more
critical observer than many, was charitable. He thought Plessen's
unremitting cheer was entirely consistent with his personality.[69]
Indeed, along with charming manners and a certain military air, Plessen's most striking characteristic was his unflagging optimism. He alone
among the men of the entourage was not worn down by the vicissi-
tudes of his master's moods, nor depressed by the increasingly peril-
ous state in which Germany found itself. His blitheness was doubtless
comforting to Wilhelm, but it became ridiculous and finally dangerous during the war, as we shall see. Plessen's optimism, his loyalty to
Wilhelm, his unimaginative patriotism, and his intellectual limits are
nicely displayed in a letter he wrote in June 1918 to former FA Wilhelm v. Dommes, who had just received the *Pour le Mérite*. Plessen's
youngest son had already been killed, his wife of forty-three years had
just died, and Plessen himself was coming to the end of four years of
gruelling pressure, which had already caused the physical collapse of
virtually everyone at the Hauptquartier except himself. Nonetheless,
he could still write:

I approach the future with firm, happy confidence! The thought of returning
home in my loneliness is difficult! With the end of the war, my life and aspi-
rations [*Leben u. Streben*] up to now end! My race is run! If my beloved wife
were still alive, it would be different! In any case, I now close my book with
inexpressible gratitude for my King and my wife! From both of them I have
received so inexpressibly much undeserved goodness![70]

Plessen's ability to retain Wilhelm's friendship was what kept him
in his position for twenty-six years. As FA Max v. Mutius described
the situation generally: 'this personal relation between Wilhelm and
his aides was, I almost want to say, unfortunately, the determining
factor, because of the Kaiser's overly great subjectivity.'[71] Wilhelm, of

course, found it perfectly proper that this should be true. When Wilhelm appointed Senden-Bibran FA in 1888, he made it clear that he had done so 'as a sign of my trust and of my friendship.'[72] Wilhelm often expressed his friendship and generosity by rewarding subjects with Court positions, in addition to the usual medals, titles, and invitations. In 1893, strictly because he liked him, Wilhelm appointed Kuno Moltke FAD. Moltke's only qualification for this post was his musicality. Even his best friends had to admit that Moltke was politically hopeless.[73] In a similar case in December 1908, the Kaiser named Major Adolf Freiherr v. Holzing-Berstett to a FAD post. Holzing-Berstett's previous experience had been at the royal stables, where he was a subordinate of Oberstallmeister Hugo von Reischach. He would doubtless have remained in that position were it not for an accident which made it difficult for him to ride a horse.[74] Wilhelm rescued Holzing-Berstett from retirement by bringing him into the innermost circle at Court, where he served as FAD for five years and as FA until Wilhelm's abdication.

Wilhelm filled the FA(D) posts for other reasons, too, which had equally little to do with qualifications needed for such a position. He occasionally used the assignment as a half-way station for officers, particularly military attachés, who were between assignments or were waiting for their future commands to become open. The monarch also honored officers for extraordinary service by making them his FAs. Such was the case of Kapitän zur See Guido von Usedom, whom Wilhelm appointed FA in 1900 out of sheer exuberance over Germany's participation in the suppression of the Boxer Rebellion in China. Usedom had actually done nothing to earn the honor, apart from having served there as a naval officer. Wilhelm's act was therefore purely symbolic and may have had patriotic propaganda value, but irritated those who felt that such honors should be saved for those who deserved them.[75]

However, even in the case where the appointee was undeniably a hero, physical valor was still not an infallible criterion for a responsible post near the monarch. Korvetten-Kapitän Nikolaus Count zu Dohna-Schlodien was commander of the auxiliary cruiser *Möwe*, which from 1915 to 1917 twice ran the British blockade to sink or capture 41 enemy ships.[76] His exploits excited the public imagination and made him the most famous naval hero of the day. Upon his second triumphal return to Kiel on 22 March 1917, Dohna-Schlodien was greeted by the following message from his Emperor: 'I heartily welcome you and your brave crew back home. In grateful recognition of your deeds, which for all time will be a page of glory for my navy, I name you to be my Flügeladjutant.'[77] This was fine so long as Dohna-Schlodien was not actually at imperial Headquarters, for his impulsiveness and eccentricity would hardly have contributed to sober decision making. As the war continued to use up FAs, Wilhelm suddenly proposed in May 1918 to bring Dohna-Schlodien to Headquarters as his FAD. By this time, power had slipped so far from the Emperor's hands that even Dohna-Schlodien's presence could pose no great threat to operations. Nonetheless, Admiral v. Müller made his disapproval known to Wilhelm. The chief of the Naval Cabinet told the Kaiser that 'on account of [Dohna-Schlodien's] somewhat one-sided gifts it is not wished even by the navy that [he serve in] positions of sharply concentrated activity, but [Müller added somewhat maliciously], his gifts would be adequate for a Flügeladjutant.'[78] Had the appointment been made during the height of personal regime, Müller would doubtless have protested more strongly. Dohna-Schlodien was duly appointed on 9 May and arrived for duty on the 22nd.[79]

Despite Wilhelm's obstinacy in these matters, he was not immune to lobbying pressures from the rest of the entourage on behalf of certain candidates. The case of Oskar von Chelius illustrates both how the lobbying took place and what its limits were. Chelius[80] had been made FA in 1899, when he took up the post of military attaché to Italy. In July 1905, Chelius returned to Germany and served as FAD for fourteen months before assuming command of the Leib-Garde-Husaren Regiment. For four years he was regimental commander and simultaneously FA. In 1909 he saw an opportunity to return to Court service. Major General Wolf Freiherr Marschall von Altengottern's[81] approaching retirement would open up a FAD position. Chelius vastly preferred this to his other alternative, a post as brigade commander in Potsdam. He therefore wrote to Max v. Fürstenberg to enlist his aid. In recent years, Fürstenberg had replaced Philipp zu Eulenburg as Wilhelm's best friend.[82] Fürstenberg and Chelius had known each other for some time because Chelius was from Baden and Fürstenberg had inherited large properties there and had become integrated into the social life of the duchy. Both were on very friendly terms with the local ruling house. Their own friendship had only recently become intimate,[83] but Chelius evidently felt safe enough to ask Fürstenberg for the favor:

I believe [Chelius wrote] that [Wilhelm intends] to appoint [me FAD] but I would be endlessly grateful to you, if you could do something for me in this matter during the *Kaisertage* at Donaueschingen.[84] It would be best if you would say something to the Kaiser when you are alone with him. He takes you and your advice very seriously and is frequently pleased when others remind him of something that he probably has in mind anyway. The Kaiser knows that Marschall wants to go, so it will be easy to bring the subject up.

Chelius then spent a page assuring Fürstenberg that Wilhelm was very well-disposed toward him (Chelius) and, of course, that Chelius wanted nothing more than to be of service.

Even so, it is frequently necessary with him [Wilhelm] to set something like this going with a word, particularly from someone whose judgment and advice are valuable and dear [to him] like yours. Apart from me, there is no old cavalry officer available who could come into question because the Kaiser will not choose anybody new. The only possibility would be [Eberhard Count von] Schmettow,[85] but he is a long distance away from commanding a brigade, and I don't believe that his marriage with H. M. was very good, even though it appeared to go well ... Plessen is an old friend of Schmettow and it's not impossible that the latter would step in for him. [Moritz Freiherr von] Lyncker[86] and Plessen are well-disposed to us both, I know, and I suggest that you might drop a word to both of them.

He reiterated that the most important point was speaking to Wilhelm alone: 'When you have accomplished this, send me a short telegram ... so that I will understand.'[87] Six months later (16 June 1910), Chelius got his wish. He then wrote to Fürstenberg to thank him, because he owed his post 'largely to ... [your] warm recommendation.'[88] Chelius remained in Wilhelm's closest entourage until the abdication.

Chelius's maneuvering was typical of the engineering which preceded every appointment to a sought-after position.[89] Chelius knew that the most important factor in appointments was Wilhelm, who could best be influenced informally, by friends, and in isolation. A distant second best would be to influence the commandant of the Hauptquartier and the chief of the Military Cabinet, whose responsibility it was to recommend a candidate to Wilhelm. Chelius's letter also reveals the psychology at work: Wilhelm was to be presented with an idea and then encouraged to believe it was his own. The influencer was to be flattered by the notion that he was a significant man whose opinions were important to the 'all-highest.' This was the standard strategy used by the men at Court, not only by irresponsible intriguers, but by the responsible advisers as well, for it did not require great insight to see that this was an effective way to handle Wilhelm's peculiarities.[90]

Even so, there was a delicate balance in operation, which the backstage machinations must not be allowed to obscure. No cabal secretly forced its puppet on the Kaiser. Wilhelm's desire for the familiar face had already narrowed the choice to two men, both of whom had already served at Court and both of whom were firmly established in the network of the high and mighty. Furthermore, once Chelius had achieved his goal, he was satisfied. He aspired to nothing further, nor is there any indication that he used his position for dark political ends. The letter-writing and subtle jockeying were part of the normal process by which the already select were elevated a half-step upward.

This selection process, which assembled a military entourage chosen according to appearance, temperament, and previous acquaintance with the monarch, resulted in a military entourage even more conservative sociologically than the Prussian officer corps at large. The following information on the sociological backgrounds of the entourage officers was gleaned from various sources.[91] It is only possible to assemble biographical information for 89 members (82 percent) of the military entourage. Except for the naval figures and the figures concerning nobility/non-nobility, both of which are complete, the calculations which follow are based on this random sample of 89 individuals. There is, however, no reason to suppose that the missing nineteen men were very different from their brother officers. The men of the entourage will be considered from the standpoints of social origin (noble/bourgeois), father's occupation, their own wealth, the social origin of their wives, education, religion, and home province.

Wilhelm's entourage differs most strikingly from the rest of the Prussian officer corps in its blue-bloodedness. The officer corps at large had been evenly divided in 1867 between persons of noble and of bourgeois descent. By 1913, it had become 70 percent bourgeois and 30 percent noble.[92] Even the General Staff, which was at least partially an instrument for the preferential treatment (quick advancement) of noble officers,[93] was half bourgeois in 1913.[94] Only 10 percent (eleven men) of Wilhelm's military entourage, however, began their careers as non-nobles, and all but one were ennobled during, or usually before, their advancement into the entourage. The extent of the imbalance is clear from the fact that there were both more barons (*Freiherren*) and more counts (*Grafen*), respectively, than there were ennobled bourgeois. In fact, the counts alone outnumbered the bourgeois almost two to one. In this respect, the entourage was a very slight improvement over the Guard Corps. The Cavalry Guard was usually 100 percent noble, while the infantry contained fewer than 5 percent bourgeois officers.[95] Almost half (45 percent) of the bourgeois serving Wilhelm came from the navy, from which it was in any case difficult to extract nobles, since they accounted for less than 15 percent of all naval officers.[96] Had Wilhelm not possessed an overweening interest in the navy, the number of bourgeois in his entourage would have slipped to the infinitesimal.

The fathers of the entourage officers were more well-to-do, more respectably employed (by noble standards), and more estranged from industry and manufacture than were the fathers of officers in other segments within the Prussian officer corps. Karl Demeter presents statistics concerning the father's occupation of entrants into the *Kriegsakademie*, which are the only detailed figures of this sort available for the army. *Kriegsschüler* were chosen strictly according to ability,[97] and one might expect that the bourgeoisie would be better represented here than in other parts of the army. Down to the war the trend was toward fewer sons of landowners and officers and toward more sons of higher civil servants, merchants, factory owners, and the like.[98] If one averages Demeter's figures for the period 1888–1913, the following are the results: 10 percent of the fathers of the *Kriegsschüler* were landowners, 29 percent were officers, 33 percent were higher civil servants, and 15 percent were merchants or factory owners.[99]

A comparison with the entourage figures is instructive. The characteristics of the fathers of the entourage officers do not, however, fit into the system of classification used by Demeter. Demeter was able, though he does not explain how, to make clear distinctions between, for example, landowners and officers. Not infrequently, however, the biographical sources noted above list persons as both, and sometimes even as higher civil servants as well. These sources show 14 percent of the fathers of entourage officers to have been exclusively landowners. If one counts those landowners who are cross-listed as officers and civil servants, the number leaps to 37 percent. Thirty-one percent of the fathers were exclusively officers (with those cross-listed, 43 percent). Twenty-two percent were higher civil servants (37 percent counting those cross-listed). Only 4 percent of the fathers were merchants, bankers, or factory owners. None was cross-listed.[100] Despite the complications presented by the cross-listing, the conclusions are still clear. Industry-connected occupations were vastly underrepresented, higher civil servents were slightly so; the officer corps was somewhat overrepresented and the landowners considerably so.

There are other indications that the men of the entourage were slightly more well-to-do than their brother officers. The preponderance of cavalrymen alone would suggest this, since the expenses

incurred in the cavalry were enough to make membership in it pro-
hibitive to many nobles. In addition, the men of the entourage seem
to have married earlier than their counterparts in regular service, a
situation which suggests that entourage officers were wealthier than
their fellows. In order to forestall early marriages, all of the German
armies demanded that young officers prove they have independent
financial means sufficient to lead a respectable married life. A sliding
scale was developed, according to which the youngest officers had to
have more money than did older ones. The sums demanded could be
quite large – one case in the navy for a lieutenant, junior grade,
amounted to 60,000 M for each family.[101] The entourage's average
age of thirty and a half at marriage appears to be several years younger
than was usual (although comparable figures unfortunately exist only
for the Bavarian army).[102]

The men of the entourage were moving toward greater exclusivity
in yet another way. They were marrying 'better' than their fathers
had. Whereas 32 percent of the group had bourgeois mothers, only
20 percent of them chose bourgeois wives.[103] The frequently voiced
fears that penury was forcing noblemen to marry 'beneath them' were
clearly not the case in the entourage. Since most of the men married
before they became Flügeladjutanten, it would seem that their choice
of spouse might have been a consideration in their appointment. Wilhelm had, of course, already approved their marriages, because as
officers they were obliged to receive imperial permission to marry.
One might add that the conspicuous absence of divorce (there was
one, the Kaiser's close friend, Kuno Moltke, who divorced while in
the entourage) fitted well with Auguste Viktoria's abhorrence of that
practice.

We must now turn to the educational backgrounds of the entourage, for education is often an important clue to social and political
behavior. The leaders of the Prussian army realized this as much as
later social scientists have and were caught in a dilemma during the
latter part of the nineteenth century.[104] On the one hand, the increasing technical demands of modern weaponry and warfare demanded
better-educated officers. On the other hand, those who possessed this
education tended to come from the (upper) middle class rather than
from the nobility. Preservation of social caste thus flew in the face of
the requirements of military efficiency. The army pursued an uneven
course between the two extremes by preserving lower standards to
ensure a sufficient number of noble recruits, while also admitting an
every increasing number of more highly qualified personnel.

The complex Prussian school system[105] produced young officers with widely varying education backgrounds. In ascending order of general education (*Allgemeinbildung*) the recruits were: (1) persons exempted from educational standards by order of the Kaiser (an increasingly smaller percentage of noble scions), (2) pages of the Court (also a very small number), (3) persons from the cadet schools, (4) persons who had attended either a *Realgymnasium* or a *Gymnasium.* Categories three and four are further divisible into three rough groups: (a) those who left school three years before graduating (possessing the so-called *Sekundareife*), (b) those who left school without passing their final exams (*Primareife*), and (c) those who had passed their exams (*Abitur*), usually at the age eighteen or nineteen.

Although the Bavarian army had required the *Abitur* since 1872,[106] the Prussian army could not bring itself to do so lest it lose the officer corps as a bastion of noble power.[107] It continued throughout Wilhelm's reign to accept *Primaner,* survivors of the cram courses (*Pressen*), and to prefer persons from the Cadet schools, which provided a vastly inferior education to that of the *Gymnasium.*[108] Nonetheless, the demands of the modern age could not be entirely circumvented: the *Abiturienten* in the Prussian, Saxon, and Württembergian armies rose steadily from 35 percent in 1890 to 65 percent in 1912.[109] The navy, where technical expertise was even more essential than in the army, and which in any case could not attract a large number of nobles to its ranks, experienced an even more precipitious rise, from 40 percent in 1894 to 90 percent in 1914.[110]

Educational information for the military entourage is available for only 55 of its 108 members. This information is, furthermore, not always clear. In particular, it is difficult to determine at precisely which stage the men left their various schools before joining the military. Of the 55, 43 were 18 or over when they entered the service and were therefore old enough to have achieved the *Abitur,* but there is no certainty that they had actually done so. What is certain is that half (27) had received purely military educations in the *Kadettenkorps.* The other half (25) had gone almost exclusively to *Gymnasien.* Only one person had been privately tutored and two had attended *Realgymnasien.* A rather high number (11) of the *Gymnasiasten* had gone on to hear lectures at a university. Demeter, alas, did not separate his figures according to *Kadettenkorps* versus *Gymnasium* and *Realgymnasium,* so it is impossible to know whether the entourage had fewer or more persons with strictly military backgrounds than the rest of the army. An educated guess, however, is possible and would conclude that the entourage was probably fairly representative of the Prussian officer corps in general. Thirty-nine percent of the 1905 General Staff, for example, had been *Kadetten* (51 percent were from *Gymnasien, Real-gymnasien,* and *Oberrealschulen*).[111] Since the *Generalstäbler* were better educated than their fellow officers, one would expect the *Kadetten* figure to be slightly lower than what was in the officer corps at large. Furthermore, in Bavaria, whose officers were overwhelmingly bourgeois and better educated than the Prussians, the percentage of majors in 1911 who were graduates of the *Kadettenkorps* was still 31 percent.[112]

These data all indicate that the entourage was less of an exception within the army-wide officer corps in educational background than it was in other respects. The ignorance of the military entourage, particularly in political matters, which was the target of frequent complaints by civilian diplomats, cannot be ascribed to peculiarities in the way the men were chosen, but is due rather to the nature of the entire pool from which they came. Even had the number of *Gymnasiasten* been higher, one cannot conclude that the milieu would have been liberalized. As Rumschöttel rightly points out, 'the contents and worth of a humanistic education [*Gymnasialbildung*] conformed to the ideology represented by the officer corps; the higher schools fulfilled a social and political function, of which the officers, with their conservative convictions and their reactionary goals, could only approve.'[113]

The same conservative convictions are evident in the religious composition of the military entourage, which reflected perfectly the prejudices of the army and the Emperor. It was overwhelmingly Protestant. There seem to have been only three Roman Catholic FAs. One was inherited from Wilhelm I's entourage. That was Ernst Freiherr v. Hoiningen gen. Hüne, who was military attaché to France. Another, Count Karl v. Kageneck, was also military attaché to a Catholic country, Germany's ally Austria-Hungary. Oskar Chelius, Fürstenberg's friend, seems to have been the only Catholic actually to serve in the entourage.

The only other FA of non-Protestant background was Walter Mossner, whose parents were Jewish. It is not clear whether Mossner himself later converted.[114] Even had he done so, he would have been a conspicuous exception to the rule. Although Jews had served as officers in the wars of unification and would again in the First World War, they were systematically excluded from the corps during peacetime, in Bavaria as well as in Prussia.[115] It was possible for a few Jews to break the barrier through conversion, but their numbers were small. Mossner's acceptance into the officer corps was the result of historical accident. His father, a Berlin banker, had been instrumental in King Wilhelm I's escape from the revolutionary forces in 1848. Years later, when asked by Wilhelm if there were nothing the King could do for him, Mossner replied that his son, Walter, was a fine horseman and wished to join the cavalry. Wilhelm overrode the strenuous objections of the Husaren Regiment 7 and forced them to accept Mossner as an officer. The King's grandson, Wilhelm II, ennobled Mossner in 1890 and in 1892 appointed him FA. He remained in that position for five years, although, again, he never performed service at Court. As is frequently the case when an outsider suddenly becomes part of the in-group, Mossner went out of his way to prove his *monarchischen Sinn*. Bülow reckoned him among the finest of Germany's cavalry officers. He distinguished himself in the wars of unification and went on to become governor of Strasbourg. Mossner's second wife, whom he married in 1883, was of impeccably blue blood.

A final sociological facet of the entourage is place of origin. As one might expect, the men were mostly from north Germany, although by no means exclusively or even mostly from east of the Elbe. Three Badener and one Bavarian were, however, the sole representatives of southern Germany. Because of the high number of officer's children in the entourage, the figures for Brandenburg are inflated. The rest of the men were evenly distributed from East Prussia to the Rhine, with Pomerania, Posen, Silesia, and the Rhineland slightly better represented than the other areas. If there was a strong Prussian tone to the entourage, however, it came through the officer corps itself, through the fathers of the FAs and through the regiments in which the sons had already served, rather than through their home provinces.

It was the officer's life itself which more than any other factor determined the peculiar characteristics of Wilhelm's entourage. The newly appointed FA had, as a rule, already spent twenty-five years in the officer corps. Since his acceptance by the regiment, he had undergone a process which would not end even with his retirement, and which, by encouraging some traits and discouraging others, was designed to fashion a uniform product, the officer. As Schaible, author of a famous manual for young officers, put it:

within the company, through the equality of living standards in general, there will evolve in time an agreement of conviction, a similarity in action of the individual, so that, when one has come to know the individual one may aptly know his entire *Stand*.[116]

This is not to argue that Schaible's prescriptions are always descriptions. Nonetheless, the molding process was more successful than not. The officer was a type, a character with easily recognized features, as a brief glance through the pages of *Simplicissimus* (which exaggerated the type) or of any contemporary novel will confirm.[117] The process was successful because it was not so much a negative as a positive one. That is, the standards of the officer corps were basically the standards of the nobility tightly focussed and made more explicit. 'The so-called *Standesgefühl* can be described as class consciousness.'[118] Thus, the officers' honor code, while rigid and repressive, basically reflected the values that the candidate brought with him to the corps. The enormous status of the officer in Wilhelminian society ensured that the young would be willing to undergo the rigors of garrison life, to deny themselves freedom and certain comforts in order to wear the select and gaudy plumage of the defenders of order.

It was the imprint of the officer's life that largely determined the tone and the prejudices of the entourage as a whole. No other experience had such a far-reaching effect upon the way in which the members of the entourage viewed themselves or their society. No other experience directed their political reactions as much as did their socialization in the officer corps. To understand the peculiar mixture of arrogance and foreboding, of self-confidence and insecurity that informed the thoughts and actions of most members of the entourage, one must examine the guidelines which defined their class consciousness. These guidelines were incorporated into the officer's honor code.

That which distinguished the officer from others was his honor. The idea of honor for the officer corps developed from the honor of knights and may have served originally to prevent soldiers from deserting in battle.[119] But an equally powerful function of honor was self-definition. Behavior in all spheres could be controlled by labelling it either honorable (approved by the group) or dishonorable. Transgression against the laws of the group, that is, loss of honor, resulted in expulsion. The boundaries separating the group from the rest of society were then clear. Other *Stände* of society were defined as having less value because they possessed less honor. Honor, which consisted in rigid adherence to the group's dictates, became the central principle of one's life.

The honor code was the distillation of the values of the officer. The two institutions for enforcement of the code were the duel and, later, the military courts of honor. The extent to which the concept of honor had actually produced a separate *Stand* is clear from the unsuccessful efforts of the state to prevent duelling. The state naturally wished to deny individuals the right to resort to violence, thus reserving force for its own exclusive use. As early as 1651, the Hohenzollerns forbad duels outright, a prohibition which remained legally in force forever after. Despite the opposition of crown and state, the practice continued, because failure to duel always equalled dishonor. Up until World War I men continued to be driven from their regiments for refusing to duel. Too weak to win the battle head on, the Hohenzollerns were forced, in succeeding centuries, to try to coopt the authority of the honor code by containing it within a state-sanctioned institution, the military honor court. This court was to adjudicate disputes which would otherwise end up on the duelling field. The autonomy of the officer corps was so strong, however, especially after the prestige it had garnered in 1864–71, that the Crown finally capitulated. In 1874, it weakened the role of the honor court by allowing it only to judge whether a duel should take place, instead of using it to replace the duel altogether. A second attempt at cooption was the formulation of the idea that it was dishonorable to force a duel.[120] A duel-happy officer, it was said, was disgracing the honor of his *Stand*. It was hoped that this redefinition of honor would dilute the rigidity of the original conception and discourage the illegal practice stemming from it.

On 1 January 1897, Wilhelm II ordered that all disputes had to come first before the honor court and, further, that it was the duty of the court to intervene on behalf of the person who had not initiated the challenge, in order to try to arrange a compromise. Because the courts were considered to fall under Wilhelm's power of command, this order had the effect of making the Kaiser, rather than the officer corps itself, the highest instance of appeal,[121] thus weakening the power of the *Stand* against that of the crown. The AKO of 1 January 1897 resulted in a decline in the number of duels in the active officer corps. The honor court became gradually an acceptable alternative to duelling, and more and more young officers came to decide their cases on the basis of personal, rather than of collective honor. This last trend marks a belated victory for bourgeois over noble or *Stand* values, which always placed the honor and reputation of the group over that of the individual.[122]

If this brief examination of the duel has illustrated the strength of the officer corps, not only vis-à-vis other *Stände*, but even against the Crown/State, then a look at the contents of the honor code will show the corps' social isolation. The honor code may indeed have assured valor on the battlefield, but it could hardly have been more perfectly designed to produce poor political advisers.

The essence of the honor code, as we have seen, lay in its group character. The worth of the individual derived solely from his membership in the group. 'The judgment . . . of his peers [*Genossenschaft*],' wrote Schaible, the expert on the honor code, 'must immediately be regarded as complete and decisive.'[123] Total adherence to peer judgment would finally yield homogeneous officers, perfectly interchangeable one with the other, in attitude, opinion, and deed.[124] The first duty of the individual was, then, to submit to the group. 'The sense of freedom of the individual must always retreat before the generally binding laws of the corps-spirit, which stands in the first line.'[125]

Within the corps, rigid hierarchy was to be observed. Younger officers were to speak only when spoken to. They were advised to exercise great care in their intramural conversations lest the harmony of the whole be disturbed.[126] Schaible's discussion of critical thinking (*das Räsonniren* [*sic*]) is particularly interesting in this connection. He distinguished two meanings to the word. The first meaning, critical thinking, Schaible admitted was good, but only so long as it did not lead one to fail to carry out orders or to criticize 'legitimate military regulations.'[127] He did not explain how one could recognize a legitimate regulation without questioning it. Schaible intimated that *Räsonniren* was a fine attribute in a senior officer, but not in a subordinate. Again, how one was to develop this faculty without practicing it, he did not divulge. The overuse of critical thinking, Schaible feared, led to its second meaning, disputatiousness, and finally to negativism, one of the characteristics Kaiser Wilhelm II hated most: '*Ich dulde keine Schwarzseher!* [I will not tolerate pessimists]'. 'This *Räsonniren*, criticism, and fault-finding,' Schaible concluded, 'is one of the most striking and ruinous diseases in a corps; it undermines discipline and mocks all obedience.'[128]

In case these injunctions were not clear enough, Schaible went on expressly to include (staff) adjutants among those who must be careful in their criticism:

Furthermore, the younger adjutants are admonished as they take up their duty [as adjutant] to make this the rule: never utter ill-intentioned criticism of the commander, even should he have his weaknesses. An adjutant must never misuse these [weaknesses], nor presume to command more than lies in his area. The necessary, requisite tact, which precisely the adjutant must possess, will guard him from such mistakes.[129]

With this sort of training, it is hardly surprising that the FAs were disinclined to question Wilhelm's orders, regardless of how choleric or absurd they might have been.

The enforced suppression of critical thinking and individual responsibility would have been quite serious enough without those other major defects of the officer corps, political ignorance and social arrogance. These two unhappy qualities were the result of the compulsory isolation in which the officers lived. By the late nineteenth century, the honor code had become so rigorous and so specific that living one's life was a hazardous and complex operation. To preserve the purity of one's honor, one could not have any dealings whatsoever with the lower class, which possessed no honor and was therefore incapable of giving satisfaction by a duel. One was not to engage in conversation with workers, nor enter inns, taverns, or other public establishments which catered to them, nor was one to read their newspapers, sing their songs, or even listen to them singing their songs. Above all, one was to avoid contact with their political organizations or any manifestation thereof. The proper officer shared a 'conservative viewpoint' and 'strong monarchical convictions.' He must be ready to fight the forces of revolution 'internally and externally.'[130]

The bourgeoisie, or at least the upper portions of it, possessed more honor than did the lower class, but still tolerated activities forbidden by the officer's honor code, and therefore was less honorable than the *Offiziersstand*. Care was necessary in dealing with it as well. Officers were admonished not to have too much to do with bourgeois society, lest they neglect their own comrades.[131] Even respectable public establishments should be visited only infrequently, otherwise the officer was likely to fail 'to appear in the [noble] ball-room, to seek social intercourse with well-brought-up ladies and to mix in society altogether.'[132] Schaible's fears betray his silent (and justified) suspicions that the officers' own society was deadening compared even to bourgeois events, which themselves were not notoriously lively in this period.

Another danger to the officer stemming from the bourgeoisie was the contagion of politics. Even in cases where the ideas themselves were conservative enough to be innocuous, the peril came from the notion of party politics per se. It all smacked too much of bargaining and brawling [*Parteihader*]. It was unharmonious and therefore threatening. Should the unwary officer suddenly find himself surrounded by political discussion, he should leave as quickly as possible.[133]

The safest place for the officer, after all, was with his own. The officer's *Kasino* provided him with 'comradely intercourse, at the same time it always maintained good manners.'[134] It insulated him from politics, and 'imposed upon him a closet for his own health and for the general good of the state.'[135] The *Kasinos* had been instituted in the mid-nineteenth century at least partly to provide young, unmarried officers with an inexpensive place to eat. By the late nineteenth century, there was much pressure applied to force everyone to eat there. The younger officers were then more exposed to the opinions of their elders. In addition, politics was seldom discussed. The usual subjects were 'women, horses, dogs, and chances for promotion.'[136]

The isolation of the officer from any social situation from which he might have learned something about the society, economics, and politics of Germany was complete. His ignorance was not mitigated by what he learned either in the schools or in army training. Since 1871 the military schools had concentrated more and more on technical knowledge to the exclusion of *Allgemeinbildung* and politics.[137] This was true also at the *Kriegsakademie,* where Scharnhorst's emphasis on *Bildung* was replaced by military subjects, while languages, history, and mathematics became peripheral. Applicants to the *Kriegsakademie* were crammed in tactics and technica by members of the General Staff, but were expected to tutor themselves in history, languages, and geography.[138] Their conversations among themselves reflected this bias. According to General Groener, the only controversial subject discussed with any frequency was religion, particularly the pros and cons of Stöcker's attempt to wean the workers from socialism to anti-Semitic Christianity. Politics interested only the military attachés.[139] The upshot was monumental political ignorance. Worse, 'this isolation had the result, that officers did not recognize their deficiencies in general knowledge, and did not see the necessity to repair matters through further study.'[140] Instead, they felt that, as part of the exclusive officer corps, they had reached the pinnacle of perfection. Those things they did not know did not interest them. F. C. Endres, that ascerbic but astute observer within the army, noted later that one could find truly educated persons in the army only with the aid of a magnifying glass.[141]

The rigidly prescribed life of the officer had other negative effects, too. It was generally observed that, in the last part of the nineteenth century, the honor code had petrified into a collection of petty details, or as Schaible put it, 'we know that these days . . . the true perception of honor by the officer has refined itself extraordinarily.'[142] More and more things were forbidden as dishonorable. 'From shoes to letters, from dancing to speech: at base there was nothing which one could question.'[143] The number of duels fought shot up in the 1880s, at least partly because the number of forbidden acts had so increased.[144] Galloping rigidity was part of the rearguard action taken by the officer corps against the social trends which treatened it. If the bourgeoisie was becoming richer than the nobility, if the working class was organizing, then the officer corps would protect its integrity by heightening its exclusiveness, by cutting itself off even more from dangerous social waves. Paradoxically, the more the nobility and its most purified sector, the officer corps, raised its standards, the harder the bourgeoisie tried to live up to them, particularly in the form of the reserve officer.

Regardless of the evanescent success of the tactic of inflexibility, it had devastating effects on the individuals subject to it. In a world where everything is already prescribed and nothing can be questioned, life becomes next to impossible. Exercise of commonsense is prohibited. Not only that, the ability to make distinctions is shattered:

The all-highest word continues [wrote Schaible]: 'true honor cannot exist without devoted fulfillment even of the *apparently smallest* duties.' It is not accidental that these are called *apparently* smallest duties because especially in the soldier's profession, there are no small duties. The fulfillment of every soldierly duty, even the smallest, will be, in recognition of its worth and meaning, of the highest importance, whether it be in a purely military matter, or considered from an ethical or didactic viewpoint.[145]

This was a world which regarded the soiled glove as a harbinger of the failed campaign. It provided for an excessively symbolic interpretation of the world at large. It promoted fear by extrapolating from the insignificant, the accidental, or the irrelevant to the universal. The fear which the overvaluation of petty events produced fed the mania for control. If everything could only be regulated, then nothing, not even a furtive symbol, could ruin the harmony and order of the *ancien régime*. What could not be tolerated was confusion. The obverse of control-mania is an apocalyptic vision of the world in which, once control has broken down (or, rather, is perceived to have broken down), then nothing remains except a huge, symbolic fight to the finish. The forces of confusion must destroy or be destroyed in an Armageddon. Manfred Messerschmidt has observed that these twin tendencies reached even into the war planning itself:

The insulation of the army from social development, from new forces and political factors affected indirectly even the war-planning of the General Staff by narrowing its perspective to numbers, strength relationships, and tailored attack plans – always with a view toward the 'annihilation' of potential enemies. . . . It appeared, that [the nation] would only be served by 'absolute' decisions.[146]

Surrounded by a thicket of unqualified regulations, the officer tiptoed along the thread which separated the honorable from the dishonorable. His existence was a nervous one, for he lived knowing that the slightest misstep would hurl him from the social pinnacle to black-est disgrace.[147] His nervousness was increased by the demands that certain regulations placed upon his private life. Marriage before the age of 30–35 was highly discouraged. The navy, in fact, perferred its officers never to marry at all.[148] Every officer had to apply to the Kaiser personally for permission to wed. At that time, his superiors would make sure that he had enough money, was old enough and that his fiancée and her family were respectable enough for an officer. Until he was married, he was officially expected to remain celibate. Although this provision was doubtless honored more in the breach than in the observance, it still made the life of the younger officer uncomfortable.

Natural desires, which could not be satisfied in the normal ways within the total institution of the officer corps, became sublimated under the feeling of honor. The 'exemplification of the *Stand*' and honor 'motivation coming from the higher mind' provided compensatory satisfaction. These did not, how-ever, defuse aggressions, but only strengthened them. These aggressions were used, among other things, to fulfill their professional duty, 'the use of deadly, organized force.'[149]

Many of the regulations were not actually meant for the officers, but for the public. They provided both a reason for the privileges and status of the corps and a model for the behavior of other classes. The external purpose of the code was so overwhelming that the unwritten rule became: sins could be forgiven so long as they were kept quiet, so long as the public did not hear of them.[150] The honor code was, in fact, a potent form of noble propaganda. Schaible makes this clear in his homily on the uniform: 'On duty [the officer] is always to be well-dressed, off duty [he is to be] immaculate.'[151] The obsessive concern with externality, which increased for the same reasons that the honor code stiffened, had three effects on the officers, all of them harmful. It caused them to waste time on ceremonies and *Kleinigkeiten*. It sur-rounded them with a sense of hypocrisy. Everyone knew that mis-tresses, homosexuality, debts, drunkenness, and adultery, to name a few things, were far commoner than one was allowed to admit. It would be an interesting research project indeed to discover the effects of prolonged hypocrisy on human behavior. They are doubtless not good. The same could be said about repression, too, of course. And the officers were trapped between them both.

The third result of the value placed on external effect was expense. Many scions of the upper bourgeoisie used their abundant funds to elevate themselves to a style befitting their conception of the noble life. The nobility was, in fact, less wealthy than the bourgeoisie imagined. Faced with the bourgeois challenge, however, the nobility within the officer corps did its best to compete. The result was the rapid spread of expensive dinners, horse races, and gala evenings, which numerous officers could ill afford. Wilhelm II contributed mightily to this trend by his own curiously unPrussian, almost *parvenu* taste for the sumptuous. He continually changed the regimental uniforms, which the officers were obliged to buy;[152] he encouraged expensive *Abschiedsdiners,* horse races, fancy hunts, and other events. Despite repeated injunctions by the officer's manuals,[153] commanders, and occasionally by Wilhelm himself, the trend continued,[154] with the result that many officers were driven either into debt or at the very least into stupefaction by the continuing round of obligatory reciprocal dinners, dances and fêtes. One often wonders when during the *Saison,* military matters were accomplished at all.

The FAs and FADs had perfectly realized the officer's life, with all its brittleness and tension. This was, of course, a prerequisite for becoming a FA in the first place. Added to the burdens of the officer corps were the burdens of the Court.

The milieu created and shared by the FA(D)s was as narrow and stuffy as their own limited experience would be expected to produce. The imperial day unfolded mechanically. The FADs were most in evidence during the walks and rides which Wilhelm undertook at least twice daily, and during lunch and dinner, when the chief duty of the FADs was to provide conversation. For the visitor at Court who had a humanistic education or interests, these conversations were tedious and frustrating. When women were not present, the tone was 'coarse,' sprinkled with dirty stories,[155] to which Wilhelm contributed.[156] When this *Herrenklub* was invaded by women, that is, by the Kaiserin and her *Hofdamen,* talk became labored and stiff, as the FADs struggled to find something to say.[157] The Kaiserin herself was usually silent and gave the impression that she resented the military men who prevented her from being alone with Wilhelm.[158]

The FADs joined the Empress in her silence whenever the conversation turned to subjects about which they were mostly ignorant. Unfortunately, these subjects included art, literature, music, architecture, and archeology, to name a few.[159] Unlike his FAs, Wilhelm found these topics engrossing and consequently filled the vacuum himself. He would speak uninterruptedly on a wide variety of matters,[160] but even his speaking gifts were not adequate to vanquish the boredom incubated by the narrow entourage. This was one of the reasons that Wilhelm travelled so often. Wilhelm, said his friend Admiral von Hollmann, was attracted to Cowes, for example, not by the sailing, but

especially by the unrestrained conversation with distinguished English society in which he finds what he values most and searches for in Germany in vain, because the great majority here [in Germany] bend before the Kaiser like a grainfield before the approaching storm; he finds at Cowes unselfish exchange of opinion with independent, strongly formed characters and personalities.[161]

This was also the reason that Wilhelm found Philipp Eulenburg and the Liebenberg Circle so appealing.[162] In fairness to the men of the entourage, it must be said that Wilhelm made it difficult for them to be outspoken. He pronounced his own opinions in no uncertain terms. His vehemence made even strong characters hesitate to disagree with him, particularly in matters which were not directly of concern to them. It was better to save one's eloquence for substantive questions.[163] Their training as officers had schooled them to be unobtrusive and to defer whenever possible to their commanders, and, most of all, to their supreme commander.

If Wilhelm found his military servants boring, they were not always pleased with their monarch or with their position, either. The FAD post was an unsettling mixture of the dull and the terrifying. The life could be easy because one had whole days off. Even on duty, one could be lulled into tedium because everything, people, places, times, were interchangeable.

In the end [one FAD wrote], it was all the same, where one lived, ate and slept – in one of the imperial castles, in the provinces, at a foreign court, in a large private house, or in the special train. Everything was arranged in advance to the smallest detail, in a short time the most various things were accomplished, the Kaiser came last and went first. That spared much time and energy. Our own servants looked after the many changes of clothes.[164]

The 'many changes of clothes' for instance were part of the stiffness of Court life, which may have added to its sense of security but did not make it particularly comfortable. The relentless publicity which surrounded the courtiers froze them into a formality that some found difficult to accept. Even on imperial vacations one could never relax. 'One simply must get used to the fact that one is always in society,' wrote Eulenburg during the *Nordlandreise,* after FAD Kuno Moltke had complained about the constant pomp.[165]

The sense of certainty borne of routine and formality could be destroyed in an instant, however, by the impulsive Kaiser or by world events. Wilhelm would change firmly laid plans almost literally at the last minute and wrench his companions into the helter skelter world of his own whims. Alfred von Kiderlen-Wächter, the sometime representative of the Foreign Office on Wilhelm's trips during the mid-1890s, experienced once what was common fare for the FADs. Kiderlen's plans to visit his mistress were abruptly shattered by an imperial telegram ordering him to Berlin to accompany Wilhelm on a trip. 'I don't even know when the trip begins,' he lamented. 'According to the newspapers it is to go to Wartburg, Schliz [*sic*] (zu Goertz) and Karlsruhe. More I don't know, not even if another trip is planned.'[166]

Worse than the last minute alterations were the consequences of Wilhelm's trust. The Kaiser routinely confided in whomever happened to be near him. He discussed weighty matters of a non-military nature with his young officers and expected them to have opinions and to offer advice. Such continuous pressure was difficult to bear even for persons trained in high politics. Even a bright, ambitious, politically astute diplomat like Kiderlen found that 'the responsibility which one takes for *each* word of [Wilhelm's] confidence is frequently a burden on one!'[167] The position of the FAD was even more difficult than that of the Foreign Office representatives or of those officers tied to the Cabinets, for the FADs were less generally well-informed and therefore less able to give Wilhelm the kind of advice he demanded from them. Many of them, perhaps even most, tried to avoid becoming implicated in imperial decisions by restricting their spoken opinions strictly to military questions.[168] But Wilhelm made this strategy difficult by the way he treated them. Wilhelm's FAs were both his comrades and his close friends.[169] He was more intimate with his FAs than he was with his own sons.[170] Under these circumstances it was hard for a FA to refrain from fulfilling Wilhelm's expectations and instead to adhere rigorously to his duties (which were in any case ill-defined).

FAs were made further uncomfortable by a psychological trait of Wilhelm's that curiously mirrored the duality of duty–friendship in which they already found themselves. Wilhelm was in many respects overly friendly and trusting of his FAs,[171] but his moodiness and bad nerves made him incapable of the steadiness and consideration which a reciprocal friendship demands. One of his FAs, who was well-disposed to Wilhelm, later wrote that 'the Kaiser was basically a nervous sort, very pointed and sharp in his quick judgment and, despite all of the personal good will, inwardly cool.'[172] He rarely asked personal questions about his FAs' families or problems and seemed uninterested in the human factors which affected their lives and the performance of their duties.[173] Despite the rigidity which surrounded them, the FAs could never count, ultimately, on either the routine of duty or on the mood of the monarch.

Nor could a FA count on his fellow courtiers. The Court was never free from the atmosphere, if not always the fact, of intrigue. This is unavoidable in any situation where a handful of people inhabit a summit of power or prestige solely by virtue of a personal relationship to one man. The slope is steep, the sides are slippery, and the clawing hands are more numerous than are secure holds on which to rest them. Wilhelm's Court seems to have been rather better in this respect than many. Still, one lived with the uncomfortable knowledge that one was being watched by hawks only too ready to swoop down upon the slightest misstep. Eulenburg's spectacular fall illustrated the possibilities all too graphically.

Despite its glamor, then, the life of the FA was not entirely enviable. Senden-Bibran wrote that the worst part about it was the loss of personal freedom which it entailed. He had been fairly outspoken before he accepted the position, and he wondered if he could find the 'right tone,' strike a properly deferential attitude toward the 'elevated person' of the Kaiser.[174] Court life was not particularly enjoyable either for a man like Deines, who hated the company of Court 'larvae,'[175] or for a Wedel, who chafed at the 'creatures' whom Wilhelm favored.[176] Even men who were known for their accommodation if not servility, found the *Hofluft* distasteful. Admiral Hollmann is a case in point.[177] Or FAD Gustav von Neumann-Cosel, who distinguished himself by obsequiously kissing his Emperor's hand. Neumann-Cosel found duty at Court so dreadful that at the end of each tour he would return to his room, swear loudly several times to exorcise the too-civil restraint he had been forced to practice, and would then sleep for twenty-four hours.[178] These two examples raise the possibility that some FADs cultivated submissiveness as a defense against the anxiety that their personal service produced. The frustrations of Court life drove other FADs from the rarified imperial air altogether to the life outside, which was perhaps more bumptious, but also more real. It is legitimate to wonder whether a truly strong and independent person could long have tolerated the fetters which Court life forged.[179]

The inner and outer restraints, the demands made by Wilhelm specifically and by his temperament generally, the combination of certainty and uncertainty placed an enormous burden on the FAs. 'In the end,' FAD Mutius records, 'one found oneself while on duty in a continuous, if often unconscious, tension.'[180] One felt as though one were sitting on a powder keg which threatened to explode. Unlike Mutius, who liked that feeling, many of his colleagues found the pressure simply unbearable. Until they could bring themselves to leave,[181] their nervousness joined Wilhelm's to create the peculiar, edgy atmosphere that distinguished the Berlin Court.

8

The politics of the military entourage

The role of the military in German politics has been the subject of much discussion by both the Wilhelminians and later historians.[1] Wilhelm II's military entourage was the institution which, to a large extent, defined, controlled, and expressed the military's political viewpoints, and attempted to act upon them. Political leadership within the military entourage oscillated between the chief of the General Staff and the Military Cabinet chief, depending in peacetime largely upon the personality and political conceptions of the incumbents.[2] From Wilhelm's accession through 1890, Chief of Staff General Alfred v. Waldersee marked the political course. His successor from 1891 to 1905, General Alfred v. Schlieffen, left politics to Cabinet Chief v. Hahnke, who expanded the Military Cabinet's power without in the slightest modifying its bedrock conservatism.[3] The ascendancy of 'the most conservative institution of the Empire' continued until Cabinet Chief Dietrich v. Hülsen-Haeseler's death in 1908, after which the pendulum swung back to the Chief of Staff (now in the person of Helmuth v. Moltke), where it stayed until the monarchy collapsed in 1918. While overt political leadership usually emanated from these two positions, the rest of the military entourage was hardly inactive. It participated, particularly in drawn-out campaigns, in the form of smaller networks centered around friendship or shared conviction.

The military entourage's political pretensions did not go unchallenged. The Reichstag, Bundesrat, Staatsministerium, Foreign Office, south German governments and public opinion all tried to curb its influence. But the power of the military entourage (as the central expression of the military altogether) rested upon the Kaiser's exclusive right to command the armed forces (*Kommandogewalt*). This, in turn, was the ultimate locus of the Crown's concrete power, and was thus untouchable. Not surprisingly then, none of the institutions that challenged the military men at Court succeeded in eroding Wilhelm's *Kommandogewalt*,[4] and therefore none could uproot, although they might prune, the political potential of the military entourage. *Kommandogewalt* and the struggle against it form one external structural aspect of the military entourage's influence. The other was the Kaiser himself. For, despite the symbiotic relation between the military entourage and the Crown, they were not a unit and they did not always agree. Wilhelm, through support, acquiescence or opposition, set the possible range for the military entourage's political activity. The following discussion does not exhaust every facet of that activity. It does, however, examine four controversies that describe the scope and characteristic patterns of the military entourage's politics, ranging from foreign through domestic to personnel policy, and with opposition running from public institutions to the Kaiser.

The most consistent domestic source of worry for Wilhelm's responsible foreign policy advisers came from the military attachés.[5] The task of the military and naval attachés was difficult because it was ill-defined and highly sensitive. They were supposed to 'become acquainted with all the important events in the army or navy of the foreign state to which they were accredited. . . . [They were] to become thoroughly familiar with their spirit and arrangements, to observe personnel and materiel, organization and laws, training and technology.'[6] The instructions, however, found it 'impossible to define . . . [their position] completely' and left it to the attachés' own tact, or in especially difficult cases, to the advice of the diplomatic head of the mission to decide what was proper behavior.[7]

The relation of the attaché to his mission chief was equally difficult. The attaché, while accredited to the embassy or legation and possessing the same rights of immunity as the diplomats, was not so much of the mission as next to it. He was subordinate to the mission chief in his attaché duties, but in all other capacities was still under the authority of his superiors in the military. The mission chief could not punish an attaché, and both the mission chief and the attaché could complain about one another to higher authorities (the chancellor and then the Kaiser). Attachés had to submit their reports to the mission chief, who then forwarded them to the chancellor, who sent them on to the War Ministry or the Naval Office, whence they might go further to the General Staff, Admiralty, or Kaiser. The reports were not supposed to contain political observations, except 'when such observations were inextricably mixed with the military content.'[8] This exception opened the way for a political role which was expressly forbidden them in other parts of the instructions.

The strength of the military and naval attachés vis-à-vis their civilian diplomatic chiefs was increased by Wilhelm's overestimation of the capabilities of officers and by the fact that many of them were simultaneously FAs and, thus, privileged members of the royal entourage. Almost a quarter of all the FAs and FADs who served Wilhelm during his reign were at one time military attachés. [9] The only time they played a consistent role in foreign affairs, however, was at the beginning of Wilhelm's reign when they were directed by General Waldersee, Chief of Staff, from 10 August 1888 to 28 January 1891, thereafter Commander of the IX Army Corps in Hamburg-Altona. In order for the military entourage to wreak methodical damage on policies set by civilians, a strong leader or orchestrator was required. Waldersee was just such a man.

Helmuth von Moltke, Waldersee's predecessor at the General Staff, had lacked political ambition and hence had been content to allow Bismarck to run foreign policy. As Moltke's long-time assistant, Waldersee had chafed at the latter's modest restraint. Neither Waldersee's character nor the ideas that he strove so mightily to put into practice were in the least modest or restrained. The general was a thoroughly unashamed and bumptious reactionary. His opinions were a virtual parody of the Junker *Weltanschauung*. He believed that the strength and goodness of Germany lay in agrarian Prussia led by unbending officers of the evangelical nobility. The threat to the old order, which Waldersee preferred to think of as civilization, came from the social by-products of industrialism, the working class in particular. This class, in his view, was grasping, insatiable, godless, unpatriotic, and immoral. If current trends continued, Waldersee saw bloody revolution as inevitable. The subversive proletariat would be joined in an Armageddon by Jews, Catholics, non-conservatives and non-Prussians on the domestic front, and by Russia and France in the foreign arena.[10]

Waldersee's paranoia led him to prefer to bring on the Last Fight before the forces of order deteriorated still further in moral and physical strength. His anxiety to fight was so great that he was indifferent in his choice of enemies. He grasped at any opportunity to develop a small event into a *casus belli*. In rapid succession he advocated preventive wars, now against France, now against Russia, against them both, or against striking workers in Germany.[11] Although they had been acquainted for some years previously,[12] Wilhelm and Waldersee began meeting frequently only in 1884 at the general's military lectures.[13] Waldersee's outspoken bellicosity, which Wilhelm interpreted as masculinity, made him attractive to the young Prince.

At the same time that Waldersee was cementing his relationship with Prince Wilhelm,[14] he was breaking away from the Bismarcks. Waldersee considered a war with Russia inevitable and found the Bismarcks' policy of friendship with that country little short of criminal. He did his best to wean Wilhelm from pro-Russia sentiment and to build up instead his regard for Germany's Austrian allies and for increased armaments for the coming war.[15] Waldersee's major tools in his struggle against the Bismarcks were Military Attachés Adolf von Deines (Austria, 1887–94), Ernst Frhr von Hoiningen gen. Hüne (France, 1886–93), Maximilian Graf Yorck von Wartenberg (attached to the German Military Plenipotentiary in Russia), Karl von Villaume (Russia, 1887–93), and Karl von Engelbrecht (Rome, 1882–95). These men kept Waldersee well supplied with military reports and private letters, which detailed the presumed belligerent actions of Russia and France, the strength of Austria, the perfidy of Italy, and the stupidity of Germany's ambassadors to each of these countries. Waldersee collected their reports and fed them to Prince (then Kaiser) Wilhelm in such a way as to discredit official foreign policy and especially its creators, Otto and Herbert von Bismarck.

Otto von Bismarck retaliated by setting the precedents by which the *Nebenpolitik* of the military attachés was finally curbed. He went so far as to forbid the attachés any political role whatsoever.

While Bismarck tried to rein in the military attachés, Waldersee was busy trying to upgrade their status and influence permanently. The system by which military attachés were chosen was not unlike that which produced FAs. In the army, the General Staff combed its qualification reports for persons with suitable education, experience, financial means, social standing, and manners. Once candidates agreed to have their names on the list, it was winnowed down and sent to the Military Cabinet, which presented it to Wilhelm and in consultation with him chose the attachés. In contrast to the army General Staff, the Admiralty had a lesser role in choosing the navy's candidates. Instead, the Naval Cabinet reserved to itself this task.[16] Though unreliable qualification reports and royal interference presented roughly the same problems for the selection of military attachés and FAs, the military attachés nevertheless tended to be more intelligent than the average officer.[17] They were also more interested in politics than the FAs, although they were not necessarily much more enlightened.

At the end of January 1889 Waldersee proposed to Wilhelm that the military attachés no longer be accountable to the chancellor, as had been the case since 1867, but directly and exclusively to the

Kaiser.[18] Waldersee thought that Deines and Hüne, for example, should be encouraged to write directly to the Emperor in their capacity as FAs.[19] This would have been a huge step toward personal regime, and Wilhelm naturally agreed. Waldersee probably did not intend this step to benefit Wilhelm so much as to weaken Bismarck. Waldersee was already fairly critical of Wilhelm's work habits[20] and doubtless assumed that he, Waldersee, not Wilhelm, would end up in control of the more powerful military attachés.

In order to make the plan attractive, Waldersee repeatedly told Wilhelm what the Kaiser already believed:[21]

> Their [the military attachés'] reports are good not only because they are written by able people, but more important because they are produced by independent characters, who report their opinions fearlessly, while the diplomats only report what is acceptable to the chancellor.[22]

Thus Waldersee sought to further Wilhelm's contempt for civilians in general and for diplomats in particular, whose 'character' was not comparable to that of a pugnacious, hypermasculine soldier. Wilhelm knew that the proposed change would precipitate a clash with Bismarck, so he told Waldersee that he would move slowly by preparing the military attachés individually for their future role as political reporters.

Although Waldersee's machinations did weaken Bismarck's personal position with the Emperor, complete victory eluded him. Bismarck's successor, Caprivi, carried the old chancellor's struggle against the attachés to a successful conclusion in the 'General Instructions' to Military and Naval Attachés of 11 December 1890. The 'Instructions' reiterated that all reports were to proceed through the embassy and the Foreign Office and that under no circumstances was the attaché to rank before the diplomat who headed the mission, even in the absence of the regular ambassador.[23]

Waldersee was enraged. He had a stormy talk with Wilhelm on the subject (17 December 1890), but Wilhelm was satisfied with Caprivi's instructions. Waldersee was even more furious with Cabinet Chief von Hahnke, who had approved Caprivi's insistence that the chancellor see all military attaché reports.[24] Hahnke knew that the first person to benefit from Waldersee's proposal would have been the General Staff chief himself. Hahnke's own administrative energies were directed to the expansion of the power of the Cabinet, if necessary at the expense of the General Staff. He could safely oppose Waldersee on the military attaché issue because both he and Wilhelm felt that they could rely upon the direct communications of those military attachés who were also FAs to keep Wilhelm well-informed.[25]

The final blow to a concerted military attaché *Politik* came a little over a month later when Waldersee was abruptly dismissed from his post and exiled to Altona (28 January 1891). The Kaiser had not forgiven Waldersee for his harsh criticism of Wilhelm's leadership in the fall *Kaisermanöver*.[26] The Emperor had retained Waldersee for four months to hide the real reason behind the latter's dismissal. It is not impossible that Wilhelm's estrangement from Waldersee caused the Kaiser to acquiesce to Caprivi's limits on the military attachés more easily than he would have earlier. Whatever the case, those military attachés who were interested in subverting civilian policy now lacked a leader to coordinate their activities or to feed their reports to the Emperor at the psychologically correct moment. Neither Hahnke nor his successors, Hülsen and Lyncker, had specific foreign policy ambitions. They were concerned rather with the army itself and its relation to society, that is, with domestic, not foreign affairs. Hahnke succeeded, upon Waldersee's dismissal, in weakening the power of the General Staff relative to the Military Cabinet, a state of affairs which continued until around 1905/06.[27] But no subsequent General Staff chief, even after 1906, used the military attachés as Waldersee had done. In fact, Waldersee was something of an anomaly regarding the extremity of his political plans and the zeal with which he sought to effect them.[28]

After Waldersee a concerted effort was no longer made to insure that military attachés would also serve simultaneously as FAs. Altogether there were twenty-three FAs who were at one time also military attachés. Five of these held the two positions independently at different moments in their careers.[29] Another five achieved both designations simultaneously;[30] six were FAs who subsequently became military attachés as well;[31] while the remaining seven started as military attachés and were later made FAs in addition.[32] In the case of twelve of these men,[33] the FA appointment served to facilitate their contact with the Emperor and to make the relationship more intimate. Of this group, only three – Karl von Bülow, Chelius, and Deines – became long-term members of the entourage. Only Chelius, however, performed personal service for Wilhelm and therefore was in a position to exercise constant influence on the Kaiser if he so chose. It seems, however, that he did not.[34] Most of the FA military attachés had unimpeded access to Wilhelm only while they served in their positions. After they were transferred they usually ceased being FAs. Though they of course remained *hoffähig* [capable of being received at Court] and would be invited to lunches or dinners at Court,[35] their contacts with the Emperor became sporadic.

After Waldersee's fall, military attaché FAs – with the exception of Engelbrecht – submitted to Caprivi's instructions and presented no further threat to the execution of foreign policy. Holstein, who was hypersensitive to military interference in foreign affairs, complained less and less frequently of concrete examples of military meddling. The military/diplomatic front was indeed quiet until the naval attachés in London, Erich Müller and Wilhelm Widenmann, began their agitation for an aggressively anti-English policy. But neither Müller nor Widenmann were members of the entourage. Their leverage came instead from their position as representatives of the navy, Wilhelm's favorite branch of service, the branch whose prestige was further enhanced by Tirpitz's unchallenged eminence as creator of the fleet. The turn already taken by German–English relations only strengthened the influence enjoyed by the two attachés.[36]

Despite the vocal fears of the Foreign Office, the military attaché FAs created no overwhelming political disasters. The negative reports from Russia in 1888–90 contributed to the non-renewal of the Reinsurance Treaty, it is true, but they were only part of a general movement inside the upper levels of both the military and the Foreign Office to rearrange fundamentally Germany's relations to Russia. In this light the military attaché FAs' reports seem as much a symptom as a cause. Engelbrecht in Rome was the most active military attaché-intriguer against the Foreign Office, and Holstein was right to be concerned about him. But the diplomats rose to the challenge successfully. Bernhard Bülow's appointment as ambassador effectively quashed Engelbrecht's schemes, although it required a struggle.[37] On the whole, civilian vigilance guarded foreign policy well from this quarter.

Furthermore, the only country to have an unbroken string of military attaché FAs within its borders was not one of Germany's later foes, but its only ally, Austria. From the beginning of the Dreyfus Affair to the outbreak of war, no German military or naval attaché to Paris was also a FA. In Russia, however, beginning in 1904, Wilhelm tried to reestablish the old special arrangement whereby the Russian and German military attachés respectively stood in a unique position vis-à-vis the Emperors and were considered members of each other's entourage. Russo-German relations had already deteriorated to the extent that this attempt remained a fiction. Most military attaché FAs to Russia, with the exception of the gifted and perceptive Hintze,[38] seem to have been relatively untalented; they were in any case in no position to be successful intriguers.

The military attaché FAs' major impact lay not in what they actually did, but rather in what the civilian architects of foreign policy feared they might do. The specter of subterranean military meddling frightened especially Holstein, Marschall, Kiderlen-Wächter, and Caprivi. They feared loss of control on two levels. Military attachés or former officers who transferred to the diplomatic corps might be chary of following the instructions of 'mere' civilians. Worse, they might neglect the usual tools and even goals of diplomacy, in favor of bellicose solutions. But more than this, their loyalty as officers would be primarily to Wilhelm. They could easily become the conduits for a frightening expansion of Wilhelm's personal power in arenas in which the Emperor was completely incompetent. In order to forestall this eventuality, Holstein and his comrades accepted with the alacrity of desperation civilian candidates, for non-diplomatic as well as diplomatic posts, who in fact were more likely to become instruments of personal regime than were their military competitors. A not inconsiderable degree of Eulenburg's success in managing *Personalpolitik* stemmed from his brilliant manipulation of Holstein's fear of *Adjutantenpolitik*.[39]

The two clearest examples of consistent intervention by the military entourage as a whole both occurred in the realm of domestic politics. The most important instance dealt, not surprisingly, directly with the relationship between the military and society. The struggle centered on efforts to introduce a standard, reformed military code of justice (*Militärstrafgerichtsordnung* or MStGO) for the Reich. The overwhelming necessity of such a move was clear to everyone. The Reichstag had been proposing changes since 1870;[40] the Prussian army since 1881. The purpose of the MStGO was twofold: to institute uniform procedures in all states (Prussia, Bavaria, and Württemberg had different codes) and to modernize the regulations which had hitherto governed the largest army of Germany, the Prussian. The Prussian procedure dated to 1845 and was a model of illiberality. The courts were not independent. Investigations and trials were initiated (or quashed) solely by the local commander, and the trials were not public. The judges were always soldiers, selected according to the rank of the defendant, and their verdict was ineffective until confirmed by the commander.

Defense counsel was barred in many instances and even when admitted could produce only written statements. One could sue for annulment or for restitution only if one submitted new evidence; otherwise there was ordinarily no appeal. The King retained the right of pardon.

The Bavarian Code, by contrast, had been liberalized in 1869 to provide for public, oral trials, with unrestricted defense and the addition of civilian jurors. The courts were independent and subject to law, not to the whims of the commander.[41] The Bavarian Code basically reflected civil procedure and had worked with no detrimental effect on the army for twenty-six years when the MStGO battle was joined. The Prussian procedure, on the other hand, guaranteed class and blood justice, as its critics pointedly put it. Far from the prying eyes of the Reichstag or the press, the officer corps could protect its own from the consequences of their transgressions. Even Philipp Eulenburg, who was basically opposed to the reform of the MStGO[42] and who, more than anyone else, tried to postpone it to death, had to admit that some reform was necessary to curb the 'hair-raising stupidity' which had reigned under the old code.[43]

The reform efforts within the Prussian army had progressed so far that when General Walter Bronsart von Schellendorf became war minister in September 1893, he found a completed draft of a reform bill along Bavarian lines, which, however, did not include public trials. In consultation with Chancellor Hohenlohe, who had been instrumental in creating the Bavarian Code of 1869, Bronsart substituted a clause guaranteeing public trials and submitted the package to the Staatsministerium on 29 April 1895.[44] The ministry approved the bill unanimously, a stance it maintained consistently until the ensuing crisis took the matter out of its hands. Opposition at Court and in the army, however, centered around two provisions: public trials and the monarch's right to confirm or not to confirm (and thereby render unenforceable) the verdict of the courts (*Bestätigungsrecht*). The Hauptquartier was as unanimously against the MStGO as the ministry was for it. Military Cabinet Chief Hahnke led the campaign, with the unflagging support of Plessen,[45] Dietrich Hülsen,[46] and Adolf Bülow.[47] None of the lesser military lights deviated from Hahnke's course. Such unanimity was infrequent. Despite Holstein's distrust of military men, his correspondence indicates his repeated efforts to use sympathetic FAs to carry out his suggestions. In the MStGO affair, however, neither he, nor Hutten-Czapski,[48] nor the Grand Duke of Baden,[49] nor any of the other people who tried to help the measure through was able to find a single FA willing to be used in this way.

The Hauptquartier argued that if Wilhelm lost the right of confirmation, his command powers would be severely diminished. A court independent of Wilhelm's authority would remove the officers from Wilhelm's personal control and protection and also remove them from the influence of the Military Cabinet. Without imperial protection, who could tell what democratic outrages might be inflicted upon the officer corps? This was, indeed, the heart of the matter. Publicity was repugnant to Hahnke precisely because the army 'must remain an isolated body in which no one is allowed to peer with critical eyes.'[50] Hahnke was willing to open trials to other members of the military, but not to civilians or to the press.[51] If the public were treated to trials of high-ranking officers accused of mishandling their subordinates or of moral failures, 'discipline' would suffer. That is, public esteem for the nobility would fall and, consequently, recruits would not respect their officers. 'Discipline' became the euphemism for the maintenance of the unquestioned social/political standing of the officer corps.

'Discipline' in the usual sense of the word had clearly not suffered at all in Bavaria, either from the existence of public trials, or from the paucity of noble officers. Bronsart knew that the real issue was not discipline. Neither he nor the other military supporters of the bill favored it as a weapon against their own officer corps. Bronsart, in fact, offered to restrict publicity 'out of consideration for the rank of the officer.'[52] It would be interesting to know how much of the officer corps originally favored Bronsart's MStGO. The Military Cabinet was the most conservative military organ in Germany and frequently trailed the officer corps or the war ministry in its opinions. In this case, the Cabinet was probably more in tune with Prussian military opinion than was usual.[53] War Minister Bronsart at first had a substantial group behind him,[54] which, however, after the dismissals of Generals Spitz[55] and Schlichting,[56] and finally of Bronsart himself, was decidedly weakened. Few officers dared risk imperial censure or disfavor of the Military Cabinet chief – in this case, Hahnke – (who decided personnel matters) once they saw the consequences. General Loë, for instance, at first had favored the bill, along with General Albedyll.[57] He quickly covered his tracks, however, so as not to ruin his position with the influential Hahnke.[58] The case of the commanding generals was similar.[59]

Wilhelm opposed Bronsart's bill from the first, but it is not

necessary to join Hutten-Czapski in his surmise that Wilhelm's opposition was inevitable. The Emperor was not above promulgating
unpopular, modern regulations even for his army. He had, after all,
opened the officer corps to the talented bourgeoisie[60] and would in
1897 make it increasingly difficult for an officer to engage in duelling.[61] The issue of public trials did not at first engage the Kaiser's
attention, and his position on the matter remained uncertain. When
Hohenlohe first recorded Wilhelm's negative response to the bill (31
May 1895) only the right of confirmation had been mentioned,
although the major disputes that followed concerned publicity.[62] Time
and again in the years that followed, Wilhelm's behavior led Hohenlohe,[63] Bronsart,[64] Wilmowski (Chief of the *Reichskanzlei*), Tirpitz,[65]
and others[66] to believe that he was about to relent. And time and time
again, they would try to press home their advantage, only to discover
that, in the interim, his stand had hardened once more.

Hutten-Czapski discovered that Wilhelm was, in fact, ill-informed
on the MStGO; the Kaiser gave the weighty legal documents to Hahnke
and then simply incorporated Hahnke's opinions as his own.[67]
Hahnke's ideas had an immediate appeal for Wilhelm because they
were diametrically opposed to Bronsart's; opposing the bill thus presented Wilhelm with the opportunity of getting rid of a minister whom
he found highhanded, if not actually treacherous. Once Wilhelm's
hyperbolic temperament came into play, moreover, a process was
begun which was difficult to halt. 'The Kaiser,' wrote the Grand Duke
of Baden, '*after he has discussed such questions* [as the MStGO] *before his
entourage, feels himself bound in many decisive questions.* In such a situation it is doubly difficult to modify these decisions.'[68] Wilhelm was not
only afraid of losing face before his favorite officers at Court. In his
annual New Year's speech to the commanding generals, he had spoken out so vehemently against Bronsart that the latter had contemplated drawing his sword.[69] The ubiquitous and well-connected
Hutten-Czapski noted:

I have discovered from a reliable source that the Kaiser is not so horribly
opposed to the MStGO as is supposed. Since the New Year's speech, however,
he finds himself in a difficult position, out of which he can only escape, if he
himself seizes the initiative to change and then to get acceptance for a bill
drawn up by himself.[70]

The military opponents of the MStGO made clever use of Wilhelm's
pride. They had so transformed the situation that by August 1896,
Eulenburg could write without exaggeration that 'to His Majesty,
rejecting public [trials] is a matter of honor.'[71] Among officers, as we

have seen, honor was the lynchpin of existence. The MStGO had become for Wilhelm an existential, rather than a political, question. True compromise was therefore impossible.

Wilhelm's intransigence, and the role which the Military Cabinet and the Hauptquartier had in maintaining it, gave the MStGO considerably more importance than it would otherwise have had.[72] The military entourage used the MStGO to underline and even to widen the Crown's independence from other governmental organs, which of course increased the Crown's dependence upon the military basis of its power. The MStGO therefore developed into a power struggle between Wilhelm and his irresponsible advisers, such as Hahnke, on the one hand, and the responsible ministers, particularly Bronsart, Marschall, Chancellor Chlodwig Hohenlohe, and Holstein, on the other. Bronsart wanted to use the MStGO as a lever to destroy Cabinet govermment, which made 'departmental settlement[s] of daily affairs impossible.'[73] Cabinet government, as Hohenlohe put it and as everyone realized, was 'of course basically only personal regime.'[74]

Until the *Daily Telegraph* Affair of 1908, Bronsart struck the biggest blow against personal regime with the MStGO in the Köller Crisis of November 1895.[75] Köller was minister of the interior, entirely Wilhelm's man and with strong Court connections. He tried to subvert the unity of the ministry in the MStGO bill and reported the ministry's deliberations to Plessen and Hahnke. Bronsart was outraged at his uncollegial behavior and threatened to resign with the chancellor and the entire ministry if Wilhelm did not immediately dismiss Köller. Despite immense pressure, the ministers stayed firm and Wilhelm was forced to acquiesce to their power. Had they continued in this way, a limited form of parliamentary or at least of bureaucratic government would have replaced the expansion of personal regime.

Holstein, in particular, pushed hard for such a course. Three times in February and March 1896[76] and sporadically thereafter, Holstein urged Hohenlohe to force Wilhelm to accept Bronsart's bill by threatening to resign with the ministry and by whipping up public opinion until it would demand nothing less. In the end, Hohenlohe refused to do so because he did not want to rule over Wilhelm; he was no longer physically up to the struggle which that involved. Besides, he rationalized, the MStGO was really not so important and, anyway, Wilhelm was likely to give in.[77]

Little by little, first Bronsart, then Hohenlohe, the Staatsministerium, and finally Holstein made damaging concessions concerning the MStGO, which they euphemistically termed 'compromises.' Bronsart began in March 1896 by offering to limit publicity according to the rank of the accused.[78] Hohenlohe chimed in five days later by suggesting that the defendant himself could demand a closed trial.[79] Wilhelm was amenable to this, and Hohenlohe considered that he had won a victory.[80] Wilhelm, however, remained adamant that Bronsart should be dismissed because of his part in the Köller crisis. Eulenburg would just as soon have scrapped Hohenlohe, Marschall, and Holstein, too, so that he could inaugurate unfettered personal regime under Bernhard von Bülow's chancellorship.[81] But Eulenburg did not yet feel strong enough to do this, so instead he choreographed the next 'compromise.' By a combination of threats, flattery, and bribery,[82] Eulenburg and Wilhelm convinced Hohenlohe to break his solidarity with Bronsart and to remain in office while Wilhelm named a more pliable war minister (Gossler). This occurred in August 1896. Lucanus recognized immediately that without Bronsart's stubborn support Hohenlohe would surely give in on the MStGO sooner or later.[83] He was right.

Once Wilhelm was no longer threatened by the only weapon the responsible ministers had at their disposal, namely collegial solidarity, he (Eulenburg and Bülow) moved on to divide and conquer. While in office, Bronsart had capitulated far enough to suggest the addition of the following article:

Publicity can be curtailed for all or part of the proceedings by order of the court, if it is feared that public order, particularly state security or military interests or morality, would be endangered.[84]

Now, Wilhelm, through Gossler, added the phrase:

Under which conditions and in which forms curtailment of publicity shall occur for reasons of discipline[85] shall be determined by the Kaiser.[86]

Bronsart's paragraph, which was damaging enough, was accepted by the Staatsministerium. Gossler's addition became known as the second part of Paragraph 270 (§270/2) and was the major stumbling block to acceptance of the MStGO by Hohenlohe, later by the Reichstag, and finally by Bavaria.

Throughout the winter and spring of 1896/97, the battle over Paragraph 270/2 raged between Wilhelm, who stood fast, and the aged and infirm Hohenlohe, who threatened to resign as chancellor. Meanwhile, Eulenburg's plans for the massive personnel changes which would inaugurate personal regime developed and finally blossomed successfully in June 1897.[87] Hohenlohe's last remaining liberal supports, Marschall and Bötticher, were chopped away. Even Holstein collapsed, although he remained in office.[88] Hohenlohe tried desperately to hold out, but finally, on 29 October 1897, he too surrendered. The chancellor had promised the Reichstag in May 1896 that he would introduce the government's bill to that body in the fall. A year had already passed. Wilhelm had ignored Hohenlohe's promise and had consented only to presenting the MStGO to the Bundesrat, where Bavarian opposition had held the bill at a standstill. For if Hohenlohe thought he had solved the right of confirmation problem by reducing it to 'a harmless formality,'[89] the Bavarians did not see it that way.

Finally, on 29 October, Wilhelm's Cabinet government, in the persons of Hahnke and Lucanus, informed the responsible chancellor that the Kaiser had agreed to introduce the bill to the plenum of the Bundesrat and to the Reichstag. Hahnke was the moving spirit at work here, with Wilhelm (plus Lucanus and Eulenburg) trailing along in his wake.[90] In return for this seeming concession, however, Wilhelm insisted on keeping Paragraph 270/2. Though Hohenlohe spoke to him, the Kaiser did not weaken. When the chancellor then conferred with Gossler, the war minister not surprisingly told Hohenlohe to accept Wilhelm's offer. After doing so, Hohenlohe noted resignedly in his diary: 'It [the bill] will be turned down anyway in the Reichstag and perhaps also in the Bundesrat. That's possible. It would have been better to strike out Paragraph 270/2. But it isn't a misfortune, and I couldn't squeeze everything [that I wanted] out anyway.'[91]

Efforts continued to persuade Wilhelm to erase the offending paragraph,[92] but he remained firm. Gossler and Hohenlohe introduced the bill to the Reichstag on 16 December 1897.[93] To everyone's great surprise, the Reichstag had fewer qualms about Paragraph 270/2 than did the government. The debate on Paragraph 270/2 took place on 19 March 1898 before an empty, jaded parliament. Only two members spoke, both briefly, both opposed.[94] A Social Democratic motion to strike out the clauses was voted down, and Paragraph 270/1 and /2 was passed without further comment. The entire MStGO passed on 4 May 1898 by a vote of 177 to 83.[95]

Wilhelm's battle was not yet over, however. The Bavarians were reluctant to accede to a code less liberal than the one they had lived with for close to thirty years. When the MStGO was first introduced into the Bundesrat in 1896, Bavaria demanded to retain (according to its reserve rights) the separate Bavarian military courts. Wilhelm was furious over this intransigence. Eulenburg, for his part, wanted to use the issue as an excuse to drop the MStGO and to blame its demise on the south Germans. Both Wilhelm and Lucanus favored this plan briefly, the latter doubtless in order to please Wilhelm.[96] Military Cabinet Chief Hahnke, however, appears to have realized that the military was badly in need of a new law, and, so long as he was confident of controlling its provisions, he favored bringing it through the legislature and into practice. Hahnke was well aware of his strength with Wilhelm and this allowed him to play a conciliatory role at various points during the crisis. It was Hahnke (with the assistance of Lucanus) who engineered the technicality that allowed Wilhelm and Hohenlohe to come together in October 1897. The chief of the Military Cabinet combined the question of separate Bavarian courts and several other knotty details under the heading 'Execution Regulations' (*Ausführungsbestimmungen*). These did not need to be voted on, but were reserved for further negotiations between the Reich government and the Bavarians.

The Bundesrat approved the MStGO in early June 1898 with Baden and Bavaria dissenting, and the bill went into effect on 1 October 1900. But the wrangling over the *Ausführungsbestimmungen* continued for some years. Bavaria had numerous small objections, which were gradually compromised into non-existence.[97] Three large disagreements, however, remained: (1) whether Bavaria would continue to have separate courts; (2) whether Bavaria's addition to Paragraph 264 (that the day before a trial an announcement was to appear on the outside of the court building) was acceptable to Prussia; and (3) whether Wilhelm was to retain his right of confirmation, annulment, pardon, and mitigation (*Milderung*). The first of these questions was settled by a genuine compromise: the Bavarians gave up their separate court, but were granted their own senate within the Reich Military Court and the right to have their lawyers represent the other south German states.[98] The matter of Paragraph 264 was particularly thorny because it guaranteed public knowledge of trials. Wilhelm, Gossler, and Hahnke remained steadfastly opposed, despite the legal opinion of Justice Secretary Nieberding that Bavaria was legally entitled to carry out the MStGO in this way.[99] Only in 1907, after Bülow had talked War Minister Einem[100] into agreement, did the chancellor pressure Military Cabinet Chief Hülsen to convince Wilhelm to accede to this small measure of openness.[101]

Wilhelm's position on the right of confirmation had been uncharacteristically consistent since 1895. Under a compromise of 1902, Wilhelm retained that right, which he regarded as a necessity, since, as he told Eulenburg, 'Justice was spoken in *his name* and consequently he was the first *judge* and could exercise influence on law and judgments.'[102] Fortunately the Bavarians now regarded this as a formality. In practice, Wilhelm delegated the right of confirmation to the military commander in charge of the case (the *Gerichtsherr*) if it involved enlisted men whose crimes were not serious, while the Emperor still reserved for himself the right of confirmation for all officers. The Bavarians also agreed that Wilhelm could reserve the right of annulment, in return for which they (and Saxony and Württemberg[103]) would have the right of pardon and mitigation so long as they practiced it 'with the agreement of His Majesty the Kaiser.'[104] The *i*s, in fact, were not dotted nor the *t*s crossed until 6 May 1908, over thirteen years after the MStGO had been proposed by Bronsart.

The MStGO of 1898 was an improvement over the Prussian Code of 1845. The public found it somewhat easier to learn of controversial cases, and therefore the officer corps had a harder time protecting its own.[105] But the MStGO was not the progressive victory that it has been supposed.[106] Public trials could still be prohibited at the whim of the Emperor. Even when the trials were public, they were closed to men below the rank of the accused (Paragraph 274). The investigations and trials were still initiated by the military commander, who was bound by law but whose powers were still wide enough to give him overweening influence on the proceedings and on the sentences. Wilhelm could annul or simply not confirm verdicts against officers, if he so pleased. In short, the military entourage had won an overwhelming victory. It had given up nothing. It had forced the fall of the war minister (Bronsart), the utter capitulation of the chancellor (Hohenlohe), and the defeat of that most tenacious and stubborn enemy, Bavaria. Most of all, it had frustrated public opinion with complete impunity, for the bill had enjoyed wide popularity. When, in 1896, a friend of Hohenlohe's took soundings throughout Germany and spoke to people 'of all classes,' he reported that virtually everyone was convinced that Hohenlohe could bring in a progressive MStGO because practically the entire nation favored it. Only the *Konservativen*, his respondents felt, would support something less than the Bavarian Code.[107]

The military entourage had managed all of this by setting the terms of debate. Since Wilhelm would not be moved, a minister who insisted on public trials would either be dismissed or would precipitate a major crisis, probably a coup d'état from above. The Hauptquartier made the stakes of the game so high that no one wanted to play, much less to call their hand. Thus the ministers were driven to offer amazing concessions. They knew, for instance, that the entourage hated

Secretary Marschall for beginning the Tausch trial,[108] which threatened to expose the links between various high-level members of the
Hauptquartier and Bismarckian spies in the police force. Hohenlohe
asked Holstein if the government could not intervene in the wheels
of justice to bring the trial to a halt before reputations were ruined in
return for a liberal MStGO.[109] More incredibly still, Hohenlohe, who
had excellent reasons for opposing a large German navy, offered to
abandon his scruples if Wilhelm would only give in.[110] Even Tirpitz,
representative of Wilhelm's most cherished dream, the German fleet,
was powerless against the *maison militaire*.[111]

In the MStGO affair, the Military Cabinet led the entourage in a
holding action against creeping liberalization. Once the MStGO was
in effect, however, the Military Cabinet leaped to use it to expand
Wilhelm's command powers, as it had done successfully throughout
the latter part of the nineteenth century.[112] The chancellor, the imperial treasury minister, and the war minister agreed that the post of
president of the new Imperial Military Court was an imperial government position and therefore fell under the purview of the chancellor,
as did all the other imperial ministers. This meant that the president
would clear his budgets with the treasury minister and his appointments (Senate members and lawyers) with the chancellor. Military
Cabinet Chief Hahnke was enraged. '[A]ccording to the imperial military law, the president of the Imperial Military Court, together with
his court, occupy an *Immediatstellung* [i.e. were directly accountable to
the Kaiser]; besides, their subordination under the chancellor is not
indicated by anything [*durch Nichts geboten*].' He made the convo-
luted argument that only in its administrative duties was the court
under the chancellor; in all of its military duties, that is, in the majority of its dealings, it was under Wilhelm. Hahnke made his reasons as
clear as possible. 'It would mean a substantial retrogression for the
essence of the army, if the influence of the chancellor would insert
itself into the command rights and orders of the Kaiser.'[113] Gossler,
whom Wilhelm had appointed because he was tractable, immediately
came round to Hahnke's point of view.[114] Despite the fact that
Hahnke's argument was not legal and would have demanded, as
Richthofen in the Foreign Office put it, the creation of two chancellors, one civilian and one military,[115] Gossler's letter seems to have
had the last word. Thus the extension of ministerial government was
once again frustrated.

The MStGO became law, and the entourage demonstrated that,
under stubborn leadership and on issues which touched it directly, it

could wield power sufficient to fell ministers and chancellors, and to frustrate Federal states and public opinion.

The second most striking instance of political intervention by the military entourage concerned Wilhelm's relationship to Otto von Bismarck after his fall. The officer corps had, in general, not been pleased by Bismarck's abrupt dismissal. Bismarck and Moltke were the two chief gods of the officers' pantheon, and most were distinctly ill at ease when, in 1890, the guiding hand of the past thirty years was suddenly removed by the young, inexperienced, and unpredictable Kaiser. The officers who were closest to Waldersee[116] were privy to Waldersee's lurid descriptions of how the government was being paralyzed by the drawn-out struggle between the Kaiser and his chancellor. They therefore reacted with relief that the crisis was over.[117] But their relief did not prepare them for the men or the policies of the New Course that followed.

Pressure for imperial reconciliation with the Bismarcks[118] came from many different people for different reasons. The first person close to the entourage to advocate reconciliation was Waldersee. Waldersee's motives were, as usual, a mixture of the political and the personal. In that most important domestic issue, the so-called social question, not much had ever separated Waldersee from Bismarck: both opposed concessions to the working class, even at the risk of civil war. Waldersee had also, in the meantime, changed his mind on the foreign issues which had once divided him from the old chancellor. Waldersee now opposed an exclusively Austrian alliance and instead favored an understanding with the Russians.[119] In addition to these political views, the two exiles shared the desire to regain the power which had once been theirs and to punish the men of the New Course, such as Chancellor Caprivi and Foreign Office Secretary Marschall, who had ousted them. Barely six months after Waldersee's own fall, he inaugurated the campaign to rehabilitate the Bismarcks.[120]

Few members of the entourage had quite as much to gain personally from a Bismarckian resurgence as Waldersee thought he had. They supported Bismarck because he was the clear political antithesis to Caprivi, Marschall, and their too liberal policies, especially the trade treaties, which ignored Junker agrarian interests and which were incompatible with a tough stand against the Social Democrats. Deines, for instance, complained bitterly to his father that Caprivi showed no understanding for the agrarian emergency, but received his advice from a free-trade theorist. 'If the Reichstag should be dissolved,' he wrote, 'I hope that so many representatives from the *Bund der Land-wirte* and so many anti-Semites (not as eccentric as Ahlwardt) are elected, that an entirely new party-grouping occurs, and that the Russian trade treaties are defeated.'[121] Despite his reservations about Bismarck, Deines therefore warmly supported reconciliation.[122]

Three of the most outspoken men of the military entourage, Gustav von Kessel (FAD), Adolf von Wittich (Commandant of the Hauptquartier) and Carl von Wedel (FAD in the process of transferring to the diplomatic service) all had joined Waldersee by December 1891, when they urged Wilhelm to visit Bismarck in Friedrichsruh.[123] Eulenburg, at Holstein's exhortation,[124] explained to Wilhelm the political reasons behind the agitation.

The efforts to bring Your Majesty into closer touch with Prince Bismarck . . . grow with the strengthening of Caprivi's position.

Your Majesty can regard these efforts surely more as a symptom of this, than as a symptom of growing dissatisfaction in the Reich. The last two speeches of the chancellor [Caprivi] and the trade treaties have called forth astonishment at his importance. Reestablishment of relations with Bismarck by Your Majesty at this moment would destroy the desirable accomplishments of Caprivi and would bring about either an inadequate substitute for him or the [reestablishment of the] Bismarckian system.[125]

Adjutant Kessel and his fellow agitators sharpened their plans by the following April. They proposed to Wilhelm that reconciliation be achieved by replacing Marschall, who was directing the negotiations for the trade treaties, with Bernhard von Bülow, whom they considered better disposed to the agrarian viewpoint. Herbert von Bismarck would receive a major embassy. These changes would, of course, force Caprivi's resignation. The way would then be free for Waldersee to step in.[126] These plans, particularly the elevation of Bülow, preceded by one year similar plans by Eulenburg. One wonders if Eulenburg's own schemes were influenced by this earlier intrigue.[127] Waldersee pleaded his own cause again in June 1892 when he asked Wilhelm if the Kaiser would accept reconciliation if Bismarck made the first move.[128] The intrigues continued into July 1892 and, not having met with success, subsided to a persistent murmur during the following year and a half.

Meanwhile, more and more members of the entourage joined the battle as their personal networks were mobilized. Kessel was related to the Bismarcks (his mother was a von Mencken) and was personally close to Herbert von Bismarck.[129] Kessel was also more conservative than the men of the New Course and a *Draufgänger*, like Waldersee. Therefore his politics and his personal relationships not surprisingly

led him to the Bismarck camp. Kessel may have played a role in persuading Wittich and Wedel, who were friends, to join the ranks, for
neither of those two men was close to Waldersee or would have been
likely to follow him.[130]

Waldersee's network was even more far-reaching than Kessel's.
Dietrich Hülsen was a staunch admirer of his.[131] So was Adjutant
Lippe, who was Hahnke's right-hand man in the Military Cabinet.
Lippe hoped Waldersee would become chancellor expressly so that
Waldersee could end the rule of the civilians Holstein, Kiderlen, Paul
Kayser, and Eulenburg.[132] Plessen, who replaced Wittich as Commandant of the Hauptquartier in August 1892, was also in Waldersee's
camp, though he was more circumspect in his admiration for Waldersee than the general would have liked.[133] Plessen had ties of his own
to Herbert von Bismarck, which the latter used to convey 'information' to Plessen now and again.[134] Helmuth von Moltke, too, was well-
disposed toward Waldersee but, like Plessen, was careful not to expose
himself too openly.[135]

One of Waldersee's most valuable allies was August Eulenburg. The
Hofmarschall was strongly agrarian in sympathy, though he was more
clever and therefore more subtle politically than many others of similar persuasion, including Waldersee. August Eulenburg had nonetheless tried to prevent Waldersee's fall[136] and had continued to prize
the general as an asset against what he feared would be the future
revolution. In early 1894 August Eulenburg seems to have suffered
an uncharacteristic attack of impatience, which caused him to over-
play his hand. He invited Herbert von Bismarck to the annual Order
of the Black Eagle Investiture (21 January 1894), without Wilhelm's
knowledge, and then had two attendants try to present Herbert Bismarck to the Kaiser. Wilhelm was incensed and refused to speak to
him. The Bismarcks naturally assumed that Wilhelm had designed
the evening in order to humiliate them.[137] Reconciliation seemed farther off than at any time since 1890.[138]

The very next day, however, the impasse was surprisingly broken.
The constant efforts of the entourage at last showed some effect. The
breakthrough occurred through the unlikely agency of FA Kuno von
Moltke, Philipp Eulenburg's protégé.[139] A more politically naïve officer is difficult to imagine. Unlike many of his co-conspirators, whose
motives were highly political, Moltke was moved by a romantic,
muddle-headed attachment to the heroic figure of the Founder of the
German Empire.[140] Heedless of the political consequences, Moltke
joined August Eulenburg in the feverish plans to persuade the

Emperor. On 22 January 1894 they succeeded. Wilhelm sent Moltke to Bismarck's residence, Friedrichsruh, along with two bottles of wine and protestations of friendship. Marschall and Caprivi learned of the visit only after it had happened. They quickly moved to publish an official article which would make it seem that Wilhelm had acted with the approval of his responsible ministers. Wilhelm at first agreed to this and then retracted his agreement, after having spoken with Moltke, who felt that such a move would hurt Bismarck's feelings. Only after a long session with Marschall, at which Moltke was also present, did Wilhelm once more give his consent to the ministers' request.[141]

Four days later, Otto von Bismarck arrived in Berlin to return Moltke's visit. Much to everyone's relief, the afternoon passed amicably. Neither the Kaiser nor Bismarck discussed politics.[142] The 'reconciliation' had taken place. Although it damaged the political positions of Marschall and Caprivi, it did not create immediate political changes or reestablish the power of Bismarck, as many in the entourage had wished.

Why was the entourage, after three years of nearly unanimous effort, unable to accomplish its end more quickly and more completely? The answers describe clearly some of the limits to the influence and power of the entourage. The major reason is that in the Bismarck case, Wilhelm had a fully formed view, which differed completely from that of his entourage. His prejudices worked against their own. Wilhelm felt personally betrayed and mishandled by both Otto and Herbert von Bismarck. The drawn-out struggle between the Kaiser and the chancellor had eroded the awe and sympathy that Wilhelm had felt for the old man. Bismarck's vindictive activities in the press after his dismissal further enraged Wilhelm. Allegations in the 'Bismarckian Press'[143] impugned Wilhelm's honor, the Kaiser felt, and therefore Otto von Bismarck owed him an apology. It was understandable then that Wilhelm had little inclination to heed the whisperings around him. Even when he finally did so, Wilhelm's acquiescence was purely tactical.[144] When in 1896 the Bismarckian organ, the *Hamburger Nachrichten,* leaked the news of the non-renewal of the Reinsurance Treaty, Wilhelm was immediately ready to imprison Herbert and if necessary Otto von Bismarck for their misdeeds.[145]

The second reason that the entourage was not more successful was that its 'enemies,' Caprivi, Marschall, Holstein, and other civilian leaders, possessed parliamentary strength, internal cohesiveness, and an active conduit to Wilhelm through Philipp Eulenburg. Whenever the intrigues flared up, Holstein would contact Eulenburg, who would cleverly illuminate the pitfalls for Wilhelm and, thus, prevent him from falling into them.[146] Eulenburg, however, did not agree with Holstein that reconciliation would be an unmitigated disaster. In fact, he thought that it would be beneficial, so long as Wilhelm did not take Bismarck as an adviser.[147] By the beginning of 1894, Eulenburg was ready to begin jettisoning the men and policies of the New Course. He warned Wilhelm to go slowly, to make no hasty concessions which might harm the Emperor's position.[148] But Eulenburg made no secret of his basic approval of the Emperor's step,[149] which, he believed, would hasten the advent of personal regime. After the January 1894 meeting, Eulenburg continued to advise caution concerning the Bismarcks, not the least because he knew that, should either Otto or Herbert von Bismarck return to power, Eulenburg would be banished from power in the same breath with Caprivi, Marschall, Holstein, and Interior Secretary and Vice Chancellor Bötticher.[150] Eulenburg's caution, however, was probably unnecessary, given the depths of Wilhelm's continued animosity toward the old chancellor.

The final factor which slowed the fruition of the entourage's schemes to effect reconciliation and undermine the New Course was Waldersee. Waldersee's conversion to the Bismarck cause helped win it numerous converts within the Hauptquartier. However, Wilhelm was not appreciably better disposed toward Waldersee than he was toward Bismarck. Ever since Waldersee had stung Wilhelm with his criticism of the *Kaisermanöver,* he had made himself 'impossible' at Court. Hohenlohe noted in 1892 that Wilhelm was only too well aware of what Waldersee stood to gain should Bismarck return to power. Wilhelm recognized that Waldersee was an unscrupulous intriguer, and, Hohenlohe thought, Wilhelm had learned to handle the slippery general quite well.[151] Waldersee's open identification with the Bismarcks did them at least as much harm as it did good.

Even though the reconciliation had no spectacular after-effects, it did help shift power relations at the top in the direction that the military entourage wanted. Because everyone knew the first step had occurred without Caprivi's knowledge, it further marked the decline of his prestige. Holstein was so worried that he asked Philipp Eulenburg to recommend that Wilhelm give Caprivi a medal as a counterweight.[152] Marschall was even more seriously hurt, because his attitude toward reconciliation and his comportment during the affair angered Wilhelm. Since Marschall was one of the main targets of the intrigue, the FAs missed no opportunity to remind Wilhelm of

Marschall's putative misdeeds in January 1894 when he had clashed with them.[153] Marschall never recovered his position. He was thereafter *persona non grata* with Wilhelm[154] and therefore all the easier to dispose of when the time came. Finally, the reconciliation encouraged Wilhelm to exercise personal regime. Almost immediately, Wilhelm claimed that the coup had been entirely his own idea.[155] He was childishly proud that it had been accomplished ' "without the Wilhelmstrasse," which would hopefully be profoundly angry' because of it.[156] Furthermore, Bismarck's visit had been such a popular success that Wilhelm would only be tempted to try something similar in future.

The early and middle Bülow years, 1897–1905, were the halcyon days of Emperor Wilhelm II's reign. Philipp Eulenburg had made Bülow chancellor in order to inaugurate 'personal rule in the good sense.'[157] Eulenburg entrusted to Bülow the task of translating Wilhelm's wishes into politically manageable tactics, a job of which Wilhelm himself was incapable and for which Eulenburg was too tired. Despite Wilhelm's inconsistency, his basic political desires are not difficult to discern. They were: (1) to uphold the dignity, power, and repute of the Prusso-German monarchy, and (2) to make Germany the most powerful, most respected nation in the world. The first desire had several corollaries: the sanctity and isolation of the army had to be safeguarded and the chief force which threatened the monarchical status quo, namely Social Democracy, had to be suppressed. The second desire, *Weltgeltung,* had at least three parts: the construction of a navy to rival Britain's, the extension of German acquisitions and influence wherever possible (it did not matter where), and the recognition of Germany's greatness by the other major powers, particularly by Great Britain.

Bülow largely fulfilled Eulenburg's and Wilhelm's hopes. He reversed the policies of the New Course: the tariffs were raised and social legislation slowed virtually to a stop. The final outcome of the MStGO conflict protected the army's interests. Bülow confronted Social Democracy with ever-changing combinations of *Sammlungspolitik.* Most important of all, Bülow allowed Wilhelm and Tirpitz to launch *Weltpolitik* via the German navy. The navy was not only the symbol of Wilhelminian strivings, but also the means by which Germany would unseat Great Britain on the throne of world power. The prestige and economic benefits thus acquired were desirable in themselves, but they also had the incalculable advantage of bolstering the monarchical institutions even more firmly against the modern tide.

Bülow was able to do all of these things because he combined great tactical political astuteness with an unparalleled personal relationship to the Kaiser. He was the first and last chancellor intimate enough with Wilhelm to prevent him from disruptive interventions in policy. Bülow was not the only high political figure in these years whose influence rested overwhelmingly on Wilhelm's affectionate trust. Chief of Staff Helmuth Moltke and Military Cabinet Chief Dietrich Hülsen were the other two direct heirs of Eulenburg's work. For Eulenburg had discovered the secret of the Kaiser's complex character. And long years of close political work with Eulenburg had predisposed Wilhelm to try to recreate the pattern of that relationship with other advisers. Hence, Bülow, Hülsen, and Moltke were the oddly shaped pegs who fitted perfectly into the hole that Eulenburg had carved.

Bernhard von Bülow's conservative policy vis-à-vis agriculture and the army stilled the intrigues which had unsettled German high politics since 1890.[158] The hopes nurtured by *Weltpolitik* blossomed into a smug optimism. The military entourage was satisfied and therefore quiescent, because the political leadership was pulling in the direction in which the military wished to go. Chief of the Naval Cabinet Senden-Bibran had been troublesome to earlier chancellors because he pushed unceasingly for a large navy.[159] Once Tirpitz began to build Senden-Bibran's dream fleet, Senden devoted his activity wholly to this end.[160] Bülow's only trouble with Senden-Bibran came from the admiral's occasional anti-English outbursts.[161] The army contingent in the entourage was equally satisfied in this period, though for different reasons. The army leadership, having successfully safeguarded its inviolability in the MStGO conflict, was involved in another holding action during these years. In order to prevent the influx of bourgeois, putatively 'unreliable' officers, the army was not expanded in size,[162] and thus, unlike the navy, the army's needs were satisfied by the status quo.

The key army position continued to be chief of the Military Cabinet. Dietrich Hülsen-Häseler replaced the ailing Hahnke on 5 May 1901. Hülsen had been Wilhelm's FAD from 1890 through 1894, when he became military attaché to Vienna. His tenure there was cut short, probably by Philipp Eulenburg,[163] and he returned to a FA position until 1900, when he advanced to general *à la suite*. His relationship to Wilhelm was excellent: the Kaiser considered him a friend.[164] But he differed from the other adviser-friends like Eulenburg, Bülow, or Moltke who all echoed Wilhelm's soft side. Hülsen belonged instead to the 'manly,' aggressive end of the FA spectrum. About six and one-half feet tall, Hülsen's command presence was strengthened by his irrepressible Berlin wit, which, however, those who were the butts of his jokes were apt to find coarse and quite unfunny.[165] Of all the chiefs of Cabinet from 1888 to 1918, Hülsen was the most outspoken. Lerchenfeld, who was chary with compliments, called Hülsen 'the best man in [Wilhelm's] entourage,' because he always spoke his mind.[166] The discerning Austro-Hungarian military attaché Klepsch-Kloth agreed that Hülsen had filled his position 'excellently.'[167] Even Eulenburg, who hated Hülsen fiercely, had to admit that he possessed a 'sharp, sober intelligence [*Verstand*].'[168] Hülsen got away with such frankness because he could couch his criticisms in jokes which Wilhelm appreciated. It was thought that Hülsen dared to risk imperial censure because, unlike Hahnke who needed his position at Court for lack of personal funds, Hülsen 'had married money' and could easily have left the Court if necessary.[169] Hülsen's tenure was eased by four additional factors. First, he was in agreement with Wilhelm on most issues.[170] Second, he had excellent contacts with Germany's major ally, Austria-Hungary.[171] Third, he inherited from Hahnke a Military Cabinet substantially strengthened vis-à-vis competing institutions within the army.[172] And finally, Hülsen's main enemies in the army consisted of those who favored 'more intensive democratization of the officer corps.'[173] Hülsen was thus a staunch conservative, even by army standards. His purpose was to protect the army's position in society, not to upset it by expansion or by unnecessary meddling.[174] It is not surprising, then, that Bülow considered Dietrich Hülsen-Häseler one of his major 'supports.'[175]

Even Hülsen, whose relationship to both Kaiser and chancellor could hardly have been better, had definite limits on his influence over Wilhelm. The major power of the chief of the Military Cabinet lay in personnel. The most important post which he helped to fill was of course chief of the General Staff. It was precisely concerning this post in 1905 that Wilhelm overrode Hülsen. Chief of Staff General Alfred Count von Schlieffen was seventy-four in 1905. It was feared that a man of his age would not be able to withstand the pressure should a war break out. Wilhelm for some time had been thinking of appointing his close friend, Helmuth von Moltke, to the post. The general feeling in the army was that Moltke was a poor choice.[176] War Minister Einem listed five reasons for these feelings: (1) Moltke was not a hard worker; (2) he had been at Court and therefore away from tactical problems for too long; (3) while he was intelligent, Moltke lacked self-confidence and leadership ability; (4) he was lethargic, and (5) he had a tendency to become bogged down in detail.[177] Hülsen-Haeseler, who was well acquainted with Moltke, quite agreed and added a sixth reservation: 'above everything else, he is a religious phantast, [who] believes in guardian angels, faith-healing, and such nonsense.'[178] As if this were not enough, Moltke himself realized his own limitations and desperately tried to get Wilhelm to change his mind. Moltke approached Bülow and importuned the chancellor to intercede on his behalf. Bülow did so, although not very forcefully, because 'I had made it a rule not to mix in military affairs, particularly in personnel matters.'[179] Moltke even went to Eulenburg, who advised him to refuse Wilhelm. If Wilhelm insisted, then Moltke should set a condition that Eulenburg probably thought would be unacceptable, namely, that Wilhelm cease interfering in the *Kaisermanöver,* which he had been 'leading' and 'winning' for years.[180] To everyone's great surprise, Wilhelm acceded to Moltke's condition and even kept his word.[181] Hülsen threatened to resign over Moltke's appointment, but Wilhelm would not allow it.[182] Thus in January 1906, Helmuth von Moltke became chief of the General Staff.

Why did Wilhelm proceed against the objections of everyone, including the candidate himself? Moltke was, first of all, a close friend of Wilhelm's, someone with whom Wilhelm felt at ease. Wilhelm had objections of one sort or another to all the other possibilities, but these objections boiled down to comfort: the candidates made Wilhelm uneasy, or else he simply did not know them personally and could not tell if they would be *sympathisch* or not.[183] In this case Wilhelm's fear of the unfamiliar was encouraged by Plessen, who championed Moltke precisely because another candidate would have forced Wilhelm to 'accustom himself to new circumstances,' which, Plessen knew, Wilhelm hated to do.[184] In other words, Plessen picked a chief of staff whom he must have known would be incompetent strictly in order to make Wilhelm's life comfortable. Wilhelm's insistence on Moltke also proved the rule that the Kaiser was likely to be more stubborn in army personnel matters because appointments were made under his 'Command Power,' which he prided himself upon exercising alone.[185] Finally, Bernhard Bülow did not sufficiently support Hülsen's complaints against Moltke. As usual, Bülow took the road of least resistance and allowed Wilhelm full rein in the military sphere. The consequences of these failures to block Moltke's appointment will be examined in the following chapter.

The four examples which we have just examined of political intervention by the military entourage indicate both the range and the limits of its power and influence. The case of the military attachés is interesting primarily because it shows the fear with which the civilian architects of policy regarded the military, but also the extent to which a strong chancellor and alert civilian diplomats could curb military influence. The other three examples define the possible spectrum of military activity from total victory over all comers in the MStGO, through partial, or insubstantial victory over the Kaiser and his ministers in the Bismarckian reconciliation, to total defeat at the Kaiser's hands in Helmuth Moltke's appointment as chief of the General Staff.

There were several reasons for the complete victory of the military entourage in the struggle over the MStGO. First, the reform bill was a highly technical matter, the unravelling of which the impatient Kaiser gladly left to his Military Cabinet chief. This abdication of responsibility vastly strengthened Hahnke's hand because it made him sole interpreter of the matter. Second, Hahnke represented the MStGO as a purely military question of imperial command power, which Wilhelm and the rest of the military men regarded as the foundation of monarchical strength. Appealing to Wilhelm's command power made it all the easier for Hahnke to make the defeat of the MStGO reform a matter of 'honor.' It was then difficult for the Kaiser to be less emphatic, therefore less honorable, in defense of his command power than was Hahnke. The fact that the military entourage was unanimous in its support of Hahnke's position redoubled the *Zwangslage* [position of constraint] in which the Kaiser found himself. Military men who were not at Court and who supported the war minister were beaten into line by threats from Hahnke, who controlled their future careers. Finally, the civilian proponents of the MStGO were relatively crippled by three factors. The chancellor was too weak to present the civilian side forcefully enough to overcome the momentum churned up by the ubiquitous military entourage. The chancellor's younger, more energetic ministers (Marschall and Bötticher) had used up their political capital in fighting for the New Course. The only response that they were capable of eliciting from Wilhelm was distaste. And the strongest civilian voice in government, Philipp Eulenburg, cooperated fully with the military men against War Minister Bronsart and his civilian supporters, in order to topple them in favor of the more tractable Bernhard Bülow.

In the case of Wilhelm's reconciliation with Bismarck, the military entourage was once again more extreme than the Kaiser. But this time the Emperor had a decided opinion on the subject. Moreover, he did not need to study *Akten* to arrive at his opinion, since the matter was strictly personal. In addition, the civilian opponents of the military entourage, Caprivi and Marschall, had not yet irrevocably damaged their relationship with the Kaiser and were further strengthened by their excellent political standing with the Reichstag. Philipp Eulenburg was on their side too, and saw to it that Wilhelm heard their viewpoints at strategic moments.

In 1905, with Moltke's appointment as chief of staff, Wilhelm ran roughshod over both his military and his civilian advisers. Again, Wilhelm knew exactly what he wanted. Again, the reasons for his opinions were emotional and personal and therefore not amenable to objective arguments. And, finally, Wilhelm again regarded his command power as at stake, since personnel appointments fell under that rubric. Cabinet Chief Hülsen's hand was further undermined on both the civilian and military sides. Chancellor Bülow refused to second Hülsen adequately, pleading that Moltke's appointment was a strictly military matter. Commandant of the Hauptquartier Plessen sided with the Emperor in order to placate him. Military opinion thus seemed to be divided, and Wilhelm won.

All of these examples show that when the Kaiser had a definite viewpoint, and/or the civilian leadership possessed good relations with the Emperor and recognized political authority in the nation, the military entourage was considerably less likely to play a powerful political role. However, when this constellation was weakened in any way the star of the military entourage would surely rise. If Wilhelm was unsure of himself, or if his own views seemed to him to be less forceful, manly, or properly military than those of his military advisers, or if the civilian leadership was hesitant or even unvigilant, then the military entourage would take up the slack. This was even more true when the issue at hand could be construed as a purely military matter, especially if it seemed to touch the Kaiser's power of command. In that case, it became an existential question which demanded of the Emperor a tough stand compatible with his soldier's honor. Once Wilhelm's military advisers had been able to construe an issue in this manner, civilian advice was in vain.

9

The military entourage and the 'preventive war'

In 1905/06, the aura of peace and prosperity which had graced Wilhelm's reign was suddenly dashed. The great hopes of world power, of economic expansion and of conservative, domestic stability were replaced by greater fears. The Moroccan Crisis, which Germany had engineered in order to break up the newly formed *entente cordiale,* ended in a chilling demonstration of Germany's diplomatic isolation. When Britain launched the first *Dreadnought* on 10 February 1906, the perspicacious realized that Germany's challenge to English naval and world political superiority had been met. No longer could the German leaders dream of quietly overtaking the British on the seas and in the market place. Britain had found friends among foreign nations. It would build more ships. If Germany wished to displace Britain, Germany would have to pay an enormous price, a price which might very well include war. Domestic politics offered no respite from this gloomy picture. 1905 found Germany embroiled in the worst labor unrest since the beginning of Wilhelm's reign.[1] The possible culmination of such working-class dissatisfaction was all too obvious as Europe watched the revolution unfold in Russia. The government received no help from the Conservatives, who adamantly refused to make any concessions designed to ease Germany's strained finances, high food prices, or tense parliament. The domestic sphere, in short, was mired in stagnation. Germany's *Weltpolitik* had been partly designed to relieve internal frustration. That is, economic expansion and world prestige would maintain the domestic status quo against the pent-up demands for change. After 1905/06, therefore, this escape valve appeared increasingly blocked.

The resulting dilemma, the inability either to accommodate reform internally or to buy it off by foreign distractions, produced frustration, tension, fear, and a widespread crisis of leadership.[2] The important point regarding the military entourage is that it was precisely during this time of troubles that the military swung into its ascendancy vis-à-vis the civilian leadership. It is not surprising that the military should have made a resurgence when war again became a major policy alternative. The enormous popular prestige of the army, its complete independence from civilian control, and its close connection with the Emperor all made this development not in the least unexpected. Domestic stalemate and military dominance formed the background for the decision to go to war.

Twenty years have passed since the Fischer controversy broke upon German historiography.[3] Few people would now contest the primary responsibility which Germany bears for the outbreak of war in 1914. Fewer still would deny the central role that the German military establishment played in that process. Nonetheless, the decision that the imperial political leadership took in July 1914 was neither clear nor straightforward. Its complexity and self-contradiction have helped to make it the most controversial subject in German historiography. It was also the most fateful step that the entourage determined, for Germany, for the monarchy, and for itself. The handful of men at the apex of power embarked upon this ruinous course because of constraits, self-imposed but unintended, which drastically narrowed the field of policy choices. The following pages examine the process of narrowing.

We begin with the structure of the prewar entourage, specifically with the effects of Wilhelm's preference for accepting political advice from men who were his closest friends. This predilection could work in the interests of civilian policy. For friendship was the only stepping stone large enough to boost a mere civilian to the height of one of Wilhelm's military companions. For this reason, Bülow and Eulenburg were the only two civilians who could count upon influencing Wilhelm in an anti-military way if they chose. Both Eulenburg and Bülow in 1905/6[4] and Bülow in 1908/9 advocated peace against the war party. However, any possible pacific influence Eulenburg might have had ended in 1907 with his disgrace. Bülow's own power over the Kaiser was abruptly broken by the *Daily Telegraph* Affair of November 1908. Wilhelm felt that Bülow had betrayed him, and the Kaiser's former trust became undying hatred. With Bülow's dismissal in July 1909, Wilhelm was therefore left in the hands of his military friends. Though Bülow's successor, Bethmann Hollweg, earned Wilhelm's respect, the two were never close, nor did Bethmann ever learn how to 'handle' the Kaiser as Bernhard von Bülow had done.

Bethmann was a thoroughly scrupulous and honorable bureaucrat, who spent his chancellorship torn between the Conservatives, the 'natural' base of the monarchy, and more progressive elements, whose ideas, he realized, were much closer to what the modern age demanded. On the foreign front, he tried to block the military entourage's push for a preventive war. Once the war had begun, his moderation was quickly outstripped by those who pressed for even larger annexationist schemes than he favored and who advocated unrestricted submarine warfare, while they refused the call for internal political reform. Bethmann's honesty and intelligence, plus his obvious superiority to his predecessor and successor, have inclined historians to exaggerate his progressiveness in all these areas. Nonetheless, he remains an attractive, if unsuccessful, figure. The Kaiser appreciated Bethmann, too, although he found the chancellor's pessimism and reticence somewhat disturbing. It was not until the war that Wilhelm identified himself closely with his careful chancellor.[5]

Bethmann, however, was not the man to capitalize upon the opportunities that Wilhelm's character offered to him after the Kaiser's nervous collapse in November 1908 at Dietrich Hülsen-Haeseler's sudden death.[6] Wilhelm had always gone to great lengths to disguise his shaky self-confidence. During the winter of 1908/9 he briefly gave up these attempts at deception. As the shock wave slowly receded, Wilhelm returned somewhat to his earlier ways.[7] His sense of self had, however, been permanently damaged. This had two paradoxical effects. On the one hand, it increased his attempts to hide his weakness behind bellicose posturing and marginalia. So anxious was Wilhelm to prove his manly determination when the time came that on 6 July 1914, for example, in a conversation with Krupp von Bohlen und Halbach, he repeated three times that 'this time I shall not chicken out [*diesmal falle ich nicht um*].'[8] Krupp was 'embarrassed' by this display, presumably because he saw through it, as did most of the high members of government. The real effect of Wilhelm's breakdown, however, was to scare him away from taking the awesome step to a world war, which neither Wilhelm's nerves nor his sense of responsibility could stand. Wilhelm's tergiversations on this question will be followed below, but generally the remarks of Ambassador Tschirschky to the chief of the Austrian General Staff, Franz Graf Conrad von Hötzendorf, on 16 March 1914 sum up Wilhem's position. To Conrad's question whether a preventive war should not be started soon, Tschirschky replied, 'two important people hinder it, your Archduke Franz Ferdinand and my Kaiser.'[9]

If Wilhelm's nervousness basically worked to Bethmann's advan-

7 Helmuth von Moltke the younger (left) and Wilhelm von Dommes

tage, Chief of Staff Helmuth Moltke worked assiduously to develop the other side of the paradox, Wilhelm's blustering bellicosity. Moltke is the villain of Fritz Fischer's second book, *War of Illusions*,[10] and of Adolf Gasser's article, 'Deutschlands Entschluss zum Präventivkrieg 1913/14.'[11] He also emerges as the most powerful and consistent warlike force in the best contemporary account that we possess of the immediate prewar years, the diaries of Naval Cabinet Chief Admiral von Müller.[12] Moltke's overweening influence gives an X-ray picture of the way that Wilhelm's personality and the structure of his entourage interacted in those years.

Moltke was one of the last persons one would have expected to become either the most influential man in the army or the chief warmonger. Owing to the assiduous efforts at censorship of the Moltke family and the Foreign Office, the historical picture of the general must be pieced together from scraps.[13] Even so, its outlines are unmistakable. Moltke was on the 'soft' side of Wilhelm's spectrum. He was a quiet dreamer, earnest, intelligent, and reflective.[14] He lacked the military bombast of a Kessel or a Hülsen. Many of the passages in Moltke's letters to his wife recall the correspondence of Philipp

Eulenburg in their subject matter and their sensitivity to style. Moltke possessed a keen appreciation of the arts and of nature. Even while he pursued his military career, he devoted energy and concentration to artistic pleasures. He rented an atelier where he painted and practiced the 'cello. 'I . . . live entirely in the arts,' he wrote.[15] Moltke's involvement in spiritism was well-known and widely held against him.[16] In 1914 Admiral von Müller attributed Moltke's 'bloodthirstiness,' which Müller thought highly uncharacteristic, to Moltke's wife's spiritistic influences.[17] Moltke knew how many members of the entourage felt about such matters[18] and asked his wife to be more discreet about her beliefs.[19] As a condition for appointment to head the General Staff, Wilhelm demanded that Moltke himself refrain from spiritistic activities.[20] Moltke may have complied with this request. His diary and letters after his appointment contain only three references to the subject, two of which explain why he had had to distance himself somewhat from his wife's fervor.[21] However, Wilhelm's admonitions changed Moltke's mind as little as they did Eulenburg's on the same subject. Nor was Wilhelm entirely sincere in his rejection of spiritism. Moltke reports a long conversation he had with the Kaiser on 16 July 1911 about spiritual subjects. Moltke was impressed with the 'possibilities' that Wilhelm showed.[22] Indeed, Wilhelm's open-mindedness about spiritism was one of the ties which bound him to Moltke, just as it had to Eulenburg before him.

Moltke's other well-known and little-valued quality was his pessimism. Although many people thought that Moltke's spiritism and pessimism were connected (and hence if one could dispose of one, the other would follow), this does not appear to have been the case. Rudolf Steiner's philosophy is, in fact, more optimistic than the reverse.[23] Plessen indeed thought that Moltke's spiritistically inclined wife stiffened Moltke's resolve, rather than undermined it.[24] Moltke gloomily rejected his wife's prediction that a new 'spiritual era' was about to dawn: 'mankind must first go through much blood and suffering, before it reaches that far.'[25] Moltke knew that he inclined toward moody introspection, called himself a 'pessimist,'[26] and seems actually to have derived solace rather than despair from Steiner's teachings.[27]

Moltke's pessimistic world-view found expression much more in the fatalistic race theories of the day than in spiritism. Kuno Moltke (a close friend, though only a distant cousin to the General Staff chief) reported that Helmuth admired Paul de Lagarde, who, as Kuno summarized, 'proclaimed the fall of Germany.'[28] Helmuth Moltke was not uncritical of the works of Houston Stewart Chamberlain, but he none-theless basically agreed with them.[29] The idea that history was a car-ousel on which the various 'races' rose and fell in relationship to one another was not merely academic to the general. Moltke interpreted reality and planned policy according to this *Weltanschauung.* He wrote to Conrad in a famous letter of 10 February 1913.

> I am now as before of the opinion that in the long or the short run a Euro-pean war must come, in which it will basically be a war between Germandom and Slavdom. It is the duty of all states who are the banner carriers of Ger-man spiritual culture to join [this fight].[30]

But the fight might not be won, and ultimately one had to bow to the judgment of history. Thus, even though Moltke felt ashamed, he had to view the Japanese, 'these little yellow people,' with respect after they defeated Russia in 1904/5.[31]

Clearly, Moltke's racism was not the expression of exuberance. It did not come from a perception of Germany's burgeoning economic growth, nor a belief in the inevitable triumph of its latent power. Rac-ism based on such optimism existed in Germany at this time, but it was much more characteristic of the new, anti-establishment right-wing opposition and its bourgeois supporters than of their social bet-ters who actually held power. It is difficult to avoid concluding that Moltke's gloomy racism was simply the external corollary of his despairing view of Germany's internal strength and adaptability. We have already seen Moltke's black assessment of the *Kaiserreich's* instinct for survival.[32] He projected his sense of the decline of his class and its social order on to a larger whole, the 'race,' and presumed from it a general law of periodic decline.[33]

It was not merely in his racial theories that Moltke agreed with the politics of the entourage. He was disgusted by the 'idol-worship' of the Roman Catholics.[34] He wondered why all 'anarchists' were not simply locked up.[35] His vision of the future of Germany included huge continental expansion to provide for 'inner colonization' to undo some of the evil effects of industrialization and for complete economic independence from the rest of the world. Monopolies would con-tinue, although Moltke was politically astute enough to realize that some few concessions would have to be thrown to the Social Demo-crats.[36] Prior to the war, Bernhard von Bülow, that 'typical "Wilhel-minist," '[37] was Moltke's favorite chancellor as much as he was Wil-helm's or Eulenburg's. 'I like Bülow very much, ' he wrote in 1900, 'he is calm, clear, and determined.'[38] Even in 1909, Moltke still thought

Bülow was the best Germany had to offer.[39] Moltke never approved of Bethmann Hollweg, whose policies he found goalless, pacific, and unrealistic.[40]

Moltke's location in the entourage's political mainstream is shown again in his career as General Staff chief. As Schlieffen's successor, he inherited the 1905 version of the Schlieffen Plan, the sweeping western attack designed to annihilate France. After the failure at the Marne in 1914, some military men argued that Moltke had disagreed with Schlieffen's plan and had fatally 'watered it down.' Jehuda L. Wallach shows convincingly that this was not the case.[41] Moltke accepted the basic principles of the Schlieffen Plan and modified it only in order to bring it into conformity with changing circumstances.[42] While Gasser argues that Moltke gave in to the opinions of his fellow *Generalstäbler* on many points where he personally disagreed,[43] Wallach indicates that Moltke was more self-reliant.[44] Nonetheless, both agree, and Ritter concurs, that Moltke did not deviate from the basic military views current in the General Staff.

Moltke, then, was not an outstanding individual, either in personality or policy.[45] He represented faithfully most of the prejudices current in the immediately prewar entourage, but he lent them the added weight of technical military prestige and Wilhelm's friendship. For it was Moltke's relationship with Wilhelm that made him an important man. Indeed, Moltke was one of the few persons to whom the Emperor was always gracious.[46] In Wilhelm's eyes, Moltke possessed a number of Eulenburg's positive qualities, and the Kaiser tried once more to combine friendship with politics into the mix peculiar to personal regime. He may also have hoped that the magic name Moltke would secure a second victory like 1870/1, which would unite Germany once more.

In any case, Moltke was the last person in a position of responsibility during the *Kaiserreich* who was also Wilhelm's trusted friend and who therefore had access to the important lever of imperial affection. The tendency in appointments at Court and in the Cabinets after 1905 was toward earnest, sober bureaucrats. Few of these people were 'characters,' few were of the *burschikos* stamp, or were storytellers or artistic, few interested Wilhelm as people, and none became personally close to him. Between 1906 and 1908, all three Cabinet chiefs changed. Georg Alexander von Müller replaced Senden-Bibran as Naval Cabinet chief in April 1906. Rudolf von Valentini took over the Civil Cabinet in August 1908. Three months later, Moritz von Lyncker became Military Cabinet chief after Dietrich von Hülsen-Haeseler's sudden, unexpected death at Donaueschingen (14 November 1908). All three of these men served at their posts into the last year of the war.[47]

Of the three, Valentini would have been the most likely candidate as counterweight against Moltke.[48] Valentini's role in the internal balance of power before the war is not as clear as one would wish. Valentini's memoirs are blank for the years 1910 to 1918.[49] The excerpts from Valentini's diaries and other writings, which were collected by his friend Bernhard Schwertfeger and are in Schwertfeger's *Nachlass* in the Bundesarchiv (Koblenz), are too cursory to be revealing. Valentini's own *Nachlass* lies in the Zentrales Staatsarchiv (Merseburg) and therefore was inaccessible to this author.[50] Apparently, the *Nachlass* is not substantial and consists almost exclusively of Valentini's correspondence with Bülow and Bethmann.[51]

Valentini claimed in 1919 that he had known little about the foreign policy leading to war because his job was internal policy. Wilhelm, he wrote, 'never discussed questions of foreign policy with me.'[52] Valentini described in detail only one year of his tenure as chief of the Civil Cabinet, 1909. The events of that year bear out his professed isolation from decisions taken on external affairs. For example, although Valentini accompanied Wilhelm on the cruise to Björkö in June, Valentini knew nothing of the negotiations there between the Kaiser and the Czar, since both Wilhelm and the Foreign Office representative would not discuss it with him.[53] This did not prevent Valentini from having opinions, however. From his writings, it is clear that Valentini shared the racist preoccupations of his period.[54] He thought Germany's chief rival and enemy was Great Britain,[55] although he nevertheless opposed Tirpitz's naval plans, particularly the building of *Dreadnoughts*, because this provoked the English dangerously.[56] Anxiety about England, a sober, somewhat worried outlook on internal affairs, and a most critical assessment of Wilhelm's deficiencies as a ruler and as a human being[57] combined to put Valentini fully on the side of Bethmann Hollweg. To Valentini Bethmann was a relief from the lying, overly optimistic manipulations of Bülow.[58] Particularly during the war, Valentini fought tirelessly to preserve Bethmann's power against the encroachments of the military leaders.

Even before the war, Valentini appears to have been one of Bethmann's staunchest supporters (especially vis-à-vis the rabid military men),[59] but two factors lamed his effectiveness. The first was that flaw in the Bismarckian set-up, perpetuated by Wilhelm, which kept the various sectors of government rigidly separated one from another.

Although Valentini recognized that he was shut off from foreign and military affairs, he did nothing to overcome his isolation.[60] Even during the war, Valentini did not go on inspection trips to the front nor inform himself about military matters.[61] Instead of thus increasing his leverage, he continued to plead the seemingly one-sided civilian line, which the army could then override on technical grounds. Valentini's concept of duty required him to know everything in his own area and to refrain from all other comments.[62] Both the chancellor and the Foreign Office encouraged his reticence.[63]

Valentini's influence was also limited by his attitude toward Wilhelm and toward life at Court. 'Although the Kaiser was manifestly friendly toward me, I was never able to free myself enough from an overwhelmingly critical attitude toward his [Wilhelm's] personality and way of thinking.'[64] Valentini hated the demands of Court, which forced him to be dependent and silent,[65] monk-like and narrow.[66] Valentini had been trained in rational administration, not personal charm. He escaped from the courtier's style by retreating to the role of conscientious bureaucrat. To the rest of the entourage he seemed capable, but dull.[67]

An equally efficient bureaucrat was the chief of the Naval Cabinet, Georg Alexander von Müller.[68] Müller was the only important member of the military entourage of bourgeois origins. His father was a professor of agricultural chemistry, while his mother came from a church cantor's family.[69] Müller, however, married a colonel's daughter and joined the navy. There he rose quickly, through intelligence and hard work. After a stint in the statistical office of the Admiralty, Müller became naval attaché to Stockholm for a year (1885–6). His numerous sea commands thereafter were interrupted by service in the Admiralty and the Naval Cabinet. His real breakthrough seems to have come in 1896, when he was made personal adjutant to Wilhelm's brother, Heinrich, who was serving in East Asia. Prince Heinrich warmly recommended Müller to Senden-Bibran, then chief of the Naval Cabinet.[70] Senden took Müller back into the Cabinet in 1900 to groom him as Senden's own successor. To this end, Müller was ennobled that same year and then became first a FA and then a FAD, until he replaced Senden in 1906. Müller was appointed not only for his personal qualities, but also because he was expected to serve as a counterweight to Tirpitz, whom Wilhelm no longer trusted.[71]

As Georg von Müller advanced, he acquired some 'correct,' noble ballast to steady his course. Holger Herwig writes that Müller's responses to a visit he took in 1902 to the United States 'mirror[ed] all the social prejudices one would associate with the Prussian Junker.'[72] If this was true, it was anomalous, because Müller had a much more complicated view of society and politics than did most of his colleagues. These views came from three sources: Müller's bourgeois orientation, his branch of the service, and his bureaucratic duties as Naval Cabinet chief.

Müller had excellent connections to civilians active in the economic world. In 1915, Müller's daughter married Emil Georg von Stauss, a director of the Deutsche Bank. The brother of Müller's close friend and colleague, Admiral von Holtzendorff, was head of the German Oversea Service, Inc.[73] Throughout the war, Müller received this organization's 'Economic News Bulletin' [*Wirtschaftlicher Nachrichtendienst.*[74] Not infrequent guests at Müller's home were such persons as Arthur on Gwinner, also a director of the Deutsche Bank, Albert Ballin, head of the Hamburg–America Line, Gustav Krupp von Bohlen und Halbach, and State Secretary Karl Helfferich.[75] Müller thought Helfferich was 'by far the best brain in the Reich government.'[76]

Müller's interest in economics and his experience overseas propelled him into the imperialist ranks. 'World history is now dominated by the economic struggle,' he noted in 1896.[77] Like Max Weber, Müller concluded from this that Germany must either expand or decline. Remaining simply a continental power 'would admittedly bring the present nation comfortable days without serious conflicts and excitements, but as soon as our exports began noticeably to decline, the artificial economic edifice would start to crumble and existence therein would become very unpleasant indeed.'[78] Müller thus had a natural enthusiasm for *Weltpolitik* that Eulenburg, the agrarians, and many conventionally conservative army officers lacked. And the admiral was willing to risk 'serious conflicts and excitements' to achieve these goals. In this sense, Müller's bourgeois sympathies increased his potential to advocate a hardline foreign policy leading to war.

But these same bourgeois sympathies also undercut Müller's hardline potential and carried him far from the political mainstream of the military entourage. For Müller's Germany was a broad and variegated entity. He did not identify it or its future exclusively with the nobility or the military. So, for example, Müller insisted that education, including foreign languages, was a prerequisite for a good officer. He fought unceasingly in this direction against the Junker prejudice in favor of mere 'character.'[79] Similarly, he realized that political problems required political, not purely military, solutions. Müller's position, both before and during the war, was usually between the extreme militarists and the civilians.[80] He became increasingly drawn into politics, evidently against his will, because Chancellor Bethmann Hollweg and the civilians at the Foreign Office discovered that the admiral was the most sensible member of the military entourage. Müller gradually took over ' a mediator role, which became ever more difficult.'[81]

In short, Müller was considerably better integrated and in sympathy with leaders in non-military circles than most of his associates. This fact did not make him more popular. Quite the contrary. Müller was vilified at various times as a 'traitor' for not releasing the navy to fight during the war,[82] as a 'false' adviser to Wilhelm,[83] as a 'hypnotized' tool of Bethmann Hollweg,[84] as a pietist,[85] and as 'the greatest misfit' in the navy.[86] Some of these epithets may be dismissed as froth from the ire of Müller's political opponents.[87] Nonetheless, the last remark in particular echoed widely held sentiments. Müller was in fact a difficult person. Those opinions which he held, he held strongly. He was quite religious, although not conventionally so. He was a veritable crusader against the evils of alcohol, which he did not serve in his house and which he ostentatiously frowned upon in the company of others.[88] He thought bachelorhood criminal and spent off-duty hours trying to dragoon unmarried junior officers into matrimony.[89] On the whole, Müller exuded moral rigidity and *Besserwissen*. Unfortunately these qualities were not sweetened by a sense of humor. They were made worse by Müller's constitution, which responded to tension by developing stomach troubles, which caused Müller to suffer and to err even more on the abstemious side. Müller's ulcer recurred in 1907, after his appointment as Cabinet chief,[90] and during the war. In 1913 and 1914, when Wilhelm was treating him badly, Müller fell ill to a stream of complaints ranging from the common cold to mysterious fevers. These cannot have improved his humor, the gloominess of which was adequately expressed in his dairy and, presumably, to his associates. The fact that Müller was better informed and more conscientious than many of his colleagues made them hate him all the more.

The somewhat prissy qualities which made Georg von Müller unpopular with his peers made him equally unpopular with Wilhelm. When Müller became Cabinet chief, he wondered whether Wilhelm really liked him or not.[91] The answer was no. The scrupulous and censorious Müller was the embodiment of the worm of conscience. He detested Wilhelm's dilettantism as much as Wilhelm detested

Müller's earnestness. By February 1913 things had reached such a pass that Wilhelm would barely speak to Müller and then would say nothing of political importance.[92] The Kaiser effectively cut Müller out of the decisions that led to the war. Müller only stuck to his post from stubbornness and sense of duty. Wilhelm would doubtless have turned down a request to resign anyway, since Müller was an excellent Cabinet chief. Meanwhile, Müller sank deeper into despondency, a tendency which he harbored even in the best of times. 'Ah, how indifferent to me is this entire world,' he wrote about the Court in a typical moment. 'I would miss nothing from it all.'[93] Müller broke out of his isolation only in July 1914, but he was never more to Wilhelm than an accomplished bureaucrat.

The third Cabinet chief, Moritz Frhr von Lyncker,[94] was in many respects the archetypal soldier. His father was an officer, as were his two brothers and his wife's father. Two of his sons later died in the World War. As a young man Lyncker served in two of the most prestigious regiments of the Prussian army: Kaiser Franz and the 1st Foot Guard Regiment. He became briefly an adjutant to Crown Prince Friedrich, Wilhelm's father, and from there was transferred into the General Staff. Lyncker's identification with that institution seems to have been complete. Oberhof- and Hausmarschall Hugo Reischach described Lyncker as 'an old *Generalstäbler*,'[95] and certainly Lyncker's political views prior to 1914 seem virtually indistinguishable from Moltke's. Contemporaries agreed that Lyncker was the perfect soldier, 'a man of honor in the best sense of the word.'[96] His energy, directness, and bearing were of the proper military stamp. At the same time he was 'truly devoted to the Kaiser,'[97] 'a loyal and affectionate servant of his imperial master.'[98] Too loyal and too devoted, thought Müller, who felt that Wilhelm needed more criticism.[99] Although Lyncker was well-liked, even his military comrades agreed that he was not of Hülsen's caliber. Mutius wrote that 'with all his talent, his sober judgment lacked brilliance, which had effects as well on his judgment of people.'[100] War Minister Einem[101] agreed that he lacked all *Menschenkenntnis*.[102]

The quiet and serious Lyncker tried as much as possible to hold himself aloof from 'politics.' Müller claimed that he was largely successful in this endeavor.[103] In practice, this artificial distinction between military affairs and 'politics' meant, however, that Lyncker took decisions strictly according to military considerations. Former General Wedel complained to Valentini during the war that 'Herr von Lyncker's purely military viewpoint (whether it is chauvinist or not, I don't know) probably could not bring the necessary, objective understanding' to political subjects.[104] Lyncker's sympathy for the General Staff viewpoint, his political innocence, his intellectual mediocrity, and his subservient devotion to Wilhelm caused him to preside over the eclipse of his own power. After 1906, he acquiesced in the resurgence of the General Staff, which had languished in the shadow of the Military Cabinet since Waldersee's fall.[105] Moltke's voice, then, was stronger than the Cabinet chief's. Its message grew louder as time passed and, one by one, first the men of the military and then of the civilian entourage joined the chorus.

The Fischer controversy, having settled the question of Germany's primary responsibility for beginning the war, has now moved on to consider the motives which impelled it to do so. The spectrum ranges from the possibility that German leaders opted for war out of 'fear and despair'[106] to the contention that they planned the war deliberately to inaugurate German mastery over Europe. The last position is vigorously argued by Fischer himself in his second book, *War of Illusions*,[107] and by Adolf Gasser in two articles.[108] John Röhl has joined their arguments with considerably more caution.[109]

Fischer writes:

There is no doubt that the war which the German politicians started in July 1914 was not a preventive war fought out of 'fear and despair.' It was an attempt to defeat the enemy powers before they became too strong, and to realize Germany's political ambitions which may be summed up as German hegemony over Europe.[110]

Gasser, whom Fischer copiously cites, attributes German expansion to three impulses: (1) the economic ones arising from the needs of a developed capitalist, industrial society; (2) the ideological one of prestige necessary for a self-conscious nation state; and (3) the inner splits in German society which encouraged the leading classes to try to coopt the Social Democrats as they had the liberals in 1866.[111] These elements developed after 1911/12 into an 'abounding consciousness of power and pressure for victory.'[112] 'The Germans' had worked themselves into a 'boundless confidence in victory, a . . . "collective megalomania." This irrationally exaggerated consciousness of power found its most fatal expression in the almost mythical belief in one's own invincibility.'[113] Once one has understood this frame of mind, 'everything afterwards follows of itself.'[114]

Yet this coherent picture is disturbed by three elements which Fritz

Fischer, Gasser, and most other historians have found puzzling: the lack of actual planning, the irrationality which seems to characterize German policy of the late Wilhelminian period, and the fatalism of some of the central decision makers. These three elements are consistent, however, with the structure, habits, and personalities of the entourage.

More historians have not embraced the Fischer–Gasser thesis precisely because the documents reveal few preparations which could be characterized as 'plans.' Gasser admits, 'certainly the German Reich in 1914 did not go into the war with a clearly marked-out program of conquest.'[115] 'It seems unbelievable, but it is so: the German army command directed the civilian leadership toward preventive war after April 1913, without having the slightest notion of how England could be forced to declare itself beaten and to break off the war.'[116] The closest the leadership came to a decision for war before 1914 and to coherent, cohesive planning for it was in the *Kriegsrat* (War Council) of 8 December 1912. This event is the lynchpin in the argument of those who believe that Germany deliberately planned an aggressive war for the summer of 1914. The *Kriegsrat* is the subject of a more detailed discussion below,[117] but on the whole one may say that the planning it engendered was objectively inadequate and surprisingly incomplete.

In order to understand Germany's peculiar odyssey toward war and the entourage's part therein, we should examine more closely the problem of planning. It might be helpful to break down planning into three stages, somewhat along the military model of tactics, strategy, and grand strategy. The first, or tactical stage, is the most concrete. It deals with specific, well-defined situations. Such first-level planning would rarely extend itself beyond days or, rarely, a week or so. An example would be the drafting of a diplomatic note or the response to a natural disaster. Schlieffen's plan, once it had calcified into a catalogue of pre-typed telegrams and railroad schedules also falls into this category, regardless of the fact that Schlieffen regarded it as operational.[118]

The second, strategic, stage is characterized by more long-term and therefore less specific planning. The concerted anti-Russian propaganda campaign that the Empire waged in 1913 and 1914 is an instance of this middle-level planning.[119] So would be a memorandum outlining Germany's stance at a forthcoming diplomatic conference, or Eulenburg's sketch of the inauguration of personal regime.[120] Middle-level plans are not mired in tactics. In the Eulenburg case, for example, the plan comprised several alternatives, should anything go wrong. It did not specify when the changes would take effect, or even their exact sequence. The purpose of this level of planning is to create situations which will only be completely realized months or even years later. Reliable information, rational or goal-oriented evaluation of the information, and consistent application of the principles of the plan are necessary for such planning to be successful. Strategy, as Liddell Hart writes, is based upon '*a sound calculation and coordination of the end and the means.*'[121]

The third level is the highest and most abstract of the three. Perhaps we should abandon the military metaphor here, because even grand strategy tends to be more specific than what we have in mind.[122] This third level contains the vision of the ultimate goal of policy, understood in the broadest terms and usually conceived in decades. National liberation, world revolution, the Darwinian struggle, or the 'New Order' are all visions of this kind. They are the *Weltanschauungen* according to which all other planning proceeds. They are the assumptions which guide policy makers by making alternative policies simply inconceivable to them. The assumptions which characterize the third level are frequently unspoken. They rarely appear in policy documents at the other levels and are therefore ill-suited to measurement.

German historians of recent years have become quite adept at deciphering these high-level assumptions. They do so by searching for logical continuities in actions, regardless of the words which were used to cloak them. They subject the written evidence to minute scrutiny which translates code words into their real meanings. Or they focus attention upon the silences, the things not mentioned. Thus, Volker Berghahn could finally reconstruct the 'Tirpitz Plan's' aggressive intent by looking at the kind of ships Tirpitz wanted built and how these ships could actually be used, even though the ultimate goal 'admittedly was not spoken, on the contrary, was as much as possible concealed.'[123] Adolf Gasser can show that the phrase *Gleichberechtigung* [equal treatment] really meant 'World Hegemony.'[124] In the same way, one learns a great deal about the assumptions of the military from the prewar debates on *Mitteleuropa* and *Mittelafrika*. Both these schemes were actually efforts to reach world power without war. In each, Germany's preponderance would be secured by its economic power, not by military conquest or overt control. These plans were widely discussed just before the war, yet most military men were uncharacteristically silent on the subject. The few whose views we have were negative.[125] The pressure for imperialism was therefore at least split among those whose goals were primarily economic and those who conceived of struggle purely in military terms.

From the foregoing discussion it should be clear that the lack of planning so typical of the Wilhelminian era is to be found in the middle-level planning stage. Clearly, there was no dearth of grand goals or guiding assumptions. Wilhelm's goal was to uphold unchanged the monarchy and its socio-political bases by a combination of repression and nationalism within and economic and power-prestige expansion without.[126] This aim was shared by Bülow[127] and Bethmann Hollweg[128] and by the civil and military entourage, as well as by numerous other social groups, most notably heavy industry and the *Bildungsbourgeoisie*.[129] Each, of course, differed in emphasis and preferred tactics, but the end was essentially the same.

Equally, the attention lavished upon 'tactics' was astonishing. Perhaps this began with the need to play off various groups against one another or with the continuing need to build stop-gap measures against Social Democracy. At any rate, the cleverness with which domestic political maneuvering was used, especially by Bülow, has frequently been noticed.[130] Beginning in 1898, this cleverness found its way into the Navy Act. Tirpitz's design here was to create a huge navy automatically by embedding increasing fleet size and replacement of old ships into the original bill(s). Once the Reichstag approved the initial idea, the entire future development of the fleet would follow of itself.[131] Such mechanistic and minutely planned unfolding was unsurpassed until the immediately prewar elaborations of the Schlieffen Plan.

Why, then, was so little of the care and imagination spent upon tactics and grand designs directed toward the concrete, rational planning necessary for their success? Almost every structure in the monarchy contributed to this deficiency. One might sum up this overdetermination by saying that politics was practically absent from the monarchy. For what we have called middle-level planning is at base nothing else but politics, the representation, clash, and (never perfect) resolution of different aspects, viewpoints, or constituencies of the nation. There was no place for such an interchange in the Wilhelminian system. For example, there was no forum where the Reich leadership discussed foreign policy or its ramifications, that is, there was no functioning cabinet. The decline of ministerial responsibility, hastened by Wilhelm and Eulenburg in the 1890s, made matters worse. The abysmal lack of high-level coordination between the civilians and the military, or even among the various military branches themselves, was a third nail in the coffin of coherent, mid-range planning. These were all structural problems of the Bismarckian Reich.[132] A simply brilliant monarch might have overcome these problems, although it is unlikely. In fact, however, Wilhelm's incapacity for sustained work and his capacity for self-deception worsened an already bad situation. This, in turn, is a structural flaw of monarchies, insofar as a monarch becomes the head of state for reasons other than fitness.[133]

The entourage as an institution could not make good these structural defects, because it was incapable even of overcoming its own. Court life set narrow limits to the information necessary for mid-range planning and to the depth in which the information could be evaluated. Unless a Cabinet chief made special efforts to break out of the Court, he found himself surrounded day after day by the same handful of people, all of them military men or upper-level bureaucrats and almost all of them nobles. At social occasions he might meet the next larger ring of the *Hofgesellschaft,* which would include some bankers and industrialists, but these events rarely provided the opportunity to exchange more than platitudes. Wilhelm's many trips, plus the unending stream of dances, operas, and ceremonies left one with barely enough time to complete the most necessary work, much less to ruminate over larger questions of policy.[134]

The narrowness of the social milieu, its overpreponderance of Junkers, made it most difficult for radically new ideas to penetrate into the entourage. Here, again, the structural problem of monarchies intervened in the form of Wilhelm's personality. The Wilhelminian system allowed the all-powerful monarch to choose all the most important personnel, with the result that he duplicated the poles of his own character: the timid and the rash. The first group, as we have seen, was comprised either of nonentities who mirrored their surroundings without actually adding anything or of musty bureaucrats whose efficiency made the system work as well as it did. These last men were too well aware of the limits of their *Ressorts* to attempt to correct the centrifugal forces which many of them recognized were harmful. Even had they tried, their chances of success were not good, because Wilhelm endured their presence, but was not inspired by them to follow those of their counsels which differed from his own opinions.[135] Thus, the civilians declared themselves incompetent to judge the military technocrats; and Wilhelm despised and ignored the more sober-sided Cabinet chiefs, who tried to force him to work more. The other side of the personality pole, the dashing, rash 'characters,' were all military men, without political patience or training. Not surprisingly, they tended to favor drastic solutions, which Wilhelm found attractive because they were clear and ostentatious, they demanded little work on his part (or so he imagined) and no unmanly compromises.

We have so far discussed several ways in which structure (of monarchies in general, of the Bismarckian system in particular, and of the personality types collected in the entourage) hindered middle-level planning. It is now time to look at some aspects of the content of such planning. Imperialist expansion should have been intimately connected with concrete business interests which would have benefitted from it. In the course of this 'natural' expansion (Gasser's phrase),[136] Germany would have reaped enormous power-political advantages as well. This was the course of events which Bethmann Hollweg originally envisioned.[137] It was not the course which Germany followed, however.

As Norman Rich has written, 'in view of the immense if not decisive importance of German economic expansion in Germany's rise to the position of a great power, it is remarkable how small a part economic considerations played in determining the political decisions, especially in foreign policy' of the government.[138] Of all the highest decision makers, Bethmann was most focussed on economics, as his September program attests.[139] And, of course, economic leaders continued to make their wishes known to the government, especially on economic matters, and their recommendations were not infrequently incorporated into policy, particularly after August 1914. But the fact remains that to most members of Wilhelm's entourage, economic expansion and even world power were first and foremost means to maintain the domestic status quo. Their intrinsic advantages were secondary. They were meant to provide somehow enough prosperity and/or nationalist prestige to quell the pressure for reforms at home.[140] How they managed this did not matter. *Mittelafrika, Mitteleuropa*, it was all the same so long as the victory was large enough to sustain the power of the Junkers and their Kaiser. The means thus stood only in oblique relationship to the end, making it all the harder to fashion a consistent policy. The usual ways to measure success, economic growth, acquisition of territory, increase in influence, could not be used under such a system because the question was not 'have we expanded' but 'have we expanded enough' (to reach the greater goal)? How much success was enough? How much victory, expansion or influence externally would translate into internal stability or 'security'?

The upshot of this dilemma was that nothing short of overwhelming victory became acceptable, as Kiderlen-Wächter discovered to his chagrin during the second Moroccan Crisis.[141] The obsession that only total victory could save the Reich persisted through the last years of peace and even throughout the war. This perception cemented German war aims and prevented a negotiated peace, which would be the prelude to Prussian franchise reform and the end of the socio-political basis of the Wilheminian system. Ludendorff declared on 1 January 1918 that he 'would rather endure a terrible end than [the] endless terror' that internal unrest would mean.[142] The stakes, then, even before the war, were nothing less than the existence of the Reich, as it was narrowly construed by its leaders. Existential problems demand extreme solutions. This existential *Angst* is the origin of the bombastic schemes and the willingness to risk everything which are so easily misinterpreted as the products of overconfidence.

The very scale of Germany's ambitions made rational, middle-range planning difficult in another way, too, for it caused the German leadership to promote deceptions which gradually became blinding self-deceptions. Germany's desire for world power had to be kept carefully hidden from the public, lest the British or the Social Democrats find out about it. The navy was conceived as the chief instrument of expansion and internal salvation before 1911 or 1912. Its actual purpose was to unseat the British, yet if this purpose were acknowledged before Germany was strong enough to deliver the coup de grâce, the British would naturally respond by 'Copenhagening' the fleet.[143] Therefore the Germans invented an elaborate cover story to hide the truth. This deception was ultimately believed more in Berlin than in London. When the British realized the goal of German policy, they acquired allies and began arming heavily. The Germans interpreted these defensive measures as offensive ones, that is, they denied their own aggressive intentions and projected them instead upon the enemies of their own devising.[144]

This pattern was repeated when it became necessary to present the coming war, which Germany would start, as a defensive war against Russian aggression so that the Social Democrats would agree to fight.[145] This illusion was temporarily successful but ultimately costly. Again, those who had fostered the myth came more and more to believe it. Even in the absence of evidence showing Russian bellicosity,[146] Moltke and other leaders labored incessantly under the nightmare that as soon as Russia was ready, it would strike Germany. The original deception concerning Russia's putative aggressiveness and Germany's innocence had become so thoroughly transformed into self-deception that it was not seriously challenged by German historians until 1959.[147] To some extent, German policy makers disguised their intentions even from themselves. As General Groener admitted after the war, 'We aspired to world mastery unconsciously. Of course, I can only say this in the most intimate circles, but whoever looks at the subject somewhat clearly or historically cannot doubt it.'[148] Under these circumstances it is unlikely that they would have been able to plan rationally how to realize those intentions or to decide whether they had been successful.

The lack of coherent, middle-level planning was thus overdetermined in both structure and content. Its absence caused the Wilhelminians to revert directly to the tactical level in their attempts to put their *Weltanschauungen* into practice. At this level they could entrust policy to experts who could control every detail and thus, presumably, guarantee a victory of the magnitude necessary to perpetuate the Wilhelminian order. The building of the battle fleet, with its unalterable building tempos, designed to expand automatically regardless of the Reichstag or the response of Great Britain, is the first major example of the substitution of tactics for middle-level planning. The fleet combined the audacity characteristic of the third level of planning (or better, wish-fulfillment), with the narrowmindedness of the tactical level. The former consisted of the idea that Germany could build from scratch a navy powerful enough to defeat the British, and that this could be accomplished in a single battle of annihilation.[149]

An even more glaring example of the use of mere tactics to realize *Weltanschauungen* is provided by the Schlieffen Plan. Although it was originally the brainchild of Schlieffen, Moltke embraced it and so did practically all the younger staff officers,[150] the naval leaders,[151] and insofar as they did not struggle much against it, Bernhard von Bülow, Bethmann, and Foreign Minister Jagow, too.[152] The Schlieffen Plan was intoxicating precisely because it promised to achieve total victory, the absolute defeat of both France and Russia, and furthermore to do so automatically. Schlieffen held out 'prescriptions for victory,' 'simple dogmas,' which, if correctly applied, unfolded themselves like immutable laws immune to failure.[153] The Schlieffen Plan was even grander in scale than Tirpitz's design, and like it, hung from the outcome of a single battle.

Just as the Wilhelminian demand for European hegemony did not arise from bubbling optimism, neither did Schlieffen's daring plan. Both it and its reliance on the battle of annihilation were Schlieffen's technical response to insecurity, specifically to Germany's numerical inferioritiy vis-à-vis France and Russia.[154] From the fact of this inferiority, Schlieffen culled two lessons: (1) that Germany could only hope to win by relentless attack, and (2) that only a complete victory would suffice, otherwise the enemy could continue the war and ultimately make its superior weight felt.[155] Put another way, the perception of insecurity pushed Schlieffen, as it had Tirpitz, to embrace both aggressiveness and total victory. Successful defense was no longer enough.[156] Schlieffen had thus traversed the same ground as the Wilhelminian leadership had done and had arrived at essentially the same conclusions. It is only fitting that his plan, in promising to save the Reich, should have helped to destroy it.

The role played by insecurity in the Schlieffen Plan did not end with its conception. The rigidity of tactical thinking left its mark in farcical overplanning.[157] Schlieffen's heirs, Moltke and Ludendorff, spent eight years cementing every last detail. Chance, politics, enemy troop movements, nothing was to affect even the most minute parts of the grand scheme. This unreal attitude toward war is particularly surprising coming from officers who considered themselves students of Clausewitz, who had written, 'There is no human affair which stands so constantly and so generally in close connection with chance as war. But together with chance, the accidental, and along with it good luck, occupy a great place in war.'[158]

The General Staff was trying to control the inherently uncontrollable. It wanted to master chaos by sheer technical maneuvering. It tried on the military level what Tirpitz implanted at the very heart of German naval strategy,[159] what the Reich and Prussian governments had once attempted on the political level vis-à-vis the Social Democrats, what the noble officer corps had already done by refining and petrifying the honor code,[160] and what the Court had done by dividing its days among rigidly planned, never-changing ceremonies.[161] The impulse to control threatening situations by discounting alternatives in order to rely on technique alone was too strong for the Wilhelminians to resist. As Moltke's Quartermaster General[162] explained, because it was a time 'in which so much was uncertain [*da so vieles schwankte*],' Moltke decided 'in case of war to give the Reich leadership a buttress for its will in the form of an unchangeable offensive.'[163] The Wilhelminian inclination to repress immanent chaos (social or political change, war, emotion) by overcontrol was one of the hallmarks of the age, one of the reasons that the Wilhelminians found solace in technical planning. Indeed, Houston Stewart Chamberlain elevated German technical facility and organization to mythic proportions and predicted that they would assure Germany's victory in the war, provided that political considerations did not fatally dilute them.[164] Divorced from political planning, however, technical or tactical solutions simply disregard the causes of the difficulty in favor of controlling the effects.

The consequence of taking the technical way out in the years before 1914 was that the persons who controlled the technique received an increasing amount of power. This meant, of course, the army and the chief of staff, in particular. This process was enhanced by the fact that Moltke was the last 'friend' of Wilhelm's who was in a position of real power. Civilian influence diminished further as Moltke and his staff honed their plan. In April 1913, they increased the speed of the military timetable so that, once the army mobilized, actual war followed quickly and almost inevitably. This robbed the diplomats of days of possible negotiating time and thus put them more firmly into the hands of the military.[165] At the same time (April 1913), the General Staff abandoned its alternative plans for an eastern offensive. Thus, a war which actually started in the east had to be fought by way of Paris.[166] Finally, Bethmann Hollweg's efforts to keep Britain neutral were useless from the beginning because the Schlieffen Plan dictated a march through Belgium, which almost certainly would (and ultimately did) bring Britain into the war. To these ever tightening constrictions on the civilians in government one must add the cost of armaments which seriously overstrained the budget and in 1913 completed the stalemate in the Reichstag.[167]

By 1912, then, the military and its narrow considerations had become the dynamic force in high-level politics. To the civilians, Bethmann Hollweg, Jagow in the Foreign Office, and Valentini, was left the negative role of opposition. One by one, Moltke's opponents relinquished this fight. The mechanism which allowed them to do so without actually admitting it was the belief in the inevitability of a coming war. This idea was current in all the European countries prior to 1914 and would be worth comparative study. In the meantime, it can be said that in Germany the idea had a specific content: if war is inevitable, then it should be fought under the most favorable circumstances possible. These circumstances would be measured militarily, not politically. Germany's military position vis-à-vis France and Russia had reached its zenith in 1905/6, when Russia was traumatized from the Russo-Japanese war and the revolution of 1905. Germany's advantage declined with every passing year as France and Russia expanded their armies and as Russia built military railroads toward Germany's eastern border. Upon completion of these railroads, Russia could launch an attack quickly enough to destroy the Schlieffen Plan, which required at least four weeks to wipe out France before German armies could be freed for the eastern front. Russia's railroads would be finished in 1917. The Germans were convinced that they would lose a major war which began after that date. The logic of this is inescapable. If war were inevitable, if the only 'prescription for victory' were the Schlieffen Plan, and if the Allies would not begin the war until they were ready, then Germany had to begin the war before the balance tipped in its disfavor. The combination, inevitability of war plus the Schlieffen Plan, led inexorably to the idea of preventive war. This is, of course, an unusual way to use that word, for, as far as we know, Germany's enemies did not really intend to attack it. Nonetheless, World War I was a preventive war 'in a peculiar,' subjective sense.[168] The Reich leadership never admitted to itself or to anybody else its part in creating the enemies ringed around it. The leaders persisted in interpreting their own actions as defensive (an idea consonant with the underlying attempt to preserve and defend the Empire). Therefore, the reactions of threatened nations appeared to them as offensive acts, and they moved to cut their enemies short. That was their reality; so to them, but to no one else, the war they began was 'preventive.'[169]

By and large, the entourage embraced preventive war earlier than Wilhelm did. Predictably, the military led this movement. Schlieffen had advocated war in 1905. Holstein's seeming agreement with Schlieffen was the immediate reason that Bernhard von Bülow removed him from office. The next opportunity for war occurred in spring 1909 after Austria-Hungary annexed Bosnia-Herzogovina. There was already a 'war party' in Berlin, as the Russian ambassador, Osten-Sacken, reported:

> The war party, tempted by the unquestionable military preparedness of the army and of the other classes of society, hurt in its feelings of traditional loyalty to the Supreme Commander, regards war as the only possible means of restoring in the eyes of the masses the monarchy's shaken prestige.
>
> Feeling in military circles is moving towards the conviction that the superiority of the army at the present moment promises the greatest prospects of success for Germany. Such a conviction might tempt this Emperor and give his foreign policy a militant character.

Moreover, a victorious war could, at least at first, reduce the pressure of the radical movement among the people for a change of both the Prussian and the Imperial constitution on more liberal lines. These – in general terms – are the symptoms of domestic life in Germany which can explain the reasons for the military preparations.[170]

The war party consisted at least of Moltke and Chief of the Military Cabinet Lyncker. According to Hofmarschall Zedlitz-Trützschler, Lyncker thought Germany's chances against France and Russia were good, and he went so far 'as to regard war at the present moment as desirable in order to escape from difficulties at home and abroad.' Both Lyncker and Moltke feared, however, that Wilhelm's nerves would not stand up to a war.[171]

Two years later the war party had grown. Moltke and Lyncker were itching to take advantage of the second Moroccan Crisis and both were angry at Wilhelm for 'giving in.' Lyncker said that Wilhelm was 'big in words and weak in deeds.'[172] Moltke wondered gloomily about the future of the Empire 'if we cannot pluck up the courage to take an energetic line which we are prepared to enforce with the sword.'[173] Hans Plessen, the commandant of the Hauptquartier, added his voice to theirs, although he may have spoken more softly. In mid-August, Plessen sent Admiral von Müller a 'serious sounding letter,' which Müller mentions in the same breath as one from Tirpitz, which referred to Morocco as an 'Olmütz.'[174] Later on Plessen seems to have accommodated himself somewhat to the crisis's peaceful end. He wrote to Max von Fürstenberg that he was not particularly pleased by the outcome in Morocco, but he admitted that getting 300,000 kilometers [*sic*] in Africa without paying for it was certainly a success.[175]

The last member of the Eulenburg Circle who was still *hoffähig* and in an official position had also decided that war was inevitable. Axel von Varnbüler, Wüttemberg's diplomatic representative to Berlin, reflects perfectly the movement of opinion in the entourage. By the end of 1905, Varnbüler was gripped by a profound pessimism about Germany's future. He considered Bernhard von Bülow a complete failure, who had allowed the internal situation to become dangerous. In foreign affairs Germany stood completely isolated, 'the only and last representative of the monarchical principle.' Varnbüler's response was, quoting Wilhelm, 'to keep our powder dry and our weapons sharp, because we can only depend on ourselves alone.'[176] In a dispatch from 1910, Varnbüler considered the question of preventive war. He expected, from sources near Tirpitz, that German naval strength would reach its zenith vis-à-vis England between 1912 and

1915, after which it would experience a relative decline. 'Will the coincidence of internal difficulties with the culmination of external[ly directed] instruments of power produce . . . the results of external diversion, of warlike *Machtpolitik* [i.e. war]?' Varnbüler, as was his custom, answered his own question obliquely, but nonetheless clearly. The idea of such a war was not 'obsolete,' even in a 'Europe inclined to effeminacy.' Some persons thought that Wilhelm, particularly after his nervous collapse in 1908, would never allow 'a dare-devilish adviser' to push him into a war which was not absolutely necessary. 'I would question the validity of this opinion precisely as regards the question of using the fleet and the army at a time of internal crisis.'[177]

By 1911, Varnbüler had come down decisively on the warlike side.

Hopefully we'll hold tight [he wrote about Morocco]. Kiderlen I trust to do it, he's got nerves of steel [*wie Batzenstricke*]. But the other one, who writes this motto all too often on photos and in golden books. . . . That's the question! Bethmann – for a chancellor he isn't spoken of much in this affair; but he needs a foreign victory for his Reichstag elections too much to leave the State Secretary [Kiderlen-Wächter] in the lurch. [178]

In the next years, Varnbüler continued to press for war, because, as he explained to Kuno Moltke, Germany had to use the strength 'of our army and officer corps' 'before it really does rust.'[179]

It is safe to assume that at least two other long-time members of the military entourage also pushed for war.[180] They were General Gustav von Kessel, the military governor of Berlin, general *à la suite* and old friend of Wilhelm's,[181] and General Adjutant Alfred von Löwenfeld. Kessel was an old comrade of Military Cabinet Chief Lyncker from the days when both had been young adjutants to Kaiser Friedrich III. Lyncker used to relay Kessel's messages to Holstein in the Foreign Office.[182] During the war both Kessel and Löwenfeld belonged to the rabidly annexationist, anti-Bethmann Hollweg fronde around Admiral Tirpitz.[183] Löwenfeld was known as a good soldier, although he was unpopular because of his frankness.[184] The few letters of Löwenfeld which one runs across all leave the impression of a typically *forsch* soldier.[185] One would be very surprised to learn that these two did not support Moltke and Lyncker.

The navy officers were still holding back because the navy was not nearly ready to take on the British. Both in 1911 and in 1912, Admiral Tirpitz spoke out strongly in favor of peace.[186] Admiral von Müller in 1911 agreed with Tirpitz, but his words show that he was beginning to move toward the war party. Müller told Wilhelm: 'I myself am fully convinced that a military conflict with England cannot be avoided in the long run.[187] But I am equally convinced that the present moment is the most unfavorable one imaginable for the navy.'[188]

The next crisis, the first Balkan war, strengthened the war party again. Plessen now dropped whatever reserve he had shown in 1911. This time, he wrote:

> I believe that no decision will come this winter, but in the spring the big *Krach* will break out, because the English will do their utmost to see Austria-Hungary engaged in the east so that they can take us on with France by ourselves! Now, I wish it would come to this! The earlier, the better! The great liquidation must come sometime![189]

'The earlier, the better.' These were the same words Moltke used two months later at the 'War Council' of 8 December 1912. The *Kriegsrat* was a psychological dress-rehearsal for the decision of July 1914. It represented a sharp shift in the Kaiser's position and was the last time that the navy could play its peace card. Up until the autumn of 1912, Kaiser Wilhelm had stuck with stubborn consistency to a policy of 'non-intervention at any price,'[190] that is, he refused to support Austria-Hungary in the Balkans, for fear of beginning a major war. Indeed, the Kaiser's position was so categorical that it threatened Germany's alliance with the Austrians and robbed Bethmann and the Foreign Office of needed diplomatic maneuvering room. Consequently, the Austrians, Bethmann, Kiderlen and Admiral Müller were among those who pressed Wilhelm to adopt a more pro-Austrian, and thus, more potentially warlike stand. This Wilhelm began to do on 9 November 1912 and succeeding days.[191] So far, the chancellor and his diplomats had shown a willingness to risk war, not a positive urge to begin one.[192] They had begun to give in to Moltke's inexorable logic and had persuaded the Kaiser to give in with them. Suddenly, in December, Wilhelm overshot this delicate mark and came down with a crash into Moltke's camp.

Wilhelm was moved by his fury at England, which on the 8th had let him know that it could not stand by and watch France destroyed as a great power in a war betweeen Germany and France. This was a British effort to convince Germany to curb Austria in the Balkans and thus to prevent war. Wilhelm's 'excited misreaction'[193] interpreted this as British duplicity. He summoned Moltke, Müller, Tirpitz, and Admiral von Heeringen to a meeting that Bethmann later dubbed a 'war council.' There Moltke expressed his usual opinion: 'I believe a war is unavoidable, and the sooner, the better.'[194] The Kaiser quite agreed, but 'reluctantly'[195] gave in to Tirpitz's request to allow the navy eighteen more months to prepare.[196] That would have set the date at June 1914.

Did the *Kriegsrat* signify a decision to begin war in the summer of 1914? One way to try to answer this question is to see what preparations came out of the council and how conscientiously they were carried out. Predictably, the military results were strongest. The army bill of 1913, containing huge increases, was the major outcome of the *Kriegsrat*. Wilhelm had also ordered a large naval increase, but the chancellor managed to stifle that. The Kaiser also ordered work on plans to invade England, and these seem to have been begun.[197] In addition, the usual term of the War School was cut from nine to seven months, and officers deemed unsuitable for wartime service were hastily pensioned.[198] The Prussian war minister told a Bavarian colleague that shortening the War School course was not a war measure, however, and had nothing to do with the *Kriegsrat*.[199] Finally, the army began experiments to stock conserves, oats, and hay.[200]

Preparations in the civilian sector were uneven. The Foreign Office pressed harder to round up Balkan allies. Moltke had suggested a propaganda campaign to prepare the German people for a war against Russia. Wilhelm agreed, Müller informed Bethmann, and both the chancellor and Kiderlen launched appropriate articles in the press.[201] The military men remained dissatisfied with the civilians' handiwork, however.[202] They should have been more pleased with the Imperial Bank, which, beginning in 1913, added twenty million pounds sterling to its gold stock by buying at a loss.[203] Consultations inside government and between it and both industry and agriculture increased after December 1912, but, as Fischer admits, 'these activities did not lead to new measures, but at the same time they reflected the increasing preoccupation with war both in the domestic and the international sphere.'[204] Cooperation among the state agencies, the Foreign Office, the business community, and the military did not really begin until 1914, and remained virtually without results.[205]

The difficulty with assessing these events is that preparations for an 'inevitable' war and preparations to launch a war are hard to distinguish, particularly if in both cases hostilities are expected to be short. The *Kriegsrat* evidence alone does not prove the contention that Wilhelm and his military advisers in December 1912 reached a firm decision to provoke war and stuck to that resolve for one and a half years before actually doing so.[206] Obviously something important had happened at the council, because it had too many effects, however incomplete. But Admiral Müller's summary notation on the *Kriegsrat* makes clear that resolution and adamantine timetables were not the order of the day:

General Moltke: I believe a war is unavoidable, and the sooner the better. But we ought to do more through the press to prepare the popularity of a war against Russia, as suggested in the Kaiser's discussion. H.M. agreed to this and ordered the State S[ecretary] [Tirpitz] to use his press connections in this way. T[irpitz] then remarked that the navy would gladly see the great struggle put off for one and a half years. Moltke said, the navy would not even be ready then, and the army would come into an ever more unfavorable situation, because the enemies were arming more strongly than we [were], because of our financial straits. That was the end of the meeting. The result was pretty much zero.

Müller went on to explain why the result was zero:

The Chief of the General Staff says: War the sooner the better, but he doesn't draw the logical consequence from this, which would be to present Russia or France or both with an ultimatum which would unleash the war with right on our side.[207]

Müller recognized in the *Kriegsrat* that characteristic at Court which his bureaucrat's heart so despised, unprofessional inconsequence.[208] The press campaign and the navy were simply excuses to shrink from acting according to the imperative to which everyone paid lip service. Müller was by no means a conventional warmonger. Even as an early imperialist, he had eschewed war as a goal, or even a necessary means to world power.[209] But the admiral was trapped by the logic of inevitable war, plus the Schlieffen Plan. Müller agreed with Moltke that war was unavoidable. He also knew that the navy would never be prepared. This meant that naval considerations should no longer prevent Germany from entering a war if the army's position relative to other powers demanded it. And yet Wilhelm had still decided against immediate war, and Moltke had acquiesced.

The way they had done so, however, made the *Kriegsrat* different from earlier policy discussions. For the *Kriegsrat* in a sense allowed Wilhelm and his military advisers to choose war without taking responsibility for it, that is, without having to fight at once. Wilhelm put his imprimatur on Moltke's logic, and then delayed the inevitable explosion, not in order to use every last opportunity to prepare for it (that the Germans did not do), but to allow the last important stragglers (Bethmann, Wilhelm himself, and the naval officers) to 'accustom' themselves to 'the idea of war.'[210] Not only to accustom themselves, but almost to force themselves to embrace it. In this regard, the *Kriegsrat* performed the same function that the Schlieffen Plan did: it relieved uncertainty by automatic mechanism. The decision for war was a strictly military one, briefly delayed by other military (naval) considerations. When these considerations disappeared, the original decision more or less automatically went into effect, and wriggling out of it a second time really would have seemed 'chickening out.' In the meantime, one needed neither to ponder all the complex policy choices which the military decision a priori cut through and discarded, nor did one have to pay the price for this simple, but violent solution.

This was the sort of comfortable non-decision that Wilhelm always preferred. And there were other patterns, too, that cropped up in December 1912. First, the War Council contained no civilians, nor did the civilian leaders ever get a complete report of what went on there, particularly regarding military decisions.[211] Second, the news that England would definitely join Germany's enemies in a war elicited from Wilhelm and his advisers only one response: attack. Conciliation, even reconsideration of Germany's dangerous foreign policy never entered their heads. Their response to adversity remained rigid aggression. Finally, when the chancellor received whatever direct account of the *Kriegsrat* he obtained, he got it from Admiral Müller, which marks the beginning of Müller's role as go-between for the civilian leaders. Müller was absolutely right: the *Kriegsrat* was one more example of the pattern of decision making within Wilhelm's entourage.

In the eighteen months between December 1912 and July 1914, Bethmann Hollweg and his diplomats did indeed 'accustom themselves to the idea of war.' So did Admiral Müller, although he had no influence on the course of events because right up until mid-July 1914 he was in Wilhelm's bad graces and politically quarantined.[212] Indeed, the straggler who had the most difficulty with the decision for war was Wilhelm himself. Even in the week of his greatest rage at Great Britain, the Kaiser was still capable of pacific statements. Austria's Ambassador Szögyényi reported a conversation with Wilhelm on 11 December 1912, in which 'despite all the warlike noise, His Majesty assured me that he certainly hoped that peace would be maintained.'[213] Nonetheless, Wilhelm never retreated to his pre-October 1912 position of 'non-intervention at any price.' On 30 January 1913 Wilhelm assured Szögyényi that Germany did not want war, 'but in the case that the [Austro-Hungarian] monarchy became involved in war, he [Wilhelm] would absolutely join it with the strength of the entire Reich.'[214] On 4 March 1913, Wilhelm told Varnbüler that the past crisis had shown him that in the next one Germany might very well have to fight for its life.[215].

These dark thoughts can never have been far from Wilhelm's mind. He let them escape again in a flurry of warlike enthusiasm in October 1913.[216] This excitement was, however, short-lived. All the rest of the reports on Wilhelm from December 1912 to 3 July 1914 dwell upon the Emperor's peaceable inclinations[217] (which most observers attributed to his bad nerves and abhorrence of work and responsibility). Moltke, who never ceased to worry about Russia and its railroad building, continuously tried Wilhelm's nerves.[218] His and the Kaiser's own racism haunted their imaginations with the specter of racial Armageddon.[219] Wilhelm mentioned to Lerchenfeld-Köfering in January 1914 that good relations with Russia were impossible in the long run because 'the Slavic race is caught up in an expansionist fever.'[220] The next month the Austrian military attaché reported how worried Wilhem was about the Russian railroads.[221] This problem surfaced again in a discussion Wilhelm had with Max Warburg, the banker, on 21 June 1914. Wilhelm was worried enough to consider 'whether it might not be better to attack than to wait.'[222] One week later Archduke Franz Ferdinand was assassinated. On 3 July Wilhelm followed the consequences of Moltke's logic: 'Now or never.'[223] Bethmann Hollweg approved of Wilhelm's position on 5 July 1914 and the war began to unfold.

Wilhelm did not rest easy with his decision. For all his bluster, he did not want war. He did not trust himself enough. But Moltke and the entourage shamed him into it through fear: fear of being abandoned by Austria-Hungary if Germany failed to support its ally, fear that if the 'inevitable war' were postponed much longer Russia and France would destroy Germany, and fear that Wilhelm would be thought unmanly, a coward, by those whose high opinions he valued so highly, the military. 'This time I shall not give in.' '[N]obody could again accuse him [Wilhelm] of irresolution.'[224] Indeed, Wilhelm did not give in. At the end of July he wavered, but so did the other stragglers, Bethmann and even Admiral Müller. When Müller learned of George V's 'Halt-in-Belgrade' proposal, he agreed with Tirpitz that there was no reason for war. But it was too late now, and Müller could at least be pleased that the populace accepted the end of peace so well.[225] Thus began the ill-planned 'preventive war' and with it the end of the monarchy.

10

The war years

Wilhelm's nerves reacted to the war exactly as everyone had feared they would: they broke down. It was the strain of war, not the possibility that Germany might lose, which caused the problem. Wilhelm's depression was already in full swing by 6 August 1914. He suddenly found it necessary to sleep far into the morning. As Auguste Viktoria made sure that no one disturbed him, Plessen was already urging that 'one must keep His Majesty's mood up by all means.'[1] This was hardly easy. The Cabinet chiefs used to take long walks with Wilhelm, to take his mind off his troubles. At the end of one of these walks, Wilhelm sat down on a bench and motioned for his companions to be seated as well. Since the bench where the Kaiser sat was too short, they pulled up another. Wilhelm then turned to them and cried, 'Do you already despise me so much that nobody will sit next to me?'[2] This outburst occurred on 21 August 1914, before the battle of the Marne.

As the war became more serious, Wilhelm's nervous condition became more pronounced. He experienced troughs of depression at crisis points, particularly during personnel changes (Moltke in September 1914, Falkenhayn in July–August 1916 and the weeks preceding Bethmann's resignation in July 1917).[3] Well before the German army in the west began to suffer its string of defeats in August 1918, Wilhelm's condition slipped once more. He refused to work, to leave his haven in Wilhelmshöhe and finally, to leave his bed.[4] A few days later he admitted to Admiral v. Müller that 'he had recently had a small nervous breakdown [on account of] his wife's illness and the news from the front, but he had gone to bed, slept for twenty-four hours and now he was like new.' Müller, who had witnessed numerous such episodes, commented in his diary: 'well, well.'[5]

Almost worse than his depressions, were the periods of over-elation which alternated with them. Wilhelm would become stridently over-confident: 'No peace before England is defeated and destroyed. Only amidst the ruins of London will I forgive Georgy.'[6] In such 'unbearable'[7] moods, Wilhelm would tell grisly war stories, whose bloody details he magnified with each telling. He could tell officers to take no prisoners[8] or plan the starvation of 90,000 Russian prisoners of war.[9] Wilhelm's bloodthirstiness was actually a cover for weakness. It was part of his never-ending quest to be 'manly.' He fooled no one. When Wilhelm was in such moods, Admiral Müller wondered 'how it looks inside the head of this man, to whom war is, at base repulsive.'[10] Wilhelm could also puff himself up so far that he would claim to have participated in battles[11] or even to have won them.[12]

In his efforts to rid himself of depression, then, Wilhelm drove himself deeper and deeper into unreality. He misread dispatches, always in a positive way,[13] he denied events to which he had been party the very day before.[14] 'He lived in illusion,' wrote the Austrian military attaché Klepsch-Kloth.[15] His entourage wondered if he acted from 'ignorance of the facts or [from] duplicity. One stands before an insoluble riddle.'[16]

The first response of the entourage to Wilhelm's nervous ills was to shield him from bad news or hardship. The Kaiserin and General Plessen were the worst offenders if only because they continued this tack throughout the war.[17] They, together with Oberhofmarschall Reischach and Hausmarschall Gontard, arranged Wilhelm's life so that it was virtually untouched by war. His various quarters were entirely redone, at costs ranging from 70,000 to 80,000 M.[18] His table reflected war conditions not a jot. When Admiral Müller asked Wilhelm to omit some of the richer portions, Wilhelm answered that he had tried but that Auguste Viktoria had insisted for his health that he have 'a somewhat richer table.'[19] It was no wonder that Wilhelm could not understand the effects that the blockade and bad harvest had on civilian morale.[20] In any case, the Kaiserin did her best to prevent such news from reaching his ears.[21]

Wilhelm was no better informed by his many 'trips to the Front.' Plessen encouraged these, not so that Wilhelm would learn something, but because it made Wilhelm feel better to move around.[22] This was the old cure for Wilhelm's restlessness. In fact, the Kaiser rarely saw actual fighting. He passed his days at the Grosses Hauptquartier (GHQ), far removed from both the front and Berlin. He worked as little as possible; he was surrounded by the same group of military men plus two civilians, the Civil Cabinet chief and the representative of the Foreign Office. Under these conditions Wilhelm sank quickly into bored and nervous isolation.

The Kaiser welcomed this state of affairs, however. His nerves had made concentrated work impossible. Decision making became a torture. Klepsch-Kloth reported that 'H.M. less than [was] usual [before the war] thinks or judges for himself, he now almost exclusively takes up the ideas of "others." '[23] Barely two weeks into the war, Wilhelm had let the Supreme Command [Oberste Heeresleitung, or OHL] know that running the war was its responsibility, not his.[24] Although Wilhelm complained now and again that he was being bypassed, basically 'he [was] quite satisfied with this.'[25]

Generals Falkenhayn, Ludendorff, and Hindenburg were satisfied, too. Without Wilhelm's interference they could do what they pleased. All three generals took pains to keep Wilhelm as ignorant and isolated as possible. They succeeded well.[26] In a sense, the Supreme Command only continued a palpable prewar trend. For although Wilhelm made a great show of his exclusive right to command power, a show which became all the more insistent as seemingly ungovernable political troubles loomed on the horizon,[27] the Kaiser had in fact stopped exercising that power after around 1900.[28] Wilhelm's wartime impotence was thus quite predictable.[29] But the dynamics of war changed the context of this fact and therefore its meaning. Before 1914, the cleft between the military and the Crown[30] remained hidden, bridged over by the myth that the two were inseparable and by the common internal enemy, the Social Democrats. In addition, the Kaiser's power was spread out among other institutions, like the civilian government and the secret Cabinets, whose chiefs were bound to the monarch's person, as well as to the institutions they represented.

After August 1914, this constellation changed. The state of seige that went into effect on 31 July 1914 knocked the pins from underneath the civilian government.[31] Administration of all areas except Bavaria reverted by law to the various army corps commanders. At the top of the civilian hierarchy, Bethmann Hollweg, like Bernhard Bülow before him, did not help his cause by studiously refusing to 'interfere' with 'purely military' matters. Thus, from the beginning of war, the main non-military foundation of imperial power lay lamed. And as this process continued, it affected the Cabinets as well, for they were only as strong as the monarch they served.

The military did not merely cut loose from the Kaiser institutionally, but also ideologically, and this turned out to be the most dangerous trend of all for the monarchy. The two, of course, are not unrelated. When the monarch himself failed as the symbol for loyalty and the justification for action, he was replaced by something more abstract, but infinitely more flexible and thus more useful: the future Germany, its security, its greatness.[32] In short, nationalism finally triumphed over monarchism. It did not happen smoothly, consistently, or all at once, but it happened nonetheless. As the war dragged on, the officer corps joined other leading segments of prewar Wilhelminian society in embracing the radical nationalism that had previously been the joint preserve of heavy industry and the national, antiestablishment opposition.[33] The radical nationalists (such as the Pan-Germans, sections of the Navy League, and so forth)[34] came mostly from the bourgeois strata and had been unstintingly critical of the Reich's elevated, but too cautious caretakers. As we have seen, the caretakers themselves came to doubt their own abilities. It must have been with relief that they finally abandoned their own pessimism for the heady exuberance of their social inferiors and the greedy optimism of their aims.

The new converts to radical nationalism (Tirpitz, Ludendorff, and Colonel Max Bauer[35] are among the most notorious) brought with them three idées fixes from the old Wilhelminian officer corps: technical military considerations far outweighed mere politics in decisions affecting the nation, compromise with enemies (domestic or foreign) was unthinkable, and preparations must begin now (even in the midst of World War I) for the next inevitable war. The goal these gentlemen pursued was a huge victory, won by force of arms, to establish a German-ruled autarkic fortress on the continent. No sacrifice was too great to achieve this end. Not even the Kaiser. As Colonel Bauer put it, 'the Kaiser must be almost completely shut out as well, because his wavering weakness would ruin everything in all the major decisive questions.'[36] Bauer wanted a dictatorship.[37] So did Tirpitz, who, as early as April 1915, tried to get Wilhelm declared incompetent so that a regency under Crown Prince Wilhelm could carry out the far right-wing program. Before the plan failed, Tirpitz had contacted at least one heavy industrialist and even the Kaiser's doctor, Niedner.[38] In the next year and a half, Tirpitz evidently concluded that a formal regency was unnecessary; like Bauer, he thought merely shoving the Kaiser aside would do nicely. In October and November 1916, while Bauer nurtured similar plans, Tirpitz secured Ludendorff's backing for his own. The admiral then conferred with Bülow and with August Eulenburg, who was horrified.[39] The plot eventually fell through.

The Supreme Command and its ardent supporters were not the only people to move right during the war, of course. This was a general phenomenon afflicting the chancellor, the ministries, the Foreign Office, even the entourage.[40] It would be a mistake, however, to think there were no differences among them, although from the allied or left-wing perspective, this often seemed to be the case. In general, three issues described the difference between the radical nationalists and the old-fashioned conservatives. First, the conservatives would have dearly loved a victory as smashing as the one the nationalists proposed, and, whenever the war news was bright, their war aims were barely, if at all, distinguishable from the nationalists'. However, the conservatives were prepared to settle for less if they felt that was all they could get. In other words, their ideology, while hardly transparent, was at least somewhat permeable to disappointing reality. A corollary to this marks the second difference: the conservatives of the older observance allowed politics (economics, parties, social problems) to influence their stand on how the war should be run. Although they were as hesitant during the war as before to accept the full consequences of this position, they nevertheless were far removed from the military purists who dismissed political considerations altogether. Finally, the conservatives were appalled at the radicals' ruthless, instrumental attitude toward the sovereign, an attitude they recognized as completely inimical to monarchism. They tried to subvert Supreme Command by forcing Wilhelm back into the decision making process, and, when that failed, by keeping him in the public light, so that people would not forget that 'after all, we do have a Kaiser.'[41] These three issues were so fundamental, that they split the wartime entourage into two deeply hostile factions.

There are several ironies involved in this process. First, if before the war the military had been the guarantor of the Kaiser's personal power, after 1914 it was the civilian government. As the military usurped more and more power, the old conservatives in the entourage turned to the chancellor and the Foreign Office to try to stem the tide. Not surprisingly the conservatives were not entirely happy with this situation. For one thing, they approached impending domestic reform with even less alacrity than Bethmann did. For another, Bethmann was not confident or energetic enough in the struggle with Supreme Command. Müller noted in May 1916, 'once again the Cabinet chiefs are united in the judgment that Bethmann is, despite everything, a pitiable fellow [*doch ein erbärmlicher Kerl ist*].'[42] Nonetheless, Bethmann was their best instrument to save the monarchy and the country. This became even clearer after the summer of 1916. Up until then, the radical nationalists lacked an obvious military alternative to the chancellor. General Erich von Falkenhayn,[43] who had succeeded Helmuth Moltke as chief of the General Staff in late

1914, was relatively unpopular. Not so his successor, Paul von Hindenburg,[44] or the latter's partner, Erich Ludendorff.[45] After these two had inaugurated the third Supeme Command in August 1916, the radical nationalists focussed adulation on these leaders, while they vilified Bethmann for sabotaging their extreme ambitions. This clarified the split in the entourage to a single question: Bethmann, for or against?

The second irony is a familiar one. Those who served Wilhelm's interests best, liked him least. Personal fealty did not move them, but rather loyalty to monarchy in the abstract and to the efficient, bureaucratic functioning of its institutions. Consequently, the pro-Bethmann group consisted of the three heads of Cabinet, but particularly Civil Cabinet Chief Valentini and Naval Cabinet Chief Müller, plus the representatives of the Foreign Office, Karl Georg von Treutler[46] and his successor Werner Frhr von Grünau.[47] Oberhof- und Hausmarschall Hugo Reischach and General Adjutant Oskar Chelius were sympathetic to the Bethmann camp, but not really active in it. Military Cabinet Chief Lyncker's position in this schema is also something of a problem. Müller, Valentini, and Treutler usually counted him on their side.[48] Lyncker did support Bethmann against OHL, although he always wavered under pressure.[49] For in the end, it was not politics, or devotion to bureaucratic duty which placed Lyncker with the pro-government group, but tragedy. Lyncker remained the one-sided, military naïf which he had always been,[50] but the death of both his sons, in September 1914 and February 1917, destroyed Lyncker's will to live by his military credo. He was completely broken[51] and retired to virtual inactivity.[52] While the more energetic and equally one-sided Ulrich Frhr Marschall gen. Greiff[53] ran Cabinet business, Lyncker lapsed into melancholia much more appropriate to the pessimism of the Bethmann supporters than to the grandiose optimism of the other side.[54]

Ranged against the 'pessimists' was practically everybody else at headquarters, led by the redoubtable Plessen, the Kaiserin, and the young FA and FADs. Hausmarschall Hans v. Gontard[55] tried to keep aloof from the intrigues.[56] Gontard, however, was in a key position. As erstwhile educator of the Kaiser's sons, he was practically a member of the family and the only one to get along with everyone in it. Auguste Viktoria's sudden political prominence during the war is not least due to Gontard's unparalleled position as pipeline to Wilhelm. August Eulenburg, Minister of the Royal House back in Berlin, was also part of the anti-Bethmann faction. Eulenburg's adamantine

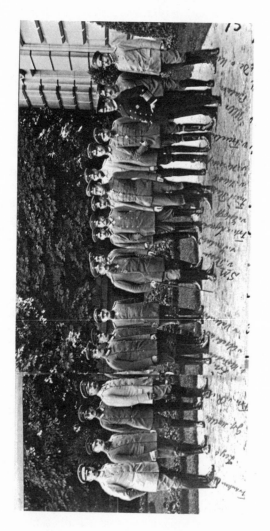

8 The entourage during the war, taken in September 1915. Left to right: Frankenberg, Zeys, Moltke, Richthofen, Münchhausen, Chelius, Valentini, Kaiser Wilhelm II, Plessen, Gontard, Lyncker, Estorff, Pless, Scholl, Hirschfeld, Treutler, Müller, Balzer, Niedner

opposition to domestic reform seems to have been chiefly responsible for his political alignment. As we have seen, however, the old courtier found the schemes to isolate Wilhelm completely repellent.[57] Even so, August Eulenburg unwittingly contributed to the monarchy's dissolution behind the scenes. Only once, in his anxiety to remove Valentini, was Eulenburg so incautious as to be caught intriguing,[58] but it is unlikely that this was the only time he was active in this way.

Like Eulenburg, the other gravediggers of the monarchy did so blindly, without understanding the consequences of their actions. The FADs and FAs were for the most part too inexperienced to grasp where military purity was leading them. It is doubtful, however, that mere age would have saved them. It certainly did not save Hans v. Plessen, whose case is emblematic of the fatal convergence of military training and personal fealty. Displacing the Kaiser from the center of power was the furthest thing from Plessen's mind, yet more than any other figure in Wilhelm's entourage, Plessen's actions worked to this end. Throughout the war, Plessen and Admiral Müller skirmished over aspects of this problem. Müller and his comrades tried constantly to persuade Wilhelm to go more frequently to Berlin, to get OHL to move Supreme Headquarters from out-of-the-way places like Pless, Charleville or Spa to a central location accessible to civilian influence, and, finally, to bring economists and politicians to the Emperor's attention. Müller hoped these three tactics would end 'the rotten inactivity [*Versumpfung*] of the Kaiser and his entire entourage.'[59]

In a typical interchange in 1916, Müller told Plessen of 'the necessity to raise the Emperor's participation in the course of things.' Plessen agreed and went on to suggest that Wilhelm needed a vacation.[60] Plessen's first thoughts were always for Wilhelm's ease and comfort. Knowing that difficult decisions made the Kaiser positively ill, and knowing that the toughest decisions were those that pitted the Supreme Command against the diametrically opposed civilian government, Plessen relieved his beleaguered master by simply trying to shut out the civilian half of the clashing opinions, with which in any case he did not agree. Plessen's talent for this sharpened, once Hindenburg and Ludendorff lent him their full support. The Austrian military plenipotentiary at German headquarters complained repeatedly how 'especially' Plessen 'tried to shut H. M. off completely from every contact.'[61] Plessen's success at this endeavor made impossible the sort of government that Valentini and the other Court bureaucrats wanted: 'It must be agreed, that each [adviser] presents his side, and that *H. M. decides.* Otherwise, the Kaiser will be shut out and we will have a dictatorship.'[62] Against this, Plessen followed Hindenburg's maxims, 'internal politics does not belong at headquarters,'[63] and the Kaiser did not belong anywhere else, otherwise the 'pessimists' would get to him.[64]

The direct struggle to bring Wilhelm into the center of decision making therefore failed. Wilhelm's ignorant indolence forced even the Cabinet chiefs to take over a great deal of his own work by default, the origin of many wartime complaints about the all-powerful Cabinets. Just how powerful they were and in what direction becomes clearer if we examine three of the most debated issues of the war: war aims, unrestricted submarine warfare, and Prussian electoral reform.[65] These problems tried the unity of the pro-Bethmann faction in the entourage and sharpened its differences not only with the Supreme Command, but also with the chancellor and his allies from the Foreign Office. Finally, the infighting over these issues showed how much Wilhelm stood under the influence of each group.

Despite the fact that Germany began the war without a defined or agreed upon list of objectives, war aims did not emerge as an issue for the Empire's leadership in the first year and a half.[66] Bethmann's September (1914) Program, with its call for 'security for the German Reich in west and east for all imaginable time,' summed up what most leaders in government and the military wanted to win.[67] By December 1915, however, Bethmann had begun to doubt seriously that Germany could unilaterally force the world to accede to its terms.[68] The chancellor began to develop an arsenal of alternative tactics designed to achieve as many of Germany's goals as possible. For the ever receding possibility of military breakthrough, Bethmann substituted separate peace negotiations; for outright annexations in east and west, he suggested indirect control through economic ties and military conventions. Fritz Fischer is quite right to insist that the difference between Bethmann and his supporters, on the one hand, and the third OHL (Ludendorff and Hindenburg) and their vocal fans, on the other, was a difference in method or form.[69] Both tried to cement the largest, most secure German victory possible, and both of their visions of the future were unacceptable to their neighbors and incompatible with a quick or a lasting peace. But it would be incorrect to deduce from this that the difference between (broadly) the political and the military leaders was therefore unimportant. To the contemporaries, it was as important and as stark as the difference between night and day. It was in fact the axis around which politics revolved at the apex of power during the last three years of war.

That a mere difference in tactics should have struck the contemporaries as so crucial is less surprising if we remember the Wilhelminian tendency to use tactics to solve existential problems. The movement from the minute to the grand level was practically immediate and thoughts followed this pattern as easily as actions. Bethmann's tactical shift contained a seed which any trained Wilhelminian recognized as a mighty tree. For the chancellor's doubts about an overwhelming military victory held within them a double critique of the military. First, they questioned the technical infallibility of the army even in military matters. The General Staff, after all, had promised 'prescriptions for victory' and had not delivered. From this flowed the second critique. The military had justified its claim to be beyond civilian reach and entitled to interfere in politics by referring to its victorious role in German unification and generally to its historical expertise and loyalty as the strongest support of Crown and monarchy. Civilian chancellors, diplomats, and ministers had one by one bowed to this logic and abandoned the political stage to the military experts. When these failed to rescue Germany in the manner which they had promised, their own logic suggested that the military be removed from its special position. Bethmann Hollweg followed through by trying to reinsert the civilian arts of politics and diplomacy into decision making, whence the military had banned them. This would have represented an enormous change in the prewar Wilhelminian system and a terrific shock for the military. But Bethmann's seed held worse in its kernel.

The Wilhelminian leaders had convinced themselves that only an overwhelming military victory could save the monarchy unchanged. Bethmann's tactical shift tacitly acknowledged that such a victory was unlikely. Again, their own logic dictated that anything less made dreaded internal reform inevitable. Even a negotiated peace (including a relatively favorable one), 'minor' annexations, or major German economic, military, or cultural advantages short of direct annexation were inadequate, because it was the very magnitude and prestige of victory that counted. Bethmann knew perfectly well that his tactical shift presaged major reforms. In a memorandum from December 1915, the chancellor wrote:

The limits within which we will have to lead our postwar national life are already given, and even a more or less happy arrangement of the conclusion of peace will hardly be able essentially to widen them. . . . The justifiable sense of self-worth that all classes of people have acquired on the battlefields will tend toward the feeling that after such experiences the old is finished and something new must come, and it will turn its criticism not only on the war and its history and prehistory, but also on the entire existing order [*auf die gesamten bestehenden Zustände*].

The Social Democrats would have to be truly integrated into political life, not just manipulated as scapegoats, and the parties would all take an active part in governing.[70]

In fact, Bethmann's view of the future after a limited victory was much more optimistic than what heavy industry, Pan-Germans, or wide circles of the military and the bourgeoisie had in their mind's eye. They demanded 'far-reaching territorial expansion in the west as in the east,' not just for Germany's external security, but also 'to distract [the people] from internal dissension, which [after a so-called "rotten peace"] would doubtless set in again.'[71] As the Pan-Germans' chairman explained to the Crown Prince the same year: 'if at this fateful hour, an unsatisfying peace were concluded, then not just the Empire, but above all the monarchy and the Hohenzollern dynasty – with all the other dynasties – would be called into question . . . . Then revolution would be only a question of time.'[72] The astute Lerchenfeld wrote that if it were not revolution, it would at the very least be 'a huge dissatisfaction . . . that would occur at the cost of the Kaiser's position and indeed that of the current leading strata.'[73]

This was the very nightmare that the Wilhelminian leaders had gone to war in order to circumvent. To succumb to this nightmare before the very last drop of blood compelled one to, was unthinkable. It was doubly unthinkable to the military, which held itself up as the epitome of the unchanged Wilhelminian system, and whose very honor ('*viel Feind, viel Ehr'*) was at stake. These were the reasons that a difference 'only of degree'[74] between Bethmann and his opponents made all the difference in the world.

The first cracks in the entourage on the war aims question began to appear in April 1915, when the three Cabinet chiefs and the representative of the Foreign Office agreed that continuous offensives were unlikely to produce a breakthrough leading to victory. They believed, with General Staff Chief Falkenhayn, that Germany should conduct a defensive war and wait for stalemate and time to work against the allies.[75] (It was not until later that the Germans recognized that time in fact worked the other way.) During the next two years, this generally sober-sided approach characterized the views of the pro-Bethmann men. There were differences among them, however. Treutler hewed unswervingly and exactly to Bethmann's position.[76]

Valentini was as usual slightly to the right, particularly concerning Belgium, which he felt the chancellor had relinquished without receiving anything in return.[77] Nonetheless, Valentini supported Bethmann's struggle against the rabid annexationists with a loyalty so complete that his enemies never perceived any disagreement between the Cabinet chief and the chancellor.[78]

Neither Müller nor Lyncker was as directly involved with war aims discussions as Treutler (the chancellor's direct representative) or even Valentini (whose second master, after the Kaiser, Bethmann was). War aims did not properly fall in the bailiwicks of either the Naval or the Military Cabinets, and Lyncker in particular scrupulously avoided being drawn into decisions outside his competence.[79] Müller was more vocal, although it appears from his diary that he, too, was only an onlooker during the meetings at which actual decisions were made. His opinions, however, were such that he was invariably lumped with the other 'pessimists,' Bethmann and Valentini.[80] There is some reason to believe that Müller may in fact have held an even darker view. In November 1916, Austria-Hungary finally forced Germany to list its war aims. This was done in a two-stage process. First, Bethmann composed a list and submitted it to OHL. Hindenburg expanded and detailed the demands and returned them. The chancellor softened these somewhat before the Austrians (and the Emperor) saw them. When Müller learned of them, he remarked that they were 'not consonant with the military situation.' He found them 'incomprehensible.'[81] But of the six demands that Müller mentioned, at least three and parts of two others were the chancellor's original suggestions.[82]

By spring 1917, OHL's dictatorship was advanced enough to permit it to set war aims practically unilaterally. It did so at the Kreuznach conference of 23 April 1917.[83] Hindenburg and Ludendorff took Bethmann's September Program and widened it still further. Had Germany been capable of realizing these goals, Bethmann, the Cabinet chiefs, and Treutler would have cheerfully greeted them. As it was, they acquiesced in bitter frustration. Müller recorded his impression:

completely immoderate, in east and west alike . . . . Valentini was quite right when he described the whole thing as 'childish.' One could read Bethmann's and Zimmermann's thought from their eyes: 'it does no harm if we lay down maximum goals. It will work out differently anyhow.'[84]

This was precisely Bethmann's tack. He agreed to OHL's demands with the mental reservation 'if we are able to dictate the peace.'[85]

Otherwise, and it would obviously be otherwise, 'he declared himself not obliged to continue the war, under all circumstances, until these aims should have been achieved.'[86]

After Bethmann's dismissal in July 1917 and until the end of the war, Müller, Treutler's successor Grünau, Valentini (until his ouster in January 1918), and seemingly also Lyncker continued to side with the civilians against OHL. The civilian position tended toward greater flexibility, more solicitude for Austria-Hungary, fewer direct annexations, and a desire for a quicker peace.[87] OHL (and Germany policy) remained little affected by these tendencies.

Did the Cabinet chiefs, Treutler, and Grünau have any stronger effect upon Kaiser Wilhelm in the war aims problem? The answer to this question, as with submarine warfare and Prussian electoral reform, is a difficult one. As we have seen, Wilhelm's mental condition during the war was extremely unstable. The extent of his paralysis, indolence, suggestibility, and inconstancy came as a shock to people who had served him for years. Consequently, the Kaiser's conversations and marginalia cover every side of every issue that cropped up during the war. This is equally true for war aims, where Wilhelm swung quickly between the civilian and the OHL position and back again, and once even adopted as his own (without consulting a soul) the demands he found in a letter from some grain merchant.[88] In general, however, it could be said that Wilhelm favored more hyperbolic war aims than the Cabinets or chancellor. Their main effect upon him was to curb his flights of fancy. This was no small service, for, as soon as OHL had stilled the civilian voice at headquarters by forcing Valentini out, Wilhelm lost all control. At a February 1918 conference on the future peace treaty with Russia, for example, the Kaiser demanded continued war in order to break the forces of international Jewry and the freemasons.[89] Such fantastic outbursts multiplied in the ensuing months, although Wilhelm's impotence fortunately robbed them of direct effect.

The war aims controversy had been difficult for the chancellor to get leverage on, because of the inadmissible consequences of his tactics and because, except for Treutler, Bethmann's allies in the entourage were not supposed to give their opinions on the subject, since it did not technically concern the Cabinets. Such was not the case with submarine warfare.[90] Even though this did not come directly under the purview of the Naval Cabinet chief, it was nonetheless a naval matter. Admiral Müller, who, together with Treutler, was the most critical member of the entourage, could and did (for a time) bring his entire weight to bear on Bethmann's side. In addition, the issue was much more clear cut than the war aims tangle had been. This was only proper, since, in a sense, everyone had been this route before. For the decision to launch unrestricted submarine warfare replicated in many ways the original decision to go to war in 1914. And it had the same result.

As the 1914 war was supposed to smash the domestic and external stalemate in which Germany found itself, unrestricted submarine warfare was to do the same for the war, which after August 1914, had bogged down into bloody immobility. The term unrestricted submarine warfare meant simply that Germany's U-boats would sink without warning merchant or passenger ships, armed or unarmed, neutral or enemy, sailing in the 'war zone' around England. Restricted submarine warfare meant that one or another of these categories might be spared altogether, or that submarines before firing would surface, warn their victims and give them time to abandon ship.[91] Most naval officers supported unrestricted submarine warfare, and beginning in 1915, Tirpitz and others launched a huge propaganda campaign that mobilized for submarines the same groups who favored gigantic annexations and, later on, a Ludendorff–Hindenburg 'dictatorship.'[92] The two sides on the issue were thus nearly what they had been in the war aims controversy.

Supporters of unrestricted U-boats argued consistently that they were a decisive miracle-weapon that would snap the British continental blockade (physical encirclement) and turn the tables on England by cutting off its food supply. In January 1916, Chief of the Admiral Staff Holtzendorff claimed that submarines would knock Britain out of the war in six to seven months,[93] and Tirpitz agreed.[94] As the war dragged on, another argument appeared. Since Germany could not achieve a breakthrough on land, and since its own supplies and its ally's fighting spirit were dwindling, submarines must be unleashed soon.[95] In reply to worries that neutral countries, chief among them the United States, would enter the war on the allied side, the naval enthusiasts replied that (1) it would never happen,[96] (2) if it did, the war would be over before Germany would feel any effects,[97] and (3) even if it did and the war continued, the United States was not strong enough to harm Germany.[98] The combination of nervous haste and bombastic promises is a familiar one.

Opponents argued just as consistently on the other side. First, unrestricted U-boats could not sink as much tonnage as they claimed, and thus would not provide a breakthrough, much less win the war. Second, they would, however, ruin Germany's position with the neutrals, and the United States would enter the war. That had three further consequences: (1) chances for a negotiated peace would disappear; (2) the war would lengthen; and (3) Germany would be starved into submission.[99]

No sooner had the war entrenched itself in immobility than the Admiral Staff began pressing the Kaiser to order submarine attacks on freighters.[100] This pressure foundered upon a solid beachhead of opposition from Falkenyahn, Bethmann, Treutler, Müller, Valentini, all the senior diplomats, most ministers, and even Reischach.[101] Admiral Hugo von Pohl,[102] chief of the High Sea Fleet, nevertheless managed to get Wilhelm alone in February 1915 and convinced him to establish a war zone around Great Britain and to allow submarines to sink enemy freighters there. The order was already public before any other advisers even knew about it.[103] This was indeed a setback (which the opponents of submarine warfare soon corrected), but it was an isolated event. The rest of 1915 brought a string of unbroken victories against the Admiral Staff. So, in three crises with the United States, the first occasioned by the mere announcement of submarine warfare, and the second and third over the sinking of the *Lusitania* in May and the *Arabic* in August, the chancellor and his allies drafted Germany's notes and the Kaiser's new orders to his U-boats. These were all designed to mollify the United States and amounted to severe restrictions on Germany's U-boats.[104] When Admiral Gustav Bachmann, [105] chief of the Admiral Staff, protested, the Kaiser replaced him with Admiral Henning von Holtzendorff,[106] whom Bethmann and Müller considered more tractable.[107] Holtzendorff, an opponent of Tirpitz, did for a time lay even greater limits on submarine activity.[108] In addition, Wilhelm exiled Tirpitz from headquarters, although he did not yet relieve him of office altogether.

These were all substantial victories, but each one had been successively harder to win. The combat began to tell on Bethmann's two workhorses, Müller and Treutler. Müller drafted many of the notes and orders himself and acted as Treutler's expert go-between.[109] The admiral was somewhat spared the negative effects of his toil, because he could make his work seem like compromise between the two sides, but Treutler stood in the full blast of the Admiral Staff's fury. He noted later that

because of my immediate stand against the false use of U-boats and the circumstances that this created, I was more frequently than anyone else drawn personally into the battle with the navy, and I may say that these conflicts slowly ground down my position, until in 1916 I could no longer be a support for the chancellor and had to leave headquarters.[110]

It took another year, 1916, to wear down or convert the navy's opponents. The year began badly when Falkenhayn, grasping at straws, embraced unrestricted submarine warfare after land combat had failed to break the allies.[111] Holtzendorff, too, gradually succumbed to the magical promise, and later, when Tirpitz was finally removed altogether, his successor at the Navy Office, Capelle, likewise hopped aboard the growing bandwagon. At the end of January, Holtzendorff claimed that Germany had enough submarines to bring England to heel in six to seven months. Time was running out, and he pressed Wilhelm for a decision.[112] Wilhelm gave an interim order for 'intensified,' rather than unrestricted submarine warfare (passenger steamers, even armed ones, would be spared), while the final decision on limitless warfare would fall in several weeks. In fact, prompted by another United States note, discussion went on until May 1916, when even the intensified U-boat war was cancelled. This left Germany's submarines with a variety of restrictions which fluctuated during the remainder of the year.[113]

The discussions of February–May 1916 were only an ephemeral victory for the pro-Bethmann faction; they intimated strongly the defeat to come. For one thing, although Bethmann and Treutler remained steadfast in their opposition, Müller began to pull away. Holtzendorff had convinced him that the new crop of improved U-boats really were militarily capable of dispatching Great Britain.[114] Falkenhayn's arguments added more weight to the balance. As Germany's and its allies' conditions became ever worse, it seemed truly criminal to abstain from the one weapon that might mean rescue. On the other hand, America's entry into the war would seal defeat. 'A desperate situation!' Müller wrote in his diary.[115]

Müller responded in three ways. First, he began to contemplate unrestricted submarine warfare as a real possibility, 'but I do not presume to make a judgment on what political results U-boat war would have for us . . . or on whether the war situation on land is such that we must grasp at such a desperate measure.'[116] Second he adopted an interim middle course between unrestricted and completely restricted submarine warfare. This compromise staved off the extremists, but it also made it impossible to return to the position that the civilians wanted. When in November 1916 Bethmann and Grünau asked Müller to help them tighten the reins further while delicate negotiations with the Unized States proceeded, Müller refused.[117] Third, Müller tried to win time, during which he hoped some of the question marks that hung over the decision would be resolved. Some of the items that Müller, Treutler, and Grünau specifically mentioned were: the outcome of Verdun, whether Romania would join the war as an ally or an enemy, the German harvest (which would make the central powers more or less vulnerable to possible United States entry into the war), and whether the allies would accept the German peace offer of late 1916.[118]

The way stations along Müller's odyssey form a familiar pattern. It began with reliance on the prescriptions for victory of technical experts. Their insistence persuaded Müller to think the unthinkable, at first from a purely military standpoint. Whenever he included extra-military considerations (and Müller always did so), he became nervous and uncertain. So he put off the final reckoning until certain interim conditions had been fulfilled, or questions answered. Meanwhile, however, he grew accustomed to the final decision, until it had assumed inevitability. The step could then be dared with a kind of relief, tempered by melancholy.

While Müller floated along this stream, Bethmann lost his other strongest ally, Treutler. Treutler's unbending opposition to the navy had ruined his health, and the doctors packed him off on a seven-week rest cure at the beginning of May 1916. His replacement, Grünau, was a young man, who lacked Treutler's self-confidence, experience, military background, and personal ties to the Kaiser. He was therefore less combative, and also less effective, which 'certain parties found pleasant.'[119] By the time Treutler returned on 16 June 1916, the intrigue to remove him was under way. It was Wilhelm's psychological state that enabled it to succeed, however. The U-boat fight and Falkenhayn's dismissal had beaten the Kaiser into another of his minor nervous breakdowns. He complained that 'he suffers so from loneliness. He has the impression that the older men at headquarters avoid him.'[120] Wilhelm's old schoolfriend, Prussian War Minister Wild von Hohenborn, an ardent enthusiast of unrestricted submarine warfare, took advantage of these sentiments to discredit Treutler as 'a dreadful pessimist,' and 'recommended absolutely his removal, under the pretext of as yet insufficiently strong health.'[121] Wilhelm leapt at the idea, because Treutler was making him 'completely sick.' The Emperor then lied to Treutler, telling him the doctors had ordered him back on rest cure.[122] Under these melodramatic circumstances, the most vocal anti-submariner departed the entourage.

With his main support gone, Bethmann began to swim in Müller's waters. Two of Müller's conditions for turning loose the submarines, certainty about Romania (which joined the allies on 27 August) and a good German harvest,[123] were fulfilled in late summer 1916. Bethmann, carried along by Müller's logic, began to relinquish absolute opposition to ruthless U-boat war.[124] He roused himself enough, and Müller with him, to set one further condition: the outcome of Germany's peace offensive in December 1916.[125] When that failed, Müller took the plunge: 'the general war situation demands our ultimate weapon [*letzte Kampfmittel*] and our political situation, much improved through our peace offer and its sharp rejection by the Entente, allows the use of this means a reasonable chance of success.'[126] Müller then went to work on Bethmann, calming him down, persuading him that if Müller, who had been on the chancellor's side all these years, thought unrestricted U-boat warfare was necessary, then it really was. Bethmann surrendered: 'not approval, but acquiescence to a fact.'[127]

Wilhelm, who had at least formally the final word, had in the U-boat question also mimicked his part in the decision to go to war. He wavered, often from day to day, depending on whose advice he heard last.[128] But since the summer of 1916, the Kaiser had been consistently on Bethmann's side; he thought ruthless submarine warfare would be 'suicide.'[129] The forces behind his 'unexpected, sudden' conversion[130] were basically the same ones operating in 1912/14. Austria's military observer at German headquarters described the surface phenomenon well. He thought that 'these decisions are always difficult for the Kaiser, because [his] military sentiment always leans toward the energetic naval side, which promises a positive goal and success, rather than toward the usually hesitant view of the Foreign Office.'[131] As we know, Wilhelm's military sentiments were in fact an enormous, self-imposed burden that he assumed in order to hide the more vulnerable reality beneath. Treutler knew this, too. A year before the final decision, he explained to Bethmann the Kaiser's paralyzing inner dilemma:

The Kaiser is happy that in the meantime something has happened which spares him the necessity of decision. The question obviously weighs upon him like a burden, because he is inwardly against [unrestricted submarine warfare], but he believes that he must follow the soldiers' advice unless some special occurrence intervenes.[132]

In January 1917, all the special occurrences advanced by the chancellor and his allies had run out. The tension broke. With 'psychotic haste,'[133] Wilhelm signed the order releasing the submarines, exclaiming, 'U-boat war is a purely military matter which does not concern the chancellor at all.'[134]

The year 1917 thus started with an act of desperation and was shortly to see another, Prussian electoral reform. As we have seen, domestic reform was a necessary corollary to Bethmann Hollweg's politics after December 1915, not because he wanted it that way, but because the logic of Germany's situation (and its decision to begin war) demanded it.[135] The poor military outlook, tremendous casualties, worsening economy, and finally, the first phase of revolution in Russia forced Bethmann's hand. Prussian electoral reform was the most popular reform issue. If the Crown did not announce an immediate end to the three-class voting system in Prussia, the chancellor felt, the people might very well try to end it (and everything else) themselves. The more conservative Prussian ministers blocked such an announcement. The most Bethmann could wring out of them and the Kaiser was the promise that sometime in the future, it would happen. Wilhelm proclaimed this in the famous Imperial Easter Message of 7 April 1917. Bethmann's aim was to forestall genuine democratic reform efforts from the bottom up, as is clear from his (and Wilhelm's) chilly response to the Reichstag Constitution Committee's reform proposals.[136] But even Bethmann's hesitant steps toward change were too much for the broad, right-wing phalanx led by OHL. In their eyes, anyone who supported Bethmann's brand of conservatism was a 'chancellor democrat,'[137] who, far from preserving Germany by inaugurating small changes, was actually destroying its essence.

As usual, OHL's view did not correspond to reality. Bethmann's supporters represented a spectrum of opinion on electoral reform. Müller believed that it was absolutely necessary as early as October 1914.[138] Consequently, he was pleased at the Easter Message. Unfortunately, Müller could not do much to help Bethmann against his opponents, because electoral reform was a domestic matter that did not properly concern the Naval Cabinet chief. Furthermore, political disagreements had by this time split the entourage into thoroughly hostile factions, and none of the hardliners designed to discuss politics with Müller.[139]

The chancellor must have missed Müller and Treutler even more, because Civil Cabinet Chief Valentini was not in complete agreement with him. Valentini would only allow that he was 'in no way an opponent of the leftward orientation' of Bethmann's politics in general, but the Easter Message was as far as he could comfortably go.[140] He opposed actual reform while the war continued, so as not to distract people from the war effort. And he rejected Bethmann's idea to have the Kaiser appoint party leaders as ministers (an effort to coopt the Reichstag). Valentini feared such a step would enrage the right, whet the left's appetite and ruin the chancellor's position with Wilhelm.[141] The worst part about Valentini's misgivings was that he could think of no alternatives to recommend. 'What else can save us, then,' he asked, 'except some unforeseeable occurrences in the environment [*Umwelt*]? That was clear to me from the beginning, when this huge force [the war] fell upon us. I have not allowed even the occasional victories of our weapons to cloud this conviction.'[142]

The third Cabinet chief was even slightly to Valentini's right. At least in the beginning, Lyncker did not like the Easter Message, but Grünau 'hope[d] to change [Lyncker's mind].'[143] It appears that Grünau's hopes were not misplaced. Lyncker cooperated with the other Cabinet chiefs when Bethmann made his final effort to force through suffrage reform, and he strongly backed both Bethmann and Valentini when both were driven from their offices in good measure because they had championed domestic change.

It was finally Bethmann himself who worked most effectively for suffrage reform and who became most identified with it, while the Cabinet chiefs worked softly in the background. Wilhelm as usual vacillated. Wilhelm's vision of himself as a reformer emerged from time to time, even in the war. Klepsch-Kloth reported a conversation from June 1915, in which the Kaiser 'talked a lot about his own projects, reform of the suffrage and other institutions, in order to accommodate the people at large, who have accomplished so much with sacrifice; in short, he was preparing a more social reform [*sozialere Reform*], regardless of the opposition of the Conservatives or the nobility.'[144] One heard little of this in the intervening years. When it came time to act on these words, Wilhelm was more hesitant. Prodded by Bethmann, Wilhelm delivered the Easter Message and was quite pleased with the results,[145] but balked at actually introducing reforms during the war.[146] The chancellor pushed on, however, and finally forced a decision to fall in the first week of July 1917 in Berlin, after the Kaiser had consulted with his ministers and state secretaries. The three Cabinet chiefs made sure that as soon as Wilhelm arrived in Berlin he would meet with Bethmann and thus stand the best chance of remaining under the chancellor's influence.[147] They succeeded, and so did Bethmann. The Kaiser approved immediate introduction of suffrage reform (on which the Prussian parliament then had to vote). The Kaiser even gave his imprimatur to the Reichstag's Peace Resolution.[148] With these two steps, Wilhelm moved farther left than he had ever been, or would ever be again.

For an instant, Bethmann and the moderates in the entourage had shown what was possible with this Kaiser. The peculiar circumstances of war had helped them. The Kaiser was shaken and suggestible as never before, the entourage smaller and in firmer control, because there were no distracting trips and few ceremonies. But most of all, the serious times heightened, or perhaps even created the difference between the conservatives of the nineteenth century and the conservative revolutionaries of the twentieth. Even Wilhelm, for all his phantasy and unsteadiness, could be brought to understand this difference. He recognized that Hindenburg, Ludendorff, heavy industry, and their other supporters were engaged in a 'revolutionary undermining of Crown rights and the institution of [the Emperor's] supreme command, that flies in the face of all Prussian tradition.'[149] The Kaiser held strongly to Bethmann as a trusted counterweight against this movement, and he could be moved to hear what was necessary if it came from this source. And Bethmann had finally convinced Wilhelm that some political change was necessary, that is, that 'even a new chancellor would have to demand equal suffrage and the acceptance of parliamentarians into the government.'[150] In other words, Bethmann cast change as a necessary prerequisite to a continued monarchy, rather than as the inimitable chief enemy of the Crown, as the military and agrarians had always done. This was a step not towards progressive government, which neither Bethmann, the Cabinet chiefs, nor Wilhelm wanted, but towards some modicum of reality and reasonableness. It came too little and too late. But it did show that in the monarchy's death throes there were a few people who were, in Wehler's phrase, 'capable of learning.'[151] The bureaucrats, whose job was to mediate efficiently between Wilhelm and the different parts of official Germany, the outsiders, whether by social background, temperament or idiosyncrasy, and the merely melancholy, proved more adept at learning than others. But there were not enough of them.

If Bethmann and his workhorses had shown what one might accomplish with Wilhelm, their defeat soon showed how little one could do with the entourage as a whole, or with the other institutions that it supported and which were reflected in it. For Bethmann's triumph lasted only a few days, before the OHL, the entourage, and the

Reichstag combined to topple him. The precipitating factor, for the entourage, officer corps, and the Crown Prince at least, had been suffrage reform. This struck at the very heart of the privilege system they were fighting to maintain. Ludendorff, Hindenburg, the Prussian war minister, and most of the officer corps rejected reform out of hand. The officers poisoned the air at headquarters with scurrilous remarks about the chancellor, and the infighting took on a grim and hate-filled tone.[152] The motto in the entourage was *Gegen Demokraten helfen nur Soldaten,* 'only soldiers help against democrats.' This was Plessen's enlightened maxim, which the Empress gleefully repeated.[153] Müller tried to reason with her, but gave up. 'It is hopeless.'[154] While the bourgeois parties in the Reichstag abandoned Bethmann,[155] Ludendorff and Hindenburg threatened to resign if the chancellor were not removed. Bethmann bowed to the inevitable on 13 July 1917. The Conservatives in the Prussian parliament defeated suffrage reform the following year. Nothing remained of Bethmann's brief victory.

The third OHL and its allies in the entourage moved quickly to eradicate what remained of Bethmann's influence. The first victim was Civil Cabinet Chief Valentini. The Kaiserin and Plessen had begun serious lobbying against Valentini in May 1917.[156] The Crown Prince chimed in during the summer and in the fall was joined by August Eulenburg.[157] Hindenburg himself delivered the coup de grâce on 16 January 1918 in a letter to Wilhelm in which he claimed that Bethmann and Valentini were solely responsible for the spread of radicalism in Germany. Neither he nor Ludendorff could serve any longer with this man.[158] Valentini left the same day.[159] Before he had gone, however, Valentini confronted the Crown Prince and explained what this action meant and, indirectly, what the Cabinet chiefs had been trying all along to prevent. 'What an undermining of the monarch's authority!' he told Crown Prince Wilhelm. 'This time it is his generals who force the Kaiser to a change in the person of one of his nearest advisers; the next time it will be the Parliament!'[160]

The quality of the entourage changed overnight.

Since you are no longer with us, [Müller wrote to Valentini] a very affected tone reigns among us. The most important questions . . . of domestic politics are mentioned at most once, by the young Messrs Mewes, Hirschfeld and Co [FADs Friedrich Mewes and Georg Ernst Edler v. Hirschfeld] in insolent expressions, to which no answer is given. Mars rules the hour.[161]

Grünau and Reischach noticed a change for the worse in Wilhelm's marginalia a bare two weeks after Valentini's departure: 'continued saber rattling, disdain of diplomats, and anti-Semitism.'[162] The man who could take credit for this change was the new chief of the Civil Cabinet, Friedrich v. Berg.[163] Since June 1917 Plessen, middleman for Ludendorff and Hindenburg, had been pushing Berg to replace Valentini.[164] Once Berg was installed he repaid his benefactors well. 'Berg conceives of his position with H. M. not as a support for the civil government, but goes instead through thick and thin with the Supreme Command.'[165] Berg's mission was to forge the strongest ties between Wilhelm and OHL. These ties had been sundered because the Kaiser, directed by the 'pessimists,' had followed policies which the OHL abhorred. Undoing the damage meant 'that I [Berg] gradually had to bring him [Wilhelm] around to my opinion.'[166] Berg's opinions had once been merely ultra-conservative, stereotypically Junker. During the war, he moved steadily right, until he entered the never-never land of conservative radicalism. He supported Ludendorff's wildest annexationist schemes. He opposed Prussian suffrage reform.[167] He thought that Germany's diplomats 'did not think or feel German, but rather international.'[168] His ties with the rabid agrarians could not have been closer. As Admiral Müller put it, 'Berg bursts with *Kastendünkel.*'[169] Berg achieved in weeks what the Lyncker–Valentini–Müller–Treutler foursome had labored for years to avoid. Despite Wilhelm's backsliding and moments of megalomania, the fact remains that his own policies were never so close to those advocated by the civilians in government as they were during the war. Wilhelm had been held on Bethmann's civilian path only with difficulty, however. He swung easily back into military-induced unreality once the obstacles had been removed. Berg was appalled at Wilhelm's non-Conservative opinions, which Berg labelled pessimistic or lacking in confidence.[170] 'My efforts,' Berg later recalled, 'were directed towards winning self-confidence for the Kaiser. Through trust in the army and in the Oberste Heeresleitung, he [Wilhelm] would come to trust absolutely in victory.'[171] And so he did, throughout the months when Germany was losing the war. Thus, it was Berg, Plessen, and the OHL who set the tone which Müller noted.

By 1918, the sheer duration of the war, the frustrating claustrophobia of headquarters ('our cloud cuckoo land,' as Müller called it[172]), nervous exhaustion, the edgy, boring evenings with the Kaiser, and the acidic infighting had ground everyone except Plessen into anxious shadows of their prewar selves. Without Valentini, the two original Cabinet chiefs sank into silent despair. Lyncker began to bend toward the stronger side,[173] but he soon fell ill and was replaced in July by Ulrich Frhr von Marschall,[174] because he was still too 'doubtingly pessimistic' for the General Staff.[175] Under the stress of war, Müller's gastric ulcer flared up again. His enemies in the navy started to intrigue. Müller stopped fighting. He became resigned to the 'stupidity' which surrounded him, and contented himself with noting the outrages in his diary. Müller must have retired quickly, because Berg 'never noticed that his influence was disrupting.'[176] Had Müller had any influence left, 'disrupting' would have been the least that Berg would have found it. So, 'Mars ruled the hour' and presided over the tragi-comic end of monarchy and entourage, the abdication of 9 November.

By the end of October 1918, the personnel of the entourage had changed. Clemens v. Delbrück,[177] formerly Vice Chancellor and State Secretary of the Interior (1909–16), had succeeded Berg as chief of the Civil Cabinet on 12 October 1918. The 'revolution from above' of October 1918[178] had created a government too democratic for Berg to tolerate.[179] Kapitän zur See Karl v. Restorff[180] became acting Naval Cabinet chief on 28 October 1918.[181] Wilhelm spent the last ten days of his reign with the following members of the entourage: Grünau, Paul v. Hintze, who was now State Secretary of the Foreign Office, Delbrück, Plessen, Marschall, FAs Ilsemann, Hirschfeld, Moltke, Münchhausen, and Dohna-Schlodien, Dr Niedner and Gontard. Hindenburg and Wilhelm Groener, Ludendorff's successor,[182] were the other two conferees in the last week. The tone and mood of the entourage were unchanged. 'There are still so many people in his [Wilhelm's] entourage who tell the Kaiser that he has the people behind him,' Lerchenfeld, the Bavarian representative in Berlin, reported on 30 October.[183] 'H. M. is simply not informed.'[184]

At least since President Woodrow Wilson's Note of 23 October, if not before, every politically aware person knew that Wilhelm must abdicate. The new chancellor, Prince Max von Baden, the ministers, and the minister presidents of the state governments agreed. They realized that the allies would not treat with the Kaiser, that the broad mass of the people blamed Wilhelm for prolonging the war. If Wilhelm abdicated quickly enough, some thought, it might be possible to save the monarchy. Every day lost diminished that possibility. By 30 October Under Secretary Wahnschaffe thought it was already too late to save it.[185]

Not surprisingly, the pro-Bethmann group and those with links to the civil government (Grünau and Hintze) were the first in the entourage to realize that Wilhelm must go. Treutler performed his last service for Wilhelm by trying to persuade him to abdicate voluntarily. Wilhelm and most of the entourage reacted with disgust to Treutler's 'disloyalty.'[186] Knowing Wilhelm too well, Müller tried to convince Military Cabinet Chief Marschall that since abdication was inevitable, it was better to do so with grace, voluntarily, than to wait to be forced later. Marschall refused to hear of such a thing.[187] Both Hintze and Grünau worked tirelessly for abdication. Hintze, however, tried to do so in small stages, to take Wilhelm by surprise.[188] Wilhelm's old friend Max Fürstenberg, who always knew which way the wind was blowing, also favored abdication.[189]

Wilhelm was not inclined to listen to such counsel. He relied completely on his military advisers,[190] whose opinions ranged from the rabid to the unreal. Fanatics like Berg, Ludendorff, and Schulenburg thought Wilhelm should rush to his troops and find a hero's death fighting either against the allies or against the 'bolsheviks' at home. However, 'there was no man there' to advise Wilhelm in this way, lamented Berg. 'Life does not count, only honor, the monarchy, and the Fatherland.'[191] In fact, Schulenburg, who accompanied the Crown Prince to Spa on 9 November, did advise Wilhelm to do precisely this, to stage a military showdown. To Hintze's question, would German troops loyal to Wilhelm actually shoot German civilians or troops disloyal to him, Schulenburg was forced to reply, no.[192] The Crown Prince presumably agreed with Schulenburg, but was careful to arrive so late and to leave so early that he did not have to share responsibility either for Schulenburg's plan or for the decision actually taken.[193] Groener later claimed that he, too, had recommended this aggressive course to Plessen and Gontard, who rejected it. Plessen denied the whole story.[194]

Plessen and Marschall favored a slighly less drastic solution. Since they operated under the delusion that the army was still loyal, risk of death would not be involved. Wilhelm could simply put himself at the head of an army and march triumphantly back to Berlin and create order there. This was the course which Wilhelm favored steadfastly until the 9th. The FAs, for their part, believed that Wilhelm should simply stay at his post in Spa. None of them addressed himself to what might come after that.[195]

Several weeks earlier, on 2 October, Wilhelm had arrived in Berlin. There, the Kaiser was open to increasing pressure from the government and political parties to abdicate. To forestall this, the military entourage, led probably by Plessen and Marschall,[196] spirited Wilhelm back to GHQ in Spa on 29 October. From afar, the chancellor and the Foreign Office tried repeatedly to bring Wilhelm to abdicate.[197] Buoyed by the 'optimists,' however, Wilhelm remained unmoved.

The first crack in the united military front did not appear until late on 8 November, when General Groener changed his mind about the state of the army. Until then he thought that the officer corps and enough troops still supported the monarchy to make abdication not only unnecessary, but in fact harmful, because it would precipitate the army's dissolution.[198] Now, however, Groener declared that Wilhelm could not use the army reliably against revolutionaries, because it could not feed itself and would not fire on Germans. Plessen was unimpressed; Hindenburg was unsure.[199] The next morning Hindenburg succumbed to Groener's arguments after they were substantiated by fifty officers from the front whom Groener had shipped in to give their opinions.[200] These developments moved Plessen and Marschall only to agree that Wilhelm should abdicate as Kaiser, but not as King of Prussia. Wilhelm followed their advice. When Hintze phoned Berlin to despatch this news, he learned that Prince Max had already been forced to announce Wilhelm's complete abdication two hours before.[201]

Plessen and Marschall at last gave in to the *fait accompli*. The question now was what would happen to the ex-Kaiser? Groener, Hindenburg, Grünau, Hintze, Plessen, and Marschall conferred and decided Holland was the safest place to guard Wilhelm from the hands of revolution. Groener, Hindenburg, and Hintze finally convinced Wilhelm of this plan and set the departure for the next morning.

During the next few hours Wilhelm changed his mind several times. After the war the Court-in-exile tried to orchestrate the various eye-witness accounts of 9 November to heap responsibility for Wilhelm's flight first on Hindenburg and Groener and ultimately on Hintze.[202] According to this line, Wilhelm rejected Groener's advice, wavered, but ultimately made up his mind to stay and fight. Only Hintze's remonstrance (delivered by Grünau) that if Wilhelm delayed any longer he would be cut off and surrounded by revolutionaries, only this moved the Kaiser to reconsider.[203] Despite the best efforts of the exiled monarchists, however, the eye-witness accounts do not agree.[204] Even the disagreements cannot obscure the fact that Wilhelm abdicated because he no longer had military support sufficient to force himself back into power; he fled to Holland to escape death at the hands of revolutionaries. The advice which he received from Groener and Hintze, though tardy, was quite right.

The 'criminal shortsightedness,' as Fürstenberg called it,[205] of the military entourage was pierced not by Grünau's or Hintze's entreaties, not by information, not by political thinking or even by common sense, but only by a *fait accompli*. Groener recognized that

most [German] generals during the entire war were prisoners of a dangerous self-delusion. They did not recognize the true strategic or political situation. They clung to their thoughts of the fine victories which their troops had won on the battlefields. They did not think at all about the[ir] strategic or political effects.[206]

Wilhelm and the military entourage, who had clearly learned nothing from the war, learned nothing from the abdication either. They quickly reverted to their old thought that abdication had not been necessary at all. If only Wilhelm had found loyal troops and marched on Berlin. This is the burden of their attempt to rewrite history.[207] Groener and Hintze had given bad advice. After all, Groener was a Württemberger,[208] and Hintze, according to Wilhelm, was a tool of the Jews and the Roman Catholic Church.[209]

Sadder but no wiser, Wilhelm arrived at the Dutch border on the morning of 10 November 1918. He was accompanied by seventy men. German Ambassador Rosen turned back forty servants and technicians, lest Wilhelm wear out his welcome.[210]

11

The entourage: its influence and responsibility

The preceding chapters have examined the interdetermination of several structures. On the most general level, the structure of the semi-autocratic monarchy itself defined the basic contours of political and social life in the Reich. It reserved effective political action for the Junkers and their monarch by preserving institutions which could not be penetrated by social groups unwilling to assume the characteristics and adopt the political interests of the ruling Junker class. These institutions were the army, officer corps, the upper bureaucracy, including the diplomatic corps, and the Court and Cabinets. As far as possible, the monarch and the Junkers strove to restrict information gathering and decision making to these institutions. The economic elite, the men of industry, finance, and commerce, largely accepted this division of labor, because their primary interest was business, not politics, because they shared more of the noble world view than they rejected, and because they feared Social Democracy more than they disliked the Junkers. The acquiescence of the economic elite strengthened monarchical institutions immeasurably.

This study has focussed on two monarchical institutions in particular: the Court and the Cabinets. Both Court and Cabinets served as bureaucratic arms of the monarch. They were simply to carry out his orders, never to initiate policy. Although their tasks and organization were bureaucratic, however, the Court and Cabinets were still personal institutions. Personnel recruitment continued in the late nineteenth century to follow two guidelines appropriate to personal institutions: loyalty to the particular monarch and 'character.' 'Character' as we have seen, was the Prussian code word for a constellation of qualities which included good birth, correct upbringing, propriety, and adherence to noble values and judgments. There were a sufficient number of bureaucratic virtues, like efficiency, duty, and service, which had become part of the Prussian noble ethos, to ensure that selection according to 'character' did provide personnel who could successfully expedite business, so long as they were not called upon to help create policy.

Both proximity to the monarch and the personal relationship between him and his servants in the Court and Cabinets conspired, however, from the beginning to implicate the latter in policy formation. This tendency became more marked as the alternate source of advisers, the ministries, became associated with efforts to curb the power of the monarch, either on the part of the ministers themselves or, via interpellation, of the parliament. After 1871 it seemed in the interest of the monarch to rely more on his personal suite than on trained bureaucrats, whose loyalty might be to the *gute Sache* rather than to the Kaiser. The use of the Court and Cabinets as a reactionary counterweight to bureaucratic independence or parliamentary influence meant that the monarch valued them precisely for their old-fashioned qualities. That is, there was little chance that the Court and Cabinets would ever be modernized either in organization or personnel. They were the last reliable (because controllable) enclave of Junker power. The structure of quasi-autocratic monarchy thus resulted in the paradox that the monarch continued to consult people who were neither trained nor chosen for decision-making abilities.

This paradox created a palpable tension within Wilhelm's entourage, as it became harder to reconcile personal service with bureaucratic or political duty. The entourage tended to divide into those who had regular, defined bureaucratic work and those who did not. The former consisted broadly of the Cabinet chiefs, the representatives of the Foreign Office, the Ober- and Hofmarschälle, and the minister of the royal house. The men in these offices identified themselves more and more with their work, rather than with their personal relationship with the monarch. The bureaucratic process pulled them inexorably in its tow. We have noticed how, as the reign wore on, the appointments to these positions advanced individuals, like Müller or Valentini, who were preeminently bureaucratic in their outlook and, to that degree, distanced from Wilhelm. The relentlessness of this process is clear also in the careers of Paul von Hintze, Carl von Wedel, and Karl von Treutler. All began their careers as officers and built personal relationships with Wilhelm on that basis. For different reasons, each transferred into the diplomatic corps. All subsequently became critical of Wilhelm and the military entourage, Treutler and Hintze to such an extent that Wilhelm considered that they had betrayed him.

Ranged against these gentlemen were those whose duties were

strictly personal. These people were mostly in the Hauptquartier, that is, they were mostly officers whose narrow outlook had certainly not been broadened by the necessity to provide imperial instructions with the appearance of coherence and continuity. The officers of the Hauptquartier could content themselves with pleasing Wilhelm, without regard to the longer-range effects of his pleasure. The 'bureaucrats,' even when they too were officers, were thus more likely to be in sympathy with the stand of the real bureaucrats – the chancellor, his ministers, the Foreign Office – than was the Hauptquartier. At the very least the 'bureaucrats' were more apt to understand why the chancellor or the ministers felt forced to take a position unpopular with the Kaiser.

The structure of the entourage itself smothered even this modicum of enlightenment. The personal bond between the Kaiser and the men of the entourage forbad behavior consistent with the bureaucratic outlook. Personal servants of the Emperor were supposed to lighten his burden by transmitting orders without fuss. They were not supposed to argue or contradict, to bend the Emperor to their schedules, to 'lie in wait,' in short, to do any of the things which concern for the *gute Sache* might require. Only three courses were open to men who longed to transgress these bounds: they could resign (or be dismissed), like Hofmarschall Robert von Zedlitz-Trützschler (Treutler, Alfred von Kiderlen-Wächter, or Rudolf Valentini); they could transfer out of Court service, like Wedel or Hintze; or they could criticize occasionally but for the rest maintain frustrated silence, like Müller, who sublimated his anger into an ulcer and a diary. The failure to restrain Wilhelm in the way in which responsible ministers might have done was the chief criticism levelled at the men of the entourage. This failure, however, owed more to the structure of personal entourage than to individual cowardice or sycophancy.

If monarchy, which is a system of personal loyalty writ large, determined the limits of the entourage as a political organization, the social class system reinforced these limits and imposed still others. The monarchy and the nobility were involved in an inextricable, symbiotic relationship with one another. Each one was the other's mainstay, its chief raison d'être. At the end of the nineteenth century this was more true than it had ever been. As social, economic, and political changes increasingly threatened both institutions, they clung the more desperately to each other. The identification of the nobility with the monarchy changed the content of the noble ethos in at least two ways, which had significant effects, in turn, upon the men of the entourage:

it became militarized, and it became almost monomaniacally concerned with self-preservation.

The militarization of the Prussian nobility was, of course, an old process. By the Wilhelminian era, however, it meant that the nobility as a whole had assumed the ethos of a small part of itself, namely, of the officer corps. This process did not occur to the same extent in other countries. In Prussia–Germany it was helped along by the prestige of the officer corps throughout society, by the hope that identification with the strongest part of the monarchy would shore up the nobility, and by the fact that virtually every nuclear family had at least one member in the military.[1] Because the military demanded absolute propriety not only of its officers but also of their families, the military played an even more all-pervasive role in defining and maintaining class norms than did the Court itself.

The military ethos, embodied in its officer's honor code, was more rigid, more exclusive, and more specific than civilian standards of behavior. It was also, of course, stereotypically masculine. The virtues it touted were hardness, decisiveness, strength, obedience, and control. Under this scheme of things the merits of diplomacy and politics were suspect as manifestations of indecision or weakness. As we have seen, the overvaluation of military manliness predisposed a contingent within the entourage to vigorous or bellicose policies. This was equally if not more true for men who feared that they did not measure up to the masculine ideal. Wilhelm himself is the most perfect single example of this paradox.

The minute prescriptions of the honor code exercised a decisive influence in determining the terms in which the nobility conceived of its struggle for self-preservation. Self-preservation was a natural enough concern for the nobility to have in an industrialized world, and there were several different ways in which it might have gone about securing its position. Under German circumstances, with the preponderant military influence on the nobility, the preeminent role of the nobility in the main institutions of government, and the speed of industrialization – which made the process seem so much more relentless and frightening – the Prussian nobility preferred, not the route of creative adaptation or gradual compromise (as in Britain), but that of repression, rigidity, and control. This tactic did not use the nobility's strength to its best advantage. Unlike the French nobility prior to the French Revolution, the Prussian nobility had not been excluded by the Crown from the exercise of political power.[2] It was, on the contrary, in an unparalleled position to direct social, political, and economic compromises so that it would ultimately benefit from them. Furthermore, the other social classes were more than willing to engage in compromises which would have increased their own participation in politics, but which would by no means have ended the control that the nobility exercised over key positions. Instead, however, the nobility stood fast, clutching every facet of its power.

Standing pat put the nobility in a purely defensive position. Thus having robbed itself of mobility, it could only wait for the impending onslaught. The determination to preserve every vestige of its mastery soon blinded it to distinctions between the important and the petty. The honor code stiffened. The high and mighty retreated to their own enclaves, their *Kasinos,* their newly resegregated regiments. There they darkly wondered about the portents they saw around them. What did it mean that young people insouciantly preferred to live at hotels rather than with their parents,[3] that homosexuality seemed to be spreading, that officers were no longer punctilious in their comportment at social occasions? All of these details were taken as symbolic of the larger state of German affairs.

Symbolic interpretation thus elevated insignificant detail to significance. The defensive stance of the nobility contributed to this process by fostering a mania for control. The more aspects of social and political life which could be repressed, controlled, regimented, or overseen, the less could changes in these spheres threaten the nobility and its monarchy. Again, the close identification between the nobility and the army supported this obsession with control, which was the peacetime army's raison d'être. Together, the concerns for control and for symbol produced a characteristic which the nobles themselves, oddly enough, identified as typical of the modern age: preoccupation with 'externality' (*Äusserlichkeit*), or with mere appearance. This preoccupation was more typical, however, of those who opposed the modern age than of those who felt comfortable with it. The burden which fixation upon symbolic, external detail placed upon the monarch and his entourage was a heavy one. Wilhelm spent all too much time executing, and his entourage all too much time planning for, celebrations designed to spread propaganda for the monarchy and its social order. The planning which Wilhelm, the entourage, and even under secretaries devoted to parades, swearings-in, unveilings, anniversaries, and so forth was as meticulous as that which went into the Schlieffen Plan.

The rigidity of social expectations, the obsession with control, the prison of detail, the all-pervading repression, these products of the noble ethos at the end of the nineteenth century contributed one other element to the atmosphere of the entourage: tension. It is not that standards were too high to live up to, but that they were too precise. The luxuriant growth of specific regulations made self-contradiction inevitable. Hyprocrisy was the only refuge, for too much was demanded and too much forbidden. Outwardly, the men of the entourage were more successful than most at meeting their class's standards. They had had to prove that they possessed 'character,' manly attributes, unexcelled monarchical feeling. These were prerequisites for Court positions, where one would, among other things, continuously represent the monarchy. In a sense, courtiers were on twenty-four-hour-a-day ceremonial call. But past success, which propelled one farther into the public eye, only increased the pressure. The men of the entourage were in unceasing bondage to the noble code. Not a few left Court positions to try to regain (in private life) what they had lost.

The structure of monarchy, of personal government, delimited the entourage organizationally, while the noble ethos and, more specifically, the officer's honor code regulated the behavior of its members through socialization and peer pressure. The third force which imposed itself on these two others was the monarch himself. The dissection of Wilhelm's personality is not merely a biographical exercise, or a lapse into the great man theory of history (in German: *Personalisierung*). On the contrary, Wilhelm's character had wide-ranging structural implications for the constitution and operation of the entourage and for decision making in the monarchy.

On the most general level, the Prusso-German monarchy concentrated enormous power into the hands of the King-Emperor. Much of that power was expressly reserved for the Kaiser alone; it could not be limited by other institutions. The greatest flaw in the system was precisely that the monarch received this power by virtue of birth, not talent. Once Wilhelm became Kaiser, the system's inertia worked to keep him in that position, despite his obvious deficiencies. Regencies were not lightly embarked upon, because they disturbed the continuity of the monarchy and thus damaged one of its claims to legitimacy. In addition, the two obvious regents for Wilhelm were Wilhelm's brother Prince Heinrich, before the majority of Wilhelm's son the Crown Prince, and the Crown Prince himself thereafter. Both Prince Heinrich and the Crown Prince were thought to be even worse than Wilhelm, so that regency was not a popular solution to the problems that Wilhelm's character created.

The monarchical form of government itself is thus to blame for creating a situation in which Wilhelm's personality could wreak such havoc and for offering no easy remedy for the condition once it had been recognized. The social class structure was also implicated in the catastrophe. Wilhelm was in some ways a casualty of the rigid expectations of his day. In what ways social structure, via Wilhelm's family and upbringing, produced the flawed character of the last Kaiser is beyond the purview of this book. What is clear, however, is that the prevailing social norms could not have been more ill-suited to the Kaiser nor better designed to prevent him from helping himself. Hardest on him was the unrelenting demand that he be 'manly,' shorthand for a congeries of qualities, most of which Wilhelm did not possess. In order to hide his inadequacy, Wilhelm forced himself to become a public caricature of masculinity. He listened more closely to advice proffered by the tough-minded soldiers of his military suite and, given a choice, he inclined toward policies which seemed more vigorous, courageous, or strong, against those from which observers might deduce that Wilhelm was a coward. Wilhelm thus reflected on the personal level the same obsessions with control and strength that the nobility at large revealed in its ideology.

The double-binding nature of the overvaluation of masculinity made matters worse. Beginning at the age of ten, Wilhelm was brought up strictly in the company of men. They were his friends, teachers, and models. Masculine virtues were the only ones that counted. Women might well have been another species, so undervalued and little regarded were they. It is no wonder that Wilhelm disliked them or that his emotional life revolved around male friends. But having thus encouraged homoeroticism in every way, the noble ethos then excoriated its overt manifestation as decadent weakness and disgusting perversion. This hardly encouraged Wilhelm to understand himself or to live his life in a way that might have satisfied him. The Kaiser was by no means alone in this predicament, as the number of similarly conflicted persons whom he collected around himself at Court shows.

Broadly speaking, Wilhelm's peculiar personality affected the entourage in three ways: by his choice of personnel to fill Court, Cabinet, and Hauptquartier positions (which in turn changed the patterns these institutions followed); by the limits which his character placed upon the effectiveness of entourage members in dealing with him; and by widening the entourage to include friends like Philipp Eulenburg, whose influence then became immense.

We have seen how Wilhelm's *Personalpolitik* carefully reduplicated the two sides of his personality. There were the tough-acting, brusque military men, whom Wilhelm admired, and the softer types, whom Wilhelm could dominate in emulation of the others and with whom he could empathize. There were also the 'bureaucrats,' whose devotion to duty and careful routine tended in Wilhelm's mind to place them with the 'soft' group. In policy terms, the 'bureaucrats' – often with the exception of the Military Cabinet chief – were usually closer to the spokesmen for civilian policy (the chancellor, ministers, and Foreign Office representatives), while the tougher sorts pleaded for more reactionary policies characteristic of the military. The 'soft' group was likely to shift to whatever position Wilhelm seemed most likely to adopt. The 'bureaucrats,' thus isolated, would then surrender, salvaging what they could.

Most of the tough characters dated from the early years of Wilhelm's reign, and many had even been placed in Wilhelm's military entourage by Chancellor Bismarck and Military Cabinet Chief Albedyll in order to ensure that Wilhelm did not follow in his liberal father's footsteps.[4] Thus Wilhelm's entourage directly reflected the reactionary policies of the Bismarckian system. The existence of the 'characters' in the entourage guaranteed that in each policy issue there would be spokesmen for a hard line. The existence of the 'soft' group, plus Wilhelm's fear of 'chickening out' meant that the hardliners were likely to win the day. The hardliners were outmaneuvered by the civilians only twice: by Eulenburg in the 1890s, and during the first years of the war. Eulenburg managed this by virtue of his friendship with Wilhelm and his adroit manipulation of various political allies. Wilhelm inclined to the politics of the civilians during the war for several reasons: because Bethmann had acquired Naval Cabinet Chief Müller as an ally, while the Military Cabinet chief acquiesced and sometimes even supported them; because the entourage was smaller, and thus the few advocates of civilian policy were proportionately stronger; and because Wilhelm finally saw that the alternative to civilian policy was the Supreme Command, which would rob him of decision-making authority altogether.

Wilhelm's personality limited the effectiveness of the entourage in other ways besides the selection of personnel. Those entourage members who had regular bureaucratic work to perform suffered the most from Wilhelm's erratic lifestyle and impulsive character. Wilhelm physically exhausted them by constant travelling, which interrupted their scheduled *Vorträge* and separated them from their files. They performed many hours of ceremonial duty that the Emperor usually ended by several more hours of conversation, all while standing: this was the much dreaded *Herumstehen,* which appears in almost everyone's memoirs. Uninterrupted standing was especially hard on the older men, of whom, however, the Kaiser took no notice whatsoever.

Wilhelm's peripatetic habits might have been supportable had he not also been prone to surprising (and often contradictory) interventions in policy, usually in the form of impromptu speeches, conversations, interviews, or telegrams. The energy which the men of the entourage had left over after trying to prevent such outbursts was promptly consumed by efforts to undo what could not be prevented. Speeches had to be rewritten for newspaper publication, witnesses to what was actually said had to be hushed up or, failing that, their eyewitness reports discreetly denied. Flurries of telegrams and letters had to be dispatched to calm the waves excited by a single imperial *Brieftelegram.* Wilhelm's inappropriate conversations often included members of his entourage and, to their credit, many spent much effort trying to avoid being placed in the position of giving advice in an area outside their *Ressort.* The entourage naturally tired of these Sisyphean labors.

Finally, the effectiveness of the men of the entourage was hindered by their very awareness of Wilhelm's fragility and weakness. A short acquaintance with the Emperor sufficed to show that his nerves could withstand neither prolonged work nor disappointment. Here again, both social class and the monarchical system combined to make the situation worse. The members of the entourage were trained to deal with the monarch as they found him, to work efficiently, and to please him. They were not trained either to chide or to change their superiors, much less their Emperor. They thus tried whenever possible to work around him. They shortened their *Vorträge* as much as possible, so that Wilhelm would not impatiently cut them off. They tried to give in to the imperial whim in matters which did not seem important, so that they would be in a stronger position to protest on graver subjects. In periods when Wilhelm's nerves seemed dangerously overstrained, they avoided giving him news which might send him whirling into depression.

These ploys have been labelled 'Byzantinism.' This term is appropriate so long as it refers to the product of a system or systems, and not merely to the isolated moral failings of individuals. However, 'Byzantinism' is still a misleading term because it implies that the entourage allowed Wilhelm to do whatever he pleased. This ignores that large part of entourage activity which sought to save Wilhelm from his own follies. In fact, there were two alternatives to handling the difficult Emperor in the manner called 'Byzantine': one could have fought the Kaiser at every turn and thus have been quickly dismissed or irrevocably exhausted, or one could simply have let matters slide. The results of the latter course would soon have been a catastrophe of uncertain proportions, with the certain byproduct, however, of an imperial nervous breakdown. The severity of that breakdown would have determined whether Wilhelm merely lapsed into docility, or was so severely damaged that only a regency could have functioned in his stead. This is not merely idle speculation. Friedrich von Holstein outlined the same alternatives in the early 1890s and for several years seriously contemplated allowing Wilhelm to destroy himself. But in the end even Holstein, who could not possibly be called a toady, who met Wilhelm only once, and whose loyalty was entirely to the *gute Sache,* could not bring himself to this step. The consequences were too awful to risk.[5] So Holstein too chose the path of amelioration, just as nearly everyone in the entourage and most of Wilhelm's friends did as well.

The person most adept at the policy of amelioration was Wilhelm's friend Philipp zu Eulenburg. Wilhelm's intense need for sympathetic, protective, male companionship opened him up to Eulenburg's many charms. Eulenburg, moved by love and pity for the young Kaiser, began trying to make ruling easier for Wilhelm. The count was guided by a vision of personal regime. That is, if Wilhelm ruled himself, he would suffer no disappointments caused by ministers, chancellors, or parliament. Wilhelm's peculiarities soon forced Eulenburg to modify this scheme, however. Wilhelm's ideas would form the basis of government policy, but the actual political maneuvering would be done by an utterly loyal chancellor, Bernhard Bülow.

Eulenburg was at first helped in his project by Holstein at the Foreign Office. Holstein assisted Eulenburg because the latter successfully smoothed over innumerable rough spots that Wilhelm had created and because Eulenburg was the strongest proponent of civilian policy in the entourage. Again and again, Eulenburg thwarted the military entourage's wild plans for a revolution from above or for proroguing parliament. Holstein soon learned, however, that Eulenburg was only a civilian in the choice of his means, but not of his ends. Eulenburg shied away from *Krachpolitik* because he thought it would harm Wilhelm. Therefore he favored slower changes, sweeter words, more diplomatic maneuvering. But the goal which these devices would ultimately reach was personal regime 'in the good sense,' that is, the inauguration of policy chosen by Wilhelm. This goal was eminently acceptable to the men in the military entourage, because they agreed with Wilhelm's larger objectives. Ironically, Eulenburg later had doubts about the wisdom of personal regime. Partly, these stemmed from disappointment at how Wilhelm treated him, and worries about Wilhelm's mental condition. But some of Eulenburg's misgivings arose because the future which he envisioned was considerably less expansionist and bellicose than the one toward which Germany seemed to be heading.

Eulenburg's doubts came too late. He had already removed the two strongest advocates of actual civilian policy, Chancellor Caprivi and Foreign Minister Marschall. Bülow did just what Eulenburg had originally hoped: he put Wilhelm's ideas to work. These ideas were *Weltpolitik* externally and the repression of social change internally. Those military men who did not already favor the former acquiesced to it as a means to achieve the latter, their real goal. For the military entourage and Wilhelm were unanimous in wanting primarily the maintenance of the status quo and, where possible, the extension of reactionary institutions (like the Cabinets) against modern ones (like the ministers or the Reichstag). *Weltpolitik* was a means to this goal and a symbol of it, but the fruits of *Weltpolitik* were nonetheless sweet or desirable for that. Eulenburg, the civilian, by preparing personal regime, thus helped to enhance the power of the military entourage. His disgrace in 1907/8 only brought that process to its logical conclusion.

By observing the actions of the entourage over time, we have seen the horizon bounding the politically possible become narrower, step by step. At the most general level, the monarchical form of government presented limits to political action, which were then further restricted by the expectations and prejudices of social class. The horizon narrowed still further under the baleful effects of Wilhelm's personality. Under these circumstances, pinpointing the nature of the 'influence' of the entourage is not merely a matter of discovering who whispered what advice into the monarch's ear at what time. The influence exercised by the entourage formed a pattern, which was the result of the interaction among three levels of structure: the entourage as an organizational form, the types of personalities who belonged to the entourage, and the character of the monarch himself. These structures constrained each other in such a way that two aspects of the entourage came to predominate in policy. These two aspects were its position as the preserver of the monarch's power and its overwhelming military tone. The first made it highly unlikely that policies would progress much beyond the reactionary. The second ensured that these policies would be executed in the most forthright, not to say clumsy, manner possible.

Put in another way, the entourage considered as a whole had two major effects on the conduct of affairs in the Wilhelminian Empire. First, the entourage was more conservative than Wilhelm was. We will never know how far Wilhelm's modern potential might have been developed in other surroundings. We do know, however, that the Emperor had no sympathy for the agrarians, that he was fascinated by industrialism and technology and that he was at base not in favor of war. That he could be moved to support some degree of change became clear during the first years of the war under the active tutelage of the Valentini–Treutler–Müller group. But Wilhelm also harbored reactionary potential and it was this which the entourage fostered year in, year out. Because the German governmental system concentrated so much power into the hands of the quasi-autocratic Emperor, the entourage's activity in pushing Wilhelm to the right was of immense political importance. In effect, the entourage established the limits to progressive change emanating from the top. Those limits could hardly have been narrower. Even moderate reform was too dangerous for the entourage to allow. Eulenburg's success in ousting the men who represented the relatively progressive New Course is simply unimaginable without the enthusiastic support that he received from the entourage. Similarly, the liberal reform typified by the MStGO was quashed single-handedly by the military entourage against the protests of practically the entire country.

The second effect which the entourage as a whole had on policy was more radical than the mere holding action described above. The entourage was the direct conduit between the Emperor and the army. It was the mechanism which perfected the well-nigh untrammelled power which that reactionary institution possessed in the Prusso-German state. And it was through the entourage that the leap forward to 'preventive war' was made. 'Preventive war' as the only solution to the monarchy's problems was an idea which began with the General Staff and was based upon a narrowly military assessment of Germany's position. The idea gained currency first among the other military men in the entourage, while the Kaiser and the civilians resisted it. Only after years of increasingly strident urging by Moltke and others in the military entourage, did the Kaiser, the chancellor and the civilians embrace, however reluctantly, the 'necessity' of war. This is not to say that the military is solely responsible for the war. We have seen the great extent to which the patterns of Wilhelminian society, military and civilian, prepared the way for such an idea: the mania for control, the anxious rigidity, the reluctance to rule except by repression, the hypersensitivity to weakness, and so forth. 'Preventive war' was attractive to the Wilhelminian establishment because it was a purely tactical solution to the monarchy's ills. Nonetheless, the army was the discoverer of and the driving force behind the idea, and the entourage was the institutional means through which it reached acceptance.

What do these two effects say about the relationship between the entourage and the Kaiser? Whose influence was overriding? It is impossible to answer this question perfectly, but the pattern seems reasonably clear. Wilhelm's desires held a basic contradiction. He wanted simultaneously to change everything (German industrial power, the European state constellation, world colonial divisions) and to keep everything the same (his personal power, the army's position inside Germany, Prussia's heritage). The entourage wanted the second part of this program, but became increasingly convinced that adopting sections of the first part might be most useful in cementing the second. Even so, the entourage as a whole interpreted Wilhelm's goals in a less flexible, less imaginative and less grandiose way than he did, and to this extent, thwarted him. Unless Wilhelm was really prepared, in deed as well as word, to become a nationalistic caesar, however, the entourage still represented more of Wilhelm's program than any other contemporary institution could have done. But for it, the emphasis was on preservation. This produced the peculiar decision-making technique which arrived at crucial decisions by more or less backing into them. Two of the most important stages in the decision-making process were often short-circuited, which had two results: first, the a priori exclusion of most solutions to a problem as simply inconceivable, and second, the inadequate assessment of the real consequences or costs of the few solutions that were left. The short-circuiting was unacknowledged and often unconscious, so that at the end of the process, the entourage (and Wilhelm) thought they faced inevitable conclusions. In this way, the product of their own limitations appeared to them to be external coercion.

Indeed, the entourage was especially in its limitations the perfect Wilhelminian institution. It represented in a single unit the larger, agrarian nobility, the army, and the monarchy. It reflected intensely the biases and preoccupations of all three. It mediated among them and hammered their different impulses into a single direction. Its

duty was to preserve the status quo, and it did so in the manner peculiar to the most dynamic factor of the three, the army. Bismarck had
purposely filled Wilhelm's entourage with hypermartial men precisely
in order to foster the reactionary potential of the entourage as an
institution. He was eminently successful in this endeavor. It is no wonder, then, that the entourage did not rise above its milieu, that it
responded to the crises of the *Kaiserreich* in the rigid pattern characteristic of the upper stratum of society.

The critics who blamed the men of the entourage for personal failure were in general wrong. The vast majority tried their utmost to
fulfill their duty as they understood it. Their failure was overdetermined by their class, their training as officers, and their position within
the monarchy. They remained prisoners of these structures up to 9
November and even beyond. Thus all their efforts to preserve and
control produced only destruction. The end they tried so mightily to
circumvent, they in fact created. It is appropriate that the last word
should belong to a long-time member of the military entourage,
Generaladjutant Oskar von Chelius. Two weeks after Wilhelm's abdication, surveying the wreckage of his world, he wrote:

Our beloved Kaiser no longer there. Everything lost a[nd] destroyed! Unfortunately I came too late to Spa [General Headquarters], otherwise I would
have stayed by him. As it was, I didn't get to see him any more in that frightful
moment, and my heart bleeds when I think of him. . . . What will happen
now? The French are demanding [his extradition] from Holland! The poor,
poor, beloved Kaiser, to whom my whole life belonged! . . . I will remain for
the time being here [in Berlin] a[nd] hand in my resignation. How good it
was to be the Generaladjutant of the beloved Kaiser. Now everything is finished! My sons have fallen, my worldly possessions [remain] in [St] Petersburg[6]
– only a life of remembrance with my wife remains, until we may follow our
sons. The future lies in deepest darkness, and from every prospect looms
chaos [*jeder Ausblick wird zum Chaos*]![7]

Notes to the text

Chapter 1, pp. 1–14

1 Cited in Volker Berghahn, *Germany and the Approach of War in 1914* (London, 1973), p. 167. Berghahn's volume contains the best, broad exposition of this theme.
2 See pp. 248–65, for a more complete discussion of this subject.
3 Fritz Fischer, *Griff nach der Weltmacht* (Düsseldorf, 1961), English translation: *Germany's Aims in the First World War* (New York, 1967).
4 See, among others, John A. Moses, *The Politics of Illusion: The Fischer Controversy in German Historiography* (New York, 1975) and Arnold Sywottek, 'Die Fischer-Kontroverse,' in Imanuel Geiss and Bernd-Jürgen Wendt (eds.), *Deutschland in der Weltpolitik des 19. und 20. Jahrhunderts* (Düsseldorf, 1973), pp. 19–47.
5 Fritz Fischer, *Krieg der Illusionen. Die deutsche Politik von 1911 bis 1914* (Düsseldorf, 1969), English translation: *War of Illusions. German Policies from 1911 to 1914* (New York, 1975).
6 Fritz Fischer, *Bündnis der Eliten. Zur Kontinuität der Machtstrukturen in Deutschland 1871–1945* (Düsseldorf, 1979).
7 James Sheehan's words, *Journal of Modern History*, vol. 48, no. 3 (Sept. 1976), p. 567, cited in Richard J. Evans, 'Introduction: Wilhelm II's Germany and the Historians,' in Richard J. Evans (ed.), *Society and Politics in Wilhelmine Germany* (New York and London, 1978), p. 16. Joachim Remak uses the phrase, too, in *American Historical Review*, vol. 82, no. 1, (Feb. 1977), p. 130.
8 Eckart Kehr, *Battleship Building and Party Politics in Germany, 1894–1901* (Chicago, 1975; German original Berlin, 1930) and *Der Primat der Innenpolitik. Gesammelte Aufsätze zur preussisch-deutschen Sozialgeschichte im 19. und 20. Jahrhundert*, ed. Hans-Ulrich Wehler (Berlin, 1965).
9 Hans-Ulrich Wehler, *Das Deutsche Kaiserreich 1871–1918* (Göttingen, 1973).
10 Arthur Rosenberg's *Imperial Germany. The Birth of the German Republic 1871–1918* (Boston, 1964; German original Berlin, 1930) also concentrates on structural problems, but is incomplete and uneven, although intelligent and insightful.
11 Wehler, *Kaiserreich*, p. 229.
12 Richard Evans isolates five ways in which the Junkers exercised control according to Wehler: repression, manipulation, diversion, compensation, and indoctrination. See Evans, 'Wilhelm II's Germany,' p. 20.
13 See Thomas Nipperdey, '1933 und Kontinuität der deutschen Ge-

schichte,' in *Historische Zeitschrift*, vol. 227, no. 3 (Aug. 1978), pp. 87–111, and Hans-Günther Zmarzlik, 'Das Kaiserreich in neuer Sicht?,' *Historische Zeitschrift*, vol. 222, no. 1 (Feb. 1976), pp. 105–26.

14 For example Roman Catholics. See David Blackbourn, *Class, Religion, and Local Politics: The Centre Party in Württemberg Before 1914* (New Haven/London, 1980).

15 This is one of Geoff Eley's main complaints: *Reshaping the German Right. Radical Nationalism and Political Change after Bismarck* (New Haven/London, 1980).

16 Zmarzlik, 'Das Kaiserreich,' p. 125.

17 Thomas Nipperdey, 'Wehlers "Kaiserreich": Eine kritische Auseinandersetzung,' in Nipperdey, *Gesellschaft, Kultur, Theorie. Gesammelte Aufsätze zur neueren Geschichte* (Göttingen, 1976), pp. 366–7; and Nipperdey, '1933 und Kontinuität,' p. 110.

18 Evans, 'Wilhelm II's Germany,' pp. 22–3.

19 *Ibid.*, and Hans-Ulrich Wehler, 'Einleitung,' Wehler (ed.), *Moderne Deutsche Sozialgeschichte* (Cologne/Berlin, 1970), pp. 9–16, and Jürgen Kocka, *Sozialgeschichte* (Göttingen, 1977).

20 Eley, *German Right*, pp. 160–7.

21 Despite protestations to the contrary. See *ibid.*, ch. 9 and Evans, 'Wilhelm II's Germany,' pp. 30–1.

22 J. H. Clapham, *The Economic Development of France and Germany, 1815–1914*, 4th edn (Cambridge, 1966), p. 278.

23 Wehler, *Kaiserreich*, p. 47. For further statistics see Walther G. Hoffmann, *et al.*, *Das Wachstum der deutschen Wirtschaft* (Heidelberg, 1965).

24 Hanna Schissler, *Preussische Agrargesellschaft im Wandel. Wirtschaftliche, gesellschaftliche und politische Transformationsprozesse von 1763 bis 1847*. Kritische Studien zur Geschichtswissenschaft, Band 33 (Göttingen, 1978), and Ernst Klein, *Geschichte der deutschen Landwirtschaft im Industriezeitalter*. Wissenschaftliche Paperbacks, Bd 1 (Wiesbaden, 1973), p. 119. We badly need a social history of the Prussian nobility in the nineteenth and twentieth centuries.

25 For statistics concerning the diplomatic corps see Lamar Cecil, *The German Diplomatic Service 1871–1914* (Princeton, 1976), pp. 58–103; for the army officer corps see Karl Demeter, *Das deutsche Offizierkorps in Gesellschaft und Staat, 1650–1945* (Frankfurt, 1962), chs. 1 and 2; for the navy see Holger H. Herwig, *The German Naval Officer Corps. A Social and Political History 1890–1918* (Oxford, 1973), ch. 3; for the bureaucracy see John Röhl, 'Higher Civil Servants in Germany, 1890–1900,' *Journal of Contemporary History*, vol. 2, no. 3 (July 1967), pp. 101–21, and Lysbeth W. Muncy, *The Junker in the Prussian Administration under William II, 1888–1914* (Providence, Rhode Island, 1944).

26 See, for example, Eckart Kehr, 'Zur Genesis des Königlich Preussischen Reserveoffiziers,' in Kehr, *Der Primat der Innenpolitik*, pp. 53–63; Hans Rosenberg, 'Die Pseudodemokratisierung der Rittergutsbesitzerklasse,' in Rosenberg, *Probleme der deutschen Sozialgeschichte* (Frankfurt am Main, 1969; the essay originally appeared in 1958), pp. 7–50; and Hermann Rumschöttel, *Das Bayerische Offizierkorps 1866–1914*. Beiträge zu einer historischen Strukturanalyse Bayerns im Industriezeitalter, Bd 9 (Berlin, 1973), pp. 94–7.

27 See the studies listed in note 25. The literature on the officer corps is tremendous and growing. A recent book in English is Martin Kitchen's study, *The German Officer Corps, 1890–1914* (Oxford, 1968). For the bureaucracy see also Paul Robert Duggan, 'Currents of Administrative Reform in Germany, 1907–1918' (unpublished Harvard doctoral dissertation, 1969) and John Gillis, *The Prussian Bureaucracy in Crisis* (Stanford, 1971).

28 See Wilhelm Schüssler, *Die Daily Telegraph Affaire: Fürst Bülow, Kaiser Wilhelm und die Krise des Zweiten Reiches 1908* (Göttingen, 1952).

29 Erich Eyck, *Das persönliche Regiment Wilhelms II* (Erlenbach/Zürich, 1948).

30 John C. G. Röhl, *Germany Without Bismarck* (London, 1967).

31 John Röhl discusses these and other aspects of governance in more detail in his 'Introduction' to John C. G. Röhl and Nicolaus Sombart (eds.), *Kaiser Wilhelm II: New Interpretations* (Cambridge, 1981), pp. 13–17.

32 *Ibid.*, p. 14.

33 See pp. 10–11.

34 Konrad Jarausch, *The Enigmatic Chancellor: Bethmann Hollweg and the Hubris of Modern Germany* (New Haven, 1973).

35 Wehler, *Kaiserreich,* pp. 68–72. Wehler confuses the issue by not always distinguishing between the agrarians and the industrialists and by using the term 'elite' in both the eingular and plural. One is not sure what distinction he means to make by this.

36 Wolfgang J. Mommsen, 'Domestic Factors in German Foreign Policy before 1914,' in *Central European History,* vol. 6, no. 1 (March 1973), p. 41.

37 Eley, *German Right.*

38 Among them: Dirk Stegmann, *Die Erben Bismarcks, Parteien und Verbände in der Spätphase der Wilhelminischen Deutschlands Sammlungspolitik 1897–1918* (Cologne/Berlin, 1970); Peter-Christian Witt, *Die Finanzpolitik des Deutschen Reiches von 1903–1913, eine Studie zur Innenpolitik des Wilhelminischen Deutschland* (Lübeck/Hamburg, 1970); Hans-Jürgen Puhle, *Agrarische Interessenpolitik und preussischer Konservatismus im Wilhelminischen Reich, 1893– 1914* (Hannover, 1967); Hartmut Kaelble, *Industrielle Interessenpolitik in der Wilhelminischen Gesellschaft: Centralverband Deutscher Industrielle, 1895–1914* (Berlin, 1967); Hans Jaeger, *Unternehmer in der deutschen Politik, 1890– 1914* (Bonn, 1967); and Eley, *German Right.*

39 Wehler, *Kaiserreich,* p. 184.

40 Thus, General Alfred Waldersee, at least in the early years of Wilhelm's reign, is a member of the *Umgebung,* but Admiral Tirpitz, despite his indubitable importance, is not. Chancellor Bernhard Bülow is a problematic case which will be considered later.

41 Bavarian Representative v. Lerchenfeld-Köfering to Minister President v. Lutz, 21 June 1889, in BGSA Munich, Gesandtschaft Berlin, volume 1059, and Philipp Eulenburg to Friedrich v. Holstein, 8 November 1888, BA Koblenz, Nl. Eulenburg 4/p. 172.

42 Deines to his father, 31 December 1895, MA Freiburg, Nl. Deines 13/p. 62.

43 Holstein to Chancellor Chlodwig Hohenlohe, 8 March 1896, BA Koblenz, Nl. Hohenlohe, Rep. 100 xxii/a/7.

44 Eulenburg to Holstein, 31 January 1897, BA Koblenz, Nl. Eulenburg 45/ p. 27.

45 Maximilian Harden, editor of *Die Zukunft*, was author of the scandals of
   1907–9 (see p. 12). He seems to have been convinced that homosexuals
   were linked in some sort of international brotherhood. He was also convinced that Eulenburg's homosexual connection to a French diplomat,
   Raymond Lecomte, was the cause of Germany's setback in the Morocco
   Affair. See pp. 133–7.
46 Good moral character was, of course, one of the prerequisites for candidacy as a Flügeladjutant or other permanent companion. Admiral v.
   Müller, chief of the Naval Cabinet (1908–18), was frequently outraged at
   the obscenities and drunkenness of the members of the *Umgebung* (Müller
   in Walter Görlitz [ed.], *Der Kaiser* [Göttingen/Berlin/Frankfurt/Zürich,
   1965], pp. 24–35). Harden's revelations about the sexual preferences of
   some of the higher-ups did nothing to improve their moral reputations.
47 Bethmann Hollweg in 1893, cited in Jarausch, *Enigmatic Chancellor*, p. 40.
48 This was Wilhelm's view, which he told General Morgen on 23 August
   1919. MA Freiburg, Nl. Morgen 37 (9-page memorandum).
49 A frequent complaint of Eulenburg's, in Eulenburg, *Mit dem Kaiser als
   Staatsmann und Freund auf Nordlandreisen*, 2 vols. (Dresden, 1931), II, 119–
   20, 324.
50 For example, Harden referred to Eulenburg as 'the Harpist' and mocked
   the musical and poetic interests of the other members of the Liebenberg
   Circle, Harden, 'Praeludium,' in *Die Zukunft*, 17 November 1906.
51 The Kladderadatsch Affair is the expression of this all-pervasive attitude.
   See Helmuth Rogge, 'Die Kladderadatschaffäre,' *Historische Zeitschrift*, vol.
   195 (1962), pp. 90–130.
52 Holstein to Eulenburg, 8 January 1897, BA Koblenz, Nl. Eulenburg 45.
53 This is an underlying assumption of most of the above criticism.
54 Admiral v. Müller in Görlitz, *Der Kaiser*, p. 60.
55 Mommsen, 'Domestic Factors,' p. 36.
56 Wehler considers this question so important that he devotes the epilogue
   of his history of the *Kaiserreich* to the *Lernfähigkeit* of this group, Wehler,
   Kaiserreich, pp. 227–39.
57 See Harry F. Young's account in ch. 5 of *Maximilian Harden: Censor Germaniae; the Critic in Opposition from Bismarck to the Rise of Nazism* (The Hague,
   1959).
58 Crown Prince Wilhelm, *Memoirs of the Crown Prince of Germany* (New York,
   1922), pp. 99–101; and Robert v. Zedlitz-Trützschler, *Zwölf Jahre am
   deutschen Kaiserhof. Aufzeichnungen des Grafen Robert Zedlitz-Trützschler,
   ehemaligen Hofmarschalls Wilhelms II* (Stuttgart/Berlin/Leipzig, 1925), pp.
   216–18.

Chapter 2, pp. 15–44

1 Friedrich von Holstein to Philipp zu Eulenburg, 4.4.90, in John C. G.
   Röhl, *Philipp Eulenburgs Politische Korrespondenz*, 3 vols. (Boppard am Rhein,
   1976), I, no. 379. Dates will be written day·month·year.
2 21st ed. (Leipzig, n.d. [1894]).
3 See also Helmut Rogge, 'Affairen im Kaiserreich, Symptome der

Staatskrise unter Wilhelm II, *Die politische Meinung*, LXXXI (1963), 58, 64–5.

4 Holstein to Eulenburg, 6.12.90 in Röhl, *Eulenburgs Korrespondenz*, I, no. 452.

5 Diary entry of 28.4.17 in MA Freiburg, Nl. Müller 5/p. 364. The original calls the Emperor 'this miserable egotist [*diesem elenden Egoisten*].' In the published version the phrase reads 'the Kaiser.' See Georg von Müller, *Regierte der Kaiser? Kriegstagebücher, Aufzeichnungen und Briefe des Chefs des Marine-Kabinetts Admiral Georg Alexander von Müller 1914–1918*, ed. Walter Görlitz (Göttingen/Berlin/Frankfurt, 1959), pp. 280–1.

6 General Hans von Plessen about Wilhelm in Admiral Alfred von Tirpitz's diary, 28.11.03 in MA Freiburg, Nl. Tirpitz 20/pp. 304–6.

7 Bülow's notes of a conversation with Admiral Friedrich (von-1900) Hollmann on 28.4.97 in BA Koblenz, Nl. Bülow 30. Hollmann (1842–1913) was head of the Reichsmarineamt from 1890 to 1897. Bülow (1849–1929) was Foreign Secretary (1897–1900) and then Chancellor (1900–9).

8 Bülow's notes of a conversation with Eulenburg, 7.4.97, *ibid.*, 76, and Eulenburg to Holstein, 6.8.89, Röhl, *Eulenburgs Korrespondenz*, I, no. 230.

9 See pp. 185–6, 266–7, 273–4 and 290. Hans von Plessen (1841–1929), Prussian general and Commandant of the Hauptquartier, 1892–1918.

10 See pp. 47–8, 63–4, 68–70, 111–14.

11 John C. G. Röhl, 'The Emperor's New Clothes: A Character Sketch of Kaiser Wilhelm II' in John C. G. Röhl and Nicolaus Sombart (eds.), *Kaiser Wilhelm II: New Interpretations* (Cambridge, 1981).

12 See pp. 112–14.

13 See pp. 266–8.

14 Bülow's marginal comment to Crown Prince Wilhelm's memoirs (type-script) in BA Koblenz, Nl. Schwertfeger 293/p. 32.

15 Walter Bronsart von Schellendorff (1833–1914), Prussian General and War Minister, 1893–6.

16 Diary entry of 3.1.96, Chlodwig zu Hohenlohe-Schillingsfürst, *Denkwürdigkeiten der Reichskanzlerzeit*, ed. Karl A. von Müller (Stuttgart, 1931), p. 151. Hohenlohe (1819–1901) was Minister President of Bavaria (1866–70), Ambassador to Paris (1874–85), Statthalter of Alsace-Lorraine (1885–94), and Chancellor and Minister President of Prussia (1894–1900).

17 Holstein to Bülow, 2.4.97, BA Koblenz, Nl. Bülow 90/pp. 286–9.

18 On Klepsch's qualifications see Peter Brouczek, 'Der k.u.k. Delegierte im Deutschen Grossen Hauptquartier Generalmajor Alois Klepsch-Kloth von Roden und seine Berichterstattung 1915/1916,' *Militärgeschichtliche Mitteilungen*, 1/74 (1974), pp. 109–26.

19 Emphasis in the original. Alois Frhr Klepsch-Kloth von Roden, 'Erinnerungen,' ÖKrA Vienna, Nl. Klepsch-Kloth, p. 106.

20 Bethmann Hollweg to Rudolf von Valentini, 11.12.20, translated in Konrad Jarausch, *The Enigmatic Chancellor: Bethmann Hollweg and the Hubris of Imperial Germany* (New Haven, 1972), p. 396. Bethmann (1856–1921) was Imperial Secretary of the Interior and Vice Chancellor (1907–9), and Chancellor from 1909 to 1917.

21 The two best biographies of Wilhelm are Michael Balfour, *The Kaiser and*

His Times (New York, 1972 [1964]), and Wilhelm Schüssler, *Kaiser Wilhelm II, Schicksal und Schuld* (Göttingen/Berlin/Frankfurt/Zürich, 1962). Despite the number of biographies (see the bibliography in Ernst R. Huber, *Deutsche Verfassungsgeschichte seit 1789*, vol. 4: *Struktur und Krisen des Kaiserreichs* [Stuttgart/Berlin/Cologne/Mainz, 1969], pp. 178–9) and their newness (there were two in English in 1977 and 1978 alone: Alan Palmer, *The Kaiser: Warlord of the Second Reich* [New York, 1978] and Tyler Whittle, *The Last Kaiser: A Biography of Wilhelm II, German Emperor and King of Prussia* [New York, 1977]), a definitive biography remains to be written. John Röhl's essay 'The Emperor's New Clothes' offers a provocative thumbnail character analysis of the last Kaiser. The volume in which it appears (see note 11) provides a mosaic portrait of Wilhelm. In addition, Lamar Cecil is preparing a scholarly biography, which one awaits with interest.

22 Eulenburg to Hohenlohe, 1.10.95, in BA Koblenz, Nl. Eulenburg 38/p. 704.

23 Chancellor Leo von Caprivi to Eulenburg, 28.2.92, *ibid.*, 17/p. 120.

24 Georg Alexander (von-1900) Müller (1854–1940), Chief of the Naval Cabinet from April 1906 to October 1908.

25 Georg v. Müller, *Der Kaiser . . . Aufzeichnungen des Chefs des Marinekabinetts Admiral Georg Alexander von Müller über die Ära Wilhelms II*, ed. Walter Görlitz (Göttingen/Berlin/Frankfurt/Zürich, 1965), p. 36.

26 See pp. 266–8 and 282.

27 Walther Rathenau, *Der Kaiser. Eine Betrachtung* (Berlin, 1923), p. 27. Walther Rathenau (1867–1922), industrialist and later Foreign Minister (1922). See James Joll's biographical essay in James Joll, *Three Intellectuals in Politics* (New York, 1965 [1960]), pp. 59–132.

28 Herbert von Bismarck to Eulenburg, 11.8.86 in BA Koblenz, Nl. Eulenburg 1/p. 48.

29 Diary entry of 4.3.11, MA Freiburg, Nl. Müller, 4/p. 30.

30 Karl von Einem, *Kriegsminister unter Wilhelm II. Erinnerungen eines Soldaten 1853–1933* (Leipzig, 1933), p. 126.

31 Marie von Bunsen, *Zeitgenossen die ich Erlebte 1900–1930* (Leipzig, 1932), p. 194.

32 *Ibid.*, p. 192.

33 Baronin Spitzemberg, *Das Tagebuch der Baronin Spitzemberg geb. Freiin v. Varnbüler. Aufzeichnungen aus der Hofgesellschaft des Hohenzollernreiches*, ed. Rudolf Vierhaus (Göttingen, 1960), 2.2.85, p. 213.

34 Bernhard von Bülow, *Denkwürdigkeiten*, 4 vols. (Berlin, 1930–1), I, 262–3.

35 Thus, Max Egon Fürst zu Fürstenberg, diary entry of 13.4.08, in FFA Donaueschingen, Nl. Fürstenberg.

36 Spitzemberg mentions the 'airless room of boredom' that the future Empress and her female relatives created, *Tagebuch*, 4.3.85, p. 214. See also Bunsen, *Zeitgenossen*, p. 193.

37 Ladislaus Graf von Szögyényi-Marich to Agenor Graf von Goluchowski, private 12.12.02, ÖStA Vienna PA III 158.

38 Bülow, *Denkwürdigkeiten*, I, 264.

39 See pp. 271 and 287.

40 Deines to his father, 3.9.96, MA Freiburg, Nl. Deines 13/pp. 106–7.

41 Mathilde Gräfin von Keller, *Vierzig Jahre im Dienst der Kaiserin. Ein Kultur-bild aus den Jahren 1881–1921* (Leipzig, 1935), 27.7.83, p. 45.
42 August Eulenburg to Philipp Eulenburg, 27.12.97, BA Koblenz, Nl. Eulenburg 49/pp. 728–9. 'This whole business is certainly nothing new to me,' Deines remarked to his father, 31.12.97, MA Freiburg, Nl. Deines 13/pp. 173–173b.
43 Deines to his father, 4.5.97, *ibid.*, p. 136b.
44 Philipp Eulenburg to his wife, Augusta, 4.7.99, BA Koblenz, Nl. Eulenburg 53/p. 101.
45 Gräfin Dönhoff, born Marie Princess di Camporeale in 1848, divorced her first husband, diplomat August von Dönhoff, and married Bernhard Bülow, the later Chancellor.
46 Wilhelm to Marie Gräfin von Dönhoff, Bonn, 20.2.79, BA Koblenz, Nl. Bülow 173/p. 17.
47 Eulenburg to Holstein, 4.8.90, BA Koblenz, Nl. Eulenburg 12/pp. 519–20.
48 Kiderlen-Wächter to Hedwig Kypke, 7.7.94, Yale University, Nl. Kiderlen-Wächter, Box 1. Ernst Jäckh, *Kiderlen-Wächter der Staatsmann und Mensch. Briefwechsel und Nachlass*, 2 vols. (Stuttgart/Berlin/Leipzig, 1925), I, 122 changes the phrase, 'it is downright awkward,' which refers to the situation of having the Empress aboard, to 'she is downright awkward [*sie ist doch recht genierlich*].'
49 Eulenburg to his wife, 4.7.99, in Philipp zu Eulenburg, *Mit dem Kaiser als Staatsmann und Freund auf Nordlandreisen*, 2 vols. (Dresden, 1931), II, 118. See also Bernhard Schwertfeger, *Kaiser und Kabinettschef. Nach eigenen Aufzeichnungen und dem Briefwechsel des Wirklichen Geheimen Rats Rudolf von Valentini* (Oldenburg i.O, 1931), p. 160.
50 Wilhelm to Marie Gräfin von Dönhoff (in English), 11.12.78, BA Koblenz, Nl. Bülow, 173/p. 12.
51 Philipp zu Eulenburg, 'Drei Freunde' (unpublished manuscript, courtesy of John Röhl), pt I, sect. 3, pp. 165–6 [I/3/pp. 165–6].
52 German ranks, titles, and offices will not be italicized.
53 Eulenburg gives a sensitive description of their friendship in 'Im neuen Palais,' 10.10.89, BA Koblenz, Nl. Eulenburg 6/pp. 146–57.
54 The friendship between Wilhelm and Eulenburg, their relationship, its nature and political effects are the subjects of chapters 3, 4, and 5.
55 See chapter 5 for Maximilian Harden's surmises.
56 Philipp Eulenburg, 'Drei Freunde,' I/4/p. 307.
57 Röhl, 'The Emperor's New Clothes,' pp. 43–7.
58 Hugo Graf von Lerchenfeld-Köfering to Krafft Frhr von Crailsheim, 25.1.01, in BGSA Munich, Gesandtschaft Berlin 1073.
59 *Ibid.*
60 Diary entry of 3.7.13, in MA Freiburg, Nl. Müller 4/p. 196.
61 Michael Balfour, *The Kaiser and His Times* (New York, 1972), pp. 76–9.
62 Adolf von Deines to his father, 24.9.94, MA Freiburg, Nl. Deines 12/pp. 128–128b.
63 Eulenburg, 'Drei Freunde,' I/4/p. 306.
64 There are innumerable examples in Müller, *Regierte der Kaiser?*, 17.1.15,

9.4.15, pp. 82 and 97 and in the entry of 28.1.16, MA Freiburg, Nl. Müller 5/p. 130, which is omitted in *Regierte der Kaiser?*, p. 150.

65 Eulenburg to Bülow, 1.10.01, BA Koblenz, Nl. Eulenburg 58/pp. 184–5.

66 Klepsch-Kloth to Conrad von Hötzendorf, 10.11.08, ÖKrA Vienna, Chef des Generalstabs 1908, 25:1/18.

67 Müller, *Der Kaiser*, p. 164.

68 Otto Fürst zu Stolberg-Wernigerode (1837–96) was Oberstkämmerer, 1888–94. He was succeeded by Christian Kraft Fürst zu Hohenlohe-Oehringen (1848–1926) until 1899, when Friedrich Fürst zu Solms-Baruth (1853–1920) replaced him and remained until 1918.

69 Wilhelm von Wedel-Piesdorf (1836–1915) was minister from 1888 to 1907. From 1907 to 1913 August Graf zu Eulenburg (1838–1921) managed this post in combination with several others. From 1914 through 1918 this was his sole position.

70 1888–90, Eduard von Liebenau; 1890–1914, August zu Eulenburg; 1914–18, Hugo von Reischach (1854–1934).

71 1888–94, Graf von Schwerin; 1894–1901, Heinrich Frhr von und zu Egloffstein (1848–1914); 1901–3, Ulrich von Trotha (1854–1946); 1903–10, Robert von Zedlitz-Trützschler (1863–1942); 1910–18, Hans von Gontard (1861–1931).

72 1888–1914, Maximilian Frhr von Lyncker (1845–1923); 1914–18 Gontard performed these duties although the actual position was not filled.

73 For descriptions of how the Court operated see Herzogin Viktoria Luise, *Im Glanz der Krone. Erinnerungen* (Munich, 1975, orig. 1967), pp. 225–40; Hugo von Reischach, *Unter Drei Kaisern* (Berlin, 1925), pp. 268–70 and Robert von Zedlitz-Trützschler, *Zwölf Jahre am deutschen Kaiserhof* (Stuttgart/Berlin/Leipzig, 1925), p. 143.

74 August Eulenburg was the brother of Botho Eulenburg (1831–1912; Prussian Minister of the Interior 1878–81; Minister President of Prussia 1892–4) and the cousin of Philipp Eulenburg.

75 Cited by Eulenburg in BA Koblenz, Nl. Eulenburg 11/p. 469.

76 See, for example, Maximilian Harden in *Die Zukunft*, 61 (5.10.07), p. 15; Bülow, *Denkwürdigkeiten*, I, 73–5; Müller, *Der Kaiser*, p. 181; and Bogdan von Hutten-Czapski, *Sechzig Jahre Politik und Gesellschaft*, 2 vols. (Berlin, 1936), I, 407.

77 August Eulenburg to Philipp Eulenburg, 17.12.94, Röhl, *Eulenburgs Korrespondenz*, II, no. 1066 and Müller, *Der Kaiser*, p. 181.

78 *Ibid.*

79 Szögyényi to Gustav Graf von Kálnoky, 31.1.94, ÖStA Vienna PA III 145 Varia; and p. 227.

80 August Eulenburg to Philipp Eulenburg, 5.2.94, Röhl, *Eulenburgs Korrespondenz*, II, no. 894; Holstein to Eulenburg, 19.3.94, BA Koblenz, Nl. Eulenburg 28/pp. 245–6.

81 (1831–99), Prussian General; Head of the Reichsmarineamt, 1883–8; Minister President of Prussia, 1890–2; Chancellor and Prussian Foreign Minister, 1890–4.

82 (1842–1912), Imperial Foreign Secretary, 1890–7; Prussian Foreign Minister, 1894–7.

83 (1845–1932), Imperial Justice Secretary, 1893–7; Imperial Vice Chancellor and Secretary of the Interior, 1897–1907.

84 (1833–1907), Imperial Secretary of the Interior, 1880–97; Imperial Vice Chancellor, 1881–97; Prussian Vice President, 1888–97.

85 For Caprivi's tenure and policies see J. Alden Nichols, *Germany After Bismarck: The Caprivi Era 1890–1894* (New York, 1968, orig. 1958); Karl Erich Born, *Staat und Sozialpolitik seit Bismarcks Sturz. Ein Beitrag zur Geschichte der innenpolitischen Entwicklung des Deutschen Reiches 1890–1914* (Wiesbaden, 1957); and Kenneth Barkin, *The Controversy over German Industrialization, 1890–1902* (Chicago, 1970).

86 On tariffs see Barkin, *Controversy*, pp. 211–52; on tendencies within the bureaucracy, see John C. G. Röhl, 'Higher Civil Servants in Germany, 1890–1900,' *Journal of Contemporary History*, vol. 2, no. 3 (July 1967), pp. 115–21.

87 Philipp Eulenburg, Notes of a talk with Wilhelm on 29.8.03 in 'Zur Psyche und Politik Kaiser Wilhelms II' (unpublished manuscript, courtesy of John Röhl).

88 Hutten-Czapski, *Sechzig Jahre*, I, 407.

89 Max von Mutius, 'Lebenserinnerungen, 1865–1918,' MA Freiburg, Nl. Deines 2/p. 185.

90 Reischach to Fürstenberg, 31.12.08, FFA Donaueschingen, Nl. Fürstenberg.

91 See their correspondence, which goes up to 1900, in PA Bonn, Nl. Holstein 10.

92 Anonymous, *Am Hofe der Kaiserin Auguste Victoria* (Berlin, n.d., probably 1893), p. 124.

93 (1832–1904) General Fieldmarshal; Chief of the General Staff, 1888–91; Commander of the allied troops in China, 1900–1.

94 Waldersee to Philipp Eulenburg, 28.11.89, Röhl, *Eulenburgs Korrespondenz*, I, no. 261.

95 See *ibid.*, nos. 259–64 and no. 259, footnote 3.

96 Liebenau to Holstein, 21.10.88, PA Bonn, Nl. Holstein 10.

97 For a typical 'Liebenau story,' a genre that August Eulenburg never elicited, see Kiderlen-Wächter to Holstein, 19.7.90, in Norman Rich and M. H. Fisher (eds.), *Die geheimen Papiere Friedrich von Holsteins*, 4 vols. (Göttingen/Berlin/Frankfurt, 1961), III, no. 324.

98 August Eulenburg to Valentini, 24.7.15, BA Koblenz, Nl. Schwertfeger 206/p. 21.

99 Schwertfeger, *Kaiser und Kabinettschef*, p. 159.

100 *Ibid.*, p. 160 and below, p. 287.

101 Schwertfeger, *Kaiser und Kabinettschef*, pp. 184–5 and below, p. 287.

102 Müller's diary, 7.11.18 in Müller, *Regierte der Kaiser?*, p. 446 and Bülow, *Denkwürdigkeiten*, I, 76.

103 Prinz Max von Baden, *Erinnerungen und Dokumente* (Stuttgart/Berlin/Leipzig, 1927), pp. 526–7, 530, 540.

104 Müller, *Regierte der Kaiser?*, p. 275.

105 Reischach to Fürstenberg, 31.12.08, FFA Donaueschingen, Nl. Fürstenberg.

106 Viktoria Luise, *Im Glanz der Krone,* pp. 159–68.
107 Bülow, *Denkwürdigkeiten,* I, 248.
108 Karl-Heinz Janssen (ed.), *Die graue Exzellenz. Zwischen Staatsräson und Vasallentreue. Aus den Papieren des kaiserlichen Gesandten Karl Georg von Treutler* (Frankfurt/Berlin/Vienna, 1971), p. 107, and Keller, *Vierzig Jahre,* p. 18.
109 Janssen, *Die graue Exzellenz,* p. 107.
110 Still the best discussion of this is Heinrich Otto Meisner, 'Zur neueren Geschichte des preussischen Kabinetts,' in *Forschungen zur brandenburgischen und preussischen Geschichte,* no. 36 (1924), pp. 39–66 and 180–209. Heinrich Potthoff follows Meisner in his introduction to *Friedrich v. Berg als Chef des Geheimen Zivilkabinetts 1918. Erinnerungen aus seinem Nachlass* (Düsseldorf, 1971), pp. 3–36. On the Military Cabinet see Rudolf Schmidt-Bückeburg, *Das Militärkabinett der preussischen Könige und deutschen Kaiser. Seine geschichtliche Entwicklung und staatsrechtliche Stellung 1787–1918* (Berlin, 1933). The Naval Cabinet has not yet found its historian, but for brief discussions of its jurisdiction and effects see Walther Hubatsch, *Der Admiralstab und die obersten Marinebehörden in Deutschland 1848–1945* (Frankfurt, 1958), pp. 49–59 and 77–80; and Jonathan Steinberg, *Yesterday's Deterrent. Tirpitz and the Birth of the German Battle Fleet* (London, 1965), pp. 53–5.
111 Allerhöchste Kabinettsorder (AKO) of 28.3.89.
112 For the Civil Cabinet, see the next page, and for a more complete explanation of jurisdiction for the Military and Naval Cabinets, see pp. 176–8; Meisner, 'Kabinetts,' pp. 190–7; Potthoff, *Berg,* pp. 15–36; Schmidt-Bückeburg, *Das Militärkabinett,* pp. 152–3, 183, 190–1, 222–3, 239–40; and Holger Herwig, *The German Naval Officer Corps: A Social and Political History, 1890–1918* (Oxford, 1973), p. 24.
113 Thus the official description of the Civil Cabinet duties from 1889, in Schmidt-Bückeburg, *Das Militärkabinett,* pp. 190–1, which follows Meisner, 'Kabinetts,' pp. 190–7.
114 Schmidt-Bückeburg, *Das Militärkabinett,* p. 191.
115 (1831–1908), entered the Prussian Ministry of Culture in 1859; 1881, Under State Secretary in the Prussian Ministry of Culture; 1888 ennobled (by Friedrich III); 1888–1908, Chief of the Civil Cabinet.
116 Bülow, *Denkwürdigkeiten,* I, 63–72.
117 Lucanus denied it, *ibid.,* I, 173, 381. See also Alfred Graf von Waldersee, *Denkwürdigkeiten des Generalfeldmarschalls,* ed. Heinrich Otto Meisner, 3 vols. (Stuttgart/Berlin, 1923), II, 6.
118 Eulenburg to Holstein, 22.6.95, BA Koblenz, Nl. Eulenburg 36/p. 446.
119 Lucanus to Eulenburg, 20.1.97, *ibid.,* 45/p. 85, and Bülow, *Denkwürdigkeiten,* I, 381.
120 Axel von Varnbüler to Hermann Frhr von Mittnacht, 10.1.97, in HStA Stuttgart E-73, Verz. 61, 12e.
121 Meisner, 'Kabinetts,' p. 207 n. 1; Schmidt-Bückeburg, *Das Militärkabinett,* p. 197.
122 Fritz Hartung, 'Verantwortliche Regierung, Kabinette und Nebenregierungen im konstitutionellen Preussen 1848–1918,' in *Forschungen zur brandenburgischen und preussischen Geschichte,* no. 44 (1932), p. 317. The

Civil Cabinet papers are located in the German Democratic Republic in the Zentrales Staatsarchiv in Merseburg.

123 Szögyényi to Lexa Graf von Aehrenthal, 13.8.08, ÖStA Vienna, PA III 166.

124 See pp. 83–98, and John C. G. Röhl, *Germany Without Bismarck* (London, 1967), ch. 6.

125 See *ibid.*, pp. 181–2, 215–17.

126 Holstein to Eulenburg, 15.6.97, BA Koblenz, Nl. Eulenburg 47/pp. 338–41.

127 Bülow, *Denkwürdigkeiten*, I, 362.

128 Eulenburg feared that Lucanus would press the reactionary Botho Eulenburg for chancellor, Philipp Eulenburg to Bülow, 7.7.97, BA Koblenz, Nl. Eulenburg 47/pp. 406–8.

129 Bernhard Bülow to Karl Bülow, 20.5.07, BA Koblenz, Nl. Bülow 15/pp. 1–4.

130 Schwertfeger, *Kaiser und Kabinettschef*, p. 47, and Bülow, *Denkwürdigkeiten*, I, 63.

131 *Ibid.*, pp. 205–6.

132 *Ibid.*, p. 95.

133 (1855–1925).

134 Schwertfeger, *Kaiser und Kabinettschef*, pp. 23–31.

135 *Ibid.*, p. 45.

136 BA Koblenz, Nl. Schwertfeger 215/p. 70, emphasis in the original.

137 MA Freiburg, Nl. Mutius 2/p. 187.

138 For Valentini's role against the military see pp. 271–87.

139 August Eulenburg to Philipp Eulenburg, 27.3.89, Röhl, *Eulenburgs Korrespondenz*, I, no. 332.

140 For the personnel and duties of the *Militärisches Gefolge* see pp. 175–95.

141 1888–92, Adolf von Wittich (1836–1906); 1892–1918, Hans von Plessen (1841–1929).

142 Civilians, it is true, reported first to the Hofmarschall.

143 The duties of the FADs are detailed at the beginning of chapter 7.

144 (1797–1888), King of Prussia, 1861–88; German Emperor, 1871–88.

145 For the 'Wilhelm the Great' campaign see Isabel V. Hull, 'Prussian Dynastic Ritual in the German Empire' (forthcoming).

146 Viktoria Luise's account in Viktoria Luise, *Im Glanz der Krone*, pp. 330–3.

147 For Wilhelm I's habits see Meisner, 'Kabinetts,' pp. 184–9, and Hutten-Czapski, *Sechzig Jahre*, I, 37–40.

148 Meisner, 'Kabinetts,' p. 190 n. 1.

149 FA Gustav Frhr von Berg to Marinekabinett, Telegram, 20.1.99, and Memorandum of Kapitän zur See von Müller, 3.4.01, both in MA Freiburg, RM2/58. See also Schmidt-Bückeburg, *Das Militärkabinett*, pp. 178–9.

150 Discussion with Caprivi reported in Lerchenfeld to Crailsheim, 30.3.90, BGSA Munich, Gesandtschaft Berlin 1068.

151 Müller, *Der Kaiser*, pp. 28–31.

152 Holstein to Eulenburg, 15.11.93, Röhl, *Eulenburgs Korrespondenz*, II, no. 843.

153 Schwertfeger, *Kaiser und Kabinettschef,* p. 59.
154 Diary entry of 25.2.05, in MA Freiburg, Nl. Müller 3/p. 228.
155 Zedlitz-Trützschler, *Zwölf Jahre,* p. 235.
156 Viktoria Luise, *Im Glanz der Krone,* p. 143.
157 Waldersee, *Denkwürdigkeiten,* II, 153.
158 Zedlitz-Trützschler, *Zwölf Jahre,* pp. 230–1.
159 Wedel-Piesdorf to State Secretary of the Foreign Office Heinrich von Tschirschky und Bögendorff, 14.4.07, PA Bonn, Preussen 1, 1d *secr.* Bd 3.
160 Maximilian Harden to Holstein, 5.4.08, PA Bonn, Nl. Holstein 42, omitted from Rich, *Die geheimen Papiere,* IV, 471.
161 Diary entry of 11.4.08, FFA Donaueschingen, Nl. Fürstenberg.
162 (1859–1918).
163 (1864–1931).
164 (1857–   ).
165 Plessen to Fürstenberg, who had escaped in 1914, 1.4.14, *ibid.*
166 Diary entry of 3.5.12, MA Freiburg, Nl. Müller, 4/pp. 135–6.
167 MA Freiburg, RM2/385.
168 Müller to Tirpitz, Corfu. 29.4.14, MA Freiburg, Nl. Tirpitz 18.
169 Diary entry of 12.4.08, FFA Donaueschingen, Nl. Fürstenberg.
170 *Ibid.*
171 (1851–1914).
172 MA Freiburg RM2/333.
173 (1857–1918), Director of the Hamburg–America Line.
174 (1836–1905), industrialist.
175 (1826–1903), Director of the Disconto-Gesellschaft.
176 (1837–1912), industrialist.
177 (1858–1917), Silesian coal magnate.
178 Varnbüler to Julius Frhr von Soden, 8.7.04, HStA Stuttgart E-73, Verz. 61, 12e.
179 Tirpitz to Artur Graf von Posadowsky-Wehner, 5.7.12, MA Freiburg, Nl. Tirpitz 27/p. 188.
180 (1840–1920).
181 (1847–1923).
182 (1863–1948).
183 (1868–1948).
184 Descriptions of the *Nordlandreisen* may be found in: Philipp zu Eulenburg, *Mit dem Kaiser;* Janssen, *Die graue Exzellenz,* pp. 101–11, and Müller, *Der Kaiser,* pp. 171–4.
185 August Eulenburg to Philipp Eulenburg, 7.6.98 in BA Koblenz, Nl. Eulenburg 51/p. 111.
186 Müller, *Der Kaiser,* p. 172.
187 Eulenburg to Bülow, 1.8.99, BA Koblenz, Nl. Eulenburg 54/p. 196.
188 MA Freiburg, Nl. Mutius 2/p. 181.
189 Müller, *Der Kaiser,* p. 32.
190 Helmuth von Moltke, *Erinnerungen, Briefe, Dokumente, 1877–1916* (Stuttgart, 1922), p. 349.
191 See p. 72 and pp. 161–3.
192 Eulenburg to Auguste Viktoria, Rominten, 1.10.97, BA Koblenz, Nl.

Eulenburg 48/p. 543; see also Johannes Haller, *Aus dem Leben des Fürsten Philipp zu Eulenburg-Hertefeld* (Berlin/Leipzig, 1926), pp. 48–50.
193 Eulenburg's phrase, Eulenburg to Holstein, Prökelwitz, 20.5.90, Röhl, *Eulenburgs Korrespondenz,* I, no. 396.
194 See p. 70.
195 See pp. 147–9.
196 Szögyényi to Goluchowski, 3.12.01, ÖStA Vienna, PA III 156.
197 Bülow, *Denkwürdigkeiten,* II, 425.
198 See Helmuth Rogge, 'Die Kladderadatschaffäre. Ein Beitrag zur neueren Geschichte des Wilhelminischen Reiches,' *Historische Zeitschrift,* vol. 195 (1962), pp. 108, 113, 117, 122–3, and Rich, *Die geheimen Papiere,* III, nos. 405–7 and IV, nos. 664–5.
199 Harry F. Young, *Prince Lichnowsky and the Great War* (Athens, Georgia, 1977), p. 28.
200 Varnbüler to Soden, 14.12.01, HStA Stuttgart E-73, Verz. 61, 12e.
201 MA Freiburg, Nl. Mutius 2/p. 178.
202 Müller, *Der Kaiser,* p. 171.
203 For a more complete discussion of official ceremonies and their effects in this period see Hull, 'Prussian Dynastic Ritual.'
204 Karl von Einem, *Erinnerungen,* pp. 124–5.
205 Spitzemberg, *Tagebuch,* pp. 392–3.
206 Moltke, *Erinnerungen,* p. 353.
207 Moltke's diary of 25.8.05, *ibid.,* pp. 337–8.
208 Plessen to Fürstenberg, Bonn, 11.10.13, FFA Donaueschingen, Nl. Fürstenberg.
209 Instruction for the Parade of 27.8.10 in MA Freiburg RM2/105.
210 'Akten Vermerk' of 1.2.09 in MA Freiburg RM2/77/p. 221.
211 Norbert Elias, *Die höfische Gesellschaft. Untersuchungen zur Soziologie des Königtums und der höfischen Aristokratie mit einer Einleitung: Soziologie und Geschichtswissenschaft* (Neuwied/Berlin, 1969), pp. 63–4.
212 George L. Mosse, *The Nationalization of the Masses: Political Symbolism and Mass Movements in Germany from the Napoleonic Wars through the Third Reich* (New York/Scarborough, Ontario, 1977), pp. 90–3.
213 Volker Plagemann, 'Bismarck Denkmäler,' in Hans-Ernst Mittig and Volker Plagemann, *Denkmäler im 19. Jahrhundert, Deutung und Kritik* (Munich, 1972), pp. 244–5.
214 Meisner, 'Kabinetts,' p. 201.
215 MA Freiburg, Nl. Mutius 2/p. 171.
216 Austrian Military Attaché Karl Frhr von Bienerth to Conrad von Hötzendorf, Feb. 1912, ÖKrA Vienna Militär-Attaché Berlin, Fasz. 12.
217 *Freisinnige Zeitung* no. 251, 24.10.08 in MA Freiburg RM2/90.
218 'Allerhöchste Bestimmungen über die am 2. Mai 1889 stattfindende Nagelung und Weihe der dem 1. Bataillon 1. Garde Regiments zu Fuss zu verleihenden neuen Fahne,' in MA Freiburg RM2/80.
219 Mosse, *Nationalization,* pp. 82–3 and 91–2.
220 Adolf von Trotha to Müller, 1.10.12; Baudissin to Müller, 10.10.12, in MA Freiburg RM2/88.
221 Thus, a Mrs Leishman to Müller on the occasion of the Ambassador's Dinner of 12.2.13, MA Freiburg, Nl. Müller, 4/p. 184.

222 Deines to his father, 14.1.93, MA Freiburg, Nl. Deines, 12/pp. 3–4; Gustav von Senden-Bibran, 'Erlebnisse als Chef des Marinekabinetts' (unpublished manuscript), MA Freiburg, Nl. Senden-Bibran 11/p. 14, and Spitzemberg, *Tagebuch,* 21.1.00, p. 393.

223 See Moltke, *Erinnerungen,* p. 316 and Bienerth to Conrad, 21.6.13, ÖKrA Vienna, Militär-Attaché Berlin, Fasz. 13, and Szögyényi to Goluchowski, priv., 19.2.04, ÖStA Vienna, PA III 160.

224 See pp. 195–203.

Chapter 3, pp. 45–75

1 Wilhelm to Eulenburg, 28.7.88, in John C. G. Röhl (ed.), *Philipp Eulenburgs politische Korrespondenz,* 3 vols. (Boppard am Rhein, 1976–), I, no. 187. Röhl notes (p. 303 n. 2) that 'Hokan' was the more 'energetic' of the two. Röhl's introduction to this volume is the finest piece of scholarship to date on Eulenburg.

2 Eulenburg to Wilhelm, 10.1.88 and 15.6.88 in BA Koblenz, Nl. Eulenburg 3/p. 2 and 4/p. 119.

3 Wilhelm to Eulenburg, 11.8.86, in Röhl, *Eulenburgs Korrespondenz,* I, no. 88.

4 Cited in Philipp Eulenburg, 'Drei Freunde' (unpublished manuscript in the possession of John Röhl), vol. I, pt 4, p. 302, italics in the original. Hereafter cited as I/4/p. 302.

5 Friedrich von Holstein to Eulenburg, 15.1.97, BA Koblenz, Nl. Eulenburg 45/p. 36.

6 Wilhelm, when he introduced Eulenburg to Hinzpeter on 17.1.89, *ibid.,* 5/p. 16.

7 Eulenburg to Wilhelm, 15.11.98, to appear in Röhl, *Eulenburgs Korrespondenz,* vol. 3.

8 Register of books removed when the yacht was sold, 23.4.07, in MA Freiburg, RM2/317.

9 Wilhelm's phrase, cited by Eulenburg in a 'Notiz' from 5.7.99, BA Koblenz, Nl. Eulenburg 53/p. 103.

10 Philipp Eulenburg, *Mit dem Kaiser als Staatsmann und Freund auf Nordlandreisen,* 2 vols. (Dresden, 1931), I, 114, 159, 203, 260.

11 Although Wilhelm used the familiar 'Du' to Eulenburg from early on, it is not clear what Eulenburg called Wilhelm in conversation. In letters Eulenburg (and later Fürstenberg) referred to Wilhelm as 'Your Majesty.' After 1900 Eulenburg frequently used 'Sie.'

12 Philipp's Uncle Fritz was Bismarck's Minister of the Interior from 1862 to 1878.

13 Reinhold Conrad Muschler, *Philipp zu Eulenburg, Sein Leben und seine Zeit* (Leipzig, 1930), pp. 53–4.

14 See his continuous battle with his father over money in Röhl, *Eulenburgs Korrespondenz,* I, nos. 42, 124, 125, 127, 204. It was said that Wilhelm did not want Eulenburg to become Minister of the Royal House because he thought Eulenburg a spendthrift (Holstein to Hohenlohe, Nov. 1894, BA Koblenz, Nl. Hohenlohe, Rep. 100 XXII/A1). If this is true, Wilhelm had, for once, shown good judgment.

15 Ladislaus Szögyényi-Marich to Agenor Graf Goluchowski, Private, 2.1.00, ÖStA Vienna, PA III 154, and Hans von Tresckow, *Von Fürsten und anderen Sterblichen. Erinnerungen eines Kriminalkommissars* (Berlin, 1922), p. 155. Eulenburg also worried that he had not enough money for such a title, see Eulenburg to Wilhelm, 5.12.99, to appear in Röhl, *Eulenburgs Korrespondenz*, vol. 3.

16 Adolf von Deines to his father, 14.3.94, MA Freiburg, Nl. Deines 12/p. 79b.

17 Eulenburg to Ludwig von Hirschfeld, 24.3.89, in Röhl, *Eulenburgs Korrespondenz*, I, no. 215.

18 Axel von Varnbüler, 'Memoiren' (unpublished manuscript, courtesy of John Röhl), p. 106.

19 Friedrich von Holstein to Eulenburg, 23.12.92, in Röhl, *Eulenburgs Korrespondenz*, II, no. 753.

20 Eulenburg to Auguste Viktoria, 21.10.02, BA Koblenz, Nl. Eulenburg, 59/p. 96.

21 Eulenburg to Herbert von Bismarck, 27.5.88 (emphasis in the original), BA Koblenz, Nl. Eulenburg, 3/p. 105.

22 (1843–1942).

23 Emil Görtz to his mother, 21.4.76, HStA Darmstadt, Nl. Görtz, F 23 A Korr., emphasis in the original.

24 Alfred von Bülow to Görtz, 18.1.77, *ibid.*, F 23 B.

25 Varnbüler's 'Memoiren,' cited in Röhl, *Eulenburgs Korrespondenz*, I, p. 110, n. 3.

26 Eulenburg to Varnbüler, 25.7.75, *ibid.*, I, no. 18.

27 Eulenburg to Varnbüler, 13.8.77, *ibid.*, I, no. 20.

28 Eulenburg to his sister, 19.9.81, *ibid.*, I, no. 36.

29 '*Hochideal gestimmten, oft schwärmerischen Männerfreundschaften,*' in his 'Memoiren,' cited *ibid.*, I, no. 18, n. 3.

30 The best example of such letters may be found in Philipp Eulenburg, *Fünf Jahre der Freundschaft in Briefen von Fritz von Farenheid-Beynuhnen und Graf Philipp zu Eulenburg-Hertefeld* (n.p., 1897).

31 Eulenburg's notes to his correspondence are replete with characterizations on the model: 'my good friend,' 'my very good friend,' etc. Eulenburg called the typescript of his correspondenz 'Eine preussische Familiengeschichte: Haus Liebenberg.' See Röhl, *Eulenburgs Korrespondenz*, I, pp. 53–73, for a discussion of the typescript and its authenticity.

32 Holstein to Eulenburg, 22.1.94, BA Koblenz, Nl. Eulenburg 27/p. 57.

33 Count Wedel was Kammerherr and Zeremonienmeister to Wilhelm. He was also homosexual and became one of the many victims of the Eulenburg scandal. See Tresckow, *Fürsten*, pp. 140–3.

34 Muschler, *Philipp zu Eulenburg*, p. 44.

35 (1847–1923). FAD to Wilhelm II, 1893–7; Military Attaché to Vienna, 1897; FA, 1897–1902; Military Commandant of Berlin, 1905–7.

36 (1851–1937). Varnbüler was the brother of Baronin Spitzemberg, the diarist of the *Hofgesellschaft*.

37 (1851–1891). Botschaftsrat in Tokyo, 1889; in Rome, 1889–90; and in St Petersburg, 1890–1.

38 (d. 1885).

39 (1850–1917). Private Secretary to Queen Olga of Württemberg and Imperial Russian Kammerherr and Staatsrat.

40 (1851–1916), Envoy to Switzerland.

41 (1851–1914).

42 (1843–1926).

43 This group consisted of Friedrich Eulenburg, Philipp's brother (until Friedrich's disgrace in 1898), Leopold Graf von Kalnein (Philipp's brother-in-law), Paul von Leszczynski (infantry general), and Heinrich von Keszycki (Eulenburg's cousin).

44 (1846–1905).

45 (1858–1922), brother of Dietrich Count von Hülsen-Haeseler, Chief of the Military Cabinet, 1901–8. Georg was Intendant of the Court Theater in Wiesbaden, 1894–1903, and Intendant of the Berlin Court Theater, 1903–18. He appears to have acquired the title 'Count' and the appendage Haeseler to his last name after Dietrich's death in 1908.

46 (1848–1916), FAD 1891–6; General *à la suite*, 1899–1916; Chief of the General Staff, 1906–14.

47 (1849–1923), see also pp. 188–9.

48 (d. 30 July 1909).

49 (1846–1918), FAD 1888–93; General *à la suite*, 1893–1918.

50 (1853–1914), Deputy Master of the Imperial Stables, 1900–14.

51 (1861–1927), editor of *Die Zukunft* and author of the Eulenburg scandal.

52 See 'Praeludium,' in *Die Zukunft*, 17.11.06 (vol. 57), p. 265; 'Moritz und Rina,' *ibid.*, 30.3.07 (vol. 58), p. 475; 'Monte Carlino,' *ibid.*, 13.4.07 (vol. 59), p. 44; and Harden to Holstein, 8.6.08, PA Bonn, Nl. Holstein 42.

53 (1857–1921), Secretary to the French Legation in Munich, 1884–7; in London, 1887–93; at the Vatican, 1893–5; in Berlin, 1895–9; in Egypt, 1899–1905; First Secretary in Berlin, 1905–7; Acting Ambassador to Berlin, January to June 1907.

54 (1858–1916), Imperial Foreign Secretary, 1906–7; thereafter, Ambassador to Austria-Hungary.

55 See pp. 122–3.

56 (1854–1930), FA, 1898–1903; General *à la suite*, 1905–7; forced to resign his commission in 1907.

57 (1854–1925), diplomat, First Secretary in Paris, 1897–9; Vortragender Rat (Councillor) at the Foreign Office, 1904–7; resigned from the diplomatic service, 1 May 1907.

58 (1859–1934), Major in the Garde du Corps, forced to resign in 1907; sentenced in 1908 to fifteen months in prison.

59 Letters were still being disposed of as late as 1917. 'Enclosed is a touching old letter of yours, which I came across yesterday as I was putting my correspondence in order. I did not want to rip it up, it is too touching for that, but it had better remain in your hands.' Eulenburg to Varnbüler, 7.12.17, HStA Stuttgart, Nl. Varnbüler xxxvi/9.

60 Norman Rich and M. H. Fisher (eds.), *Die geheimen Papiere Friedrich von Holsteins*, 4 vols. (Göttingen/Berlin/Frankfurt, 1963), IV, no. 1092, n. 3.

61 See pp. 138–9.

62 See Carroll Smith-Rosenberg, 'The Female World of Love and Ritual:

Relations between Women in Nineteenth-Century America,' *Signs,* vol. 1, no. 1 (Autumn 1975), pp. 7–8, for a perceptive and sensitive discussion of homosocial relations and love in the nineteenth century.

63 Varnbüler to Moltke, 15.4.98, HStA Stuttgart, Nl. Varnbüler xxxvi/9. For a fuller citation see pp. 55–6.

64 Kuno Moltke to Varnbüler, 31.3.91, 5.5.91 and 19.6.91; Varnbüler to Moltke, no date, probably 1889, HStA Stuttgart, Nl. Varnbüler xxxvi/9.

65 Moltke to Varnbüler, 31.3.91, *ibid.* (italics added).

66 Eulenburg disapproved of the wives of all his close friends, including the Kaiser. Eulenburg was not alone, however. All the Liebenbergers tended to dislike the women whom their male friends married. See, for example, the responses to Augusta Eulenburg, p. 50; and Alfred Bülow to Görtz, 30.1.76, misdated 1875, HStA Darmstadt, Nl. Görtz F 23 B.

67 Eulenburg, 'Notiz' to a letter of 12.3.96, BA Koblenz, Nl. Eulenburg 40/pp. 129–30, Eulenburg's italics. This 'Notiz' was written after the trials.

68 Eulenburg to his mother, 22.11.96, BA Koblenz, Nl. Eulenburg 44/ p. 735.

69 (1854–1908), FAD, Chief of Military Cabinet, 1901–8.

70 For Eulenburg's view see his papers 48/p. 487. The Austrian view is given by the Austrian Military *Bevollmächtigter* Klepsch-Kloth to the Chief of the Austrian General Staff, 20.9.05, ÖKrA Vienna, Chef des Generalstabes 1905, 25: 1/28.

71 Eulenburg to his wife, 30.8.97, BA Koblenz, Nl. Eulenburg 47/p. 442.

72 Eulenburg to his mother, 22.11.97 and 14.12.97, *ibid.,* 49/pp. 635, 697.

73 Cited in Harry F. Young, *Maximilian Harden: Censor Germaniae* (The Hague, 1959), p. 104.

74 Varnbüler to Moltke, 15.4.98. Original in HStA Stuttgart, Nl. Varnbüler xxxvi/9, partially cited in the introduction to Röhl, *Eulenburgs Korrespondenz,* 1, pp. 39–40. 'Gelichtet' is a forestry term meaning 'thinned.'

75 For example, John Addington Symonds, Karl Ulrichs, and Oscar Wilde.

76 Diary entry for 20.2.94, BA Koblenz, Nl. Eulenburg 28/p. 178.

77 See for example his letter to Nathaniel Rothschild, 17.9.04, Röhl, *Eulenburgs Korrespondenz,* 1, pp. 36–7, cited below, p. 131.

78 Eulenburg, 'Aus der Art,' in *Nord und Süd,* vol. xxviii, no. 83 (Feb. 1884), pp. 147–70.

79 E. Hollock, *Nachrichten über die Grafen Eulenburg* (n.p., n.d.), p. 115.

80 See Admiral Georg v. Müller's comments in Georg von Müller, *Der Kaiser ... Aufzeichnungen des Chefs des Marinekabinetts Admiral Georg Alexander von Müller über die Ära Wilhelms II,* ed. Walter Görlitz (Göttingen/Berlin/Frankfurt/Zürich, 1965), p. 176.

81 Eulenburg to Moltke, 10.7.07, in 'Aufzeichnungen des Fürsten Philipp zu Eulenburg-Hertefeld' (unpublished manuscript), pt 1, vol. 1, pp. 80–5, courtesy of John Röhl (hereafter: part/volume/pp.). Partially cited in Muschler, *Philipp zu Eulenburg,* p. 630.

82 See Philipp Eulenburg, 'Mein Freund Jan (Freiherr von Wendelstadt), Weihnachten 1909,' in Deutsches Zentrales Staatsarchiv Potsdam, Nl. Eulenburg, no. 623. (My thanks to John Röhl for this reference.)

83 Tresckow, *Fürsten,* pp. 161–2.

84 Maximilian Harden, *Köpfe*, 3 vols. (Berlin, 1913), III (*'Prozesse'*), 180.
85 Alfred Bülow to Görtz, 30.10.75, HStA Darmstadt, Nl. Görtz F 23 B.
86 *Ibid.*
87 Alfred Bülow to Görtz, 30.1.76, misdated 1875, *ibid.*
88 Alfred Bülow to Görtz, 7.7.76, *ibid.*
89 Alfred Bülow to Görtz, 18.1.77, *ibid.*, emphasis in the original.
90 Bernhard Bülow, *Denkwürdigkeiten*, 4 vols. (Berlin, 1931), IV, 642, reports a gathering of old friends in 1890.
91 Alfred Bülow to Görtz, 30.1.76, HStA Darmstadt, Nl. Görtz F 23 B.
92 Alfred Bülow to Görtz, 18.1.77, *ibid.*
93 *Ibid.*, emphasis in the original.
94 Alfred Bülow to Görtz, 11.1.86, *ibid.*
95 Alfred Bülow to Eulenburg, 8.3.93, BA Koblenz, Nl. Eulenburg 23/p. 113, omitted in Röhl, *Eulenburgs Korrespondenz*, II, no. 780.
96 Alfred Bülow to Varnbüler, 16.6.07, HStA Stuttgart, Nl. Varnbüler XXXV/20; and Eulenburg to Bernhard Bülow, telegram, 29.6.16, BA Koblenz, Nl. Bernhard Bülow 14/p. 533.
97 Hinzpeter to Anna Gräfin Görtz, 17.7.89, HStA Darmstadt, Nl. Görtz F 23 A. Korr.
98 Hinzpeter to Karl Graf Görtz, 6.12.75, *ibid.*
99 See Hinzpeter to Karl Görtz, 24.4.81 and 6.6.85, *ibid.*
100 Varnbüler to Kuno Moltke, 17.10.92, in Röhl, *Eulenburgs Korrespondenz*, II, no. 716.
101 Harden to Holstein, 15.11.08, PA Bonn, Nl. Holstein 42, also cited by Röhl, *Eulenburgs Korrespondenz*, I, 47.
102 John C. G. Röhl has catalogued some examples of this sort of behavior in Röhl. 'The Emperor's New Clothes: A Character Sketch of Kaiser Wilhelm II,' in John C. G. Röhl and Nicolaus Sombart (eds.), *Kaiser Wilhelm II: New Interpretations* (Cambridge, 1981), pp. 34–5. See also Philipp Eulenburg, 'Drei Freunde,' II/1/pp. 47–50, for how frequently Wilhelm touched the male entourage members.
103 Eulenburg to Wilhelm, 22.12.88, in Röhl, *Eulenburgs Korrespondenz*, I, no. 208.
104 Eulenburg to Wilhelm, 15.2.91, BA Koblenz, Nl. Eulenburg 14/pp. 40–1.
105 'Gottgewollte,' in a 'Notiz' from 5.3.89, *ibid.*, 5/pp. 74–5.
106 Diary entry of 15.7.89, in Eulenburg, *Mit dem Kaiser*, I, 47 and elsewhere.
107 Eulenburg, Varnbüler, and Moltke all referred to Wilhelm as *'das Liebchen'* among themselves. Varnbüler to Moltke, 4.6.98 and 17.5.98, HStA Stuttgart, Nl. Varnbüler XXXVI/9, and Moltke to Eulenburg, 1.3.97, BA Koblenz, Nl. Bülow 76/pp. 153–60; see also Holstein's diary entry, 11.11.06, in Rich and Fisher, *Die geheimen Papiere*, IV, no. 1004, cited in Röhl, *Eulenburgs Korrespondenz*, I, p. 40, n. 126.
108 Eulenburg to Wilhelm, 25.3.93, BA Koblenz, Nl. Eulenburg 24/pp. 163–4.
109 Eulenburg to Wilhelm, 10.3.92, in Röhl, *Eulenburgs Korrespondenz*, II, no. 604, Eulenburg's italics.
110 For Moltke's personality and career at Court, see pp. 103–5; for his politics, see pp. 104–5 and 227–8.

111 Eulenburg to his mother, 27.1.94, BA Koblenz, Nl. Eulenburg 27/p. 90.
112 Eulenburg, 'Aufzeichnungen,' I/1/p. 92.
113 Varnbüler to Moltke, November 1890, in Röhl, *Eulenburgs Korrespondenz,* I, no. 442.
114 See his criticism of Kiel Week, above, p. 35 and his remarks about Wilhelm's war-leadership, 'Memoiren,' pp. 635–8. For Varnbüler's career, see below, pp. 101–3.
115 Eulenburg, *Mit dem Kaiser,* II, 157.
116 Eulenburg, 'Drei Freunde,' II/2/p. 127.
117 This was the Hochberg–Pierson affair, detailed on pp. 118–19.
118 Bogdan von Hutten-Czapski, *Sechzig Jahre Politik und Gesellschaft,* 2 vols. (Berlin, 1935), I, 411.
119 Hinzpeter to Karl Görtz, 24.7.73, HStA Darmstadt, Nl. Görtz F 23 A Korr.
120 Hinzpeter to Karl Görtz, 28.9.74, *ibid.*
121 Hinzpeter to Karl Görtz, 28.9.76, *ibid.*
122 Hinzpeter to Anna Görtz, 17.7.89, *ibid.*
123 Hinzpeter to Anna Görtz, 22.6.89, *ibid.*
124 Hinzpeter to Anna Görtz, 9.7.89, *ibid.*
125 Hinzpeter to Emil Görtz, 4.9.89, *ibid.*
126 It pleased the gossip mill, too, which hoped to discover something scandalous in the relationship. See Varnbüler, 'Memoiren,' p. 574.
127 Emil Görtz to Anna Görtz, 3.5.80, HStA Darmstadt, Nl. Görtz F 23 A Korr., emphasis in the original.
128 Hinzpeter to Emil Görtz, 5.6.90, *ibid.*
129 List of events for 30.7.91, *ibid.,* F 23 A Fasz. 296, Bd 3, '*Reiseangelegenheiten (Nordlandreise 1898/99).*'
130 Georg Hülsen to Emil Görtz, 17.10.92, *ibid.,* F 23 H, partly cited in Röhl, *Eulenburgs Korrespondenz,* II, p. 953, n. 3.
131 Hülsen to Görtz, 19.10.91, *ibid.,* p. 953, n. 4.
132 Hülsen to Görtz, 19.10.91, HStA Darmstadt, Nl. Görtz F 23 H, not cited in Röhl, *Eulenburgs Korrespondenz,* II, p. 953, n. 4.
133 Robert Zedlitz-Trützschler, *Zwölf Jahre am deutschen Kaiserhof. Aufzeichnungen des Grafen Robert Zedlitz-Trützschler ehemaligen Hofmarschalls Wilhelms II* (Berlin/Leipzig, 1925), diary entry for 8.2.09, p. 216.
134 Varnbüler to Julius Frhr von Soden, 17.11.00, HStA Stuttgart, E-73, Verz. 61, 12e.
135 Müller's diary entry from 12.2.05, MA Freiburg, Nl. Müller 3/p. 226.
136 The doctor attending Eulenburg at his trial complained to Police Commissioner Tresckow that it was difficult to treat Eulenburg because he and the whole family believed in spiritistic cures and would only call a regular doctor when the symptoms became unbearable. Tresckow, *Fürsten,* pp. 209–10.
137 Muschler, *Philipp zu Eulenburg,* p. 29 and Eulenburg, *Mit dem Kaiser,* I, 206–8.
138 Eulenburg to Wilhelm, 27.3.88, in Röhl, *Eulenburgs Korrespondenz,* I, no. 165, emphasis in the original.
139 Eulenburg to Klara Baronin von Esebeck, 22.3.91, *ibid,* no. 492.
140 Diary entry, 21.8.96, BA Koblenz, Nl. Eulenburg 43/pp. 539–40.

141 Eulenburg to Auguste Caroline Grossherzogin von Mecklenburg, 8.4.89, in Röhl, *Eulenburgs Korrespondenz*, I, no. 217.
142 Eulenburg to Nathaniel Rothschild, 17.9.04, *ibid.*, pp. 36–7, and below, p. 131.
143 Eulenburg to his sister, 23.2.89, *ibid.*, no. 212.
144 Admiral Friedrich von Hollmann was an ardent spiritist and delighted the Kaiser with his stories, Eulenburg to Bülow, 25.9.99, BA Koblenz, Nl. Eulenburg 56/pp. 258–60.
145 Prince Heinrich's diary, vol. I, p. 216, courtesy of Dr Max Bruecher, Freiburg i. Br.
146 Eulenburg to Wilhelm, 25.4.87, in Röhl, *Eulenburgs Korrespondenz*, I, no. 112.
147 See Heinrich Otto Meisner (ed.), *Denkwürdigkeiten des General-Feldmarschalls Alfred Grafen von Waldersee*, 3 vols. (Stuttgart, 1923), II, 222, cited in Röhl, *Eulenburgs Korrespondenz*, I, no. 538, n. 3, and Otto von Bismarck, *Gedanken und Erinnerungen*, 3 vols. (Stuttgart/Berlin, 1921), III, 125–6.
148 Eulenburg, 'Aufzeichnungen,' I/2/p. 137.
149 Eulenburg to Wilhelm, 9.8.87, in Röhl, *Eulenburgs Korrespondenz*, I, no. 120, emphasis in original.
150 Eulenburg to Wilhelm, 15.10.88, *ibid.*, no. 199.
151 Eulenburg to Bernhard Bülow, 25.9.00, BA Koblenz, Nl. Eulenburg 56/p. 258.
152 Waldersee's diary entry of 18.11.91, in Waldersee, *Denkwürdigkeiten*, II, 222. There is no mention of this in Eulenburg's papers.
153 See, however, Röhl, *Eulenburgs Korrespondenz*, I, no. 208, n. 2.
154 Harden, *Köpfe*, III, 174.
155 Wolfgang Stribrny, 'Kaiser Wilhelm II. und die Burg Hohenzollern,' *Zeitschrift für Religions- und Geistesgeschichte*, vol. 13, no. 1/2 (1971), pp. 129–34.
156 Wilhelm had begun his speech by favorably comparing the Berlin Sculptor School to the Renaissance. The speech is reprinted in E. Schröder (ed.), *Zwanzig Jahre Regierungszeit. Ein Tagebuch Kaiser Wilhelms II. Vom Antritt der Regierung, 15. Juni 1888 bis zum 15. Juni 1908 nach Hof- und anderen Berichten* (Berlin, 1909), pp. 394–400.
157 Houston Stewart Chamberlain, *Die Grundlagen des Neunzehnten Jahrhunderts*, 2 vols. (Munich, 1899).
158 Eulenburg, 'Notiz' of 29.10.01, BA Koblenz, Nl. Eulenburg 58/p. 218.
159 *Ibid.*, p. 215.
160 See Houston Stewart Chamberlain, *Briefe* (Munich, 1928), pp. 131–275.
161 See, for example, pp. 278 or 292.
162 Varnbüler to Soden, 14.12.01, HStA Stuttgart, E-73, Verz. 61, 12e.
163 Eulenburg, *'Ein Kaiserbesuch* und *Houston Stewart Chamberlain*. [*sic*] Auch eine Jagd in Liebenberg. Oktober 1891,' BA Koblenz, Nl. Eulenburg 58/p. 191.
164 Hinzpeter to Emil Görtz, 12.2.75, HStA Darmstadt, Nl. Görtz F 23 A Korr.
165 That was Friedrich von Holstein, see below, p. 92.

166 See his famous letter to Bernhard Bülow, *Denkwürdigkeiten*, I, 4–5, cited below, p. 107.

Chapter 4, pp. 76–108

1 Cited by John C. G. Röhl (ed.) *Philipp Eulenburgs Politische Korrespondenz*, 3 vols. (Boppard am Rhein, 1976–), I, p. 315, n. 5, and Walter Bussmann (ed.), *Staatssekretär Graf Herbert von Bismarck, Aus seiner politischen Privatkorrespondenz* (Göttingen, 1964), p. 524, n. h (marginal comment to a letter from Herbert von Bismarck to Otto von Bismarck, 5.10.88).

2 Holstein advised Eulenburg on 15.6.86 to write shorter reports, because the Bismarcks preferred them that way. If the reports were good, they would be sent directly to the Chancellor (BA Koblenz, Nl. Eulenburg 1/p. 18). From this time on, Holstein wrote Eulenburg almost daily.

3 On 1.11.88.

4 Alfred von Bülow to Bernhard von Bülow, 9.1.86, BA Koblenz, Nl. Bülow 14/pp. 234–5.

5 See Philipp Eulenburg to Herbert von Bismarck, 5.2.86, in Röhl, *Eulenburgs Korrespondenz*, I, no. 64.

6 Ladislaus Graf von Szögyényi-Marich to Agenor Graf von Goluchowski, private, 11.11.00, ÖStA Vienna, PA III 154; Alexander von Hohenlohe to Friedrich von Holstein, 25.8.01, PA Bonn, Nl. Holstein 9; and Anton Monts to Heinrich von Tschirschky und Bögendorff, 27.11.06, in Anton Monts, *Erinnerungen und Gedanken des Botschafters Anton Graf Monts*, ed. Karl F. Nowak and Friedrich Thimme (Berlin, 1932), p. 430.

7 Johannes Haller, 'Bülow und Eulenburg,' in Friedrich Thimme (ed.), *Front Wider Bülow. Staatsmänner, Diplomaten und Forscher zu seinen Denkwürdigkeiten* (Munich, 1931), p. 35.

8 Chlodwig zu Hohenlohe to Alexander zu Hohenlohe, 7.1.00, BA Koblenz, Nl. Hohenlohe Rep. 100 XXVII/3, reprinted in Fürst Chlodwig zu Hohenlohe-Schillingsfürst, *Denkwürdigkeiten der Reichskanzlerzeit*, ed. by Karl Alexander von Müller (Stuttgart/Berlin, 1931), p. 554. The printed version omits the word 'Erzlump' from the concluding sentence which reads in the original: 'Es ist erschreckend, dass dieser Erzlump der Freund des Kaisers ist [It is dreadful that this complete lout is the friend of the Kaiser].' (Hereafter, this volume of Hohenlohe's memoirs will be cited as *Denkwürdigkeiten*, III). See also Baronin Spitzemberg, *Das Tagebuch der Baronin Spitzemberg geb. Freiin v. Varnbüler. Aufzeichnungen aus der Hofgesellschaft des Hohenzollernreiches*, ed. Rudolf Vierhaus (Göttingen, 1960), 5.1.00, pp. 392–3.

9 Eulenburg to Wilhelm, 5.12.99, to appear in Röhl, *Eulenburgs Korrespondenz*, III.

10 Eulenburg to Holstein, 16.7.86, in Norman Rich and M. H. Fisher (eds.), *Die geheimen Papiere Friedrich von Holsteins*, 4 vols. (Göttingen/Berlin/Frankfurt, 1961), III, 145–6. Holstein noted in the margin: 'So, Eulenburg would like to go himself. That would not be bad.' Georg Frhr von Werthern-Beichlingen, who had been Prussia's envoy to Bavaria since 1867, was due to retire shortly. See also Röhl, *Eulenburgs Korrespondenz*, I, no. 84, n. 2.

11 (1843–1917).
12 Eulenburg to Wilhelm, 19.2.88, Röhl, *Eulenburgs Korrespondenz*, I, no. 154.
13 *Ibid.*, and Eulenburg to Holstein, 29.2.88, *ibid.*, no. 159.
14 Eulenburg to Herbert von Bismarck, 20.6.87, *ibid.*, no. 115.
15 *Ibid.*
16 Holstein to Eulenburg, 27.11.90, *ibid.*, no. 444. Eulenburg did not actually take over the post until May 1891.
17 See Lerchenfeld-Köfering's reports of 17.2.91 and 20.2.91 in BGSA Munich, Gesandtschaft Berlin 1061.
18 (1842–1919), Prussian General; FAD, 1889; 1891 transferred into the diplomatic corps; Envoy to Sweden, 1892–4; Ambassador to Italy, 1899–1902; Ambassador to Austria-Hungary, 1902–7; Statthalter of Alsace-Lorraine, 1907–14.
19 Caprivi may have supported the idea in order to get Eulenburg out of Munich after Eulenburg's recent controversial role in the defeat of the School Bill. See Röhl, *Eulenburgs Korrespondenz*, I, p. 25.
20 Eulenburg's Protocol of a conversation between Wilhelm and Eulenburg aboard the *Hohenzollern* in Norway on 11.7.92, in BA Koblenz, Nl. Eulenburg 20/pp. 504–6.
21 (1832–98), Austrian Minister of Foreign Affairs and Minister of the Imperial and Royal House, 1881–95.
22 (1825–1906), German Ambassador to St Petersburg, 1867–76; German Ambassador to Vienna, 1878–94.
23 Bülow to Eulenburg, 6.9.92, Röhl, *Eulenburgs Korrespondenz*, II, no. 699.
24 (1852–1912), Diplomat; Envoy to Mecklenburg and the Hansa cities, 1894–5; to Copenhagen, 1895–9; sometime Representative of the Foreign Office on Wilhelm's trips; Envoy to Romania, 1900–10; Secretary of the Foreign Office, 1910–12.
25 Bülow to Eulenburg, 4.5.93, Röhl, *Eulenburgs Korrespondenz*, II, no. 801.
26 Eulenburg to Holstein, 29.6.93, *ibid.*, no. 809.
27 Eulenburg note to his letter to Wilhelm of 27.8.93, *ibid.*, p. 1102, n. 4.
28 For Lichnowsky's relation to Bülow, see Harry F. Young, *Prince Lichnowsky and the Great War* (Athens, Georgia, 1977), pp. 9–11, 195–6, n. 5.
29 Eulenburg diary entry for 16–18 December 1893, BA Koblenz, Nl. Eulenburg 26/pp. 578–81; and Eulenburg to his mother, 18.12.93, Röhl, *Eulenburgs Korrespondenz*, II, no. 864.
30 This report is printed in Johannes Lepsius *et al.* (eds.), *Die Grosse Politik der Europäischen Kabinette, 1871–1914. Sammlung der Diplomatischen Akten des Auswärtigen Amtes*, 40 vols. (Berlin, 1926), IX, 105–9, no. 2138.
31 Eulenburg to Bülow, 29.12.93, Röhl, *Eulenburgs Korrespondenz*, II, no. 873.
32 *Ibid.*, I, p. 26.
33 Erhardt Graf von Wedel (ed.), *Carl Graf von Wedel, Zwischen Kaiser und Kanzler, Aufzeichnungen aus den Jahren 1890–1894* (Leipzig, 1943), pp. 199–200.
34 Deines to his Father, 11.2.94, MA Freiburg, Nl. Deines 12/pp. 71–2. At the time, Deines was Military Attaché to the German Embassy in Vienna.
35 Wedel, *Kaiser und Kanzler*, p. 200.
36 Max Ratibor to Holstein, 22.10.94, in Rich and Fisher, *Die geheimen Papiere*, III, no. 424.

37 Eulenburg to Wilhelm, 3.11.94, Röhl, *Eulenburgs Korrespondenz*, II, no. 1042.
38 See John Röhl, *Germany Without Bismarck* (London, 1967), ch. 1; Röhl, 'Staatsstreichplan oder Staatsstreichbereitschaft? Bismarcks Politik in der Entlassungskrise,' *Historische Zeitschrift* (Dec. 1966); Röhl, 'The Disintegration of the Kartell and the Politics of Bismarck's Fall from Power, 1887–1890,' *The Historical Journal*, vol. IX, no. 1 (1966), pp. 60–90; and Martin Reuss, 'Bismarck's Dismissal and the Holstein Circle,' *European Studies Review*, vol. 5, no. 1 (1975).
39 Bülow thought Wilhelm was to blame. See Bernhard von Bülow, *Denkwürdigkeiten*, 4 vols. (Berlin, 1930), I, 148; but Hinzpeter, who was directly on the scene, agreed with Eulenburg: Hinzpeter to Karl Görtz, 2.2.84, HStA Darmstadt, Nl. Görtz F 23 A Korr.
40 Diary entry of 13.1.90, Röhl, *Eulenburgs Korrespondenz*, I, pp. 406–7, n. 3.
41 (1845–98), jurist who had served in the civil administration and in the Foreign Office; Vortragender Rat in the Justice Section of the Foreign Office, 1885–90; Director of the Colonial Section of the Foreign Office, 1890–6; President of the Reichsgericht, 1896.
42 Eulenburg to Wilhelm, 7.2.90 in Röhl, *Eulenburgs Korrespondenz*, I, no. 311, and Eulenburg to Holstein, 9.2.90, *ibid.*, no. 316. Kayser was not appointed.
43 Eulenburg to Gustav von Kessel, 23.2.90, BA Koblenz, Nl. Eulenburg 9/pp. 145–6, reprinted in Johannes Haller (ed.), *Aus 50 Jahren, Erinnerungen, Tagebücher und Briefe aus dem Nachlass des Fürsten Philipp zu Eulenburg-Hertefeld* (Berlin, 1923), pp. 291–2.
44 Eulenburg to Holstein, 28.2.90, Röhl, *Eulenburgs Korrespondenz*, I, no. 326.
45 Eulenburg to Wilhelm, 7 and 8.3.90, *ibid.*, nos. 336 and 339; and Eulenburg to Holstein, 18.3.90, BA Koblenz, Nl. Eulenburg 10/p. 279.
46 Philipp Eulenburg, 'Graf Herbert Bismarck,' originally published in *Deutsche Rundschau*, vol. 49, no. 6, reprinted in Haller, *Aus 50 Jahren*, pp. 81–107; the quotation is on p. 85.
47 Eulenburg to Bülow, 29.1.90, BA Koblenz, Nl. Eulenburg 8/pp. 69–73.
48 *Ibid.*
49 Eulenburg was Prussia's representative to Oldenburg from November 1888 to Spring 1890, when he was accredited to Stuttgart. In April 1891, Eulenburg was back in Munich at the head of the legation, where he remained until Spring 1894, when he became German Ambassador to Austria. Eulenburg kept this post until his resignation in Winter 1902.
50 Eulenburg to Wilhelm, 11.5.92, BA Koblenz, Nl. Eulenburg 19/pp. 305–6.
51 Eulenburg to Wilhelm, 6.3.97, *ibid.*, 46/pp. 177–81.
52 Eulenburg to Holstein, 2.12.94, PA Bonn, Nl. Holstein 37, reprinted in Johannes Haller (ed.), *Aus dem Leben des Fürsten Philipp zu Eulenburg-Hertefeld* (Berlin/Leipzig, 1926), pp. 178–82. See also Röhl, *Germany without Bismarck*, pp. 127–8, and Norman Rich, *Friedrich von Holstein: Politics and Diplomacy in the Era of Bismarck and Wilhelm II*, 2 vols. (Cambridge, 1965), II, 487–8.
53 See Hartmut Pogge von Strandmann and Imanuel Geiss, *Die Erforderlichkeit des Unmöglichen* (Frankfurt, 1965), pp. 8ff.; for conservative pressure for a coup and the government's response after 1900, see Klaus Saul,

Staat, Industrie, Arbeiterbewegung im Kaiserreich. Zur Innen- und Aussenpolitik des Wilhelminischen Deutschland 1903–1914 (Düsseldorf, 1974), pp. 13–50.

54 Eulenburg to Holstein, 2.12.94, see note 52, above.

55 *Ibid.*

56 For a detailed account of the Caprivi years see Röhl, *Germany Without Bismarck;* J. Alden Nichols, *Germany After Bismarck: The Caprivi Era 1890–1894* (New York, 1968; 1958); and Peter Leibenguth, 'Modernisierungskrisis des Kaiserreichs an der Schwelle zum Wilhelminischen Imperialismus. Politische Probleme der Ära Caprivi (1890–1895)' (Unpublished Ph.D. dissertation, Köln, 1975).

57 Eulenburg memorandum for Kaiser Wilhelm II, 20.3.94, Röhl, *Eulenburgs Korrespondenz,* II, no. 933.

58 See p. 20, note 45.

59 See Röhl, *Eulenburgs Korrespondenz,* I, nos. 50, 62, 68, 110, 140, 188, 226, 267 (an exception), 331, 386, 410, 473, 517.

60 Eulenburg to Bülow, 28.2.93, *ibid.,* no. 776.

61 Eulenburg to Bülow, 29.1.90, in Haller, *Aus 50 Jahren,* pp. 288–90, and Röhl, *Eulenburgs Korrespondenz,* I, no. 331, n. 2.

62 Bülow to Eulenburg, 13.3.93, *ibid.,* II, no. 785.

63 Bülow, *Denkwürdigkeiten,* IV, 487.

64 Bülow to Eulenburg, 28.9.95, in Haller, *Aus dem Leben,* p. 235.

65 Bülow to Eulenburg, 10.7.89, Röhl, *Eulenburgs Korrespondenz,* I, no. 226.

66 Bülow to Eulenburg, 2.3.90, *ibid.,* no. 331.

67 Bülow to Eulenburg, 28.5.91, *ibid.,* no. 517.

68 There are particularly bombastic examples in letters to Eulenburg of 19.12.93 (*ibid.,* II, no. 866), 15.12.94 (*ibid.,* no. 1065), and 15.2.98, in Kurt Zentner, *Kaiserliche Zeiten. Wilhelm II und seine Ära in Bildern und Dokumenten* (Munich, 1964), pp. 58–9. 15.2.98 also appears in facsimile in Thimme, *Front Wider Bülow,* pp. 8ff.

69 Bülow to Eulenburg, 13.3.93, Röhl, *Eulenburgs Korrespondenz,* II, no. 785.

70 Bülow to Eulenburg, 23.7.96, cited in Röhl, *Germany Without Bismarck,* p. 194.

71 Eulenburg to Wilhelm, 12.3.92, in Röhl, *Eulenburgs Korrespondenz,* II, no. 605.

72 Eulenburg to Bülow, 28.2.93, *ibid.,* no. 776.

73 Bülow to Eulenburg, 24.4.93, *ibid.,* no. 797.

74 Bülow to Eulenburg, 28.9.93, *ibid.,* no. 826.

75 See Röhl, *Germany Without Bismarck,* pp. 106–7.

76 Eulenburg to Bülow, 9.3.94, in Röhl, *Eulenburgs Korrespondenz,* II, no. 924.

77 Röhl, *Germany Without Bismarck,* p. 107.

78 (1828–1901), Prussian Finance Minister, 1890–1901; Vice President of the Prussian Staatsministerium, 1897–1901.

79 See Haller, *Aus dem Leben,* pp. 172–8, and Eulenburg to Bülow, 7.5.94, in Röhl, *Eulenburgs Korrespondenz,* II, no. 963.

80 For detailed accounts of the crisis see Nichols, *Germany After Bismarck,* pp. 329–57, and Röhl, *Germany Without Bismarck,* pp. 110–17, and their footnotes for further secondary works. Nichols considerably underestimates Eulenburg's role in unseating Caprivi.

81 Nichols, *Germany After Bismarck,* p. 349; and Röhl, *Germany Without Bismarck,* p. 115.
82 See Holstein to Eulenburg, 27.11.94, BA Koblenz, Nl. Eulenburg 33/pp. 920–2; Eulenburg's answer of 2.12.94, Holstein to Eulenburg, 4.12.94 and 24.12.94 plus Eulenburg to Holstein, 27.12.94, in Haller, *Aus dem Leben,* pp. 178–84.
83 Holstein to Eulenburg 24.12.94, *ibid.*
84 Eulenburg to Holstein, 27.12.94, *ibid.*
85 Holstein to Eulenburg, 17.2.95, BA Koblenz, Nl. Eulenburg 34/pp. 115–17.
86 Holstein to Eulenburg, 9.2.96, Rich and Fisher, *Die geheimen Papiere,* III, 530–2, and Holstein to Eulenburg 21.12.95, *ibid.*, pp. 516–17.
87 Eulenburg to Holstein, 14.2.96, BA Koblenz, Nl. Eulenburg 40/pp. 90–1.
88 Eulenburg to Hohenlohe, 20.3.96, in Hohenlohe, *Denkwürdigkeiten,* III, 201–3.
89 See Eulenburg's note of 27.10.96, BA Koblenz, Nl. Eulenburg 44/p. 722 in which he remarks upon Holstein's friendliness. Also Holstein to Bülow, 10.6.96 and 31.3.97, BA Koblenz, Nl. Bülow 90/pp. 154–9 and 278–85; and Eulenburg's note of 11.11.96, BA Koblenz, Nl. Eulenburg 44/p. 757.
90 See the discussion below of the events of November 1895 and June 1897.
91 See Rolf G. Weitowitz, *Deutsche Politik und Handelspolitik unter Reichskanzler Leo von Caprivi: 1890–1894* (Düsseldorf, 1978); Kenneth D. Barkin, *The Controversy over German Industrialization 1890–1902* (Chicago, 1970), ch. 2. There is a short but intelligent discussion of the social basis and effects of the tariffs in Peter Leibenguth, 'Modernisierungskrisis des Kaiserreichs,' ch. 5.
92 The Tausch scandal involved the political police of Berlin, whom Marschall found to be unresponsive to the current government because it was peopled by Bismarckians. Marschall won considerable public acclaim by prosecuting some of them and their spies in the Tausch trial. See Dieter Fricke, 'Die Affaire Leckert–Lützow–Tausch und die Regierungskrise von 1897 in Deutschland,' *Zeitschrift für Geschichtswissenschaft,* VIII (1960), 1579–1603, and Helmuth Rogge, 'Affairen im Kaiserreich. Symptome der Staatskrise unter Wilhelm II,' *Die Politische Meinung,* LXXXI (1963), 58–72.
93 Eulenburg to Wilhelm, 3.11.94, in BA Koblenz, Nl. Eulenburg 32/p. 862.
94 *Ibid.*
95 See Röhl, *Germany Without Bismarck,* pp. 132–6, of which the following account is a paraphrase.
96 (1846–1922), Prussian General; FAD, 1893–6.
97 Eulenburg to Hohenlohe, 16.2.95, BA Koblenz, Nl. Hohenlohe Rep. 100 XXII/A/2, reprinted in Hohenlohe, *Denkwürdigkeiten,* III, 39–42.
98 Translation by Röhl, *Germany Without Bismarck,* p. 135.
99 See Eulenburg, 'Tagebuch Notiz (für Bülow),' (February 1895), BA Koblenz, Nl. Eulenburg 34/pp. 153–4. For a discussion of Bismarck's visit to Berlin in 1894 and the Court intrigues behind this see below, pp. 225–30.

100 See pp. 219–20.
101 Eulenburg to Bülow, 6.12.95, BA Koblenz, Nl. Bülow 75/pp. 285–6, and Eulenburg to Bülow, 13.1.96, *ibid.*, 76/pp. 1–11.
102 Walther Bronsart von Schellendorff (1833–1914), Prussian General; Prussian War Minister, 1893–6.
103 Wilhelm to Eulenburg, 25.12.95, BA Koblenz, Nl. Eulenburg 39/p. 940.
104 See pp. 215–25.
105 Eulenburg, 'Notizen zur Besprechung' from 1.8.96, reprinted in Röhl, *Germany Without Bismarck*, pp. 196–7.
106 (1841–1927), served as Prussian War Minister from 1896 to 1903.
107 Wilhelm to Eulenburg, 13.8.96, cited in Röhl, *Germany Without Bismarck*, p. 198.
108 Holstein to Eulenburg, 24.11.96, Rich and Fisher, *Die geheimen Papiere*, III, 584–7.
109 Eulenburg to Wilhelm, 26.11.96, BA Koblenz, Nl. Eulenburg 44/pp. 784–5.
110 See note 92.
111 Bülow to Eulenburg, 23.7.96, cited in Röhl, *Germany Without Bismarck*, p. 194.
112 Eulenburg to Bülow, 24.4.97, *ibid.*, p. 230.
113 Eulenburg promised that Wilhelm would intervene with his cousin the Czar in the matter of Hohenlohe's huge, Russian estate, Werki.
114 Lerchenfeld to Crailsheim, 17.6.97 (no. 284), BGSA Munich, Gesandtschaft Berlin 1068. He was also anxious not to prejudice his eight children's chances for success by ending his career in political disgrace.
115 See Röhl, *Germany Without Bismarck*, p. 234.
116 *Ibid.*, pp. 231–2.
117 Eulenburg to Wilhelm, 8.4.97, BA Koblenz, Nl. Eulenburg 46/pp. 240ff., and Bülow's marginal comment on Holstein to Bülow, 5.4.97, BA Koblenz, Nl. Bülow 90/pp. 298–308.
118 Eulenburg to Bülow, 18.12.97, BA Koblenz, Nl. Eulenburg 49/p. 714, Eulenburg's italics.
119 *Ibid.*
120 See p. 55.
121 This is reflected in the number of pages for each year:

1886	54	1892	813	1898	348
1887	112	1893	622	1899	257
1888	222	1894	1012	1900	319
1889	258	1895	972	1901	257
1890	714	1896	832	1902	123
1891	396	1897	730		

BA Koblenz, Nl. Eulenburg 60/p. 188.
122 *Ibid.*, 60/pp. 149, 178.
123 Eulenburg to Bülow, 2.5.99, *ibid.*, 53/p. 78.
124 Eulenburg to Bülow, 20.10.00, *ibid.*, 56/p. 285. Italics in the original.
125 See Eulenburg's account in 'Drei Freunde' (unpublished manuscript, courtesy of John Röhl), pt II, sec. 2, pp. 192–5 (hereafter II/2/pp. 192–5).
126 See, for example, Hutten-Czapski's appraisal of Bülow as the 'most suitable' candidate for Secretary of the Foreign Office, Bogdan von Hutten-

Czapski, *Sechzig Jahre Politik und Gesellschaft,* 2 vols. (Berlin, 1935), I, 328.
127 Eulenburg to Wilhelm, 8.3.90, Röhl, *Eulenburgs Korrespondenz,* I, no. 339.
128 Holstein to Eulenburg, 23.10.90, *ibid.,* no. 424.
129 Holstein to Eulenburg, 6.12.90, *ibid.,* no. 452, and Bülow, *Denkwürdig-keiten,* IV, 642.
130 See Röhl, *Eulenburgs Korrespondenz,* I, p. 23, and Hans Philippi, *Das Königreich Württemberg im Spiegel der Preussischen Gesandtschaftsberichte 1871–1914.* Veröffentlichungen der Kommission für geschichtliche Landeskunde in Baden-Württemberg, Reihe B, Forschungen, vol. 65 (Stuttgart, 1972), pp. 104–22.
131 Eulenburg to Holstein, 5.1.87, Röhl, *Eulenburgs Korrespondenz,* I, no. 101, and p. 206, n. 6.
132 Hugo Graf von und zu Lerchenfeld-Köfering (1843–1925) was Bavaria's diplomatic representative in Berlin and in the Bundesrat from 1880 to 1918.
133 Eulenburg to Marschall, 2.12.90, Röhl, *Eulenburgs Korrespondenz,* I, no. 450, especially n. 3.
134 Eulenburg to Wilhelm, 14.8.92, *ibid.,* II, no. 693.
135 Kiderlen-Wächter to Caprivi, 19.9.93, PA Bonn, Württemberg 35 *secr.,* vol. 2, and Eulenburg to King Wilhelm II of Württemberg, 2.2.94, in Röhl, *Eulenburgs Korrespondenz,* II, no. 892.
136 Hermann Freiherr von Mittnacht (1825–1909), Minister President of Württemberg 31.7.76 to 10.11.1900. See Georg H. Kleine, *Der württembergische Ministerpräsident Freiherr Hermann von Mittnacht.* Veröffentlichungen der Kommission für geschichtliche Landeskunde in Baden-Württemberg, Reihe B, Forschungen, vol. 50 (Stuttgart, 1969).
137 Friedrich Rudolf Karl von Moser (1840–1909), Württemberg's diplomatic representative to Berlin and in the Bundesrat from 11 February 1890 to 19 February 1894.
138 See note 135.
139 Moltke to Varnbüler, 4.10.93, HStA Stuttgart, Nl. Varnbüler XXXVI, Karton 9.
140 King Wilhelm II of Württemberg (1848–1921) ruled from 6.10.91 to 29.11.18.
141 See note 135.
142 See Helmuth Rogge, 'Die *Kladderadatsch-*Affäre. Ein Beitrag zur neueren Geschichte des Wilhelminischen Reiches,' *Historische Zeitschrift,* CXCV (1962), 90–130, and Norman Rich, *Friedrich von Holstein,* 2 vols. (Cambridge, 1965), I, 403–15.
143 Holstein to Eulenburg, 2.2.94, Röhl, *Eulenburgs Korrespondenz,* II, no. 893.
144 Eulenburg to Wilhelm, 27.11.93, *ibid.,* no. 850. Varnbüler would simultaneously be Württemberg's representative to the Bundesrat.
145 See note 135.
146 Philippi, *Das Königreich Württemberg,* p. 122.
147 Wilhelm's marginal comment on report No. 61 of 13.11.00, cited in *ibid.,* pp. 137–8.
148 This is how he described Varnbüler to King George V in 1913. Varnbüler to Weizsäcker, 28.5.13, HStA Stuttgart E-73, Verz. 61, 12e.
149 See Hans-Ulrich Wehler, 'Der Fall Zabern. Rückblick auf eine Verfas-

sungskrise des wilhelminischen Kaiserreiches,' *Die Welt als Geschichte,* no. 23 (1963), pp. 27–46; Kurt Stenkewitz, *Gegen Bajonette und Dividende. Die politische Krise in Deutschland am Vorabend des Weltkrieges* (Berlin, 1960).

150 Varnbüler to Weizsäcker, 4.12.13, HStA Stuttgart, E-73, Verz. 61, 12e.
151 Philippi, *Das Königreich Württemberg,* p. 121.
152 See Varnbüler's letter to Moltke of 15.4.98 cited in the preceding chapter, pp. 56–7.
153 Georg von Müller, *Der Kaiser . . . Aufzeichnungen des Chefs des Marinekabinetts Admiral Georg von Müller . . .* , ed. Walter Görlitz (Göttingen, 1965), p. 189.
154 Eulenburg diary entry for 24.5.92, BA Koblenz, Nl. Eulenburg 19/pp. 351–2.
155 Philipp Eulenburg, *Mit dem Kaiser als Staatsmann und Freund auf Nordlandreisen,* 2 vols. (Dresden, 1931), I, 203.
156 Eulenburg to Wilhelm, 12.8.92, in Röhl, *Eulenburgs Korrespondenz,* II, no. 691.
157 Eulenburg to Wilhelm, 15.4.93, *ibid.,* no. 790.
158 Eulenburg to Varnbüler, 19.4.93, *ibid.,* no. 796.
159 Among the pro-Bismarckians were Deines (Deines to his Father, 11.2.94, MA Freiburg, Nl. Deines 12/pp. 67–72), Kessel, Wittich, Wedel (Holstein to Eulenburg, 7.12.91, Röhl, *Eulenburgs Korrespondenz,* I, no. 561), Waldersee (Holstein to Eulenburg, 9.6.92, *ibid.,* II, no. 671) and August Eulenburg (Kiderlen-Wächter to Eulenburg, 22.1.94, BA Koblenz, Nl. Eulenburg 27/pp. 54–5).
160 Moltke to Eulenburg, 25.1.94 (Röhl, *Eulenburgs Korrespondenz,* II, no. 889), 27.1.94 (BA Koblenz, Nl. Eulenburg 27/pp. 84–90) and 28.1.94 (Röhl, *Eulenburgs Korrespondenz,* II, no. 890).
161 See p. 228.
162 Eulenburg to Wilhelm, 5.2.94, Röhl, *Eulenburgs Korrespondenz,* II, no. 895.
163 Moltke sent Adm. v. Müller a book by Chamberlain during the war: Müller's diary for 14.4.15, MA Freiburg, Nl. Müller 5/p. 9, omitted from Walter Görlitz (ed.), *Regierte der Kaiser? . . . Kriegstagebücher, Aufzeichnungen und Briefe des Chefs des Marine-Kabinetts Admiral Georg Alexander von Müller 1914–1918* (Göttingen/Berlin/Frankfurt, 1959), p. 97.
164 See pp. 55–6.
165 Eulenburg to Wilhelm, 9.5.99, to be printed in Röhl, *Eulenburgs Korrespondenz,* III.
166 Görlitz, *Regierte der Kaiser?,* p. 122. Deines had remarked upon the same thing in 1897 (Deines to his Father, 17.6.97, MA Freiburg, Nl. Deines 13/p. 144b). In peacetime, mediocrities will do. After the war started the complaints became louder and more frequent: see Wild von Hohenborn to his wife, 13.4.15, MA Freiburg, Nl. Wild von Hohenborn 3/p. 104b, and Lerchenfeld to Hertling, 7.2.15 and 24.3.17 in Ernst Deuerlein (ed.), *Briefwechsel Hertling–Lerchenfeld 1912–1917,* 2 vols. (Boppard am Rhein, 1973), I, no. 156 and II, no. 358.
167 Rich, *Friedrich von Holstein,* I, p. 95.
168 Eckart Kehr, 'Das soziale System der Reaktion in Preussen unter dem Ministerium Puttkamer,' in Hans-Ulrich Wehler (ed.), *Der Primat der Innenpolitik.* Veröffentlichungen der historischen Kommission zu Ber-

lin beim Friedrich-Meinecke-Institut der Freien Universität Berlin, vol. 19 (Berlin, 1970), pp. 64–87.

169 P. Robert Duggan, 'Currents of Administrative Reform in Germany, 1907–1918' (Unpublished Ph.D. dissertation, Harvard, 1969).

170 Holstein recognized this. It is doubtless the main reason he held on to Eulenburg for so long. Holstein to Eulenburg, 14.3.92, Röhl, *Eulenburgs Korrespondenz*, II, no. 606.

171 For example, Eulenburg to Wilhelm, 3.6.93 (BA Koblenz, Nl. Eulenburg 24/pp. 280–1) or 6.3.97 (*ibid.*, 46/pp. 177–81).

172 Eulenburg 'Notiz' of late March 1894, *ibid.*, 28/pp. 258–9.

173 Eulenburg to Wilhelm, 1.11.94, *ibid.*, 32/p. 857.

174 Eulenburg to Marschall, 2.5.92, *ibid.*, 19/pp. 293–4. Holstein suggested this technique, though perhaps for other reasons, Holstein to Eulenburg, 27.4.92 and 7.5.92, in Röhl, *Eulenburgs Korrespondenz*, II, nos. 646 and 650.

175 Bülow, *Denkwürdigkeiten*, I, 4–5.

176 I say 'some' successes, because even Eulenburg was by no means always able to sway Wilhelm in the directions he wanted.

Chapter 5, pp. 109–45

1 (1850–1914).

2 (1856–1909), they married in 1875.

3 Szögyényi to Goluchowski, 18.4.98, ÖStA Vienna, PA III 151 (Varia).

4 Eulenburg to Wilhelm, 8.10.97, BA Koblenz, Nl. Eulenburg 48/pp. 548–9. Friedrich had served as a staff officer in the 1. Garde Dragoner Regiment.

5 Austrian Ambassador Szögyényi reported that Wilhelm was 'highly irritated' about Friedrich Eulenburg [*in hohem Grade aufgebracht*]. Szögyényi to Goluchowski, 18.4.98, ÖStA Vienna, PA III 151 (Varia).

6 Eulenburg claimed that Wilhelm regarded the FAs as 'a particular extract of the essence of everything excellent,' cited in Rudolf Schmidt-Bückeburg, *Das Militärkabinett der preussischen Könige und deutschen Kaiser. Seine geschichtliche Entwicklung und staatsrechtliche Stellung, 1787–1918* (Berlin, 1933), p. 195.

7 Eulenburg to Wilhelm, 8.10.97, BA Koblenz, Nl. Eulenburg 48/pp. 548–9.

8 *Ibid.*

9 In a note written later to Bülow's letter of 27.5.98, Eulenburg wrote that 'I saw no reason ... to turn from my poor brother [*von meinem armen Bruder abzuschwenken*],' *ibid.*, 50/p. 108.

10 Contained in the same note, *ibid.*

11 See Bernhard von Bülow, *Denkwürdigkeiten*, 4 vols. (Berlin, 1930), I, 450–1.

12 Eulenburg to Bülow, 3.5.98, BA Koblenz, Nl. Eulenburg 50/p. 91.

13 Bülow to Eulenburg, 27.5.98, *ibid.*, pp. 108–9.

14 Eulenburg to Bülow, 20.7.98, BA Koblenz, Nl. Bülow 76/pp. 300–2.

15 *Ibid.*

16 Eulenburg to Bülow, 21.7.99, BA Koblenz, Nl. Eulenburg 54/p. 177.

17 Eulenburg to Bülow, 27.7.99, *ibid.*, 54/pp. 183–6.
18 *Ibid.*
19 See Eulenburg to Bülow, 8.3.97, BA Koblenz, Nl. Bülow 76/p. 162 for Eulenburg's earlier outrage at the Foreign Office for the skepticism there about Wilhelm's mental condition.
20 Eulenburg to Bülow, 15.7.00, *ibid.*, 77/pp. 1–11.
21 Eulenburg to Bülow, 21.7.03, in Eulenburg, 'Zur Psyche und Politik Kaisers Wilhelm II' (unpublished manuscript, courtesy of John Röhl), pt II, pp. 3–18, citation from p. 4.
22 *Ibid.*, p. 12.
23 *Ibid.*, p. 15.
24 Eulenburg to Bülow, 9.8.03, BA Koblenz, Nl. Bülow 77/pp. 275–6 and Bülow, *Denkwürdigkeiten*, I, 616–17.
25 Eulenburg to Bülow, 9.8.03, BA Koblenz, Nl. Bülow 77/p. 277.
26 Eulenburg to Bülow, 21.7.03, in 'Psyche und Politik,' p. 5.
27 *Ibid.*, p. 12.
28 Compare 'Psyche und Politik,' p. 17 with the original in BA Koblenz, Nl. Bülow 77/p. 281.
29 Eulenburg to Bülow, 15.7.00, BA Koblenz, Nl. Bülow 77/pp. 5–6.
30 Eulenburg to Caprivi, 24.2.93, in John C. G. Röhl (ed.), *Philipp Eulenburgs politische Korrespondenz*, 3 vols. (Boppard, 1976–), II, no. 773.
31 Eulenburg to Bülow, 29.9.99, BA Koblenz, Nl. Eulenburg 54/pp. 205–7.
32 Eulenburg to Kiderlen-Wächter, 4.10.93, *ibid.*, 25/p. 432.
33 Eulenburg's diary entry of 10.8.93, *ibid.*, 25/p. 369.
34 Protocol of a conversation between Wilhelm and Eulenburg on 9.7.96, BA Koblenz, Nl. Eulenburg 42/pp. 479–80.
35 Eulenburg to Wilhelm, 18.8.97, *ibid.*, 48/pp. 451–2, and Eulenburg to Wilhelm, 22 and 28.8.97 and 23.12.97, DZA Merseberg, Rep. 53 J, courtesy of Röhl. Also, Eulenburg to Bülow, 22.3.98, to Wilhelm 25.3.98 and 4.4.98, in BA Koblenz, Nl. Eulenburg 50/pp. 74, 78, and 84–5.
36 Eulenburg to Wilhelm, 18 and 28.8.97. See preceding note.
37 Eulenburg to Bülow, 22.3.98, *ibid.*, 50/p. 74.
38 Agenor Count Goluchowski (1849–1921), Minister of the Royal House and of External Affairs (1895–1906).
39 Bülow's notes of his talk with Eulenburg in Venice, 7.4.97, BA Koblenz, Nl. Bülow 76/pp. 171–4.
40 Holstein to Bülow, 31.3.97, *ibid.*, 90/pp. 278–84.
41 Eulenburg 'Notiz,' 13.2.99, BA Koblenz, Nl. Eulenburg 53/pp. 40–1.
42 See, for example, Eulenburg to Bülow, 15.12.98 and 20.12.98, *ibid.*, 52/pp. 344, 348.
43 Eulenburg to Prof. Kurt Breysig, September 1919, in John Röhl (ed.), *1914: Delusion or Design? The Testimony of Two German Diplomats* (London, 1973), p. 127.
44 Eulenburg's 'indolence' meant he was not always effective when present. See Thurn to Goluchowski, Private, 19.2.02, in ÖStA Vienna, PA III 158, and Szögyényi to Goluchowski, 3.12.01, no. 48-D, *ibid.*, 156.
45 Eulenburg to August Eulenburg, 30.8.02, BA Koblenz, Nl. Eulenburg 59/pp. 83–4, emphasis in the original.
46 For a sketch of Fürstenberg see pp. 147–57.

47 Eulenburg to Max Egon Fürstenberg, 31.8.02, FFA Donaueschingen, Nl. Fürstenberg.
48 Szögyényi to Goluchowski, Private, 2.1.00, ÖStA Vienna, PA III 154.
49 Which was untrue, see Röhl, *Eulenburgs Korrespondenz*, I, 49–50.
50 Eulenburg to Bülow, 18.2.02, BA Koblenz, Nl. Eulenburg 59/pp. 26–7.
51 Harden, 'Liebenberg,' *Die Zukunft*, 9.11.01, pp. 203–12. Bülow mentions the incident as well, Bülow, *Denkwürdigkeiten*, I, 605.
52 See Maximilian Harden, 'Die Ära Hochberg,' in BA Koblenz, Nl. Harden 130/pp. 3–13.
53 Perhaps he destroyed it when a trial seemed inevitable. See Philipp Eulenburg, 'Drei Freunde' (unpublished manuscript, courtesy of John Röhl), II/2.2/p. 267.
54 Eulenburg's version of the Hochberg–Pierson affair, *ibid.*, pp. 206–56.
55 Eulenburg to Bülow, 14.1.02, BA Koblenz, Nl. Bülow 77/p. 158; this paragraph is reprinted with omissions in Bülow, *Denkwürdigkeiten*, I, 605. For Dohna's letter see above, p. 61. Harden cites the letter in Harden, *Köpfe*, 3 vols. (Berlin, 1913), III, 180. Eulenburg destroyed his copy.
56 Eulenburg to Lucanus, 16.2.02, in Eulenburg, 'Drei Freunde,' II/2.2/p. 256 (Beiblatt), and Eulenburg to Lucanus, 17.11.02 and 20.2.03, to appear in Röhl, *Eulenburgs Korrespondenz*, III.
57 Eulenburg to Bülow, 14.1.02, BA Koblenz, Nl. Bülow 77/p. 155. Eulenburg deleted this paragraph, among others, from his papers, *ibid.*, Nl. Eulenburg 59/pp. 6–7. Bülow reprints the sentence cited above correctly, but silently omits several other passages in his *Denkwürdigkeiten*, I, 604–5.
58 B. Uwe Weller, *Maximilian Harden und die 'Zukunft'* (Bremen, 1970), p. 169, and Bogdan Graf von Hutten-Czapski, *60 Jahre Politik und Gesellschaft*, 2 vols. (Berlin, 1936), I, 467.
59 Harden, 'Moritz und Rina,' in *Die Zukunft*, 17.12.02, p. 477; Helmuth Rogge, *Holstein und Harden Politisch-Publizistisches Zusammenspiel zweier Aussenseiter des Wilhelminischen Reichs* (Munich, 1959), pp. 59f., and Weller, *Harden*, p. 169.
60 Eulenburg's account in Philipp Eulenburg, *Mit dem Kaiser als Staatsmann und Freund auf Nordlandreisen*, 2 vols. (Dresden, 1931), II, 314–19.
61 Tirpitz's Diary entry for 26.9.04 in MA Freiburg, Nl. Tirpitz 21/pp. 22–3.
62 Tirpitz's Diary entry for 4.1.05, *ibid.*, 21/pp. 45–6.
63 Eulenburg to Wilhelm, 26.8.05, to appear in Röhl, *Eulenburgs Korrespondenz*, III.
64 (1849–1915), Russian statesman; Finance Minister, 1892–1903; Minister President, 1903–5.
65 See Norman Rich, *Friedrich von Holstein: Politics and Diplomacy in the Era of Bismarck and Wilhelm II*, 2 vols. (Cambridge, 1965), II, 725–7.
66 Terence Cole has recently asserted that Eulenburg 'was clearly playing a crucial role' in the diplomatic maneuvering around Morocco, Cole, 'Kaiser versus Chancellor: The Crisis of Bülow's Chancellorship 1905–6,' in Richard J. Evans (ed.), *Society and Politics in Wilhelmine Germany* (London/New York, 1978), pp. 52–3. But Cole cites no new sources and the old ones upon which he relies (notes 42–45) do not substantiate that claim.
67 Rich, *Holstein*, II, 746–53.

68 Marie von Bülow told Eulenburg's wife this: Eulenburg, 'Drei Freunde,' II/2/p. 195; see also Bülow, *Denkwürdigkeiten*, II, 261.

69 See Rich's account, *Holstein*, II, 774–5.

70 See, for example, Eulenburg to Wilhelm, 23.5.02, BA Koblenz, Nl. Eulenburg 59/pp. 57–9, and most of Eulenburg's letters to Bülow throughout the late spring and early summer of 1897. Bülow does not discount the possibility that Eulenburg was genuinely concerned about Bülow's health, see Bülow, *Denkwürdigkeiten*, I, 262.

71 Harden, 'Praeludium,' in *Die Zukunft*, vol. 57, 17.11.06, p. 265.

72 See the report of the Bavarian Gesandter, no. 43/vi, 22.1.06, BGSA Munich, Gesandtschaft Berlin 1078.

73 Anglophobia was a common bond between them.

74 Szögyényi to Aehrenthal, Private, 5.6.07, ÖStA Vienna, PA III 165.

75 Lerchenfeld to Podewils, no. 236, 22.4.07 in BGSA Munich, Gesandtschaft Berlin 1079.

76 'How did Harden arrive at that?' he asked Tschirschky. Monts to Tschirschky, 27.11.06, in Anton Monts, *Erinnerungen und Gedanken des Botschafters Anton Graf Monts*, ed. Karl Nowak and Friedrich Thimme (Berlin, 1932), p. 430.

77 Tschirschky to Monts, 18.11.06, *ibid.*, pp. 446–7.

78 Personal communication from John Röhl.

79 Bülow, *Denkwürdigkeiten*, II, 262–3. For the newspaper accounts see Rogge, *Holstein und Harden*, pp. 101–3.

80 Lerchenfeld to Podewils, no. 531, 9.11.06, BGSA Munich, Gesandtschaft Berlin 1078.

81 This was Helmuth Rogge's carefully considered conclusion, Rogge, *Holstein und Harden*, pp. 99–103; Cole agrees, 'Kaiser versus Chancellor,' pp. 58–9.

82 Harden knew of a number of intrigues: Harden to Holstein, 28.5.08, PA Bonn, Nl. Holstein 42, omitted from Norman Rich and M. H. Fisher (eds.), *Die geheimen Papier Friedrich von Holsteins*, 4 vols. (Göttingen/Frankfurt/Berlin, 1961), IV, no. 1091; Harden to Holstein, 4.7.08, in Rich and Fisher, *Die geheimen Papiere*, IV, no. 1105 (under 9 July); and Harden to Holstein, 1.8.08, PA Bonn, Nl. Holstein 42. Tschirschky wrote to Monts that the major intriguer was Wilhelm himself, who felt Bülow had lost much political support and was no longer up to the job. Tschirschky to Monts, 18.4.07, in Monts, *Erinnerungen*, pp. 448–9.

83 The representatives of foreign governments accurately reported the bases of the rumors: Szögyényi to Aehrenthal, 5.6.07, ÖStA Vienna, PA III/165; Lascelles to Grey, no. 483, 31.10.07, PRO London FO 371/260/36332/p. 375, Cartwright to Grey, no. 16, 18.6.07, *ibid.*, FO 371/260/20482/p. 339, and de Salis to Grey, 28.6.01, *ibid.*, FO 371/260/21539/pp. 361–5. Holstein told Bülow the same thing, Holstein to Bülow, 4.8.01, reprinted in Rich and Fisher, *Die geheimen Papiere*, IV, no. 783.

84 See pp. 126–7.

85 So, for example, Eulenburg to Bülow, 14.1.02, BA Koblenz, Nl. Bülow 77/pp. 153–60, where Eulenburg declares: 'This whole business must find an end. It is the *least* I can do for you out of deep thankfulness: to give you some peace on my account. You are probably right to like me, because in the entire world there are only a *very few people* who love you as I do.'

(Eulenburg's italics). Reprinted with unindicated omissions in Bülow, *Denkwürdigkeiten*, I, 604–5.

86 See his friendly letter to Bülow of 21.10.09, original in BA Koblenz, Nl. Bülow 88/pp. 285–96, reprinted with occasional changes and omissions in Bülow, *Denkwürdigkeiten*, III, 26–8.

87 See Guttenberg to Crailsheim, Private, 18.9.01, BGSA Munich, Gesandtschaft Berlin 1073.

88 See Eulenburg to Bülow, 8.3.02 with Bülow's marginalia, BA Koblenz, Nl. Bülow 77/pp. 167–80. Eulenburg's most critical letter (21.3.02) ends with the assurance that Bülow should not think that Eulenburg was irritated with him. 'That is *not the case* – it could never happen with you, [my] *best, truest friend.' Ibid.*, pp. 187–202, italics are Eulenburg's.

89 See pp. 121, 126–7.

90 Cole, 'Kaiser versus Chancellor,' pp. 57–9.

91 See Eulenburg's letters to Bülow during the *Nordlandreise* of 1899 (especially 21 to 27 July 1899), in BA Koblenz, Nl. Eulenburg 54/pp. 173–86; again the next summer (especially 14, 15, 18 and 21 July 1900), *ibid.*, 56/pp. 234–9 (originals for 14 and 15.7.00 in BA Koblenz, Nl. Bülow 77/pp. 1–11); and during the *Nordlandreise* in 1903 (21, 26, 28, 29 July and 9 August 1903), Eulenburg, 'Zur Psyche und Politik,' II/pp. 3–18, original of 9.8.03 in BA Koblenz, Nl. Bülow 77/pp. 273–83, which Bülow reprints with changes in his *Denkwürdigkeiten*, I, 616–17.

92 Szögyényi to Goluchowski, Private, 29.8.02, ÖStA Vienna, PA III 158.

93 Eulenburg's letters were querulous and Bülow's marginalia waspish. See, for example, Eulenburg to Bülow, 8.3.02 and 21.3.02, in BA Koblenz, Nl. Bülow 77/pp. 175–80 and 187–202.

94 Tschirschky to Monts, 18.4.07, in Monts, *Erinnerungen*, p. 449.

95 See note 81, above.

96 Monts, who was well aware of Eulenburg's pre-1898 intrigues, wrote that Eulenburg would not have tried to undermine Bülow, if only because Bülow had too much damaging information about Eulenburg that he might have used publicly. Monts to Tschirschky, 27.11.06, Monts, *Erinnerungen*, p. 431. See also Haller's refutation in 'Bülow und Eulenburg,' in Friedrich Thimme (ed.), *Front Wider Bülow. Staatsmänner, Diplomaten und Forscher zu seinen Denkwürdigkeiten* (Munich, 1931), pp. 35–6, and Johannes Haller, *Aus dem Leben des Fürsten Philipp zu Eulenburg-Hertefeld* (Berlin/Leipzig, 1926), pp. 335–6.

97 The Statthalter charge was fairly common in 1900 and 1901: Szögyényi to Goluchowski, Private, 11.11.00, ÖStA Vienna, PA III 154 and Alexander Hohenlohe to Holstein, 25.8.01, PA Bonn, Nl. Holstein 9. The charge reappeared in the same form in November 1906: Monts to Tschirschky, Monts, *Erinnerungen*, p. 430, and Lerchenfeld to Podewils, no. 333, 31.5.07, BGSA Munich, Gesandtschaft Berlin 1079. Cole believes that Eulenburg wanted the post in 1906 for financial reasons, Cole, 'Kaiser versus Chancellor,' p. 58.

98 Cole takes the press rumors seriously because he claims that two diplomatic reports, one by Berkheim to Karlsruhe, and the other by Lerchenfeld to Munich, offer independent confirmation (Cole, 'Kaiser versus Chancellor,' p. 58). Lerchenfeld's report, however, merely paraphrases 'one part of the press here' and goes on to disagree with the conclusions

the press reached. Lerchenfeld to Podewils, no. 531, 9.11.06, BGSA Munich, Gesandtschaft Berlin 1078. See also note 81, above.

99 Raymond Lecomte (1857–1921) had been attached to the French embassy in Munich while Eulenburg was there. Lecomte had become First Secretary in Berlin on 28 July 1905. He was removed on 13 June 1907 because of the Eulenburg scandal.

100 See Rich, *Holstein*, II, 726, n. 3. Rich gives a very detailed and judicious account of the first Moroccan Crisis, who made what decisions and why. This discussion follows his interpretation.

101 *Ibid.*, pp. 736–45.

102 Maurice Baumont, *L'Affaire Eulenburg* (Geneva, 1973, revised from the 1933 edn), p. 180.

103 Haller, *Aus dem Leben*, p. 327, and Reinhold Muschler, *Philipp zu Eulenburg, Sein Leben und seine Zeit* (Leipzig, 1930), p. 609.

104 It was when Harden learned of the 1906 visit, that he began his campaign, Rich and Fisher, *Die geheimen Papiere*, IV, no. 1004, n. 5. On Lecomte's presence or absence see Haller, *Aus dem Leben*, pp. 315–16, and *Norddeutsche Allgemeine Zeitung*, no. 257, 1.11.07. Young, who believes Lecomte was present in 1905, discusses the sources (none of them firsthand) which substantiate that account, Young, *Maximilian Harden: Censor Germaniae. The Critic in Opposition from Bismarck to the Rise of Nazism* (The Hague, 1959), pp. 96 and 116–17. It was Wilhelm who invited Lecomte in 1906, not Eulenburg. Politics was not discussed. Eulenburg to Varnbüler, 17.6.07, HStA Stuttgart, Nl. Varnbüler xxxv/20, and Robert von Zedlitz-Trützschler, *Zwölf Jahre am deutschen Kaiserhof* (Berlin/Leipzig, 1925), p. 174. See also Walther Rathenau, *Tagebuch 1907–1922*, ed. Hartmut Pogge von Strandmann (Düsseldorf, 1967), p. 149.

105 The speech is reprinted in E. Schröder, *Zwanzig Jahre Regierungszeit. Ein Tagebuch Kaiser Wilhelms II. Vom Antritt der Regierung, 15. Juni 1888 bis zum 15. Juni 1908 nach Hof- und anderen Berichten* (Berlin, 1909), Second Part, pp. 133–5.

106 Lerchenfeld to Podewils, no. 201 xiv, 26.3.05, BGSA Munich, Gesandtschaft Berlin 1077. See also Richard von Kühlmann, *Erinnerungen* (Heidelberg, 1948), p. 253.

107 Zedlitz-Trützschler, *Zwölf Jahre*, p. 174, and Baumont, *L'Affaire Eulenburg*, p. 123.

108 A. J. P. Taylor, *The Struggle for Mastery in Europe, 1848–1918* (London, 1971; 1954), p. 441.

109 Volker Berghahn, 'Zu den Zielen des deutschen Flottenbaus unter Wilhelm II,' *Historische Zeitschrift*, vol. 210 (1970), p. 96, n. 34, and his very perceptive discussion on pp. 93–100.

110 Varnbüler to Soden, 25.6.05, HStA Stuttgart, E-73, Verz. 61, 12e.

111 Zedlitz-Trützschler, Diary entry for 13.3.06, *Zwölf Jahre*, p. 145.

112 The conversation took place on 16 March 1906. *Ibid.*, pp. 146–7.

113 Findlay to Grey, Dresden, 27.6.08, PRO London FO 371/460/ 22750/21713.

114 Described by Jonathan Steinberg in his perceptive article, 'The Copenhagen Complex,' *Journal of Contemporary History*, vol. 1, no. 3 (1966), pp. 23–46.

115 Fairfax Cartwright to Grey, June 1908, PRO London FO 371/460/ 22750/21713.
116 Szögyényi to Aehrenthal, Private, 24.6.08, ÖStA Vienna, PA III 167.
117 Berghahn, 'Zu den Zielen,' p. 97. See also Lydia Franke, 'Die Randbemerkungen Wilhelms II in den Akten der auswärtigen Politik als historische und psychologische Quelle' (Dissertation, Berlin, 1932), pp. 45–7, and Peter G. Thielen, 'Die Marginalien Kaiser Wilhelms II,' *Die Welt als Geschichte,* vol. 20 (1960), p. 253, for discussion of Wilhelm's quick changes between optimism and pessimism.
118 Berghahn, 'Zu den Zielen,' p. 97.
119 Klepsch-Kloth to Conrad, 8.1.07, ÖKrA Vienna, Chef des Generalstabs 1907, 25:1/1.
120 Lascelles to Grey, 20.12.06, PRO London FO 371/80/42951/42951, and Lascelles' annual report for 1906, *ibid.*, 260/17091/17091/pp. 264–6.
121 See for example, the *Kladderadatsch* affair, which concentrated on the advisers, and the Caligula affair, which focussed on Wilhelm's personality: Helmuth Rogge, 'Die *Kladderadatsch*affäre. Ein Beitrag zur neueren Geschichte des Wilhelminischen Reiches,' *Historische Zeitschrift,* CXCV (1962), 90–130, and, more generally, Rogge, 'Affairen im Kaiserreich. Symptome der Staatskrise unter Wilhelm II,' *Die politische Meinung,* LXXXI (1963), 58–72.
122 See Harden, 'Prozess Eulenburg,' in *Die Zukunft,* vol. 64, 25.7.08, p. 125.
123 Harden, *Köpfe,* III, 175, 178 and 272.
124 Chlodwig Hohenlohe to Alexander Hohenlohe, 7.1.00, BA Koblenz Nl. Hohenlohe, Rep. 100 XXVII/3, reprinted with an omission in Fürst Chlodwig zu Hohenlohe-Schillingsfürst, *Denkwürdigkeiten der Reichskanzlerzeit,* ed. Karl Alexander von Müller (Stuttgart/Berlin, 1931), p. 554. See above, p. 110, note 9.
125 Alexander Hohenlohe to Chlodwig Hohenlohe, 12.1.00, BA Koblenz, Nl. Hohenlohe, Rep. 100 XXII/A/20.
126 Holstein to Eulenburg, 1.5.06, Rich and Fisher, *Die geheimen Papiere,* IV, no. 973.
127 *Ibid.,* no. 974, n. 1 and no. 975; and Varnbüler memorandum of May 1906, courtesy of John Röhl.
128 Bülow, *Denkwürdigkeiten,* II, 291, and Bülow's memorandum, undated, BA Koblenz, Nl. Bülow 32/p. 33, partially reprinted in Rogge, *Holstein und Harden,* pp. 157–8.
129 Bülow's marginal comment to Eulenburg's letter to him of 8.3.02, BA Koblenz, Nl. Bülow 77/p. 180.
130 Bülow's wife reported at least part of Renvers' diagnosis to Axel Varnbüler a scant two months later, Varnbüler to Moltke, 12.5.02, HStA Stuttgart, Nl. Varnbüler XXXVI/9.
131 Anton Monts to Bernhard Bülow, 23.7.08, PA Bonn, D 122/3g/3/pp. 83–4.
132 Eulenburg to Nathaniel Rothschild, 17.9.04, in Röhl, *Eulenburgs Korrespondenz,* I, 36–7.
133 This is a common theme in the Austrian diplomatic reports. See particularly Hohenlohe to Aehrenthal, 6.11.07 (no. 59-B), ÖStA Vienna, PA III 165.

134 See Police Commissioner Tresckow's statement of his own innocence when he was first put on the vice squad. Hans von Tresckow, *Von Fürsten und anderen Sterblichen, Erinnerungen eines Kriminalkommissars* (Berlin, 1922), p. 107.

135 Bülow's marginal comment on the Crown Prince's Memoirs in BA Koblenz, Nl. Schwertfeger 293/p. 8. Bülow is incorrect, the police merely refused to give him any information, see Tresckow, *Von Fürsten*, p. 190.

136 See pp. 169–71.

137 Harden, 'Prozess Moltke wider Harden,' *Die Zukunft*, vol. 67, 1.5.09, p. 162.

138 Zedlitz-Trützschler, *Zwölf Jahre*, p. 145.

139 Hirschfeld (1868–1935), Moll (1862–   ), and Krafft-Ebing (1840–1902) were pioneers in the scientific study of sexuality. Kraepelin (1856–1926) was the author of the most widely used textbook on psychiatry in the Wilhelminian period.

140 See John Lauritsen and David Thorstad, *The Early Homosexual Rights Movement (1864–1933)* (New York, 1974), and James Steakley, *The Homosexual Rights Movement in Germany* (New York, 1975).

141 See Jürgen Baumann, *Paragraph 175* (Berlin/Neuwied am Rhein, 1968) for the history of the law.

142 Harden, 'Nur ein Paar Worte,' in *Die Zukunft*, vol. 59, 15.6.07, p. 372.

143 Harden's address to the court in the first Moltke–Harden trial, reprinted in *Die Zukunft*, vol. 61, 9.11.07, p. 185.

144 *Ibid.*, p. 209; 'Nur ein Paar Worte,' *ibid.*, vol. 59, 15.6.07, p. 372; 'Die Freunde,' *ibid.*, vol. 59, 22.6.07, p. 421, and Harden, *Köpfe*, III, 244–5.

145 It reached its eighth revised edition in 1915 (Leipzig). See Kurt Kolle, *Kraepelin und Freud, Beitrag zur neueren Geschichte der Psychiatrie* (Stuttgart, 1957).

146 Harden, *Köpfe*, III, 201–2.

147 Harden, 'Nur ein Paar Worte,' *Die Zukunft*, vol. 59, 15.6.07, pp. 372–3.

148 Harden to Holstein, 7.5.07, Rich and Fisher, *Die geheimen Papiere*, IV, no. 1027.

149 Harden, *Köpfe*, III, 182–3.

150 Harden to Holstein, 10.10.08 in PA Bonn, Nl. Holstein 42. See also his letters of 1.8, 16.9, and 12.10.08, *ibid.*

151 Young, *Harden*, ch. 5; Rogge, *Holstein und Harden*, pp. 1–73, and Rich, *Holstein*, II, 757–97.

152 Muschler, *Eulenburg*, p. 622.

153 *Ibid.*, p. 623.

154 August Eulenburg to Philipp Eulenburg, 12.5.07, *ibid.*

155 Cited in Haller, *Aus dem Leben*, p. 351.

156 Varnbüler to Laemmel, 22.4.08, in Röhl, *Eulenburgs Korrespondenz*, I, 42, Varnbüler's italics.

157 *Ibid.*

158 Varnbüler to Moltke, 24.10.12, *ibid.*, p. 43, Varnbüler's italics.

159 Loebell to Bülow, telegram, 23.10.07, BA Koblenz, Nl. Bülow 178/pp. 78–9.

160 Lascelles to Grey, 9.1.08, PRO London FO 371/457/1188.

161 Moltke to Varnbüler, 3.12.18, HStA Stuttgart, Nl. Varnbüler XXXVI/9.

162 Rogge, *Holstein und Harden*, p. 11.
163 Monts to Tschirschky, 27.11.06, Monts, *Erinnerungen*, pp. 430–1.
164 Eulenburg had sent one of these letters to Bülow himself: Moltke to Eulenburg, 1.3.97, now in BA Koblenz, Nl. Bülow 76/pp. 153–60.
165 Tresckow, *Von Fürsten*, p. 190.
166 Holstein to his cousin, 25.11.07, in Rogge, *Holstein und Harden*, pp. 13–14. Bülow may have been trying to direct attention away from himself.
167 Varnbüler's information supports this conjecture, Varnbüler to King Wilhelm II of Württemberg (handwritten copy), 30.5.07 and 16.6.07, HStA Stuttgart, Nl. Varnbüler xxxv/20.
168 Bülow to Wilhelm, telegram, 26.10.07 in Rich and Fisher, *Die geheimen Papiere*, IV, no. 1057.
169 *Ibid.*, and Bülow to Holstein, 10.10.08, *ibid.*, no. 1140.
170 See Harden to Holstein, 23.3.08, *ibid.*, no. 1080; 31.5.08 (no. 1093); 1.6.08 (no. 1094); 16.6.08 (no. 1098); 27.6.08 (no. 1100); and Holstein to Bülow, 7.10.08 (no. 1137).
171 Harden to Holstein, 15.11.08, PA Bonn, Nl. Holstein 42.
172 Harden to Holstein, 16.9.08, *ibid.*, omitted in Rich and Fisher, *Die geheimen Papiere*, IV, no. 1130.
173 Harden to Holstein, 15.11.08, *ibid.*, no. 1151, also cited by Röhl, *Eulenburgs Korrespondenz*, I, 47.
174 Holstein to Bülow, 7.10.08, Rich and Fisher, *Die geheimen Papiere*, IV, no. 1137; 10.10.08 (no. 1139), and 11.10.08 (no. 1141).
175 Bülow to Holstein, 10.10.08, *ibid.*, no. 1140, and 20.10.08, no. 1144.
176 Young, *Harden*, p. 120, and Rogge, *Holstein und Harden*, chs. 4 and 6.
177 Varnbüler to Weizsäcker, 19.11.08, HStA Stuttgart, E-73, Verz. 61, 12e.
178 Rich, *Holstein*, II, 771.
179 Klepsch-Kloth to Conrad, 12.6.07, ÖKrA Vienna, Chef des Generalstabs 1907, 25:1/21.
180 Muschler, *Eulenburg*, p. 621, and Bülow memorandum in BA Koblenz, Nl. Bülow 32/p. 33.
181 Alfred von Löwenfeld (1848–1935), Prussian General; FAD, 1896–8; General *à la suite* to the Kaiser, 1901–18.
182 Eulenburg, 'Aufzeichnungen,' I/2/p. 234.
183 D. Hülsen to Fürstenberg, July 1908, FFA Donaueschingen, Nl. Fürstenberg.
184 Löwenfeld to Fürstenberg, 22.7.08, *ibid.*
185 Plessen to Fürstenberg, 8.11.07, *ibid.*
186 Zedlitz-Trützschler, *Zwölf Jahre*, pp. 183–4.
187 August Eulenburg to Philipp Eulenburg, 12.5.07, cited in Muschler, *Eulenburg*, p. 623.
188 Bülow (for the Kaiser) to Eulenburg, 31.5.07, *ibid.*, p. 624.
189 Varnbüler to King Wilhelm II of Württemberg, handwritten copy, 16.6.07, HStA Stuttgart, Nl. Varnbüler xxxv/20. Varnbüler's source of information was Bülow, who gave him a memorandum, in the Kaiser's handwriting, recounting Hülsen's report and the Kaiser's reaction to it. See also Bülow, 'Meine Haltung gegenüber den Harden Prozessen,' undated memorandum, probably late 1920s, in BA Koblenz, Nl. Bülow 32/p. 33, partially cited in Rogge, *Holstein und Harden*, pp. 157–8 and 170.

190 Wilhelm's marginalia to the *Tägliche Rundschau* of 27 and 29 October 1907 in PA Bonn D 122/3g/Bd 2.
191 Zedlitz-Trützschler, *Zwölf Jahre*, pp. 181–8.
192 *Ibid.*, p. 184.
193 Harden to Holstein, 5.4.08, PA Bonn, Nl. Holstein, omitted in Rich and Fisher, *Die geheimen Papiere*, IV, no. 1085.
194 Hülsen described him as 'grieved,' Hülsen to Fürstenberg, 28.4.08, FFA Donaueschingen, Nl. Fürstenberg.
195 Wilhelm to Bülow, 18.7.08, telegram, in Rogge, *Holstein und Harden*, p. 314.
196 Gottfried Prinz von Hohenlohe to Aehrenthal, 3.9.07, Private, ÖStA Vienna, PA III 165, and Lerchenfeld to Podewils, no. 57 lxxi, 8.11.07 in BGSA Munich, Gesandtschaft Berlin 1079.
197 Zedlitz-Trützschler, *Zwölf Jahre*, p. 171.
198 Hohenlohe to Aehrenthal, 5.11.07, no. 59 A–G, in ÖStA Vienna, PA III 165.
199 Klepsch-Kloth to Conrad, 10.12.07, ÖKrA Vienna, Chef des Generalstabs 1907, 25:1/3 and Müller to Tirpitz, 4.12.07, MA Freiburg, Nl. Tirpitz 227.
200 Georg von Müller, *Der Kaiser . . . Aufzeichnungen des Chefs des Marinekabinetts Admiral Georg Alexander von Müller über die Ära Wilhelms II,* ed. Walter Görlitz (Göttingen/Berlin/Frankfurt/Zürich, 1965), p. 176.
201 Monts to Bülow, 23.7.08, PA Bonn D 122/3g/3; Hohenlohe to Aehrenthal, 30.10.07, Private, ÖStA Vienna, PA III 165; Fairfax Cartwright to Grey, 20.3.08, PRO London FO 371/459/9959.
202 Velics to Aehrenthal, no. 55, 1.11.07, ÖStA Vienna PA IV 55.
203 Spitzemberg, *Tagebuch*, pp. 476–7.
204 Tresckow, *Von Fürsten*, p. 172.
205 Reischach to Fürstenberg, 20.4.09, FFA Donaueschingen, Nl. Fürstenberg.

Chapter 6, pp. 146–74

1 (1863–1941).
2 Karl Egon IV Fürst zu Fürstenberg died childless on 27 November 1896.
3 These lands centered around Donaueschingen and included estates at Stühlingen, Heiligenberg, Werdenberg, Gundelfingen, Kinzigtal, Mösskirch, Hohenhöwen, Wildenstein, Waldsperg, Werenwag, and Immendingen. His Bohemian lands are listed in Friedrich Lanjus, *Die erbliche Reichsratswürde in Österreich* (Langenlois, 1939), p. 92.
4 This is clear from Fürstenberg's response, Max Egon Fürstenberg to Wilhelm, telegram, 14.10.00, FFA Donaueschingen, Nl. Fürstenberg.
5 Wilhelm to Fürstenberg, 13.10.01, *ibid.* It is not clear that Fürstenberg called Wilhelm 'Du' in conversation. On paper he always referred to the Kaiser at 'Your Majesty.'
6 Wilhelm to Fürstenberg, Doorn, 3.10.21, *ibid.*
7 Wilhelm to Fürstenberg, 17.11.10, *ibid.*
8 Wilhelm to Fürstenberg, telegram, 16.11.08, *ibid.*
9 Max von Mutius, 'Lebenserinnerungen,' MA Freiburg, Nl. Mutius 2/p. 189.

10 Axel von Varnbüler to Karl Frhr von Weizsäcker, 27.2.14, HStA Stuttgart, E-73, Verz. 61, 12e.
11 Wilhelm to Fürstenberg, telegram, Achilleion, 13.4.12, FFA Donaueshingen, Nl. Fürstenberg.
12 Hugo von Reischach to Fürstenberg, 20.4.00, and Hans von Plessen to Fürstenberg, 28.4.05, *ibid.*
13 Georg Alexander von Müller, *Der Kaiser . . . Aufzeichnungen des Chefs des Marinekabinetts Admiral Georg Alexander von Müller über die Ära Wilhelms II,* ed. Walter Görlitz (Göttingen/Berlin/Frankfurt/Zürich, 1965), pp. 176–7.
14 MA Freiburg, Nl. Mutius 2/pp. 189–90.
15 (1860–1933).
16 Philipp Eulenburg's footnote, written after 1908, to his letter to Wilhelm of 4.4.00 in BA Koblenz, Nl. Eulenburg 56/p. 154. On Fürstenberg's good looks see Bernhard von Bülow, *Denkwürdigkeiten,* 4 vols. (Berlin, 1930), II, 122.
17 Viktoria Luise, *Im Glanz der Krone, Erinnerungen* (Munich, 1967), p. 227.
18 Diary entry, 18.4.09, FFA Donaueschingen, Nl. Fürstenberg.
19 Diary entry, 12.4.08, *ibid.*
20 Reischach to Fürstenberg, Schloss Friedrichshof, Cronberg, 19.9.97, *ibid.*
21 1887–1947, born Princess Reuss ältere Linie, widowed Princess von Schönaich-Carolath. Auguste Viktoria died in Doorn in April 1921 of the heart ailment from which she had suffered for many years. A year and a half later, in November 1922, Wilhelm remarried.
22 Hermine von Hohenzollern to Fürstenberg, 11.6.25, FFA Donaueschingen, Nl. Fürstenberg.
23 Diary entry, 12.9.11, *ibid.*
24 Cited in diary, 26.4.09, *ibid.*
25 Diary entry, 15.3.08 and 18.4.09, *ibid.*
26 MA Freiburg, Nl. Mutius 2/p. 189.
27 Bogdan von Hutten-Czapski, *Sechzig Jahre Politik und Gesellschaft,* 2 vols. (Berlin, 1936), I, 249 and II, 169–70.
28 Rudolf Vierhaus (ed.), *Das Tagebuch der Baronin Spitzemberg geb. Freiin v. Varnbüler. Aufzeichnungen aus der Hofgesellschaft des Hohenzollernreiches* (Göttingen, 1960), pp. 389–402, and Maximilian Harden to Friedrich von Holstein, 16.11.08, in Helmuth Rogge (ed.), *Holstein und Harden. Politisch-publizistisches Zusammenspiel zweier Aussenseiter des Wilhelminischen Reichs* (Munich, 1959), p. 388.
29 Varnbüler to Weizsäcker, 27.2.14, HStA Stuttgart, E-73, Verz. 61, 12e. Two *Vorträge* which Fürstenberg presented to Wilhelm on 16.12.09 are clearly biased in Fürstenberg's favor and are therefore inconclusive in assigning blame for the catastrophe, FFA Donaueschingen, Nl. Fürstenberg.
30 Varnbüler to Weizsäcker, 27.2.14, HStA Stuttgart, E-73, Verz. 61, 12e.
31 Ladislaus Graf von Szögyényi-Marich to Leopold Graf Berchtold, 8.5.14, ÖStA Vienna, PA III 171.
32 Spitzemberg, *Tagebuch,* Diary entry, 14.12.13, p. 565.
33 Szögyényi to Berchtold, 8.5.14, ÖStA Vienna, PA III 171.
34 Joseph M. Baernreither, *Verfall des Habsburgerreiches und die Deutschen, Fragmente eines politischen Tagebuches, 1897–1917,* ed. Oskar Mitis (Vienna, 1939), pp. 181–6.

35 (1848–1925).
36 (1863–1931).
37 (1853–1914).
38 (1872–1932).
39 (1863–1932).
40 Verständigungsconferenz, 5–20 February and 19–22 March, 1900.
41 Baernreither, *Verfall*, p. 117.
42 Fürstenberg to Karl Buquoy, Lana, 19.10.07, FFA Donaueschingen, Nl. Fürstenberg.
43 Baernreither, *Verfall*, p. 119, n. 1.
44 Bülow, *Denkwürdigkeiten*, I, 153–4.
45 Szögyényi to Fürstenberg, 28.1.99, FFA Donaueschingen, Nl. Fürstenberg.
46 Wilhelm to Fürstenberg, 13.2.09 and Franz Ferdinand to Fürstenberg, 12.2.10, copy, *ibid.*
47 They did not use the familiar 'Du.'
48 Eulenburg to Bülow, 24.4.00, BA Koblenz, Nl. Eulenburg 56/pp. 158–60; Eulenburg to Wilhelm, 4.4.00 and 13.5.00, *ibid.*, 56/pp. 150 and 169, and Baernreither, *Verfall*, p. 119.
49 Heinrich von Tschirschky und Bögendorff to Fürstenberg, 26.1.06, FFA Donaueschingen, Nl. Fürstenberg.
50 Theobald von Bethmann Hollweg to Fürstenberg, 6.1.13, *ibid.*
51 Bethmann Hollweg to Fürstenberg, 8.1.13, *ibid.*
52 Diary entry, 22.4.09, *ibid.*
53 Diary entry, 31.3.12, *ibid.*
54 Bülow, *Denkwürdigkeiten*, I, 154.
55 1908 Diary, p. 18, FFA Donaueschingen, Nl. Fürstenberg.
56 Fritz Fischer, *War of Illusions: German Policies from 1911 to 1914*, trans. Marion Jackson (New York, 1975), pp. 153–9.
57 (1859–1913).
58 Johannes Lepsius *et al.*, *Die Grosse Politik der Europäischen Kabinette 1871–1914. Sammlung der Diplomatischen Akten des Auswärtigen Amtes*, 40 vols. (Berlin, 1926), XXXIII, 360–1, footnote, and Szögyényi to Berchtold, 20.11.12, in Kommission für neuere Geschichte Österreichs, *Österreich-Ungarns Aussenpolitik von der bosnischen Krise 1908 bis zum Kriegsausbruch 1914. Diplomatische Aktenstücke des österreich-ungarischen Ministeriums des Äussern* (Vienna/ Leipzig, 1930), IV, p. 941.
59 Alfred von Kiderlen-Wächter to Tschirschky, telegram, 19.11.12, *Grosse Politik*, XXXIII, 360–1.
60 Tschirschky to Fürstenberg, Budapest, 19.11.12, FFA Donaueschingen, Nl. Fürstenberg.
61 Fischer, *War of Illusions*, p. 158.
62 John C. G. Röhl, 'Admiral v. Müller and the Approach of War, 1911/1914,' *The Historical Journal*, Vol. XII, no. 4 (1969), pp. 659–60, and Fischer, *War of Illusions*, pp. 218–19. Kiderlen and Bethmann soon got over their fear that Wilhelm had gone too far in his reassurances.
63 Plessen to Fürstenberg, 31.7.14, FFA Donaueschingen, Nl. Fürstenberg.
64 See his apologetic telegram, Wilhelm to Fürstenberg, 14.8.14, *ibid.*
65 Diary entry, 3.8.14, *ibid.*
66 Baernreither, *Verfall*, pp. 262–9, and Alois Frhr Czedik von Bründlsberg

und Eysenberg, *Zur Geschichte der k. k. österreichischen Ministerien 1861–1916*, 4 vols. (Teschen/Wien/Leipzig, 1920), IV, 453–7.
67 Moritz von Lyncker to Fürstenberg, GHQ, 9.12.15, FFA Donaueschingen, Nl. Fürstenberg.
68 Diary entry, 2.5.16, *ibid.*
69 Alois Frhr. Klepsch-Kloth von Roden to Army High Command, GHQ, 19.6.16, ÖKrA Vienna, MKSM Sep. Fasz. 69–6/2.
70 Diary entry, 20–25.6.18, FFA Donaueschingen, Nl. Fürstenberg.
71 Wilhelm to Fürstenberg, Brieftelegram, 13.10.40, on Fürstenberg's birthday, *ibid.*
72 (1858–1918).
73 (1854–1902).
74 Fischer, *War of Illusions*, pp. 13–14.
75 There is no definitive study, either of the Krupp firm or of the Krupps themselves. Willi A. Boelcke, *Krupp und die Hohenzollern in Dokumenten. Krupp-Korrespondenz mit Kaisern, Kabinettschefs und Ministern 1850–1918* (Frankfurt, 1970, revised and expanded from *Krupp und die Hohenzollern* [East Berlin, 1956]) contains the most reliable commentary so far on the firm and its owners. There is a great need for a thorough study of the symbiotic relationship between Fr. Krupp and the German government.
76 Boelcke, *Krupp und die Hohenzollern*, pp. 108–9, 114, and Bernt Engelmann, *Krupp. Legenden und Wirklichkeit* (Munich, 1969), pp. 272–3.
77 Boelcke, *Krupp und die Hohenzollern*, p. 161, n. 1, and, below, pp. 170–1.
78 Alfred Krupp to Fritz Krupp, 8.1.85, Aktennotiz in Historisches Archiv Fried. Krupp GmbH, Essen, A IV 2 e.
79 v. Jacobi to Fritz Krupp, Bonn, 14.7.78, *ibid.*, FAH III C 226/pp. 5–6.
80 See Jacobi to Fritz Krupp, 6.7.80, *ibid.*, pp. 17–18.
81 This is the first surviving invitation, Liebenau to Krupp, 14.1.85, *ibid.*, p. 19.
82 *Ibid.*, FAH III E 1.
83 Krupp to Ardenne, 6.2.96, signed carbon copy, *ibid.*, FAH III C 60.
84 Krupp to Hollmann, Capri, 26.3.01, pencilled copy in Krupp's hand, *ibid.*, FAH III C 234.
85 Krupp to Ardenne, Essen, 3.6.98, carbon copy, *ibid.*, FAH III C 60.
86 Richard Owen, 'Military–Industrial Relations: Krupp and the Imperial Navy Office,' in Richard J. Evans (ed.), *Society and Politics in Wilhelmine Germany* (London/New York, 1978), p. 81.
87 Wilhelm to Bertha Krupp, 12.12.02, original, HA Krupp Essen, FAH IV E 782/p. 141, partially cited in Owen, 'Military–Industrial Relations,' p. 81.
88 Wilhelm Berdrow, 'Friedrich Alfred Krupp' (unpublished manuscript), HA Krupp Essen, FAH III L 8.
89 Boelcke reads these documents to mean that the *Direktorium* managed the firm. Boelcke, *Krupp und die Hohenzollern*, pp. 114–15.
90 Krupp to *Direktorium*, Berlin, 19.3.96, HA Krupp Essen, WA 41/2/p. 117.
91 Krupp to *Direktorium*, copy, 27.7.91, *ibid.*, FAH III B 102.
92 Krupp to *Direktorium*, Kiel, 2.6.99, *ibid.*, FAH III B 103.
93 See p. 72.
94 Hollmann to Krupp, Berlin, 13.3.99 (about the torture of dining with officers of the Alexander Guard Regiment); and Hollmann to Krupp,

Berlin, 20.5.99 (about avoiding a wedding invitation from similar circles), both in *ibid.*, FAH III C 233.

95 Hollmann to Krupp, Berlin, 21.10.01, *ibid.*, FAH III C 234.
96 Hollmann to Krupp, 5.8.94, *ibid.*, FAH III C 58.
97 The Kaiser 'thanked Hollmann for bringing him together with such interesting people (two Rathenaus, Staby, Delbrück, Carl Fürstenberg, etc.),' so Harden to Holstein, 13.3.09, PA Bonn, Nl. Holstein 42.
98 Ballin to Harden, Hamburg, 5.11.09, BA Koblenz, Nl. Harden 4.
99 See pp. 244–7.
100 Hollmann to Krupp, Berlin, 6.3.00, HA Krupp Essen, FAH III C 233, emphasis in the original. See also Hollmann to Krupp, 17.9.01, *ibid.* FAH III C 234, for similar sentiments.
101 So, for example, Hollmann to Krupp, 27.10.99, *ibid.*, FAH III C 233.
102 Hollmann to Krupp, 29.3.00, *ibid.*
103 Berdrow, 'Krupp,' pp. 39–44, *ibid.*, FAH III L 8 and Hollmann to Krupp, 17.3.92, *ibid.*, FAH III C 58.
104 Boelcke, *Krupp und die Hohenzollern*, pp. 99–100.
105 Hollmann to Krupp, 24.6.92, HA Krupp Essen, FAH III C 58/pp. 17–19.
106 Hollmann to Krupp, 12.11.97, *ibid.*, pp. 112–15.
107 Hollmann to Krupp, postcard, Berlin, 5.8.97, *ibid.*, p. 102.
108 Hollmann to Krupp, 28.2.93, *ibid.*, p. 28.
109 Hollmann to Krupp, 18.8.95, *ibid.*, p. 67.
110 Hollmann to Krupp, 22.11.01, *ibid.*, FAH III C 234/p. 64.
111 Hollmann to Krupp, 31.8.97, *ibid.*, FAH III C 58.
112 Helena Hollmann to Krupp, 11.1.98, *ibid.*, pp. 123–4.
113 Hollmann to Krupp, 18.4.99 and 26.4.99, *ibid.*, FAH III C 233/pp. 11–14 and 22–3.
114 For the purposes of the Navy League see Geoff Eley, *Reshaping the German Right. Radical Nationalism and Political Change after Bismarck* (New Haven/London, 1980), pp. 73–85, and Wilhelm Deist, *Flottenpolitik und Flottenpropaganda. Das Nachrichtenbureau des Reichsmarineamtes 1897–1914* (Stuttgart, 1976).
115 Hollmann to Krupp, 18.4.99, HA Krupp Essen, FAH III C 233/pp. 11–14.
116 Krupp to Hollmann, Capri, 22.4.99, pencilled copy in Krupp's hand, *ibid.*, pp. 18–18a.
117 Eley, *German Right*, p. 144, n. 122.
118 Krupp to Hollmann, Capri, 22.4.99, pencilled copy in Krupp's hand, HA Krupp Essen, FAH III C 233/p. 19, and Krupp to Barandon, Capri, 24.4.99, draft, *ibid.*, FAH III B 146.
119 Hollmann's account of a personal report to the Kaiser, Hollmann to Krupp, 8.10.00, *ibid.*, FAH III C 233.
120 Hollmann to Krupp, 19.8.00, *ibid.*, p. 118a.
121 Engelmann, *Krupp*, pp. 257–8.
122 Owen considers the rumor 'apocryphal,' Owen, 'Military–Industrial Relations,' p. 88, n. 64.
123 Especially Marschall v. Bieberstein, Krupp to Ardenne, 8.1.97, copy, HA Krupp Essen, FAH III C 60.
124 Boelcke, *Krupp und die Hohenzollern*, pp. 109–10.

125 Krupp to *Direktorium*, 4.2.90, copy, HA Krupp Essen, FAH III B 38/p. 15.
126 Krupp to Ardenne, 24.1.93, signed copy, *ibid.*, FAH III C 60.
127 Owen, 'Military–Industrial Relations,' p. 82.
128 Boelcke, *Krupp und die Hohenzollern*, pp. 109, 184.
129 *Ibid.*, p. 174.
130 Krupp to Jencke, 22.1.96, HA Krupp Essen, FAH III B 117.
131 Wilhelm to Krupp, telegram, 1.11.02, *ibid.*, FAH III C 227, and Krupp to *Direktorium*, 19.1.96, *ibid.*, FAH III B 117.
132 Krupp to Ardenne, 8.3.92, *ibid.*, FAH III C 60, and Wilhelm to Krupp, 7.1.93, telegram, *ibid.*, FAH III C 226.
133 Krupp to Wilhelm, 22.12.92, copy in Jencke's hand, *ibid.*, FAH III B 188.
134 Boelcke, *Krupp und die Hohenzollern*, p. 102.
135 Owen, 'Military–Industrial Relations,' p. 83.
136 *Ibid.*, p. 76, and Roderich Grunow to Geh. Rat Korn, 6.9.96, HA Krupp Essen, FAH III B 178.
137 Wilhelm Gussmann, one of the directors, expressed surprise at the speed and completeness of the turnaround, Gussmann to Krupp, 11.9.96, HA Krupp Essen, FAH III C 98.
138 Krupp to Gussmann, 6.9.96, draft in Krupp's hand, *ibid.*
139 Hollmann to Krupp, 25.8.96, *ibid.*, FAH III B 178.
140 Owen, 'Military–Industrial Relations,' p. 76.
141 Boelcke, *Krupp und die Hohenzollern*, pp. 26–34.
142 Krupp to Ardenne, Berlin, 24.1.93, signed carbon copy, HA Krupp Essen, FAH III C 60.
143 See p. 97.
144 Krupp to Ardenne, Essen, 1.5.92, signed carbon copy, HA Krupp Essen, FAH III C 60.
145 Gossler to Krupp, Sept. 1893 (excerpts sent to Ardenne), *ibid.*
146 Julius von Schütz (citing Col. Gisevius in the Technical Department) to Fr. Krupp, 10.5.95, and 6.11.95, *ibid.*, WA IV 1077.
147 Berdrow, 'Krupp,' pp. 60–5, *ibid.*, FAH III L 8.
148 Fritz Krupp's notes for his personal report to Wilhelm of 8.5.00, cited in Owen, 'Military–Industrial Relations,' p. 78, Owen's translation.
149 Owen is impressed by the hypocrisy, *ibid.*, pp. 76, 78; so is Boelcke, *Krupp und die Hohenzollern*, p. 105.
150 *Direktorium* to Krupp, Essen, 3.12.98, HA Krupp Essen, FAH III B 81/pp. 21–5.
151 Fritz Krupp's marginalia to *ibid.*
152 Wilhelm to Fr. Krupp *Direktion*, 11.7.00, *ibid.*, FAH III B 35/p. 11.
153 Hollmann to Krupp, 30.9.00, *ibid.*, FAH III C 233/pp. 131–3.
154 Hollmann to Krupp, 5.1.00, *ibid.*, FAH III C 233.
155 Dreger to Menshausen, 8.9.97, *ibid.*, FAH III B 117.
156 Hollmann's notes for a personal report to Wilhelm of May 1901, *ibid.*, FAH III B 186.
157 Hollmann to Krupp, 8.10.00, *ibid.*, FAH III C 233.
158 See Boelcke, *Krupp und die Hohenzollern*, p. 106.
159 See pp. 219–20.
160 Berdrow, 'Krupp,' p. 62, HA Krupp Essen, FAH III L 8.

161 See Owen's account in Owen, 'Military–Industrial Relations,' pp. 77–82.
162 *Ibid.*, p. 78. Owen discounts the company's claim that it did so 'very unwillingly.'
163 Berdrow, 'Krupp,' pp. 179–80, HA Krupp Essen, FAH III L 8, and Ludwig Delbrück to Hartmann, 20.3.06, *ibid.*, FAH III C 9/pp. 227–32.
164 Jencke to Krupp, 1.4.00, *ibid.*, FAH III B 36/pp. 44a–44f.
165 Such as the decision to sell the firm, if Tirpitz's campaign did not cease. See Krupp to Hollmann, 13.8.00, carbon copy, *ibid.*, FAH III C 233/pp. 116–17.
166 As Carl Fürstenberg and Georg v. Siemens did in 1901. Hollmann to Krupp, 13.7.01, *ibid.*, FAH III C 234/pp. 36a and 45a.
167 For Krupp's sexual reputation see Hans von Tresckow, *Von Fürsten und anderen Sterblichen. Erinnerungen eines Kriminalkommissars* (Berlin, 1922), pp. 126–9. Harden emphatically disagreed with Tresckow, Maximilian Harden, 'Krupp,' in *Die Zukunft*, vol. 41, 29.11.02, p. 333.
168 The first person to use the article was Bernhard Menne in his *Blood and Steel. The Rise of the House of Krupp* (New York, 1938; Zürich, 1936), pp. 212–13. See also Norbert Muhlen, *The Incredible Krupps, The Rise, Fall, and Comeback of Germany's Industrial Family* (New York, 1959), p. 94; William Manchester, *The Arms of Krupp, 1587–1968* (New York, 1970), pp. 264–5; Boelcke, *Krupp und die Hohenzollern*, p. 161, n. 1; and Engelmann, *Krupp*, pp. 283–4.
169 Harden also got wind of a rumor to the effect that Wilhelm had abandoned Krupp. See Harden, 'Krupp,' p. 335 and Menne, *Blood and Steel*, p. 213.
170 Boelcke, *Krupp und die Hohenzollern*, p. 161, n. 1.
171 Manchester, *The Arms of Krupp*, p. 265.
172 Hollmann to Krupp, postcard, 31.10.02, HA Krupp Essen, FAH III C 234.
173 Hollmann to Krupp, 3.10.02, *ibid.*, p. 98.
174 Krupp to Wilhelm, 13.10.02, in Boelcke, *Krupp und die Hohenzollern*, no. 87.
175 *Ibid.*, and Krupp to v. Studt, 25.10.02, Boelcke, *Krupp und die Hohenzollern*, no. 88.
176 Binswanger's correspondence with Frau Krupp goes until 1920, HA Krupp Essen, FAH III D 112 and Vogt's goes to 1914, *ibid.*, FAH III D 169.
177 Boelcke reprints the article in *Krupp und die Hohenzollern*, pp. 164–6.
178 *Ibid.*, pp. 166–7, n. 1.
179 The speech is reprinted in *ibid.*, no. 93. For public opinion see Bülow, *Denkwürdigkeiten*, I, 586.
180 See Boelcke, *Krupp und die Hohenzollern*, pp. 173–87.
181 Ballin's life and influence has been relatively well documented. There are three useful biographies: Bernhard Huldermann, *Albert Ballin*, trans. W. J. Eggers (London, 1922); Peter F. Stubmann, *Ballin, Leben und Werk eines deutschen Reeders* (Berlin, 1926); and Lamar Cecil, *Albert Ballin: Business and Politics in Imperial Germany 1888–1918* (Princeton, 1967). Cecil's book is specifically concerned with Ballin's effect on high politics, so it is the foundation for the discussion which follows.
182 Cecil, *Ballin*, pp. 102–3.

183 *Ibid.*, p. 107.
184 *Ibid.*, p. 108.
185 *Ibid.*, p. 106, n. 15.
186 *Ibid.*, pp. 48–58, 78–9, 246–7 and 353.
187 Bernhard Huldermann, cited in *ibid.*, p. 106.
188 *Ibid.*, pp. 108–9; for Müller, see pp. 244–7.
189 This is the theme of Cecil's book, *ibid.*
190 *Ibid.*, p. 212.
191 *Ibid.*, p. 338.

Chapter 7, pp. 175–207

1 The Schlossgardekompagnie, composed of venerable non-commissioned officers, guarded the royal residences and surroundings. The Leibgendarmerie guarded the monarch's person and performed orderly duties for the Hauptquartier. See Wilhelm Deist, 'Kaiser Wilhelm II in the Context of his Military Entourage,' in John C. G. Röhl and Nicolaus Sombart (eds.), *Kaiser Wilhelm II: New Perspectives* (Cambridge, 1981), p. 191, n. 58.
2 A copy of the AKO is in MA Freiburg RM2/72.
3 'In Verfolg Meiner Ordre von 7. Juli d. Js.' of 3.12.88 in *ibid.*
4 Rudolf Schmidt-Bückeburg, *Das Militärkabinett der preussischen Könige und deutschen Kaiser. Seine geschichtliche Entwicklung und staatsrechtliche Stellung 1787–1918* (Berlin, 1933), pp. 16–20; Gordon Craig, *The Politics of the Prussian Army, 1640–1945* (New York, 1955), pp. 52–3; and Manfred Messerschmidt, *Die politische Geschichte der preussisch-deutschen Armee. Handbuch zur deutschen Militärgeschichte*, vol. IV, pt 1 (Munich, 1975), 297–302.
5 Schmidt-Bückeburg, *Das Militärkabinett*, pp. 143–4.
6 H. L. von Schweinitz, cited in *ibid.*, pp. 157–8.
7 *Ibid.*, p. 143.
8 Ernst Müller-Meiningen in 1914, cited in *ibid.*, p. 236. See also Deist's discussion in Deist, 'Kaiser Wilhelm II in the Context of his Military Entourage', in Röhl and Sombart (eds.), *Kaiser Wilhelm II*, pp. 170–9.
9 Hermann Rumschöttel, *Das bayerische Offizierkorps, 1866–1914*, vol. 9 of Beiträge zu einer historischen Strukturanalyse Bayerns im Industriezeitalter (Berlin, 1973), pp. 68, 77, 154–5; and Karl Demeter, *Das deutsche Offizierkorps in Gesellschaft und Staat, 1650–1945* (Frankfurt, 1962), pp. 94, 250–1.
10 (1833–1912).
11 Unpublished essay by Klaus Schlegel, 'Wilhelm von Hahnke,' courtesy of the author.
12 Wilhelm II, *Aus meinem Leben, 1859–1888* (Berlin and Leipzig, 1927), p. 237.
13 *Ibid.*, pp. 236–7.
14 *Ibid.*
15 *Ibid.*
16 Johannes Haller (ed.), *Aus 50 Jahren. Erinnerungen, Tagebücher und Briefe aus dem Nachlass des Fürsten Philipp zu Eulenburg-Hertefeld* (Berlin, 1923), p. 240.
17 Waldersee's diary entries of 26.8.88, 11.12.89, and 30.8.90, in Heinrich

Otto Meisner (ed.), *Denkwürdigkeiten des Generalfeldmarschalls Alfred von Waldersee*, 3 vols. (Stuttgart/Berlin, 1923), II, 1, 82, 141, and Adolf von Deines to his father, 12.7.94 and 29.1.96, MA Freiburg, Nl. Deines 12/p. 111 and 13/pp. 63–4.

18 Lerchenfeld to Crailsheim, 31.3.01, BGSA Munich, Gesandtschaft Berlin 1073.

19 For Hahnke's political role see pp. 216–25. Hahnke's successors, Dietrich von Hülsen-Haeseler and Moritz von Lyncker, are discussed on pp. 231–3, 247–8, 259, 277–8, and 285–9.

20 See Deist, 'Kaiser Wilhelm II in the Context of his Military Entourage,' in Röhl and Sombart (eds.), *Kaiser Wilhelm II*, pp. 178–9.

21 Draft entitled 'Marine-Kabinet [*sic*]' in Admiral von Senden-Bibran's handwriting in MA Freiburg, RM2/1 and Holger Herwig, *The German Naval Officer Corps: A Social and Political History, 1890–1918* (Oxford, 1973), p. 24.

22 (1847–1909).

23 Bernhard von Bülow, *Denkwürdigkeiten*, 4 vols. (Berlin, 1930), I, 68.

24 Eckart Kehr, *Schlachtflottenbau und Parteipolitik, 1894–1901* (Berlin, 1930), p. 57, n. 102.

25 Holstein to Bülow, 6.6.96, BA Koblenz, Nl. Bülow 90/p. 146.

26 Fürst Chlodwig zu Hohenlohe-Schillingsfürst, *Denkwürdigkeiten der Reichskanzlerzeit*, ed. Karl Alexander von Müller (Berlin, 1931), pp. 288–9 (hereafter cited as Hohenlohe, *Denkwürdigkeiten*, III).

27 Volker Berghahn, *Der Tirpitz-Plan. Genesis und Verfall einer innenpolitischen Krisenstrategie unter Wilhelm II* (Düsseldorf, 1971), pp. 181, 184.

28 (1820–1902), Ambassador to France, 1885–1900.

29 Cited in Berghahn, *Der Tirpitz-Plan*, p. 189, n. 79.

30 Eulenburg to Holstein, 16.7.96, PA Bonn, Nl. Holstein 39.

31 Hohenlohe to Eulenburg, 25.3.97. This sentence appears in Eulenburg's typescript in BA Koblenz, Nl. Eulenburg 46/p. 212, but is not printed in Hohenlohe, *Denkwürdigkeiten*, III, 322–3.

32 Eulenburg to Wilhelm, 12.11.96, BA Koblenz, Nl. Eulenburg 44/pp. 764–7.

33 Berghahn, *Der Tirpitz-Plan*, pp. 291–2.

34 *Ibid.*, pp. 189–90, 223.

35 Senden-Bibran's successor, Admiral Georg von Müller, is discussed on pp. 244–7.

36 See John Röhl, *Germany Without Bismarck* (London, 1967), pp. 280–2.

37 MA Freiburg, Nl. Mutius 2/p. 167.

38 'Ausführungsbestimmungen zur AKO von 7.7.88,' signed by General Major Adolf von Wittich, copy in MA Freiburg, RM2/72.

39 Senden-Bibran to Wilhelm, 9.5.88, MA Freiburg, RM2/1 and Nl. Senden-Bibran 11/p. 38.

40 MA Freiburg, Nl. Mutius 2/p. 167.

41 Georg v. Müller, *Der Kaiser . . . Aufzeichnungen des Chefs des Marinekabinetts Admiral Georg Alexander von Müller über die Ära Wilhelms II*, ed. Walter Görlitz (Göttingen/Berlin/Frankfurt/Zürich, 1965), pp. 187–8.

42 Schmidt-Bückeburg, *Das Militärkabinett*, pp. 229–30.

43 Magnus von Levetzow to Prince Guidotto Henckel von Donnersmarck,

16.2.28, cited in Herwig, *German Naval Officer Corps,* p. 74. Emphasis in the published version.

44 Schmidt-Bückeburg, *Das Militärkabinett,* pp. 229–30.

45 Franz Carl Endres, 'Soziologische Struktur und ihre entsprechende Ideologien des deutschen Offizierkorps vor dem Weltkriege,' *Archiv für Sozialwissenschaft,* vol. 58 (1927), p. 296.

46 See, for example, Karl von Einem, *Erinnerungen eines Soldaten 1853–1933* (Leipzig, 1933), pp. 148–51, on General v. Moltke, and Deist, 'Kaiser Wilhelm II in the Context of his Military Entourage.'

47 Eulenburg's diary entry on Carl Wedel, 6.7.94 in BA Koblenz, Nl. Eulenburg 30/p. 568.

48 Hutten-Czapski on Villaume in Bogdan v. Hutten-Czapski, *60 Jahre Politik und Gesellschaft,* 2 vols. (Berlin, 1936), I, 85; and Mutius on Plessen, MA Freiburg, Nl. Mutius, 2/p. 185.

49 Müller (and everyone else) on Scholl MA Freiburg, Nl. Müller 3/Diary entry for 1.4.05.

50 Ingenohl's Qualification Report in MA Freiburg, RM2/2037.

51 Eulenburg on Hülsen, Philipp Eulenburg, 'Drei Freunde,' II/2/pp. 163–4, courtesy of John Röhl.

52 Eulenburg on Bissing, BA Koblenz, Nl. Eulenburg 11/p. 441.

53 Eulenburg, 'Drei Freunde,' I/1/p. 50.

54 'Bestimmungen über die Besetzung S.M. Jacht "Hohenzollern" und der Königlichen Lustwasserfahrzeuge zu Potsdam mit Mannschaften' of 25.2.89, in MA Freiburg RM2/230.

55 Freiherr v. Bodenhausen to the Kiel Station, 23.9.98, in MA Freiburg RM2/230, and Platen to Müller, 18.12.08, RM2/233.

56 Austria's Military Attaché to Germany, Alois Klepsch-Kloth in 1902 on the *Kaisermanöver,* page 71 of a manuscript put together from Klepsch-Kloth's letters to the Austrian Haus- Hof- und Staatsarchiv of September 1956, in ÖKrA Vienna, Nl. Klepsch-Kloth.

57 (1836–1906), General Adjutant of the Kaiser, 1888–1906.

58 (1841–1929), Prussian General, Commandant of the HQ, 1892–1918.

59 BA Koblenz, Nl. Eulenburg 10/p. 333.

60 FA Adolf von Deines to his Father, 4.9.92, MA Freiburg, Nl. Deines 11/pp. 140–1.

61 Hugo v. Lerchenfeld-Köfering to Minister President Johann Frhr v. Lutz, 9.1.89, BGSA Munich, Gesandtschaft Berlin, 1059.

62 Deines to his father, 4.9.92, MA Freiburg, Nl. Deines 11/pp. 140–1.

63 MA Freiburg, Nl. Mutius 2/p. 185.

64 *Ibid.*

65 Carl v. Wedel, *Zwischen Kaiser und Kanzler, Aufzeichnungen des Generaladjutanten Grafen Carl von Wedel aus den Jahren 1890–1894* (Leipzig, 1943), diary entry of 17.5.91.

66 MA Freiburg, Nl. Mutius 2/p. 186.

67 Müller, *Der Kaiser,* pp. 184–5.

68 MA Freiburg, Nl. Mutius 2/p. 186.

69 See note 67.

70 Plessen to Dommes, *Grosses Hauptquartier* (GHQ), 13.6.18, MA Freiburg, N1. Dommes 5.

71 MA Freiburg, Nl. Mutius 2/p. 188.
72 Wilhelm to Senden-Bibran, copy, 13.11.88, MA Freiburg, Nl. Senden-Bibran 11/p. 33.
73 See pp. 103–5 and 227–8.
74 Reischach to Fürstenberg, 22.12.08, FFA Donaueschingen, Nl. Fürstenberg.
75 Helmuth von Moltke, *Erinnerungen, Briefe, Dokumente 1877–1916* (Stuttgart, 1922), p. 243.
76 His exploits are detailed in Eberhard von Mantey, *Der Kreuzerkrieg in den ausländischen Gewässern*, vol. 3: *Die deutschen Hilfskreuzer* (Berlin, 1937), pp. 138–210.
77 *Ibid.*, p. 208.
78 Georg von Müller, *Regierte der Kaiser? Kriegstagebücher, Aufzeichnungen und Briefe des Chefs des Marine-Kabinetts Admiral Georg Alexander von Müller 1914–1918*, ed. Walter Görlitz (Göttingen/Berlin/Frankfurt, 1959), p. 374; cf. MA Freiburg, Nl. Müller 6/p. 59A.
79 MA Freiburg, Nl. Müller 7/p. 2.
80 (1858–1923).
81 (1855–1930).
82 See pp. 147–57.
83 This is the first surviving letter in which Chelius addresses Fürstenberg with the familiar 'Du.' As late as April 1908 they were still on formal terms.
84 Donaueschingen was Fürstenberg's Baden estate where Wilhelm went hunting each November/December beginning in 1905.
85 (1861–1935), FAD from 1903 to 1906, FA from 1907 to 1913.
86 (1853–1932), Chief of the Military Cabinet, 1908–18.
87 Chelius to Max von Fürstenberg, Potsdam, 7.11.09, FFA Donauestingen, Nl. Fürstenberg.
88 Chelius to Max Fürstenberg, 21.6.10, *ibid.*
89 Endres, 'Soziologische Struktur,' p. 318.
90 See, for example, Philipp Eulenburg's general advice to Bülow when Bülow became State Secretary of the Foreign Office in 1897, Bülow, *Denkwürdigkeiten*, 1, 4–5, cited above, p. 107.
91 Biographies in *Wer Ist's?* and in Kurt von Priesdorff, *Soldatisches Führertum*, 10 vols. (Hamburg, 1937–41), are quite helpful because they give the officers' service, promotion records, and educational data. The *Gotha Taschenbücher* often include employment and landowning entries. Unfortunately, the *Taschenbücher* are rather more capricious than one would like. They sometimes omit family members with no indication when or why they have done so, and not infrequently they contain misinformation. Under these circumstances one regrets more acutely the loss of the army personnel records during World War II. The survival of the naval records makes the sea officers more accessible to the historian. Personal papers, the records of the German Foreign Office, memoirs, newspapers, and ambassadorial reports partially fill the gaps left by the other records.
92 Demeter, *Das deutsche Offizierkorps*, p. 26.
93 Gerhard Papke, 'Offizierkorps und Anciennität,' in Oberst I. G. Dr Meier-Welcker (ed.), *Untersuchungen zur Geschichte des Offizierkorps, Anciennität und Beförderung nach Leistung* (Stuttgart, 1962), p. 193.

94 Demeter, *Das deutsche Offizierkorps*, p. 27. See also Daniel J. Hughes, 'Occupational Origins of Prussia's Generals, 1871–1914,' *Central European History*, vol. 13, no. 1 (March 1980), pp. 3–33, which appeared too late to be incorporated here.

95 Endres, 'Soziologische Struktur,' p. 296.

96 Herwig, *The German Naval Officer Corps*, p. 42.

97 Hansgeorg Model, *Der deutsche Generalstabsoffizier. Seine Auswahl und Ausbildung in Reichswehr, Wehrmacht und Bundeswehr* (Frankfurt, 1968), p. 18.

98 Demeter, *Das deutsche Offizierkorps*, p. 23.

99 *Ibid.*, p. 22.

100 The cross-listings are: 11 men listed as both upper-level civil servants and landowners (13% of total); 8 listed as both officers and landowners (10%); 2 as both officers and upper-level civil servants (2%).

101 Herwig, *German Naval Officer Corps*, p. 82, n. 2.

102 Rumschöttel, *Das bayerische Offizierkorps*, pp. 141–2.

103 Ninety percent of the men were married and 90 percent of these had children.

104 See Manfred Messerschmidt's detailed account in 'Militär und Schule in der wilhelminischen Zeit,' in *Militärgeschichtliche Mitteilungen*, vol. 23 (1/1978), pp. 51–76.

105 See Holger Herwig's helpful chart, *German Naval Officer Corps*, p. 41, n. 1, and his discussion, pp. 41ff.

106 See Rumschöttel, *Das bayerische Offizierkorps*, pp. 41–61, for an excellent account of the discussions surrounding this move.

107 Demeter, *Das Deutsche Offizierkorps*, ch. 2.

108 Endres, 'Soziologische Struktur,' pp. 295, 298; Herwig, *German Naval Officer Corps*, p. 46; and Rumschöttel, *Das bayerische Offizierkorps*, p. 47.

109 Demeter, *Das deutsche Offizierkorps*, p. 89.

110 Herwig, *German Naval Officer Corps*, p. 47.

111 Demeter, *Das deutsche Offizierkorps*, p. 92.

112 Rumschöttel, *Das bayerische Offizierkorps*, p. 48.

113 *Ibid.*, p. 61. See also Messerschmidt, 'Militär und Schule,' pp. 52 and 56.

114 Demeter thinks not: *Das deutsche Offizierkorps*, p. 202, n. 17. Bülow mentions only that Mossner's *parents* were Jewish: Bülow, *Denkwürdigkeiten*, IV, 233. Martin Kitchen writes in *The German Officer Corps 1890–1914* (Oxford, 1968), p. 39, that in 1878 there were no Jewish officers in the Prussian army, by which he must mean non-converted Jews. If this were the case, then Mossner must have converted.

115 Demeter, *Das deutsche Offizierkorps*, pp. 202–5, Kitchen, *German Officer Corps*, pp. 22–48, and Rumschöttel, *Das bayerische Offizierkorps*, pp. 238–54.

116 Camill Schaible, *Standes- und Berufspflichten des deutschen Offiziers. Für angehende und jüngere Offiziere des stehenden Heeres und des Beurlaubtenstandes*, 3rd edn (Berlin, 1896), p. 27.

117 See also Endres, 'Soziologische Struktur,' pp. 285, 303.

118 Rumschöttel, *Das bayerische Offizierkorps*, p. 173.

119 Demeter, *Das deutsche Offizierkorps*, p. 110.

120 This was first argued in 1808: *ibid.*, p. 123.

121 *Ibid.*, pp. 132–8.

122 Rumschöttel, *Das bayerische Offizierkorps*, pp. 180, 205.

123 Schaible, *Berufspflichten*, p. 15.
124 *Ibid.*, p. 84.
125 *Ibid.*, p. 53.
126 *Ibid.*, pp. 58–9.
127 *Ibid.*, pp. 66–7.
128 *Ibid.*, p. 68.
129 *Ibid.*, p. 69.
130 *Ibid.*, pp. 34–5.
131 *Ibid.*, pp. 62–3.
132 *Ibid.*, p. 64.
133 *Ibid.*, pp. 59–60.
134 *Ibid.*, p. 65.
135 *Ibid.*, p. 66, also Herwig, *German Naval Officer Corps*, p. 90.
136 Endres, 'Soziologische Struktur,' p. 304.
137 Manfred Messerschmidt, 'Die Armee in Staat und Gesellschaft – Die Bismarckzeit,' in Michael Stürmer (ed.), *Das Kaiserliche Deutschland. Politik und Gesellschaft 1870–1918* (Düsseldorf, 1970), p. 103.
138 Model, *Generalstabsoffizier*, pp. 15–18.
139 Wilhelm Groener, *Lebenserinnerungen. Jugend, Generalstab, Weltkrieg* (Göttingen, 1957), pp. 59–60, and Demeter, *Das deutsche Offizierkorps*, p. 152.
140 Endres, 'Soziologische Struktur,' p. 304.
141 *Ibid.*
142 Schaible, *Berufspflichten*, p. 17.
143 Rumschöttel, *Das bayerische Offizierkorps*, p. 198.
144 *Ibid.*, p. 167.
145 Schaible, *Berufspflichten*, p. 25.
146 Messerschmidt, 'Die Armee,' p. 105.
147 See Rumschöttel, *Das bayerische Offizierkorps*, p. 189, on nervousness.
148 Herwig, *German Naval Officer Corps*, p. 79.
149 Rumschöttel, *Das bayerische Offizierkorps*, p. 150. See also Endres on the erotic meaning of the uniform, Endres, 'Soziologische Struktur,' p. 289.
150 *Ibid.*, p. 303, and Rumschöttel, *Das bayerische Offizierkorps*, pp. 190–1.
151 Schaible, *Berufspflichten*, p. 70.
152 Demeter, *Das deutsche Offizierkorps*, p. 219.
153 See Schaible, *Berufspflichten*, pp. 41–7.
154 Endres, 'Soziologische Struktur,' pp. 299–300.
155 Robert Count von Zedlitz-Trützschler, *Zwölf Jahre am deutschen Kaiserhof* (Stuttgart/Berlin/Leipzig, 1925), p. 138, and Wedel, *Kaiser und Kanzler*, p. 193.
156 Müller, *Der Kaiser*, p. 35, n. 30.
157 MA Freiburg, Nl. Mutius 2/p. 172.
158 MA Freiburg, Nl. Senden-Bibran 11/p. 39.
159 Eulenburg to his wife, 7.7.03, in Philipp zu Eulenburg-Hertefeld, *Mit dem Kaiser als Staatsmann und Freund auf Nordlandreisen*, 2 vols. (Dresden, 1931), II, 324.
160 Zedlitz-Trützschler, *Zwölf Jahre*, p. 230.
161 Axel von Varnbüler (citing Hollmann) to Freiherr v. Mittnacht, 2.4.96, HStA Stuttgart, E-73, Verz. 61, 12d.
162 Zedlitz-Trützschler, *Zwölf Jahre*, pp. 231–2.

163 *Ibid.*, pp. 226–7.
164 MA Freiburg, Nl. Mutius 2/p. 180.
165 Eulenburg's diary entry for 6.7.93 in Eulenburg, *Mit dem Kaiser*, I, 282.
166 Alfred von Kiderlen-Wächter to Hedwig Kypke, Stuttgart, 19.4.95, Yale University, Kiderlen-Wächter Papers, Box I.
167 Kiderlen to Hedwig Kypke, Stavanger, Norway, 4.7.94, *ibid.* Italics in the original.
168 Philipp Eulenburg to Wilhelm, 12.11.96, BA Koblenz, Nl. Eulenburg 44/pp. 764–7.
169 MA Freiburg, Nl. Senden-Bibran 11/p. 41.
170 MA Freiburg, Nl. Mutius 2/pp. 167–8.
171 See Einem, *Erinnerungen eines Soldaten*, pp. 141–2, on Wilhelm's absolute trust in his 'friends.'
172 MA Freiburg, Nl. Mutius 2/p. 168.
173 MA Freiburg, Nl. Senden-Bibran 11/pp. 35–6.
174 MA Freiburg, Nl. Senden-Bibran 11/p. 37.
175 Deines to his father, 22.9.92, MA Freiburg, Nl. Deines 11/p. 146. This was his reaction to the court at Vienna where he was military attaché, but his later letters betray no overweening sympathy for the Berlin Court, either.
176 Wedel, *Kaiser und Kanzler*, p. 193.
177 See p. 161.
178 Müller, *Der Kaiser*, pp. 188–9.
179 Endres thinks decidedly not, Endres, 'Soziologische Struktur,' p. 311.
180 MA Freiburg, Nl. Mutius 2/p. 171.
181 If Wilhelm liked a person or if he were doing a good job, permission to transfer was not easy to acquire. See Zedlitz's story, Zedlitz-Trützschler, *Zwölf Jahre*, pp. 249–50.

Chapter 8, pp. 208–35

1 The literature on this subject is voluminous. One might begin by consulting Gerhard Ritter, *Staatskunst und Kriegshandwerk: Das Problem des 'Militarismus' in Deutschland*, 4 vols. (Munich, 1956–); Gordon A. Craig, *The Politics of the Prussian Army 1640–1945* (London/New York, 1955); Manfred Messerschmidt, *Die politische Geschichte der preussisch-deutschen Armee. Handbuch zur deutschen Militärgeschichte 1648–1939*, IV, 1 (Munich, 1975); Bernd F. Schulte, *Die deutsche Armee 1900–1914. Zwischen Beharren und Verändern* (Düsseldorf, 1977); and Michael Geyer, 'Die Geschichte des deutschen Militärs von 1860 bis 1945. Ein Bericht über die Forschungslage (1945–1975),' in Hans-Ulrich Wehler (ed.), *Die moderne deutsche Geschichte in der internationalen Forschung 1945–1975* (Göttingen, 1978).
2 Wilhelm Deist, 'Kaiser Wilhelm II in the Context of his Military Entourage,' in John C. G. Röhl and Nicolaus Sombart (eds.), *Kaiser Wilhelm II: New Interpretations* (Cambridge, 1981), pp. 179–80.
3 Hermann Rumschöttel, *Das bayerische Offizierkorps, 1866–1914*, vol. 9 of Beiträge zu einer historischen Strukturanalyse Bayerns im Industriezeitalter (Berlin, 1973), pp. 68, 77, 154–5, and Karl Demeter, *Das Deutsche*

Offizierkorps in Gesellschaft und Staat, 1650–1945 (Frankfurt, 1962), pp. 94, 250–1.

4 Deist, 'Kaiser Wilhelm II in the Context of his Military Entourage,' in Röhl and Sombart (eds.), *Kaiser Wilhelm II*, pp. 179–81.

5 For a good, general discussion of military attachés see Alfred Vagts, *The Military Attaché* (Princeton, New Jersey, 1967), especially chs. 15 and 16.

6 'Instruktion für die zu den auswärtigen Missionen kommandirten Offiziere,' 11.12.90, in MA Freiburg, RM4/36.

7 *Ibid.*

8 *Ibid.*

9 23 of 94, or 24.5 percent.

10 The best single statement of this is in his letter to Wilhelm of 22.1.97, Alfred Graf von Waldersee, *Denkwürdigkeiten*, ed. Heinrich Otto Meisner, 3 vols. (Stuttgart/Berlin, 1923), II, 386–9. Other interesting opinions are well expressed in diary entries of 15.12.87 (I, 343), 11.10.88 (II, 6), 3.2.90 (II, 99–100) and 9.11.90 (II, 158–60).

11 *Ibid.*, diary entries of 15.10.85 (I, 263), 16.11.86 (I, 303), 1.1.87, (I, 309), 25.2.87 (I, 337–8), 16–28.5.88 (I, 399–401) and 23.6.88 (I, 408).

12 Alson J. Smith, *A View of the Spree* (New York, 1962), pp. 63–4.

13 Waldersee, *Denkwürdigkeiten*, I, 274.

14 The friendship between Waldersee and Wilhelm was encouraged by their respective wives. Both Wilhelm and Auguste Viktoria were quite taken with Mary Waldersee, who was an American *bourgeoise*, ambitious, clever, and fanatically religious. Some newspapers of the time and her biographer Alson J. Smith (*Spree*, pp. 82–4) asserted that the Countess was briefly Wilhelm's mistress. These wisps of gossip emanated from the fact that Wilhelm frequently dined with the Waldersees and was heavily influenced by them. Titillating parallels with Madame de Pompadour immediately were suggested, but no further evidence was adduced either then or since. Smith's book is lively but mistaken on too many counts to be reliable. The private source which he used, the letters of the Countess's mother, who lived with the Waldersees in Berlin, does not support the contention. If there was an affair it escaped the attention of Auguste Viktoria, whose well-developed capacity for jealousy was more correctly focussed on Wilhelm's male friends. The future Kaiserin was worried that Wilhelm was too young for the throne to which he would soon accede (Waldersee, *Denkwürdigkeiten*, I, 328). She implored Waldersee to 'visit Wilhelm often in order to stand by the Prince with advice' (*ibid.*, I, 271), which the ambitious Waldersee was only too happy to do. Auguste Viktoria was further impressed by the extreme piety of the two Waldersees, and she encouraged them in their efforts to persuade Wilhelm to support the strident, anti-Semitic campaign of Court Chaplain Stöcker.

15 Waldersee, *Denkwürdigkeiten*, I, 281.

16 Note by Admiral Senden-Bibran 5.4.02 in MA Freiburg RM2/966.

17 Gerhard Ritter, 'Die deutschen Militär-attachés und das Auswärtige Amt. Aus den verbrannten Akten des Grossen Generalstabs,' in *Sitzungsberichte der Heidelberger Akademie der Wissenschaften*, phil.-hist. Klasse, 1959, Abh. 1 (Heidelberg, 1959), p. 6.

18 Waldersee, *Denkwürdigkeiten*, II, pp. 30–1.

19 *Ibid.*, II, 30.
20 *Ibid.*, I, 412, and II, 1, 14.
21 Ritter, 'Militär-attachés,' pp. 6–9.
22 Waldersee, *Denkwürdigkeiten*, II, 42.
23 For a discussion of Caprivi's instructions see Ritter, 'Militär-attachés,' pp. 23–4. The instructions themselves are reprinted in Heinrich O. Meisner, 'Militärattachés und Militärbevollmächtigte in Preussen und im Deutschen Reich,' *Neue Beiträge zur Geschichtswissenschaft*, vol. 2 (Berlin, 1957).
24 Waldersee, *Denkwürdigkeiten*, II, 166–7.
25 *Ibid.*
26 *Ibid.*, II, 145–6.
27 See Wilhelm Deist, 'Die Armee in Staat und Gesellschaft, 1890–1914,' in Michael Stürmer (ed.), *Das kaiserliche Deutschland* (Düsseldorf, 1970), pp. 332–4.
28 Ritter, 'Militär-attachés,' p. 25.
29 They were: Mutius, Rebeur-Paschwitz, Schulenberg, Senden, and Pritzelwitz.
30 Karl Bülow, Chelius, Kageneck, Lambsdorff, and Massow.
31 Alfred Dohna-Schlobitten, Dietrich Hülsen-Haeseler, Jacobi, Lauenstein, Kuno Moltke, Seckendorff.
32 Deines, Engelbrecht, Hintze, Hüne, Morgen, Schwartzkoppen, and Villaume.
33 Those listed in notes 29 and 31 above.
34 See pp. 189–90.
35 Hüne, for example, was invited as late as May 1913.
36 For the naval attachés see Klaus-Volker Giessler, *Die Institution des Marineattachés im Kaiserreich*, vol. 21 of *Wehrwissenschaftliche Forschungen* (Boppard am Rhein, 1976).
37 For the correspondence surrounding the Engelbrecht affair see John C. G. Röhl, *Philipp Eulenburgs politische Korrespondenz*, 3 vols. (Boppard am Rhein, 1976–), I, nos. 408, 444, 464, and II, nos. 777, 785, 789, 857, 875, 882, 884, 930, 963 and 1080. See also Deist, 'Kaiser Wilhelm II in the Context of his Military Entourage,' in Röhl and Sombart (eds.), *Kaiser Wilhelm II*, pp. 180 and 190 n. 50.
38 Paul (von-1906) Hintze (1864–1941), Military Plenipotentiary to Russia, 1908–11; Foreign Secretary, 9 July 1918–3 October 1918.
39 See p. 105, and n. 37 above.
40 For the early history of the reform efforts see Helge Berndt, 'Zur Reform der Militärstrafgerichtsordnung 1898. Die Haltung der Parteien im Reichstag,' in *Militärgeschichtliche Mitteilungen* (2/73), pp. 7–11.
41 Oskar Ehrl, 'The Development of the German Military Criminal Procedure during the 19th Century,' *Revue de Droit Pénal Militaire et de Droit de la Guerre*, vol. VII, no. 2 (1968), pp. 241–50.
42 Eulenburg to Holstein, 29.2.96 in BA Koblenz, Nl. Eulenburg 40/pp. 111–12.
43 Philipp Eulenburg, 'Aufzeichnungen,' II/2/p. 116 (unpublished manuscript, courtesy of John Röhl).
44 Bogdan v. Hutten-Czapski, *Sechzig Jahre Politik und Gesellschaft*, 2 vols. (Berlin, 1935), I, 280–2.

45 B. Bülow to Eulenburg, 30.11.95 in BA Koblenz, Nl. Eulenburg 39/p. 842.

46 Eulenburg, 'Aufzeichnungen,' II/2/p. 161.

47 B. Bülow to Eulenburg, 30.11.95 in BA Koblenz, Nl. Eulenburg 39/p. 842 and Hutten-Czapski, *Sechzig Jahre*, I, 292.

48 Bogdan Count von Hutten-Czapski (1851–   ), Schlosshauptmann from Posen and member of the Prussian Herrenhaus, was a close political friend of Chancellor Hohenlohe and an extremely astute and well-connected figure in Berlin.

49 Friedrich I, Grand Duke of Baden (1826–1907).

50 Hohenlohe, Journal of 2.11.95, in Chlodwig zu Hohenlohe-Schillingsfürst, *Denkwürdigkeiten der Reichskanzlerzeit*, ed. K. A. von Müller (Stuttgart, 1931), p. 116. (Hereafter cited as Hohenlohe, *Denkwürdigkeiten*, III.)

51 Hohenlohe's Journal, 2.11.95, *ibid.*, pp. 116–17.

52 Hohenlohe's Journal, 2.3.96, *ibid.*, p. 186.

53 Museum Director Schricker (Strassburg) to Hohenlohe, 2.8.96, *ibid.*, p. 247.

54 Hohenlohe to Eulenburg, early August 1896, *ibid.*, pp. 253–4.

55 Holstein to Eulenburg, 16.5.96, BA Koblenz, Nl. Eulenburg 41/p. 309.

56 Hohenlohe, *Denkwürdigkeiten*, III, 221.

57 Hohenlohe Journal, 2.11.95, *ibid.*, p. 115.

58 Hutten-Czapski, *Sechzig Jahre*, I, 282.

59 Hohenlohe to Eulenburg, early August 1896, Hohenlohe, *Denkwürdigkeiten*, III, 253–4.

60 In March 1890.

61 AKO 1.1.97.

62 Hohenlohe, *Denkwürdigkeiten*, III, 74.

63 On 31.5.92, *ibid.;* around 10.5.96, *ibid.*, p. 220; and on 15.6.96, *ibid.*, p. 235.

64 2.3.96, *ibid.*, p. 186, and Hutten-Czapski to Holstein, 15.11.96, in Norman Rich and M. H. Fisher (eds.), *Die geheimen Papiere Friedrich von Holsteins*, 4 vols. (Göttingen/Berlin/Frankfurt, 1961), III, 501–3.

65 24.8.97, Hohenlohe, *Denkwürdigkeiten*, III, 379.

66 Waldersee, for example, 8.6.96, Waldersee, *Denkwürdigkeiten*, III, 370.

67 Hutten-Czapski to Alexander v. Hohenlohe, Kassel, 16.3.96, in Hohenlohe, *Denkwürdigkeiten*, III, 199.

68 Grand Duke of Baden to Eulenburg, 24.10.95 in BA Koblenz, Nl. Eulenburg 38/p. 756. Emphasis in the typescript.

69 John C. G. Röhl, *Germany Without Bismarck* (London, 1967), p. 179.

70 Hutten-Czapski to Hohenlohe, 6.3.96 in Hohenlohe, *Denkwürdigkeiten*, III, 186–8.

71 Eulenburg to Holstein, Alt Aussee, 4.8.96 in Rich and Fisher, *Die geheimen Papiere*, III, no. 576.

72 Holstein to Lindenau, 27.7.96, *ibid.*, no. 572.

73 Hutten-Czapski to Holstein, 15.11.95, *ibid.*, no. 500.

74 Diary entry 24.8.96 in Hohenlohe, *Denkwürdigkeiten*, III, 256.

75 See Röhl, *Germany Without Bismarck*, pp. 142–6.

76 Diary entries of 1.2.96, 28.2.96 and 2.3.96 in Hohenlohe, *Denkwürdigkeiten*, III, 164, 181–2 and 186.

77 Diary entry of 2.3.96, *ibid.*, p. 186.

78 See note 52.
79 Diary entry for 7.3.96, in Hohenlohe, *Denkwürdigkeiten*, III, 191.
80 *Ibid.*
81 See p. 96, and Röhl, *Germany Without Bismarck,* pp. 183–4.
82 Eulenburg to Hohenlohe, 5.7.96, BA Koblenz, Nl. Eulenburg 43/p. 475; August Eulenburg to Philipp Eulenburg 11.8.96, *ibid.,* 43/pp. 571–2, and Eulenburg to Wilhelm, 24.8.96, *ibid.,* 43/p. 590.
83 Kiderlen-Wächter to Eulenburg, 10.8.96 in Rich and Fisher, *Die geheimen Papiere*, III, no. 581.
84 Hohenlohe, *Denkwürdigkeiten*, III, 373.
85 See Paragraph 8 of the Imperial Military Law of 2 May 1874, which made the Emperor responsible for military discipline.
86 Hohenlohe, *Denkwürdigkeiten*, III, 373.
87 See p. 97, and Röhl, *Germany Without Bismarck,* pp. 230–40.
88 For the odd reasons behind Holstein's behavior, see *ibid.,* p. 234.
89 Hohenlohe, *Denkwürdigkeiten*, III, 373.
90 *Ibid.,* pp. 336 and 399.
91 Hohenlohe, *Denkwürdigkeiten*, III, 397–8.
92 Frhr von Watter's report of about 2.11.97 in HStA Stuttgart, E-130a/1116.
93 The Bill is printed in *Stenographische Berichte über die Verhandlungen des Reichstags,* IX Legislationperiode, V Session 1897/98, Anlage 1, pp. 90–206.
94 Oertel, SPD, and Beckh, Progressives, *Sten. Ber.,* II, 1618–20.
95 *Ibid.,* III, 2155–84. For the Reichstag's role and reaction, see Berndt, 'Zur Reform der Militärstrafgerichtsordnung,' pp. 7–29.
96 Hohenlohe, *Denkwürdigkeiten*, III, 382 and 392.
97 A complete discussion of these and other matters must wait for a history of the MStGO. A dissertation by Wolfgang Mecklenburg, 'Die Neuordnung der Militärstrafprozessordnung im Kaiserreich' (Freiburg i. Br.) is being completed.
98 Hohenlohe to the Prince Regent, 29.10.98 in PA Bonn D 121/24/*secr.* Bd 4; Monts to Auswärtiges Amt and Bülow to Auswärtiges Amt, both of 24.11.98, *ibid.,* and Ehrl, 'Criminal Procedure,' p. 253.
99 Nieberding to Bülow, 9.2.01 in PA Bonn D 121/24/*secr.* Bd 6.
100 Gossler left office on 15.8.03 and was succeeded by Karl von Einem (1853–1934), who served until 11.8.09.
101 Bülow to Dietrich Hülsen-Haeseler, 15.6.07, PA Bonn D 121/24/*secr.* Bd 7.
102 Eulenburg to Bülow, 13.7.98 in BA Koblenz, Nl. Eulenburg 51/p. 152.
103 Bülow to Wilhelm, 21.10.07 and Oertzen to Bülow, 24.10.07, PA Bonn D 121/24/*secr.*Bd 7.
104 Gossler to Oswald Frhr von Richthofen, 19.7.02, *ibid.;* the Bavarian verbal agreement: 2.8.06, *ibid.*
105 In the von Krosigk case of 1902, the military was forced to rescind a death sentence which had been rigged in order to impress upon enlisted men the inviolability of the officer corps. *New York Evening Post,* 13.5.02 in PA Bonn D 121/24/*secr.* Bd 7.
106 Hutten-Czapski, *Sechzig Jahre,* I, 296–7, and Ehrl, 'Criminal Procedure,' pp. 256–7.
107 Schricker to Hohenlohe, 2.8.96 in Hohenlohe, *Denkwürdigkeiten*, III, 247.

108 Holstein to Eulenburg, 12.1.97 in BA Koblenz, Nl. Eulenburg 45/p. 29; Holstein to Eulenburg, 23.1.97, *ibid.*, 45/p. 58; Holstein to Eulenburg, 29.3.97, *ibid.*, 46/p. 219; Diary entry 30.3.97 in Hohenlohe, *Denkwürdigkeiten*, III, 327. An account of the trial is in Dieter Fricke, 'Die Affäre Leckert–Lützow–Tausch und die Regierungskrise von 1897 in Deutschland,' *Zeitschrift für Geschichtswissenschaft*, VIII (1960), 1579–1603.

109 Hohenlohe to Holstein, 29.4.97, Hohenlohe, *Denkwürdigkeiten*, III, 333.

110 Diary entry of 12.10.97 and 17.10.97, *ibid.*, pp. 390 and 392.

111 He tried twice, with Senden-Bibran, to convince Wilhelm to relent, for Wilhelm's intransigence threatened the passage of the first Naval Bill. Tirpitz to Grand Duke of Baden, 14.11.97 in MA Freiburg Nl. Tirpitz 4/pp. 173–5.

112 Manfred Messerschmidt, *Militär und Politik in der Bismarckzeit und im Wilhelminischen Deutschland. Erträge der Forschung*, vol. 43 (Darmstadt, 1975), pp. 33, 39, 93–4.

113 Hahnke's marginalia (19.2.00) to a note from Gossler of 10.2.00 in PA Bonn D 121/24/*secr.* Bd 5.

114 Gossler to Hohenlohe, 14.4.00, *ibid.*, Bd 6.

115 Richthofen memorandum of 5.3.00, *ibid.*, Bd 5.

116 See p. 211.

117 Deines to his father, 20.3.90, MA Freiburg, Nl. Deines 11/pp. 13–16.

118 After his father had been dismissed by the Emperor, Herbert von Bismarck (1849–1904) himself resigned from his post as Imperial Foreign Secretary, which he held from 1886 to 1890.

119 Waldersee Diary, 3.7.91, Waldersee, *Denkwürdigkeiten*, II, 211.

120 Despite initial discouragement, he kept at it. *Ibid.*, pp. 211, 223, 243–6.

121 Deines to his Father, 29.3.93, MA Freiburg, Nl. Deines 12/pp. 14–14b; also his letter of 27.11.93, *ibid.*, pp. 53–4. The *Bund der Landwirte* was the conservative, anti-Semitic, agrarian organization which, after 1893, acted as the chief lobbying group for the Junkers: see Hans-Jürgen Puhle, *Agrarische Interessenpolitik und preussischer Konservatismus im Wilhelminischen Reich, 1893–1914. Ein Beitrag zur Analyse des Nationalismus in Deutschland am Beispiel des Bundes der Landwirte und der Deutsch-Konservativen Partei* (Hannover, 1967), and Sarah R. Tirrell, *German Agrarian Politics after Bismarck's Fall: The Formation of the Farmer's League* (New York, 1951). Hermann Ahlwardt was a major, rather hysterical figure of political anti-Semitism in the 1890s. See Peter Pulzer, *The Rise of Political Anti-Semitism in Germany and Austria* (New York, 1964), pp. 112–13, 115–17.

122 Deines to his Father, 11.2.94, MA Freiburg, Nl. Deines 12/pp. 67–72.

123 Holstein to Eulenburg, 7.12.91, in Röhl, *Eulenburgs Korrespondenz*, I, no. 561.

124 Holstein to Eulenburg, 12.12.91, in Johannes Haller, *Aus dem Leben des Fürsten Philipp zu Eulenburg-Hertefeld* (Berlin/Leipzig, 1926), pp. 104–5.

125 Eulenburg to Wilhelm, 13.12.91, *ibid.*, pp. 106–8.

126 Holstein to Eulenburg, 27.4.92, 3.5.92 and 7.5.92, Röhl, *Eulenburgs Korrespondenz*, II, nos. 646, 648 and 650.

127 See Röhl, *Germany Without Bismarck*, p. 104.

128 Holstein to Eulenburg, 9.6.92, Röhl, *Eulenburgs Korrespondenz*, II, no. 671.

129 Eulenburg to Holstein, 27.4.92, BA Koblenz, Nl. Eulenburg 19/pp. 286–7.
130 Diary entries of 30.8.90 and 29.8.92, Waldersee, *Denkwürdigkeiten*, II, 141 and 264.
131 Eulenburg note of 3.8.98 in BA Koblenz, Nl. Eulenburg 52/p. 263.
132 Diary entry of 5.8.93, Waldersee, *Denkwürdigkeiten*, II, 292.
133 *Ibid.*, II, 275, 277–8.
134 Kiderlen to Eulenburg, 27.11.93, Röhl, *Eulenburgs Korrespondenz*, II, no. 851.
135 Waldersee, *Denkwürdigkeiten*, II, 275.
136 August Eulenburg to Philipp Eulenburg, 1.2.91, Röhl, *Eulenburgs Korrespondenz*, I, no. 469.
137 Kiderlen to Eulenburg, 22.1.94, in BA Koblenz, Nl. Eulenburg 27/pp. 54–5.
138 Hugo v. Lerchenfeld-Köfering to Frhr von Crailsheim, 22.1.94 and 23.1.94, in BGSA Munich, Gesandtschaft Berlin 1064.
139 For Moltke's life and relationship to Wilhelm and the entourage see pp. 103–5.
140 Eulenburg to Wilhelm, 5.2.94, Röhl, *Eulenburgs Korrespondenz*, II, no. 895.
141 See Marschall's diary, 22.1.94, cited in *ibid.*, pp. 1197–8, n. 3 and Marschall to Eulenburg, 23.1.94, BA Koblenz, Nl. Eulenburg 27/pp. 70–3.
142 Eulenburg note of 26.1.94, BA Koblenz, Nl. Eulenburg 27/pp. 90–1; MA Freiburg, Nl. Deines 12/pp. 68–70, and Lerchenfeld Report no. 53 of 27.1.94, in BGSA Munich, Gesandtschaft Berlin 1064.
143 A term which Kuno Moltke succeeded in getting banned at Court, Moltke to Eulenburg, 28.1.94, Röhl, *Eulenburgs Korrespondenz*, II, no. 890.
144 Eulenburg to Moltke, 23.6.95, *ibid.*, BA Koblenz, Nl. Eulenburg 36/pp. 447–50.
145 Wilhelm to Hohenlohe, 28.10.96, BA Koblenz Nl. Hohenlohe, Rep. 100 XXII/A/9, vol. 19. Hohenlohe restrained Wilhelm from this spectacular course, Hohenlohe to Wilhelm, 29.10.96, *ibid.* Compare Admiral v. Müller, *Der Kaiser . . . Aufzeichnungen des Chefs des Marinekabinetts Admiral George Alexander v. Müller über die Ära Wilhelms II*, ed. Walter Görlitz (Göttingen/Berlin/Frankfurt/Zürich, 1965), p. 17. Görlitz is mistaken (note 24) that Wilhelm's ire subsided by itself.
146 See for example Haller, *Aus dem Leben*, pp. 104–8; or the brouhaha over how to handle Herbert von Bismarck's wedding in June 1892 in Röhl, *Eulenburgs Korrespondenz*, II, nos. 667, 669, 671, 674–83, 685–6.
147 Eulenburg's progress from a supporter to an enemy of the Caprivi system is detailed on pp. 79–86.
148 Eulenburg to Wilhelm, 23.1.94, Röhl, *Eulenburgs Korrespondenz*, II, no. 887.
149 Haller, *Aus dem Leben*, pp. 174–5.
150 Eulenburg to Moltke, 15.6.95, BA Koblenz, Nl. Eulenburg 36/pp. 433–42.
151 Diary of 19.6.92, BA Koblenz, Nl. Hohenlohe, Rep. 100 XXVII, vol. 1.
152 Holstein to Eulenburg, 23.1.94, BA Koblenz, Nl. Eulenburg 27/pp. 67–9.

153 Eulenburg Note: 'Einiges aus meinen Gesprächen mit dem Kaiser, 26. Jan. 1894,' *ibid.*, pp. 90–1.

154 Axel Varnbüler to Frhr v. Mittnacht, 29.10.94, HStA Stuttgart, E-73, Verz. 61, 12d.

155 Lerchenfeld Report Nr. 60, 28.1.94 in BGSA Munich, Gesandtschaft Berlin 1064.

156 This is what he told Eulenburg, Eulenburg note, 'Einiges aus meinen Gesprächen,' BA Koblenz, Nl. Eulenburg 27/pp. 67–9.

157 See pp. 86–9.

158 Bismarck's death in 1898 also robbed the reactionaries of a focus for their schemes.

159 Röhl, *Germany Without Bismarck*, pp. 166–71; Eulenburg to Holstein, 16.7.96 in PA Bonn, Nl. Holstein 39; Holstein to Bülow, 6.6.96, BA Koblenz, Nl. Bülow 90/pp. 138–53, and Hohenlohe to Eulenburg, 25.3.97, BA Koblenz, Nl. Eulenburg 46/p. 212.

160 Bernhard von Bülow, *Denkwürdigkeiten*, 4 vols. (Berlin, 1930), I, 68–9.

161 *Ibid.*, II, 440.

162 Eckart Kehr, 'Klassenkämpfe und Rüstungspolitik im kaiserlichen Deutschland,' in Eckart Kehr, *Der Primat der Innenpolitik. Gesammelte Aufsätze zur preussischdeutschen Sozialgeschichte im 19. und 20. Jahrhundert*, ed. Hans-Ulrich Wehler, 2nd edn (Berlin, 1970), pp. 99–102.

163 See p. 55.

164 Velics to Kálnoky, 24.10.94, in ÖStA Vienna, PA III 144.

165 Eulenburg Note in BA Koblenz, Nl. Eulenburg 42/p. 377.

166 Lerchenfeld Report Nr 552 of 18.11.08 in BGSA Munich, Gesandtschaft Berlin 1080.

167 Klepsch-Kloth to General Staff Chief 20.9.05, ÖKrA Vienna, Chef des Generalstabs 1905, 25:1/28.

168 Monts agreed. Monts to Bülow, 20.5.95, BA Koblenz, Nl. Bülow 106. Philipp Eulenburg, 'Drei Freunde,' II/2/pp. 163–4 (unpublished manuscript, courtesy of John Röhl).

169 Lerchenfeld Report Nr 177, 31.3.01, in BGSA Munich, Gesandtschaft Berlin 1073.

170 Except the Moltke question and the Eulenburg Affair (see p. 142).

171 Klepsch-Kloth to General Staff Chief, 20.9.05, in ÖKrA Vienna, Chef, des Generalstabs 1905, 25:1/28.

172 Deist, 'Kaiser Wilhelm II in the Context of his Military Entourage,' in Röhl and Sombart (eds.), *Kaiser Wilhelm II*, pp. 178–9.

173 Klepsch-Kloth to General Staff Chief, 20.9.05, OKrA Vienna, Chef des Generalstabs 1905, 25:1/28.

174 Volker Berghahn, *Germany and the Approach of War in 1914* (London, 1973), p. 8.

175 Bülow, *Denkwürdigkeiten*, II, 440.

176 Klepsch-Kloth to General Staff Chief, 4.10.04, ÖKrA Vienna, Chef des Generalstabs 1904, 1/23.

177 Karl von Einem, *Kriegsminister unter Wilhelm II. Erinnerungen eines Soldaten 1853–1933* (Leipzig, 1933), pp. 148–51.

178 Hutten-Czapski, *Sechzig Jahre*, I, 410.

179 Another reason why Bülow and Hülsen got on so well. Bülow, *Denkwürdigkeiten*, II, 183–5.

180 Haller, *Aus dem Leben*, p. 335, n. 2.
181 Helmuth v. Moltke, *Erinnerungen, Briefe, Dokumente 1877–1916* (Stuttgart, 1922), p. 313, and Waldersee, *Denkwürdigkeiten*, III, 219, 226.
182 Hutten-Czapski, *Sechzig Jahre*, I, 246 and 410.
183 Bülow, *Denkwürdigkeiten*, II, 184.
184 Einem, *Erinnerungen*, pp. 148–9.
185 Bülow, *Denkwürdigkeiten*, II, 185.

Chapter 9, pp. 236–65

1 See Carl E. Schorske, *German Social Democracy, 1905–1917: The Development of the Great Schism* (New York, 1955), pp. 36–7.
2 The characteristics, causes, and first fruits of the growing pessimism are discussed on pp. 127–30; and Volker Berghahn, *Germany and the Approach of War in 1914* (London, 1973), chs. 7–9.
3 For a bibliography of Fritz Fischer's works and books about the controversy see Imanuel Geiss and Bernd–Jürgen Wendt (eds.), *Deutschland in der Weltpolitik des 19. und 20. Jahrhunderts* (Düsseldorf, 1973), pp. 585–7.
4 Bülow wavered, but finally came down on the side of peace. See Norman Rich, *Friedrich von Holstein: Politics and Diplomacy in the Era of Bismarck and Wilhelm II*, 2 vols. (Cambridge, 1965), II, 696–753.
5 For Bethmann see Hans Günther Zmarzlik, *Bethmann Hollweg als Reichskanzler, 1909–1914* (Düsseldorf, 1957); Eberhard Vietsch, *Bethmann Hollweg, Staatsmann zwischen Macht und Ethos* (Boppard am Rhein, 1969); Konrad Jarausch, *The Enigmatic Chancellor: Bethmann Hollweg and the Hubris of Modern Germany* (New Haven, 1973); and Fritz Stern, 'Bethmann Hollweg and the War: The Limits of Responsibility,' in Fritz Stern and Leonard Krieger (eds.), *The Responsibility of Power: Historical Essays in Honor of Hajo Holborn* (New York, 1967), pp. 271–308. Klaus Hildebrand, *Bethmann der Kanzler ohne Eigenschaften? Urteile der Geschichtsschreibung–Eine kritische Bibliographie* (Düsseldorf, 1970) is a short and engaging guide to Bethmann's changing fortunes at the hands of historians. It is regrettable that Wolfgang Mommsen's *Habilitationsschrift* on Bethmann has never been published.
6 For Wilhelm's mental condition, see p. 12, note 58.
7 Robert von Zedlitz-Trützschler, *Zwölf Jahre am deutschen Kaiserhof* (Berlin/Leipzig, 1925), pp. 229–30.
8 Fritz Fischer, *War of Illusions: German Policies from 1911 to 1914* (New York, 1975; German edn, 1969), p. 478. 'Chicken out' is Berghahn's translation in Berghahn, *Germany and the Approach of War*, p. 193.
9 Franz Conrad von Hötzendorf, *Aus meiner Dienstzeit 1906–1918*, 7 vols. (Vienna/Berlin/Leipzig/Munich, 1921–5), III, 597.
10 See note 8.
11 Adolf Gasser, 'Deutschlands Entschluss zum Präventivkrieg 1913/14,' in Marc Sieber (ed.), *Discordia Concors. Festgabe für Edgar Bonjour zu seinem siebzigsten Geburtstag am 21. August 1968*, 2 vols. (Basel/Stuttgart, 1968), I, 173–224.
12 John C. G. Röhl, 'Admiral von Müller and the Approach of War, 1911–1914,' *The Historical Journal*, vol. XII, no. 4 (1969), p. 672.

13 John C. G. Röhl, *1914: Delusion or Design? The Testimony of Two German Diplomats* (London, 1973; German edn, 1971), pp. 37–8.

14 Georg Alexander von Müller, *Der Kaiser . . . Aufzeichnungen des Chefs des Marinekabinetts Admiral Georg Alexander v. Müller über die Ära Wilhelms II*, ed. Walter Görlitz (Göttingen/Berlin/Frankfurt/Zürich, 1965), p. 186.

15 Moltke to his Wife, 29.5.88 in Helmuth von Moltke, *Erinnerungen, Briefe, Dokumente 1877–1916* (Stuttgart, 1922), p. 139.

16 See Hülsen's remarks, p. 233, n. 178.

17 Müller, *Der Kaiser*, p. 187.

18 Moltke to his Wife, 17.7.04, in Moltke, *Erinnerungen*, pp. 295–6.

19 31.3.03, *ibid.*, p. 278.

20 Karl von Einem, *Kriegsminister unter Wilhelm II. Erinnerungen eines Soldaten 1853–1933* (Leipzig, 1933), pp. 148–51.

21 Letters of 19.5.07 and 18.7.07, Moltke, *Erinnerungen*, pp. 334–45 and 349. The brutal editing of these documents by his wife and Rudolf Steiner calls into question the reliability of these entries. Rudolf Steiner (1861–1925) was the founder of Anthroposophy, a spiritistic movement which was quite popular at the beginning of this century and is still active. See the documents and bibliography in Johannes Hemleben, *Rudolf Steiner in Selbstzeugnissen und Bilddokumenten* (Reinbek bei Hamburg, 1974).

22 Moltke, *Erinnerungen*, p. 361.

23 See Robert Carroll Galbreath, 'Spiritual Science in an Age of Materialism: Rudolf Steiner and Occultism' (Ph.D. dissertation, University of Michigan, 1970) for a complete discussion of Steiner's philosophy.

24 Müller, Diary for 13.9.14, in MA Freiburg, Nl. Müller, 4/p. 296. This section omitted in Müller, *Regierte der Kaiser? Kriegstagebücher, Aufzeichnungen und Briefe des Chefs des Marine-Kabinetts Admiral Georg Alexander von Müller 1914–1918*, ed. Walter Görlitz (Göttingen/Berlin/Frankfurt, 1959), p. 57.

25 Moltke to his Wife, 20.2.05, Moltke, *Erinnerungen*, p. 318.

26 Diary entry of 7.7.00, *ibid.*, p. 241.

27 Compare his despondency over Christianity, pp. 280–1, with his reactions to Steiner, pp. 290–1, 294–5 and 300–1, *ibid.*

28 Kuno Moltke to Axel Varnbüler, 20.9.19 in HStA Stuttgart, Nl. Varnbüler xxxvi, Karton 9.

29 Moltke, *Erinnerungen*, pp. 282–3, 300–1.

30 Conrad, *Aus meiner Dienstzeit*, iii, 147. Also Fischer, *War of Illusions*, pp. 169–74 and 190–5.

31 Moltke, *Erinnerungen*, p. 322.

32 See p. 41.

33 Moltke was not alone in doing so. See Isabel V. Hull, 'Prussian Dynastic Ritual and the End of Monarchy' (forthcoming).

34 Moltke, *Erinnerungen*, p. 245.

35 *Ibid.*, p. 244.

36 Moltke to Minister Director Dr Freund, 29.6.15, MA Freiburg, Nl. Moltke 36.

37 This happy phrase is Peter Winzen's in *Bülows Weltmachtkonzept. Untersuchungen zur Frühphase seiner Aussenpolitik 1897–1901* (Boppard am Rhein, 1977), p. 22.

38 Diary entry 4.7.00 in Moltke, *Erinnerungen,* p. 239.
39 *Ibid.,* p. 351.
40 Müller, *Der Kaiser,* p. 186.
41 Jehuda L. Wallach, *Das Dogma der Vernichtungsschlacht* (Munich, 1970; English edn, 1967).
42 Wallach, *Vernichtungsschlacht,* pp. 132–50, and Gerhard Ritter, *Der Schlieffenplan. Kritik eines Mythos* (Munich, 1956), pp. 55–6, and, as one example among many, Moltke to Conrad, 10.2.13, in Conrad, *Aus meiner Dienstzeit,* III, 144–7.
43 Gasser, 'Präventivkrieg,' p. 187.
44 Wallach, *Vernichtungsschlacht,* pp. 157–8.
45 He was also not a 'complete nothing,' as Wallach rightly points out, *ibid.,* p. 153.
46 Moltke, *Erinnerungen,* pp. 286–7.
47 Valentini was forced out in January 1918, Lyncker in July, and Müller resigned in October.
48 See pp. 29–30 for a discussion of Valentini and his conception of the duties of the Civil Cabinet chief.
49 Bernhard Schwertfeger, *Kaiser und Kabinettschef. Nach eigenen Aufzeichnungen und dem Briefwechsel des Wirklichen Geheimen Rats Rudolf von Valentini* (Oldenburg i. O., 1931), p. 125.
50 My request to use the East German Archives was rejected three times, as were two further attempts to use intermediaries.
51 Renate Endler, 'Nachlässe in der Historischen Abteilung II des Deutschen Zentralarchivs,' *Zeitschrift für Geschichtswissenschaft,* XIX, 9 (1972), 1161.
52 Valentini to Major von Harbou, 28.1.19 in Schwertfeger, *Kabinettschef,* p. 126.
53 *Ibid.,* pp. 118–19.
54 *Ibid.,* p. 78.
55 *Ibid.,* p. 71.
56 *Ibid.,* p. 110.
57 *Ibid.,* pp. 50, 73 n. 1, and 83.
58 *Ibid.,* p. 73.
59 Fischer, *War of Illusions,* p. 284.
60 Schwertfeger, *Kabinettschef,* pp. 126–7.
61 Müller, *Der Kaiser,* pp. 183–4.
62 Schwertfeger, *Kabinettschef,* pp. 48–9, 110 and 114.
63 *Ibid.,* p. 126.
64 *Ibid.,* p. 83.
65 *Ibid.,* p. 50.
66 *Ibid.,* pp. 83–4.
67 MA Freiburg, Nl. Mutius 2/p. 187.
68 (1854–1940).
69 Holger Herwig, *The German Naval Officer Corps: A Social and Political History 1890–1918* (Oxford, 1973), p. 77.
70 Prince Heinrich to Senden-Bibran, 30.7.99, MA Freiburg, Nl. Senden-Bibran 4/pp. 24–7.
71 Müller, *Der Kaiser,* pp. 26, 63–4.
72 Herwig, *Naval Officer Corps,* p. 77.

73 The German Oversea Service was begun by Albert Ballin, head of the Hamburg–America Line, after the war began, to disseminate reliable information about the war. See Lamar Cecil's excellent discussion of Ballin's wartime network in his *Albert Ballin: Business and Politics in Imperial Germany, 1888–1918* (Princeton, New Jersey, 1967), pp. 248–57.

74 Deutscher Überseedienst, GmbH to Müller, 9.11.17, in MA Freiburg RM2/5.

75 These names are sometimes deleted without indication in Görlitz's published editions of Müller's papers.

76 Diary entry of 3.5.16, in Müller, *Regierte der Kaiser?*, p. 174. Karl Helfferich (1872–1924), economist; director of the Deutsche Bank; State Secretary of the Treasury, 1915–16; State Secretary of the Interior, 1916–17.

77 Admiral v. Müller, 'Germany's Future Policy, 1896,' in Müller, *Der Kaiser*, pp. 36–41, reprinted and translated by John C. G. Röhl, *From Bismarck to Hitler. The Problem of Continuity in German History* (London, 1970), pp. 56–60.

78 *Ibid.*, p. 59.

79 *Ibid.*, pp. 48–9, 58–9 and 65.

80 Müller, *Der Kaiser*, p. 68.

81 Müller, *Regierte der Kaiser?*, p. 397.

82 Müller, *Der Kaiser*, p. 223.

83 Reported in MA Freiburg, Nl. Mutius 2/p. 187.

84 Capelle to Tirpitz, 20.8.12, MA Freiburg, Nl. Tirpitz 27/pp. 272–3.

85 Reported by Hugo von Reischach, *Unter drei Kaisern* (Berlin, 1925), p. 242.

86 So said Adm. Schröder, who thought Müller was in league with the Foreign Office. Cited by Herwig, *Naval Officer Corps*, p. 229, n. 3.

87 Reischach, *Unter drei Kaisern*, p. 242.

88 Herwig, *Naval Officer Corps*, pp. 82 and 88.

89 *Ibid.*, pp. 34 and 82.

90 Professor Doctor W. Korte to Wilhelm, 13.7.07, MA Freiburg, RM2/14.

91 Müller, *Der Kaiser*, p. 26.

92 *Ibid.*, p. 128, and Röhl, 'Adm. v. Müller,' p. 667.

93 Diary entry of 15.2.13, MA Freiburg, Nl. Müller, 4/p. 181.

94 (1853–1932), Military Cabinet Chief, 1908–18.

95 Reischach, *Unter drei Kaisern*, p. 242.

96 MA Freiburg, Nl. Mutius 2/p. 186.

97 Reischach, *Unter drei Kaisern*, p. 242.

98 Einem, *Erinnerungen*, p. 122.

99 Diary entry of 23.3.17 MA Freiburg, Nl. Müller 5/p. 341, where Müller remarks that 'even Lyncker' thought Wilhelm's long, social evenings were too much. Görlitz has unaccountably substituted the word '*Hoffrömmste*' for Lyncker's name in *Regierte der Kaiser?*, p. 267.

100 MA Freiburg, Nl. Mutius 2/p. 187.

101 Karl von Einem (1853–1934), Prussian General; War Minister, 1903–9.

102 Einem, *Erinnerungen*, p. 122.

103 Diary entry of 24.7.18 in Müller, *Regierte der Kaiser?*, pp. 396–7.

104 Wedel to Valentini, 27.6.16 (copy) in BA Koblenz, Nl. Schwertfeger 209/p. 11.
105 Wilhelm Deist, 'Die Armee in Staat und Gesellschaft 1890–1914,' in Michael Stürmer (ed.), *Das kaiserliche Deutschland* (Düsseldorf, 1970), pp. 333–4.
106 This phrase was originally coined by Hermann Kantorowicz, *Gutachten zur Kriegsschuldfrage 1914,* ed. Imanuel Geiss (Frankfurt, 1967), pp. 289–91 and 322, and reused by the historian Karl-Heinz Janssen in *Die Zeit,* 21.3.1969, both cited in Adolf Gasser, 'Der deutsche Hegemonialkrieg von 1914,' in Geiss and Wendt, *Deutschland in der Weltpolitik,* p. 337.
107 See note 35.
108 Gasser, 'Präventivkrieg' (see note 11) and 'Hegemonialkrieg,' pp. 307–39.
109 In his introduction to *Delusion or Design* (see note 13) and more recently in 'An der Schwelle zum Weltkrieg: Eine Dokumentation über den "Kriegsrat" von 8. Dezember 1912,' *Militärgeschichtliche Mitteilungen,* 1/1977, pp. 77–134, and his 'Die Generalprobe. Zur Geschichte und Bedeutung des "Kriegsrates" vom 8. Dezember 1912,' in Dirk Stegmann, Bernd-Jürgen Wendt, Peter-Christian Witt (eds.), *Industrielle Gesellschaft und politisches System. Beiträge zur politischen Sozialgeschichte.* Schriftenreihe des Forschungsinstituts der Friedrich-Ebert-Stiftung, Bd 137 (Bonn, 1978), pp. 357–73.
110 Fischer, *War of Illusions,* p. 470.
111 Gasser, 'Hegemonialkrieg,' p. 324.
112 Gasser, 'Präventivkrieg,' p. 209.
113 Gasser, 'Hegemonialkrieg,' p. 326.
114 *Ibid.,* p. 328.
115 Gasser, 'Präventivkrieg,' p. 211.
116 *Ibid.,* p. 208.
117 Pp. 261–4.
118 See Jehuda Wallach's intelligent discussion of this problem in *Vernichtungsschlacht,* pp. 67 n. 17, 97–9 and 115.
119 See Fischer, *War of Illusions,* pp. 192, 195–6, and Röhl, 'An der Schwelle,' pp. 90–1.
120 See pp. 96–7, and John Röhl, *Germany Without Bismarck* (London, 1967), pp. 196–8.
121 Emphasis in the original. B. H. Liddell Hart, *Strategy* (New York, 1954), p. 336.
122 *Ibid.,* pp. 335–6, 366–72.
123 Volker Berghahn, *Der Tirpitz-Plan. Genesis und Verfall einer innenpolitischen Krisenstrategie unter Wilhelm II* (Düsseldorf, 1971), p. 200. See also pp. 184–201 and 222–6.
124 Gasser, 'Präventivkrieg,' p. 211; Gasser, 'Hegemonialkrieg,' p. 334; Röhl, 'An der Schwelle,' pp. 87 and 132 n. 149; and Fischer, *War of Illusions,* p. 165.
125 Fischer, *War of Illusions,* ch. 12, pp. 259–71. Only Müller (one sentence) and Bernhardi are mentioned.
126 Dieter Groh, ' "Je eher, desto besser!" Innenpolitische Faktoren für die

Präventivkriegsbereitschaft des Deutschen Reiches 1913/14,' *Politische Vierteljahresschrift,* vol. 13 (1972), pp. 501–21.

127 This is the theme of Winzen, *Bülows Weltmachtkonzept.*

128 Historians still debate when exactly Bethmann abandoned the hope of reaching this goal by peaceful means. See Fischer, *War of Illusions,* pp. 164–8, and Röhl, *Delusion or Design?,* pp. 22–7.

129 Klaus Wernecke, *Der Wille zur Weltgeltung. Aussenpolitik und Öffentlichkeit im Kaiserreich am Vorabend des Ersten Weltkrieges* (Düsseldorf, 1970).

130 Bülow's maneuvering has often been interpreted as planlessness. See Winzen, *Bülows Weltmachtkonzept,* pp. 13–16.

131 Berghahn, *Der Tirpitz-Plan,* pp. 157–61 and 169–73.

132 See Hans-Ulrich Wehler, *Das deutsche Kaiserreich, 1871–1918* (Göttingen, 1973), pp. 60–78.

133 Dirk von Pezold, 'Cäsaromanie und Byzantinismus bei Wilhelm II' (Inaugural-Dissertation, Cologne, 1971), pp. 255–65, and Zedlitz-Trützschler, *Zwölf Jahre,* p. 249.

134 Müller's diary is studded with such complaints.

135 This was Müller's experience and also Zedlitz-Trützschler's, *Zwölf Jahre,* p. 210.

136 Gasser, 'Hegemonialkrieg,' p. 325.

137 Jarausch, *The Enigmatic Chancellor,* p. 147; and Alfred v. Tirpitz, *Erinnerungen* (Leipzig, 1920), p. 233.

138 Rich, *Friedrich von Holstein,* II, 840.

139 Fritz Fischer, *Germany's Aims in the First World War* (New York, 1967; German original, 1961), pp. 103–05.

140 Berghahn, *Der Tirpitz-Plan,* pp. 592–604.

141 Fischer, *War of Illusions,* pp. 71–94.

142 Cited in Hans W. Gatzke, *Germany's Drive to the West* (Baltimore, 1966; orig. 1950), pp. 250–1.

143 See Jonathan Steinberg, 'The Copenhagen Complex,' *Journal of Contemporary History,* vol. 1, no. 3 (1966), pp. 23–46.

144 Gasser, 'Präventivkrieg,' p. 215; Ludwig Dehio, *Germany and World Politics in the Twentieth Century* (New York, 1959), pp. 72–108; and Berghahn, *Der Tirpitz-Plan,* pp. 380–1.

145 Fischer, *War of Illusions,* pp. 190–9, 370–88 and 461–8.

146 Neither Wilhelm, Bethmann nor Moltke expected Russia to begin war in 1914. Bienerth to Conrad, 21.3.14, ÖKrA Vienna, Militär-Attaché Berlin, Fasz. 13; Hertling 'Unterredung mit Bethmann Hollweg' of 13.4.14, in BGSA Munich, Gesandtschaft Berlin 1086, and Moltke to Conrad, 13.3.14, in Conrad, *Aus meiner Dienstzeit,* III, 613.

147 Eckart Kehr and Ludwig Dehio are exceptions to this rule. See Berghahn, *Der Tirpitz-Plan,* pp. 11–12.

148 Cited in Gasser, 'Hegemonialkrieg,' p. 335.

149 Berghahn, *Der Tirpitz-Plan,* p. 66.

150 Wallach, *Vernichtungsschlacht,* pp. 66, 108.

151 Müller succumbed after 24.12.12, Müller, *Der Kaiser,* p. 186, and Röhl, 'An der Schwelle,' p. 100.

152 Fischer, *War of Illusions,* pp. 389–403; Ritter, *Der Schlieffenplan,* pp. 95–

102. Gottlieb von Jagow (1863–1935), State Secretary of the Foreign Office, 1913–16.
153 The first phrase is Schlieffen's, the second Wallach's in Wallach, *Vernichtungsschlacht*, p. 124 and also pp. 82–3.
154 *Ibid.*, p. 75.
155 *Ibid.*, pp. 75, 87–9 and 121.
156 *Ibid.*, p. 81.
157 *Ibid.*, pp. 97–9.
158 Carl von Clausewitz, *On War*, ed. Anatol Rapoport (London, 1968), p. 116.
159 He expected sheer technical, tactical virtuosity to defeat the seasoned, more powerful British. See Volker Berghahn, 'Zu den Zielen des deutschen Flottenbaus unter Wilhelm II,' *Historische Zeitschrift*, vol. 210 (1970), p. 90.
160 See pp. 195–203.
161 See pp. 41–4.
162 Georg Graf von Waldersee was German Quartermaster General after 1912. As such, his job was to coordinate supplies for the entire army.
163 Georg Graf von Waldersee, *Von Kriegführung, Politik, Persönlichkeit und ihrer Wechselwirkung aufeinander* (Berlin, 1927), p. 445, cited in Gasser, 'Präventivkrieg,' p. 182 n. 30.
164 Houston Stewart Chamberlain, 'Deutschland als führender Weltstaat' (written 9 September 1914), printed in Chamberlain, *Kriegsaufsätze*, 9th edn (Munich, 1915), pp. 36–43. I thank John Röhl for calling this essay to my attention.
165 Gasser, 'Hegemonialkrieg,' p. 318.
166 Wilhelm had announced this maxim in November 1912, see Röhl, 'Generalprobe,' p. 360.
167 Berghahn, *Germany and the Approach of War*, pp. 104–24 and 145–64.
168 *Ibid.*, p. 167.
169 See Berghahn's sensitive explanation, *ibid.*, pp. 167–8.
170 Fischer, *War of Illusions*, p. 62.
171 Zedlitz-Trützschler, *Zwölf Jahre*, p. 226, translated in Fischer, *War of Illusions*, p. 61.
172 Rudolf Vierhaus (ed.), *Das Tagebuch der Baronin Spitzemberg. Aufzeichnungen aus der Hofgesellschaft des Hohenzollernreiches* (Göttingen, 1960), entry for 7.8.11, p. 531.
173 Moltke to his wife, 19.8.11, Moltke, *Erinnerungen*, p. 362, translated in Fischer, *War of Illusions*, p. 88.
174 Entry of 12.9.11, MA Freiburg, Nl. Müller 4/p. 77. See also Röhl, 'Adm. v. Müller,' p. 654, and Müller, *Der Kaiser*, p. 88.
175 Plessen to Max Egon Fürstenberg, 8.1.12 in FFA Donaueschingen, Nl. Fürstenberg. France had ceded to Germany part of the French Congo and some land adjacent to the German Cameroons.
176 Varnbüler to Julius Frhr von Soden, 5 December (Varnbüler erroneously wrote 'November') 1905, HStA Stuttgart E-73, Verz. 61, 12e.
177 Varnbüler to Karl Frhr von Weizsäcker, 28.7.10, pp. 7–10, HStA Stuttgart, E-73, Verz. 61, 12e.

178 Spitzemberg, *Tagebuch*, 2.8.11, p. 531.
179 Varnbüler to Kuno Moltke, 18 November, no year (probably 1912), in Röhl, *Delusion or Design?*, p. 53.
180 A Cavalry General von Deines is listed by Fischer as a member of the Army League (*War of Illusions*, p. 105). This could not be Adolf v. Deines, earlier FAD and MA, who died on 17 November 1911, 2½ months before the League was founded.
181 Zedlitz-Trützschler, *Zwölf Jahre*, p. 231.
182 Moritz Lyncker to Holstein, San Remo, 10.2.88, PA Bonn, Nl. Holstein vol. 11.
183 Entry of 10.9.12, Müller, *Regierte der Kaiser?*, p. 128.
184 Klepsch-Kloth to Conrad, 4.3.08, ÖKrA Vienna, Chef des Generalstabs 1908, 25:1/5, and MA Freiburg, Nl. Schulenburg, 1/p. 20.
185 Some of these letters may be found in FFA Donaueschingen, Nl. Fürstenberg.
186 Berghahn, *Germany and the Approach of War*, pp. 98, 169–70, and Müller diary of 8.12.12, in Röhl, 'An der Schwelle,' p. 100.
187 This marks a distinct change from his position in 1896, when he wanted Germany to avoid a confrontation with England. See Müller, 'Germany's Future Policy,' p. 59.
188 Röhl, 'Adm. v. Müller,' p. 654, and Müller, *Der Kaiser*, p. 91.
189 Plessen to Fürstenberg, 12.10.12, FFA Donaueschingen, Nl. Fürstenberg.
190 Röhl, 'Adm. v. Müller,' p. 659.
191 Röhl, 'Generalprobe,' pp. 360–3.
192 Röhl disagrees, *ibid.*, p. 359.
193 Röhl's phrase, 'An der Schwelle,' p. 97.
194 Müller diary of 8.12.12, *ibid.*, p. 100.
195 This is how Bavarian Military Plenipotentiary General v. Wenninger described it, Wenninger to Bavarian War Minister Freiherr Kress v. Kressenstein, 15.12.12, *ibid.*, no. 22.
196 Müller's diary, 8.12.12, *ibid.*, no. 4.
197 Wenninger to Kress v. Kressenstein, 14.12.12, *ibid.*, no. 21; Bethmann Hollweg's memorandum of 20.12.12, *ibid.*, no. 34.
198 Wenninger to Kress v. Kressenstein, 14.12.12, *ibid.*, no. 21.
199 *Ibid.;* compare Röhl, 'Generalprobe,' p. 373.
200 Wenninger to Kress v. Kressenstein, 24.12.12, in Röhl, 'An der Schwelle,' no. 38.
201 *Ibid.*, nos. 9 and 10.
202 *Ibid.*, pp. 90–1.
203 Röhl, 'Generalprobe,' p. 371.
204 Fischer, *War of Illusions*, p. 204.
205 *Ibid.*, pp. 439–42.
206 Fischer (throughout *War of Illusions*), Gasser (in the two articles cited above) and Röhl ('Generalprobe,' p. 373) all believe this to have been the case. Groh, 'Je eher, desto besser!,' and Berghahn (*Germany and the Approach of War*) both have advanced interpretations closer to the one that this author holds.
207 Entire entry in Röhl, 'An der Schwelle,' p. 100.

208 Müller's diary is replete with frustrated outbursts about the illogicality and undirected nature of German policy and its leaders. See an example from 19.10.12, MA Freiburg, Nl. Müller 4/p. 159, omitted in Müller, *Der Kaiser*, pp. 121–2.

209 Müller, 'Germany's Future Policy,' p. 59.

210 Wilhelm's phrase about Bethmann, Müller's diary, 14.12.12, MA Freiburg, Nl. Müller 4/p. 172, cited in Röhl, 'Generalprobe,' p. 362.

211 Röhl, 'Generalprobe,' p. 369.

212 Röhl, 'Adm. v. Müller,' p. 669.

213 Szögyényi to Berchtold, 17.12.12, ÖStA Vienna, PA III 170 Varia 1912.

214 Bienerth to Conrad, 26.2.13, in Conrad, *Aus meiner Dienstzeit*, II, 152.

215 Varnbüler to Weizsäcker, 4.3.13, HStA Stuttgart E-73, Verz. 61, 12e.

216 Wedel to Foreign Office, 17.10.13, PA Bonn Preussen I/1d/secr. Bd 4.

217 See for example, reports on Wilhelm for 27.4.13, 4.1.14 and 16.1.14 in Conrad, *Aus meiner Dienstzeit*, III, 275, 596 and 597; and Fischer, *War of Illusions*, p. 215 (1.7.13).

218 Reports of 13.3.14 and 12.5.14 in Conrad, *Aus meiner Dienstzeit*, III, 613 and 671.

219 See Röhl, 'Generalprobe,' pp. 365–6.

220 Lerchenfeld to Hertling, 8.1.14, in BGSA Munich, Gesandtschaft Berlin 1086.

221 Bienerth to Conrad, 21.3.14, ÖKrA Vienna, Militär-Attaché Berlin, Fasz. 13.

222 Cited in Fischer, *War of Illusions*, p. 471.

223 Wilhelm's marginalia on Amb. Tschirschky's report to Bethmann of 30.6.14, in Imanuel Geiss (ed.), *July 1914, The Outbreak of the First World War: Selected Documents* (New York, 1967; German original, 1965), p. 64.

224 Report of a conversation with Krupp-Bohlen on 6 July 1914, cited in Fischer, *War of Illusions*, p. 478.

225 See Röhl, 'Adm. v. Müller,' pp. 669–70.

Chapter 10, pp. 266–92

1 Georg v. Müller, *Regierte der Kaiser? Kriegstagebücher, Aufzeichnungen und Briefe des Chefs des Marine-Kabinetts Admiral Georg Alexander von Müller 1914–1918*, ed. Walter Görlitz (Göttingen/Berlin/Frankfurt, 1959), p. 44.

2 *Ibid.*, p. 50.

3 See diary entry of 14.9.14, *ibid.*, p. 59; entry of 15.9.14 in MA Freiburg, Nl. Müller 4/p. 298; entries for the month of July 1916 in Müller, *Regierte der Kaiser?*, pp. 198–207; Karl-Heinz Janssen (ed.), *Die Graue Exzellenz. Zwischen Staatsräson und Vasallentreue. Aus den Papieren des kaiserlichen Gesandten Karl Georg von Treutler* (Frankfurt/Berlin/Vienna, 1971), pp. 216–17; Klepsch-Kloth to Austrian High Command, Pless, 4.8.16, ÖKrA Vienna, Militär Kanzlei Seiner Majestät (hereafter MKSM) Sep. Fasz. 69-6/2; and entry for 30.4.17, Müller, *Regierte der Kaiser?*, pp. 281–2.

4 3.9.18, *ibid.*, pp. 406–7.

5 6.9.18, *ibid.*, p. 410. Müller's response was omitted by Görlitz, see MA Freiburg, Nl. Müller 7/p. 26A.

6 Bülow's notes of a conversation with Wilhelm from December 1914, in BA Koblenz Nl. Bülow 140/p. 3.
7 Müller's phrase, 22.6.15, Müller, *Regierte der Kaiser?*, p. 110.
8 14.10.14, MA Freiburg, Nl. Müller 4/p. 311, omitted in Müller, *Regierte der Kaiser?*, p. 65.
9 4.9.14, MA Freiburg, Nl. Müller, 4/p. 292, omitted in Müller, *Regierte der Kaiser?*, pp. 54–5. My thanks to John Röhl for pointing this passage out to me.
10 MA Freiburg, Nl. Müller 4/p. 311. Also Nl. Mutius 2/p. 199.
11 Entry of 28.10.14, Müller, *Regierte der Kaiser?*, p. 67.
12 Görlice – 3.12.15 in Fürstenberg's Diary, FFA Donaueschingen, Nl. Fürstenberg, and Craonne, 1.6.18 in Müller's diary, Müller, *Regierte der Kaiser?*, p. 381.
13 18.9.16, MA Freiburg, Nl. Müller 5/p. 244, not in Müller, *Regierte der Kaiser?*, p. 222.
14 For example Treutler's dismissal. See Janssen, *Die graue Exzellenz*, pp. 215–17, and Müller, *Regierte der Kaiser?*, pp. 201–2.
15 Klepsch-Kloth, 'Erinnerungen,' p. 105 in ÖKrA Vienna, Nl. Klepsch-Kloth.
16 Entry of 27.10.17, MA Freiburg, Nl. Müller 6/p. 25, omitted in Müller, *Regierte der Kaiser?*, p. 327.
17 Janssen, *Die graue Exzellenz*, p. 176.
18 Entries of 12.10.15 and 14.3.17 in MA Freiburg, Nl. Müller, 5/p. 91, and Müller, *Regierte der Kaiser?*, p. 265.
19 Entries of 5.4.17 and 2.6.17, *ibid.*, pp. 271 and 290.
20 Entries of 8.6.15 and 11.6.18, *ibid.*, pp. 108 and 383.
21 Entry of 6.9.16, *ibid.*, p. 220.
22 Klepsch-Kloth to Army High Command, 8.10.16, ÖKrA Vienna, MKSM Sep. Fasz. 79/42.
23 Klepsch-Kloth to Army High Command, Pless, 11.10.16, *ibid.*
24 Janssen, *Die graue Exzellenz*, p. 162.
25 Entry of 8.2.17, Müller, *Regierte der Kaiser?*, p. 259.
26 Klepsch-Kloth to Army High Command, 31.10.16, ÖKrA Vienna MKSM 69-6/2; Klepsch-Kloth to Army High Command, 8.8., 5.10. and 6.10.18, ÖKrA Vienna, Armeeoberkommando Fasz. 600.
27 Gerhard Ritter, *The Sword and the Scepter. The Problem of Militarism in Germany*, 4 vols. (Coral Gables, Florida, 1969–73), II, 134.
28 Wilhelm Deist, 'Kaiser Wilhelm II in the Context of his Military Entourage,' in John C. G. Röhl and Nicolaus Sombart (eds.), *Kaiser Wilhelm II: New Interpretations* (Cambridge, 1981), p. 179.
29 Lerchenfeld to Hertling, 2.5.15, in Ernst Deuerlein (ed.), *Briefwechsel Hertling–Lerchenfeld 1912–1917. Dienstliche Privatkorrespondenz zwischen dem bayerischen Ministerpräsidenten Georg Graf von Hertling und dem bayerischen Gesandten in Berlin Hugo Graf von und zu Lerchenfeld, Erster Teil. Deutsche Geschichtsquellen des 19. und 20. Jahrhunderts Herausgegeben von der Historischen Kommission bei der Bayerischen Akademie der Wissenschaften, Bd 50/1* (Boppard am Rhein, 1973), pp. 430–1.
30 Wilhelm Deist, *Militär und Innenpolitik im Weltkrieg 1914–1918*, 2 Parts. Quellen zur Geschichte des Parlamentarismus und der politischen Parteien, Zweite Reihe (Militär und Politik), Bd 1 (Düsseldorf, 1970), I, p. xv.

31 See Deist's dissection of the state of siege law and its effects, *ibid.*, pp. xxxi–li.
32 Prussian War Minister Wild v. Hohenborn in a speech on 27.1.17, in *ibid.*, II, no. 251, p. 661.
33 Andreas Hillgruber, 'Kontinuität und Diskontinuität in der deutschen Aussenpolitik von Bismarck bis Hitler,' in his *Grossmachtpolitik und Militarismus im 20. Jahrhundert. 3 Beiträge zum Kontinuitätsproblem* (Düsseldorf, 1974), pp. 21–2.
34 On radical nationalism see Geoff Eley, *Reshaping the German Right. Radical Nationalism and Political Change after Bismarck* (New Haven/London, 1980).
35 (1869–1929), Chief of Operations in Dept II at Supreme Command.
36 Bauer cited by Hermann Ritter (Colonel) Mertz v. Quirnheim, December 1916, in Deist, *Militär und Innenpolitik*, II, no. 246, p. 652. On similar worries during the July crisis, see Fritz Fischer, *Bündnis der Eliten. Zur Kontinuität der Machtstrukturen in Deutschland 1871–1945* (Düsseldorf, 1979), p. 19.
37 See previous note.
38 Müller's diary, 18.4.15, in Müller *Regierte der Kaiser?*, pp. 97–9; and Alfred von Tirpitz, *Erinnerungen* (Leipzig, 1920), pp. 459–60 (diary entry of 27.3.15.)
39 Deist, *Militär und Innenpolitik*, I, 424, n. 27.
40 Hillgruber, 'Kontinuität,' pp. 21–2.
41 General Karl von Einem to his wife, 17.9.18, in Deist, *Militär und Innenpolitik*, II, 1268, n. 7.
42 Müller's diary, 16.5.16, MA Freiburg, Nl. Müller 5/p. 180, not reprinted in Müller, *Regierte der Kaiser?*, p. 178.
43 (1861–1922), Lt General; Prussian War Minister, 1913–15; Chief of the General Staff, 1914–16.
44 Paul v. Beneckendorff und v. Hindenburg (1847–1934), Field Marshal; Chief of the General Staff, August 1916–18; President of the Weimar Republic, 1925–34.
45 (1865–1937), General; First Quartermaster General, 1916–18.
46 (1858–1933).
47 (1874–1957). Fritz Fischer, *War of Illusions. German Policies from 1911 to 1914* (New York, 1975), p. 378, and Janssen, *Die graue Exzellenz*, p. 268, list him incorrectly as Curt v. Grünau.
48 Müller to Valentini, Spa, 5.7.18, BA Koblenz, Nl. Schwertfeger 213.
49 Bernhard Schwertfeger (ed.), *Kaiser und Kabinettschef. Nach eigenen Aufzeichnungen und dem Briefwechsel des Wirklichen Geheimen Rats Rudolf von Valentini* (Oldenburg i. O., 1931), pp. 138, 152, 166.
50 Entry of 2.2.18, MA Freiburg, Nl. Müller, 6/p. 40A, omitted in Müller, *Regierte der Kaiser?*, p. 350.
51 Adolf Wild v. Hohenborn to his wife, 15.11.14, MA Freiburg, Nl. Wild v. Hohenborn 3/p. 59b.
52 Klepsch-Kloth to Army High Command, 8.6.15, ÖKrA Vienna, MKSM Sep. Fasz. 79/42.
53 (1863–1923).
54 MA Freiburg, Nl. Mutius 2/p. 187; Janssen, *Die graue Exzellenz*, p. 168; and Friedrich v. Berg, *Friedrich v. Berg als Chef des Geheimen Zivilkabinetts*

1918. Erinnerungen aus seinem Nachlass, ed. Heinrich Potthof. Quellen zur Geschichte des Parlamentarismus und der politischen Parteien, Erste Reihe, Bd 7 (Düsseldorf, 1971), p. 96.

55 (1861–1931).
56 Schwertfeger, *Kabinettschef,* pp. 184–5.
57 See p. 269.
58 Schwertfeger, *Kabinettschef,* p. 186.
59 Müller's diary, 8.1.17, Müller, *Regierte der Kaiser?,* p. 247.
60 Müller's diary, 22.7.16, *ibid.,* p. 204.
61 Klepsch-Kloth to Army High Command, 8.12.17, ÖKrA Vienna, Armeeoberkommando Fasz. 600; see also *idem,* 25.3.18 and 3.6.18, *ibid.*
62 Valentini's pencilled memorandum, 'Gedanken, die ich bei Konferenz mit Hindenburg und Ludendorff am 11 Jan. 1917 in Pless entwickelt: mit Erfolg!,' BA Koblenz, Nl. Schwertfeger 212/pp. 1–3, emphasis in original.
63 Müller's diary, 16.10.16, Müller, *Regierte der Kaiser?,* p. 213.
64 Müller's diary, 8.1.17, *ibid.,* p. 247.
65 The discussion of these three problems will be far from exhaustive. They will merely be used to illustrate the lines along which the wartime entourage operated.
66 For German war aims see Fritz Fischer, *Germany's Aims in the First World War* (New York, 1967; German original, 1961), and Hans Gatzke's older, but still worthwhile, *Germany's Drive to the West (Drang nach Westen). A Study of Germany's Western War Aims during the First World War* (Baltimore, 1950).
67 Fischer, *Germany's Aims,* p. 103.
68 *Ibid.,* p. 215 and Bethmann's memorandum to Valentini, 9.12.15, in Deist, *Militär und Innenpolitik,* I, no. 119.
69 Fischer, *Germany's Aims,* pp. 376–7.
70 Bethmann's memorandum of 9.12.15, Deist, *Militär und Innenpolitik,* I, no. 119, pp. 273–7.
71 General Frhr v. Gayl to Bethmann, 23.6.15, *ibid.,* I, no. 105, pp. 244–5.
72 General v. Gebsattel to Crown Prince Wilhelm, 27.4.15, *ibid.,* p. 245, n. 6.
73 Lerchenfeld to Hertling, 21.3.15, in Deuerlein, *Briefwechsel Hertling–Lerchenfeld,* no. 163, p. 415.
74 Fischer, *Germany's Aims,* p. 377.
75 Müller's diary, 9.4.15, Müller, *Regierte der Kaiser?,* pp. 96–7.
76 See, for example, Treutler's marginal comments on Hatzfeldt's memorandum of 2.6.16, BA Koblenz, Nl. Schwertfeger 210/p. 24.
77 Schwertfeger, *Kabinettschef,* p. 171.
78 *Ibid.,* and Vice Admiral Hipper's diary entry of 24.6.15, in Deist, *Militär und Innenpolitik,* I, 244, n. 4.
79 Lyncker to Tirpitz, 20.12.26, in Janssen, *Die graue Exzellenz,* pp. 182–5.
80 For example, Müller's diary of 22.1.18, Müller, *Regierte der Kaiser?,* p. 348.
81 Müller's diary of 8.11.16, *ibid.,* p. 234.
82 Fischer, *Germany's Aims,* pp. 313–15.
83 See *ibid.,* pp. 347–51.
84 Müller's diary of 23.4.17, Müller, *Regierte der Kaiser?,* pp. 278–9, partially cited in Fischer, *Germany's Aims,* pp. 349–50, 350, n. 1. The translation is partly from the English edition.
85 Fischer, *Germany's Aims,* p. 350, n. 1.

86 *Ibid.*, p. 350.
87 See, for example, Kühlmann's position at Brest-Litovsk, *ibid.*, pp. 492–93, and Müller's diary, 19.12.17, 10.2.18, 12.2.18, 13.2.18, Müller, *Regierte der Kaiser?*, pp. 339, 351–5.
88 Müller called them 'absolutely stupid' and 'too crazy,' diary entry of 11.5.17, Müller, *Regierte der Kaiser?*, pp. 286–7.
89 Müller's diary, 13.2.18, *ibid.*, pp. 354–5.
90 For a more detailed account of unrestricted submarine warfare see Ritter, *Sword and Scepter*, III, 119–77 and 264–318.
91 See *ibid.*, pp. 121–4 for the state of international law and custom.
92 Janssen, *Die graue Exzellenz*, p. 205, and Fischer, *Germany's Aims*, p. 308.
93 Müller's diary, 15.1.16, Müller, *Regierte der Kaiser?*, p. 147.
94 Tirpitz to Wilhelm, copy, 27(24?).4.16, MA Freiburg, Nl. Tirpitz 192.
95 This was Falkenhayn's view, Müller's diary, 24.1.16 and 9.2.16, Müller, *Regierte der Kaiser?*, pp. 149, 153–4.
96 See Müller's diary, 9.2.16, *ibid.*, pp. 153–4.
97 So Falkenhayn and Wild v. Hohenborn, Müller's diary, 15.1.16, *ibid.*, p. 148, and Ritter, *Sword and Scepter*, III, 306.
98 So, Capelle, *ibid.*, p. 334. See also Wilhelm's outburst, Müller diary, 16.1.17, Müller, *Regierte der Kaiser?*, p. 251, and Ludendorff's remark, 'I don't give a hoot about America! [*Ich pfeife auf Amerika*],' cited in Janssen, *Die graue Exzellenz*, p. 210.
99 Bethmann's memorandum of about 29.2.16 in BA Koblenz, Nl. Schwertfeger 208; Müller's diary, 9 and 10.2.16, Müller, *Regierte der Kaiser?*, pp. 154–5, and elsewhere; and Treutler's memorandum of 3.3.16, in Janssen, *Die graue Exzellenz*, pp. 196–204.
100 Janssen, *Die graue Exzellenz*, p. 190.
101 Fürst Pless joined the opponents when the Kaiser's headquarters moved to Pless in May 1915, *ibid.*, pp. 190–1, 211, and Schwertfeger, *Kabinettschef*, p. 145.
102 (1855–1916), Chief of the Admiral Staff, 1913–15; Chief of the High Sea Fleet, 1915/16.
103 Janssen, *Die graue Exzellenz*, pp. 192–3; and Ritter, *Sword and Scepter*, III, 166.
104 The United States was only partly satisfied. See Ritter, *Sword and Scepter*, III, 129–34, 145–9.
105 (1860–1943), Chief of the Admiral Staff, 2 February 1915–3 September 1915.
106 (1853–1919), Chief of the Admiral Staff, 1915–18.
107 Janssen, *Die graue Exzellenz*, p. 195; and Müller's diary, 1.9.15, Müller, *Regierte der Kaiser?*, p. 126.
108 Ritter, *Sword and Scepter*, III, 149.
109 See Müller's diary entries for 27.5.15, 29–31.5.15, 5–6.6.15, 22.6.15, 24–25.6.15, 29–30.6.15, 1–6.7.15, 27.8.15 and 6.9.15, Müller, *Regierte der Kaiser?*, pp. 104–7, 110–15, 125, and 127.
110 Janssen, *Die graue Exzellenz*, p. 194.
111 Ritter, *Sword and Scepter*, III, 157.
112 Müller's diary, 24.1.16, Müller, *Regierte der Kaiser*, p. 149.
113 See Ritter, *Sword and Scepter*, III, 264–87.

114 Müller's diary, 6.1.16, Müller, *Regierte der Kaiser?*, p. 146.
115 10.2.16, *ibid.*, p. 155.
116 9.2.16, *ibid.*, p. 153.
117 30.11.16, *ibid.*, pp. 237–8.
118 See Müller's diary of 3.10.16 and 8.1.17, *ibid.*, pp. 225–6 and 247; and Treutler's memorandum of 3.3.16, in Janssen, *Die graue Exzellenz*, pp. 196–204.
119 Treutler in *ibid.*, p. 212.
120 Müller's diary, 4.7.16, Müller, *Regierte der Kaiser?*, p. 201.
121 Wild v. Hohenborn's diary entry for 5.7.16, MA Freiburg, Nl. Wild v. Hohenborn 2/p. 163, cited in Janssen, *Die graue Exzellenz*, p. 215.
122 Müller's diary of 5.7.16, Müller, *Regierte der Kaiser?*, p. 201.
123 It seemed better in August and September 1916 than it actually was.
124 Ritter, *Sword and Scepter*, III, 266–7.
125 For the peace overtures see Fischer, *Germany's Aims*, pp. 295–302; for the Reichstag's role as a condition in the submarine question see Ritter, *Sword and Scepter*, III, 271–5.
126 Müller's diary entry of 8.1.17, Müller, *Regierte der Kaiser?*, p. 247.
127 Müller diary, 9.1.17, *ibid.*, pp. 248–9.
128 Compare, for instance, Müller's entry of 3.3.16, *ibid.*, p. 161 with Ritter, *Sword and Scepter*, III, 168.
129 Müller's diary, 3.10.16, Müller, *Regierte der Kaiser?*, pp. 225–6.
130 Müller's words, 8.1.17, *ibid.*, p. 247.
131 Klepsch-Kloth to Army High Command, 9.3.16, ÖKrA Vienna, MKSM Sep. Fasz. 69-6/2.
132 Treutler to Bethmann, 17.1.16, in Janssen, *Die graue Exzellenz*, p. 196.
133 Jarausch's expression, Konrad Jarausch, *The Enigmatic Chancellor: Bethmann Hollweg and the Hubris of Imperial Germany* (New Haven, 1973), p. 300.
134 Müller's diary, 8.1.17, Müller, *Regierte der Kaiser?*, p. 247. Müller noted caustically that this was a 'curious standpoint.'
135 See the discussion above, pp. 274–6.
136 Arthur Rosenberg, *Imperial Germany. The Birth of the German Republic 1871–1918* (Boston, 1968; German original, 1930), p. 159. See also Wilhelm to Bethmann, telegram, 12.5.17, in Deist, *Militär und Innenpolitik*, II, no. 296.
137 This was the entourage's label for Admiral v. Müller, Müller's diary, 8.4.17, Müller, *Regierte der Kaiser?*, p. 273.
138 Naval Captain Hopmann to Imperial Navy Office, 27.10.14, in Deist, *Militär und Innenpolitik*, I, no. 87.
139 Müller's diary, 8.4.17, Müller, *Regierte der Kaiser?*, p. 273.
140 Valentini to Loebell, copy, 1.7.17, BA Koblenz, Nl. Schwertfeger 210/p. 81.
141 *Ibid.;* see also Schwertfeger, *Kabinettschef*, p. 183.
142 Valentini to Loebell, copy, 1.7.17, BA Koblenz, Nl. Schwertfeger 210/p. 81.
143 Grünau to Bethmann, 11.4.17, in Deist, *Militär und Innenpolitik*, II, no. 281.
144 Klepsch-Kloth to Army High Command, Pless, 8.6.15, ÖKrA Vienna, MKSM Sep. Fasz. 79/42.

145 Müller's diary, 8.4.17, Müller, *Regierte der Kaiser?*, p. 273.
146 Wilhelm to Bethmann, telegram, 12.5.17, in Deist, *Militär und Innenpolitik*, II, no. 290.
147 Müller's diary, 7.7.17, Müller, *Regierte der Kaiser?*, p. 300.
148 Bethmann memorandum, copy, of 14.7.17, BA Koblenz, Nl. Schwertfeger 119/p. 3.
149 Wilhelm to Lyncker, copy, 27.2.17, BA Koblenz, Nl. Schwertfeger 212/p. 30.
150 Bethmann memorandum of 11.7.17, copy, *ibid.*, 119/p. 2.
151 TANS/Ulrich Wehler, *Das Deutsche Kaiserreich 1871–1918* (Göttingen, 1973), pp. 227–38; see also p. 12, n. 56.
152 See Deist, *Militär und Innenpolitik*, II, 700–4.
153 Müller's diary, 8.4.17, Müller, *Regierte der Kaiser?*, p. 273.
154 Müller's diary, 14.4.17, *ibid.*, p. 275.
155 See Rosenberg, *Imperial Germany*, pp. 171–4; Bethmann's memorandum of 11–14.7.17, BA Koblenz, Nl. Schwertfeger 119/pp. 1–6; Schwertfeger, *Kabinettschef*, pp. 157–72; and Müller's diary entries in Müller, *Regierte der Kaiser?*, pp. 300–6.
156 Schwertfeger, *Kabinettschef*, p. 153.
157 *Ibid.*, pp. 184–5.
158 Hindenburg to Wilhelm, 16.1.18, in Deist, *Militär und Innenpolitik*, II, 1124–7 and footnotes.
159 Müller, *Regierte der Kaiser?*, p. 344. See the good discussion by Potthoff in Berg, *Erinnerungen*, pp. 43–52.
160 Valentini memorandum, copy, Potsdam, 10.10.18, BA Koblenz, Nl. Schwertfeger 206/p. 55.
161 Müller to Valentini, 30.3.18, in BA Koblenz, Nl. Schwertfeger 213/p. 6; also the entries of 2.2.18 and 27.2.18 in Müller, *Regierte der Kaiser?*, pp. 350 and 359.
162 Müller's diary, 27.2.18, Müller, *Regierte der Kaiser?*, p. 359; see also Müller's entry of 31.1.18, *ibid.*, p. 349.
163 (1866–1939). See Potthoff on Berg's life and politics, Berg, *Erinnerungen*, pp. 37–73.
164 *Ibid.*, p. 45.
165 Entry 10.3.18, Müller, *Regierte der Kaiser?*, p. 362.
166 Cited by Potthoff in Berg, *Erinnerungen*, p. 54 n. 14.
167 *Ibid.*, pp. 99–100.
168 *Ibid.*, p. 105.
169 Müller to Valentini, 29.8.18, BA Koblenz, Nl. Schwertfeger 213/p. 7.
170 Berg, *Erinnerungen*, pp. 98–9, 107.
171 *Ibid.*, p. 105.
172 Müller to Valentini, Spa, 5.7.18, BA Koblenz, Nl. Schwertfeger 213.
173 Entry of 2.2.18, Müller, *Regierte der Kaiser?*, p. 350.
174 (1863–1923).
175 Entry of 20.7.18, Müller, *Regierte der Kaiser?*, p. 395.
176 Berg, *Erinnerungen*, p. 104.
177 (1856–1921).
178 Wehler, *Das Kaiserreich*, pp. 216–18.
179 Berg, *Erinnerungen*, pp. 189–95.
180 (1871–1946).

181 Müller, *Regierte der Kaiser?*, pp. 439–40.
182 Ludendorff resigned on 27.10.18.
183 Lerchenfeld to Otto Ritter von Dandl, 30.10.18, BGSA Munich, MA 973.
184 Lerchenfeld to Dandl, 28.10.18, *ibid.*; also Treutler in Janssen, *Die graue Exzellenz*, p. 219, and Bethmann to Treutler, 29.9.18, *ibid.*, p. 253.
185 Entry of 30.10.18 in Müller, *Regierte der Kaiser?*, p. 442.
186 Janssen, *Die graue Exzellenz*, pp. 218–21, and Magnus v. Levetzow, 'Kurze Aufzeichnung von Angaben, die der frühere deutsche Gesandte Herr von Treutler gelegentlich eines Besuches bei Guidotto [Henckel-Donnersmarck] in Egern am Juli 1928 gemacht hat' in MA Freiburg, Nl. Levetzow 82. My thanks to Dr Gerhard Granier for bringing the *Nachlass* to my attention.
187 Entry from 28.10.18, Müller, *Regierte der Kaiser?*, p. 440.
188 Grünau to Foreign Office, 15.12.18 (copy), pp. 10–11. This is his official report on the abdication. In MA Freiburg, Nl. Levetzow vol. 38.
189 Fürstenberg's diary of 8.11.18 in Spa. FFA Donaueschingen, Nl. Fürstenberg.
190 Grünau to Foreign Office, 15.12.18 (copy), p. 9, MA Freiburg, Nl. Levetzow 38.
191 Berg, *Erinnerungen*, pp. 196–7.
192 Grünau to Foreign Office, 15.12.18 (copy), pp. 21–2, MA Freiburg, Nl. Levetzow 38.
193 Groener memorandum of 1.6.22 in *ibid.*, 38/p. 224.
194 *Ibid.*, and Plessen's press release of 14.11.25 in MA Freiburg, Nl. Dommes vol. 18. See also note 199, below.
195 Nikolaus Graf zu Dohna-Schlodien, to Levetzow 19.10.? (copy), in MA Freiburg, Nl. Levetzow vol. 37, pp. 77–80; Sigurd v. Ilsemann Notes of 18.6.19 (copy 3), *ibid.*, vol. 37, and Georg Edler v. Hirschfeld 8.10.19 (copy), *ibid.*
196 Heinrich Scheüch to Schwertfeger, 17.12.27 in BA Koblenz, Nl. Schwertfeger 545.
197 Chancellor to Grünau, 30.10.18; Bussche to Grünau, 31.10.18; Solf to Grünau, 31.10.18; Wahnschaffe to Grünau, 8.11.18; Chancellor to Grünau 8.11. (Nr 1455); Chancellor to Grünau, 8.11.18 (not numbered), which arrived on 9.11.18; Solf to Grünau, 31.10.18. These are the most important telegrams. They are all in PA Bonn General Hauptquartier 36/Bd 4. See also Prince Max von Baden, *Erinnerungen und Dokumente* (Stuttgart, 1927), pp. 531, 535, 605, 613, 619, 625.
198 Bavarian Military Plenipotentiary to Bavarian War Minister, 1.11.18, in Deist, *Militär und Innenpolitik*, II, no. 500.
199 Plessen, Marschall, Schulenburg, 'Die Vorgänge des 9. November 1918 im Grossen Hauptquartier in Spa' (2nd copy), MA Freiburg, Nl. Levetzow 37/pp. 24–5.
200 *Ibid.*, pp. 25–6; and Grünau to Foreign Office, 15.12.18, pp. 16–17 (see note 190, above).
201 Max Prince von Baden, *Erinnerungen und Dokumente*, chs. 10–14.
202 Wilhelm Dommes Memorandum of 26.2.26, MA Freiburg, Nl. Dommes 18.
203 Plessen to Wilhelm, 6.1.27, *ibid.*

204 Compare Grünau's report (note 190) with Ilsemann's notes of 18.6.19 (note 195), with Plessen *et al.*, 'Die Vorgänge' (note 199), with the 'Ergänzungen' to 'Die Vorgänge,' signed by Hindenburg, Plessen, Marschall, Schulenburg, Gontard, and Niemann, undated, copy in MA Freiburg, Nl. Levetzow vol. 37.
205 Diary entry of 8.11.18, FFA Donaueschingen, Nl. Fürstenberg.
206 Groener Memorandum of 1.6.22, MA Freiburg, Nl. Levetzow 38/pp. 227–8.
207 See the sources cited above in notes 194, 195, 199, 202, 203 and 204.
208 Hirschfeld Letter of 8.10.19 in MA Freiburg, Nl. Levetzow 37/p. 83.
209 Wilhelm to Cramon, Postcard, 4.1.27, MA Freiburg, Nl. Cramon 34.
210 Ambassador Friedrich Rosen to Foreign Office, 17.11.18 (copy), BA Koblenz, Nl. Solf 128.

Chapter 11, pp. 293–306

1 See H. L. von Schweinitz's comment, cited above, pp. 176–7 and in Rudolf Schmidt-Bückeburg, *Das Militärkabinett der preussischen Könige und deutschen Kaiser. Seine geschichtliche Entwicklung und staatsrechtliche Stellung 1787–1918* (Berlin, 1933), pp. 157–8.
2 See Nikolaus von Preradovich, *Die Führungsschichten in Österreich und Preussen 1804–1918, mit einem Ausblick bis zum Jahre 1945* (Wiesbaden, 1955), and Lysbeth Walker Muncy, *The Junker in the Prussian Administration under William II, 1888–1914* (Providence, Rhode Island, 1944).
3 Baronin Spitzemberg, *Das Tagebuch der Baronin Spitzemberg. Aufzeichnungen aus der Hofgesellschaft des Hohenzollernreiches,* 4th edn, ed. Rudolf Vierhaus (Göttingen, 1976), p. 519.
4 Schmidt-Bückeburg, *Das Militärkabinett,* pp. 158–9.
5 See pp. 92–3.
6 Where Chelius had been Military Plenipotentiary at the outbreak of war.
7 Chelius to Fürstenberg, Berlin, 25.11.18, FFA Donaueschingen, Nl. Fürstenberg.

Bibliography

The historiography of the entourage of Kaiser Wilhelm II has until recently revolved around two issues: personal regime (the problem of whether or not Wilhelm ruled personally) and cabinet politics (the constitutional and political importance of the non-responsible royal cabinets). Erich Eyck, in *Das persönliche Regiment: politische Geschichte des Deutschen Kaiserreichs von 1890 bis 1914* (Erlenbach/Zürich, 1948), argued that Wilhelm had indeed ruled, but he did not present enough documentation to persuade his critics, who responded with a flood of articles which argued the opposite. Ernst Rudolf Huber's 'Das persönliche Regiment Wilhelms II,' *Zeitschrift für Religions- und Geistesgeschichte*, vol. 3 (1951) is probably the best of these early replies, although Fritz Hartung, 'Das persönliche Regiment Kaiser Wilhelms II,' *Sitzungsberichte der deutschen Akademie der Wissenschaften zu Berlin*, no. 3 (1952) is the most vociferous. In 1967 John C. G. Röhl came to Eyck's defense in an excellent, closely argued book, *Germany Without Bismarck: The Crisis of Government in the Second Reich* (London, 1967), which was based upon the voluminous papers of Wilhelm's closest friend and political adviser, Philipp zu Eulenburg. Many historians are still unable to accept the idea of personal regime, because they insist that Wilhelm had no basic plan and was in any case too unsteady to follow one consistently, despite Röhl's demonstration of the consistency underlying the political machinations in the 1890s. Others reject personal regime because they feel that history is the product of larger, mainly economic trends, which vastly overshadow the actions of individuals: thus, Hans-Ulrich Wehler, *Das Deutsche Kaiserreich 1871–1918* (Göttingen, 1973).

The scholarly products of the second line of inquiry, that of cabinet politics, have been less polemical. Heinrich Otto Meisner, 'Zur neueren Geschichte des preussischen Kabinetts,' *Forschungen zur brandenburgischen und preussischen Geschichte*, vol. 36 (1924), pp. 39–66 and 180–209, is still fresh and informative. It forms the basis for Heinrich Potthoff's good introduction to *Friedrich von Berg als Chef des Geheimen Zivilkabinetts 1918. Erinnerungen aus seinem Nachlass*, ed. Potthoff (Düsseldorf, 1971). Fritz Hartung's article, 'Verantwortliche Regierungen, Kabinette und Nebenregierungen im konstitutionellen Preussen 1848–1918,' *Forschungen zur brandenburgischen und preussischen Geschichte*, vol. 44 (1932), pp. 1–45 and 302–73, is now dated and interesting more as a collection of contemporary prejudices than as a scholarly work. The Military Cabinet found an excellent historian in Rudolf Schmidt-Bückeburg, author of *Das Militärkabinett der preussischen Könige und Deutschen Kaiser. Seine geschichtliche Entwicklung und staatsrechtliche Stellung, 1787–1918* (Berlin, 1933). This critical book is a wonderful source not only for the constitutional history of the Military Cabinet, but also for the subtle, political question of its overweening influence on policy making. The Naval Cabinet has not yet become the subject of such a study. In the meanwhile see Walther Hubatsch, *Der Admiralstab und die obersten Marinebehörden in Deutschland, 1848–1945* (Frankfurt, 1958), and Jonathan Steinberg, *Yesterday's Deterrent. Tirpitz and the Birth of the German Battle Fleet* (London, 1965) for brief descriptions of how the Naval Cabinet worked.

The Wilhelminians considered the entourage itself a fit object of study and debate, quite apart from the questions of personal regime or Cabinet politics. The theme runs through the memoir literature and is even the subject of whole books, such as Ernst Graf von Reventlow's tendentious *Kaiser Wilhelm II. und die Byzantiner* (Munich, 1906) and Dr Fritz Friedmann's gossipy but informative *Der deutsche Kaiser und die Hofkamarilla* (Zürich, 1896). Unfortunately, much of the material on the entourage written by contemporaries was published anonymously or pseudonymously and, even in cases where the authors could be verified, the rumor-ridden information which they repeated often cannot be. For these reasons, the major sources for this study have been primary ones.

Recently, some scholars have begun to focus on the entourage. The sociologist Norbert Elias has written *Die höfische Gesellschaft. Untersuchungen zur Soziologie des Königtums und der höfischen Aristokratie* (Neuwied/Berlin, 1969). This work concerns primarily the French aristocracy at court just prior to the French Revolution. Conditions both among the Junkers and at the German Court one hundred years later were so different from those in France in 1789 that Elias's book is frequently irrelevant to our concerns. This is regrettable, since Elias's study is intelligent. Dirk von Pezold studied the entourage for his dissertation, 'Cäsaromanie und Byzantinismus bei Wilhelm II' (Cologne, 1971). He did not use primary sources, nor did he consider aspects of the problem beyond those presented by the monarchical institutions. Ekkehard-Teja P. W. Wilke, *Political Decadence in Imperial Germany: Personnel-political Aspects of the German Government Crisis 1894–1897*, vol. 59 of the Illinois Studies in the Social Sciences (Urbana/Chicago/London, 1976) is a pedantic and unsuccessful attempt to argue against John Röhl's *Germany Without Bismarck*, using the same sources but without insight.

From this brief overview of the books directly and indirectly concerning the entourage, one can see that the best sources for such a study are primary ones: letters to and from the entourage members, their own diaries, or the reports of clever observers of the goings-on at Court. The most important single collection is the Eulenburg papers in the BA Koblenz. John C. G. Röhl is currently engaged in publishing the most important of these letters under the title *Philipp Eulenburgs politische Korrespondenz* (Boppard am Rhein, 1976–). Only the first two volumes had been published in time to be incorporated into the notes to this study. Friedrich von Holstein's *Nachlass* (PA Bonn) must be used to supplement the published edition of his papers, Norman Rich and M. H. Fisher (eds.), *Die geheimen Papiere Friedrich von Holsteins*, 4 vols. (Göttingen/Berlin/Frankfurt, 1956–63), which unaccountably omits important parts of letters exchanged by Holstein and Maximilian Harden, particularly concerning the Eulenburg scandal. Rich's edition, which is on the whole excel-

lent, is also weighted toward foreign policy at the expense of domestic policy,
and thus many letters to and from Holstein dealing with the entourage are
not included. Bernhard Bülow's papers (BA Koblenz) contain many letters
from Holstein and Eulenburg, as well as a wealth of other material. Another
civilian of interest to the historian of the entourage is Max Egon Fürst zu
Fürstenberg, whose papers lie, unordered, in the FFA in Donaueschingen.
Despite the fact that the papers were not preserved systematically, they are
most important because they contain letters from various members of the
entourage, from Wilhelm himself, from important Austrian officials, plus
Fürstenberg's sketchy diary. This collection represents practically the only
reliable information we possess about Fürstenberg.

The *Militärarchiv* (Freiburg i. Br.) houses numerous *Nachlässe* which have
some information on the entourage. By far the most important of these is the
diary of Georg Alexander von Müller, Chief of the Naval Cabinet. Alongside
Eulenburg's letters, the Müller diary is the best source on the Kaiser and his
entourage. Walter Görlitz has edited the diary into two volumes: *Regierte der
Kaiser? Kriegstagebücher, Aufzeichnungen und Briefe des Chefs des Marinekabinetts
Admiral Georg Alexander v. Müller, 1914–1918* (Göttingen/Berlin/Frankfurt,
1959) and *Der Kaiser . . . Aufzeichnungen des Chefs des Marinekabinetts Admiral
Georg Alexander v. Müller über die Ära Wilhelms II* (Göttingen/Berlin/
Frankfurt/Zürich, 1965). Unfortunately, Görlitz's transcription contains
numerous small misreadings and occasional deliberate falsifications of names
and facts (see John C. G. Röhl, 'Admiral von Müller and the Approach of
War, 1911–1914,' *The Historical Journal*, XII, 4 [1969], 651–73). In addition,
Der Kaiser, which covers the years prior to 1914, is much too thin to do the
diary justice. Anyone seriously interested in learning what Müller thought of
his surroundings must return to the original document. Gustav von Senden-
Bibran's papers, while not politically revealing, are nonetheless interesting
because they describe the daily routine at Court so well. The *Nachlässe* of
Adolf von Deines and Max von Mutius are both important from this regard.

It is fortunate for the historian that the Kaiser and his entourage were the
objects of the perceptive scrutiny of several contemporaries. One of these was
the Bavarian representative to Berlin, Hugo Graf von Lerchenfeld-Köfering.
His reports in the BGSA Munich are consistently astute and well-balanced.
They would have been more revealing still had he been less reticent about
sexual matters or perhaps more inclined to informed speculation. Five years
of his correspondence with Hertling has been published by Ernst Deuerlein
(ed.), *Briefwechsel Hertling–Lerchenfeld, 1912–1917. Dienstliche Privatkorrespondenz zwischen dem bayerischen Ministerpräsidenten Georg Graf von Hertling und dem
bayerischen Gesandten Hugo Graf von und zu Lerchenfeld*, 2 vols. (Boppard am
Rhein, 1973). Perhaps because he was a military man and therefore less
inclined to use diplomatic language, the reports of the Austrian Military Plenipotentiary in Berlin, Alois Frhr Klepsch-Kloth, are even more valuable than
those of Lerchenfeld. Klepsch-Kloth's reports and his memoirs are in the
ÖKrA Vienna. Axel von Varnbüler was Württemberg's diplomatic representative to Berlin from 1894 to 1918. Since he was also a close friend of Wilhelm's, Varnbüler's reports (in the HStA Stuttgart) often contain inside
information unavailable even to well-informed persons. Unlike Lerchenfeld,
Varnbüler did not shrink from including long-winded gossip in his baroque

messages to the Württemberg government. The British ambassadors seem to have been largely in the dark about how the German government was run, but the reports of their younger colleagues in Dresden and Munich (chiefly Cartwright and de Salis) are always intelligent and insightful.

Of the many memoirs of the period, the following are the most informative and the most reliable: Rudolf Vierhaus (ed.), *Das Tagebuch der Baronin Spitzemberg. Aufzeichnungen aus der Hofgesellschaft des Hohenzollernreiches* (Göttingen, 1960), for social matters; both Chlodwig Fürst zu Hohenlohe-Schillingsfürst, *Denkwürdigkeiten der Reichskanzlerzeit*, ed. Karl A. von Müller (Stuttgart, 1931), and Bogdan von Hutten-Czapski, *Sechzig Jahre Politik und Gesellschaft*, 2 vols. (Berlin, 1935) are indispensable for an understanding of high politics. Alfred Graf von Waldersee, *Denkwürdigkeiten des Generalfeldmarschalls*, ed. Heinrich Otto Meisner, 3 vols. (Stuttgart/Berlin, 1922–3) contains a wealth of information on the military entourage, especially at the beginning of Wilhelm's reign. Three inside members of the Kaiser's entourage have left us very good accounts of life and politics there: Karl-Heinz Janssen (ed.), *Die graue Exzellenz. Zwischen Staatsräson und Vasallentreue. Aus den Papieren des Kaiserlichen Gesandten Karl Georg von Treutler* (Frankfurt/Berlin/Vienna, 1971), Robert von Zedlitz-Trützschler, *Zwölf Jahre am deutschen Kaiserhof* (Berlin, 1924), and Bernhard Schwertfeger (ed.), *Kaiser und Kabinettschef, nach eigenen Aufzeichnungen und dem Briefwechsel des Wirklichen Geheimen Rats Rudolf von Valentini* (Oldenbourg, 1931). For a good overview of the personages of the Court and the way in which it functioned see Herzogin Viktoria Luise, *Im Glanz der Krone. Erinnerungen* (Munich, 1975). Three other books by entourage members are generally valuable, but each is less revealing than one would like: Hugo Frhr von Reischach, *Unter drei Kaisern* (Berlin, 1925), Carl Graf von Wedel, *Zwischen Kaiser und Kanzler. Aufzeichnungen aus den Jahren 1890–1894*, ed. Erhardt Graf von Wedel (Leipzig, 1943), and Helmuth von Moltke's heavily edited but nonetheless interesting *Erinnerungen, Briefe, Dokumente 1877–1916* (Stuttgart, 1922).

Since the men of the entourage were primarily nobles and officers, the scholarship concerning these two groups helps explain the attitudes and preoccupations of the entourage. Unfortunately there is no thorough, scholarly treatment of the Prussian nobility which combines economic, political, demographic, and social dimensions. Until such a book exists, one must be content with Walter Görlitz's, *Die Junker: Adel und Bauer im deutschen Osten. Geschichtliche Bilanz von sieben Jahrhunderten*, 3rd rev. edn (Limburg, 1964). Two older, but still useful studies handle the activities of the Junkers in the bureaucracy: Lysbeth Walker Muncy, *The Junker in the Prussian Administration under William II 1888–1918* (Providence, Rhode Island, 1944), and Nikolaus von Preradovich, *Die Führungsschichten in Österreich und Preussen, 1804–1918* (Wiesbaden, 1955). On the recruitment of new nobles see Lamar Cecil, 'The Creation of Nobles in Prussia, 1871–1918,' *American Historical Review*, vol. 75, no. 3 (Feb. 1970), pp. 757–95. Otto Graf zu Stolberg-Wernigerode's *Die unentschiedene Generation: Deutschlands konservative Führungsschichten am Vorabend des ersten Weltkrieges* (Munich/Vienna, 1968) is an idiosyncratic, but highly interesting and suggestive account of the attitudes of the Wilhelminian establishment before the war.

The most famous historical treatment of the German army is Gerhard Ritter's *The Sword and the Scepter, The Problem of Militarism in Germany,* 4 vols., trans. Heinz Norden (Coral Gables, Florida, 1969–73), of which the second volume treats the prewar Wilhelminian period. Both Wiegand Schmidt-Richberg, *Von der Entlassung Bismarcks bis zum Ende des Ersten Weltkrieges (1890–1918)*, vol. 5 of the Handbuch der deutschen Militärgeschichte, 1648–1939 (Frankfurt, 1969), and Martin Kitchen, *The German Officer Corps, 1890–1914* (Oxford, 1968), are disappointing volumes because they are neither critical nor analytical enough. Fortunately Manfred Messerschmidt, *Handbuch zur Militärgeschichte, 1814–1890*, vol. 4 (Munich, 1975) and his *Militär und Politik in der Bismarckzeit und im Wilhelminischen Deutschland*, vol. 43 of the Erträge der Forschung (Darmstadt, 1975), as well as Wilhelm Deist's article, 'Die Armee in Staat und Gesellschaft, 1890–1914,' in Michael Stürmer (ed.), *Das kaiserliche Deutschland* (Düsseldorf, 1970), pp. 312–39, more than fill the gaps left by Kitchen and Schmidt-Richberg. Holger Herwig's book, *The German Naval Officers Corps: A Social and Political History, 1890–1918* (Oxford, 1973), handles that subject well.

There are four works which are simply indispensable for an understanding of the *Weltanschauung* and social position of the officer in German society, and which, hence, formed the background of the chapters on the military entourage. The most famous of these works is Karl Demeter's *Das deutsche Offizierkorps in Gesellschaft und Staat, 1650–1945* (Frankfurt, 1962), which is a wonderful social history of the corps based upon sources which were destroyed during World War II. Hermann Rumschöttel is an able young successor to Demeter. His *Das bayerische Offizierkorps, 1866–1914*, vol. 9 of the Beiträge zu einer historischen Strukturanalyse Bayerns im Industriezeitalter (Berlin, 1973), is a model of careful scholarship in primary sources combined with analysis and imagination. The acerbic contemporary critic, Franz Carl Endres, wrote an essay in 1927 which is still fresh, exciting and suggestive, 'Soziologische Struktur und ihre entsprechende Ideologien des deutschen Offizierkorps vor dem ersten Weltkriege,' *Archiv für Sozialwissenschaft*, vol. 58 (1927), pp. 282–319. Finally, one primary source which no one who is interested in the officer corps can afford to ignore is the famous manual for young officers written by the Freiherr von Knigge of the corps, Camill Schaible, *Standes- und Berufspflichten des deutschen Offiziers. Für angehende und jüngere Offiziere des stehenden Heeres und des Beurlaubtenstandes*, 3rd edn (Berlin, 1896).

There are several good articles, but no single, all-inclusive volume to which the historian might turn, who seeks to map the mentality of the entourage or of the Wilhelminian establishment. Volker Berghahn has done the best job so far. See the many pointed psychological insights he makes in his article, 'Zu den Zielen des deutschen Flottenbaus unter Wilhelm II.,' *Historische Zeitschrift*, vol. 210 (1970), pp. 34–100, and his excellent interpretive overview *Germany and the Approach of War in 1914* (London, 1973). In ' "Neujahr 1900" Die Säkularwende in zeitgenössischer Sicht,' *Archiv für Kulturgeschichte*, vol. 53, no. 2 (1972), pp. 335–81, Michael Salewski draws clever conclusions from the ways in which the Germans celebrated the dawn of the new century. Eberhard Kessel, in 'Zur inneren Entwicklung Deutschlands unter Wilhelm II und in der Weimarer Republik: Ein Literaturbericht,' *Archiv für Kulturgeschichte*, no. 2 (1962), pp. 253–80, discusses the memoir and diary literature well, but one wishes he had been more synthetic in his analysis of the meaning of what he has found. Similarly, Georg Steinhausen, 'Verfalls-stimmung im kaiserlichen Deutschland,' *Preussische Jahrbücher,* vol. 194 (1923), pp. 153–85, attempts too much and leaves the reader unsatisfied. Ludwig Dehio has a number of intelligent comments upon the Wilhelminians' pessimism in his article, 'Gedanken über die deutsche Sendung, 1900–1918,' *Historische Zeitschrift,* vol. 174 (1952), trans. Dieter Pevsner and reprinted in Ludwig Dehio, *Germany and World Politics in the Twentieth Century* (New York, 1967), pp. 72–108.

The following pages list all of the primary sources consulted for this project and all secondary sources cited in the notes.

I. Unpublished sources

1 Geheimes Staatsarchiv Preussischer Kulturbesitz, Berlin-Dahlem, Nachlässe:
Leo von Caprivi
Theodor Schiemann

2 Politisches Archiv des Auswärtigen Amtes (PA), Bonn
Deutschland 121 Angelegenheiten der deutschen Armee, vols. 1–18
     121 *secr.* Angelegenheiten der deutschen Armee, vols. 1–2
     121 Nr 7   *secr.* Personalien von Offizieren und Beamten, vols. 1–7 and 3a.
     121 Nr 24 *secr.* Die deutsche Militärstrafprozessordnung, vols. 1–7
     122 Nr 2F Staatssekretär Bernhard von Bülow, 1897–1900, vols. 1–4
     122 Nr 2H Staatssekretär Heinrich von Tschirschky, 1906–1907
     122 Nr 3B Prozess Leckert–Lützow–Tausch, 1896–1913, vols. 1–3
     122 Nr 3G Harden und *Die Zukunft,* 1891–1919, vols. 1–4
     122 Nr 8   Reichskanzler Caprivi, 1890–1894, vols. 1–4
     122 Nr 10 General von Wedel, 1891–1920
     134 *secr.* Geheime Berichte des Reichskanzlers an Seine Majestät, 1886–1906
     149 Nr 2   Behandlung der beim Auswärtigen Amt eingehenden Militär- und Marineberichte (1896–1917)
Preussen I Nr. 1d Kaiser Wilhelm II, 1888–1920, vols. 1–28
    I Nr 1d *secr.* Kaiser Wilhelm II, 1888–1919, vols. 1–5
    I Nr 3L   Korrespondenz Wilhelms II mit dem Grossherzog von Baden, 1888–1917
    I Nr 4K   Korrespondenz Wilhelms II mit dem Grossherzog von Baden, 1888–1917, vols. 1–2
Württemberg 35 *secr.* Militärische Angelegenheiten, 1890–1895, vols. 1–4
England 78 Nr 2 *secr. Daily-Telegraph*-Affaire, vols. 1–5
     78 Nr 2 *secretiss. Daily-Telegraph*-Affaire, vols. 1–2
Österreich 90 Das diplomatische Corps in Wien, 1892–1903, vols. 2–4
Generalhauptquartier 36 Seine Majestät, 1915–1919, vols. 1–4
Nachlass: Friedrich von Holstein

3 Hessisches Staatsarchiv, Darmstadt
Nachlass: Emil Graf von Schlitz genannt von Görtz

4 Fürstlich Fürstenbergisches Archiv, Donaueschingen
Nachlass: Maximilian Egon II Fürst zu Fürstenberg

5 Historisches Archiv der Fried. Krupp GmbH, Essen
Nachlass: Friedrich Alfred Krupp

6 Bundesarchiv-Militärarchiv (MA), Freiburg i. Br.

Kaiserliches Marinekabinett (RM2)
RM2 vol. 1 Errichtung, Zuständigkeit und Geschäftsgang des Marinekabinetts (1888–1918)
RM2   9 Personalangelegenheiten der Offiziere, Beamten und Mannschaften des Marinekabinetts (1913–1918)
RM2 10–15 Allgemeine Personalien d. Offiziere des Marinekabinetts
RM2 57–60 Schriftwechsel und Unterlagen zu Vorträgen und Audienzen bei S.M. (1889–1918)
RM2   61–64 Übersicht über Besichtigungen von Truppenteilen des Garde-Korps (1891–1912)
RM2   72–74 Flügeladjutanten, persönliche Adjutanten und Militär-Gouverneure (1889–1918)
RM2   75–76 Vertretung d. Kaisers und Königs bei Feierlichkeiten (1894–1913)
RM2   77–79 Bestimmungen über Paraden, Paroleausgaben, Geburtstagsfeier des Kaisers und bei Hofempfängen (1889–1917)
RM2   80–82 Bestimmungen über Jubiläumsfeiern, Fahnen- und Kirchenweihen (1897–1915)
RM2   83–84 Jubiläen in der kaiserlichen Marine (1894–1919)
RM2   85–88 Gedenktafeln, Gedenkblätter und Denkmäler (1894–1917)
RM2   89–93 Teilnahme Kaiser Wilhelms II. an Rekrutenvereidigungen (1900–1914)
RM2   94–108 Herbstmanöver von Armee und Marine (1894–1914)
RM2   114 Vortrag Kaiser Wilhelms II. an der Kreigsakademie über den Ausbau der deutschen Flotte (8.2.94)
RM2   115 Konzepte zum Vortrag von 8.2.94
RM2   116 Schiffspredigten (1896–1908)
RM2   117 Akten gemischten Inhalts über persönliche Angelegenheiten Kaiser Wilhelms II. (1899–1912)
RM2   118–119 Schriftwechsel Kaiser Wilhelms II. (1887–1919)
RM2   120 Schriftwechsel Kaiser Wilhelms II. und Lord Salisbury (1893)
RM2   121 Briefen des Vizeadmiral Heinrich Prinz von Preussen an Kaiser Wilhelm II. aus Ostasien (1897–1900)
RM2   122 Briefe von König Wilhelm von Württemberg an Kaiser Wilhelm II.
RM2   123 Montagu Briefe 1901–1913
RM2   150–159 Bücher und Schrifte für Seine Majestät (1.1903–12.1918)
RM2   226 Silberhochzeit des Kaiserpaares (1905–1912)

RM2   227 25 Jähriges Regierungsjubiläum des Kaisers an 15.6.13 (1912–1914)

RM2   228 Bau der kaiserlichen Jacht *Hohenzollern* (1889–1893)

RM2   230–236 Indiensthaltung der kaiserlichen Jacht und ihrer Begleitschiffe

RM2   237–257 Erwerb und Indiensthaltung der privaten Segeljachten des Kaisers (1891–1908)

RM2   258–259 Kosten derselben (1891)

RM2   280 Kosten derselben (1901)

RM2   304–320 Bau und Indiensthaltung der kaiserlichen Privatjacht *Meteor III* (1901–1910)

RM2   321–331 Bau und Indiensthaltung der kaiserlichen Privatjacht *Meteor IV* (1908–1914)

RM2   332–333 Bau und Indiensthaltung der kaiserlichen Privatjacht *Meteor V* (1913–1919)

RM2   334 Instruktionen für den Führer der kaiserlichen Privatjacht *Meteor*

RM2   335 Schiffsführer der kaiserlichen Privatjacht *Meteor* (1906–1918)

RM2   336–339 Indiensthaltung der kaiserlichen Privatjacht *Iduna*

RM2   340–342 Indiensthaltung der kaiserlichen Privatjachten *Samoa I, II, III* und *Niagara* (1899–1912)

RM2   351 Miete fremder Jachten für Kaiser Wilhelm II. (1902–1903)

RM2   353 Reisedaten des Kaisers 1889–1913

RM2   354 Verzeichnis der Reisen Kaiser Wilhelms II. zur Begegnung mit fremden Monarchen 1908

RM2   365 Kaiser Reisen

RM2   367–381 Kaiser Reisen

RM2   386 Kaiser Reisen

RM2   394 Kaiser Reisen

RM2   395–396 Akten gemischten Inhalts über persönlichen Angelegenheiten des Prinzen Friedrich Wilhelms (1900–1918)

RM2   397–406 Akten gemischten Inhalts über persönlichen Angelegenheiten des Prinzen Heinrich

RM2   470 Personalbogenbestimmungen über das Offizierskorps der kaiserlichen Marine (1902–1918)

RM2   476 Bestimmungen über Offizierpatente (1854–1918)

RM2   528–529 Adelsprädikate der Eingestellten Seekadetten (1891–1918)

RM2   530–531 Bestimmungen über Offizierbeförderungen (1890–1918)

RM2   833 Auszüge aus den Qualifikationsberichten der Kapitäne zur See von 1.12.06–1.12.17.

RM2   965–971 Attachés bei deutschen Botschaften und Gesandtschaften

RM2   1934 Kieler Woche 1907

RM2   1940 Kieler Woche 1914

RM2   1941 Kieler Woche 1915

RM2   1942 Kieler Woche 1916

RM2 2006–2007 Personalakte-Capelle

RM2   2009 Personalakte-Hollmann

RM2   2010 Personalakte-Hintze

RM2   2014 Personalakte-Karl Müller

RM2   2015 Personalakte-Pohl

RM2   2018 Kosten des Erwerbs und der Indiensthaltung der privaten
                 Segeljachten des Kaisers (1911)
RM2   2019 Personalakte-Scheer
RM2   2021 Personalakte-Trotha
RM2   2030 Personalakte-Galster
RM2   2031 Personalakte-Hintze
RM2 2036–2037 Personalakte-Ingenohl
RM2 2040–2041 Personalakte-Ritter von Mann
RM2   2055 Personalakte-Zeye
RM2 Shelf Nr 3682, VII 2–14 Ehrengerichtliche Angelegenheiten (1905–1911)
RM2 Shelf Nr 3682, VII 2–15 Orden und Ehrenzeichen
RM2 Shelf Nr 3683, VII 2–16 Allerhöchste Kabinettsordres
RM2 Shelf Nr 3683, VII 2–17 Allerhöchste Kabinettsordres

Reichsmarineamt (RM3)
RM3 2732   Ehrengerichtliche Angelegenheiten (4.13–12.16)
RM3 10119   Anzug und Verhalten der Offiziere und Mannschaf-
                     ten in Berlin (1899–1919)
RM3 10211–10214   Marine Attachés (1899–1917)
RM3 10217   Marine Attachés
RM3 MGFA DZI M46 vols. 24–25 Personalakte-Rebeur-Paschwitz
RM3 MGFA DZI M46 vol. 33   Personalakte-Usedom
RM3 832 D vols. 313–314   Allerhöchste Kabinettsordres
                            (4.05–17.9.17)

Kaiserliches Oberkommando der Marine (RM4)
RM4 vol. 24 Organization der Marine-Kabinett
RM4   36 Instruktionen für Marine- und Militär-Attachés

Admiralstab der Marine (RM5)
RM5 vols. 132–134 Allerhöchste Dispositionsfond
RM5   287–288   Marine- und Militär-attachés (1903–1918)
RM5   290–303   Allerhöchste Kabinettsordres (1899–1918)
RM5   559   Offizielle Besuche und Etikette (1900–1918)
RM5   940–941   Marine- und Militärattachés (1902–1919)
RM5   5307   Immediatvorträge (7.1905–1.1915)

Nachlässe:
     Paul Behncke
     Wilhelm von Büchsel
     Edward von Capelle
     August von Cramon
     Adolf von Deines
     Wilhelm von Dommes
     Hans-Hubert von Durant de Sénégas
     Heinrich von Gossler
     Konrad von Gossler
     Wilhelm von Hahnke
     Adolf Wild von Hohenborn

Magnus von Levetzow
Helmuth von Moltke (the younger)
Kurt von Morgen
Georg von Müller
Max von Mutius
Alfred von Schlieffen
Friedrich von der Schulenburg-Tressow
Gustav von Senden-Bibran
Alfred von Tirpitz
Detlof von Winterfeldt

7 *Bundesarchiv (BA), Koblenz*
Nachlässe:
Max Bauer
Otto von Bismarck
Karl Heinrich von Bötticher
Bernhard von Bülow
Philipp zu Eulenburg-Hertefeld
Johannes Haller
Maximilian Harden
Chlodwig zu Hohenlohe-Schillingsfürst
Eberhard von Schmettau
Bernard Schwertfeger
Wilhelm Solf
Friedrich Thimme
Rudolf von Valentini

Kleine Erwerbungen:
Wilhelm Dörpfeld
Georg Graf von Hülsen
Wilhelm II

8 *Bayerisches Geheimes Staatsarchiv (BGSA), Munich*

Gesandtschaft Berlin vols. 1058–1096 Politische Berichte und Instruktionen, teilweise Politische Akten, besonders Berichte

MA I 697	Stellung des Reichskanzlers beim Kaiser, 1905
MA I 698	Bericht aus 28.3.03 über Berlin
MA I 699	Aussöhnung zwischen dem Kaiser und Reichskanzler Bülow, 1909
MA I 700	Unterredung zwischen Podewils und Bülow, 1908
MA I 739	Beschwerde Philipp zu Eulenburgs über Presseangriffe, 1894
MA I 865	Deutscher Botschafter in Wien, 1894
MA I 995	Lerchenfeld- private politische Berichte an den Staatsminister Graf Hertling
MA I 957a–957b	Diplomatische Korrespondenz zwischen Lerchenfeld und Hertling

MA I 958   Diplomatische Korrespondenz zwischen Lerchenfeld und
                        Hertling
MA I 959–960   Politischer Briefwechsel mit Hertling
MA I 970   Konflikte zwischen oberster Heeresleitung und Reichs-
                        leitung
MA I 973   Abdankung des Kaisers
MA I 76032   Kaiserrede in Döberitz
MA I 76075–76076 Kaiserreden, 1899–1918
MA I 76129   Hohenlohe wird Reichskanzler
MA I 76135   Bülow wird Reichskanzler
MA I 76140   Bülows Krankheit, 1906
MA I 76145   Bethmann Hollweg wird Reichskanzler
MA I 95310   Philipp zu Eulenburg: Erhebung in den Fürstenstand,
                        Feier der silbernen Hochzeit, strafrechtliche Untersu-
                        chung, 1900–1909

9 Hauptstaatsarchiv (HStA), Stuttgart

Ministerium der auswärtigen Angelegenheiten III:
   E-46 Hauptfaszikel IV 1202 Militärbevollmächtigter, 1867–1910
   E-46   V 1204–1205 Ernennungen der Gesandter
   E-46   V 1206 Prozesssachen Axel von Varnbüler, 1909–1916
   E-46   III 1066, 1067 Familien Angelegenheiten des preus-
                        sischen Hauses
   E-73 Verz. 61 vols. 12c–12i Gesandtschaft Berlin
Nachlässe:
   Conrad Haussmann
   Axel von Varnbüler

10 Österreichisches Haus- Hof- und Staatsarchiv (ÖStA), Vienna

Politisches Archiv des Ministeriums des Äussern (PA):
   PA III Preussen 144–171 Berichte, Weisungen und Varia (1897–1915)
   PA IV Bayern   55–56   Berichte, Weisungen und Varia (1907–1910)
Nachlass: Franz Ferdinand

11 Österreichisches Kriegsarchiv (ÖKrA), Vienna

Chef des Generalstabs 1898–1912 25
Militär Kanzlei Seiner Majestät Sep. Fasz. 69 Nr 6/2 and 6/3
                                  Sep. Fasz. 78 Nr 33
                                  Sep. Fasz. 79 Nr 9, Nr 42
                                  Fasz. 600
Militär Attaché Berlin vols. 5–9 (1897–1915)
                        Fasz. 10–14 (1897–1915)
Nachlässe:
   Arthur von Bolfras
   Alois Klepsch-Kloth von Roden
   Karl Steininger

12 *Public Record Office, London (PRO)*

Foreign Office (FO 371)
FO 371 vols.   75–80   1906 Germany
FO 371   257–263 1907 Germany
FO 371   457–463 1908 Germany
FO 371   670–677 1909 Germany
FO 371   901–907 1910 Germany
FO 371   1121–1129 1911 Germany
FO 371   1370–1379 1912 Germany
FO 371   1647–1654 1913 Germany

13 *In the possession of John C. G. Röhl, Sussex*

From Philipp zu Eulenburg's Papers:
   'Reisen mit dem Kaiser,' 4 vols.
   'Drei Freunde'
   'Aufzeichnungen des Fürsten Philipp zu Eulenburg-Hertefeld'
   'Freundschaft und Kaisertum'

14 *Houghton Library, Harvard University, Cambridge, Massachusetts Waldersee–
Lee Papers*

15 *Sterling Memorial Library, Yale University, New Haven, Connecticut Kiderlen-
Wächter Papers*

II. Published sources

A. Periodicals
   Die Norddeutsche Allgemeine Zeitung
   Die Zukunft

B. Books, articles and dissertations
Baernreither, Joseph M. *Verfall des Habsburgerreiches und die Deutschen. Fragmente eines politischen Tagebuches, 1897–1917*. Edited by Oskar Mitis. Vienna, 1939
Balfour, Michael. *The Kaiser and His Times*. New York, 1974 (1964)
Barkin, Kenneth. *The Controversy over German Industrialization, 1890–1902*. Chicago, 1970
Baumann, Jürgen. *Paragraph 175*. Berlin/Neuwied, 1968
Baumont, Maurice. *L'Affaire Eulenburg*. Geneva, 1973, revised from the 1933 edition
Berghahn, Volker. *Germany and the Approach of War in 1914*. London, 1973
   Der Tirpitz-Plan. Genesis und Verfall einer innenpolitischen Krisenstrategie unter Wilhelm II. Düsseldorf, 1971
   'Zu den Zielen des deutschen Flottenbaus unter Wilhelm II.' *Historische Zeitschrift*, vol. 210 (1970), pp. 34–100
Bismarck, Otto von. *Gedanken und Erinnerungen*. 3 vols. Stuttgart/Berlin, 1921

Boelcke, Willi (ed.). *Krupp und die Hohenzollern. Krupp-Korrespondenz mit Kaisern, Kabinettschefs und Ministern 1850–1918.* Frankfurt, 1970

Brouczek, Peter. 'Der k.u.k. Delegierte im Deutschen Grossen Hauptquartier Generalmajor Alois Klepsch-Kloth von Roden und seine Berichterstattung 1915/1916.' *Militärgeschichtliche Mitteilungen,* 1/74 (1974), pp. 109–26

Bunsen, Marie von. *Zeitgenossen die ich erlebte, 1900–1930.* Leipzig, 1932

Bussmann, Walter (ed.). *Staatssekretär Graf Herbert von Bismarck. Aus seiner politischen Privatkorrespondenz.* Deutsche Geschichtsquellen des 19. und 20. Jahrhunderts herausgegeben von der Historischen Kommission bei der Bayerischen Akademie der Wissenschaften, Bd 44. Göttingen, 1964

Cecil, Lamar. *Albert Ballin, Business and Politics in Imperial Germany, 1888–1918.* Princeton, New Jersey, 1967

'The Creation of Nobles in Prussia, 1871–1918.' *American Historical Review,* vol. 75, no. 3 (February, 1970), pp. 757–95

The German Diplomatic Service, 1870–1914. Princeton, New Jersey, 1976

Chamberlain, Houston Stuart. *Briefe.* Munich, 1928

Die Grundlagen des Neunzehnten Jahrhunderts. 2 vols. Munich, 1899

Clapham, J.H. *The Economic Development of France and Germany, 1815–1914.* Cambridge, 1966

Clausewitz, Carl von. *On War.* Edited by Anatol Rapoport. London, 1968

Conrad von Hötzendorf, Franz. *Aus meiner Dienstzeit, 1906–1918.* 7 vols. Vienna/Berlin/Leipzig/Munich, 1921–1925

Craig, Gordon. *The Politics of the Prussian Army, 1640–1945.* New York, 1955

Czedik von Bründlsberg und Eysenberg, Alois Frhr. *Zur Geschichte der k. k. österreichischen Ministerien, 1861–1916.* 4 vols. Teschen/Vienna/Leipzig, 1920

Dehio, Ludwig. 'Gedanken über die deutsche Sendung, 1900–1918.' *Historische Zeitschrift,* vol. 174 (1952). Translated by Dieter Pevsner and reprinted in Ludwig Dehio, *Germany and World Politics in the Twentieth Century.* New York, 1967, pp. 72–108

Deist, Wilhelm. 'Die Armee in Staat and Gesellschaft, 1890–1914.' In *Das kaiserliche Deutschland,* edited by Michael Stürmer. Düsseldorf, 1970

Flottenpolitik und Flottenpropaganda. Das Nachrichtenbureau des Reichsmarineamtes, 1897–1914. Stuttgart, 1976

'Kaiser Wilhelm II in the Context of his Military Entourage.' In *Kaiser Wilhelm II: New Interpretations,* edited by John C. G. Röhl and Nicolaus Sombart. Cambridge, 1981

(ed.). *Militär und Innenpolitik im Weltkrieg, 1914–1918.* 2 vols. Düsseldorf, 1970

Demeter, Karl. *Das deutsche Offizierkorps in Gesellschaft und Staat, 1650–1945.* Frankfurt, 1962

Deuerlein, Ernst (ed.). *Briefwechsel Hertling–Lerchenfeld, 1912–1917. Dienstliche Privatkorrespondenz zwischen dem bayerischen Ministerpräsidenten Georg Graf von Hertling und dem bayerischen Gesandten Hugo Graf von und zu Lerchenfeld.* 2 vols. Boppard am Rhein, 1973

Duggan, P. Robert. 'Currents of Administrative Reform in Germany, 1907–1918.' Dissertation, Harvard, 1969

Ehrl, Oskar. 'The Development of the German Military Criminal Procedure during the 19th Century.' *Revue de Droit Pénal Militaire et de Droit de la Guerre*, VII, 2 (1968), pp. 241–50

Einem, Karl von. *Kriegsminister unter Wilhelm II. Erinnerungen eines Soldaten, 1853–1933.* Leipzig, 1933

Elias, Norbert. *Die höfische Gesellschaft. Untersuchungen zur Soziologie des Königtums und der höfischen Aristokratie.* Neuwied/Berlin, 1969

Endler, Renate. 'Nachlässe in der Historischen Abteilung II des Deutschen Zentralarchivs.' *Zeitschrift für Geschichtswissenschaft*, XX, 9 (1972), pp. 1160–5

Endres, Franz Carl. 'Soziologische Struktur und ihre entsprechende Ideologien des deutschen Offizierkorps vor dem ersten Weltkriege.' *Archiv für Sozialwissenschaft*, vol. 58 (1927), pp. 282–319

Engelmann, Bernt. *Krupp. Legenden und Wirklichkeit.* Munich, 1969

Eulenburg, Philipp zu. 'Aus der Art.' *Nord und Süd*, XXVIII, 83 (Feb. 1884), pp. 147–70

Aus fünfzig Jahren. Erinnerungen, Tagebücher und Briefe aus dem Nachlass des Fürsten. Edited by Johannes Haller. Berlin, 1923

Aus dem Leben des Fürsten Philipp zu Eulenburg-Hertefeld. Edited by Johannes Haller. Berlin/Leipzig, 1926

Fünf Jahre der Freundschaft. n.p., 1897

Mit dem Kaiser als Staatsmann und Freund auf Nordlandreisen. 2 vols. Dresden, 1931

Eyck, Erich. *Das persönliche Regiment: politische Geschichte des Deutschen Kaiserreichs von 1890 bis 1914.* Erlenbach/Zürich, 1948

Fischer, Fritz. *War of Illusion: German Policies from 1911 to 1914.* New York, 1975. German original, 1969

Franke, Lydia. 'Die Randbemerkungen Wilhelms II. in den Akten der auswärtigen Politik als historische und psychologische Quelle.' Dissertation, Berlin, 1932

Fricke, Dieter. 'Die Affäre Leckert–Lützow–Tausch und die Regierungskrise von 1897 in Deutschland.' *Zeitschrift für Geschichtswissenschaft*, VIII (1960), 1579–1603

Friedmann, Fritz. *Der deutsche Kaiser und die Hofkamarilla.* Zürich, 1896

Friedrich von Berg als Chef des Geheimen Zivilkabinetts 1918. Erinnerungen aus seinem Nachlas. Edited by Heinrich Potthoff. Düsseldorf, 1971

Galbreath, Robert Carroll. 'Spiritual Science in an Age of Materialism: Rudolf Steiner and Occultism.' Dissertation, University of Michigan, 1970

Gasser, Adolf. 'Der deutsche Hegemonialkrieg von 1914.' In *Deutschland in der Weltpolitik des 19. und 20. Jahrhunderts*, edited by Imanuel Geiss and Bernd-Jürgen Wendt, pp. 307–39. Düsseldorf, 1973

'Deutschlands Entschluss zum Präventivkrieg 1913/14.' In *Discordia Concors. Festgabe für Edgar Bonjour zu seinem siebzigsten Geburtstag am 21. August 1968*, edited by Marc Sieber, I, 173–224. 2 vols. Basel/Stuttgart, 1968

Gatzke, Hans W. *Germany's Drive to the West.* Baltimore, 1966 (originally, 1950)

Geiss, Imanuel (ed.). *July 1914: The Outbreak of the First World War. Selected Documents.* New York, 1967. German original, 1965

Geiss, Imanuel and Wendt, Bernd-Jürgen (eds.). *Deutschland in der Weltpolitik des 19. und 20. Jahrhunderts.* Düsseldorf, 1973

Geyer, Michael. 'Die Geschichte des deutschen Militärs von 1860 bis 1945.

Ein Bericht über die internationalen Forschungslage (1945–1975).' In *Die moderne deutsche Geschichte in der internationalen Forschung, 1945–1975,* edited by Hans-Ulrich Wehler. Göttingen, 1978

Giessler, Klaus-Volker. *Die Institution des Marineattachés im Kaiserreich.* Wehrwissenschaftliche Forschungen, vol. 21. Boppard am Rhein, 1976

Görlitz, Walter. *Die Junker: Adel und Bauer im deutschen Osten. Geschichtliche Bilanz von sieben Jahrhunderten.* 3rd rev. edn Limburg, 1964

(ed.). *Der Kaiser . . . Aufzeichnungen des Chefs des Marinekabinetts Admiral Georg Alexander v. Müller über die Ära Wilhelms II.* Göttingen/Berlin/Frankfurt/Zürich, 1965

(ed.). *Regierte der Kaiser? Kriegstagebücher, Aufzeichnungen und Briefe des Chefs des Marinekabinetts Admiral Georg Alexander v. Müller, 1914–1918.* Göttingen/Berlin/Frankfurt, 1959

Groener, Wilhelm. *Lebenserinnerungen. Jugend, Generalstab, Weltkrieg.* Göttingen, 1957

Groh, Dieter. ' "Je eher, desto besser!" Innenpolitische Faktoren für die Präventivkriegsbereitschaft des Deutschen Reiches 1913/14.' *Politische Vierteljahresschrift,* vol. 13 (1972), pp. 501–21

Haller, Johannes. 'Bülow und Eulenburg.' In *Front Wider Bülow: Staatsmänner, Diplomaten und Forscher zu seinen Denkwürdigkeiten,* edited by Friedrich Thimme. Munich, 1931

Harden, Maximilian. *Köpfe.* 3 vols. Berlin, 1913

Hartung, Fritz. 'Das persönliche Regiment Kaiser Wilhelms II.' *Sitzungsberichte der deutschen Akademie der Wissenschaften zu Berlin,* no. 3 (1952)

'Verantwortliche Regierungen, Kabinette und Nebenregierungen in konstitutionellen Preussen 1848–1918.' *Forschungen zur brandenburgischen und preussischen Geschichte,* vol. 44 (1932), pp. 1–45 and 302–73

Hemleben, Johannes. *Rudolf Steiner in Selbstzeugnissen und Bilddokumenten.* Reinbek bei Hamburg, 1974

Herwig, Holger. *The German Naval Officers Corps: A Social and Political History, 1890–1918.* Oxford, 1973

Hildebrand, Klaus. *Bethmann Hollweg der Kanzler ohne Eigenschaften? Urteile der Geschichtsschreibung. Eine kritische Bibliographie.* Düsseldorf, 1970

Hoffmann, Walther G., *et al. Das Wachstum der deutschen Wirtschaft.* Heidelberg, 1965

Hohenlohe-Schillingsfürst, Chlodwig Fürst zu. *Denkwürdigkeiten der Reichskanzlerzeit.* Edited by Karl A. von Müller. Stuttgart, 1931

Hubatsch, Walther. *Der Admiralstab und die obersten Marinebehörden in Deutschland, 1848–1945.* Frankfurt, 1958

Huber, Ernst R. *Deutsche Verfassungsgeschichte seit 1789.* vol. 4, *Struktur und Krisen des Kaiserreichs.* Stuttgart/Berlin/Cologne/Mainz, 1969

'Das persönliche Regiment Wilhelms II.' *Zeitschrift für Religions-und Geistesgeschichte,* vol. 3 (1951)

Huldermann, Bernhard. *Albert Ballin.* Translated by W. J. Rogers. London, 1922

Hutten-Czapski, Bogdan von. *Sechzig Jahre Politik und Gesellschaft.* 2 vols. Berlin, 1935

Ilsemann, Sigurd von. *Der Kaiser in Holland. Aufzeichnungen aus den Jahren 1918–1941.* Munich, 1971

Jäckh, Ernst (ed.). *Alfred von Kiderlen-Wächter. Briefwechsel und Nachlass.* 2 vols. Berlin, 1925

Jaeger, Hans. *Unternehmer in der deutschen Politik, 1890–1914.* Bonn, 1967

Janssen, Karl-Heinz (ed.). *Die graue Exzellenz. Zwischen Staatsräson und Vasallentreue. Aus den Papieren des Kaiserlichen Gesandten Karl Georg von Treutler.* Frankfurt/Berlin/Vienna, 1971

Jarausch, Konrad. *The Enigmatic Chancellor: Bethmann Hollweg and the Hubris of Imperial Germany.* New Haven, 1973

Joll, James. *Three Intellectuals in Politics.* New York, 1965. Original, 1960

Kaelble, Hartmut. *Industrielle Interessenpolitik in der Wilhelminischen Gesellschaft: Centralverband Deutscher Industrielle, 1895–1914.* Berlin, 1967

Kehr, Eckart. 'Klassenkämpfe und Rüstungspolitik im kaiserlichen Deutschland.' In *Eckart Kehr. Der Primat der Innenpolitik. Gesammelte Aufsätze zur preussisch-deutschen Sozialgeschichte im 19. und 20. Jahrhundert,* edited by Hans-Ulrich Wehler, pp. 87–110. 2nd edn Berlin, 1970

Schlachtflottenbau und Parteipolitik, 1894–1901. Berlin, 1930

'Das soziale System der Reaktion in Preussen unter dem Ministerium Puttkamer.' In *Der Primat der Innenpolitik,* edited by Wehler, pp. 64–87

Keller, Mathilde Gräfin von. *Vierzig Jahre im Dienst der Kaiserin. Ein Kulturbild aus den Jahren 1881–1921.* Leipzig, 1935

Kessel, Eberhard. 'Zur inneren Entwicklung Deutschlands unter Wilhelm II. und in der Weimarer Republik: Ein Literaturbericht.' *Archiv für Kulturgeschichte,* no. 2 (1962), pp. 253–80

Kitchen, Martin. *The German Officer Corps, 1890–1914.* Oxford, 1968

Koch, J. W. (ed.). *The Origins of the First World War.* London, 1972

Kolle, Kurt. *Kraepelin und Freud. Beitrag zur neueren Geschichte der Psychiatrie.* Stuttgart, 1957

Kommission für neuere Geschichte Österreichs. *Österreich-Ungarns Aussenpolitik von der Bosnischen Krise 1908 bis zum Kriegsausbruch 1914. Diplomatische Aktenstücke des österreichischen-ungarischen Ministeriums des Äussern.* 8 vols. Vienna/Leipzig, 1930

Kraepelin, Emil. *Psychiatrie.* Leipzig, 1915

Kühlmann, Richard von. *Erinnerungen.* Heidelberg, 1948

Lauritsen, John and Thorstad, David. *The Early Homosexual Rights Movement, 1864–1933.* New York, 1974

Leibenguth, Peter. 'Modernisierungskrisis des Kaiserreichs an der Schwelle zum wilhelminischen Imperialismus. Politische Probleme der Ära Caprivi, 1890–1894.' Dissertation, Cologne, 1975

Lepsius, Johannes, *et al.* (eds.). *Die Grosse Politik der Europäischen Kabinette, 1871–1914. Sammlung der Diplomatischen Akten des auswärtigen Amtes.* 40 vols. Berlin, 1922–7

Liddell Hart, B. H. *Strategy.* New York, 1954

Manchester, William. *The Arms of Krupp, 1578–1968.* New York, 1968

Mantey, Eberhard von. *Der Kreuzerkrieg in den ausländischen Gewässern.* vol. 3, *Die deutschen Hilfskreuzer.* Berlin, 1937

Maximilian, Prince of Baden. *Erinnerungen und Dokumente.* Stuttgart, 1927

Meisner, Heinrich Otto. 'Zur neueren Geschichte des preussischen Kabinetts.' *Forschungen zur brandenburgischen und preussischen Geschichte,* vol. 36 (1924), pp. 39–66 and 180–209

'Militärattachés und Militärbevollmächtigte in Preussen und im Deutschen Reich.' *Neue Beiträge zur Geschichtswissenschaft*, vol. 2. Berlin, 1957

Menne, Bernhard. *Blood and Steel. The Rise of the House of Krupp*. Zürich, 1936. New York, 1938

Messerschmidt, Manfred. 'Die Armee in Staat und Gesellschaft – Die Bismarckzeit.' In *Das kaiserliche Deutschland. Politik und Gesellschaft, 1870–1918*, edited by Michael Stürmer. Düsseldorf, 1970

Militär und Politik in der Bismarckzeit und im Wilhelminischen Deutschland. Erträge der Forschung, vol. 43. Darmstadt, 1975

'Militär und Schule in der wilhelminischen Zeit.' *Militärgeschichtliche Mitteilungen*, 1/78 (1978), pp. 51–76

Die Politische Geschichte der preussisch-deutschen Armee. Handbuch zur deutschen Militärgeschichte, IV, 1. Munich, 1975

Mittig, Hans-Ernst and Plagemann, Volker (eds.). *Denkmäler im 19. Jahrhundert. Deutung und Kritik*. Munich, 1972

Model, Hansgeorg. *Der deutsche Generalstabsoffizier. Seine Auswahl und Ausbildung in Reichswehr, Wehrmacht und Bundeswehr*. Frankfurt, 1968

Moltke, Helmuth von. *Erinnerungen, Briefe, Dokumente 1877–1916*. Stuttgart, 1922

Mommsen, Wolfgang J. 'Domestic Factors in German Foreign Policy before 1914.' *Central European History*, vol. 6 (1973), pp. 3–43

Monts, Anton. *Erinnerungen und Gedanken des Botschafters Anton Graf Monts*. Edited by Karl F. Nowak and Friedrich Thimme. Berlin, 1932

Mosse, George L. *The Nationalization of the Masses: Political Symbolism and Mass Movements in Germany from the Napoleonic Wars through the Third Reich*. New York/Scarborough, Ontario, 1977

Muhlen, Norbert. *The Incredible Krupps. The Rise, Fall, and Comeback of Germany's Industrial Family*. New York, 1959

Muncy, Lysbeth Walker. *The Junker in the Prussian Administration under William II 1888–1918*. Providence, Rhode Island, 1944

Muschler, Reinhold Conrad. *Philipp zu Eulenburg. Sein Leben und seine Zeit*. Leipzig, 1930

Nichols, J. Alden. *Germany After Bismarck: The Caprivi Era, 1890–1894*. New York, 1958

Palmer, Alan. *The Kaiser: Warlord of the Second Reich*. New York, 1978

Papke, Gerhard. 'Offizierkorps und Anciennität.' In *Untersuchungen zur Geschichte des Offizierkorps, Anciennität und Beförderung nach Leistung*, edited by I. G. Meier-Welcker. Stuttgart, 1962

Pezold, Dirk von. 'Cäsaromanie und Byzantinismus bei Wilhelm II.' Dissertation, Cologne, 1971

Philippi, Hans. *Das Königreich Württemberg im Spiegel der preussischen Gesandtschaftsberichte 1871–1914*. Veröffentlichungen der Kommission für geschichtliche Landeskunde in Baden-Württemberg Reihe B Forschungen, vol. 65. Stuttgart, 1972

Plagemann, Volker. 'Bismarck-Denkmäler.' In *Denkmäler im 19. Jahrhundert. Deutung und Kritik*, edited by Hans-Ernst Mittig and Volker Plagemann, pp. 217–52. Munich, 1972

Pogge von Strandmann, Hartmut (ed.). *Walther Rathenau. Tagebuch 1907–1922*. Düsseldorf, 1967

Pogge von Strandmann, Hartmut and Geiss, Imanuel. 'Staatsstreichpläne, Alldeutsche und Bethmann Hollweg.' In *Die Erforderlichkeit des Unmöglichen*. Hamburger Studien zur neueren Geschichte, vol. 2. Frankfurt, 1965

Potthoff, Heinrich (ed.). *Friedrich von Berg als Chef des Geheimen Zivilkabinetts 1918. Erinnerungen aus seinem Nachlass.* Düsseldorf, 1971

Preradovich, Nikolaus von. *Die Führungsschichten in Österreich und Preussen, 1804–1918.* Wiesbaden, 1955

Puhle, Hans Jürgen. *Agrarische Interessenpolitik und preussischer Konservatismus im Wilhelminischen Reich, 1893–1914. Ein Beitrag zur Analyse des Nationalismus in Deutschland am Beispiel des Bundes der Landwirte und der Deutsch-Konservativen Partei.* Hannover, 1967

Pulzer, Peter. *The Rise of Political Anti-Semitism in Germany and Austria.* New York, 1964

Rathenau, Walther. *Der Kaiser. Eine Betrachtung.* Berlin, 1923

Reischach, Hugo Frhr von. *Unter drei Kaisern.* Berlin, 1925

Reuss, Martin. 'Bismarck's Dismissal and the Holstein Circle.' *European Studies Review,* vol. 5, no. 1 (1975)

Reventlow, Ernst Graf von. *Kaiser Wilhelm II. und die Byzantiner.* Munich, 1906

Rich, Norman. *Friedrich von Holstein: Politics and Diplomacy in the Era of Bismarck and Wilhelm II.* 2 vols. Cambridge, 1965

Rich, Norman and Fisher, M. H. (eds.). *Die geheimen Papiere Friedrich von Holsteins.* 4 vols. Göttingen/Berlin/Frankfurt, 1956–63

Ritter, Gerhard. 'Die deutschen Militär-attachés und das Auswärtige Amt. Aus den verbrannten Akten des Grossen Generalstabs.' In *Sitzungsberichte der Heidelberger Akademie der Wissenschaften.* Phil.-hist. Klasse, 1959, Abh. 1. Heidelberg, 1959

Der Schlieffenplan. Kritik eines Mythos. Munich, 1956

The Sword and the Scepter. The Problem of Militarism in Germany. Translated by Heinz Norden. 4 vols. Coral Gables, Florida, 1969–73. German original, 1956–68

Rogge, Helmuth. 'Affairen im Kaiserreich. Symptome der Staatskrise unter Wilhelm II.' *Die Politische Meinung,* LXXXI (1963), 58–72

'Die *Kladderadatschaffäre*. Ein Beitrag zur neueren Geschichte des Wilhelminischen Reiches.' *Historische Zeitschrift,* CXCV (1962), 90–130

Holstein und Harden. Politisch-publizistisches Zusammenspiel zweier Aussenseiter des Wilhelminischen Reiches. Munich, 1959

Röhl, John C. G. 'Admiral von Müller and the Approach of War, 1911–1914.' *The Historical Journal,* XII, 4 (1969), 651–73

'An der Schwelle zum Weltkrieg: Eine Dokumentation über den "Kriegsrat" von 8. Dezember 1912.' *Militärgeschichtliche Mitteilungen,* 1/77 (1977), pp. 77–134

'The Disintegration of the Kartell and the Politics of Bismarck's Fall from Power, 1887–1890.' *The Historical Journal,* IX, 1 (1966), pp. 60–90

'The Emperor's New Clothes: A Character Sketch of Kaiser Wilhelm II.' In *Kaiser Wilhelm II: New Interpretations,* edited by John C. G. Röhl and Nicolaus Sombart. Cambridge, 1981

From Bismarck to Hitler. The Problem of Continuity in German History. London, 1970

'Die Generalprobe. Zur Geschichte und Bedeutung des "Kriegsrates" vom
    8. Dezember 1912.' In *Industrielle Gesellschaft und politisches System*, ed. Dirk
    Stegmann, Bernd-Jürgen Wendt and Peter-Christian Witt. Bonn, 1978
Germany Without Bismarck: The Crisis of Government in the Second Reich. Lon-
    don, 1967
'Staatsstreichplan oder Staatsstreichbereitschaft? Bismarcks Politik in der
    Entlassungskrise." *Historische Zeitschrift*, vol. CCIII (December 1966)
(ed.). *1914: Delusion or Design? The Testimony of Two German Diplomats.* Lon-
    don, 1973
(ed.). *Philipp Eulenburgs politische Korrespondenz.* 3 vols. Boppard am Rhein,
    1976–
Rosenberg, Arthur. *Imperial Germany: The Birth of the German Republic, 1871–
    1918.* Boston, 1964. German original, 1930
Rumschöttel, Hermann. *Das bayerische Offizierkorps, 1866–1914.* Beiträge zu
    einer historischen Strukturanalyse Bayerns im Industriezeitalter, vol. 9.
    Berlin, 1973
Salewski, Michael. ' "Neujahr 1900" Die Säkularwende in zeitgenössischer,
    Sicht.' *Archiv für Kulturgeschichte*, vol. 53, no. 2 (1972), pp. 335–81
Saul, Klaus. *Staat, Industrie, Arbeiterbewegung im Kaiserreich. Zur Innen- und Aus-
    senpolitik des Wilhelminischen Deutschland, 1903–1914.* Studien zur moder-
    nen Geschichte, Bd 16, edited by Fritz Fischer, Klaus-Detlev Grothusen,
    Günter Moltmann. Düsseldorf, 1974
Schaible, Camill. *Standes- und Berufspflichten des deutschen Offiziers. Für ange-
    hende und jüngere Offiziere des stehenden Heeres und des Beurlaubtenstandes.*
    3rd edn Berlin, 1896
Schmidt-Bückeburg, Rudolf. *Das Militärkabinett der preussischen Könige und
    Deutschen Kaiser. Seine geschichtliche Entwicklung und staatsrechtliche Stellung,
    1787–1918.* Berlin, 1933
Schmidt-Richberg, Wiegand. *Von der Entlassung Bismarcks bis zum Ende des Ersten
    Weltkrieges (1890–1918).* Handbuch der deutschen Militärgeschichte,
    1648–1939, vol. 5. Frankfurt, 1969
Schorske, Carl E. *German Social Democracy, 1905–1917: The Development of the
    Great Schism.* New York, 1955
Schröder, E. *Zwanzig Jahre Regierungszeit. Ein Tagebuch Kaiser Wilhelms II. Vom
    Antritt der Regierung 15. Juni 1888 bis zum 15. Juni 1908 nach Hof- und
    anderen Berichten.* Berlin, 1909
Schulte, Bernd-Felix. *Die deutsche Armee 1900–1914. Zwischen Beharren und
    Verändern.* Düsseldorf, 1977
Schüssler, Wilhelm. *Die Daily-Telegraph-Affaire: Fürst Bülow, Kaiser Wilhelm und
    die Krise des Zweiten Reiches 1908.* Göttingen, 1952
Kaiser Wilhelm II. Schicksal und Schuld. Göttingen, 1962
Schwertfeger, Bernhard (ed.). *Kaiser und Kabinettschef, nach eigenen Aufzeich-
    nungen und dem Briefwechsel des Wirklichen Geheimen Rats Rudolf von Va-
    lentini.* Oldenbourg, 1931
Smith, Alson J. *A View of the Spree.* New York, 1962
Smith-Rosenberg, Carroll. 'The Female World of Love and Ritual: Relations
    between Women in Nineteenth-Century America.' *Signs*, I, 1 (Autumn
    1975), 1–29
Spitzemberg, Hildegard Baronin. *Das Tagebuch der Baronin Spitzemberg. Auf-*

zeichnungen aus der Hofgesellschaft des Hohenzollernreiches. Edited by Rudolf Vierhaus. Göttingen, 1960

Steakley, James. *The Homosexual Rights Movement in Germany.* New York, 1975

Stegmann, Dirk. *Die Erben Bismarcks. Parteien und Verbände in der Spätphase des Wilhelminischen Deutschlands Sammlungspolitik 1897–1918.* Cologne/Berlin, 1970

Steinberg, Jonathan. 'The Copenhagen Complex.' *Journal of Contemporary History,* I, 3 (1966), 23–46

Yesterday's Deterrent. Admiral Tirpitz and the Birth of the German Battle Fleet. London, 1965

Steinhausen, Georg. 'Verfallsstimmung im kaiserlichen Deutschland.' *Preussische Jahrbücher,* vol. 194 (1923), pp. 153–85

Stern, Fritz. 'Bethmann Hollweg and the War: The Limits of Responsibility.' In *The Responsibility of Power: Historical Essays in Honor of Hajo Holborn,* edited by Fritz Stern and Leonard Krieger. New York, 1967

Stolberg-Wernigerode, Otto Graf zu. *Die unentschiedene Generation: Deutschlands konservative Führungsschichten am Vorabend des ersten Weltkrieges.* Munich/Vienna, 1968

Stribrny, Wolfgang. 'Kaiser Wilhelm II und die Burg Hohenzollern.' *Zeitschrift für Religions- und Geistesgeschichte,* Bd XIII, Heft 1/2 (1971), pp. 129–34

Stubmann, Peter F. *Ballin, Leben und Werk eines deutschen Reeders.* Berlin, 1926

Taylor, Alan J. P. *The Struggle for Mastery in Europe, 1848–1918.* London, 1971 (1954)

Thielen, Peter G. 'Die Marginalien Kaiser Wilhelms II.' *Die Welt als Geschichte,* XX (1960), 249–59

Thimme, Friedrich (ed.). *Front Wider Bülow. Staatsmänner, Diplomaten und Forscher zu seinen Denkwürdigkeiten.* Munich, 1931

Tirpitz, Alfred von. *Erinnerungen.* Leipzig, 1920

Tirrell, Sarah R. *German Agrarian Politics after Bismarck's Fall: The Formation of the Farmer's League.* New York, 1951

Tresckow, Hans von. *Von Fürsten und anderen Sterblichen. Erinnerungen eines Kriminalkommissars.* Berlin, 1922

Vagts, Alfred. *The Military Attaché.* Princeton, New Jersey, 1967

Vietsch, Eberhard. *Bethmann Hollweg. Staatsmann zwischen Macht und Ethos.* Boppard am Rhein, 1969

Viktoria Luise, Herzogin. *Im Glanz der Krone. Erinnerungen.* Munich, 1975

Waldersee, Alfred Graf von. *Denkwürdigkeiten des Generalfeldmarschalls.* Edited by Heinrich Otto Meisner. 3 vols. Stuttgart/Berlin, 1922–3

Wallach, Jehuda. *Das Dogma der Vernichtungsschlacht.* Munich, 1970

Wedel, Carl Graf von. *Zwischen Kaiser und Kanzler. Aufzeichnungen aus den Jahren 1890–1894.* Edited by Erhardt Graf von Wedel. Leipzig, 1943

Wehler, Hans-Ulrich. *Das Deutsche Kaiserreich 1871–1918.* Göttingen, 1973

(ed.). *Eckart Kehr. Der Primat der Innenpolitik.* Veröffentlichungen der Historischen Kommission zu Berlin beim Friedrich-Meinecke-Institut der Freien Universität Berlin. Berlin, 1970

Weitowitz, Rolf G. *Deutsche Politik und Handelspolitik unter Reichskanzler Leo von Caprivi: 1890–1894.* Düsseldorf, 1978

Weller, B. Uwe. *Maximilian Harden und die 'Zukunft.'* Bremen, 1970

Wer Ist's? Berlin, 1898 and thereafter

Wernecke, Klaus. *Der Wille zur Weltgeltung. Aussenpolitik und Öffentlickeit im Kaiserreich am Vorabend des Ersten Weltkrieges.* Düsseldorf, 1970

Whittle, Tyler. *The Last Kaiser: A Biography of Wilhelm II, German Emperor and King of Prussia.* New York, 1977

Wilhelm, Crown Prince. *Memoirs of the Crown Prince of Germany.* New York, 1922

Wilhelm II, German Emperor. *Aus meinem Leben, 1859–1888.* Berlin, 1927

Wilke, Ekkehard-Teja P. W. *Political Decadence in Imperial Germany: Personnel-political Aspects of the German Government Crisis 1894–1897.* Illinois Studies in the Social Sciences, vol. 59. Urbana/Chicago/London, 1976

Winzen, Peter. *Bülows Weltmachtkonzept. Untersuchungen zur Frühphase seiner Aussenpolitik, 1897–1901.* Boppard am Rhein, 1977

Witt, Peter-Christian. *Die Finanzpolitik des Deutschen Reiches von 1903–1913. Eine Studie zur Innenpolitik des Wilhelminischen Deutschland.* Lübeck/Hamburg, 1970

Witte, Sergei. *The Memoirs of Count Witte.* New York/Toronto, 1921

Young, Harry F. *Maximilian Harden: Censor Germaniae.* The Hague, 1959

Prince Lichnowsky and the Great War. Athens, Georgia, 1977

Zedlitz-Trützschler, Robert von. *Zwölf Jahre am deutschen Kaiserhof.* Berlin, 1924

Zentner, Kurt. *Kaiserliche Zeiten. Wilhelm II. und seine Ära in Bildern und Dokumenten.* Munich, 1964

Zmarzlik, Hans Günther. *Bethmann Hollweg als Reichskanzler, 1909–1914.* Düsseldorf, 1957

Glossary

Akten	official, government files
Ausführungsbestimmungen	orders for the carrying out of a law or decree
Äusserlichkeit	superficiality
Bund der Landwirte	Agrarian League
Bundesfürsten	federal princes
Cäsarenwahnsinn	megalomania
Direktorium	Board of Directors
Draufgänger	daredevil, or reckless person
forsch	daring, bold
Freiherr	baron
Geheimrat	Privy Councillor
Generalstäbler	members of the General Staff
Gleichberechtigung	equality
Gnadensachen	matters subject to the Kaiser's grace
Graf	Count
gute Sache	the good of the cause
Gymnasium	most prestigious of the secondary schools, preparatory to the university, emphasizing Latin and Greek
Hauptquartier	headquarters (official name of the military entourage)
hoffähig	of sufficient rank or station to be presented at Court
Hofgesellschaft	proper society (presentable at Court)
Immediatstellen	positions with direct and personal access to the Kaiser
Immediatvorträge	reports presented directly before the Kaiser
Jagdgesellschaft	hunting party
Kadettenanstalt	military school
Kaiserjagd	royal hunt
Kaisermanöver	annual maneuvers at which the Kaiser was present
Kaiserreich	the German Empire
Kartell	political alignment of the Conservative, Free Conservative and National Liberal Parties, 1887–90
Kasino	officers' mess
Kladderadatsch	satirical Berlin magazine
Kommandogewalt	Kaiser's power of military command

Krautjunker	derisive term for a Prussian noble implying boorishness
Kriegsakademie	War Academy
Kriegsrat	the 'Council of War' of 8 December 1912
Kriegsschüler	officer–students at the War Academy
Kulturkampf	Bismarck's policy against the Roman Catholic Church, 1871–8
Leibkompagnie	the select Company which guarded the Kaiser's person
Männerbund	male society, or male bonding
Menschenkenntnis	insight into character or personality
Militärische Meldungen	military reports (to the Kaiser)
Nachlass	private papers
Nagelung	ceremony of nailing a military unit's colors
Nordlandreise	The Kaiser's annual Norwegian summer cruise
Oberrealschule	least prestigious second school, emphasizing only modern subjects and languages
Offizierstand	officer class
Personalpolitik	process of choosing personnel
Realgymnasium	secondary school for modern subjects, science and Latin, but not Greek. Second in prestige after the classical Gymnasium
Reichsleitung	government leadership
Ressort	bureau, or area of expertise
Sammlungspolitik	the policy of political alliance, specifically between the agrarians and the industrialists
Staatsprüfung	state examination
Stand	caste or class
Standesfehler	a failing associated with or deriving from one's class
Tageseinteilung	daily schedule
Umgebung	entourage
Vortrag	report
Weltanschauung	worldview or conception
Weltgeltung	world importance
Weltpolitik	policy designed to make Germany a world power
Zwangslage	position of constraint

Index